The Dance
of Change

PETER SENGE

ART KLEINER

CHARLOTTE ROBERTS

RICHARD ROSS

GEORGE ROTH

BRYAN SMITH

New York   London   Toronto   Sydney   Auckland

The Dance of Change

The Challenges
of Sustaining Momentum
in Learning Organizations

A Fifth Discipline Resource

A CURRENCY BOOK

PUBLISHED BY DOUBLEDAY
a division of Random House, Inc.
1540 Broadway, New York, New York 10036

Doubleday/Currency is a trademark of Doubleday, a division of Random House, Inc.

Book design by Chris Welch

Library of Congress Cataloging-in-Publication Data
　　　　The dance of change: the challenges of sustaining momentum in
　　　　learning organizations / Peter M. Senge . . . [et al.].
　　　　　　p.　　cm.
　　　　Includes index.
　　　　1. Organizational learning.　　2. Organizational change.　　I. Senge, Peter M.
　　　　HD58.82.D36　　　1999
　　　　658.4'06--DC21　　　　　　　　　　　　　　　　　　　　　　　　98-39789
　　　　　　　　　　　　　　　　　　　　　　　　　　　　　　　　　　　CIP

ISBN 0-385-493223

Contents

The Challenges of Initiating

The Challenges of Sustaining Transformation

The Challenges of Redesigning and Rethinking

Endnotes

Getting
Started

〜〜〜〜〜〜

I. Orientation

1 Toward an Atlas of Organizational Change

Look ahead twenty or thirty years. Does anyone expect the next twenty years to be less tumultuous than the last twenty years? Given the changes expected in technology, biology, medicine, social values, demography, the environment, and international relations, what kind of world might humanity face? No one can say for sure, but one thing is reasonably certain: Continuing challenges will tax our collective abilities to deal with them. Failure to rethink our enterprises will leave us little relief from our current predicaments: rising turbulence causing rising stress; increasing disconnection and internal competitiveness; people working harder, rather than learning how to work smarter; and increasingly intractable problems beyond the reach of any individual or organization. If you are an organizational leader, someone at any level concerned deeply about these challenges, then you face a daunting task. In effect, you are engaged in a great venture of exploration, risk, discovery, and change, without any comprehensive maps for guidance.

Actually, for most of human history, intrepid explorers have set out on their journeys of discovery without comprehensive maps. The "portolans" and "rutters" of the European Renaissance, for example, were hand-drawn charts describing specific routes along byways and coastlines, often derived from the hasty notes of previous travelers. No one expected them to provide more than rough guidance. Sea and land alike were turbulent, ever-changing environments. Currents and wind patterns shifted. Vegetation evident in August might be gone the following March. Storms altered the contours of sandbars and shoals.

Yet, however imperfect, maps and guides have been among humankind's most treasured artifacts—jealously guarded, often worth more than gold. The sixteenth-century explorer Ferdinand Magellan quashed an on-board mutiny because he kept his maps hidden, and thus made himself indispensable; only he knew where to pilot the ships. Even today, in an age of satellite positioning and cellular telephony, sailors and fishing fleets still regard hand-drawn rutters passed on among family and friends as their most precious cargo.

Not surprisingly, the first atlas makers, who gathered and collected those charts and notes into books and portfolios, changed history. Some, like the sixteenth-century Spanish royal court-appointed "pilot major," Amerigo Vespucci, were former explorers themselves. In Seville, Vespucci hung a giant wall chart where navigators sailing into port traced their discoveries. (Less favored map publishers had to bribe sailors and courtiers, or ply them with drink.) Vespucci's efforts did not go unrewarded: He was credited, for a time, with discovering the "Americas," and the Western Hemisphere still bears his name.

Ultimately, however, the most significant atlas maker of his time contributed something more important than just a name to history. Gerardus Mercator, a Flemish mathematician, created a medium for systematically organizing diverse data into a coherent image of the Earth as a whole. He drew the first map of the world on a grid of uniform north-south, east-west parallels. Not just Europe and the "Indies," but all of the inhabited continents could fit. To be sure, Mercator's world map was distorted: Greenland appeared almost as big as Africa (due to projecting a three-dimensional surface onto a two-dimensional map), and he placed almost two thirds of the globe above the equator, an unabashedly Eurocentric view. But Mercator's framework enabled cartographers to gradually assemble the tales of many journeys onto one global picture. The grid framework ushered in a new era of scientific mapmaking.

We, the authors of this book, likewise aspire to establish a simple and systematic way to organize the diverse tales recounted by organizational change explorers into a coherent whole.

At first glance, it appears that people seeking change in organizations have very different goals in mind. Some seek the "accelerating," "visionary," or "intelligent" organization; others, the "innovative," "living," "adaptive," or "transformational" company. They try total quality, re-engineering business processes, "boundarylessness," strategic alliances, or scenario planning. Drawing upon the predecessors to this book (*The Fifth Discipline* and *The Fifth Discipline Fieldbook*), many seek to build

See The Fifth Discipline: The Art and Practice of the Learning Organization, by Peter Senge (New York: Doubleday/Currency, 1990), and *The Fifth Discipline Fieldbook: Strategies and Tools for Building a Learning Organization*, by Peter Senge, Art Kleiner, Charlotte Roberts, Rick Ross, and Bryan Smith (New York: Doubleday/Currency, 1994).

"learning organizations." But despite the different labels, common aspirations guide most of their efforts. They are trying to respond quickly to external changes and think more imaginatively about the future. They want better relationships, with less games-playing and more trust and openness. They want to unleash employees' natural talents and enthusiasm. They hope to move genuinely closer to their customers. Through all of this, they are striving to shape their destiny, and thereby achieve long-term financial success.

Current management literature is full of practical advice and suggestions; but it lacks a way to effectively organize diverse insights. Like the portolans and rutters of yore, it can only orient people relative to a predetermined path and destination, not relative to a broader terrain. The framework developed in the following pages represents an alternative—a simple "grid." Undoubtedly, there are flaws. Like Mercator's Eurocentrism, some of these imperfections may only become evident years from now, as we see the flaws in our assumptions. Other flaws may be inherent limitations of the framework itself, like the distortion of Greenland. And it is impossible to say what measure of success will meet this new mapmaking endeavor. But without better maps, it is extremely unlikely that organizational change efforts will ever sustain themselves. Each new adventure will be the first.

We thus hope that, over time, the framework of "the dance of change" will provide a starting point, enabling all of us who care deeply about building new types of organizations to become part of a common knowledge-building process, leading gradually to better maps and healthier organizations.

Our sources on the history of mapmaking and exploration included: *The Story of Maps* by Lloyd A. Brown (Boston: Little, Brown, 1949); *History of Cartography* by Leo Bagrow (Chicago: Precedent Publishing, 1985); and *A World Lit Only by Fire* by William Manchester (Boston: Little, Brown, 1992).

2 The Life Cycle of Typical Change Initiatives

Peter Senge

Most change initiatives fail. Two independent studies in the early 1990s, one published by Arthur D. Little and one by McKinsey & Co., found that out of the hundreds of corporate Total Quality Management (TQM) programs studied, about two thirds "grind to a halt because

The many, many references about these failures include: *The Economist*, April 18, 1992 (describing the Arthur D. Little and McKinsey studies); "Why Do Employees Resist Change?" by Paul Strebel, *Harvard Business Review*, May/June 1996, p. 86 (cites a 20–50% reengineering success rate); "Leading Change: Why Transformation Efforts Fail," by John P. Kotter, *Harvard Business Review*, Mar/Apr 1995, p. 59; and "Reengineering: A Light That Failed," by James Champy, *Across the Board* , vol. 32, no. 3 , pp. 27–31, March 1995.

of their failure to produce hoped-for results." Reengineering has fared no better; a number of articles, including some by reengineering's founders, place the failure rate somewhere around 70 percent. Harvard's John Kotter, in a study of one hundred top management–driven "corporate transformation" efforts, concluded that more than half did not survive the initial phases. He found a few that were "very successful," and a few that were "utter failures." The vast majority lay ". . . somewhere in between, with a distinct tilt toward the lower end of the scale." Clearly, businesses do not have a very good track record in sustaining significant change. There is little to suggest that schools, healthcare institutions, governmental, and nonprofit institutions fare any better.

Even without knowing the statistics, most of us know firsthand that change programs fail. We've seen enough "flavor of the month" programs "rolled out" from top management to last a lifetime. We know the cynicism they engender. We have watched ourselves and others around us "salute the flag" and then say privately, "Here we go again," and "This will never work." Some companies even create their own jargon to laugh a bit at their skepticism: At Harley-Davidson, management's latest great ideas are greeted with the phrase "AFP," which is translated publicly as: "Another Fine Program."

This failure to sustain significant change recurs again and again despite substantial resources committed to the change effort (many are bankrolled by top management), talented and committed people "driving the change," and high stakes. In fact, executives feeling an urgent need for change are right; companies that fail to sustain significant change end up facing crises. By then, their options are greatly reduced, and even after heroic efforts they often decline.

Our core premise in writing this book is that the sources of these problems cannot be remedied by more expert advice, better consultants, or more committed managers. The sources lie in our most basic ways of thinking. If these do not change, any new "input" will end up producing the same fundamentally unproductive types of actions.

To understand why sustaining significant change is so elusive, we need to think less like managers and more like biologists. We can start by seeing that, over time, most change initiatives follow a generic life cycle that looks something like the diagram on the following page.

The innovative practices advocated by the initiative—be it total quality management, process redesign, or "building a learning organization"— grow for a while and then stop growing.   Maybe they cease altogether. Maybe the initiative persists at a low level, the religion of a small group of

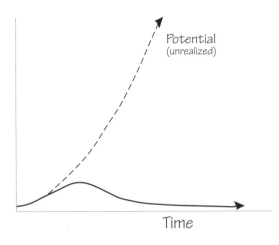

Potential
(unrealized)

Time

"true believers." Either way, the initial growth fails to realize its potential. It is understandable that many innovative new practices do not spread because they turn out never to generate sufficient benefits. But what about those that do demonstrate significant benefits and still do not spread, as occurs with a great many promising innovations that "die on the vine" in large corporations? The dashed curve on the diagram indicates the potential growth that the innovative practice could have enjoyed. Why, if the new ideas or tools or processes had real potential, did they only penetrate to 1 percent of the organization? Why was only 5 percent improvement in new product development rate achieved when there might have been a 100 percent improvement? Why did momentum die out?

As any biologist would immediately say, the curve in the diagram is not idiosyncratic to organizational change efforts. It traces the pattern followed by anything that grows in nature, even something that grows and dies "prematurely." In fact, the s-shaped growth pattern occurs so consistently in biology that it has its own name: "sigmoidal" growth. All individual organisms, from humans to beetles, likewise grow according to the same pattern: accelerating, then gradually slowing until "full" adult size is reached. Biological populations grow the same way: accelerating for a time, then gradually slowing. This pattern recurs again and again in nature because of the way nature generates and controls growth.

All growth in nature arises out of an interplay between reinforcing growth processes and limiting processes. The seed contains the possibility for a tree, but it realizes that possibility through an emergent reinforcing growth process. The seed sends out small feelers. These primitive roots draw in water and nutrients. This leads the roots to expand farther, drawing in more water and nutrients, leading to further expansion—more water, nutrients, and so on. The initial growth process is under way. But how far it progresses depends on a host of limits: water, nutrients in the soil, space for the roots to expand, warmth. Even-

For examples of change initiatives and innovations that did not realize their potential (even though they eventually became highly influential), see *The Age of Heretics,* by Art Kleiner (New York: Doubleday, 1996) or *Failure in Organization Development and Change: Cases and Essays for Learning,* by Philip H. Mirvis and David N. Berg, editors (New York: John Wiley and Sons, 1977).

tually, as the tree begins to extend beyond the surface, other limits will come into play: sunlight, space for the tree's branches to spread, insects that destroy the tree's leaves.

When growth stops "prematurely," before the organism reaches its potential, it is because the growth has encountered constraints that could be avoided, that are not inevitable. Other members of the species will grow more because they do not encounter the same constraints. Any particular limit mentioned above—not enough water, nutrients, or space for the root system—could potentially keep the seed from growing.

What, then, can biology teach us about the growth and premature death of organizational change initiatives?

First, it immediately suggests that most leadership strategies are doomed to failure from the outset. Leaders instigating change are often like gardeners standing over their plants, imploring them: "Grow! Try harder! You can do it!" No gardener tries to convince a plant to "want" to grow: If the seed does not have the potential to grow, there's nothing anyone can do to make a difference.

Second, it suggests that leaders should especially focus on understanding the limiting processes that could slow or arrest change. Above all else, the gardener must understand the constraints that can limit growth and attend to these constraints. Why should this be any different for leaders seeking to sustain significant change? Entreating people to try harder, to become more committed, to be more passionate cannot possibly have much lasting effect. The biological world teaches that sustaining change requires understanding the reinforcing growth processes and what is needed to catalyze them, and addressing the limits that keep change from occurring.

So, what types of limits might these be? What are some of the constraints that all efforts to sustain significant change encounter? One insight may lie in a phrase that became common in the heyday of TQM. I remember sitting in a meeting in the mid-1980s with a group of managers on the vanguard of TQM at a leading U.S. manufacturer. "We've picked all the low hanging fruit," one stated. When I asked what he meant, he said, "We've done all the easy things. In truth, things were so bad in many of our production facilities that it was enough just to give people a little bit of authority to fix practices that many had known needed to be changed for a long time. Now we're up against much tougher problems and the rate of improvement is declining. Now we're up against problems where the real problem is us, the management. We're pretty good at directing others to change, but not so great at changing ourselves."

Most serious change initiatives eventually come up against issues embedded in our prevailing system of management. These include managers' commitment to change as long as it doesn't affect them; "undiscussable" topics that feel risky to talk about; and the ingrained habit of attacking symptoms and ignoring deeper, systemic causes of problems.

We are limited in dealing with such issues by our collective learning capabilities. Shared commitment to change develops only with collective capability to build shared aspirations. People start discussing "undiscussable" subjects only when they develop the reflection and inquiry skills that enable them to talk openly about complex, conflictive issues without invoking defensiveness. People start seeing and dealing with interdependencies and deeper causes of problems only as they develop the skills of systems thinking. In my experience, if basic learning capabilities like these are deficient, then they represent a fundamental limit to sustaining change.

Most advocates of change initiatives, be they CEOs or internal staff, focus on the changes they are trying to produce and fail to recognize the importance of learning capabilities. This is like trying to make a plant grow, rather than understanding and addressing the constraints that are keeping it from growing. Consequently, their initiatives are doomed from the start to achieve less than their potential—until building learning capabilities becomes part of the change strategy.

But . . . there remains a problem. For the past ten years and longer, many people have been doing just that—building learning capabilities as an essential part of producing more effective work practices. We often call these "learning initiatives." Many have had great success. But just as many have failed. And, where success has been achieved, innovators continue to struggle to sustain momentum. Obviously, building learning capabilities is necessary, but not sufficient.

I have come to the conclusion that what is missing is more subtle. In practice, most learning initiatives do not reflect any deep understanding of nature's growth dynamics. In effect, they deal only with the growth processes and not with the limiting processes. Developing learning capabilities in the context of working groups and real business goals can lead to powerful reinforcing growth processes. This has been the focus of most of the "learning organization work" for the past twenty years. Activating the self-energizing commitment and energy of people around changes they deeply care about has been the key to the many successes that have been achieved. But, nothing in nature grows in the absence of limiting processes. And, we have given these limiting processes much too little attention. This is why so many learning initia-

The capabilities referred to here are embodied in the five "learning disciplines" of *The Fifth Discipline*: personal mastery and shared vision (aspiration), mental models and team learning (reflection and inquiry), and systems thinking.

I am indebted to Nitin Nohria of Harvard for pointing out how inadequate learning capabilities limit most change initiatives. — Peter Senge

The quote from Humberto Maturana is from "Biosphere, Homosphere, and Robosphere: What has that to do with business?," a presentation at the Society for Organizational Learning (SoL), June 23–24, 1998, re-created by Pille Bunnell. An edited transcript by Maturana and Bunnell is available through SoL; for access, see http://www.fieldbook.com/sol.html. Also see *The Tree of Knowledge,* by Humberto Maturana and Francisco J. Varela (Boston: Shambala/Random House, 1987, 1992); *Autopoiesis and Cognition: The Realization of the Living,* by H. R. Maturana and Francisco Varela (Boston: D. Reidel Publishing Co., 1980); the Observer Web site, dedicated to Maturana and Varela's work: http://www.informatik.umu.se/~rwhit/ AT.html and the Fieldbook referrals to Maturana's work at http://www.field book.com/maturana.html.

tives, like so many other change initiatives, ultimately fail to sustain momentum.

Sustaining any profound change process requires a fundamental shift in thinking. We need to understand the nature of growth processes (forces that aid our efforts) and how to catalyze them. But we also need to understand the forces and challenges that impede progress, and to develop workable strategies for dealing with these challenges. We need to appreciate "the dance of change," the inevitable interplay between growth processes and limiting processes. As Chilean biologist Humberto Maturana puts it, "Every movement is being inhibited as it occurs." This is nature's way. We can either work with it, or work against it.

This requires us to think of sustaining change more biologically and less mechanistically. It requires patience as well as urgency. It requires a real sense of inquiry, a genuine curiosity about limiting forces. It requires seeing how significant change invariably starts locally, and how it grows over time. And it requires recognizing the diverse array of people who play key roles in sustaining change—people who are "leaders."

3 The Leadership of Profound Change

Toward an ecology of leadership

Peter Senge

THE MYTH OF THE HERO-CEO

"Significant change only occurs when it is driven from the top."
"There is no point in going forward unless the CEO is on board."
"Nothing will happen without top management buy-in."

How many times have we all heard these familiar refrains, and simply accepted them as "the way things are"? Probably many times, and yet there are good reasons to challenge these hoary truisms. The evidence for top management's power to direct large organizations to change is thin at best. Everywhere one hears of CEOs' needing to "transform" their organizations, yet the examples of successful, sustained transformation are few. Moreover, in this "age of empowerment," doesn't it seem a bit strange that we are asked to accept the singular power of top executives so unquestionably? How can we hope to bring about less hierarchical, authoritarian organizations solely through recourse to hierarchical authority?

In fact, the myth of the omnipotent CEO is merely a special case of a deeper cultural icon, the myth of the hero-leader. According to this shared story, leaders are the few special people blessed with the capability for command and influence. They have become leaders precisely because of their unique mix of skill, ambition, vision, charisma, and no small amount of hubris. They can overcome the blocks that stymie everyone else. They make great things happen. The implication is clear: If you too want to make a difference, you had better be one of these special people.

In the world of today's organizations, this idealization of great leadership leads to an endless search for heroic figures who can come in to rescue the rest of us from recalcitrant, noncompetitive institutions. But might this very thinking be a key reason such institutions prevail? Might not the continual search for the hero-leader be a critical factor in itself, diverting our attention away from building institutions that, by their very nature, continually adapt and reinvent themselves, with leadership coming from many people in many places, not just from the top?

I have come to see our obsession with the hero-CEO as a type of cultural addiction. Faced with the practical needs for significant change, we opt for the hero-leader rather than eliciting and developing leadership capacity throughout the organization. A new hero-CEO arrives to pump new life into the organization's suffering fortunes. Typically, today, the new leader cuts costs (and usually people), and boosts productivity and profit. But the improvements do not last. Many of the leader's grand strategies never get implemented; instead, people cling to habitual ways of doing things. New ideas do not spring forth from people at the front lines because they are too intimidated to stick their neck out. Energies are not released to create new products or new ways to meet customer needs because people are too busy competing with one another to please their bosses. Sooner or later, new crises ensue, giving rise to the search for new hero-leaders. In effect, the myth of the hero-leader creates a reinforcing vicious spiral of dramatic changes imposed from the top, and diminished leadership capacity in the organization, leading eventually to new crises and yet more heroic leaders.

Worshipping the cult of the hero-leader is a surefire way to maintain change-averse institutions. In fact, one can hardly think of a better strategy to achieve precisely this goal. The price that we all pay, in the long run, is incalculable: institutions that lurch from crisis to crisis, continual stress on the members of those institutions, mediocre (at best) long-term financial performance, and a subtle, pervasive reinforcement of the point of view that "common people" are powerless to change things.

In the business world, the vicious addictive spiral extends into the investment community. Investor pressures for improved short-term financial performance lead to calls for more aggressive top management. New hero-leaders come forward who can boost short-term performance. But their strategies typically preclude long-term investments in developing collective capacities to innovate, thereby guaranteeing long-term mediocre financial results. This, in turn, leads to more pressures from investors and more hero-leaders. In other words, the investment community paradoxically colludes in sustaining a system guaranteed to undermine creation of wealth in the long run.

A DIFFERENT VIEW OF EXECUTIVE LEADERSHIP

Now consider a different set of statements:

> "Little significant change can occur if it is driven only from the top."
> "CEO proclamations and programs rolled out from corporate headquarters are a great way to foster cynicism and distract everyone from real efforts to change."
> "Top management buy-in is a poor substitute for genuine commitment and learning capabilities at all levels in an organization. In fact, if management authority is used unwisely, it can make such commitment and capability less likely to develop."

These views are not just heard at lower levels in the hierarchy; they are echoed by senior executives in organizations that have achieved some sustained success.

"When I first came in as CEO," Shell Oil's Phil Carroll has said, "everyone thought, 'Phil will tell us what to do.' But I didn't have the answer, thank goodness. If I had, it would have been a disaster."

Harley-Davidson chairman Rich Teerlink has commented: "Anyone who thinks a CEO can drive this kind of change is wrong."

And Charles Szulak, former President of Visteon Automotive Systems at Ford Motor Company, has said, "Carrying significant change through an organization of eighty-two thousand people cannot possibly be done by a handful of people at the top."

There are good reasons why these executives, and others like them, have come to hold more humble views about the powers of executive leadership. First, they know that people, especially in large organizations, have become cynical about "flavor of the month" management fads.

Second, they appreciate the fundamental differences between compliance and commitment. The word "commitment" has become fashionable because it is widely believed that "high commitment" work environments are more productive, and probably also because many managers feel uncomfortable telling people to "comply" with management's directives. But the simple fact is that most management-driven change efforts do not require commitment. They are built around compliance. Either people comply with the new reorganization, or they know they will be at odds with their bosses. Knowing that it is difficult to discern visions from commands when they travel down the hierarchy, savvy senior managers use the power of their position with great care—because they seek to foster more than just compliance.

Deep changes—in how people think, what they believe, how they see the world—are difficult, if not impossible, to achieve through compliance. Reflecting on twenty years of leading change toward more value-based work environments, retired Hanover Insurance CEO Bill O'Brien says, "What people pressuring for management to 'drive' cultural change don't understand is: A value is only a value when it is voluntarily chosen."

Last, thoughtful executives know that many top management initiatives are not just ineffective, they often make matters worse. This is not just true for short-term financially driven changes that increase fear and internal competitiveness. It is equally true for many management efforts to improve organizational effectiveness. For example, Harvard's Chris Argyris has shown how management efforts to improve internal communications—like employee surveys, focus groups, and "360 feedback"—can give people anonymous ways to "tell management what is wrong" without assuming any responsibility for improving matters. The feedback process thereby subtly reinforces the view that management is the source of problems and only management has the power to fix them.

If the power of top management is in fact limited, why then do people in organizations continue to cling to the belief that only the top can drive change? As Argyris suggests, this belief allows us all to continue to

For more about the relationship between "commitment" and "compliance," see *The Fifth Discipline*, p. 218.

See "Good Communication that Blocks Learning," by Chris Argyris, Harvard Business Review, July/August 1994, p. 77.

hold the top responsible for whether or not change happens. While that view might be disempowering on one level, it provides a convenient strategy if our real goal is to preserve the status quo. Moreover, there are different types of change, some of which—like reorganizing or creating a new corporate strategy—can only be brought about by top management. Such top-driven changes are familiar to most of us—but they do not reduce fear and distrust, nor unleash imagination and creativity, nor enhance the quality of thinking in the organization. When people confuse top-driven change and profound change, it's easy to hold an exaggerated view of the power of top management, a confusion that no doubt persists among some top managers as well. Finally, we simply have no strategy for escaping the cultural addiction to the myth of the hero-leader. In the U.S., especially, it seems to be part of our cultural DNA. One goal of this book is to contribute toward such a strategy.

CHANGE, TRANSFORMATION, AND PROFOUND CHANGE

The original meaning of the old French word *changer* was "bend," or "turn," like a tree or vine searching for the sun. The idea that "the only constant is change" has been a truism of life since at least the time of Heracleitus, circa 500 B.C.

Today, in business and organizations, the word "change" means several often-contradictory things. It sometimes refers to external changes in technology, customers, competitors, market structure, or the social and political environment. ("We know our world will change, and we have to adapt along with it.") "Change" also refers to internal changes: how the organization adapts to changes in the environment. The timeless concern is whether these internal changes—in practices, views, and strategies—will keep pace with the external change.

Concerns over the pace of internal change lead executives to intervene. Hence today, "change" can also mean top-down programs like reorganizing, reengineering, and many other "re's." Because these change programs are typically imposed from the top, many in the organization feel threatened or manipulated by them—even if they support in principle the intent or rationale behind the management change agenda. As organizational change pioneer Richard Beckhard once put it, "People do not resist change; people resist being changed."

Today, some managers use the word "transformation" to describe comprehensive organizational change initiatives, such as those at General Electric and Shell Oil. We chose not to do that in this book. We recognize that transformation can mean many things to many people. As W. Edwards Deming said, "Nothing changes without personal transformation." Yet, perhaps because of the tradition of top-down change programs, we worry a bit about "corporate transformation" coming to mean "really large changes" imposed from top management. (The original Latin word *transformare* simply means "to change shape.") We also worry about the word's connotation of a singular episode of change, "transforming" the organization from one state to another. (Inventor Joseph Henry chose the term in 1830 to name his device for changing the voltage of electric current from one steady-state to another.)

In this book, we use the term "profound change" to describe organizational change that combines inner shifts in people's values, aspirations, and behaviors with "outer" shifts in processes, strategies, practices, and systems. The word "profound" stems from the Latin *fundus*, a base or foundation. It means, literally, "moving toward the fundamental." In profound change there is learning. The organization doesn't just do something new; it builds its capacity for doing things in a new way—indeed, it builds capacity for ongoing change. This emphasis on inner *and* outer changes gets to the heart of the issues that large industrial-age institutions are wrestling with today. It is not enough to change strategies, structures, and systems, unless the thinking that produced those strategies, structures, and systems also changes.

WHAT IS LEADERSHIP AND WHO ARE THE LEADERS?

In business today, the word "leader" has become a synonym for top manager. When people talk about "developing leaders" they mean developing prospective top managers. When they ask, "What do the leaders think?" they are asking about the views of top managers.

There are two problems with this. First, it implies that those who are not in top management positions are not leaders. They might aspire to "become" leaders, but they don't "get there" until they reach a senior management position of authority. Second, it leaves us with no real definition of leadership. If leadership is simply a position in the hierarchy, then, in effect, there is no independent definition of leadership. A person is either an executive or is not. There's nothing more to say about leadership. End of story.

We will look at leadership differently in this book.

We will view leadership as the capacity of a human community to shape its future, and specifically to sustain the significant processes of change required to do so. This is an unusual definition of leadership today, but actually not a new one. It is a definition that we think comes closer to most people's actual experience of leadership.

We believe, specifically, that leadership actually grows from the capacity to hold creative tension, the energy generated when people articulate a vision and tell the truth (to the best of their ability) about current reality. This also is not a new idea. "Leadership is vision," says Peter Drucker. Or, as expressed in Proverbs 29:18, "Where there is no vision, the people perish."

Most great leaders intuitively appreciate the principle of creative tension. Martin Luther King Jr. expressed the idea beautifully in his famous "letter from the Birmingham jail": "Just as Socrates felt that it was necessary to create a tension in the mind, so that individuals could rise from the bondage of myths and half-truths . . . so must we . . . create the kind of tension in society that will help men rise from the dark depths of prejudice and racism." While Dr. King is famous for his "dream," his leadership practice centered around "dramatizing the present situation" so that people could see the current reality of racism.

By this definition, any organization has many leaders because there are many people at many levels in the hierarchy who play critical roles in generating and sustaining creative tension. Consequently, we will focus on leadership communities rather than hero-leaders. This view of leadership communities has arisen gradually over the past ten years, as we have seen again and again, diverse people in diverse positions contribute vitally to the way that an enterprise shapes its future.

In particular, we have come to appreciate the interplay between three types of leaders:

■ **Local line leaders:** We have rarely seen any successful change initiatives that did not involve imaginative, committed local line leaders. By "local line leaders," we mean people with accountability for results and sufficient authority to undertake changes in the way that work is organized and conducted at their local level. This local level may be limited to a few people or involve a few thousand people. Local line leaders can be plant managers, heads of product develop-

66 ❧ etter from the Birmingham Jail," by Martin Luther King, Jr., written April 16, 1963, published at http://www.ai.mit.edu/~isbell/HFh/black /events and people/008.letter from jail.

ment teams, or sales managers. They can also be teachers or princi-pals, or nurse shift managers. Local line leaders are vital because only they and their colleagues, not executives, can undertake meaningful organizational experiments to test the practical impact of new ideas and approaches.

> Some of the line leaders telling their story in this book include Bob Womac at Ford Visteon (page 164), Dave Marsing at Intel (page 214), plant managers at British Petroleum (page 444), developers of practice fields at several organizations (page 91), Ehud Matya of Eskom (page 221), and the "mentors" at Covenant Insurance (page 128).

■ **Internal networkers, "network leaders," or community builders:** Likewise, we have never seen any examples of broad diffusion of new learning practices without the enthusiastic participation of effective internal networkers. Indeed, many studies of the diffusion of innova-tive practices show the importance of the informal networks through which new ideas and innovative practices spread organically in and across organizations. Internal networkers may be internal staff peo-ple, such as internal consultants or people in training or executive development departments. They may also be front line people—salespeople, manufacturing supervisors, or engineers who participate in ongoing "communities of practice."

See, for example, *Communities of Practice: Learning, Meaning, and Identity*, by Etienne Wenger (New York: Cambridge University Press, 1998).

Internal networkers are a natural counterpart to local line leaders. The great strength of local line leaders is their passion for creating better results within their unit; their limitation is that they often have limited contact beyond their unit. Internal networkers complement the provincialism of local line leaders. Their strength is their ability to move about the larger organization, to participate in and nurture broad networks of alliances with other, like-minded individuals, and to help local leaders, both by assisting directly and by putting them in contact with others who share their passions and from whom they can learn. They are the natural "seed carriers" of new ideas and new practices. Because they carry ideas, support, and stories through the organization, internal networkers can also help make executive lead-ers more aware of the support that change initiatives in the company need from them.

The role of internal networkers or community builders is tangible, but difficult to specify; because it belongs much more to the informal social networks of the company than it does to the hierarchy. In some ways, paradoxically, their lack of hierarchical authority makes them effective. When a "boss" calls a meeting, everyone has to show up.

The three types of leaders was originally discussed in "Leading Learning Organizations; The Bold, the Powerful, and the Invisible," in The Drucker Foundation's *The Leader of the Future*, by F. Hesselbein, M. Goldsmith, R. Beckhard, eds. (San Francisco: Jossey-Bass, 1996).

When a boss visits a local operation, everyone reacts. The boss may ask: "Who is committed to the new plan?" Everyone will respond affirmatively. By contrast, when someone without hierarchical authority organizes a meeting, only those who are interested show up. When she or he asks who wants to learn more, only those who are genuinely interested respond affirmatively.

The art of internal networking is described in this book by Ford's Vic Leo on page 167, by Shell's Linda Pierce on page 177, by David Meador of Detroit Edison (writing about his experience at Chrysler) on page 298, and by many others.

■ **Executive leaders:** None of the above implies that effective executive management is unimportant. If anything, it is more necessary today than ever, because the changes that institutions confront are long-term and "deep," in the sense of entailing shifts in hitherto taken-for-granted assumptions and norms, and in traditional organizational structures and practices. Effective executive leadership is probably more challenging today than ever before, especially because of the combination of the demands of profound change and extraordinary external pressures, like the investor pressures discussed above.

This role of executive leaders is complicated by the fact that they are one step removed from the organization's direct value-producing activities. They have overall accountability for organizational performance but less ability to directly influence actual work processes. They may be corporate presidents, vice presidents and directors, school superintendents, or hospital CEOs. They are vital to profound change through their efforts to create an organizational environment for continual innovation and knowledge generation.

They do this in many ways: through investing in new infrastructure for learning, through support and inquiry, and ultimately through "leadership by example," establishing new norms and behaviors within their own teams. They become mentors, coaches, and stewards. They focus on design more than on making key decisions. They work to push decisions down to more local levels, unless they are the only ones who can make those decisions.

We have found that the most effective executive leaders start by recognizing that "this is a new ballgame," and many of their own most trusted traditional skills and behaviors may be their biggest obstacles. To foster a more learning-oriented culture, they must give up feeling that they have to have all the answers. They must become more comfortable with, and capable of, asking questions that do not have easy answers. And they must realize that they cannot do this alone, that they need partners, that becoming isolated heroes will cut them off from the support and assistance that they must have to be effective.

Some of the executive leaders whose work is featured in this book include Fluor Corporation President and CEO Phil Carroll (formerly Shell Oil CEO) on page 203, former Eskom President Ian McRae on page 539, Mark Moody-Stuart, chairman of the Royal Dutch/Shell Committee of Managing Directors, on page 523, and retired General Gordon Sullivan, former Chief of Staff of the United States Army, on page 475.

Undoubtedly, this simple tripartite categorization of different types of leaders oversimplifies the reality of leadership communities. But at least it heads us in a direction away from isolated hero-leaders and toward a view of different people leading in different ways, who need each other to sustain significant change. In essence, leaders are people who "walk ahead," people genuinely committed to deep changes, in themselves and in their organization. They naturally influence others through their credibility, capability, and commitment. And they come in many shapes, sizes, and positions.

This taxonomy of "three leaders" has been influenced by Edgar Schein's analysis of the complementary role of executives, engineers, and operators in corporations. See Edgar H. Schein, "The Three Cultures of Management," *Sloan Management Review*, Fall 1996.

WHAT DO LEADERS DO ?

There is one other way in which we will look at leadership differently in this book. We will concentrate more on leadership activities in sustaining deep change processes, and less on leadership characteristics. Character matters. Moral formation matters. Conceptual skills matter. But so much has been written about the "characteristics and stories of great leaders," it is hard to see what more can be added. Moreover, books on great leaders and on leadership development tend, all too often, to subtly (or not so subtly) reinforce the hero-CEO myth. Instead we will concentrate on what leaders of all sorts do to sustain significant change. Ultimately, we believe this is more likely to help real people confronting real challenges.

The danger in focusing on leaders' actions is the temptation to resort to superficial "formulas" for how to lead effectively. In this book, we will use the biological perspective of growth processes and limiting processes to talk about leaders' actions strategically.

In particular, we will develop a systemic theory of the forces that naturally come into play to generate and to limit profound change in organizations. In doing this we will draw on the insights of practitioners,

The background for these ideas comes from many long-term change experiments that began in 1991 with the founding of the MIT Center for Organizational Learning (OLC), a consortium of corporations working together to advance the state of the art in organizational learning. In 1977, the OLC evolved into the broader-based Society for Organizational Learning (SoL). Experiments fostered at the OLC and then at SoL have occurred in cross-functional teams and in diverse functional areas—product development, sales, and manufacturing. They have occurred at many levels, from local operations, to engineering and sales teams, to business units, to top management teams. Most have been conducted in business organizations, but many have taken place in healthcare, education, and governmental organizations. Some of the experiments have been dramatically successful, in business and human terms. Others have failed to generate any meaningful change. Through them all, certain recurring lessons about leadership keep emerging.

We are indebted to Arie de Geus, Tom Johnson, Fritjof Capra, and a great many others for helping us realize the implications of seeing the organization as a living system. See the review of de Geus' book, *The Living Company*, p. 503; and Tom Johnson's contribution on p. 291.

consultants, and researchers who have been living with and studying such changes during the past two decades. This will enable us to examine in depth how different types of leaders work with these forces—the awareness they develop, the strategies they follow, and the lessons they have learned.

It will also enable us to understand how different types of leaders need one another. Ultimately, each of the three types of leadership can only function effectively when the others function effectively. While any one type may be sufficient to produce some meaningful changes, over the long term, the diversity of forces at play require all three types of leadership. A deficiency in any of the three will ultimately limit the effectiveness of the other two.

Also, exploring how leaders work with the forces that shape change will shed unique light on how people grow in their capabilities to lead. Leadership development constitutes an important concern in many organizations. But it also often focuses on classroom training and other traditional "learning" approaches. Here, our focus will be "OJT": on-the-job training. We believe that, ultimately, the most important learning occurs in the context of our day-to-day life, the aspirations we pursue, the challenges we face, and the responses we bring forth. Thus, the contributors to this book describe their "leadership development" in context: the real-life settings in which they face particular challenges and develop new capabilities, individually and collectively, to meet those challenges.

We call the perspective that emerges from thinking about leadership in this way an "ecological perspective" because it illuminates how diverse leaders' actions interact with one another and with the forces at play. It leads us to see leadership as a systemic phenomenon inseparable from its context. From this vantage point, leadership and sustaining change become two sides of the same coin.

As a great science teacher once said, "There is a world of difference between studying what a cell is, and studying how a cell functions." The former leads to memorizing an endless series of boring facts about membranes, nuclei, ectoplasm, and endoplasm. The latter leads to discovering that the cell is alive, continually interacting with its environment, generating the internal conditions for the DNA to do its mysterious dance of protein formation, maintaining the integrity of its cell wall, and continually rebuilding itself. In this same sense, we want to understand how a healthy leadership community in an organization functions, and how it enables people to shape their future.

While there is a great deal to be explored about how effective leadership communities function, there is also a clear starting point for the exploration. We are seeking to understand how people nurture the reinforcing growth processes that naturally enable an organization to evolve and change, and how they tend to the limiting processes that can impede or stop that growth.

The rest of this book will elaborate this perspective. Specifically:

■ What are the specific "reinforcing growth processes" that make profound change possible? Leaders nurture these reinforcing processes through their understanding and participation. How, specifically, do they do this?

■ What are the limiting forces that impede growth? What are the specific limits or constraints that come into play? How do they manifest themselves? What strategies do effective leaders pursue to relieve, or work around, the limits?

This represents a radical shift from thinking of leaders as heroes at the top who "drive change." You drive a car. It is a machine that you control, with the aim of getting to where you want to go. The car takes you there. You do not "drive" a plant to grow. Nor do you "drive" your teenager. Nor, we would argue, do leaders "drive" their organization. The organization is a human community. It is a living system, like the plant or the teenager. There is no one driving it. But there are many tending the garden.

4 The Challenges of Profound Change

Art Kleiner, Charlotte Roberts, Rick Ross, George Roth, Peter Senge, Bryan Smith

"THIS LEARNING STUFF" CAN WORK

In 1988, the *Harvard Business Review* carried an article called "Planning as Learning," by Arie de Geus, coordinator of group planning at Royal Dutch/Shell. Though he was not well known outside of Shell, his article resonated with a great many people—particularly this line:

The de Geus quote comes from "Planning as Learning," by Arie de Geus, *Harvard Business Review* (March/April, 1988): p. 74. The Welch quote comes from "Letter to Shareholders," by Jack Welch, in the *General Electric Annual Report* (Stamford, CT, 1996).

"We understand that the only competitive advantage the company of the future will have is its managers' ability to learn faster than their competitors."

Eight years later, the American CEO most admired by his peers, Jack Welch of General Electric, showed that he had come to the same conclusion. Welch made this statement in a GE annual report:

"Our behavior is driven by a fundamental core belief: The desire, and the ability of an organization to continuously learn from any source— and to rapidly convert this learning into action—is its ultimate competitive advantage."

⟩⟩ See the review of Arie de Geus' book *The Living Company*, on page 503. For more on the General Electric "culture change" initiative, see page 74.

Several other large companies—including Coca-Cola, First National Bancorp, Chevron, Mead Industries, Shell Oil, and Tenneco—have also featured the "learning organization" concept in recent annual reports. These and other corporate statements echo the theme that learning is the only infinitely renewable resource. Competitors can gain access to other resources: capital, labor, raw materials, and even technology and knowledge (for example, they can hire away your people). But no one can purchase, duplicate, or reverse-engineer an organization's ability to learn.

By now, there are many years of experience to draw upon from organizations that have explicitly sought to enhance their capacity to learn. While the gains from downsizing, reengineering, and "slash and burn" retrenchments often fail to sustain themselves, the gains from enhancing learning capacity have proven to be sustainable, cumulative, and self-reinforcing. Here are just a few examples described in this book:

- The Ford Motor Company's Electrical and Fuel Handling Division (EFHD, now part of Ford/Visteon, a freestanding Ford operation that combines all Ford's components businesses) had been a poorly regarded division, losing $50 million in 1991. It changed into a "successful learning community" that made more than $150 million in 1996. The division's sales doubled, and it expanded from three United States plants to ten around the world, with an unprecedented style of collegiality across international boundaries. "We talk about problems openly, without penalty, so the problems don't happen again," said one senior manager.

⟩⟩ See page 167 for more about fostering the effective development of change initiatives throughout Ford Motor Company.

■ "Transformation" endeavors at the Shell Oil Company in Houston, and more recently within the Royal Dutch/Shell group of companies worldwide, have been credited with sparking a renaissance of business initiative and innovation. Shell Oil has evolved a "federalist" governance structure, in which formerly bureaucratic entities like Shell Chemicals and Shell Services (formerly the "Administration" department, responsible for information technologies and other centralized services) have become new global businesses independent and viable in their own right.

⟩⟩ See pages 177, 203, 211, and 523 for more about Shell Oil and Royal Dutch/Shell.

■ The U.S. Army's highly innovative National Training Center uses elaborate practice fields, simulations, and "After Action Reviews" to build a sophisticated organizational self-awareness involving officers and enlisted men. The success of tactical operations in Desert Storm, Haiti, and Bosnia has been attributed to this new approach—and so has a recognizable leap in soldiers' capabilities and commitment.

⟩⟩ For more about the U.S. Army, see page 470.

Similar stories in this book cover a wide range of organizations: Detroit Edison, British Petroleum, Burch-Lowe, Chrysler, Covenant Insurance, Eskom, Harley-Davidson, Intel, Hewlett-Packard, Mitsubishi Electric, Scania, Springfield Remanufacturing Company, Toyota, Xerox, and many others. There are enough similar stories about schools to fill an entire Fifth Discipline Fieldbook on education (which is scheduled to appear early in the year 2000).

What about not profits?

Ultimately, these learning initiatives are judged through the lens of business results. People learning in business settings have no difficulty defining meaningful indicators of real progress—like time to market, customer loyalty, quality, and long-term profitability and growth. But people also ascribe meaning to the satisfaction of the journey itself. "This was the first time in [my long career] with this company that I, as an individual, felt valued by management," commented an engineer involved in a multiple-year learning initiative. "I felt that they had an absolute trust in me and in the team. Because I had trust from them, I

Quoted from Roth and Kleiner, *A Car Launch With Heart: The Story of AutoCo Epsilon*, by George Roth, Art Kleiner, et al. (New York: Oxford University Press, 1999) pp. 25–26.

put a lot of trust in my team. On other programs, I was constantly double checking and telling people what to do—not asking them, 'What do you think we should do?' It's enthused a lot of people who have not been enthused at this company for twenty years."

Each of the authors of this book has had the experience of being pulled aside by a manager or executive. "I just want to tell you," the manager will say, "what I appreciate more than anything else about this work. I've rediscovered my love of learning."

LEARNING VERSUS "TRAINING" AND "TEACHING"

To many people in business, "learning" means "training." They seem to see learning as a frill, with no link to business results (or other desired results). At worst, learning means "taking in information"—listening to a lecture or reading an assigned text, with no relevance to the future you are creating.

This view may come from the passive style of rote learning that many people associate with school. The word "training" originally meant "directing the course of a plant": to be trained is to be controlled.

But the word "learning" derives from the Indo-European *leis*, a noun meaning "track" or "furrow." To "learn" means to enhance capacity through experience gained by following a track or discipline. Learning always occurs over time and in "real life" contexts, not in classrooms or training sessions. This type of learning may be difficult to control, but it generates knowledge that lasts: enhanced capacity for effective action in settings that matter to the learner.

All organizations learn—in the sense of adapting as the world around them changes. But some organizations are faster and more effective learners. The key is to see learning as inseparable from everyday work. (Training, by contrast, is typically episodic and detached from the context in which results are produced.)

THIS "LEARNING STUFF" CAN BE DANGEROUS (THE CHALLENGES OF SUSTAINING PROGRESS)

But amid all of the success and satisfaction, there are also many stories of failure, setbacks, and organizational backlash. Some learning initiatives never seem to get off the ground, despite interest, resources, and a compelling business case. In other cases, initial success is never recognized. Innovators who expected to be rewarded and promoted lose their jobs instead. Or they just move on, searching for organizational settings more open to their ideas. Even after years of success, learning-oriented cultures can come under relentless attack from new bosses, new members who don't appreciate their benefits, or sudden changes in the business environment that lead to a perceived need for tighter controls. Unexpected problems seem to come from nowhere. We who have been working in the field of organizational learning for many years have experienced all of the above problems, and a few more. Indeed, leaders of innovation have faced these sorts of setbacks for the two-hundred-year history of modern corporations, and throughout human history.

Recognizing that learning is not just a matter of good intentions, some leaders seek to reinforce those intentions with shifts in governance structures or top-down policies. Jack Welch, in his 1997 letter to GE shareholders, pointed to "critical enablers," such as new compensation and appraisal mechanisms, as essential mechanisms "if the rhetoric [of organizational learning] is to become reality."

While changes in measurement and performance appraisal mechanisms might be important, we are skeptical about whether they are sufficient. In fact, inappropriate measurement of people's performance is but one of several limits to learning. There are equally deep and difficult impediments to change. For example, an unspoken attitude that "managers should never present problems—only solutions" could ensure, if unchallenged, that all reward systems promote "lone ranger–style" heroics and discount team learning. Unless this assumption is openly examined and unless it eventually shifts, any new performance appraisal mechanism that managers design will simply reproduce the same chronic problems that plagued the company before.

⟩⟩ For more on this issue, see the challenge of "Walking the Talk," page 193.

So far, we have identified ten distinct challenges—sets of forces that oppose profound change (as well as three growth processes that sustain such changes). Each grows from distinct limits to learning and change. Although we have encountered these challenges in the context of "learning initiatives"—change initiatives in which enhancing learning capability was an overt part of the strategy—we believe they will just as likely come into play in all initiatives aimed at deep and extensive change.

For more of the historical perspective on corporate change, see *The Age of Heretics*, by Art Kleiner (New York: Doubleday, 1996).

They are, as best we can tell, the organizational analogs to water, soil nutrients, sunlight, and space for roots to spread. They are the limits to any profound change process, and any one of them can be sufficient to thwart such change.

All of these challenges are predictable. They arise as natural counter-pressures to generating change, just as the need for soil, sunlight, and water arise as natural limits when plants start to grow. Though they often appear as seemingly independent events, they are interconnected and interdependent. There are high-leverage strategies that can help teams and individuals deal with each challenge separately. But the greatest leverage comes from understanding them as an ensemble of forces.

Failure to understand these limits and the challenge they generate is the source of countless frustrations for committed leaders. For those readers who have struggled with the norms of control and intimidation in traditional cultures, who have coped with being judged as ineffective amid abundant evidence that new innovations are working, and who have had to protect subordinates from the larger corporate culture, it is easy to become discouraged. It seems like the harder you push, the harder "the system pushes back."

In fact, this is exactly correct—the system *is* pushing back. The organizational limiting processes naturally represent the "homeostatic" forces of industrial-age organizations. The fundamental flaw in most innovators' strategies is that they focus on their innovation, on what they are trying to do—rather than on understanding how the larger culture, structures, and norms will react to their efforts. Based on the experience of those who seem to be sustaining progress, we have come to the view that no progress is sustainable unless innovators learn to understand why the system is pushing back, and how their own attitudes and perceptions (as well as other forces) contribute to the "pushback." When they see this, they start to develop systemic strategies for sustaining profound change.

TEN CHALLENGES

The challenges of initiating change develop as soon as any "pilot group" (which could be a local team or business unit, or a senior management team) begins to conduct its work in unfamiliar ways:

- "We don't have time for this stuff!"—The challenge of control over one's time. People involved in change initiatives need enough flexibility to devote time to reflection and practice (page 67).

- "We have no help!"—The challenge of inadequate coaching, guidance, and support for innovating groups, and of ultimately developing internal resources for building capacity (page 103).
- "This stuff isn't relevant!"—The challenge of relevance: making a case for change, articulating an appropriate business focus, and showing why new efforts, such as developing learning capabilities, are relevant for business goals (page 159).
- "They're not walking the talk!"—The challenge of management clarity and consistency: the mismatch between behavior and espoused values, especially for those championing change (page 193).

The challenges of sustaining momentum take place within a pilot team as it achieves early success, and between the team and the larger organizational culture.

- "This stuff is _____."—The challenge of fear and anxiety: concerns about exposure, vulnerability, and inadequacy, triggered by the conflict between increasing levels of candor and openness and low levels of trust among pilot group members (page 241).
- "This stuff isn't working!"—The challenge of negative assessment of progress: the disconnect between the organization's traditional ways of measuring success (both metrics and time horizon) and the achievements of a pilot group (page 281).
- "We have the right way!"/"They don't understand us!"—The challenge of isolation and arrogance, which appears when the "true believers" within the pilot group confront their "nonbeliever" counterparts outside the group; the pilot group and the rest of the organizational system consistently misinterpret each other (page 319).

The challenges of redesigning and rethinking appear when change initiatives gain broader credibility and confront the established internal infrastructure and practices of the organization:

- "Who's in charge of this stuff?"—The challenge of the prevailing governance structure, and the conflicts between pilot groups seeking greater autonomy, and managers concerned about autonomy leading to chaos and internal fragmentation (page 361).
- "We keep reinventing the wheel!"—The challenge of diffusion, the inability to transfer knowledge across organizational boundaries, making it difficult for people around the system to build upon each others' successes (page 417).

The blank represents the wide range of comments people might make to mask fear and anxiety they feel: "This stuff is a waste of time," or, "This stuff is out of control," or, "This stuff is very interesting . . ."

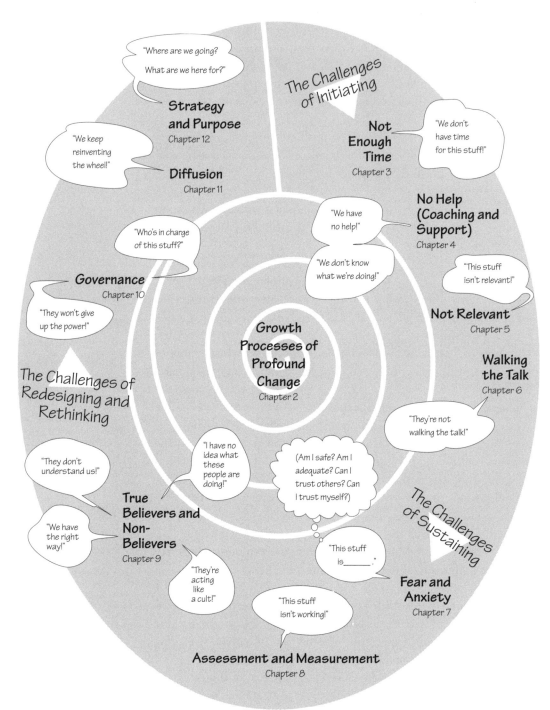

■ "Where are we going?" and "What are we here for?"—The challenge of organizational strategy and purpose: revitalizing and rethinking the organization's intended business focus, its contribution to its community, and its identity (page 487).

CHALLENGES

It is customary, in the West at least, to hear the term "challenges" and immediately gear ourselves to "overcoming" hurdles. Indeed, the word's roots come from the Latin *calumnia*, or "deception." But there is an alternative meaning, suggested by natural systems, where "challenges" are simply the conditions of the environment that regulate growth.

As more complex organisms, like human systems, evolve and grow, they contribute to their own limits or challenges. Historian Arnold Toynbee, for instance, proposed the influential theory of "challenge and response": that civilizations sustain their existence through their creative development in response to new large-scale challenges, which in turn are often the consequence of their prior development. In that spirit, challenges are opportunities to improve—by exercising our attention, understanding, and ultimate creativity. This is not dissimilar to the Chinese notion of crisis: two symbols meaning "danger" and "opportunity."

See *A Study of History*, by Arnold Toynbee, vol. 1 (London: Oxford University Press, 1934), and the abridgement of vols. 1–6, edited by D. C. Somervell (London: Oxford University Press, 1947).

There is no guarantee that you will encounter all ten challenges. You will likely encounter others we have not yet identified. But we believe that leaders seeking to sustain profound change should at least understand these limits.

In this book, we start with the challenges of initiating (such as "not enough time") because, by and large, these challenges must be confronted at the outset. After some progress has been achieved, one is likely to encounter the challenges of sustaining momentum. The challenges of redesigning and rethinking may be present from the beginning, but they will tend to manifest as obvious impediments after some success and legitimacy have been achieved. Within that general pattern, each organization will encounter its challenges in its own sequence.

Although the symptoms may appear isolated from one another, the challenges are fundamentally interdependent. Success in one challenge may make it easier, or harder, to deal with others.

The spiral at the center of the "Ten Challenges" diagram on the opposite page represents the source of momentum for a change initiative: the basic growth processes that reinforce and spread significant organizational learning. This momentum, however, is offset by a variety of contrary forces, each seeking to maintain a balance that might be disrupted by change. These "challenges" are arrayed in clockwise order around the outside of the circle. Dialogue represents symptoms that appear when the challenge emerges.

}} For a full discussion of these interdependencies, see page 561.

See Virginia O'Brien's book *Success on Our Own Terms* (New York: John Wiley, 1998). The report was "A Solid Investment: Making Full Use of the Nation's Human Capital," by the U.S. Department of Labor Glass Ceiling Commission (Washington, D.C.: U.S. Government Printing Office, 1995). Available online at *http://www.ilr. cornell.edu/library/e_archive/ glassceiling.*

As noted above, these challenges occur not just in "learning organization" initiatives, but in any organizational change movement aimed at making deep changes in systems and practices, and in people's attitudes and behavior. Writer Virginia O'Brien, for example, points out that they have all been visible in efforts by women and minority members to establish an equitable presence in the workplace. According to one prominent report, successful initiatives had to include the following elements: support from the CEO (to meet the challenge of "walking the talk"); research on the barriers created by clashing assumptions (the challenge of true believers); programs to recruit and develop new behaviors (the challenge of "no help"); reducing barriers between different parts of the organization (diffusion); linkage initiatives to business plans (not relevant); goals and managerial accountability for progress (measurement); gender-neutral rewards and promotions (governance); and other provisions that resonated with other challenges described here.

The stronger a learning or change initiative, the stronger the challenges seem to be, because they represent natural systemic responses to maintaining balances threatened by the initiative. At the same time, the earlier and more clearly that you can anticipate these challenges, the easier it becomes to deal with them. You don't have to wait until the challenges become visible; the best time to prepare for them is before they have appeared. They require investments of time and energy that may not be possible once you are facing the problems directly.

As leaders at all levels deal with these challenges (and others) regularly, they may gradually cease to appear as challenges at all. They will become aspects of life, episodes that bolster and strengthen those committed to genuine change, bringing new capabilities and new understanding. For each of us, the authors, dealing with them has helped us to see things about ourselves—like a tendency to blow up or get discouraged in the face of resistance. Ultimately, as a wise advisor once suggested, "reality is not the adversary."

QUESTIONS FOR CONSIDERING CHALLENGES

As you read about the challenges in this book, these questions can help you link them to your own experience and future.

1. Do I see the challenge in my situation? Am I aware of the set of forces that might be working counter to my efforts? Many chal-

lenges to sustaining significant organizational change are invisible at first.

2. Do I understand the nature of the challenge? How do I tend to see it? Can I see it differently? How do others see me when this challenge is encountered? These questions establish an orientation of inquiry toward important developments that we might otherwise see only as barriers blocking our path. Blaming "barriers" tends to evoke our most habitual, not our most creative, responses.

3. Who can best help me in understanding and dealing with this challenge? How might we help each other? Many of us set out to conquer our problems single-handedly. But most of the time, these challenges do not impact us as individuals. We can operate much more effectively by sharing our efforts with colleagues who are part of the same "system," or whose abilities and interests complement our own.

4. What would constitute effective action in dealing with this challenge? What capabilities might we want to develop? All too often, people's actions represent reactions to circumstances rather than considered strategies aimed at deep aspirations. This question helps you look strategically at your actions over the next several years.

5. How will I know if I am making progress? No strategy is ever completely apt, so all courses of action need to be continually assessed. But most people, when acting, stop paying attention to what is going on around them. Focused on moving forward, they lose sight of the effects they are having, especially those on the periphery of attention. Because the challenges of profound change are complex, it is pivotal to remain open to continually see them more clearly.

The background of this book

IN PREPARING THIS BOOK, THE AUTHORS HAVE DRAWN UPON THE FIELDS OF ORGANIZATIONAL learning, system dynamics, action science, "double-loop learning," process consultation, the creative orientation, dialogue, governance design, scenario planning, quantum physics, and ecology. We have listened closely to the insights of countless corporate practitioners, consultants, and academic researchers who have wrestled with the challenges of profound change. And we have built upon our own work and research over the last two decades.

In 1990, Peter Senge's book *The Fifth Discipline* codified much of this experience into a set of practices (the five "learning disciplines") for building learning capabilities in organizations. Each of the five disci-

See *The Fifth Discipline* by Peter Senge (New York: Doubleday/Currency, 1990), particularly pp. 5–13.

plines represents a lifelong body of study and practice for individuals and teams in organizations:

- **Personal Mastery:** This discipline of aspiration involves formulating a coherent picture of the results people most desire to gain as individuals (their personal vision), alongside a realistic assessment of the current state of their lives today (their current reality). Learning to cultivate the tension between vision and reality (represented in this icon by the rubber band) can expand people's capacity to make better choices, and to achieve more of the results that they have chosen.

- **Mental Models:** This discipline of reflection and inquiry skills is focused around developing awareness of the attitudes and perceptions that influence thought and interaction. By continually reflecting upon, talking about, and reconsidering these internal pictures of the world, people can gain more capability in governing their actions and decisions. The icon here portrays one of the more powerful principles of this discipline, the "ladder of inference" depicting how people leap instantly to counterproductive conclusions and assumptions.

- **Shared Vision:** This collective discipline establishes a focus on mutual purpose. People learn to nourish a sense of commitment in a group or organization by developing shared images of the future they seek to create (symbolized by the eye), and the principles and guiding practices by which they hope to get there.

- **Team Learning:** This is a discipline of group interaction. Through techniques like dialogue and skillful discussion, teams transform their collective thinking, learning to mobilize their energies and actions to achieve common goals, and drawing forth an intelligence and ability greater than the sum of individual members' talents. The icon symbolizes the natural alignment of a learning-oriented team as the flight of a flock of birds.

- **Systems Thinking:** In this discipline, people learn to better understand interdependency and change, and thereby to deal more effectively with the forces that shape the consequences of our actions. Systems thinking is based upon a growing body of theory about the behavior of feedback and complexity—the innate tendencies of a system that lead to growth or stability over time. Tools and techniques such as system archetypes and various types of learning labs and simulations help people see how to change systems more effectively, and how to act more in tune with the larger processes of the natural and economic world. The circle in this icon represents the fundamental building block of all systems: the circular "feedback loop" underlying all growing and limiting processes in nature.

}} There are several different kinds of systems thinking; see page 137.

After *The Fifth Discipline* was published, many readers wanted to know more about getting started. "What should we do Monday morning?" they asked. To answer, the authors of this book created *The Fifth Discipline Fieldbook* (1994, Doubleday/Currency)—a compendium of practice guides, exercises, stories, resource reviews, and short essays, all aimed at helping people implement the disciplines on a day-to-day basis in a wide variety of settings. Like *The Dance of Change*, *The Fifth Discipline Fieldbook* was organized as a fieldbook of "notes from the field," giving voice to dozens of leading practitioners. It was not intended primarily as a book of theory, but it embodied a key theoretical argument:

- Organizations are products of the ways that people in them think and interact.
- To change organizations for the better, you must give people the opportunity to change the ways they think and interact.
- This cannot be done through increased training, or through command-and-control management approaches. No one person, including a highly charismatic teacher or CEO, can train or command other people to alter their attitudes, beliefs, skills, capabilities, perceptions, or level of commitment.
- Instead, the practice of organizational learning involves developing tangible activities: new governing ideas, innovations in infrastructure, and new management methods and tools for changing the way people conduct their work. Given the opportunity to take part in these new activities, people will develop an enduring capability for change. The process will pay back the organization with far greater levels of diversity, commitment, innovation, and talent.

Since *The Fifth Discipline Fieldbook* appeared, we have been increasingly aware of the challenges facing change initiatives. With this theme in mind, a series of intensive working sessions were conducted by the Massachusetts Institute of Technology (MIT) Center for Organizational Learning (now the Society for Organizational Learning, or SoL), during 1994 and 1995. Some sessions involved senior executives; others, mid-level staff people; and still others, line leaders. Meeting together from a variety of companies and organizations, they reflected on their common experiences and approaches to leadership. In particular, they focused on understanding: "What forces seemed to propel organizational learning efforts forward or to slow them down?"

Peter Senge brought the results of these sessions to the rest of *The Fifth Discipline Fieldbook* authors, and invited us to consider their insights in the light of our own experience and thinking. As we critiqued and expanded upon that body of work, we developed the ten challenges enumerated in this book. We then set out to find stories of organizations and thinkers who had dealt effectively with them.

This book is just a beginning. If the framework it presents is effective, like Mercator's grid, it will only be so as part of a new era of exploration and learning.

For ongoing information and inquiry, see the Web site maintained for *The Dance of Change* and *The Fifth Discipline Fieldbook*: http://www.fieldbook.com.

5 How to Read This Book

START ANYWHERE. GO ANYWHERE.

We have designed the book to reward browsing in any direction. Cross-references embedded in the text, for example, point out meaningful links to follow.

MAKE THE BOOK YOUR OWN.

Mark up the pages. Write answers to the solo exercises in the margins. Draw. Scribble. Daydream. Note the results of what you have tried, and ideas of what you would like to try. Over time, as your field notes accumulate, they will become a record of effective practices—and a tool for reflecting on the design of the next stage of your change initiative.

USE THE EXERCISES AND TECHNIQUES.

Exercises and techniques produce a different kind of learning than simply reading about the work. If you feel "I already know that," ask yourself, honestly: Does your knowledge about these skills and methods show up in your performance? If not, then we suggest trying the approaches, techniques, and exercises that seem useful.

ENGAGE OTHERS IN THINKING ABOUT CHANGE.

Organizations, like all human groups, operate through conversation. The ideas in this book gain most of their value not as "answers" to take in by yourself, but as starting points for conversation with others. Through talking, testing, and choosing your next actions together, you can create your own answers.

Margin icons.

To MAKE BROWSING THROUGH THE BOOK EASIER, WE USE ICONS (SMALL GRAPHIC SYMbols) to indicate different types of material. In addition to icons for the five learning disciplines (shown on page 32), these icons will appear in the margins regularly:

- **Local line leaders:** Material of particular interest to organizational leaders with accountability for results at the local level and sufficient authority to undertake the way work is organized and conducted.
- **Executive leaders:** Material of particular interest to senior leaders, removed from the organization's direct value producing activities, but accountable for overall organizational performance.
- **Internal networkers and community builders:** Material of particular interest to organizational "seed carriers" and exchangers of knowledge and information about learning and change.

〉〉 For more about the three types of leaders, see page 16.

- **Tool kit:** A practical device or technique.

- **Solo exercise:** An exercise that you practice alone—to deepen your understanding and capability, to bring forth an example from your own experience, to set personal direction, or to provoke an "aha!"

■ **Team exercise:** An exercise for a group of people working together, sometimes conducted by a facilitator or team leader.

■ **Lexicon:** A guide to the roots of the words we use, and the way we use them now. Staking out the precise meaning of words is important in a field like management, where so much jargon is used so loosely.

■ **Resource**: Recommendations of books, articles, videotapes, and Web sites that we have found valuable.

■ **Roundtable:** A group of several people in conversation (or collective comment) on a single subject.

■ **Guiding idea:** A principle (or set of principles) that we find meaningful as a philosophical source of light and direction.

The "systems diagrams"

THE "LIMITS TO GROWTH" ARCHETYPE AT THE HEART OF THIS BOOK IS GROUNDED IN A body of theory, simulation, and practices called "system dynamics," with its own diagramming language. Many people find the diagrams useful because they represent interrelationships that are difficult to describe in text: nonsequential, nonlinear relationships that interact over time, complete with delays and mental models. The diagrams also provide a way to sketch out systemic interrelationships in your own situation.

For example, consider the simple act of filling a glass of water. In text, you might write: "I turn on the faucet, and water comes out."

But in a systems diagram, as shown here, filling the glass is not just an event. It's part of an ongoing water-regulation system, involving your mind, the faucet, and the glass. There is a desired water level in your mind (since you're thirsty). This creates a gap between your desire and

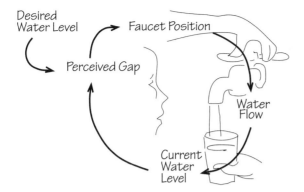

the current water level in the (empty) glass. That gap, through the medium of your hand, changes the faucet position. That, in turn, influences the water flow, which affects the current water level in the glass. The glass's water level also influences the perceived gap in your mind (your thirst); once again, through your hand, the perceived gap changes the water level.

In this book, we illustrate systems concepts in both the diagrams and in the text. Whether you use the diagrams or not, please recognize that a systems understanding can help you recognize the presence of growth forces carrying you forward, and limiting forces that may constrain your growth.

The authors wish to thank Michael Goodman, director of the systems thinking practice at Innovation Associates, for his consultation on the systems material in this book.

HOW TO READ A SYSTEMS DIAGRAM

The diagram on the next page, based on one of the initial "growth processes" of profound change, shows the basic symbols used in all the systems diagrams in this book. To read any diagram like this, follow these steps.

1. **Pick an element to start with**, one representing a part of the system you know well or can take some action in. For instance, you might start with "Investment in change initiatives."
2. **Any element may go up or down at various points in time.** Try to describe the movement of this element: "As the investment in change initiatives goes up . . ." ("increases," "rises," etc.). Then describe the impact this movement produces on the next element. ". . . The result, after some delay, is a rise in learning capabilities . . ."
3. **Continue the story back around the loop.** Use phrases that show causal interrelationship: "This in turn causes an increase in 'personal

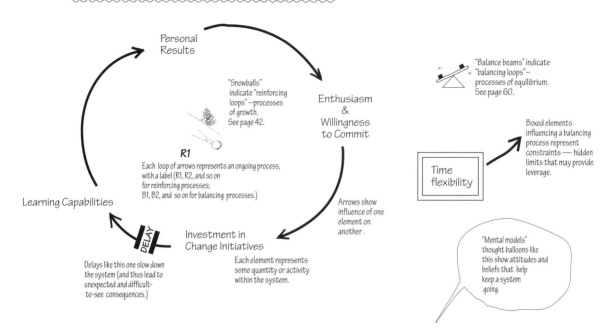

This diagram, adapted from the diagram on page 54, shows a basic reinforcing process endemic to profound organizational change. Each element of the diagram is identified. Around the right side of the diagram are three more elements (mental models thought balloons, balancing loops, and constraints), not part of this process, that will appear in other diagrams throughout this book.

results' (feelings of excitement, authenticity, and connectedness) that lead to higher levels of enthusiasm and willingness to commit. As a result, investments in change initiatives are further increased . . ."

4. **Test your understanding with a group of people.** Systems thinking is not best conducted as a solitary practice, because each person brings new insights and new perspectives about the reasons for these underlying dynamics.

See: The growth processes of profound change, page 42, "Limits Ahead," page 60; and "Five Kinds of Systems Thinking," page 137.

II. Generating Profound Change

1 Establishing a Pilot Group

Peter Senge

All living systems start small. Each of us once began as an embryo, smaller than a fingernail. The mighty sequoia tree begins in the humblest seed. It is no different in growing a new organizational culture. Once we surrender the myth that a "heroic CEO creates change," we understand that all great things have small beginnings—and we begin thinking naturally in terms of "pilot groups."

Unless some kind of pilot group can coalesce, new ideas in an organization have no incubator, no place where concept can become capability, where theory can meet practice. Thus, for at least the first several months, more likely than not, most of the action in a profound change initiative will take place at a pilot group level.

Pilot groups may be as small as five people or as large as a business unit of a thousand or more people. A pilot group could be a cross-functional team, working on a particular project; a functional team, like a product development team; or a team of the CEO and other senior executives, intending to lead by example, rather than by proclamation. Sometimes, the pilot group may comprise an informal network of people, with no hierarchical authority or mandate—but influence based on their credibility and commitment.

But while many aspects of a pilot group may vary, the line leaders who create pilot groups have a certain kind of predisposition. They are typically not "true believers" in systems thinking or "learning organiza-

The idea of "predisposition" is borrowed from an unpublished work by Vic Leo, Ford Motor Company.

tions." They are usually open-minded pragmatists. Sometimes they have an innate curiosity in a particular set of ideas like mental models or scenario thinking. Sometimes notions like building shared vision or dialogue resonate deeply with their prior experiences. Sometimes they bring a background from the quality movement, their college studies, or time in another culture that predisposes them to look differently at their current situation. Always they are people with deep concerns about practical problems and an openness to experiment. They are like former Ford product development manager Fred Simon, who says: "I wasn't convinced that this learning stuff would work, but I knew we would never achieve our goals if we kept working the way we were working."

There may be several pilot groups in an organization, often with little or no knowledge of one another. At the Shell Oil Company in Houston, in the early 1990s, one group in Exploration and Production applied the ideas of Steven Covey to their work; several groups experimented with self-managed teams at refineries and other facilities; other "skunk works"–style groups carried out relatively small, self-contained projects aimed at instilling new skills and approaches. In 1994, the work of all these pilot groups found a corporate context when the new CEO, Phil Carroll, and his senior management team embarked on a companywide transformation, starting with their own ways of working. This "Leadership Council" became, in effect, another pilot group. Soon, the top two hundred managers began to convene annually for reflection and conversation, out of which new pilot groups gradually formed, headed by local line leaders. At the same time, another pilot group emerged of key network leaders, intent on raising the quality of Shell's in-house coaching and capacity-building (see page 177).

In other organizations, such as Ford and BP, one or two pilot groups, operating more or less autonomously, achieved noticeable business results. While the presence of results wasn't compelling enough to spark immediate interest from the rest of the organization as a whole, it intrigued other leaders who fostered their own pilot groups.

Pilot group organizers may also find much of value in The Fifth Discipline Fieldbook, particularly: "The Wheel of Learning" (p. 59); "Opening Moves" (p. 77); "Exploring Your Own Story" (p. 103); the Reflection and Inquiry material on pp. 242–73; the Team Learning chapter, especially "Skillful Discussion" (p. 385); "Operating Principles for Building Community" (p. 525); and the Lincoln Continental story (p. 554).

Some particularly effective articles for people organizing pilot groups include: "Limits Ahead," page 60; "A Cadre of Coaches," page 111; "What Are We Doing This For?," page 166; "The Pinecone Strategy," page 174; "After Fixing the Crisis," page 183; and "Four Futures," page 187.

THE FIRST BASIC CHOICE: AUTHORITY- OR LEARNING-DRIVEN?

Even at this earliest stage of initiating change, a subtle choice will set the ongoing tone. Will it be authority-driven? Will the impetus and planning come from the energy of the original authors of the initiative alone—charismatic hero-leaders propelling the activities of others? Or will the change effort be driven by widespread commitment, involving the aspirations and capabilities of the many people involved in it? The former approach characterizes most change initiatives. The latter characterizes the strategies of leaders who appreciate the development of learning capabilities.

Change driven by authority is more efficient to organize, often more effective in the short run, and more immediately comfortable for people in many organizations. If all goes well, great results may occur; productivity and profitability may soar. So may morale, as employees recognize that "things are getting better." But even in this "best of all possible authoritarian initiatives," the change effort is powerful only so long as it is pushed. Success often depends entirely on a single leader's continued effort to feed the system with enthusiasm, ideas, and initiative. When the leader moves on or loses interest or energy, or actions fail to produce desired results for some reason, then the force of the initiative begins to decelerate. A few failures or setbacks, and the energy for change might dissipate altogether.

But what if the initiative is driven by learning?

To succeed, it would need to involve repeated opportunities for small actions that individuals could design, initiate, and implement themselves. First on a small scale, and then with increasingly larger numbers of people and activities, participants would articulate the goals they would like to achieve, experiment with new projects and initiatives, learn from their successes and mistakes, and talk with each other, candidly and openly, about the results. This would build commitment through participation and action. It would also naturally draw in new people who share similar values and aspirations.

This type of change process can become self-perpetuating. If one of its executive sponsors or charismatic leaders disappeared halfway through, the initiative might change somewhat, but it would keep going, because its vitality would not depend on any one individual. A learning-oriented strategy aims to produce self-sustaining change in a way that continually accelerates its own growth and development. In systems terms, it operates as a "virtuous reinforcing cycle."

i.e. Diversity

2 The Growth Processes of Profound Change

Nothing can grow in a self-sustaining way unless there are reinforcing processes underlying its growth. Therefore, thinking strategically about initiating, sustaining, and spreading fundamental management innovations over time requires appreciating the reinforcing processes that could cause such growth. In our experience, most effective leaders have tacit theories of growth, and these theories guide their actions, for better or worse.

Probably the most common tacit theory of why change initiatives should spread is the "better mousetrap theory": If an innovation or change initiative is successful, interest will spread, and, as the old adage goes, "the world will make a beaten path to our door." We've heard the better mousetrap theory invoked countless times, especially from innovative local line leaders. As one engineering manager put it, "Our approach was to let the results speak for themselves."

But there are real reasons to question the better mousetrap theory in organizations. First, the number of proven managerial innovations that never spread is legion. Innovations like process improvements or high-performance teams often die out after a few years, or chug along for decades unseen by the rest of the organization. Second, even when innovators produce a visible, influential success, they are often at risk within their organizations—sometimes because of their success and visibility. Rather than being welcomed with open arms and asked to share their insights and methods, they are often a source of threat and embarrassment to others. Third, the better mousetrap theory often causes people to focus exclusively on the "low-hanging fruit," to show quickly the practical consequences of their new ideas. While there is nothing inherently wrong with building momentum in this way, it often blinds champions of change efforts to the deeper issues that their changes will eventually reveal, and to their inability to deal with these issues. Consequently, they may fail to develop the learning capabilities needed to sustain change; they may harvest some easy victories only to find the energy behind their efforts faltering.

We believe there are at least three fundamental reinforcing processes that sustain profound change by building upon each other, only one of which is concerned explicitly with improved business results:

The "mousetrap quote" derives from a lecture by Ralph Waldo Emerson, quoted in *Borrowings* by Sarah S. B. Yule and Mary S. Keene (1889). The original passage reads: "If a man can write a better book, preach a better sermon, or make a better mouse-trap than his neighbor, though he build his house in the woods, the world will make a beaten path to his door." The "results" quote comes from Roth and Kleiner, *A Car Launch With Heart: The Story of AutoCo Epsilon*, by George Roth, Art Kleiner, et al. (New York: Oxford University Press, 1999).

For more about reinforcing cycles, see *The Fifth Discipline*, p. 79, and *The Fifth Discipline Fieldbook*, p. 114.

- enhancing personal results
- developing networks of committed people; and
- improving business results.

To understand these reinforcing processes, it is easiest to start where most leaders start: investing themselves in profound change initiatives.

INVESTMENT IN CHANGE INITIATIVES

Profound change requires investment—of time, energy, and resources. It requires at least an initial core pilot group, genuinely committed to new organizational purposes, methods, and working environments.

The most important change initiatives seem to have these qualities:

Investment
in Change
Initiatives

- They are connected with real work goals and processes;
- They are connected with improving performance;
- They involve people who have the power to take action regarding these goals;
- They seek to balance action and reflection, connecting inquiry and experimentation;
- They afford people an increased amount of "white space": opportunities for people to think and reflect without pressure to make decisions;
- They are intended to increase people's capacity, individually and collectively; and
- They focus on learning about learning, in settings that matter.

This list is adapted from "Assessing to Learn and Learning to Assess," *Report of the First Forum on the SoL Assessment Initiative,* January 1998, Society for Organizational Learning, Cambridge, MA (available from the SoL Web page: *http://www.SoL-NE.org*).

Such change efforts don't just approach business issues as onetime problems needing a solution. They see many business problems as symptomatic of deeper issues. Often, for example, nearly everyone in an office is aware of a chronic problem consuming resources and destroying morale, but no one does anything about it. The "problem" in such a case is not the obvious symptoms that need to be "fixed": The real problem is the forces that have kept people from doing anything about these symptoms for so long. Tackling such fundamental issues requires time for reflection, a deliberate focus on challenging difficult "undiscussable" issues, and an attempt to bridge internal boundaries to help grapple with systemwide problems.

Profound change initiatives come in many shapes and sizes. They can be as simple as a series of meetings on a crucial business objective or as complex as a corporatewide "transformation." They are often linked to other types of corporate change activities: in-depth quality improvement efforts, "sociotechnical" high-performance team projects, marketing reorganizations, and participative process redesign efforts. Many corporate environmentalism efforts represent serious change initiatives, because their success depends upon the ability of participants to rethink their basic business processes and their underlying purpose.

In our experience, the most effective initiatives create environments for learning by incorporating three cornerstones:

■ **New guiding ideas:** "The problem with most organizations," says retired CEO Bill O'Brien, "is that they are governed by mediocre ideas." When articulated and talked about openly, compelling new ideas help people think and act in new ways. The quality movement, for example, took much of its power from a guiding idea introduced first in Japan and then in the U.S.: Increasing quality did not necessarily mean increasing cost; in fact, low quality and high costs may both be the consequence of poor processes. Similarly, ideas like "openness" (developing a genuine spirit of inquiry and trust), "localness" (decisions should be made at the lowest possible level of the hierarchy), and "intrinsic motivation" (people are naturally motivated to learn) often play critical roles in profound change processes.

■ **Innovations in infrastructure**: New practices, policies, and resources are needed to channel activity in new directions. These might include new governance structures, new vehicles for exchanging information across boundaries, new systems for measuring success, and new ways to integrate learning and working. An example of the latter is the U.S. Army's After Action Reviews (AARs). This involves a carefully designed process for bringing together a vertical cross section of a combat unit, either after simulated or real battles, to collectively analyze decision making at all levels. AARs provide a valuable example of infrastructure because they combine extensive data (gathered through ingenious use of information technology) with skillful facilitation, to create a nonhierarchical environment for reflection and collaborative inquiry.

⟩⟩ See the material on the U.S. Army's AARs beginning on page 470.

■ **Theories, methods, and tools**: These represent bodies of knowledge that guide effective practice. For example, the five "learning disciplines" mentioned on page 32 represent a combination of theory, methods, and tools, which makes them particularly appropriate for

For more about the architecture of organizational learning, see *The Fifth Discipline Fieldbook*, p. 15ff and especially p. 21ff.

getting started in learning initiatives. Regardless of what theories, methods, and tools are employed, they must be practical; they must enable work on important issues; and they must have potential to lead to significant progress on those issues.

DEVELOPMENT OF LEARNING CAPABILITIES

"The most tangible change I observed in the first few years after the organizational learning work began at Harley was at meetings," said Harley-Davidson CEO Jeff Bleustein. "People stopped saying, 'This is the way it is,' and started saying, 'This is the way I see it.'"

That kind of small, subtle shift in language may be the only visible sign of a highly significant new capability. People who say, "This is the way I see it," may be much more effective at handling ambiguous, messy issues. They will be more comfortable with differences of opinion. They understand that their personal view doesn't necessarily represent the absolute truth, that other people will see things differently, and that everyone's assumptions are open to inquiry. They can resolve difficult issues and "solve" confrontational problems themselves, without resorting to bosses or lawyers.

We define "learning capabilities" as skills and proficiencies that, among individuals, teams, and larger communities, enable people to consistently enhance their capacity to produce results that are truly important to them. In other words, learning capabilities enable us to learn.

We continue to see the five learning disciplines of *The Fifth Discipline* as a foundation for every organization, no matter how large or small, because the capabilities they nurture support so many other capabilities:

These capabilities are covered in more detail on p. 21 in *The Fifth Discipline Fieldbook*. Also see "Five Kinds of Systems Thinking," p. 137.

- aspiration: the capability to orient, individually and collectively toward creating what people truly desire, rather than just reacting to circumstances (based on Personal Mastery and Building Shared Vision);
- reflective conversation: the capability to converse in ways that nurture reflection and inquiry, to build shared understanding, and to coordinate effective action (based on Mental Models and Team Learning); and
- understanding complexity: the capability to see patterns of interdependency underlying problems, and to distinguish short- from long-term consequences of actions (based on Systems Thinking).

Learning capabilities cannot be forced, rushed, or imposed on others. Learning takes time. (This is why there is a "delay" symbol in the link between "Investing in Change Initiatives" and "Learning Capabilities.") It takes practice. There is reason to be suspicious if you hear people say, "We've all changed our fundamental attitudes around here." Such change just doesn't happen that easily. But learning also depends upon people's choices. The first rule of all learning is that learners learn best what learners want to learn. This simple rule is often lost on busy managers driven by urgent business needs who insist that, "We must become a learning organization."

The pilot group in this early stage, like a primitive root pushing its way through the shell of an oak seed, is beginning a reinforcing growth process. Just as the small initial roots enable more water and nutrients to flow, so do new learning capabilities enable a team to begin to produce results that, in turn, enable future growth. There are three different growth processes set in motion at this time. Each is represented in the diagram on page 54 by a different reinforcing circle or "loop," labeled R1, R2, and R3.

R1: "BECAUSE IT MATTERS" (PERSONAL RESULTS)

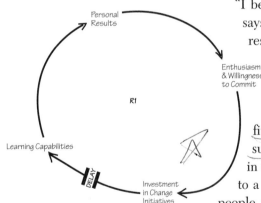

"I believe that people do have passion to produce results," says consultant and writer Fred Kofman, "but not business results. Sure, they care about business results, but they really have passion for the quality of their life. Once they experience living their lives more closely to the way they really want to live, that passion will emerge."

We have consistently found that direct personal benefits constitute the first source of reinforcing energy for sustaining deep change. It is inherently satisfying to work in a team where people trust one another and feel aligned to a sense of common purpose. Given the choice, very few people would not elect to be part of a team where there is excitement, commitment, perseverance, willingness to experiment, genuine appreciation of one another's gifts (and limitations), and the ability to effectively tackle complex issues. As Dr. W. Edwards Deming used to say, "People seek joy in work." In this day of "bottom line focus," when people often assume that personal needs are subservient to the business's needs, it is liberating to discover that the two can be aligned rather than in opposition.

Personal results are equally important for men and women, and for top managers and front line employees alike. A steelworker in a labor-management dialogue project remarked that, "For the first time in my life I am thinking, and my wife says I am listening to her." An engineer observed, "Recently, I was at a committee meeting at my church. After making my own case, I moved into inquiry mode to try and get people to explain their points more deeply. I do that consciously now. My level of skill is probably only an inch deep, but it has opened up a new world to me." And an Executive Vice President in a Fortune 50 company said, "All my life I've learned what it took to climb the ladder. The only problem was that I grew to like less and less the person I was becoming. I guess I assumed that this was just the price of success. It was a revelation to discover that the games-playing and politics we all had grown accustomed to would have to change if we were really serious about transforming the organization."

As this last comment suggests, we all hold certain taken-for-granted assumptions about "the way work needs to be" and the compromises it requires. Central to these assumptions is the industrial-age model of the employee as an input to the production process. This model hasn't changed much from the time, fifty or a hundred years ago, when many employees were called "hands." Today, we have the "enlightened" term "human resources," which literally means humans "standing in reserve," waiting to be used. Either way, the message is the same: At work, we are "employees" first and people second. If anything, our work and personal lives have become more fragmented in recent years, with increasing workloads, stress, and compromises to personal and family values.

Efforts to foster profound change do not share the view of "humans" as "resources." Rather, they assume that the key to significant, sustainable business improvement lies in harnessing the commitment, imagination, excitement, and energy of an organization's members, and that this cannot be sustained if people's personal and family lives are sacrificed.

Indeed, people's enthusiasm and willingness to commit themselves naturally increase when they realize personal results from a change initiative; this in turn reinforces their investment, and leads to further learning (the R1 loop in the diagram). If this reinforcing process is not activated, a significant force for building momentum is lost, one that reinforces each of the other forces. That is why most change initiatives fail to activate this source of reinforcing growth; they are not based on harnessing learning capabilities.

But, as in each of the reinforcing processes underlying profound change, there are also difficulties with growth through enhanced per-

I like this term!

For more about the "deep learning cycle" of learning capabilities, see *The Fifth Discipline Fieldbook*, p. 17.

Issues

sonal results. First, committed people differ from compliant people. They have their own ideas, their own passions. This can be scary for bosses used to being in control.

Second, as personal commitment increases, so too must the ability to set boundaries and make healthy life choices. Genuine "high commitment" workplaces can become unhealthy if, for example, highly ambitious people keep following their instincts and work harder and harder—at the expense of their personal lives and their relationships.

Third, the larger corporate environment doesn't change just because the climate in a pilot group changes. Personal results are often among the "undiscussables" in some business environments; people who forget this often cross over a line that undermines their credibility outside the pilot group. As one person outside a highly successful pilot group said, "Those people in the pilot group are too enthusiastic. Nobody is that enthusiastic about coming to work."

Last, there is a difference between passion and narcissism. Recognizing the importance of personal results does not mean obsessing about ourselves. If that happens, otherwise innovative teams can become isolated from business purposes. Gradually, such teams will fragment, as some members conclude that the learning effort has too little effect on business results. In our experience, the most meaningful personal results arise in groups that are deeply committed to improving their work results. Those who elevate personal results disproportionately over work results often fail to generate either.

Many of these difficulties will be explored in more depth as we examine the challenges confronted by leaders of profound change. For now, it's important to recognize the power of this reinforcing process, why it is often neglected—and the dangers it can pose.

R2: "BECAUSE MY COLLEAGUES TAKE IT SERIOUSLY" (NETWORKS OF COMMITTED PEOPLE)

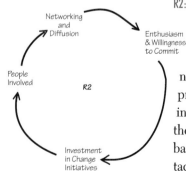

Over the past few years, British Petroleum's site managers from refineries around the world have met regularly in a "Global Refinery Network" (GRN) to share ideas and insights in ongoing advisory networks. As members encountered challenges they could bring up problems in the larger group, and the fact that other people were involved in learning efforts throughout the organization has helped them maintain credibility. When declining oil prices forced budget cutbacks in 1998, formal GRN meetings slowed down, but the informal contacts continued—and even deepened. Those, it turned out, were a highly compelling and vibrant part of BP's continuing breakthroughs in organizational learning.

}} For more about BP's learning diffusion infrastructure, see page 444.

Informal networks of managers interested in learning and quality initiatives have similarly played key roles over many years at Ford, Intel, Shell Oil, AT&T, and many other companies. Their presence lent institutional legitimacy to projects at times when there was little direct executive support, and they have provided a vital link for sharing and diffusing learning. In the mid-'90s, a reengineering team at Hewlett-Packard used organizational learning tools to cut $30 million worth of costs out of order entry and shipping in the printer business. How did they learn about organizational learning? Through HP's "Work Information Network," one of several internal networks connecting thousands of HP members over the past five years.

Studies of the ways in which innovations diffuse within large organizations have consistently pointed to the importance of informal networks and professional communities. These networks, much more than the formal management structures, seem vital to how people learn about new ideas, coach one another in trying them out, and share practical tips and lessons over time. "Organizations are webs of participation," says Xerox Vice President John Seely Brown, "Change the participation and you change the organization." Seely Brown and his colleagues at Xerox Palo Alto Research Center (where Seely Brown is director and chief scientist at Xerox) have found that "Communities of Practice" exist throughout all organizations: networks of people who rely on one another in the execution of real work. They are bound together by "a common sense of purpose and a real need to know what each other knows." Seely Brown regards them as "the critical building block of a knowledge-based company."

Such informal networks are almost always superior to hierarchical channels for spreading new innovations. First, these informal networks already exist; they are already essential for doing daily work. Spreading new ideas through them is a natural extension of current practice. Second, the information that passes laterally through them has credibility. When people whom we know and rely on talk about something new they are doing, we naturally pay attention. We might not always listen so carefully to information that comes through the management hierarchy. Third, experimenting with new ideas requires help and counsel in a safe context. Such support is more likely to come from trusted colleagues than from the hierarchy. The "help" that comes from bosses is often a mixed blessing.

The Work Information Network is described in "Corporate Networks" by Vicki J. Powers, in *Continuous Journey Magazine*, April 1995, p. 34.

66 "The People are the Company," by John Seely Brown and Estee Solomon Gray, *Fast Company*, Vol. 1, No. 1, November 1995, p. 78.

Ultimately, we know of no company that has generated significant momentum in profound change efforts without evolving spirited, active, internal networks of practitioners, people sharing progress and helping one another. As more people involved in change initiatives become part of these extended networks, information about the initiatives spreads more widely, giving rise to more interest, and potentially to more initiatives. This is the second basic reinforcing growth process (R2). This does not mean that people automatically jump on every bandwagon that they hear about. More often they wait until they learn more about the results that new ideas have achieved. But this is why R1 is most important in concert with the other reinforcing processes. If people learn about new ideas from others they trust and who have no authority over them, they are not threatened and more likely to remain open-minded.

The difficulties with this growth process for new innovations stem, in part, from how much it differs from traditional management practices. In the increasingly networked world, "managers shouldn't try to gain control," says Seely Brown. "They should surrender it." This is easy to say, but management *is* control in traditional organizations. In facing the daunting task of spreading innovative processes, traditional managers are overwhelmingly predisposed to the "roll-out." They create a plan and then set in place control processes to achieve the plan—just as they have always been trained to do as "good managers." Informal networks cannot grow in this manner. They can be encouraged, supported, enabled, thwarted, even disabled perhaps—but not "rolled out."

This can be sobering even for "enlightened managers," who don't see themselves as trying to control. "We worked for four years to develop an informal network of upper-level managers who could meet regularly, share knowledge, and help each other with their respective change efforts, only to watch the whole network decline in a few months when people just stopped coming to meetings," lamented a frustrated staff person. We all have a great deal to learn about how informal networks and communities of practice grow, decline, and either successfully or unsuccessfully diffuse innovative practices. But, if John Seely Brown is right and these networks hold a key to effectiveness in the "Knowledge Era," they may also hold a key to understanding a critical frontier of management and leadership.

> For more perspectives on the value of networks of committed people, see the article on communities of practice at Xerox, page 477. Also see the article on cultivating community at Ford, page 167, and the "study groups" roundtable, page 118.

R3: "BECAUSE IT WORKS" (BUSINESS RESULTS)

How do enhanced learning capabilities lead to greater business results? Primarily, through new business practices. This often starts with simply eliminating wasteful practices to which everyone has grown accustomed. For example, an internal report on the learning initiative at Ford's Electrical and Fuel Handling Division (EFHD) pointed out the direct effect of improvements in communication and trust:

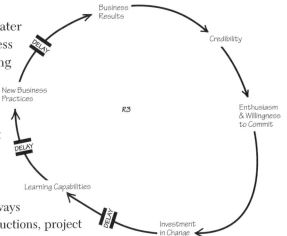

> Historical events at EFHD [had] created the collective [assumption] that management would always reduce capital funding requests. To offset these reductions, project managers [had] automatically added a "cushion" or contingency to their budgets. As division leaders began to trust their project managers, things changed. Management stopped making these reductions, and project managers stopped adding a cushion.

Now people could just talk honestly about the investments that were needed and the real constraints in funding. This saved a great deal of wasted time, "thereby allowing more funding to be allocated to other important EFHD capital and technological projects."

Over time, people invent new practices. At EFHD, a recurring theme was speed, because project leaders saw direct connections between learning capabilities and shortening delays in many practices. "Trust equals speed," said one operating committee member. "I don't have to worry about whether or not these guys are going to deliver or whether one of them is creeping up behind me. I can just focus and go on." According to an engineering manager, "Before PLST [product launch success team] a series of [launch] reviews took up to a year. Now, you present a project to this same group of people and, in one review, it's 'Does everybody agree with this? Yes or no?' and you go." As similar changes unfolded in other business practices, the costs of production (domestic and overseas) dropped, and the amount of management oversight needed went down.

As new business practices lead to better results in initial pilots, credibility increases and more people are willing to commit themselves to similar changes (reinforcing process R3 in the diagram). This process unfolded over several years at EFHD, leading gradually to more and more change initiatives, and more and more new business practices. In December 1992, there were two learning teams with thirty-two mem-

This passage comes from *Learning for Operational Excellence at EFHD, 1992–1996*, by Dave Berdish, et al. (Detroit, MI: Visteon Automotive Systems, 1997), p. 9–5. This work is also available online from the Society for Organizational Learning. See *http://www.fieldbook.com/resources.html* for details.

bers. By December 1993, there were twelve learning teams with 132 members. By December 1994, there were twenty teams with 500 members, which grew to twenty-seven teams with 1,200 members by December 1995. Gradually, innovations in business practices extended from product launch, to test runs in manufacturing (joint innovations between engineers and production people), to delivery and shipping specification and oversight, to the general managers' weekly dialogue sessions with operations managers, to joint learning sessions with suppliers. Along the way, EFHD's growth and profitability improved dramatically: Between 1991 and 1996, profits rose from negative $50 million to $150 million, sales more than doubled to $2 billion, and the division expanded from three plants in the U.S. to ten plants worldwide.

Such practical results don't just provide credibility outside the pilot team—they are crucial for the team members themselves. A change initiative is only worth its time and trouble if it demonstrably moves the participants closer to their aspirations, and to the organization's aspirations. Saying, "We spend three hours a week, now, talking about our shared vision, and we feel much better about it" is meaningless unless you can also say something like, ". . . and that made it possible to redesign the billing process and implement it in four weeks." Such statements are no less meaningful in the nonprofit or government world: People will simply not invest themselves in initiatives they don't see as leading to meaningful practical consequences.

Focusing on practical results also matters for learning. Results provide a context for experimentation, adaptation, and feedback. When members of a pilot group can see the consequences of their efforts they can reflect upon their actions and adjust them. If the members of a "committed" pilot group do not commit themselves to tangible outcomes and then assess their progress relative to those desired outcomes, learning becomes difficult or impossible.

People often believe that reinforcing growth through demonstrated business success is not just a highly significant key to sustaining change, but the only key. They ask, for example, "Why is this not the first engine of growth, rather than the third?" The answer is that there are also problems with growth through better results.

First, assessing improvement in business results is not always as clear-cut as it might seem. The people at EFHD might believe that their improvements can be traced to their commitment to organizational learning, but others might differ. Attributing causality in any complex system is never simple. "All this learning stuff had nothing to do with it," said one outsider about another change initiative. "They got results because Tom is a tough boss and he let his people know that he would not tolerate underachievers." Even within a pilot group, it is common for people's assessments to differ: "Most of the learning tools are nothing new. The key to our success was that we had great people."

〉〉 See "The Black Box of Assessment" (page 303) for more on the issues of evaluating and
〉〉 talking about business results.

Second, innovative pilot groups typically generate a mixture of results, including results that might be less clearly seen as an improvement. For example, we have seen many cases where some traditional measures got worse while others got better. Naturally, advocates for the innovations tended to focus on the measures that improved, while opponents focused on those that were getting worse.

Third, there are often significant delays between developing new learning capabilities, establishing new business practices, and achieving significant improvements in results. (These delays are indicated on the R3 diagram.) During these delays, business results may not improve—indeed, they may get worse—and the pilot group is vulnerable. People know they are trying out new ideas, and it is easy to conclude that they are not working, given the mixed results.

For all these reasons, the goal of achieving "demonstrated tangible improvements measured by common business indicators" often proves elusive. The "hard results" are often anything but hard. They are often matters of highly subjective interpretation. This is especially problematic when you consider the political and cultural backlashes that innovative pilot groups can engender.

〉〉 For example, see the challenge of "true believers and nonbelievers," page 319.

Even if a pilot group becomes acknowledged for achieving significant business results, the larger organization can still respond in ways that kill the innovative process. "You developed the last product in twelve months instead of eighteen. Very good. Do the next one in six months." Such arbitrary pressures imposed from the top reflect disrespect for people and the environment of trust needed to nurture deep change. More than a few corporations have "killed the goose that laid the golden egg" out of greed for more eggs—simply because they had so little understanding of the process that generated the egg in the first place.

The Fifth Discipline Fieldbook study groups Web page is located at *http://www.fieldbook.com/studygroup. html.* For more about setting up study groups, see p. 118.

SETTING THE "GROWTH PROCESSES OF PROFOUND CHANGE" INTO MOTION

Putting all the above ideas—all three different growth processes—together creates the following picture.

This diagram shows the three reinforcing growth processes at work in generating profound change. Investment in change initiatives leads to new learning capabilities and personal results (loop R1); more people involved and aware through informal networks (R2); and eventually the learning capabilities generate new business practices, business results, and increased credibility (R3). Each of these increases people's willingness to commit themselves to change initiatives, leading to further investment . . .

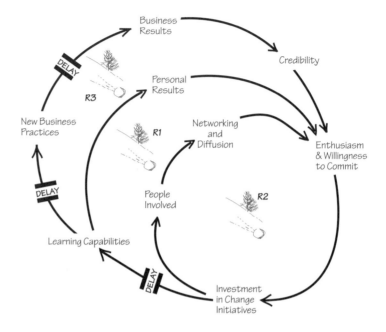

Each of these processes operates simultaneously, generating a distinct set of forces that can sustain growth, albeit with different speeds due to the different delays in each process. They are interdependent, in that changes in one can strengthen the effects of others—such as when enhanced business results further increases enthusiasm arising from personal results, or when either type of results makes people in informal networks more interested in their own learning initiatives.

But seeing all these processes for the first time, especially while considering the problems associated with each process, can create an overwhelming picture. It can be a bit paralyzing, especially to the extent that we are accustomed to simple pictures and simple solutions. What are the implications for leaders at all levels? What can effective leaders do to sustain significant change?

These questions lie at the heart of this entire book. The authors and contributors will explore them in stages, considering many different contexts and options. In particular, as we examine each of the challenges, we will consider specific strategies and tactics that people have used. These will not add up to one overall list of recommendations, but it will gradually help you develop a "gestalt" of effective leadership in sustaining profound change.

For now, it is enough to start with a few basics.

1. *While nothing happens without commitment, initial commitment is almost always limited to a handful of people.* Talk is cheap, as they say. Many "less committed" people may join and contribute to your efforts, because they are interested, have important capabilities and expertise, or are part of the "formal team."

   But in the end, everything depends on that core group of committed people. Therefore, even before you begin, find a few partners who really share your values and passions. The single biggest failing, in our experience, of many innovators is that they do not look for partners. They believe they can do it themselves, or they feel like they cannot ask for help, lest they reveal their own uncertainty. Virtually every significant change initiative we have seen starts with a genuine partnership among a small number of deeply committed individuals, often as few as two or three.

2. *Start small, grow steadily.* Don't give speeches. Find a few partners who share your values and passions. Identify key practical issues and get to work on them. Remember that profound change is a *self*-reinforcing process. As a leader you do not have to drive it. But you *do* have to participate. You must be willing to develop your own learning capabilities, and to be part of teams developing their learning capabilities. You must be open to the possibility of changing yourself.

   Even executive leaders, intent on changing the entire organization's directions, can benefit from a strategy of starting small. You might, for example, start by building better relationships and joint projects on your executive team, using that team as your pilot. Then the members of the executive team might sponsor initiatives in their organization, gradually starting other pilot groups with line projects. This new activity might percolate out into the organization, with each new pilot group using its predecessors as models to follow—and improve upon. Chances are, the more constructive the behavior of these senior executives, the more people in the company will follow that behavior as a role model.

3. *Intended results and useful tools are more important than a detailed plan.* Management writer Henry Mintzburg has noted the extent to which good management is "made up as you go along"—dependent on managers' intuitions and judgment as applied in each moment.

The same is probably even more true of a significant change initiative, where there are no answers, and experimentation, observation, and reflection are also essential. But practical tools and an approach with which to begin are also essential, whether they are "Fifth Discipline" learning tools or more traditional tools of TQM or other change approaches. Equally essential is clarity around the issues at stake and the aims of the undertaking. People will never commit fully if the goals have little real meaning to them.

4. *If you're short of time and you're up against the wall, fix the crisis first.* When the patient is hemorrhaging, that is not a good time for an in-depth reflective consultation on personal purpose. But be mindful that reacting to the crisis is not enough. It will not lay a foundation for sustained learning. More crises are likely to follow unless you use the first crisis as an opportunity to shift attention to deeper issues.

5. *Remember that leverage lies in the limits and that they will come.* While creating new personal and business results and participating in extended networks of innovators are exciting and naturally motivating, they can also distract leaders' attention from issues that will ultimately determine the fate of their efforts. Effective leaders understand intuitively that rather than driving change, they need to participate, being willing to change themselves. As they participate they also know that there will be challenges ahead, and that their greatest internal resources will be devoted to dealing with the forces that can limit the momentum they have helped to unleash.

We know of no leaders who have been involved in genuinely transformational initiatives who feel like they are "a walk in the park." Conditions typically get harder, not easier, over time. The challenges you face tend to be emotionally charged. They may make people feel overwhelmed, cynical, and lousy. If leaders expect the initiatives to go smoothly, or make promises that they think will bear fruit quickly, then they are, in effect, predisposing themselves to react in ways that may undermine the trust that may be slowly building.

But challenges are not intrinsically bad. Being blocked is a powerful incentive to creativity and innovation. The Europeans of the age of exploration took to the sea only after the Mongols challenged their land routes to China. In recent times, the Japanese quality movement represented a farsighted response to the challenge of having their political, military, and business establishment decimated during World War II.

Challenges are no less important in the evolution of organizations. The challenges of profound change tend to be signals of hidden impera-

It won't be easy!

tives built into the organizational system. They arise from the "homeo-static forces" maintaining core elements of the traditional culture and functioning of industrial-age organizations. Though they may appear idiosyncratic to individual organizations, we believe most are near universal to all contemporary large enterprises. They can't be overcome through sheer brute force or willpower; rather, they require understanding and often counterintuitive strategies. Our success in developing those strategies will determine the degree to which we can sustain profound change processes, and the degree to which real "postindustrial"-age institutions will emerge.

3 Rethinking Time

Peter M. Senge

People tend to neglect the power of reinforcing growth processes because we have become habituated to think in terms of the discrete beats of mechanical linear "clock time." It is important to remember that the mechanical clock was only invented five hundred years ago, in the fourteenth century. Before that, human beings did not think of time in constant, fixed increments that keep adding in a steady linear progression. Today, you can almost hear the machine's wheels grinding relentlessly: sixty minutes to each hour, then another sixty minutes make another hour, then another sixty minutes make another hour, then another, then another . . .

Nature's time is different.

CLOCK, TIME, PUNCTUAL

LEXICON

These three words, in themselves, trace the history of the shift from natural time to mechanical time. "Clock" comes from the Latin *clocca*, for "bell"; it reflects the first people to keep time by sound, the sixth-century Benedictine monks, who rang seven bells each day to mark hours for prayer. Suddenly, instead of people observing the flow of time (watching an hourglass or water-clock), time found them. The call of the bell broke the flow of attention and summoned people to mark the hour. The word "six o'clock" referred to the sixth bell-ring of the day. The word "time" came later, emerging sometime close to the invention of the mechanical clock; it derives from the Indo-European base *di*—to "cut up or divide."

In the sixteenth century, the time of Kepler and Galileo, the universe itself began to be seen as a vast piece of clockwork, with the planets moving in "epicycles" that resembled, in the descriptions of early cosmologists, the interlocking wheels of a mechanical clock. "By the late seventeenth century," writes historian Daniel Boorstin, "the word 'punctual'—which formerly had described a person who insisted upon points (from the Latin *punctus*, 'points') or details of conduct—came to describe a person who was exactly observant of an appointed time."

At the end of the nineteenth century, the machine metaphor had penetrated scientific thinking so completely that physicists and biologists assumed that they would soon be able to figure out the workings of the universe entirely. The mysteries of nature would simply be another set of cogs in the mechanical clock of the cosmos. That possibility died with the discoveries of quantum physics, but the intuitive feeling of being in a mechanical universe lives on in civilized society, propelled by the ticking of precisely measured beats and the continued use of words like "clock," "time," and "punctual."

See *The Discoverers*, by Daniel Boorstin (New York: Harry N. Abrams, 1991), Vol. I, p. 61ff and p. 110. Also see *The Wholeness of Nature*, by Henri Bortoft (Hudson, New York: Lindisfarne Press, 1996); and *Technics and Civilization*, by Lewis Mumford (New York: Harcourt Brace Jovanovich, 1934, 1963).

~~~~~

Nature's time is inseparable from the processes whereby nature produces change. Nature creates cycles such as the flow of the seasons, the migration of birds, and the cycles of human moods; and nature creates growth. Nature's growth processes inherently accelerate. To appreciate the stark contrast between linear clock time and the "time clock" implied by reinforcing growth processes, look at the graph below. It shows two change curves: one that advances linearly, growing in increments of ten every quarter. The second grows exponentially, doubling in size every quarter. Both curves start together at one. Which growth is more powerful? For the first six quarters, the linear progression wins out, easily. In fact, for the first four quarters, the exponential curve grows only a tiny fraction of the linear growth. But the exponential curve catches up after six quarters, and then there is no contest. Two quarters later, the exponential curve is four times the linear progression; by the tenth quarter, it is ten times the linear progression!

The really interesting feature of these two curves is their respective implications for achieving "scale." Everywhere, today, I see managers

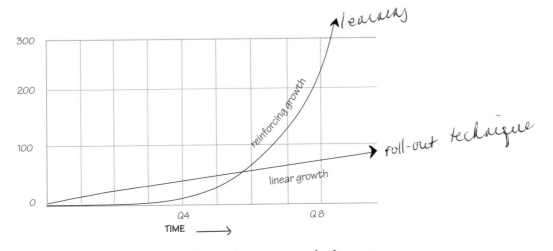

wrestling with how to achieve significant change on a scale that matters. Often these people are impatient with the "pilot group" idea. "We don't have time to just focus on a few pilot groups and then learn from them. We've got to transform two hundred production facilities around the world within the next three years." So, they opt for the "top management roll-out," a plan disconnected from any natural progression: one project, two projects, two hundred projects . . .

》》 See, for example, Vic Leo's comments about the "boom theory," page 169.

But roll-outs rarely achieve their targets—except in the most super-ficial ways—precisely because they do not activate the underlying reinforcing processes that naturally accelerate because they *are* self-reinforcing. Managers eager to meet the pressures from competitors, customers, and investors often say, "We just don't have time for this learning stuff." But, in fact, maybe they don't *not* have time for it.

But there is another old saw in biology that says, "nothing grows for-ever." While reinforcing exponential growth is nature's vehicle for expansion, it never operates unchecked. Growth in all natural systems occurs through an interplay of reinforcing processes and limiting processes. In nature, the power of limits determines the extent to which growth follows the path of acceleration. In organizational change, the power of limits similarly determines the extent to which pilot projects ever grow to realize significant impact. This is why effective leaders focus their attention on understanding and dealing with limits.

4 Limits Ahead

Using the "Limits to Growth" dynamic to meet the
challenges of profound change effectively

Michael Goodman

*Until now, this book has focused on the reinforcing processes underly-
ing profound change. The rest of this book addresses the limiting
processes that shape profound change—the challenges. Before exploring specific challenges in depth, it helps to understand their generic
nature: the interplay between reinforcing and limiting processes, and
the strategic options available to leaders in dealing with them. We
have asked Michael Goodman, director of the systems thinking practice at Arthur D. Little/Innovation Associates, to describe these
dynamics and strategies. The behavior of limits in business settings
has been a subject of his own in-depth study for the past two decades.
An alumnus of the MIT system dynamics program, Michael was also
the emcee of the "systems thinking" section of* The Fifth Discipline
Fieldbook.

If you've ever been part of a learning or change initiative, you probably
recognize the feeling of challenges. After a brilliant beginning, with
high demand, you cross a threshold. Suddenly you think, "We're not seeing any movement anymore." Your work is less effective, your support in
the organization wanes, and crosscurrents stymie your impact. The
harder you push, the harder the system pushes back.

You are part of a common systems situation known as "limits to
growth" (or "limits to success").

If you want to make any long-standing progress in that kind of situation, you need to understand where the apparent limits to your success
are coming from. Limits generally don't become visible until they're provoked, but by the time you provoke them it may be too late to deal with
them. Therefore, your highest leverage comes from anticipating them,
rather than reacting to them.

THE BASIC STRUCTURE OF "LIMITS TO GROWTH"

Limits to growth situations occur when a reinforcing process (of growth)
runs up against a *balancing process:* some form of naturally occurring

resistance. Balancing processes are the means by which systems maintain integrity, continuity, and stability. They represent the continual seeking of some natural balance point—a human body's homeostatic state, an ecosystem's balance of predator and prey, or a company's generally accepted level of stability.

Balancing points are not always obvious or explicit, but they nonetheless govern the boundaries of system activity. For example, every company has its own implicit cultural norm around the appropriate level of controversy and argument. Break that norm by speaking out too stridently, and you may well feel pressure to quiet down. Yet if you are too quiet, you might feel subtly compelled to speak out more. As members of the company cue one another this way, the system oscillates between "too much" speaking out, and "too much" silence, always approaching the group's behavioral "happy medium"—at least until some perturbation happens that throws off the balance again.

The limits described in this book together represent ten different balancing processes all operating with different time delays. Some challenges, like "not enough time," emerge quickly, while others, like the challenge of "governance" might appear more slowly. It might take years to get to a point where those forces are provoked, particularly if they have always been exclusively the domain of the boards of directors.

At the same time, the limits that drive the various challenges are all interrelated; they all affect each other in ways that probably vary from organization to organization. Tackle one challenge, and "solve" it successfully, and another may arise to compensate. In any complex system like an organization, there is a myriad of forces and tensions seeking their own setpoints, all trying to resolve one another—especially when you add in the various priorities and aspirations of the people involved.

To enter a system like this with a simple "one-size-fits-all" programmatic effort is almost certainly going to backfire, like the organizational equivalent of a crash diet. Instead, an effective pilot group approach would "admire the system on its own terms," continually learning more and more about the forces at play. Experience with limits to growth suggests four basic strategies:

STRATEGY 1: DON'T PUSH SO HARD FOR GROWTH

Limits to growth situations tend to develop in two stages: an initial phase of accelerating growth, and then a discomfiting slowdown. When the first balancing forces confront you, it's easy to feel them as an external,

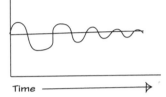

This illustration shows the typical pattern of behavior of a balancing process—oscillating toward equilibrium.

Time ——————→

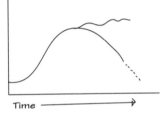

And this shows the behavior of the limits to growth structure combining reinforcing and balancing processes. First the growth accelerates. Then, after resistance kicks in, it either levels off and oscillates toward a goal, or it overshoots and collapses.

Time ——————→

disempowering nuisance, attacking you from outside. Still elated with the first flush of success, you hope to brush them aside so you can continue promoting and spreading your growth. But the limits persist. As you become more and more preoccupied with holding them off, it may become harder to look ahead. Why invest now in developing new structures of governance? You've got your hands full just getting the right help. When new challenges continue to emerge, you address them on a catch-as-catch-can basis, fighting windmills and extending yourself continually farther.

The alternative, instead of speeding up, is to slow down: Starting in the early growth phases, call time out regularly to talk together about the limits that may be facing you. This is hard to do because it goes against the grain of a deep mental model that many people hold in business: "We (and our initiative) are special. We're exempt from limits to our growth. It can't happen to us."

The truth is: Limits to growth is one of the most prevalent and powerful structures in nature. *No one is exempt.* It explains why few change efforts succeed in the long run. Having the awareness and maturity to recognize this is the first step to managing the limiting forces successfully.

STRATEGY 2: THINK ABOUT THE FUTURE TODAY

Many change initiative leaders seem to emulate Scarlett O'Hara: "I'll think about that tomorrow." Unfortunately, thanks to the delays inherent in the system, the challenges of profound change are probably already acting upon you. By the time they become visible, they will be much stronger and more difficult to manage.

The limits to growth model suggests looking *ahead* to identify the most significant challenges facing you, the sources and nature of that resistance, and its potential impact on your group. These questions may help:

■ **What do we know from experience?** Try to learn about other pilot groups in your organization, or other organizations, that have tried similar initiatives. Did they succeed? What forces did they run up against, and how did they deal with them? Even failed initiatives of the past may offer valuable lessons. There may be cases where people underestimated the force of resistance, or the length of time it would take to build capability.

- **If we succeed at first, what challenges will trouble us the most?** Which are likely to be the toughest when they arise? Which are going to appear first? Which will only appear after long delays?
- **How long will it take us to prepare for the challenges?** Building some capabilities may be relatively easy, but others may be difficult. For example, you might anticipate the challenge of strategy and purpose, and thus plan a new environmental initiative. But you may find it takes years to build the capabilities for trusting and working with competitors, community leaders, and regulators.

STRATEGY 3: CONDUCT EXPERIMENTS

No one initiating change has the answers, right off the bat, for dealing with these challenges. The answers evolve out of experience and experimentation. By designing and conducting deliberate experiments, you can develop a learning orientation where solutions are treated as plausible hypotheses, rather than as answers.

An experiment, in this case, means a new initiative set up with the clear recognition that it may not work. This might include a new approach to dealing with the "no time" challenge, or an effort to meet the challenge of "results" by establishing criteria for success. Talk through ahead of time: What results do you expect to see? What will it reveal if you achieve those results—or if you don't? Can you compare the results to another work group that did not institute the change?

Recognize that you will probably not just run one experiment. The best strategy is to run experiments in succession—reflecting each time on the results of the previous one, drawing conclusions about their meaning, planning the next effort, and then making the test.

STRATEGY 4: RESET THE GOALS BY EXAMINING YOUR MENTAL MODELS

The limits that block organizational learning initiatives have a great deal to do with the mental models embedded in the culture of your organization. Reflecting on the reasons why people find it hard to tolerate ambiguity or change, you may begin to see the priorities that keep these "set points" in place.

For example, if you intend to shake up existing governance structures, information flow patterns, or relationships with outsiders, you may trigger resistance because people are quite reasonably drawn to stability. You might need to move explicitly to show that some systems will remain predictable—for instance, the systems that allow the organization to get its products out on time and preserve quality.

TRUSTING YOURSELF

How can you be certain that you have recognized the most critical balancing processes, and have taken appropriate steps to prepare for them?

Trust, paradoxically, emerges from *not* having the answers. If you can follow these four strategies, and others in this book, you can develop a continuous process of hypothesizing, testing, and experimenting. Some of the experiments will go "wrong"—they won't achieve the results you expect. But you will be able to design new experiments based on those results. Others will "succeed" in ways you hadn't anticipated. Your understanding of the system will grow steadily, as you calibrate these results and try new endeavors, in a way that would not be possible if you were merely following someone's preconceived plan.

The
Challenges
of Initiating

In our work with organizations, we have seen many major projects begin with everything seeming right. There were line leaders committed and personally involved, with clear and important business objectives, and with significant potential benefits for the organization as a whole. Yet little was achieved, and within six months everyone involved agreed that the projects should be terminated.

As this suggests, some challenges are sufficiently strong that they can prevent growth from occurring, almost before it starts. We call these the "challenges of initiating" because they have consistently been encountered at the early stages of significant organizational change. They stem directly from the investments that pilot group members make in learning or change initiatives. These are the challenges of:

- **Not enough time**: the lack of a pilot group's flexibility and control over its own time and priorities;
- **No help**: the need for coherent, consistent knowledgeable coaching and guidance and support;
- **Not relevant**: the absence of a clear, compelling business case for learning;
- **Walking the talk**: the vulnerability and lack of reflection engendered by a gap between espoused values and actions, especially for those championing change.

Since these challenges appear relatively early in a pilot group's progress, the capabilities for addressing them cannot be built up slowly and gradually, as they can for other challenges in this book. The capabilities for managing time, help, relevance, and consistency of values and behavior must be developed under high pressure. On the bright side, managing these challenges effectively will help you develop capabilities much sooner than you would otherwise, for the other challenges down the road.

III. Not Enough Time

"We don't have time for this stuff!"

1 The Challenge

Several years ago, a promising learning project in a large corporation was abruptly terminated. It had died, people said, for lack of interest. But there had been plenty of interest; "learning" was a highly espoused priority throughout the company. The problems had started when the most senior leader—a vice president who instigated the project—missed most of the monthly working sessions.

Each time, he was determined to show up. Each time a "crisis" pulled him away. He reiterated his support for the project each time, but when the team leaders tried to reschedule, his calendar was routinely overbooked. Finally, it became apparent that—despite his seniority— he lacked enough control over his own time to continue the project. The same was true of the executives above him. Since other people took their cue from the executive leaders, the pattern cascaded down through the hierarchy. Nobody seemed to feel comfortable asking why so many managers had so little control over their calendars.

Every successful learning initiative requires key people to allocate hours to new types of activities: reflection, planning, collaborative work, and training. "Core teams" must take the time to design the next stages of the initiatives. Work groups need a day or two every month for "skillful" discussions about business issues. Being part of a network of committed people can take up a great deal of time, not just in meetings but in conversation, e-mail, and reading. Without enough time to spend on regular practice of conversational or systems thinking skills, profound change cannot occur, even if there is strong interest. People who feel trapped without enough time to meet current business demands often feel that they cannot commit themselves to new initiatives.

People facing this challenge speak of feeling disjointed; pushed and pulled from crisis to crisis, never allowed to concentrate or finish one task before being jerked away onto something new. "HR calls me and says they need reviews done by next Thursday; the budget's due Tuesday; my clients need something by Monday. I don't have time to think—and you want me to make time for learning?" One beleaguered corporate vice president lamented, "We are running a marathon at a sprinter's pace." This gentleman, responsible for a $10 billion portion of a Fortune 50 company, had regular 6:00 A.M. staff meetings. Clearly, the challenge of time is not just a problem for those at the middle levels.

The fundamental problem, in the end, is not lack of time per se, but lack of time flexibility. While everyone is busy, the real struggle is being able to prioritize one's own time. Often, people's time is so consumed with tasks and goals forced by management, they have little discretionary time to pursue what might be much more important for them, and the organization, in the long run.

THE UNDERLYING DYNAMICS OF "NOT ENOUGH TIME"

On the left of this "limits to growth" structure are the familiar reinforcing growth processes of profound change. According to this element of our theory, the greater the investment in learning initiatives, the greater the development of learning capabilities, which (through different types of "results" and through informal networks) boosts people's enthusiasm and willingness to commit to new initiatives.

But the limiting processes on the right show how limits on time can slow down growth. As a change initiative grows stronger, the time required to participate in the initiative increases. If "time flexibility" (shown as the constraint at bottom) is low, the team's time available to commit to the initiative will not increase to meet the time required, and time scarcity will limit progress. This can happen in two ways. Either the time invested in the initiative will be ineffective, for example because key people keep missing important meetings (shown as loop B1 in the diagram); or people will be unwilling to commit in the first place because they feel "there's not enough time for this stuff!" (shown as loop B2 in the diagram). Both of these processes put the brakes on new investment in learning initiatives. That, in turn, will slow or halt entirely the growth of learning capabilities (including, ironically, the ability to learn how to develop more time flexibility).

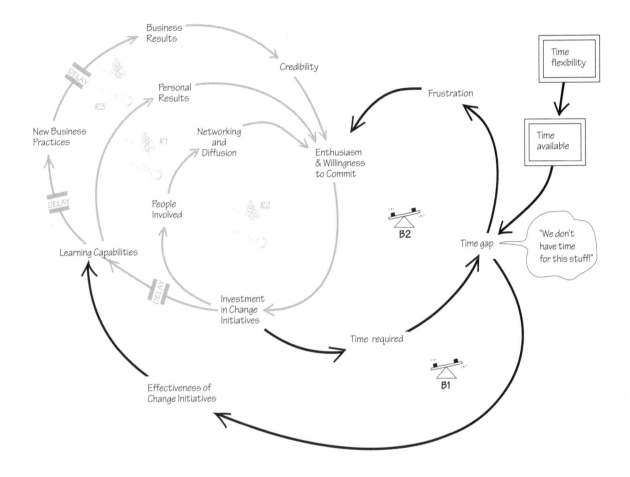

As with all the limiting processes, a range of possible scenarios can unfold as a result of "not enough time." In the extreme, with no time flexibility, little or no progress will ever occur. People will simply never commit their time because they have no time to commit, or they will try to make time, only to discover after a few months (like the VP who kept missing meetings) that there is no point in proceeding.

At the other extreme, people have high time flexibility, and this limiting process never really comes into play. Many pilot teams fall somewhere between these extremes. People may have enough control over their time that they can sustain some effort and gradually make progress, even though they are under considerable stress. Often, pilot teams eventually find that time becomes less of a constraint because they become much more efficient as they develop learning capabilities. They stop

As investments in change initiatives go up, time required of pilot team members increases. If time flexibility remains unchanged, and there is no additional time available for such initiatives, the resulting time gap has two effects: it makes the initiative less effective, thereby undermining possible growth in learning capabilities (loop B1), and it increases frustration and reduces people's willingness to commit (loop B2).

wasting time previously consumed by their ineffectiveness. They resolve issues that they had never been able to talk about before. And they stop wasteful practices like continually checking on one another or covertly trying to figure out one another's agendas, rather than inquiring directly.

Once it kicks in, the limiting process of "not enough time" can operate swiftly. If people have very little time flexibility, most change initiatives will die a quick death, never really getting started because so few are able to commit the time needed. Unfortunately, this is exactly what happens in many of today's overstressed workplaces.

STRATEGIES FOR MEETING THE CHALLENGE OF "NOT ENOUGH TIME"

the usual responses

Corporations are awash in symptomatic, quick-fix efforts to deal with the time problem—many of which only tend to exacerbate the problem by adding more distraction. "Time management" training programs, for instance, become another agenda item to shoehorn into calendars. Electronic mail, installed and supported to help people communicate more efficiently, becomes a notorious generator of time-wasting messages. (Several potential contributors to this book demurred because it took all their discretionary time to deal with routine e-mails and voicemails.) People develop informal short-term coping strategies, like scheduling themselves minute-by-minute, breaking off meetings to keep their next appointments, answering their e-mail during meetings, and catching up with routine work on weeknights and weekends—all of which have the effect of making the workplace more pressured, and making stress more difficult to deal with.

The time required for a change initiative, especially at first, will not shrink. Leverage lies in investigating the tacit assumptions and attitudes that underlie the lack of time flexibility. Approaches like these have proven most effective:

- **Integrating initiatives:** As different people get involved with organizational change, initiatives proliferate. Career planning, quality, strategy, scenario planning, human resources (HR) initiatives, and budgeting all require time and attention. When a new initiative begins, people tend to allocate another small chunk of time for that. It's far more effective to combine several different initiatives into one, even if they started with different champions and participants. Isn't the common goal to enable progress on key issues?

⟩⟩ See "Five Ways to Create Time," page 82.

■ **Scheduling time for focus and concentration:** If you hire someone to move a refrigerator up a flight of stairs, you don't stop him halfway up, to distract him with a question. You don't even interrupt him when he is investigating the stairwell, deciding which way to hold the appliance. You know that the stakes are too high; one mistake, and someone might get papered into the wall. Why, then, is it considered safe to interrupt people who are thinking through a critical issue for a business?

A great deal of leverage exists simply by rearranging time to encourage focus, concentration, and intensive work. The same activity, scheduled in a three-day block instead of three one-day blocks, can move along much farther because people can focus together.

■ **Trusting people to control their own use of time:** Conventional business practice sometimes seems based on a "chain gang" model of time management. The speed of the gang is determined by the speed of the boss. If the boss isn't visible, riding hard on the people, they won't do anything. This implicit attitude puts enormous pressure on both the formal leader of a team and the team members alike. If they're not visible, "looking busy," they might appear incompetent.

As MIT professor Lotte Bailyn points out, many work-family conflicts could be resolved simply by allowing people to schedule themselves and be rewarded for the results they produce, instead of for being visible. Letting people schedule their time is a great trustbuilder in an organization; it sends an implicit signal that people are generally regarded not as would-be slackers, but as contributors, with an interest in the future of the organization.

■ **Valuing unstructured time:** *Washington Post* cartoonist Mark Alan Stamaty was once asked why he didn't try harder to publish more cartoons per week. "I need to build in daydreaming time," he said. "The quality of my work depends upon it."

Similarly, the quality of managerial work often depends upon large amounts of unscheduled time: for "daydreaming" alone or together, for talking about significant subjects without immediate pressure to produce results, and for the impromptu conversations that help people deal with ambiguous issues like learning and change.

"Slack time" is one key benefit of dialogue, skillful discussion, practice fields, learning laboratories, and other unstructured conversational methodologies. Providing informal slack time, by giving people time to encounter one another casually in the course of their workday, represents an even higher-leverage approach.

Why do organizations find it so difficult to build in slack time? Perhaps because of the quantification of productivity. Tight measurements of time at work don't take into account the broad spectrum of thinking, conversation, decision making, research, and inquiry that constitute "work" in most organizations today. Executive leaders, conscious of numerical measurements of time, may not think to support the "unmeasurable" allowance of slack. The net result is a mismatch between flexible tasks and inflexible time requirements.

It takes courage and imagination for a time-pressured line leader to say, "We will talk about our issues, without rushing to a decision." Network leaders can help, by describing other situations where a practice field or dialogue session has contributed, or times when people slowed down, reflected together, and reached a breakthrough.

⟫ See "Managing a Practice Field," page 91.

■ **Building capabilities for eliminating busywork:** Often, the challenge of "not enough time" reflects the bitter truth of restructuring: Ten people perform work that was previously handled by fifty. Clerical and administrative work, once handled by support staff, now becomes an added managerial burden. To compensate, managers are asked to eliminate unnecessary tasks and wasted efforts. This effort, in itself, requires skill and capabilities that require time and attention to develop. Most unnecessary tasks are only obvious once people talk through their processes together.

⟫ See, for example, the efforts to accomplish this in GE's Work-Out program, on page 74.

■ **Saying "no" to political games-playing:** "If we could somehow extract all the politics, gamesmanship, and bureaucratic garbage from hierarchical organizations," says former Hanover Insurance President Bill O'Brien, "we could increase the GNP by twenty percent and reduce the workweek to three days." Asked for an example, he talks about the mental chess-playing that occupies people's attention during meetings: "'I wonder what so-and-so's agenda is? I'll be damned if I'm going to reveal my agenda before he reveals his.' Then people spend hours talking not about how to deliver more value to customers, but how to give the bosses the answer that they think the bosses want to hear."

Executive leaders often have a great deal of leverage here, through setting an example. When they visit a site, for instance, they can call ahead to eliminate the special perks and privileges that may not mean that much to them, but consume a lot of time. More fundamentally, they can also look at their own organization of time. "Look at the time calendar of any executive and you can quickly tell what type of manager he or she is," O'Brien says. Many CEOs schedule their calendars in fifteen- or thirty-minute increments. They might literally have twenty meetings in a day, or even more. When I was CEO, I would say to my direct reports, 'Look at my calendar.' It contained many half-day and longer meetings. If an issue can be resolved in fifteen minutes, why should senior management be wrestling with it?"

- **Saying "no" to nonessential demands:** Line leaders may need to deliberately say "no" to demands that come from outside. In one case, a team within Procter & Gamble began a redesign of their product "value chain," and decided that, to complete the project, they would need to deny all information requests from senior management for six months. This had to be negotiated in conversations that went all the way up to the CEO: Even after the right to deny outside requests was granted, it took constant attention to defend. Senior managers made information requests so routinely, that they were basically unconscious of it.

- **Experimenting with time:** Since "good" and "bad" effects are often interwoven in a single system, you may find that, instead of fighting the forces of resistance, it's better to start by inquiring about them. Is there some old, limiting policy that controls the amount of time flexibility? Do you know the reasons why that policy was put in place? Can another policy accomplish the same goals, while simultaneously adding control over time flexibility?

For suggestions and insights on experimenting with time flexibility and related attitudes, see "Reconceiving Balance" by Betsy Jacobson (1998), available online at *http://www.fieldbook. com/balance.html.*

Unfortunately, people often worry that talking about time flexibility makes them look contentious or unheroic. Instead of talking about how to "take excess work out of the system," or "remove political games-playing," they decide to work harder instead as individuals, thereby depleting the community-building time and reflective slack time that might actually lead to greater value.

One cultural common denominator lies behind this challenge: the mental model of people as components plugged into an industrial, mechanical machine. Components are granted no control over their time; the idea is absurd. The "machine" needs them to click in, on cue, to the place they're most needed at any given moment. But if you regard managers and employees as people with relevant aspirations for the future of the organization, then you naturally expect them to take control of their time. You would expect them to want to know how to use their time more effectively. Pulling the thread of "not enough time" leads, inevitably, to asking questions related to the tenth challenge of this book, the challenge of purpose: "What are we here to do? And if our purpose is vital, how can we avoid wasting the time we have to get there?"

2 Culture Change at General Electric

The evolution of productivity and effectiveness increases, from "Work-Out" to Six Sigma

Jacquie Vierling-Huang, Manager of Work-Out and Change Acceleration, GE Crotonville

General Electric is renowned for its pioneering approaches to organizational change—and for recognizing that significant change requires profound shifts in people's attitudes and beliefs. Herein, a senior leader from GE's famous "corporate university" at Crotonville, New York, describes how the problem of "not enough time" led to a comprehensive and thoroughly innovative initiative for organizational learning. Some readers may notice the references to crisis and heroic leadership, and wonder if GE's approach is based more on compliance than on commitment, with a sense of urgency handed down by charismatic leaders like Chairman Jack Welch. GE seems to rely on both compliance and commitment, in ways that overlap within each person and team. Wherever your organization is coming from, there's much to learn from the GE experience.

In the 1970s, General Electric was known for its strategic planning. Some say we defined the practice. In the faster-moving 1980s and 1990s, we've learned that even the most detailed plans can be blown away by a single unanticipated event—such as the fall of the Berlin Wall, the Gulf War, or the current Asian economic difficulties.

Instead of being a company governed by planning, GE is working to become an organization that values change. When a surprise occurs—

when customers make new demands, or competitors enter the marketplace—our people might not predict it. But they should be able to recognize and respond quickly, for the benefit of the whole company.

Work-Out, which was launched in 1989, was named for the idea of taking excess "work out" of the system, thus eliminating bureaucracy and freeing up people's time. It was deliberately designed to focus on the cultural side of change: helping people change their attitudes about their work and the ways they approached their jobs. We needed to involve our employees in the task of improving productivity across GE. They needed to learn how to translate companywide imperatives (such as the need to increase operating margins) into their own individual actions.

Over the years, as the diagram below shows, our learning effort has evolved through seven stages, from basic Work-Out to Six Sigma Quality. We draw upon all of these in everything we do today. All of GE's formal training programs play a key role in enabling employees to respond rapidly and effectively to change.

The name "Work-Out" is a trademark of the General Electric Corporation. It is used here only to describe the particular programs managed and marketed by General Electric. Any reference in these pages to "Work-Out" refers to that trademark.

STAGE ONE: WORK-OUTS AND THE "RAMMP" MATRIX

We started, back in 1989, with one- to three-day "town meetings"— gatherings of people focused on ending the bureaucratic, hierarchical wastes of time and productivity. We grouped people in "diagonal slice teams," including people who worked together across functions and levels, because we knew that wastes of time and effort often developed at the boundary points between functions, departments, and levels. Our teams followed a framework called RAMMP:

- **Reports:** "Is this report really necessary?" Teams noted the time it took to create and read reports, versus the number of people who valued them. There were cases where leaders routinely demanded reports, without any idea that they took three person-weeks to develop. Other reports circulated unread, every year across dozens of desks. After RAMMP sessions, people could say to their bosses, "You asked for such-and-such a document, but if you changed the requirements slightly, we could do it in half the time."
- **Approvals:** "Does this decision need to be approved by so many people?" People found purchase orders needing twelve signatures for approval; scientists trusted with enormously complex experiments, for example, were not allowed to order rubber gloves on their own.

Six Sigma Quality

Making Customers Winners: GE Tool Kit-6

Change Acceleration Process: QMI, NPI, Productivity, Globalization, etc.

Process Improvement: continuous improvement, reengineering

Productivity/Best Practices: looking outside GE

Work-Out™/ Town Meetings: empowerment, bureaucracy, busting action

- **Meetings:** "Do we need to have this meeting?" Participants asked each other whether time-consuming meetings actually accomplished anything. Was the time allotted too long? Could they set it up in a better way? Could they use videoconferencing or teleconferencing to avoid costly and time-consuming travel?
- **Measures:** Participants listed all the behaviors that they wanted to see more of, and then drew a line between their existing measures and these behaviors.
- **Policies and procedures:** Did compensation plans, incentives, appraisal methods, and other policies help people get work done more effectively? Or did they get in the way?

All the RAMMP conversations essentially focused on one question: "Do we really need to keep doing these things the same way?" These meetings encouraged a mind-set for continual questioning. At the end, in a full house session with all the subteams present, participants demonstrated their ideas for change directly to the business leaders.

We encouraged business leaders to say "yes" most of the time. We wanted them to involve and engage our employees, because we knew that the people closest to the work had the best ideas for productivity improvement. If people saw that business leaders listened to, and implemented, their ideas, they would behave differently. Partly for that reason, we started with the "low-hanging fruit"—the safe and easy changes, which business leaders could accept and which would yield quick and comfortable success.

At one manufacturing plant, for instance, when people took portable computers home, they needed elaborate security clearance requests—until 6 P.M., when the security guard went home, and they could freely take their computers home. This inconsistency had bothered many people in the plant for years, but no one had ever felt safe bringing it up. Now they finally told the plant manager, "You don't have a security system, since we can walk out after 6 P.M. with the equipment. So let's eliminate the paperwork."

There's a natural temptation to blame people: "Who instituted that security system in the first place?" But that doesn't help anyone change. Instead, we tried deliberately to talk about the original security needs. Could we remove the system without side effects—or would some other old problem reappear? Once Work-Out removed bureaucratic artifacts like that ineffective security system, we used newsletters to let everyone know what we had accomplished. This helped pave the way for further innovation.

An old GE model had told us: "Ask your manager and learn." This new model suggested: "Look everywhere—above you, below you, beside you, and outside. Your manager may be learning from you."

When we need to cut cycle time, we now go to the workers who manage a particular process. We don't tell them how to do it. We give them a goal, such as cutting their cycle time by fifty percent. Then we say: "Do a Work-Out, do whatever you need to do, and come up with an answer." Their ideas are generally better than the plant managers' ideas, because they know the situation better.

THE PAYOFF MATRIX

One of the most valuable conversational tools at RAMMP meetings was a simple matrix.

People posted their suggestions for improving "reports, approvals, meetings, measures, policies, and procedures" on this four-block grid. We wanted to identify ideas that would be easy to implement and have a big impact (Block 1). The results might show, for instance, that implementing a whole new computer system would be very difficult, but implementing just one component would be relatively easy, and produce the highest impact on the work.

After a session with this four-block grid, even if they disagreed with the final choice of priorities, everybody fully understood why the group picked the projects. We still use this matrix today, generally applying it to far more challenging issues.

Over time, we have learned to use all of the Work-Out tools, techniques, and processes in joint ventures and with major customers, to raise critical challenges for working together. Formerly, we had excluded key customers (like the railroads who purchase our locomotives) from these no-holds-barred sessions because we didn't want them to see all of our mistakes and problems. But we soon discovered that our customers already knew about those. So we began inviting them to attend Work-Out with us and talk about our problems together. This openness is a plus: I've heard large customers say, "That's exactly the kind of partner we want."

	Easy to accomplish	Difficult to accomplish
High impact on the organization	1	2
Low impact on the organization	3	4

⟩⟩ For more about external partners, see the challenge of "diffusion," page 417.

After the first couple of years of Work-Out, word began to get around within GE about its effectiveness. Now if there was a problem, people would say, "We ought to do a Work-Out on this," instead of waiting for the manager to initiate a solution.

STAGE TWO: BEST PRACTICES

Work-Out's second phase began in 1990, when, to wring "NIH" (not invented here) from our culture, we began sending people outside our businesses, and outside the company, to find the best ideas. We changed incentives to reward people for sharing ideas instead of hoarding them.

Every time we launch anything new, we study what others are doing, and we keep our antennae up. We host numerous visits from customers, partners, and other outside organizations at Crotonville. We ask about their best practices. And we listen.

We introduced the exchange of best practices at key business meetings—starting with the most senior executives of the company, who meet quarterly in the Corporate Executive Council, convened by GE CEO Jack Welch. At one session, a Wal-Mart manager described their seven-day learning cycle. Wal-Mart sends key sales managers out in the field every week, visiting their own stores and competitors' stores. They regroup at Benton, Arkansas, corporate headquarters every Friday night to compare notes. If they learn that a competitor is coming out with a new promotion, they can make the necessary decisions and announce a companywide countermove on Saturday.

"If Wal-Mart can do that," our people said, "why can't GE?" So the company instituted weekly "Quick Market Intelligence" (QMI) conferences on various topics. Some highlight critical sales issues; others deal with technology changes. People from Latin America, Asia, and Europe participate through tele- or videoconference.

> This is an example of broadening the development of strategy throughout an organization. For more examples, see the challenge of "strategy and purpose," page 487.

STAGE THREE: PROCESS MAPS

By 1991, we focused on the fact that the companies that continually increased productivity had learned to pay attention to processes. This was new for GE, whose people traditionally focused on immediate goals (like getting product out the door by the end of the month). So we began to bring multifunctional teams together to learn process mapping techniques. These techniques revealed that, in our processes (like those of most businesses), as little as 5 to 15 percent of our activities added value to our products or services. Authorizations waited for two weeks in someone's in box. Contracts languished because someone was on vacation with no backup.

So the Work-Out sessions started bringing the people who affect a process together to ask: "How would we love our processes to work? And how can we get there?" As with RAMMP, we involved customers, adding their needs and priorities to the maps. When engineers predicted, "The customers will love this new feature," we wanted to hear what the customers actually thought—and not through the filter of a focus group.

Process mapping uncovered more subtle, pervasive bottlenecks, where (unlike RAMMP) people did not already perceive blockages. No one person or group has the full perspective. People are often stunned when they finally find out what happens after they hand a project over to the next part of the process.

We instituted "stretch goals" in process mapping: goals big enough to force people to think differently. For instance, we might say: "Cut your cycle time by fifty percent." People feel stunned at first: "How will I ever get there?" Then they see that they'll need to think differently. They may not reach the goal you've set, but they'll get much farther than if it were an incremental goal. Most people will not change unless they feel a sense of crisis. A leader must create that sense of urgency, so there is time to change before it's too late. But it's not enough to give employees the sense of crisis. You have to provide them with the tools, techniques, and processes to deal with it.

STAGE FOUR: CHANGE ACCELERATION

When I joined Work-Out as a team leader in 1991, we knew that our senior leaders had not been given enough tools and techniques to initiate, lead, and manage change. Work-Out was increasing our productivity, but we felt that by training senior leaders, we could move even more quickly toward our goals.

My first assignment was to develop a change management program. We pulled together a design team that included the Work-Out team, Steve Kerr, now the head of Crotonville, and several other outside consultants. We started, in 1992, with seven in-depth workshops for the four hundred most senior people in the company. In this Change Accelera-

Other key members of the Change Acceleration Process design team included Cathy Frierson and Amy Howard of the Crotonville team, plus Dave Ulrich of the University of Michigan, Ann Arbor, Mary Anne Devanna of Columbia University, and Jon Biel, Ron Gager, and Craig Schneier.

tion Process (CAP), we tried to demystify the subject of organizational change by providing a framework or model along with a series of tools or lenses that could be used to analyze an organization.

We asked these executive leaders to come in prepared to talk about an existing strategic, "must-do" change project in their organization, where even improvements of 1 percent would pay for the training. We included material on the importance of cultural change, and the power of new ways of thinking. We coached them to become champions for change, to articulate the case for change, to develop a vision for fundamental improvement, and to shape the vision in a way that helped everybody understand it and connect it to his or her own job.

We also shared several key tools that could be used to drive successful change. For instance, in one exercise, the leaders identified all the key stakeholders who must be on board for a change process to succeed. Then they had to analyze the list: "How much does each stakeholder support this idea today? And why? Where do they need to be? What's our plan for leading them in the right direction?"

Over the years, as new CAP courses continued, we developed a cadre of "follow-through" coaches for CAP graduates. These "super facilitators," trained in CAP techniques, were charged to work with teams on an ongoing basis. Around 1994, we began bringing customers into CAP sessions. Now, when many industrial customers buy from GE, they share in our own training. Our salespeople have explicitly become facilitators to our customers' success, sometimes taking on the role that a management consultant might fill elsewhere.

STAGE FIVE: STRATEGIC INITIATIVES

Having come this far, we set up a series of in-depth initiatives, focusing on highly significant issues: developing new competence or dealing with intractable problems. For instance, we had learned from our original best-practices work that successful companies need to continually introduce new products. GE's Corporate Initiatives Group focused on identifying and sharing the best practices for new product introduction (NPI).

STAGE SIX: MAKING CUSTOMERS WINNERS

We began to share some of our integrated learning techniques with customers. Several GE businesses have "customer productivity programs," working with customers to increase the productivity of their operations. In some cases, we provide enough extra service to bill; otherwise, we are rewarded by better relationships and more capable business partners.

STAGE SEVEN: SIX SIGMA QUALITY

In 1995, Jack Welch gave GE a major stretch goal: to be a "Six Sigma" company by the year 2000. GE's interest was stimulated after Larry Bossidy (CEO of Allied Signal and an ex-GE vice chairman) suggested it. Six Sigma Quality had been developed at Motorola; it's an integrated quality process that aims at achieving no more than 3.4 defects per million opportunities. The potential advantages are enormous. Customers are demanding higher quality. Competitors have already moved in this direction. And the costs savings for GE could be billions of dollars per year.

The Six Sigma methodology, known as DMAIC (Define, Measure, Analyze, Improve, and Control) brings a rigor to identifying defects, correcting them, and controlling work processes as a whole. One key component is training. Every professional employee in GE will go through Six Sigma training, covering the DMAIC processes, along with statistical and change management tools. Each GE business has a quality leader; a quality council that meets quarterly to share best practices; and our measures and rewards include quality objectives. We're building on everything we've learned to make Six Sigma work.

THE INTEGRATED LEARNING PROCESS

We have not discarded any earlier activities. If the original Work-Out felt like weeding a garden, we've learned that weeds grow back. There are always processes to be mapped, best practices to learn, and new applications for our CAP.

Some visitors say they hope to duplicate our integrated learning process within a year or two. We wish them luck. Cultural change takes twice as long as you expect. In a sense, our learning effort started in 1981, when Jack Welch became chairman of GE. Twenty years from now, our approach will still be evolving.

If people from another company asked me how to duplicate our programs, I would not advise them to copy our approach verbatim. Instead, I would emphasize four key lessons that have emerged from our integrated learning experience, and that guide everything we do:

- Involve and engage all your employees, as well as customers, partners, and suppliers. Be boundaryless in this engagement; work to develop win-win solutions across levels, functions, businesses, and companies.
- Identify and transfer best practices from inside and outside the company. Keep your antennae tuned to anyone who can help you be more productive and successful.
- Integrate these initiatives with key human resource practices. You need to ensure that you staff, train, measure, and reward consistently with your business objectives.
- Set "stretch goals." Once employees are forced to let go of the existing conventional wisdom, they can be creative and innovative, as they design new approaches. We are constantly raising the bar.

3 Five Ways to Create Time

Rick Ross

Purpose:

To reduce overload by integrating the learning initiative with other initiatives.

Participants:

Fifteen or twenty managers, all leading organizational change in the same organization.

PRUNING YOUR CHANGE INITIATIVES.

As a group, list all the change initiatives you're engaged in right now. These might include developing a new piece of business, installing a new computer system, team building, reengineering, outsourcing, and training. If in doubt, err on the side of including it. Now look at the list. It may all be "good stuff," but chances are there's too much of it. Begin pruning it down by consolidating it. Pick the three or four highest-leverage efforts, and fold the others into them.

⟩⟩ GE's payoff matrix works well for this; see page 77.

THE DECISION STYLES LIST

Suppose that a senior leader asks your opinion of a key decision. You invest some effort and make a good case. The senior leader listens, and you feel involved—until you find out, later, that the decision had already been made. Your opinion was moot. You were asked as a kind of "white lie," a well-meaning attempt to give you the impression that you had a voice.

If you've been in that situation, how did it make you feel? Chances are, it made you wary. You felt foolish and excluded, especially if you gave the "wrong" answer.

Next time you're asked, instead of answering honestly, you'll spend your time trying to figure out the answer that's already been decided. This whole dynamic leads people to waste an enormous amount of time cycling around their decisions, considering and reconsidering them in an effort to save face, without any impact on the final result.

To avoid all this, leaders need to be clear about who's making the decision, and how. This checklist will prove helpful:

- **Telling:** "Okay, team, here's the problem. Here's the solution. Here's what I want you to do. Do it." The boss or team leader has all the clout, and makes the full decision.
- **Selling:** "Here's the problem. Here's the solution. Here's why I came to it. Now do it." The boss still has all the clout, but needs to explain why the decision has been made without inviting buy-in.
- **Testing:** "Here's the problem. Here's *my* solution. What do *you* think?" If subordinates offer some compelling arguments to the contrary, the boss will scrub the decision and come back with another.
- **Consulting:** "Here's the problem. I have no solution. I have some ideas, but I'd like to hear from you." As people talk, the poohbah listens until he or she has heard enough and says, "Hold it. I like what Joe said. We're going to do that."
- **Cocreating:** "Here's the problem. Let's make the decision together." The consensus process requires more time, more interpersonal skill, and more maturity on the part of the group. It's useful to give people a time window: "I've only got three weeks. If by then, we haven't got a true consensus, I'll have to make the call." At the end, everyone, including the leader, can say: "I've been heard, I've been understood, and I'm willing to back the decision, outside the room, with a smile."

If you believe, as I do, that people tend to be more committed to decisions when they cocreate, you may want to move in that direction, but the most critical point is: Be clear. Post the checklist and let everyone know: "If you're not sure how we're making this decision, ask me. I'll tell you." Now, when you announce a decision, your subordinates can ask: "Is this a tell, a sell, a test? Are we deciding together? What is it?"

Sometimes you'll realize that you have already made the decision. But you genuinely want their opinions. "It's a test," you say.

Or you have not yet decided. "It's a consultation."

For a different application of these five types of decision making, see "Building Shared Vision: How to Begin," by Bryan Smith, in *The Fifth Discipline Fieldbook*, p. 312. Also see the "guidelines for skillful discussion," in *The Fifth Discipline Fieldbook*, pp. 389–90.

Or you just want to get on with it. "I'm telling you." People love being told what kind of decisions they're dealing with. If it's a "telling" decision, they don't have to worry about trying to guess the correct answer anymore, and if it's a "cocreating" decision, they can feel authentically involved. Leaders who use this simple tool report that the whole team saves about 20 to 30 percent of its time, and a lot of resentment.

⟩⟩ It also helps avoid "gray stamps": see page 251.

LOOK AT YOUR CALENDAR

On a sheet of paper, write out the elements of your vision for yourself, your pilot group, and your organization. Then write the word "None" on a line by itself. Now open the primary calendar or diary in which you keep your appointments. Look at the appointments you have made for the next two months. For each appointment, make a hash mark next to the element of your vision to which it most applies. If it doesn't apply to any, mark the word "none."

What percentage of the marks have fallen next to the word "none"? If it's more than 30 to 40 percent, then you're spending this time on nonessential work. What can you do to eliminate some of that work entirely?

THE ATTENTION APPRAISAL

At the top of one side of an $8\frac{1}{2}$" x 11" sheet of paper write: "What, in your opinion, do I pay too much attention to?" On the flip side, write: "What, in your opinion, do I pay not enough attention to?" Give the sheet to each one of your team members and ask them to be candid. Collect them back, read them over, and adjust your attention accordingly. Many of my clients have found this exercise a valuable time-saver.

"RELEVANCE-TIME-RECIPROCITY" QUESTIONS (FOR YOURSELF)

■ What tasks do I wish I didn't have to bother doing, that I could delegate to someone else? What tasks shouldn't I be doing?

For example, you might be able to tell a subordinate: "You're consigned now not for just $5,000, but for $50,000. Come to me only with questions about expenses above that amount." Agree in advance that you'll try the new approach for three months. If it doesn't work, you can always go back to the old micromanagement.

■ What tasks could I handle with a lot less oversight? When I was a young manager in the San Diego city government, my boss insisted on approving all expenses. I finally asked him: "John, you always sign the ones below $50,000. Sometimes I have to wait three days for these. Why can't I just go ahead and submit them?"

Again, agree to try the new approach for three months. If it works, you and your boss will both save an enormous amount of time.

The same boss taught me how to make it work. Once, after leaving me in charge for several days, he asked why I had made a particular decision. I explained my reasoning. He had no argument with my decision. "But did you ask yourself what I would have done?"

I had to admit that the question had never occurred to me—and that if it had, I would have made a different choice.

Thereafter, whenever he left me in charge, I tried to consider the decisions that he would have made. I didn't always go the same way, but thinking about his choices always informed my decision. In retrospect, that more than any other single factor allowed me to handle tasks without oversight and save us both time.

Change delegation limits

4 Minimal Intervention

Making the most of a pilot group's limited time

Sherry Immediato, Heaven & Earth, Incorporated

We asked long-standing "learning organization" consultant Sherry Immediato to help organizations do more with less—a cornerstone of her practice.

For the last seven years, I have focused a significant part of my practice on organizations with lots of inspiration, tough choices, little capital, and virtually no discretionary time. In the process, I've learned the value of minimal intervention—designing your efforts to get the maximum results for the least effort and cost. It's all too easy to lose sight of the organization's primary priorities, and these four techniques help focus attention back there:

Special thanks to Kristin Cobble for providing extensive feedback and coaching on this article. For amplification on the ideas presented here on achieving results as simply as possible, see http://www.heaven-and-earth.com.

1. **Stop something before starting anything new:** Starting a new initiative means taking time and attention away from the rest of your work. Thus your first task is to intentionally free up energy and resources. This often means eliminating existing rules, regulations, and other infrastructure. Recently, a large petrochemical plant chose to systematically uncover opportunities for performance improvement. In the data-gathering stage, the improvement team heard numerous complaints about the organization's performance appraisal system. At best, it added meaningless paperwork; at worst, bonuses, promotions, and reprimands seemed so arbitrary that there was little incentive for good performance.

   The improvement team knew that redesigning the appraisal system woud be important later, but fixing it would distract them from more essential tasks. So they recommended that the appraisal system be suspended completely for a year with a commitment to begin redesigning it at that time. In the interim, bonuses would be based on division rather than individual performance. When the recomendation was approved, the credibility of the improvement team and the plant leadership team increased in the eyes of the employees.

   Note that this disassembly took place deliberately, not by default. By contrast, I witnessed a large healthcare system unintentionally demolish its total quality management system. The TQM leader quit, and the other senior executives were too distracted to replace him. Coordination of local initiatives stopped. Finally, quality slipped off the agenda even though the executive team still maintains that it is important.

2. **Group silence:** This is a valuable way to help groups develop a sense of the underlying forces that may benefit or impede their progress. Most groups benefit from the understanding that any member can call for a few moments of silence at any time. The board of a faith-based organization that I worked with was concerned that they were wasting time and getting off purpose too regularly. They decided to experiment for a day by requiring ten minutes of silence every hour, no matter what was happening in their conversation. The members were to use this quiet time to relax and refocus.

   Sometimes they welcomed the break, and other times they resisted it mightily. But the break revealed the hidden force that kept them from moving forward: They enjoyed one another's company too much. They used meetings to "let their hair down" and then, later, felt chagrined that they still hadn't gotten to important business. Through their experiments with silence, they began to develop the kind of relaxed focus and concentration that exists at the heart of many meditation practices and produces a deeper clarity about what really matters.

3. **The "action planning quality check":** When groups assemble "to-do lists" of action items, I ask them to consider what each action will accomplish in light of their purpose and objectives. The resulting discussion often reveals that many action items won't produce the desired results. For example, one team considered requiring its suppliers to attend a skill-building training session. Suddenly they realized that bullying the supplier would not help build the long-term partnership they wanted.

4. **Planned neglect:** Even after culling the list, a lean organization can't pursue everything that seems important. Commit to all of your desired results, but suspend specific action on some of the items for a specified period of time, such as the next six months.

There can be unanticipated benefits to deferring some priorities. Our church is now at the end of a three-phase renovation: first installing a new roof and drainage system, then repairing structural brickwork on the outside walls, and only finally renovating the water-damaged interior. This was an astute sequence: It kept people like me interested in funding yet another phase of renovation. It's hard to see chipped mortar between the bricks, but you can't miss the big white blotches on the golden wall.

Be warned that planned neglect is a double-edged tool! While it serves to focus energy, it can cause results to be compromised over time, if people are willing to "let the vision slide."

The concept of "planned neglect" was developed by Richard Beckhard; for more on his approach, see *Changing the Essence: The Art of Creating and Leading Fundamental Change in Organizations* (with Wendy Pritchard), San Francisco: Jossey-Bass, 1992.

5 Barking and Nonbarking Dogs

The strategic practice field

Rick Ross, Charlotte Roberts

In most organizations, senior managers spend far too little time talking about the "important but not urgent" strategic issues that determine success. Do they want to go global? What new markets do they want to build? How can they prepare for next year's challenges?

Purpose:

Successful teams learn to be successful through practice. This exercise establishes a practice field where teams can consider problems before they become crises, and learn to operate more effectively.

Overview:

A team meets regularly to talk candidly about strategic business issues, evaluate potential threats and opportunities, and plan collective action.

Participants:

Executive teams or teams involved in "running" a pilot group. Team members should already have some exposure to "skillful discussion" techniques.

Supplies:

A small working room with flip charts, markers, tape, and chairs (perhaps without a table).

Even if they raise these issues in staff meetings, the formal atmosphere of officially commissioned presentations gives the team members very little chance to reflect together. So they reflect separately—in huddles in corridors and restrooms, piling on attributions: "Sure, John criticized your proposal, but that's because he's working his own agenda." Or, "Fran must be trying to make me look bad in front of everybody."

A strategic practice field provides a quarterly alternative to time-wasting dysfunctionality. It gives you two days, not of "feel good" time, but of hard work on business imperatives.

STAGE ONE: "GATHERING THE DOGS"

Facilitators spend at least a day (probably two) before the practice field in preparation: by talking to each team member, and developing an agenda based upon three types of concerns:

- Barking dogs: Important and urgent items;
- Nonbarking dogs: Items that are of strategic importance, but not urgent;
- Sleeping dogs: "Undiscussable" issues that no one is willing to talk about, but that may make it difficult to proceed unless they are raised in conversation.

To help the meeting stay on track, facilitators should check the agenda with the team leader, without revealing the names of people whose comments were gathered.

STAGE TWO: THE "BARKING DOGS"

Open with a "check-in": a round-robin in which team members can briefly talk about whatever is foremost on their minds, without interruption. This sets a mood of mutual respect and interest.

Now spend a half day on the "important and urgent" issues—issues that are driving the team crazy, gleaned from preparatory interviews. Team members are expected to challenge one another's assumptions, using reflection and inquiry techniques. For instance, they might ask: "What is it that you see that leads you to make that statement?" The facilitators act as "mirrors" to the group, making impasses more evident, and raising questions that the group might miss.

The team leader of the group should be prepped to give and take as an equal member. If that isn't possible, he or she should exit for two or three hours, let the group hash out the issue, and then return.

Occasionally during this stage, the team slows down the action to look more closely at their own conversation: What types of assumptions are evident in the decisions they have made so far? What types of limits are they aware of, having listened to themselves? This segment is analogous to the practice time of a sports team or symphony orchestra. The team rehearses other potential ways of engaging challenging issues.

This stage is more akin to Dialogue than Skillful Discussion. See The Fifth Discipline Fieldbook, p. 56: "Designing a Dialogue Session."

STAGE THREE: THE "NONBARKING DOGS" PRACTICE FIELD

On the morning of the second day, take up the "important but not urgent" items. These potential threats and opportunities, if ignored, would probably turn into "barking dogs" by next year. The choice of issues is critical; the more relevant people find them, the more effective the conversation will be. Chances are, your organizational change initiative itself is a "nonbarking dog."

This second-day conversation is not a problem-solving meeting; the goal is to raise the quality of thinking. Maintain the "practice field" quality of stage two, continuing to look not just at the issues, but at the ways in which the team deals with the issues. Be willing to discover aspects of the issue that you hadn't thought about before. Look at many facets rather than quickly converging on it and moving to conclusion.

Some readers may recognize the non-barking dogs as Steven Covey's "important but not urgent" issues— "quadrant 2" issues—worth paying attention to early. See Covey, The Seven Habits of Highly Effective People, New York: Simon & Schuster, 1989, pp. 149–56.

STAGE FOUR: SLEEPING DOGS

As the team gains proficiency, you may start to introduce "sleeping dogs" —the "undiscussables" that should not be allowed to lie. "I'd like to throw a sleeping dog on the table," the facilitator might announce, "if you're all up for it. This issue came up in interviews and nobody seems to want to talk about it." The issue might involve disconnects between espoused values and actual behavior; for instance, "We talk about respect for the individual, but we're laying people off left and right."

By raising "sleeping dogs" in this safe environment, and gaining practice in talking about them, you make it easier to talk about volatile, controversial issues in the "barking dogs" section of your next session.

WHO SHOULD FACILITATE?

Teams beginning this practice generally don't have the skill to facilitate themselves. We recommend pairing an outside facilitator (drawn from a trusted consultancy) with a facilitator from the human resources or organization development staff.

External facilitators are more comfortable helping people work with unfamiliar techniques, and more apt to ask the "dumb" questions that reveal contradictions or difficult issues. They provide outside perspective. One team began to talk about moving from a product-based structure (business units) to one organized by functions (sales, marketing, etc.) "Are you aware," asked the external facilitator, "that most organizations I see are restructuring the opposite way?" This triggered an in-depth conversation about the reasoning behind the shift.

Internal facilitators bring an understanding of the organizational culture and politics, and their own biases serve as a useful counterpoint to the biases of the line leaders or executive leaders on the team. Choose the internal people carefully. They must not just have "process" training in group dynamics, but business credibility. They must be able to follow in-depth conversations about competitive strategy, costs, revenues, and business plans. Otherwise, they'll miss nuances and their insights will sound irrelevant.

Some senior teams (such as the CEO and direct reports) are too high in the hierarchy for internal consultants to handle. They will only accept an external facilitator. In one practice field, the facilitator said: "Tell me how the top executives add value to the organization." The senior vice presidents said that their job was to advise the CEO so he could make decisions. The CEO was amazed: "You're supposed to be making decisions yourselves." This conversation could not have taken place safely if an internal staff person had been in the room.

THE RESULTS

Team members gain experience in the practice fields, and then conduct their own subordinates' meetings more effectively, provoking a gradual change in leadership behavior that spreads throughout the organization. People who seemed stilted and awkward before, or who shielded themselves with a pile of overheads, now can walk into a working session and say, "Let's talk about any subject you want," and handle themselves with confidence and sensitivity. The practice field may be the first time that people below senior level are exposed to the reasoning behind corporate strategy.

VARIATIONS

Some facilitators incorporate reviews of conversational techniques, or conversations about management books into the sessions, as a way to bring in new ideas from outside.

The practice field can be accelerated, once every few sessions, by dividing into two teams, and having each tape a session with a videocamera. Then let each team view the other's tape. Members coach individual "partners" from the other team, on issues like these:

- How helpful was your partner in moving the group forward? What kind of role did he or she play? How could he or she improve?
- How did people in the group move to agreement? Did diverse points of view get voiced? Did people check in with others who had been quiet—using inquiry?
- Did anyone summarize key themes and points of disagreement?
- Did it look like people have lots of unexpressed and unvoiced views?

Then partners meet privately to give each other feedback. Later, subgroups reconvene to review their own tapes, keeping the recent feedback in mind. Then the subgroups discuss the insights they have gained about their own style, and about the subjects under discussion. Finally, in a meeting of all team members, they talk about ways to improve the next quarter's meeting.

⅋⅋ For tips on coaching and feedback, see page 108.

6 Managing a Practice Field

Nick Zeniuk (Interactive Learning Labs, Inc., formerly of Ford Motor Company); Tim Savino (Harley-Davidson); Herb Rau, Rik Glover, and Terry Johnson (Fairchild Semiconductor, formerly National Semiconductor); Harold Hillman (Amoco Management Learning Center); B. C. Huselton (Quantum Leap, formerly with GS Technologies)

By now, a decade's worth of experience exists with in-depth "practice fields" (also called learning laboratories) at certain companies. These labs help meet the challenge of "not enough time," by focusing atten-

For more about learning labs and practice fields, see *The Fifth Discipline*, p. 313, and *The Fifth Discipline Fieldbook*, p. 529. For more on the Lincoln Continental learning lab, see *The Fifth Discipline Fieldbook*, p. 554.

tion early on critical business issues and helping people develop better skills for dealing with them. Learning labs always seem to turn out differently than their designers intend. Aspects that seem immensely important at first—such as the use of computer simulations, or the evolution of a separate "room" for learning—are far less important than getting leaders involved and establishing strong links with business concerns. Here are the details from five companies where learning labs have made a difference.

WHAT'S THE MOST EFFECTIVE WAY TO INVITE PEOPLE TO JOIN?

Harold Hillman (Amoco): People should attend in intact work teams. At first, we picked people somewhat randomly. They'd go back to their business unit and other people would say, "What are you talking about?" Now we bring our managers through in teams. In the week our managers spend here at the learning center, they all work together half the week. For the other half, each intact team works together in a separate room on its own business issues.

Tim Savino (Harley-Davidson): For any given project, our goal is to try to get the "whole system" represented in the room. That might include any combination of the service organization, engineering, manufacturing, human resources, the platform teams, or others. Specific individuals generally attend out of personal interest and because they have a defined area of responsibility—for example, the product development process—and therefore a stake in any decisions that might be made.

For more about the Harley-Davidson system-mapping project, see page 468.

B. C. Huselton (re: GS Technologies): Our union and management people couldn't talk to each other. We would argue, scream, walk away from each other, and call each other names. We developed a series of gatherings—not a learning lab, per se, but a structured dialogue project where we employed many of the learning laboratory techniques. We set it up by invitation: "It's a safe environment; there's no such thing as a mistake. Do you want to join us?" We knew that anything would be better than the canned "can't-we-all-get-along-together" effective-communication programs that we had already tried. They'd brought us an incremental improvement in feeling good, but no deep changes.

We knew that institutionalizing it, or setting up mandatory learning labs everywhere, would have been frustrating and ineffective. These projects can be very effective when they build on people's curiosity:

People see that those who have been to our sessions seem to get better results, without being distraught all the time. And they wonder why.

Nick Zeniuk (re: Ford): On the Lincoln Continental project, project leader Fred Simon and I began inviting team members to spend two days onsite looking at "the problems and dilemmas that are bothering you." Over a two-year period, we brought 250 people through these learning labs, continually experimenting, trying to learn how to design practice fields that would be more effective. After we left Ford, we packaged it as a three-day "learning lab" where teams do this on their own.

WHAT ROLES DO THE SENIOR LEADER AND FACILITATOR PLAY?

Zeniuk: The leader sets the tone for learning, so it's very important that the leader is encouraging, and "walks the talk" in terms of using the techniques in day to day work. It made a difference in the Lincoln Continental learning labs that their boss (me) was doing the teaching.

On the first day, I said, "I will be learning with you. I don't know the answers, or what is going to happen here, but we will learn together to think differently about our work." Later, I heard that practically before I was even finished, it was in the halls around Ford: "Did you hear what Nick did? He stood up and said he didn't know!"

At first, it was frightening to me to stand up and act as a different kind of boss, one who is not going to tell people what to do. We bosses sometimes think that the people who work for us expect us to behave in an authoritarian way. I thought I didn't know the theories, tools, and methods well enough to facilitate the learning lab. I was wrong. I've discovered subsequently that we intuitively know most of it all already.

Savino: We have used some outside facilitators on a fairly regular basis for a couple of the ongoing learning teams. These people bring technical expertise and process skills. But the facilitation role is not limited to the facilitator. Other people, who have developed their own expertise, will sometimes stop a meeting to try new things, or will schedule time to learn about something like causal loop diagramming. It's also common for a group member to bring in someone with expertise in a particular area.

WHAT KIND OF INFRASTRUCTURE IS VALUABLE?

Terry Johnson (Fairchild Semiconductor): The most critical single factor was "dialogic conversation": conversation with a reduced pace and a more thoughtful atmosphere. The sessions evolve naturally and don't

necessarily go along a predetermined path. Nonetheless, I still plan out each session beforehand, even if I don't end up using the plan.

A computer model, in itself, is not that important. MIT researcher David Ford created a great model of our product development process, but the usage of that model was almost zero. People couldn't connect to it. They had very little patience to try to figure that out.

Huselton: Dens are vital for dialogue: open, comfortable, thoughtful physical settings where everyone can see each other. One element that inhibits learning labs is the use of the same old offices, with all the old elements and artifacts.

Zeniuk: We had a learning lab room set aside, with descriptions of all the conversational techniques on wall posters. We had chairs arranged in a circle. We said, "Don't make decisions here," because we wanted to keep the participants open to possibilities. Conceptually, the room was neat, but it turned out to be a crutch. People felt they had to go to this special room to use these techniques, and they could forget about it when they went back to their regular environment. More important, going to the "learning room" became a chore. In some ways we were still working under the model of a special place where people come to learn things that "we know," that they wouldn't ordinarily use.

We have learned how to take the learning lab to the field. We conduct it anytime, anyplace, wherever it's important. At United Technologies Automotive, during a management shakeup, the organization held up its funds for learning labs. A number of teams said, "We can't wait," and they created their own—over lunch, over dinner, on their own time.

Hillman: We have compiled a library of about four hundred learning loops, covering different dynamics. The leaders in the business units often circulate them to everyone. After they've gone through the program and are back at work, they'll develop a specific loop explanation and send it around with a note saying: "We were working on this issue, and came to this understanding, and thought you might learn from it, too." It helps people build on their knowledge. It's all available electronically to everyone in the company, and people access it regularly.

HOW DO YOU KNOW THE LEARNING LAB IS "WORKING"?

Hillman: We were really interested in finding out if people back in the business units continued to use what they learned. For the first three years, our evidence was just anecdotal: Then we had some university researchers conduct surveys. Comments showed that there had been a lot of skepticism about the "mental models" discipline. People said it was too soft and psychological: "We already know how to talk to each other." Or, "What does this have to do with business, anyway?"

But later, when we covered systems thinking along with skills of productive conversation, survey respondents said things like, "Now I get it!" They saw that the more productive their conversations, the more robust their causal loop diagrams, and the more effective their actions.

That taught us to cover all the disciplines together, instead of "mental models" one year, and "systems thinking" the next. Then people see that learning is not separate from the business.

Rik Glover (Fairchild Semiconductor): We are working on an initiative to reduce our product development cycle time from 250 days to ninety. Our first test product will come in at eighty. We can point to that as a quantitative measurable result of the learning labs, but to me, the more important result is that we are now having conversations about the kind of working environment we want to be part of in this organization.

Herb Rau (Fairchild Semiconductor): It takes time. You won't see results in six months or a year. It might take three or five years. You have to be patient and consistent if you're making change from inside.

Savino: It's very difficult to assess the impact of a single process like a learning lab. The real testimony to its value is the growing interest and membership in these learning teams. Many of the project teams at Harley-Davidson have existed for three years or more. If people did not find them valuable then they would not have been sustained this long.

Huselton: People have "life apnea"—they go on and on, in a daze, and don't take the time to learn until someone shocks them back into life again. The learning labs can provide a bit of that shock.

7 Integrating Work and Personal Life . . . in Practice

Lotte Bailyn

Professor Lotte Bailyn is considered a formidable individual around MIT's Sloan School of Management. She and her team of researchers

have developed the most informed, integrated approch that we know
of for companies that wish to boost performance by taking some of the
stress off their people. This article proposes in-depth change, evolving
from the aspirations of people in companies, who desperately want to
bring their personal lives and their work into synch.

The more productive that workplaces become, and the more they embody organizational learning, the more problems they seem to create for people. In particular, the increased involvement demanded by organizational change, and by the "learning organization," seems to require more time and energy from employees than they can easily provide—especially given the increasingly complicated pressures of their private lives.

For the past twenty years, my research has focused on exploring the apparent conflict between the pressures of work and the pressures of home. My colleagues and I use in-depth interviews, surveys, and round-table sessions to discern: What work practices interfere with people's ability to integrate their lives and to get their work done? What underlying assumptions keep those work practices in place?

We have concluded that success at home and success at work can reinforce each other. They only seem opposed because it takes such excessive effort to maintain them in isolation from each other. When business agendas clash with personal agendas, people assume that their personal needs must give in. They spend less time with their families; they give up caring for themselves; or they simply cut back on sleep.

These strategies are addictively self-perpetuating. Worse still, they do not address the fundamental problems at play—the assumptions, usually unrecognized, that guide most organizational practices. For instance, at many companies, there's a tacit assumption that successful performance does not mean producing results. It means "face time": being visibly seen at work, and always available when needed. This combines with the tacit goal of reducing headcount as much as possible. Managers tell employees to work "smarter, not harder," but their actions suggest that the managers really want employees to work smarter *and* longer. As one manager put it, "With twenty percent more efficiency, I could function with twenty percent fewer people."

As it happens, people can "work smart" for limited periods of time, but not for long hours: Fatigue, attention span, and concern over other needs all intervene. This is obvious from anyone's personal experience, and it's corroborated by research showing productivity increases when

For a more in-depth view, with more examples of practice, see Lotte Bailyn's book Breaking the Mold: Women, Men and Time in the New Corporate World (New York: The Free Press, 1993). Also see R. Rapaport, L. Bailyn, et al., Relinking Life and Work: Towards a Better Future (New York: Ford Foundation, 1996).

people job-share and work part-time. Our research also suggests that the attitudes about face time and headcount are often not based on the actual needs of the business; they're based on stereotyped, habitual organizational expectations. Until people can talk about these issues openly, and redesign the work structures that are based on them, employees will feel pressured by home and family conflict, and organizations will feel plagued by low performance. Conversely, in the cases we have studied where companies have successfully changed the work practices that stem from these traditional expectations, there is substantial performance improvement, and people begin to feel as if their work lives and home lives can come back together.

RETHINKING SUPPORT STRUCTURES

Often, a perceived "lack of time" problem is caused by the way the work is organized. In a bank we studied, the pressures from both personal and work life were so great that loan officers routinely experienced sleepless nights. When fatigued, they made poorer judgments—which heightened the pressure they felt, and threatened the bank's success.

A major reengineering effort had left the bank with thirty professional loan officers and only one administrator for office work. The officers had not only to evaluate loans and make decisions, but to obtain data and write commitment letters. Meanwhile, the bank managers demanded more loans processed, more quickly. And because the bank had recently relocated the unit, most loan officers faced much longer commutes.

Fortunately, the bank managers were willing to see this as a problem for the whole operation to solve, rather than as the fault of these individuals. Management agreed, on an experimental basis, to raise the level of administrative support, giving bank officers more time to conduct the work that only they could conduct. They taught the administrators how to write the commitment letters, and agreed to hire some temporary help. This increased costs a little, but also increased quality.

By the end of the project, the extent to which people said they were having sleepless nights had dropped dramatically. To us that was an important personal issue; to the business it was an important bottom line issue. The amount of time the loan officers put in at work had dropped slightly, perhaps an hour less per week. But the amount of time they spent performing work, instead of "spinning their wheels," dramatically increased. The administrator felt empowered and valued; her productivity jumped. The bank made the temporary help permanent because, in the end, the managers saw the benefit.

Significantly, these changes (and others) all developed out of round-table discussions among the loan officers and employees. Once given time and space to talk about it, group members came up with an approach that reorganized the work to give them the time they needed. That is true for all groups. Only the basic principle remains constant: *If everyone involved is working more hours than they reasonably choose to work, and the work is optimally organized, then more people are needed. Otherwise, the performance will suffer.*

RESTRUCTURING DAILY ACTIVITIES

For more detail see Leslie A. Perlow, *Finding Time: How Corporations, Individuals and Families Can Benefit from New Work Practices* (Ithaca: Cornell University Press, 1997).

Sometimes a different way of structuring time can make a difference. We conducted a time experiment with one product development team who worked excessively long hours. We originally proposed closing the doors at 6 P.M. and making everybody leave, but they wouldn't hear of it. They knew that this wouldn't get to the core of their problem. Individuals couldn't finish their work because they were constantly interrupted by meetings, schedule checks, and management reviews.

We worked with them to restructure the workday into "quiet times" and "interactive times." The results were astounding: The team launched the product on time and received quality rewards. Moreover, they now felt a greater sense of control, which eased some of their personal stress. The managers learned that engineers perform better without continuous surveillance. The VP even gave up his weekly ops reviews.

CREATING FLEXIBILITY

Another source of relief is increasing the flexibility of location and time: providing employees with more control and discretion over the conditions of work. Relevant benefits include flextime and "flexplace," part-time and job-sharing opportunities, and family and medical leaves. They boost productivity by retrieving time wasted in undesired commutes, and inconvenient, rigorous schedules.

Unfortunately, corporate policies tend to require managers to negotiate these benefits on a case-by-case basis, "only for the people who really need them." This extra negotiation is a real headache for most managers; and it creates dissension within the workforce. People who aren't granted flexibility feel unfairly treated. People who get it feel singled out, or no longer seen as top employees. The overall culture continues to send the message that top performers are heroes who sacrifice everything else for work. These problems can be reduced by establishing a universal flexibility design, developed collectively by the people who will be affected. There also may need to be discussion about the ongoing assumptions that people hold around time.

By encouraging people to develop their own resourcefulness, flexibility can enhance creativity and learning, and lead to unanticipated strategic benefits. In one investment firm, a relatively independent group of financial analysts felt burdened by the time they spent commuting and wanted to work from home. The organization agreed to try flexibility on an experimental basis, even finding some "loaner" computers for people who didn't have their own laptops.

A couple of weeks after the experiment began, the company's local area network (LAN) went down for four days. The only people who could get any work done were the people working from home. Some people jokingly accused us of deliberately shutting down the LAN, just to prove our point.

CULTIVATING "LEAD USERS"

Many companies operate by the implicit rule: "Never go to your superiors with a problem, only with a solution." This is a formula for creating chronic crises in organizations. Crises, in turn, lead to long and stressful hours, chaotic approaches to solving problems, and a lack of strategic orientation. No one hears about the people who *prevent* crises, solving the same problems before they get big, with much less expense, waste, and trouble. Those who wait until crises get serious, and then visibly fix them, get rewarded.

In one company, we tried to document this dynamic. We followed people and then analyzed whether their behaviors reinforced or prevented crises. The crisis preventers (whom we called "lead users") were integrated individuals. They used rationality and assertiveness but could also be empathetic and nurturing. Many of them were not very visible, but they tended to be the people who "kept the place going," helping everybody else meet his job requirements.

One manager told us about one of his engineers, the so-called "glue" in the unit. He performed support tasks that held the unit together, but he wasn't working on his own individual tasks. The manager wanted to promote him, but the "lead user" engineer didn't fit the company's pro-

See J. K. Fletcher, "A Feminist Reconstruction of Work," *Journal of Management Inquiry*, Vol. 7 (1998), pp. 163–86.

motion criteria, which were defined by individual deliverables. The manager was told, in essence, to tell the engineer, "Stop this supportive behavior and meet your own targets." Meanwhile, a top performer who always met his individual deliverables was disruptive to the group, in a way that wasted everyone's time.

If you want to avoid the draining effect of crisis-to-crisis management, you have to find ways of getting line leaders and executive leaders to see the problem. By making the contribution of "lead users" more visible we helped executives recognize the time-draining effect of an individualistic reward system.

ENSURING EQUITY FOR PEOPLE WITH PERSONAL COMMITMENTS

We always look at work not only in terms of its effectiveness and efficiency, but at its impact on people's lives. This inevitably raises questions about the deep cultural assumptions, built into corporate practice, about issues like gender roles, family, and community.

For instance, we might ask a top manager, "How did you get to where you are? Could you have gotten here if you had a wife who had a career?" Some of these men, in their fifties and sixties, realize how dependent they have always been on their wives. They begin to see their young employees, who typically have working spouses, a little differently.

At one large company, a male manager began to catch on to these connections. He had attended one meeting where, at 5:30 P.M., a female manager left to pick up her children at school, as she did every day. The next day she went to her boss, a vice president, and said, "I was upset that I had to leave. What did I miss?"

"Don't worry about it," the VP said. "We understand completely that you have to leave, and that's fine."

But the male manager protested to the VP. "That's discrimination." He explained that the VP had tacitly communicated the idea that her personal commitments made her less important. They could hold the meeting without her, and not even bring her up to speed. There was a deep inequity bred into the system—not against the female manager because she was female *per se*, but against all people who put their family commitments ahead of work, even on a previously agreed-upon basis.

In fact, employees should have the opportunity to alternate high-involvement, "fast track" phases with lower-involvement, "more time with family" phases, without being jeopardized by the periods of lower involvement.

See L. Bailyn, J. K. Fletcher, D. Kolb, "Unexpected Connections: considering employees' personal lives can revitalize your business." *Sloan Management Review*, Summer 1997, pp. 11–19.

HOW TO RAISE THE "PERSONAL" AT WORK

It's not hard to come up with ways to meet the dual agenda of work and personal lives. At one company, in a one-hour workshop session, we came up with hundreds of ideas. But then we asked: Why hasn't anybody put these ideas into effect?

Putting them into effect takes time. In our experience, you need a minimum of three months to begin to see some first-order change. Serious changes can take eight to ten years to complete, and require efforts from all sides. Individuals cannot do it alone. It's terribly important to develop these ideas in collective forums, because they nearly always involve challenging some already agreed-upon practice, and individuals generally do not have the perspective to see all sides of the issue.

Rewards and incentives should reinforce these new approaches. For instance, if people put in longer hours than actually required, it might be assumed that the person is working that extra time for its own sake. Instead of rewarding that person with higher pay and promotions, let the pleasure of the work carry the rewards.

One might expect the human resources (HR) department to advocate the use of flexible and equitable policies for improving performance. Unfortunately, many HR people (especially in older companies) tend to be resistant and negative about cultural change. Even the presence of enlightened HR people can reinforce old attitudes. Since HR is "supposed to take care of people issues," the line departments, responsible for profit and loss, can ignore them.

It is much more effective to enlist senior management to provide support and safety for experimentation. But they must be committed to share resulting productivity gains with their employees. For if they don't, they will end up with an alienated, cynical workforce, as has happened so often in response to reengineering. The dual agenda of performance and personal life needs to be kept on the table continuously. When we are invited into a company, we warn senior managers that if they are not willing to share the benefits, they'd better not even start, because they'll end up worse than they are now.

⟩⟩ See the challenge of "walking the talk," page 193.

Of course, developing new approaches to the design of work is only the first step. Beyond that lies the task of redesigning the constricting habitual patterns within families and communities. In the end, one hopes that work, family, and community will all fit together, continuously gaining from one another's presence.

TIME FOR LIFE

The Surprising Ways Americans Use Their Time, by John P. Robinson and Geoffrey Godbey,
(University Park, PA: Pennsylvania State University Press, 1997)

Important news for anyone trying to understand the challenge of "not enough time" systemically: People have *more* time, on average, than they did in 1960, even allowing for the impact of working women and surging productivity. Because people are now trying to create their own lives (as in the discipline of personal mastery) their aspirations are richer; and that makes us feel as if we haven't got enough time (and maybe never will). In the future, you and your organization will probably have more free time (albeit in smaller blocks). This eye-opening report, based on three decades of surveys and diaries, offers better perspective and advice than any time-management book. — Art Kleiner

THE TWENTY-FOUR-HOUR SOCIETY

by Martin Moore-Ede (Reading, MA: Addison-Wesley, 1993)

Based on thirty-odd years of research on the human biological clock, this book argues convincingly that human physiology is out of synch with society's round-the-clock performance demands. Reading about the role that sleep deprivation played in disasters like the Exxon Valdez oil spill and the *Challenger* explosion made them seem all the more tragic—and doubled my interest in understanding the basics of sleep-wake cycles, jet lag, alertness, and fatigue. While some of the solutions in the book seem silly and futuristic (a desk chair developed by Matsushita that lulls you to sleep, then monitors and times your body's functions, waking you with bright lights and cool air, "optimally refreshed") others are so obvious and sensible you wonder why they aren't already established practice. Moore-Ede tells how to manage your own body's cycles so you'll know when to push on finishing that big project— and when to just go home and sleep on it. — Nina Kruschwitz

IV. No Help (Coaching and Support)

"We have no help!"

1 The Challenge

A group of internal consultants and trainers first articulated this challenge in our working sessions. All of them had come up against the same "feast or famine" dynamic. During the early stages of learning initiatives, they had too little to do. They were constantly in "sales mode," trying to generate demand. But then they received more and more requests, without the capacity to meet all of them, gradually becoming overextended and overwhelmed. When this happened, the quality of the help they were able to provide declined. Under more pressure, they began to rush from client to client, taking less and less time to understand the in-depth needs of each. They dropped their least urgent tasks —including the training of new consultants who might have lightened the load. Since training new consultants might take years, there was little executive-level support for it. Executive leaders were pleased to see their existing staff used, but no one wanted to add more capacity. Instead, there was pressure to "get along with the help we have."

Without quality coaching, guidance, and support, pilot groups began to flounder. Called upon to lead new innovations, they complained of feeling like "the blind leading the blind." Often they never really accomplished anything. Ultimately, onlookers concluded that the "learning stuff" didn't work. "It would have worked," proponents replied, "but we had no help!"

"Help" can take many forms in significant change initiatives. It can

Sources of help

come through internal or external consultants. It can come from other line managers who have "been there before," and are willing to offer counsel. It can come from mentors. For example, local line leaders often know particular executives with whom they have special mentoring relationships. Sometimes, it can even come from mentors outside the organization, such as retired executives.

In all these cases, those engaged in significant change efforts need to ask for help themselves. As the old saying goes, "When the student is ready, the teacher appears." Unfortunately, there are many forces at play in contemporary organizations that discourage people from asking for help. "Macho" cultures discourage it because they foster an image that "I can do it myself." Many organizations reinforce the message that asking for help is a sign of incompetence. Managers who must continually project an air of certainty to be credible find it difficult to acknowledge in front of peers or subordinates that they do not have all the answers. Others fear that their bosses will learn what they are doing if they have outsiders helping them. All of these forces operate to create isolation among innovators, and isolation breeds blindness. Perhaps the single biggest reason managers do not ask for help is that they are unaware that they need it. They "don't know what they don't know" until it is too late to do anything about it.

Paradoxically, the challenge of "no help" often arises amid an abundance of help. Large companies retain a wide variety of internal and external consultants to help teams change their work practices. But corporate managers are often accustomed to traditional expert consulting and training practices, developed in centralized offices far from the local line leaders who need them, and focused around delivering prepackaged answers to problems. In a learning-oriented situation, this approach can be overbearing. It almost never helps in developing the capacities of pilot teams to help themselves.

THE UNDERLYING DYNAMICS OF "NO HELP"

The stronger the profound change growth processes (R1, R2, and R3 in the diagram), the greater the requirement for coaching, guidance, and support. If the help available to people is inadequate, the effectiveness of the change initiative suffers and learning capabilities fail to develop. People may say that "We don't know what to do," or, "We have no help," or more likely they just experience the frustration of spending their time on yet another initiative with minimal impact. Eventually, this dimin-

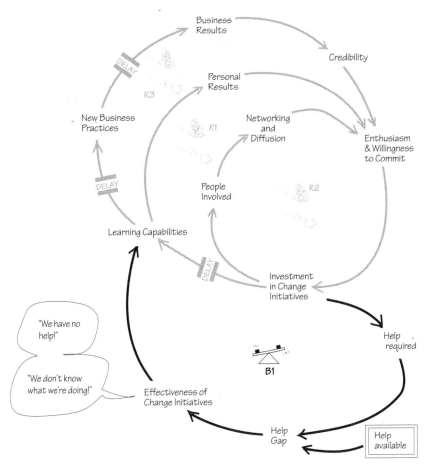

As investments in change initiatives go up, more help is required—which might include coaching, training, consultation, mentoring, or other forms of guidance for developing a change initiative. If "help available" is limited (perhaps because there isn't enough institutional support for it), the resulting "help gap" leaves people frustrated because they are investing time with little payoff: the change initiative is ineffective and learning capabilities do not develop.

ishes everyone's enthusiasm and willingness to commit and the change initiative either slows or dies out entirely.

STRATEGIES FOR MEETING THE CHALLENGE OF "NO HELP"

■ **Investing early in help:** It can take months, testing various consultants and guides, to find help that represents a reliable match for your pilot group. If you are leading a challenging initiative, you may need to find help simply to determine what kinds of help you need—in the same way that you would seek opinions from people you know before any other complex procurement task, like buying a computer. Network leaders, who are generally responsible for the organization's capacity to help itself, have a great deal of leverage in both providing and in looking for help on behalf of the organization as a whole, and its various initiatives.

■ **Creating capacity for coaching:** Learning initiative leaders need experienced, compassionate guidance from people who have "been there," and who know how to manage and design the journey. For lack of a better word, we call these people "coaches"—although their role extends beyond conventional coaching.

COACHING

The English word "coach" is derived from Kocs, the name of a village in northeastern Hungary, where carriages and carts were traditionally made. Nineteenth-century university students adopted the word as slang for "tutor." Instructors, it seems, took such an intense, personal interest in their students' progress that students felt conveyed through the exam as if driven in the instructor's carriage. We think the word, today, still conveys some of that spirit of close partnership and mutual responsibility.

A colleague at Levi Strauss with a great deal of experience in coaching notes that many people have a mental model of "coaching" from sports: Telling "players" what to do, and yelling at them through a bullhorn. Instead, she says, "The essence of coaching is listening. A good coach asks questions. Eighty percent of the job involves helping people become clearer, in their own minds, about the things they have to say."

Great coaching is artful, compassionate, and incisive. It's particularly hard to find coaches with these qualities, who can also combine "soft" (communication and teamwork) and "hard" (technical and financial) knowledge. But even if the coaching is used to develop soft skills, it must relate to the practical business issues that are driving the team to learn.

In groups, coaches often act as facilitators, helping create an atmosphere of safety. They may, for instance, show people how to confront "fancy footwork"—a term for face-saving conversational gambits that seem open and candid while actually intended, usually unconsciously, to keep some vital point hidden.

- **Finding a partner:** Executive leaders, facing the unfamiliar challenges of profound change, may need coaching more than anyone else. That is why we often advise CEOs to find a partner—someone whom they can safely confide in and to whom they can express emotional tension, including your misgivings about the very changes you may be advocating. Knowing that this "safety valve" is available, leaders can move more easily from feelings of anxiety and fear to a creative, strategic sense of purpose.

- **Building coaching into line management:** Some of the most effective coaching we've seen has come from executive and line leaders who become coaches for others. Their passion for learning inspires others around them and they tend to credit coaching itself with amplifying their own interest.

  At the American Woodmark Company, for instance, all line leaders are directly responsible for training and coaching the people who report to them. Four senior executive leaders, including chairman Bill Brandt, personally teach a five-day offsite course that 250 employees have attended, in sessions of twenty-four each, covering the culture of the company and key business processes.

  "We're committed," Brandt says, "to the idea that line leaders must be involved in not just conducting the training, but designing the training—at least the training that helps establish our values and the ways we want to do things on a broad basis." He adds that having executive leaders provide this kind of help "has given us a common language across the company and a common approach to address business situations. It's one reason why the company has done very well over the last several years."

- **Attitudes about seeking help:** As noted above, in many organizational cultures, people find it very difficult to ask for help. As one CEO put it: "I'm too old for a mentor—or maybe too young." Alternatively, some managers become dependent on outside help and its quick solutions to problems. This draws them away from seeking more fundamental solutions.

Meeting the challenge of "no help," therefore, includes building self-awareness, on both an individual and team level. Leaders need to articulate the case for help, including the gap between the group's current performance and its aspirations, and the feelings and attitudes that may make it difficult to accept the help they need, or to give it up when it is time to become more self-sufficient.

For more material on finding a partner, see *The Fifth Discipline Fieldbook*, p. 74 and (for CEOs) p. 328.

See the article on American Woodmark by former CEO Bill Brandt in *The Fifth Discipline Fieldbook*, p. 463.

This is a common systems phenomenon called "shifting the burden"; see *The Fifth Discipline Fieldbook*, p. 135.

2 From Golf to Polo

The coaching of leaders . . . and the leading of coaches

Bryan Smith and Rick Ross

Nobody is more powerful than a passionate leader, particularly in terms of his or her impact on others. That is why the coaching that leaders receive is arguably one of the highest-impact leverage points available to a team. Unfortunately, the coaching of leaders is often poorly understood. Perhaps that's because of the way most of us have been coached when learning a sport. Golf instructors, for instance, tend to teach one "correct way" to take the club back, to hold your arms, and swing. It takes all of a new player's concentration to follow the instructions—and it takes much of the fun out of the sport.

If you watch videotapes of expert players, you'll notice the individuality of their swings. The grip, backswing, and motions are all different —at least until the moment of impact. Only three or four key factors seem to hold constant, whoever is playing: the angle of the club face as it strikes the ball, the straightness of the left arm, and the turn of the hips during the final motion. No matter how creative or idiosyncratic you are, you apparently cannot avoid the irrefutable physical laws of nature.

Why, then, do instructors teach by rote? Not because the "one right way" is easier to learn. It's harder. But it is much easier to *teach*. If the player can follow a set of particular steps precisely, the probability of getting those few key factors correct will increase.

An argument has raged for years in the management literature: Is there one best style of leadership? Or is leadership different for different people in different situations? The golf analogy helps here: Just as there are many different ways to swing the golf clubs, there are many different styles of leadership, all of which may be very effective. However, there are a few seemingly irrefutable laws of leadership—and thus some fundamental skills that every leader must master.

GUIDELINES FOR LEADERSHIP COACHING

We don't presume to know for sure what the universal key factors of leadership are. But borrowing from the key factors of golf coaching, we suspect that anyone coaching a leader (or prospective leader) would want to have these conditions present:

- **A love for the game:** It's obvious when an athlete, no matter how talented, has been coerced into playing for some other reason than the intrinsic love of the sport. The athlete only learns slowly and grudgingly. Similarly, if people have taken on a leadership role in a spirit of compliance—wanting the rewards of leadership, but lacking the passion for being there—they will be hard to coach.

- **A focus on desired results:** Skilled golfers don't think consciously about the mechanics of the swing, or stare at the ball or club. They concentrate on the place you want the ball to land. Similarly, in organizations, the leader sets direction. Coaches need to help leaders keep focused on the organization's future, on their personal vision, and on the aspirations of the other people who are with them.

- **A clean, honest connection:** The critical aspects of the swing all seem to center around the moment of contact. Leadership, in that sense, is a contact sport as well. Its effectiveness depends on the connection between leaders and other people. Ask a leader: "If you lose your title and position, would people still follow you?" The answer depends upon the quality of contact the leader has made.

  The quality of coaching also depends on the quality of contact. After a meeting, leaders will often ask their coach: "Have you got any feedback for me on what I did in there?" In other words: "How did I come across? What could I do differently next time?"

High-quality coaches don't simply provide feedback, however. They take great joy in seeing people develop. They feel accountable; they know what the people they coach are trying to achieve, and why. And they manage the point of contact effectively. The coach might begin, for instance, by asking: "In that meeting, how do *you* think you did?"

If the leader says, "I thought I was a pretty good listener," the coach responds with specifics, describing particular scenes. Then the coach asks: "Is there anything that you wish you'd handled differently?"

"Well, I blew it," the leader might say, "when I cut off Joe's chance to speak." The coach can then offer his or her perception of that moment.

The coach always moves comments from the judgmental and ambiguous to the descriptive and specific, or "up and to the right" in the diagram here. People can't do anything to learn from vague accusations of "having a bad attitude" or

	Specific	"When you look at the floor when people are talking, I make the assumption that you are not interested."
Ambiguous	"You've got a bad attitude."	
	Judgmental	**Description**

"looking like you don't care." If the coaches re-create scenes with specific observations, leaders can become more observant of their own behavior—and learn to correct themselves, even when no coach is present.

FROM GOLF TO POLO

In golf coaching, there's plenty of time to reflect on your previous performance and plan your next shot. You can even go back and retake the shot, just to see how to handle it differently.

But leading an organization is more like polo. The little white ball no longer waits for you. It's always in motion. You no longer stand on firm ground; you carry a mallet and ride a galloping horse. Your teammates are also mounted on horses; and you have to coordinate your actions with them. Your opponents surround you, moving at fast speeds, intent on knocking the ball away. Horse manure flies everywhere. And the coach remains far away from you, shouting advice from the sidelines that you probably can't even hear.

Organizational change is even more complex than polo. The boundaries of the playing field keep changing. Every day, the game will be a little bit different, and probably a bit more difficult. Yet the same three critical elements seem to remain constant, in polo and in organizational change: Joy in the game is crucial. You keep your eye on the goal, not on the mechanics of the job. And your game depends on the quality of contact. In organizational change, the boundaries blur between coach and player. Leaders must give and receive help; and they must learn to be discerning about the quality of help they receive, as well as authentic in the help they give. Coaching, in short, no longer takes place before the game or from the sidelines; it is a critical part of the game itself.

WHAT DID YOU SAY?

The Art of Giving and Receiving Feedback, by Charles N. Seashore, Edith Whifield Seashore, and Gerald M. Weinberg; (Columbia, MD: Bingham House Books [410-997-2829] 1992, 1997)

Skillful coaching depends on skillful "feedback"—giving honest, candid, compelling, and *helpful* critiques of people's behavior, and effectively evaluating and learning from the things people say about you. Unfortunately, much of the time feedback "just comes out," thereby wounding or giving the wrong impression. People can learn to give feedback not just cogently, but artfully, in a way

that exalts everyone involved. This book, by three renowned author-consultants, is the best I've seen at showing how to do this, in plain inviting language. I've taken one bit of advice to heart: Feedback is often most effective not after someone has done something, but when you notice them contemplating the action.
— Art Kleiner

COACHING: EVOKING EXCELLENCE IN OTHERS
by James Flaherty (San Francisco: New Ventures West, 1997)

Sometimes a relatively finite activity, like coaching, provides a thread to a much broader body of knowledge. In that spirit, James Flaherty translates the pragmatic phenomenologies of John Dewey, Martin Heidegger, Humberto Maturana, and Fernando Flores into a comprehensive guide to working effectively with people. He never loses sight of day-to-day practice; indeed, much of the book is dedicated to the kinds of recipes that can bootstrap you out of the need for relying on recipes. But he also holds tight to essential, yet overlooked, principles for working with yourself and others; principles that take you beyond platitudes about "trust," "respect," and "frustration" (to name three), into a frame of mind and spirit from which you can help people improve. — Art Kleiner

3 A Cadre of Coaches

Charlotte Roberts

"Malcolm, you are going back over the same ground over and over. Are you repeating your ideas because you felt you weren't heard?"

Those kinds of remarks can cut sharply and alienate people. But to Malcolm, who had the irritating habit of lecturing his colleagues pedantically as if they were children, this remark opened a door. Suddenly, he understood why others in the company tended to feel bored and patronized around him. This was valuable news to him, especially because it had been so hard for him to hear it in the past. The others in the group also saw why their own responses had helped Malcolm stay in that role.

It happened during a meeting of an informal "change agents team," composed of nine managers in a Fortune 50 company. Though they came from different parts of the organization, the group had met regularly for two years. All were charged with coaching teams of managers and employees elsewhere. All of them wanted to be leaders in the company's change initiative, and to develop themselves in the process.

It had taken more than a year to build the skill and trust to challenge Malcolm constructively. Words had to be chosen with precision; members had to learn to make their views open to challenge and discussion. They had to learn, from scratch, to help each other navigate critical personal barriers that kept each of them from being effective leaders. Not bad for a team that, when they first started to meet two years before, had been virtually strangers to each other.

expansion of pilot group

Many people who feel responsible for a learning initiative recognize the value of regular informal meetings. But they generally get too little support, and pay too little attention to their mutual development. That is why deliberately casting teams as "cadres of coaches," organized for mutual support and ongoing development, is a high-leverage component of organizational change. It's particularly vital as the organization shifts its dependence away from outsiders to its own internal "learning R&D" teams. As they gain experience in this "practice field," their growing base of embedded knowledge becomes a strategic advantage for the entire company. The cadre becomes the first step toward building a capability of "shadow consultation" throughout the organization, in which people routinely learn to help each other become more effective at dealing with impasses and tough situations.

COMING TOGETHER AND GETTING STARTED

If you are the group's sponsor or initial leader, you could begin by calling together six to twelve people who are committed to the learning process, and who (in your estimation) have already developed some level of maturity or personal growth. It's preferable to recruit a mix of network leaders (staff "internal consultants") and line managers with direct responsibility for business results. Line leaders are seen as more "real," because they are already engaged in business performance issues. They can test whether the group's insights and new approaches will get results in practice. Network leaders travel in wider circles across functions.

They may offer broader experience in process improvement and aware-ness of cultural or governance issues. Both groups have a lot to learn from seeing their ideas played out in the others' milieu.

People must make a personal choice to join the cadre. A job title, or a boss's mandate to "check out this coaching thing," should not admit them, even if they are good-hearted and sincere. They will need to be open-minded and deeply committed, because their own thought process might be challenged in every session.

Intensive engagement is crucial at first; people need time to reinforce their skills and get used to coaching each other. Begin with two-day retreats, every six to eight weeks. In the first six to nine months, focus on the skills, tools, and practice of productive conversation. Use business issues—such as the budgeting or strategy development process—as the subject of conversation. Practice such conversational tools as the "ladder of inference," balancing inquiry and advocacy, the left-hand column, and various forms of systems thinking. Raise questions that may be difficult to raise elsewhere: What barriers can you expect to run into? What are the options for dealing with them? How is the organizational change ini-tiative blocking its own way?

These conversations gain strength from varied perspectives. Rather than forcing agreement, members of the cadre seek to build the broadest comprehension of current reality by looking at the assumptions and beliefs underlying each point of view.

These tools are described in *The Fifth Discipline Fieldbook*: the ladder of inference, p. 242; balancing inquiry and advocacy, p. 253; the left-hand column, p. 246; and systems thinking, starting on p. 113. Also see, in this book, "Five Kinds of Systems Thinking," p. 137.

LATER STAGES

Over time, people will bring stories of their coaching efforts to these ses-sions, so that hidden agendas and attitudes can be explored. A coach may report that she continually pushes Tom, a quiet manager, to speak more at meetings. What is her deepest agenda? Is she trying to break through a dynamic where people feel afraid to speak? Or is she acting out of self-interest, seeking the validation of "letting everyone have his say"? Is the group alienated by her efforts? Or do they appreciate her efforts? How could she sense the way she is perceived more authentically next time? Coaches need to be aware of these types of distinctions, so they can bal-ance too much intervention and too little.

The cadre will also help coaches consider whether their efforts are helping—or hindering—the company as a whole. I have seen organiza-tion effectiveness professionals schedule training sessions long before the attendees would be ready for the material, simply because the coach thinks it sounds interesting. Other coaches delay their offerings too long, because their schedule is overbooked. What is the sense of timing of your own cadre's members?

Help one another deal with the inevitable moments when someone falls back into old authoritarian behavior. In one cadre meeting a coach described how she broke in on a seemingly interminable discussion and told a group of people what to do. This, in turn, raised eyebrows and spurred mild resentment that she could feel. The cadre spent an hour or more working through the ramifications. What forces within herself (and other members) had driven behavior this time? What might she have done differently? In the future, how could she avoid backsliding (or at least land more gracefully)?

It is important to be honest to outsiders about the cadre's existence. At the same time, be aware of the danger of setting yourselves up as an elite. You don't want to be seen as "change enforcers" who meet regularly behind closed doors, and who believe themselves more skilled or dedicated than anyone else. You know you've reached that dangerous state when other people start to say things like, "The coaches are doing all the learning, so we won't need to."

SIGNS OF SUCCESS

If you are a leader, or a sponsor, of the cadre of coaches, keep an eye on your progress. By the end of the first year, the group should see a significant boost in the quality of conversation and thinking among the coaches. People should feel enough intimacy and mutual trust to express emotion without feeling threatened. In one case, we knew that a cadre of coaches had been effective when its members, all executives, openly and candidly (albeit nervously) talked about the effect of the new business environment on their own compensation. In that highly competitive environment, nearly every conversation about executive pay had been private and secretive in this past.

》》 The ability to understand and avoid "Unilateral Control" effectively is one sign of success.
》》 See page 252 for this exercise.

Ultimately, as the coaches gain skills, so will the other people who work with them. Strategic conversations will become easier because people are already used to talking about the future with their coaches. People learn from examples, and the examples initiated in a cadre of coaches may ripple out, over time, to change the ways people talk and operate throughout the company.

Dispatch from a cadre co-organizer

Tom Ryan, Shell Oil Company

In early 1995, most people at Shell Oil in Houston were still reeling from the aftermath of cutbacks, and uncertain about the company's proposed "transformation." Several of us began meeting regularly to create a practice field for transformational leaders. We carefully selected invitees in local line and senior leadership positions—excluding many of the designated "internal change agents/organizational design practitioners," for fear of being identified as "professionals." I remember worrying that invitees would think we were trying to "sell" them on corporate change. All but one of them, however, responded with encouragement and gratitude. "I have needed some place to connect," said one, "as I am very confused by a lot of things." Another wrote, "I need a safe place to ask questions."

We met every other month. Knowing that efforts at other companies had dissipated for lack of commitment, we insisted that everyone agree to show up for the first three two-day sessions, in part to justify the expense of an outside facilitator. After that, we agreed, we would evaluate our progress and decide whether or not to continue.

Later, the question of "being overwhelmed by professionals" seemed less important. We opened the group to anyone with an interest in coaching transformational activity at Shell. As of now, the membership has turned over many times. Having people come and go is not a problem, perhaps because there is a core group of four regulars (including our outside consultant), who attend every session. Even those who have left continue to express support; they credit our small group with helping them take their first personal change steps. Sharing experience in using new techniques like dialogue and systems thinking, as well as the conversational tools, all proved to be the little lagniappe that moved people along in their personal journey.

The cadre of coaches has required some financial commitment from the company, but it's paid off. Personally, I've handled some emotional lows around the group (sometimes involving anxieties about whether we would have to end it); but the main emotions I feel are satisfaction and joy. I find myself caring about the participants in ways that go beyond being colleagues: We don't agree about everything, but we are kindred spirits. We have put ourselves on the line together and learned to learn.

Like the administrator at AMC

For the techniques of drawing forth personal vision, see *The Fifth Discipline Fieldbook*, p. 201.

PURPOSE:

An exercise for coaches and pilot group leaders, helping you bring your mental models of organizational learning to the surface, and strengthen your ability to explain your commitment to help recruit others.

OVERVIEW:

Condense your view of organizational learning to a sixty-second summary, and test that answer on a sympathetic audience.

TIME:

An hour or more.

"Elevator explanation" Charlotte Roberts

1. INDIVIDUAL REFLECTION

Each individual takes ten to twenty minutes to reflect on personal reasons for involvement in the change initiative. "How does this role fit with my current situation? And with the needs of the organization?"

Write your reasons on paper. Explain the most critical points as clearly as you can, as if talking to someone about them. "I want to work in a place where I don't have to put on a mask," one person might write. Another might write, "Our competitors can offer the same products and services we do, and technology gives us only a six-month head start. Our only hope of surviving is to change the way we work—and I think the company needs my perspective."

Then expand and clarify your statement, using the techniques of "drawing forth a personal vision": If you achieved your aspiration, as part of this corporate change or transformation, what would it get you?

2. TRIADS AND DEBRIEF

Form groups of three people. Pretend that the three of you have just gotten into an elevator together. Ask one another: "Why are you involved in this learning initiative?" Imagine the doors to the elevator shutting. You each have one minute to answer before you reach your floor.

One person speaks, the second listens, and the third monitors the time. Then shift roles until each person has played each role.

Then respond back to one another: How accurate and understandable were the "elevator explanations"? What questions were left dangling? What suggestions might you offer for making them more compelling and authentic?

3. EXPLANATORY PRACTICE

To practice further, take five minutes for each person to individually refine his or her elevator explanation.

Then rearrange the groups into new trios and repeat step 2. To build sophistication, listeners may play various roles: A senior manager, a union leader, a finance auditor, or an outside journalist or stock analyst. Stay in persona as you listen and respond. Notice, as speakers, how the story shifts when you describe it to a new audience.

4. LARGE GROUP DEBRIEF

Reconvene as a large group and talk about the issues and insights that emerged. You may decide, for instance, that it's more effective to talk about outcomes (the final results) rather than processes (how the change will take place). Is it better to explain jargon, or not to use it at all? More likely than not, different precepts will apply to different situations within the company.

Blinking words Charlotte Roberts

BLINKING WORDS ARE WORDS, PHRASES, OR TONES WITH A WIDE RANGE OF POSSIBLE definitions, meanings, and connotations. Dozens of blinking words are used in business today: *Quality. Empowerment. Learning. Training. Vision-driven. Transformation. Capacity-building. Twenty-first Century Leadership.* And *Coaching.* Any of these terms or phrases may provoke reaction, like a neon sign blinking in the listener's mind: "What does the speaker really mean by this word? Are we on the same wavelength?"

1. LARGE GROUP OVERVIEW

In the full cadre, choose a sentence or example that contains many possible blinking words. Take the mission statement of your company, or a paragraph from any management book you admire. Or, if you're particularly bold, you might tape-record and transcribe a short section of your own cadre's conversation.

Start by asking one another to look for blinking words. What is the first blinking word in this sentence? What is the second? Then list several possible meanings for each word. How do you interpret "twenty-first-century" leadership? What assumptions are you making about the turn of the century? What kinds of things, by implication, would a twenty-first century leader do? What concepts do other people associate with that phrase? Explore how loaded these different meanings can be.

2. PAIRED PRACTICE FIRST ROUND

Divide into pairs. Have the members of each pair (A and B) respond to an open-ended, value-driven question such as one of these:

"What are the most important elements of leadership for your organization in the next five years?"

PURPOSE:

Jargon and ambiguous language can work against you by creating confusion and resistance. This exercise helps coaches become more conscious of their own use of "blinking words," the impact of that usage, and possible alternatives.

OVERVIEW:

Participants surface the surprising variations in their interpretations of key words.

TIME:

Two to four hours.

SUPPLIES:

Flip charts. Drafts of an existing mission statement or copies of a business book. Maybe a tape recorder.

This exercise is based on an exercise by Rick Ross and Bev Kaye.

Even the simplest business sentences are often full of blinking words. For instance: "In order for us to really change things around here, we're going to have to have better communication." Which of those words is blinking at you? Chances are, most of them. What does "change" mean? What does it mean to "communicate"? How can that be "better"? And where is "here"? Everybody looking at the chart probably has a different idea about what those words mean. — Rick Ross

"What should your team's strategic priorities be?"

In this round, As offer their opinions on the question, using the skills of high-quality advocacy and the ladder of inference. Bs interrupt, inquiring into any blinking words. B cannot offer opinions, but only ask clarifying questions: "What do you mean when you say _____?"

3. LARGE-GROUP DEBRIEF

Return to the full cadre, and talk about the experience that people felt as Bs. What was it like to listen to your partner and only focus on the tones and individual words? Many people find it tedious. Most will be surprised by how many blinking words there were. Focusing on the blinking words makes it harder to follow the main idea and difficult to listen at all. This, in fact, is the experience that many people have with your blinking words.

4. REPEAT ROUND

Switch roles in your pairs from step 2, to give everyone a chance to play both roles. Then return to the full group, debrief, and consider: How can you most effectively introduce the concepts that blinking words convey? Through stories? Through brief explanations? Or by taking the trouble to find and use less jargon-laden alternative phrasings?

Creating and managing a study group

One easy way to build your own coaching skills is to start a small reading group, in which a few people meet regularly (within an organization, or across organizations) to talk about books that they have read. On our Web site, we maintain a listing of study groups (and people interested in joining them). Web site visitor Dena Ladner e-mailed us for advice on establishing one, drawing forth stories like these:

Stephen Wehrenberg (U.S. Coast Guard, Washington, D.C.): Our group began with my casual remark on a systems dynamics e-mail list, wondering if any of the D.C.–area members had ever tried to meet. I got a flurry of interest, but nothing firm. At a system dynamics conference in 1996, Fred Affeldt (another interested D.C. resident) and I posted a notice on the bulletin board there.

We got twenty or thirty replies, and have met six or seven times since. The meetings have been diverse, but usually involve a presentation or dog and pony show by one "member" followed by discussion and mingling.

Fred Affeldt (Washington, D.C.): Since our membership includes government, nongovernment, for-profit, and not-for-profit organizations, the one hard and fast rule has been no overt marketing during our meetings. Providing an informal forum and interesting speakers has given each of us a very rich experience. Meetings have been held at a couple of member's organizations; for instance, at the Army National Guard Headquarters we received a demonstration of their new Learning Center and some of its learning technology.

Roger Breisch (MidWest Organizational Learning Network [MOLN], Chicago): I act as the hub of the network. I have e-mail addresses for about two thirds of the members and I use that list to "announce" learning events that I discover. I also publish a quarterly newsletter, *Entre Nous*, in which I create a calendar of learning events. Because of this role I tend to get many calls and e-mails about upcoming events in the area.

MOLN grew simply by networking. We are always looking for "kindred spirits," but I no longer actively promote MOLN. If I did, it would grow beyond my ability to keep up. It has grown to over four hundred people just by word of mouth.

We have experimented with a variety of learning events. My first reaction is to say that some have been successful and others have not. But then I would have to define success . . . and all my definitions would be based on traditional thinking. Measures such as, "How many people came?" are less useful than: "Did the event enable people to question their thinking?" I have not found a way to measure the latter as yet.

We have a book club that draws between five and fifteen people quarterly. We had, for a while, a Saturday night gathering called a "cocktail party with an attitude." We have a couple of ongoing groups that practice dialogue. We keep a calendar of learning events being created by other organizations in the Chicago area.

José Sánchez Alarcos (Spain): [Success] seems to be a matter of waiting for the right moment. I started our group in Spain two years ago. Our meetings were satisfactory for the attendees but I did not perceive further interest. Eventually we started to enter the mainstream in our organization. Perhaps that is why more people started to be interested a few

The study groups Web page is available at *http://www.field book.com/studygroup.html*. For more stories from people who have created study groups, see the page *studyhow.html*.

months ago. Now, I frequently receive calls from people wanting to know about our group.

4 Climbing Out of the Muck

How self-reflecting teams can help you break free of your own recurring impasses

Philip McArthur, Robert Putnam, Diana McLain Smith

The three people who look after one another in this roundtable are all partners in the consulting firm Action Design, scholars of organizational learning, and preeminent practitioners of the skills of inquiry and reflection. They have all been colleagues and friends to The Fifth Discipline Fieldbook; *Robert Putnam, for instance, helped us develop the Mental Models section of the book, Phil McArthur contributed one of the most-used segments of that section ("Opening Lines"), and Diana Smith consulted with Peter Senge on the framing of "reflection and inquiry skills" in* The Fifth Discipline. *Here, they describe the hidden dynamics that will emerge in any team of people trying to help one another learn to think and act more effectively.*

This roundtable was updated and expanded from a presentation that the three partners made to the Society for Organizational Learning in 1997. For more about Argyris's ideas and methods, see *The Fifth Discipline Fieldbook*, p. 264. For reflection and inquiry skills, see *The Fifth Discipline Fieldbook*, p. 242. Chris Argyris is the organizational learning theorist whose work (partly in collaboration with Donald Schön and the contributors of this article) provides a foundation for building skills of reflection and inquiry.

Robert Putnam (Bob): The three of us first met in fall 1979, as first-year students at the Harvard Graduate School of Education, in a course with Chris Argyris. All of us got turned on by the quality of attention and inquiry that Chris demonstrated, and by methods (such as the "left-hand/right-hand column" cases) for reflecting on our thinking and acting. The sessions ended, and we were painfully aware of how far there was to go and how much we wanted to travel farther.

So, along with several other students, we formed a consulting study group. For four years, we met faithfully every two weeks. As in our former class, one of us would write out a conversation that had taken place outside the room. Using the "left-hand column" to reveal the unspoken thoughts people might have had, and their impact on the conversation, we would diagnose the case and role-play various alternative approaches, always with a tape recorder going.

Philip McArthur (Phil): As graduate students, we didn't have the money to pay someone to transcribe our tapes. Our skill as a reflective team came in part from the time we spent listening to the conversation replay, and then writing it down. Doing this is as boring as playing scales on the piano, but perhaps just as necessary to gain proficiency.

Bob: After two years, however, the group grew stale. The same arguments and impasses recurred again and again, no matter how hard we tried to avoid them. If we wanted to keep working together, we knew we'd have to raise the ante. We'd have to learn to "get in the muck" of our meetings, and confront one another's frustrations and misunderstandings in the moment.

We already knew that there was a lot of "muck" to deal with. It was typical, for instance, for Diana to interrupt a person telling a story, and say, "You've got to stand up to people more strongly." Hearing this, I might break in and say, "Diana, you were advocating and not inquiring just now." And Phil might then tell me, "Bob, you know what? You didn't inquire with Diana, either." Around and around we would go, interrupting and misunderstanding, feeling the conversation grow choppier and the tensions escalate throughout the rest of the evening.

Our trusty tape recorder helped save us. We recorded a half-hour segment of ourselves in the muck, and I still have thirty-four pages of my handwritten transcription of that tape. We talked through the transcript and gradually realized that, while in the muck, each of us had a characteristic way of reacting that invariably made things worse.

Phil: I was the kind of person who looks for cues that I am making an impact. So I would raise a point, and Bob would sit there, impassively. I would keep making the same point, over and over again, hoping to get a reaction, thinking to myself, "How come he's not getting my point?" I could not help wondering if Bob was thinking, "Why does Phil keep repeating himself? Why can't he just get to the point?"

Bob: My own ingrained attitude was like a physician's: "First, do no harm." When I saw people interrupting and misunderstanding, I wanted to avoid making things worse. So I would hold myself back, and try to make brief interpretive "surgical strikes" to help clarify what I thought Phil or Diana had meant to point out about the other's misunderstanding. I didn't realize it, but people thought from my tone of voice that, behind my reserve, I was judging them harshly and critically. People felt dismissed, as if I thought they were "wrong, wrong, wrong."

Readers may notice that in this roundtable, unlike others in this book, we identify quotes by first name rather than last name. This reflects the highly evolved intimacy among these three colleagues and, hopefully, will give readers a better feel for this type of intensive mutual coaching.

Diana Smith: The transcript showed that I was also unwittingly following an unarticulated rule: "When others persist, view it as a sign of their uninfluenceability. When I persist, view it as a sign of my integrity." So if I saw people in trouble, I was drawn to go in and make it right. And I'd stir up the water. I often seemed to end up confronting Bob, coming on strong, like a neutron bomb: "Come on, Bob, intervene! What's your problem?"

Phil: In the heat of the moment, Diana would see Bob's diffidence as a huge vacuum in the conversation. She would rush in to fill that vacuum, trying to fix the problem, and she would see Bob as not taking responsibility for helping. Meanwhile, Bob would see her as making things worse. I would watch their disagreement turn to open war, feeling overwhelmed myself, and not seeing that I was also contributing to the situation. I gradually realized that I had to get much more involved if I was going to be a constructive bystander.

Bob: Over a six-month period, we developed an understanding of the dynamics that kept us in the muck. We realized that each of us was acting out of a sense of integrity and an intention to help. That made a big difference, and helped us to hang in together.

Diana: By our fourth or fifth year, in fact, the three of us had started a consulting practice together. But we couldn't seem to break out of those recurring patterns. We realized that we had to learn to alter the dynamics of our conversation, and change the structure of our relationship, the predictable pattern of interaction. Even when we understood the problem, we still got into nonconstructive, debilitating, seemingly self-defeating arguments. It was like being acrobats on a high wire, knowing in advance that we would fall and crash, and not being able to do anything about it. Dealing with this was much more difficult than any of us expected. Simply as human beings, we had spent all our lives in interpersonal interactions. And then we had studied it, in depth—and we were still having trouble.

"Bob, it's plain as day." You think everything's my fault, and you're motivated to get me.

Obviously Bob always disapproves of the way I do things.

Bob thinks I don't know how to handle this type of situation, but he doesn't want to say so.

Bob is expressing criticism of me.

On the tape, Bob said: "Diana, you were advocating and not inquiring just now."

We had a breakthrough one evening when Chris Argyris visited. We were working on a case with the kind of client whom Bob often struggled with: an aggressive, loud, and controlling manager. After listening to us, Chris looked very pensive and said, "You know, at one point St. Peter said, 'On this rock, I'm going to build a church.' And at some point, you've just got to say, 'On these defenses, I'm going to build a practice.'" In other words, we would never reach a standard of perfection where we could naturally master every situation. We would have to remain in our imperfect personalities and learn from there. This was a very freeing realization for me.

FOLLOWING THE MUCK UPSTREAM

Diana: We continued to bring in people from outside who could help us see our own dynamics. One evening, the systems psychologist David Kantor visited us, and Bob once again presented a case, this time with a difficult team. The line leader droned on and on, and everybody else was silent. Bob couldn't figure out how to shake up the dynamics, and, in a replay of our own habitual muck, I started pressing him to intervene more. I looked at Bob and he had a blank look on his face, almost as if he couldn't understand exactly how to take in what I was saying.

For more about David Kantor's work, see page 262.

At that moment, David said, "Bob, what does this remind you of?"

Bob said something that, to this day, represents the greatest single transformational event in my experience of his relationship with me. He told us a story about being in the third grade, when his father gave him a baseball glove. "It was old and it had no pocket; it was just a flat piece of leather," he said, "but it was my Dad's glove, and I was proud of it. I brought it to school and at the playground a bully came along and said, 'Let me have your glove.'" Bob gave him the glove. The bully started dissing the glove, calling it disgusting and making Bob feel hurt. Then the bully refused to give it back. So Bob went home to his father and told him what had happened. Rather than taking care of him and trying to help him, his father said, "You go right back to the playground now. You stand up to that guy and you get your glove back."

I had a moment of shock; I recognized that I must be Bob's worst nightmare. In all these times of trying to help my colleague and friend develop, offering my advice to him, I was doing the worst thing I could do to him. I realized that I had to stop asking Bob to be Diana; I had to learn how to help him become a better Bob.

Bob: Similarly, I had to learn that when Diana is at her most insistent and seemingly convinced, she's feeling most vulnerable and helpless inside. It doesn't show automatically, at least to me. But I have had to train myself to recognize it. Instead of arching my back and saying "No," objecting to whatever Diana insists upon, there's another move open to me. I can say, "Boy, Diana, you seem stressed. What's going on?"

Diana: There was a critical moment after that episode, where we essentially said, "We're in this for the long haul." This was very important. We no longer had to be safe, sweet, kind, or nice. It was like getting married; we knew that no matter how difficult things became, we would keep our commitment to each other's growth.

The illustration on the opposite page shows the "ladder of inference"—a conceptual device showing how different people may interpret the same situation very differently, and never know (unless they talk openly about it). The lowest rung, at the bottom, contains relatively observable data, such as a sentence uttered, that could be checked against an audiotape recording. People tend to mentally rise to more abstract, unverifiable levels—which might include the cultural meaning (as understood by anyone in the community), to conclusions and beliefs that move farther away from the original "reality" of the conversation. The "muck" is thickest at the top of the ladder. For more about the "Ladder of Inference," see *The Fifth Discipline Fieldbook*, p. 242.

People sometimes find that level of commitment daunting: "Gosh, is that what it takes?" But in terms of the learning and discovering we did, it was more than worth the price of admission. We began to really understand and see the structures of human interaction—not just on an intellectual level, but in our bones. We know, for instance, that when Bob and I get into a serious, intense conflict, even Phil is implicated. On one level, Bob represents my father, and I represent the bully in the playground. On another level, it's just the three of us, and Phil has missed his opportunity to help. He could jump in by saying, "Diana is being a bully, but Bob's not seeing the extent to which he's withdrawing in a way that leaves Diana feeling dismissed." This knowledge, that we're all implicated, has been our saving grace.

Bob: We've continued these sessions through the present day—a period of eighteen years. The value of this close, intimate learning extends beyond the boundaries of our group. It helps me deal with a number of senior executives, for instance, whose personality profiles are like Diana's. The more we recognize our own habitual limits and barriers, the more effective we seem to become.

You may wonder how this can apply to a project team with a life span of three to six months. There may indeed not be time for the deep work of a self-reflecting team. You may be better off calling in a facilitator who can help you deal with your immediate business impasses.

Diana: Even if your team is stable, you may have to deal with new members coming in. We're going through that now, as we incorporate more people into our consulting partnership. How do we help them up the learning curve? How do we develop close relationships with them? And how do we do this without creating a new stuck situation, where the "old-timers" are experts and the "newcomers" are novices?

We only know one way to deal with this: Don't cover it up. Acknowledge the difference in skill, and work on transferring that skill as quickly as possible—in all directions. It's important to recognize the natural inclination to alter your behavior, in front of the newcomers, and to keep the conversation among the old-timers private: "They really don't know us. What will they think?" If you can talk about your conversational issues openly, it sends a very powerful signal to newcomers: "Wow. You guys talk this way? That's really remarkable."

Phil: How did we do this for eighteen years? Admittedly, we had a forced structure, beginning with our graduate work and then our mutual consulting practice. And I have a lot of sympathy for people who commute forty-five minutes each way to an evening study group; we never had to do that. Nor did we have kids when we started.

Many teams in business have been together two or more years. If you've met regularly for that long, and have not taken the time to reflect on your results and your competence as a team, then you are probably perpetuating errors. The most critical constraint isn't time, but the willingness, as a group, to talk openly and candidly about your experiences. If you can retain that, then you keep your reason for showing up.

"The muck stops here." Diana McLain Smith

THESE GUIDELINES FOR HELPING OURSELVES OUT OF THE MUCK WERE FORGED OVER time, as we observed our own interactions:

- **Collect data on the things you say and do:** The biggest single differentiator between success and failure among study groups is the use of a tape recorder. People are so skilled at taking action that they are far more likely to recall what they were trying to do than what they actually did. This is a recipe for disaster. One person cries, "I was *trying* to support you!" The other retorts, "What do you mean? You were patronizing me!" Only with a tape recorder can you get reliable data on what you and others actually said and did.

  In our group, we would not talk about any especially contentious issues unless we could look at the transcript of the interchange. We would then select a couple of brief exchanges that were emotionally "hot." These provided us all the raw material we needed to see.

- **Account for what happened:** Once you have gathered direct data, each person can reflect on the events that took place and why they occurred that way. We use these four sets of questions:

  1. What "results" did I get? In other words, how did people react to my action? What did they do next?

     Beware of making attributions about people's reactions; your attributions may say far more about you than about the others. Stay with the direct data of what people actually did and said.

     Ask yourself: What do I like about the results I got? What don't I like? Did I move closer to, or farther from, my goals?

  2. What did I say or do to help create these results? Start with yourself; that's something you can change. You might see, for example, how you kept coming in to reassert your view every time a colleague said something you didn't like. Phil, Bob, and I can't count

the number of times that we discovered that the other person's "intransigence" was only matched by our own.

3. How did I see the situation, myself, and others in the room? What did I feel at that time? How did this inform my actions?

These questions help uncover how you were framing the situation to make it seem, to yourself at least, that your actions made sense, even if they were problematic.

Look closely at how you view any situation that you find tough to handle, and ask yourself: How might my actions have made sense, given the way I viewed the situation? Then ask: How does this way of viewing the situation increase, or decrease, my degrees of freedom?

4. What aspects of this particular situation did I find challenging? You might find some background factors, such as unclear roles, difficult to take. Or you might find some triggering event hard to handle, such as getting negatively evaluated or yelled at. Note the contextual factors that stretch you. This is your learning edge.

Once you have answered these questions, you have the makings of a story that can account for the results you got. In crafting the story, steer clear of evaluations. (Don't say, "I acted inappropriately or badly.") Just tell what happened and how. (For example: "When up against a strong personality, like my client Sam, who is negatively evaluating me, I see myself as helpless and Sam as holding all the cards. This makes me feel as if my only choice is to withdraw. In the end, I don't end up getting what I want or helping Sam get what he wants. This seems to make him evaluate me even more negatively.")

Keep a journal on your findings. Over time, the patterns you see, from one situation to another, will shed light on your model of the world and suggest ways to revise or extend it.

■ **Reflect with others on your accounts:** Bob, Phil, and I invariably told different stories about the same exchange. Sharing our stories, and how we arrived at them, helped us see things that each of us had missed individually. When reflecting with others, explicitly describe 1) the data you selected from the transcript and 2) how you interpreted that data. Then invite others to help you revise and elaborate your account by asking them to offer 1) new interpretations of your data, or 2) any data that you might not have seen. This data might include other things you did, your impact on them, or things they were trying to do.

Don't reject alternatives out of hand. If your view of the situation doesn't match theirs, ask how they arrived at it. Most important, ask them to help you see things you might have missed.

■ **Set conflict to work:** The challenge here is to transform "here we go-again" conflicts into ones that require each person to grow. Bob, Phil, and I are all very different. Even today, our clashes are intense and emotionally charged. Early on, we knew that we could use these differences to our advantage. We just didn't know how. It took us a while to discover that if we stopped trying to get each other to be different (i.e., easier to deal with), then we could use the very characteristics that drove us crazy to drive our own growth instead. The fact that we posed difficulties for one another became an asset, not a liability. We now see one another's downsides as an opportunity to expand our own abilities to help a much wider range of people in a wider variety of circumstances.

The phrase, "Set conflicts to work," is borrowed from Mary Parker Follett, who used it in a paper presented before a Bureau of Personnel Administration conference group in January 1925. It was reprinted in *Mary Parker Follett: Prophet of Management*, by Elliot M. Sachs (Cambridge: Harvard Business School Press, 1996).

■ **Embrace inconsistency:** No matter how competent you become, there will always be a gap between the behavior you espouse and your actions in real life. That's because the knowledge you need to act effectively is, by definition, much more complex and demanding than the knowledge you need to talk about effective action. You may believe deeply that "People should support one another and be inclusive." But you (and others) will continually run up against circumstances where that rule doesn't apply, or applies so poorly that it doesn't make sense. At that point, "real life" action judgment will always override the rule. Don't sidestep or squelch the gaps between the espoused rule and the action rule. They are telling you something about the limits to your espoused theory as well as your theory-in-use. Listen.

■ **Be humble in your efforts and compassionate toward imperfections, including your own**: While you may like some people more than others in your group, keep in mind that a range of personae live within each person. The way you operate toward them will elicit the persona you see—the sonofabitch you fear or the best person someone is capable of being.

■ **Invest in outside help—no matter how good you are or become:** Chris Argyris and David Kantor were invaluable to our group, helping us see things we could not see on our own. View consultation as an investment in excellence, not as a cure for sickness.

}} David Kantor's contribution to this book begins on page 262.

Bob, Phil, and I began our journey together almost twenty years ago. While we have touched on painful moments from our pasts, we were always much more interested in learning how we perpetuated the past in the present and how we might create a new future. That is something you can only do with a little help from your friends.

5 Precepts for Mentors . . .

. . . and for those being mentored

Bill O'Brien, Peter Collins, John Hogan, Mike Rowe; Covenant Insurance Group

Between 1979 and 1991, Bill O'Brien, as CEO of the Hanover Insurance Company, promoted an ethic of learning that included explicit emphasis on improving the quality of mentoring. A boardroom coup at Hanover prompted his resignation in 1991, but he continued to mentor people as an independent consultant, as an eminent figure in the learning organization community, and as a founding partner of the consulting firm the Centre for Generative Leadership.

Bill has also been an advisor to the Covenant Group—a property and auto insurance company based in Massachusetts and Conneticut, founded in 1995 by a group of insurance industry "discontents." Most of the work is managed through self-directed teams; claims adjusters, for instance, assign their own tasks, recruit and hire coworkers, and build their own budgets. Many Covenant people work from home. "Headquarters" is a small, informal suite of small-town offices, unpretentious and suffused with esprit de corps.

Asked for his views of effective mentorship, Bill suggested convening this group of Covenant managers: Peter Collins, who developed its products and pricing strategies; Mike Rowe, responsible for overseeing the relationships between the company, its customers, and its claims adjusters; and John Hogan, who heads the Covenant computer systems group. All four concurred: People at Covenant must learn to mentor one another effectively, or the entire operation would be at risk. Here's how they developed their practice.

Bill O'Brien: We formed the Covenant Group around three core ideas. First, we would flourish by helping people develop their fullest potential. Second, through close, long-term relationships with customers, we would build a reputation for trustworthiness—especially in the high-stress aftermath of an injury or calamity. Third, we could reduce costs by eliminating duplication and potential conflicts between agencies and company operations. We would network them through personal computers instead of expensive mainframes. These three premises contradicted the prevailing wisdom of the existing insurance business, which is based around centralized administration and short-term profits.

Mike Rowe: In establishing a culture of self-direction and team building, we have learned the value of having our people be mentors for one another. We also work hard to mentor our claims people, helping them eliminate much of the adversity that has been a part of the claims process historically. The result has been reduced stress for our claims people and the claimants that they serve, along with a very low incidence of lawsuits, compared with the industry at large.

O'Brien: A mentor relationship involves two people—who may or may not report to one another—who pay special attention to each other's development. Often, an elder will foster the growth of a younger person, but the great mentoring relationships are reciprocal. Either way, it's an extraordinarily valuable asset. If you have twenty percent of the people engaged in mentoring relationships, it will raise the thought and quality of conversation among the other eighty percent, simply because that twenty percent will begin to help create a culture of thinking about more significant things. These principles, based on our experience, may help.

NEARLY ANYONE CAN BE AN EFFECTIVE MENTOR.

O'Brien: When I first joined the insurance industry, I felt deficient in the great mystical game of actuarial mathematics. My manager, "Ralph," was a suspicious, micromanaging tyrant. But he generously spent three hours or more per month mentoring me. When the monthly and quarterly reports came out, I'd ask why the results had changed.

"Aw, it's nothing," he'd grumble. "They just monkeyed with the numbers for Wall Street." Then he'd show me how he would have done it if he were CEO. He taught me to sense discrepancies and figure out what questions to ask.

At the beginning of your career, only a few people will play things so close to their chest that you can't ask them for help. Most people will help you, particularly if you're not a threat to them, and if you can read the times when they're busy or uninterested. You need not admire everything about them to learn from them, and learning from them will tend to bring out the best in them.

tips

A MENTORING RELATIONSHIP MUST BE VOLUNTARY ON BOTH SIDES.

O'Brien: Any organizational leader should be responsible for developing his people, in a variety of different areas. But mentoring goes beyond that. A fruitful mentoring relationship requires mutual trust and respect. Two people reciprocally choose to help each other, based on affinity and chemistry. I'd guess that only twenty percent of the people in any organization will make that choice voluntarily.

That's why I don't support mentorship programs. If it's formally encouraged from the top, then eighty percent of the people in a company will join it just to look good. The rules, guidelines and official expectations would gum it up for the twenty percent who would voluntarily choose it.

John Hogan: Many people need never enter a mentoring relationship, because they're not moved to do so. They can still have completely fulfilled work lives; no one should feel pressured to "be mentored." At the same time, an organization where no mentoring takes place is probably deficient in some fundamental way.

Peter Collins: If you are ready to be mentored, you must be willing to take risks—to go through the painful process of growing. Suggestions that people make will be scary and uncomfortable. Yet, having asked for them, you can't just push them aside. There will be a delay, maybe of several months, between the time you receive advice and the time you are ready to go back to it and put it into practice.

MENTORS DON'T PROVIDE SOLUTIONS; THEY FACILITATE LEARNING.

O'Brien: Often, an older person has more conceptual experience and has thought about the dynamics of a situation. But the younger person is closer to the situation and has all the data. If one supplies the theory, and the other supplies the detailed examples, then they can come together to conceive of a solution that unscrews the mess.

Collins: A good mentor in our company doesn't go in to a local office and say, "You should raise the actuarial rates nine percent." Instead, you might say, "We think rates ought to be raised in a range from six to eleven percent. We know there are tensions. The more you raise rates, the less new business you sell." Then you lead them into a conversation that replicates the thinking that you would go through if you were in their position.

In a typical company, mentors probably emphasize technical issues: How to perform actuarial work, how to develop solutions. But I focus on cultural issues: How to think more effectively, and how the local work fits in with the values of the overall company. This type of mentoring was very valuable to me when I worked at Hanover Insurance.

O'Brien: There's got to be a shared passion around some truth to allow people to share their thoughts. I know that Mike and I have a common passion about designing a trustworthy, credible claims process. Peter and I have a shared passion about training insurance customers in safety. With that energy between us, we are willing to lay open our secrets so the other person can advise us candidly.

MENTORS CAN ONLY EXIST IN AN ORGANIZATION IMBUED WITH INTEGRITY.

Hogan: When you mentor or coach people, you advise them on their future. You represent the company to them. To take on that role when, at heart, you don't believe in the company's integrity is a no-win situation. Either you have to tell them the truth—in which case, you have to honestly ask them why they would want to stay with this company—or else you have to feed them lies, and then how can you feel good about the mentoring process? A colleague of mine left his company because he couldn't reconcile himself anymore, as a mentor, to the tension.

MENTORING RELATIONSHIPS ARE NOT PERMANENT.

O'Brien: I'd like to think that all my mentoring relationships would lead to permanent friendships, but the intensity won't last. If I am your mentor, talking with you for an hour a month, within two years you'll move on to learn from someone else, which is how it should be. I had a number of mentors during my career, and I would like to see young people in Covenant have access to a lot of different mentors.

Occasionally there may be a long-standing mentor relationship. As a senior executive at Hanover, I learned a great deal from the CEO, Jack Adam. Then, when he retired and I became CEO, I continued to learn from him. That mentorship lasted twenty two years. But we always had a subject of mutual interest, the evolving Hanover Insurance Company.

MENTORING "FAST-GROWTH" PEOPLE IS A HIGH-LEVERAGE STRATEGY.

O'Brien: When I was CEO of Hanover, I saw twenty-five to thirty percent of my job as developing the dozen or so people who reported directly to me. I was always thinking: "How do I bring Joe up a notch or two? What's his next phase of growth?"

I thought this was very high-leverage activity. If I got a high-level executive to be two notches more effective, it provided tremendous value for the company.

Now in filling high positions, I look for people with a propensity for mentoring. When considering someone for promotion, I watch how people flower under them. I ask them in interviews, "Tell me about the best person who has worked for you." If they say, "Well, he showed up on time every day, and he really knew policy coverage," then I recognize the lack of any real knowledge about mentoring. If they start talking about the way a person took on a difficult challenge, mastered it, and changed in the process, then I know they understand. Similarly, I ask about the worst person who ever worked for them. They tell me how bad that person was, and I ask, "What did you try to do to help him grow?" If the answer is short, I know I haven't found a mentor.

BEWARE OF PSEUDOMENTORING.

O'Brien: People often think of "mentoring" as the development of political connections. I have seen younger, attractive people charm older managers into making connections for them. The older manager feels needed and admired, but the younger person is simply using the contact for promotion or a recommendation and to move up the ladder.

I've also seen supposed "mentor" relationships where the older manager is trying to build a power base. The relationship is a vehicle for control, to develop a loyal group of political allies who won't cross you in a turf battle—even if they know the other side has a stronger case.

These types of relationships are disgusting to watch. Under the rubric of "learning," both sides are exploiting each other *and* the organization. They undermine the value of merit; if you can get ahead by manipulating a mentor or demanding loyalty, then you don't need to develop your capability for performance.

The only way to guard against these kinds of abuses is to cultivate an open, candid enough atmosphere that other people can see political relationships in their true light, and make their decisions accordingly.

Hogan: I get nervous when people say that the biggest attribute they want from people is loyalty. That suggests they aren't mentoring people out of a genuine commitment to development and learning. They hope to pull other people's strings. The true reward of mentoring is intrinsic: Knowing that in some intangible way, greater than the sum of its parts, you are developing yourself in helping someone else.

MENTORING IS LOVE.

O'Brien: At its deepest level, mentoring provides the energy of love. My definition of love is: helping others to complete themselves.

A few years ago, I saw an interview with Richard Rodgers, who said that the biggest mistake of his life was breaking up with Oscar Hammerstein. "We never reached the same level again," he said. "We brought out the best in each other." That, to me, is the definition of mentoring.

6 A Strategy for Building Competence

Daniel H. Kim

Author, speaker, facilitator, organizer of the annual Systems Thinking in Action conference, and publisher of the Systems Thinker *newsletter, Daniel H. Kim has been a long-standing friend of* The Fifth Discipline Fieldbook. *Here, he tackles the delicate reality that organizations seeking "help" often short-change themselves by relying on short-term training.*

There's a natural tendency, in today's fast-paced business world, to want new knowledge available quickly, in bite-size chunks, with immediate results, so it can be conveniently fit into busy schedules. Thus organizations "learn" by sending people to short skill-building workshops. This may be adequate for adding to a base of knowledge that you already possess, such as training on a new machine or a new software package. But if you are interested in developing capabilities that are different from your current base of experience, then the bite-size chunk approach will probably disappoint you in the end.

why 1 day seminars don't work

See Hubert Dreyfus's book *Mind Over Machine: The Power of Human Intuition and Expertise in the Era of the Computer,* New York: Free Press, 1986.

Philosophers Hubert and Albert Dreyfus have proposed a useful alternative approach. They suggest that skill acquisition takes place in five stages, each reflecting distinct levels of competence:

■ **Novices**: New learners have a beginning awareness of the subject area, and apply their nascent skills by following rules. With a purely intellectual understanding of the concepts and ideas, they can't easily recognize a "problem" clearly enough to be able to diagnose it.

- **Advanced beginners:** Now performance improves, to the point where learners can perform acceptably in some real settings. They are more aware of the breadth of the subject area, and they acknowledge their own lack of knowledge about the discipline as a whole. They can reliably follow the prescribed steps of a process, as long as the situation matches cases that they have studied or encountered.
- **Competent learners:** These people have had intellectual exposure to the full array of knowledge in this subject; additional instructions and tips will not make them any more competent. They can move beyond simply applying rules and procedures; they can adapt their skills to circumstance, because they have begun to internalize these skills.

    Competent learners have gone as far as they can with "know what" learning. But they still lack know-how. For instance, a competent downhill skier with know-what knowledge can follow the rules: keeping the skis parallel, leaning forward, and allowing the legs to work like shock absorbers. But this skier may still not know how to swoop gracefully down the slopes, making it look easy. That takes an ingrained, embedded, self-aware know-how.

    (Interestingly, a person can have know-how without know-what. For instance, most people know how to walk. But few can translate that knowledge into written rules and procedures that would allow someone else to replicate the skill.)
- **Proficient learners:** Direct experience with continual practice in diverse settings has given these people ingrained skill. It may be years since they relied on book learning or instruction; they can reliably meet any situation, applying the tools and practices of the field with a full grasp of the whole problem. However, they still act at a primarily conscious level.
- **Experts:** Experts break the rules to surpass the goals. They have fully internalized their practice. An expert skier does not consciously study the terrain or strategize about the best form to use. He or she just travels down the hill, making adjustments as needed. Experts continue learning through interaction with other experts—in mentoring relationships, internships, and apprenticeships.

APPLYING THE FIVE STAGES TO HELPING ORGANIZATIONS LEARN

The competencies of organizational learning involve a similar progression. For example, practitioners of systems thinking might include:

- Novices who can read simple system diagrams, understand reinforcing and balancing loops, recognize key "system archetypes" such as "limits to growth," and propose new business ideas;
- Advanced beginners who construct "causal loop" diagrams, recognize patterns in their own work, and experiment with more intricate forms of diagramming and computer modeling;
- Competent systems thinkers who have internalized the systems archetypes, can help teams deal effectively with fundamental, complex situations, can teach others to use basic systems techniques, and possess a solid working knowledge of computer modeling skills;
- Proficient systems thinkers who have developed innate judgment about systems applications to business problems; they are seasoned and capable consultants, able to grasp issues in any setting;
- Expert systems thinkers who have internalized not just the archetypes, but computer modeling principles. Where a systems archetype user might talk about "limits to growth" as a generic archetype, experts are aware of the many varieties of limits to growth, and the mathematical logic that leads some growth systems to level off, while others overshoot and collapse.

Labels can be dangerous unless they are self-assigned. And variations exist within these categories; some people may be proficient at archetype use, without even a novice's understanding of the "stocks and flows" of computer modeling. Nonetheless, these categories apply to a wide variety of skills, including the five learning disciplines.

Now consider the implications for an organization trying to develop proficiency. You might send people off to two-, three-, or five-day workshops. Most of those learners reach only a novice level of capability. Competence (the third level) might require twenty to thirty days of in-depth training and twelve to eighteen months of in-depth practice on business problems.

Sending people to additional five-day workshops might only develop their capabilities to the advanced beginner level. Sending greater numbers of people would merely spread the novice capability; it would not give anyone the in-depth skills needed to diagnose and deal with systems issues. And businesses have neither the time nor the resources, typically, to send employees into the years of training that it takes to become experts. Since it's so hard to develop proficiency, managers may conclude that something is wrong with the discipline itself.

Fortunately, organizations can bootstrap themselves into greater proficiency through a strategic approach to building expertise. In the beginning, organizations call in outside expertise, and invest in entry-level training. This leads people along the path of development, creating first a group of novices within the company, then a group of advanced beginners from the ranks of the novices.

At some point, however, the organization needs to shift its emphasis to developing a small cadre of internal people at the competent stage. This could be accomplished by partnering with external consultants and trainers. Those competent people can then, in turn, train others in the organization to become novices and advanced beginners and perhaps to reach the competent level.

To develop capacity all the way to the expert level, the organization must invest in some form of mentorship program. This can take the form of entering key people into a university master's or doctoral program (as some corporations have done) or in enrolling them in a long-term professional development program. These people can then apply their knowledge to improve results, and to help develop others' capabilities.

An organization struggling with the challenge of "not enough help" can look for help within itself by building not just entry-level talent, but an internally driven self-reinforcing growth process. Competent learners create internal coaching capability, which leads more novices and advanced beginners to become competent, while helping the competent move on to greater proficiency.

PEGASUS SYSTEMS THINKING TOOLS

A basic familiarity with systems thinking is critically important for virtually all private and public sector work, but is still rare among managers. Pegasus Communications remains the main source of material that can help remedy the gap. They publish Daniel Kim's essential reference library on causal loop diagrams and archetypes and Virginia Anderson and Luanne Johnson's self-education guide on system dynamics, with well-graduated examples and exercises. *Designing a Systems Thinking Intervention*, a short booklet by *The Fifth Discipline Fieldbook* contributor Michael Goodman and four other authors, focuses on the steps and stages from the initial question "Is this a systemic problem?" through creating agreement of all the stakeholders around a specific intervention. Pegasus' ever-expanding library is featured on its Web site, *http://www.pegasus com.com*. — Bill Godfrey

7 Five Kinds of Systems Thinking

Charlotte Roberts, with Art Kleiner

Organizational change efforts are complex systems in themselves. To lead a change effort, and maybe simply to live in one, it's essential to develop an intensive capability to see (and work with) systems. That capability, in turn, will gain strength and subtlety if you can understand systems with more than one approach.

In learning organizational work, "systems thinking" has often meant the "loops and links" of system dynamics—the notation we use in this book to depict challenges. But some people react to loops in frustration. Even after training, they can't quite figure out how to take their complex problems and translate them into a relevant, clear set of archetypal structures—let alone a systems model. And they are (rightfully) reluctant to delegate their systems insights to expert modelers.

If you've struggled to learn loops and links, then we are kindred spirits. And yet I've known that I am a systems thinker since 1981, when I was trained in family systems therapy. This has furnished me with insights that I had never seen come out of any loop.

An expanded version of this article is being published separately and may be available on-line. See *http://www.fieldbook.com/5systems.html.*

SYSTEM

A system, in this context, is anything that takes its integrity and form from the ongoing interaction of its parts. Companies, nations, families, biological niches, bodies, television sets, personalities, and atoms are all systems. Systems are defined by the fact that their elements have a common purpose and behave in common ways, precisely because they are interrelated toward that purpose.

There are probably many viable forms of systems thinking, each appropriate to different people's attitudes and learning styles. At least five are relevant to organizational change. Since system dynamics is covered throughout this book, I will concentrate on four others.

For more on system dynamics, see pages 36, 42, and 60; also *The Fifth Discipline Fieldbook,* pages 177–182 and *The Fifth Discipline,* pages 27–135.

This segment is based on *Uncommon Sense* by Mark Davidson, an in-depth biography of von Bertallanfy's life and work. Published in 1983 by J. P. Tarcher, this book, sadly, is out of print. It is also based on *The Social Psychology of Organizations*, by Daniel Katz and Robert L. Kahn (1963, 1978, Wiley), the pre-eminent textbook, with in-depth discussion of Bertallanfy's concepts—inputs, outputs, throughputs, boundary definitions, and cycles of feedback and homeostasis. Many managers will recognize open systems from the 1970s and 1980s, because the Katz-and-Kahn influence filtered out into organizational training throughout that period. Unlike most management fads of that period, it remains useful today.

Open Systems: Seeing the world through flows and constraints

BASED ON THE WORK OF VIENNESE BIOLOGIST LUDWIG VON BERTALLANFY, OPEN SYStems work starts with the idea that the whole of a system is more than the sum of its parts. "Suboptimization," a perennial issue in the quality and reengineering movements, is actually a boundary-definition issue: Define your sphere of interest too narrowly and you are apt to produce benefits for, say, your marketing function or this year's revenue goals at the expense of the whole organization's ability to respond to a looming competitive threat.

Any human organization, von Bertallanfy declared, was not a machine and should not be seen as one. It was a life-form, like a biological cell or living entity. To an open systems theorist, that meant an organization is a thing that transforms its inputs—everything it eats, breathes, perceives, absorbs, and takes in. These inputs transform the entity as well. To change an open system, you must learn to understand and influence the things that it takes in, and its relationship with its environment. Open systems researchers seek out the unconscious strategies by which the system maintains its integrity.

Right before he died in 1972 at the State University of New York at Buffalo, Bertallanfy was researching the international postal service, a truly cooperative international system that functions even in wartime, crossing political, social, and economic borders. Soldiers, no matter where they are, still get their mail. It cycles through the system. Could there be an application of this type of conflict-free operation that could help undo the friction that leads to war?

A HALF DAY ON OPEN SYSTEMS

As a team, sit down with a diagram like this and fill in each component with details about your own system:

1. What are the boundaries of the system? Is it just your team? Is it your department? Are you concerned only with one particular process or product line? Your company as a whole? Or your industry?
2. What inputs (goods, capital, labor, information) come in from outside? What transformations do these go through? What outputs (reports, products, services, numbers, waste) does the system generate? How does the world outside respond to those outputs, and how does that response affect the next round of inputs?

In a major Fortune 50 company, this exercise revealed that the market research department controlled incoming information so protectively that they kept it from R&D until after senior managers had approved it. Since that made it useless, R&D developed its own market research department (under a different name, to avoid suspicion). Neither market research department shows its results to the other; when the marketplace shifts, both groups can get blindsided.

3. Take your thinking farther out by expanding your system's boundaries one level. Bertallanfy had suggested this practice in his own writings about social change. What external people—critical stakeholders, customers, suppliers, or policy-makers—are part of your system?

4. In the system as it currently stands, who is aware of the picture you have created? Typically, most flows are privileged information. Purchasing understands the flow of raw materials and tools. Finance understands capital costs. HR understands the input of knowledge and capabilities. Sales, marketing, distribution, and product services handle different aspects of output. Only senior management looks at the entire picture of renewed input, the ways in which outputs affect inputs later. But since their view is so far removed, a great deal of waste slips through the cracks, as different members of the system duplicate or undermine one another's work.

"Open-book management" provides a very sophisticated and accessible way of carrying this understanding farther. See page 181.

5. Is the organization's attention focused disproportionately on one type of input (finance? materials?) when another type of input (human knowledge?) could yield more leverage?

ELIYAHU GOLDRATT'S BOOKS

The novels of Eliyahu Goldratt are like a set of open systems glasses that help you apply more effective approaches to flows and bottlenecks, without feeling that you are stuck in an academic treadmill. For instance, one of his narrators, a plant manager, is also a scoutmaster, who shepherds a group of kids hiking through the woods. The slowest kid, Herbie, holds the rest of them back. However fast they hike, they can't travel any faster than Herbie, or else they'll spread too far apart on the trail. The solution? Everybody divides up the gear in Herbie's pack, and then they can all move

Eliyahu Goldratt's books include: *The Goal*, with Jeff Cox (1985; a factory head rethinks production and marketing flow); *It's Not Luck* (1994; the same principles applied to corporate strategy and use of resources); *Critical Chain* (1997; on project management); and *Theory of Constraints* (1990; the underlying methodology); all from Great Barrington, MA: North River Press (800-486-2665).

much faster through the woods. The plant manager (and we readers, along with him) suddenly realize how this represents the same situation as a wasteful glut of inventory. Improving throughput offers the greatest leverage.

Each of Goldratt's books is full of stories like that, mostly in industrial or financial settings (one of his most memorable books, *Critical Chain*, is set in a business school). He spells out the theory in a slim hardback called *Theory of Constraints*. He graciously shows how various types of "systems thinking" (including *The Fifth Discipline* work and his own) all reinforce each other. And he compassionately looks at the emotional impact of "open system" problems. His books are not only valuable, but engaging, respectful, and downright generous in their intent to educate. — Art Kleiner

Social Systems: Seeing the world through human interaction

This material is based on *Seeing Systems* by Barry Oshry (San Francisco: Berrett-Koehler, 1995), a poetical and engaging guide to the principles that emerged in Oshry's experiments, and how they have been applied. The book is a mini-*Fieldbook* in itself, full of exercises, dialogues, cases, and the author's own shrewd and heartful observations. It is extremely relevant for designers of any participative enterprise; a must-read for community builders and educational reformers.

RELATIONSHIP IS EVERYTHING, WHEN YOU SEE THE WORLD AS A SOCIAL SYSTEM. A family exists with the goal of giving children a stable and nurturing place to grow. A company exists, in part, to provide a stable and rewarding livelihood for the key members of the company.

When leading a sustained change, there are three key places to look if you want to understand the influence of social systems on your potential for success. First are the social groups in your organization, and the interactions within them and among them. For instance, how effectively can your sales reps share competitive information with one another, or with your design engineering and manufacturing people?

Second are the perceptions people hold of the forces that shape their social interactions: either tangible forces, such as rules, roles, and reward systems, or intangible forces like power, pride, and attention to detail. When someone says, "I don't have any power in this system," is that an accurate description of their role and position?

Third are the purpose and goals of the system and whether they are understood and shared by everyone. If there is an implicit goal of "always show a profit," or "never lay anyone off," how does that impact people's conversations, interactions, and their willingness to belong to the system?

Barry Oshry, a long-standing researcher at Boston University and the National Training Laboratories, has developed a particularly useful approach for modeling and experiencing these three arenas. Oshry's "power systems" are recurring sets of attitudes and behavior that people adopt based on their perceived hierarchical relationships. In carefully conducted, wildly evocative seminar-experiments, he sets people up to live for a weekend in sleepaway offsites, role-playing different relationships: "tops" versus "bottoms," "ends" versus "middles," and "providers" versus "customers." In role-play after role-play, no matter what background the participants come from, people get pulled into the same roles.

Oshry's work reveals the disabilities inherent in most of our social systems. For instance, he writes about "relational blindness"—the inability to see one's self in relation to others. The elite "tops," living in remote luxury, get caught up in internecine quarrels. They never see how they look to others who must follow the rules they set. The "bottoms," with no access to the debates among the "tops," don't understand how they could constructively remove their own oppression, and the "middles," trying to make things better for everyone, get overwhelmed by competing demands. There are occasional rebellions among the "bottoms," which the "tops," perversely, appreciate—because at last they have something to work on together—without realizing the stress this places on the "middles." The customers get screwed in the process, and everyone's time and attention gets wasted.

Not every social system has to operate this way. But to break the pattern, you have to learn to understand your own subjective experiences, either with Oshry's techniques or exercises like this:

A HALF DAY ON SOCIAL SYSTEMS

1. Define the system that you care about. (As with Open Systems, identify the boundaries that affect the problem you're dealing with.)
2. Identify the different groups who belong. Who are the tops? The middles? The bottoms? The customers (demanding results from the system)? List the members of each category by name or by group.
3. Would they agree that they belong to that particular category? What responsibilities and privileges do they believe they have? Do they believe they have a voice in the system as a whole?
4. How do the groups see each other? Do they have misconceptions about one another? Do they see one another more accurately than they see themselves?

The idea of social systems goes back to Kurt Lewin's work with social psychology in the 1930s and 1940s. From Lewin, the ideas passed through the group dynamics work of the National Training Laboratories, and through the social system innovations of people like Ronald Lippitt and Dick Beckhard; other strands of this approach have emerged from gestalt theory (which influenced Lewin), family systems theory, and cultural anthropology (Lewin and Margaret Mead were close friends and colleagues during World War II). My own exposure to social systems came through sociotechnical workshops, and through a background in marriage counseling and hence family systems therapy. — Charlotte Roberts

5. What impact do those perceptions (of themselves and each other) have on each group's effectiveness?

⟩⟩ For guidance on intervening in social systems, see the review of Ron Heifetz's book, *Leadership Without Easy Answers*, on page 213.

Process Systems: Seeing the world through information flow

"INFORMATION," WROTE GREGORY BATESON, "IS ANY DIFFERENCE THAT MAKES A difference." He might have been describing the basic premise behind a family of systems approaches: sociotechnical systems, reengineering, and process mapping. Though all of them came from different roots, they all recognize that information flow is fluid, and can easily be rearranged. Thus, they boldly go where most managers fear to tread: reprogramming the flow of activity in an organization in the same way that you might reprogram a computer.

The early 1990s' management fad of reengineering revealed, often for the first time, exactly how cumbersome and self-defeating many existing office process systems are. Unfortunately, most reengineering projects were designed so that expert consultants (trained in information technology and software engineering) would come in from outside and recommend new process designs to the senior executives. The employees who resided in the process were seen as too "subjective," too wedded to old, outmoded ways of working, too invested in the political turf they want to protect (and perhaps too attached to the idea of keeping their jobs) to take part in the redesigns. The results, in many cases, were disastrous—even from the reengineers' own perspective. Often, jobs were eliminated quickly and thoughtlessly, resulting in organizations that were understaffed and tasks that didn't get done.

It is important not to throw out the process systems baby with the reengineering bathwater. The invaluable methodology of process mapping, for instance, gathers a cross-section of people together to chart the flow of work—either as it is today (in conventional process mapping) or as it could be in an ideal future (in reengineering).

⟩⟩ For examples, see articles on General Electric (page 74) and learning labs (page 91).

Just as software is tested, retested, debugged, and redesigned throughout its lifetime with the input of its customers, so should process redesign be ongoing and iterative. People who use the system must see that their

---

There are several different schools of process work, but most of them could trace their roots to the work of English researcher Eric Trist and his colleagues Fred and Merrelyn Emery. Beginning in the 1950s, they developed "sociotechnical systems": a process-based, team-oriented approach to work that came to be known as "self-organizing teams" and "high-performance teams." That story (and the story of the innovations behind social systems theory) is told in detail in Art Kleiner's *The Age of Heretics*, and in Marvin Weisbord's book *Productive Workplaces* (San Francisco: Jossey-Bass, 1987). Influences include Bertallanfy's open systems approach, Norwegian resistance teams that had fought Hitler during World War II, and the early social systems work at National Training Laboratories.

Also see "Systems Thinking With Process Mapping: A Natural Combination" in *The Fifth Discipline Fieldbook*, pp. 184–85.

reactions to problems quickly "feed back" to influence the overall design. Without this flexibility, early attempts to implement new processes will falter, and the new processes will be like "buggy" software—frustrating to use and prone to mistakes.

Good process design depends on informal information. For instance, I worked with a consumer products manufacturing plant whose fulfillment was abysmal; unnecessary errors and delays perennially made their products late. Nor could the corporate experts find any way to redesign it. Yet they had won a "vendor of the year" award from Wal-Mart. "What," I asked, "do you do when Wal-Mart calls?"

"For Wal-Mart," they said, "we trust everybody to get orders out without the usual verifications."

"And why couldn't you do that for all your customers?"

They could, and they saved $4 million the first year they tried. But they could never have conceived of the change themselves, because they had never recognized consciously that orders from Wal-Mart bypassed the normal flow until they mapped their processes.

A HALF DAY OF PROCESS SYSTEM DESIGNS

It should be agreed upon, at the beginning of this team exercise, that none of the decisions or ideas will be binding. Your goal is to reach a better understanding of the processes that exist in your organization, by comparing them to an idealized potential version.

1. Define a process in your organization that calls out for redesign—one with perennial problems.
2. What is the purpose of this process? How does it add value? What would be the purpose of this redesign? What results should the new system achieve (that it doesn't achieve now)?
3. With self-sticking notes and colored markers, construct a flow chart of your ideal process, from start to finish. Do this with a blank sheet of paper, plotting the flow of activity from one step to the next, moving from left to right across the diagram you build.
4. Using a different colored marker, plot the flow of information for each step. When a step is complete, who needs to know about it? What kinds of conversations need to happen on an irregular, informal basis?
5. Is the process robust? If there are critical bottlenecks or crises, does it crash? Or does it recover? (It will recover more easily if there are parallel processes, alternative paths for information to flow.)

   Is the new process simple and transparent? Can people grasp what the organization is asking them to do? Is it clear to them how to offer their own comments and knowledge?

Is the new process responsive? For instance, when someone notifies the next station in a process about a change, do they receive a confirmation that the next station got their message?

Is the process elegant? Does one task accomplish as many goals as possible? (For instance, if you need to arrange an approval process for placing orders, can that approval process also automatically include a check on specifications?)

6. Whose input (do you now realize) would be valuable in designing this system? How can you involve them in the next stage of redesign?

The living systems perspective is guided by several books. *The Web of Life* by Fritjof Capra (New York: Anchor Books, 1996) provides the philosophical underpinnings. It, in part, is based on a significant book with beautiful color illustrations: *What is Life?* by Lynn Margulis and Dorion Sagan (New York: Simon and Schuster, 1995). Microbiologist Margulis coauthored the "Gaia hypothesis" theory, that the Earth itself is a living organism. Both Capra and Margulis/Sagan provide intellectual histories (overlapping, complementary, and compelling) of the development of these ideas. I also drew upon *A Simpler Way*, by Meg Wheatley and Myron Kellner-Rogers (San Francisco: Berrett-Koehler, 1996), a prose poem about the way that self-organizing feels in organizations. Meg's previous book, *Leadership and the New Science*, was a sterling effort to make the concept of living systems "sing" for businesspeople.

Living Systems: Seeing the world through the interaction of its self-creating entities

NONE OF THE OTHER FORMS OF SYSTEMS THINKING, ARGUE LIVING SYSTEMS PIO-neers, see the world as it truly is: a constantly pulsing, changing, interconnected world of rapidly interacting relationships, in which order emerges naturally from chaos without being controlled.

The living systems perspective has emerged from the "new sciences" of the twentieth century: quantum physics, ecology, complexity mathematics, and chaos theory. This perspective assumes that human groups, processes, and activities are self-organizing, like ecological niches. There aren't any designers or reengineers to control the flow of information. Information courses rapidly through the organization in its own natural patterns. If the right people meet in diverse, frequent interactions, with a variety of patterns to those interactions, a beneficial reframing will emerge on its own.

Instead of looking for particular leverage points, a living systems thinker might listen for "where the system wants to go." By amplifying or intensifying people's overall awareness of that direction, new behaviors will naturally emerge, and propel the overall pattern of the system across a threshold into a new form.

When I first heard this, it reminded me of the civil rights movement, which I experienced firsthand, growing up in the South. The sit-ins and marches kept pushing and pushing, creating more and more chaos in the old system. Finally, the nation's self-awareness crossed a critical threshold and the drive for change spun the United States into a new trajectory. People became race-conscious in a completely new way. The pattern of organization around race is probably not the final pattern that any of us want. But it is still spinning into a new type of trajectory, in ever-more-hopeful ways. As people conduct their life's activities, their friendships, their work relationships, and their romances in less racially damaging ways, the pattern of organization of society gradually changes.

Organizational leaders recognize that the best moves they can make are almost nonexistent. "I walk around Motorola," Bob Galvin is said to have remarked, "and imagine I'm in a concert hall. I try to hear where there's harmony, if anyone's slightly out of tune, is anyone ahead of pace, behind pace. Is there synchronicity? I listen for the ways we're interacting with our customers. And I get some sense of how might we take that information and make the changes we want to make."

LIVING SYSTEMS ORGANIZATIONAL WORK IN PRACTICE

Living systems work is grounded in dialogue and other forms of reflective, in-depth conversations.

Facilitator:

This conversation should be ideally facilitated by someone familiar with dialogue approaches and the ideas described in Capra's book The Way of Life.

1. **What's your organization's "genetic code"?** What aspects of the organization stay constant amid the flux of people, information, and work? What values, ways of acting, or habitual beliefs reinforce your identity as "us"? (Customers, vendors, and people outside the system can help define this.)

    In Charlotte, North Carolina, the First Union Bank is customer-focused, NationsBank is more oriented to efficient transactions, and Wachovia Bank concentrates on long-term relationships. These constant characteristics affect the ways the banks recruit, develop people, and make thousands of everyday decisions.

2. **Who belongs?** Which people truly belong in this system? Do they know they belong? Have they chosen to belong? Some members of the system may not work for the organization. In a public school system, for example, members might include taxpayers and parents; in a company, they may include key customers. Some members (such as disfavored customers) may not be aware that they are members, or even aware of their influence on the whole.

3. **What is the purpose?** What "wants to happen" in this organization? Is it a desirable future?

    Thinking about living systems has changed the way I think about shared vision. Now I always ask: "Whose vision is this?" Is it only the will of the executive team? Or does it recognize the vision of customers, suppliers, employees, shareholders, and community members? What do they all want this entity to be?

When a healthcare organization asked this question recently, they recognized that there was both a social and an organizational need to find a way to care for people who made less than $15,000 per year while remaining solvent as a for-profit hospital. The need was unspoken; hospital employees seemed to fear that saying it out loud would backfire on them. Therefore, they hadn't connected it with the other goal that "wanted to happen"—serving the growing number of baby-boom customers who didn't respect bureaucracy and expected quality healthcare service at low prices, even if they had to get it from a nontraditional company entering the healthcare business.

4. **How aware is this organization of itself and its environment?** Living systems naturally adapt if their perception is unblocked. Nobody tells animals to hibernate in the winter; so why assume that people need to be told what to do? Why not just give them access to the information they need and the authority to adapt?

Does everyone in the organization know how well it is doing in the marketplace? Does everyone recognize weak signals for pending trouble? When surprising signals emerge, are they talked about . . . or are they discounted and disdained? "You think we're threatened? You must be mistaken!"

See "Conscious Oversight," page 545.

MINDWALK (1991, U.S.)

If, like me, you learn better by seeing than by reading, then you may be interested in *Mindwalk*, a two-hour filmed lecture on living systems, with Liv Ullmann and Sam Waterston. Written by Fritjof Capra and directed by his brother, Bernt Capra, it is one of the best tutorials you can ever get on living systems theory. *Mindwalk* takes more concentration than the average movie, but it repays that concentration with understanding. — Charlotte Roberts

Sustaining your effort with five forms of systems thinking

Most people in business seem to have a tacit, unspoken preference for one systems approach or another. Engineers are more comfortable with system dynamics; computer people, with information flow; biologists, with living systems; and organizational development people, with social systems. But while each has its own value in practice, they complement each other. Recently, I conducted four simultaneous systems exercises with a group of people trying to pull through a difficult merger between an American and European chemical company. (We didn't have enough people for five, so we dropped process systems.) Each subgroup talked through the situation from one systems approach—and then presented their interpretations and suggestions to the others.

- **Open systems:** Seeking inputs, the group realized that customers were the strongest force pushing the two halves of the new company together. Customers hated dealing with multiple sales reps. They wanted one price, one distribution system, and one person to call. Any call for unity would need to start with meeting customer needs.
- **Social systems:** There were still rivalries among general managers (tops), while bottoms, the salespeople, operated in isolation from one another, resisting any effort to consolidate (because they knew that they were overstaffed). Leverage would come first from involving tops in clarifying their common purpose; then, regular meetings among bottoms might lead to better coordination.
- **System dynamics:** This group settled on a "Tragedy of the Commons" interpretation. The merger had made each individual sales force more aggressive for its own products, so that they could demonstrate their competence to decision makers in the new system. But as (for instance) the Americans became more aggressive, and pushed harder on the "common pool" of customer goodwill, the Europeans became more aggressive as well, for fear that the customers would order all chemicals through the Americans. This continued to escalate, until the sales forces came to see each other as their enemy. Leverage might come from getting everyone, including customers, together to see how they worked at cross-purposes; or perhaps from increasing the prospect pool through a wider product range.
- **Living systems:** Clearly, the organization did not "want" to be divided along product lines anymore; perhaps it should organize

For more about Tragedy of the Commons, see *The Fifth Discipline Fieldbook*, p. 140.

along regional lines. Internal people and customers should have a chance to live with the new design, feel their way through it, and adjust. "We need to keep raising awareness," said one member of the group. "How are our customers responding? How are we measuring results, and what do those measurements mean?"

THE SYSTEMS THINKING PLAYBOOK:
Exercises to stretch and build learning and systems thinking capabilities, by Linda Booth Sweeney and Dennis Meadows (1995, 1998, Volumes I–III, Linda Booth Sweeney)

Compiled by prominent systems thinking innovator Dennis Meadows and educational researcher Linda Booth Sweeney (formerly at the MIT Center for Organizational Learning, now at Harvard), this book is a continually growing set of teasers, jigglers, sparkers, warm-ups, and prodders. It's particularly useful for "reframing": helping people see that reality is not quite as they imagined it. A few of the exercises go deeper, as well, to help people diagnose their situation from a variety of systems perspectives. Through their expanding looseleaf format, Web site, and CD-ROMS, these exercises keep multiplying in number. I am particularly impressed with the "Web of Life" exercise, (Vol. II, p. 16), which invites people to turn themselves, and a ball of brightly colored yarn, into a model of their organization's interrelationships. — Art Kleiner

CHOICE, CHANCE AND ORGANIZATIONAL CHANGE
Practical Insights from Evolution for Business Leaders and Thinkers, by Clay Carr (Washington, D.C.: Amacom Books, 1996)

Here is a relatively short, clearly written reflection on the choices that individuals make—separately or together—to move change forward or hold it back. Carr makes powerful use of the analogy between natural ecological systems and organizations, emphasizing the pivotal role played by information. He particularly emphasizes the importance of the periphery of the organization (those who are in daily contact with customers, suppliers, and the rest of the environment) as sources of information and leverage for necessary change.

"Brief Reality Checks," included at intervals throughout the book, invite you to reflect on the situation in your own business, with advice like this: Whenever you do adopt a new technology, ask yourself in advance how it might handicap you in the future. Technology is always less flexible than people. The second half of the book explores the concepts of complex adaptive systems—coevolution, building creativity in a world of unpredictability, internal markets, and how to finally get "self-organized."— Bill Godfrey

FEEDBACK THOUGHT in Social Science and Systems Theory, by George P. Richardson (Philadelphia: University of Pennsylvania Press, 1991)

Who made up this systems stuff, anyway? Few people recognize exactly how intricate and fascinating the answer to that question is. George Richardson goes into full detail, showing not just how the concepts emerged (from observations of thermostats, servomechanisms, economic markets, ecologies, arms races, and many other systems) but how they evolved. A dense and academic book that rewards immersion. — Art Kleiner

8 Aikido for Change Leaders

Jeff Dooley, Adaptive Learning Design, and Chris Thorsen, The Performance Edge

Managing an organizational change initiative is like trying to rebuild a large sea vessel while sailing it through unknown waters. With everything in flux, there's no solid place to stand. Typically, people overlook a readily available source of personal terra firma: their own bodies. By adopting a daily practice of physical learning, ideally involving the pursuit of mindfulness and skillful movement, people can become more physically grounded, more aware of the subtle dynamics around them, and more in touch with their own intuition.

One source of physical learning is aikido, the martial art of peace. Aikido fosters deliberate, slow, attentive movements. With time and practice, people develop a relaxed, balanced attitude within their own bodies, neither rising up to clash with resistance, nor giving in to it.

They cultivate a graceful quality of activity, one that helps them engage the trust and confidence of others during times of crisis. Whether through aikido, or some other "mindfulness"-oriented discipline, people can learn to use changes around them as a source of power, as sailors use ocean currents and the wind.

In 1985, executives of the San Francisco–based communications start-up, Cellular One, employed aikido principles to build a complex cellular network in half the time ever attempted before, without sacrificing the health of their families or the spirit of their employees. The company accomplished this by designing their own expansion to piggyback onto that of a primary competitor—stepping off the line of direct attack, and blending their effort with that of their adversary. Leadership team members at Cellular One developed this approach by practicing the "art of peace" together. Often, after an aikido demonstration, they would talk through the application of that principle to a business problem.

"Applying aikido principles in business," Cellular One president James Dixon said, "allows me to enjoy situations that, in the past, would have been painful or debilitating because the pressures were too great or the fears too strong. I was with the senior management team during the October 1987 stock market crash. Since our stock was young and volatile, it fell dramatically. As the situation worsened, we were all bombarded with phone calls, messages, and faxes. The CFO grew upbeat, even though he had lost $20 to $30 million in personal wealth. He demonstrated the ability to assess a situation, move beyond the obvious feeling of threat and danger, and take advantage of an event to which others were reacting negatively. By the end of the day, we had moved forward on three major acquisitions."

MINDFULNESS: ELEMENTARY SOLO EXERCISES

■ **For centering and grounding when a problem arises:** First, shake off the need to react to it immediately. Move to a sitting or standing position, and focus on your breathing. Do not force yourself to breathe deeply; simply allow your breathing to proceed naturally, as directed by your body. Let your awareness follow your breath deep into your stomach, and imagine that your breath is helping to dissolve any tightness or constricted places in your abdomen. As you breathe out, allow the tightness you dissolved to be expelled from your body. As you continue, let your shoulders relax and sink. Gradually feel your body sink farther into a state of relaxation and balance around your center. Imagine your body connecting with and taking root in the earth beneath you.

People emerge from this practice after a short time with a renewed awareness of balance and lightness. You may notice clear opportunities for action that you may have overlooked had you rushed headlong into generating a solution.

- **When your thoughts run away with you:** In any centering, grounding, or reflective process, as you keep your awareness focused on your breathing, you will notice that thoughts, desires, pains, and apprehensions arise in your mind. Take note of them as they arise, then let them float away or evaporate, while you stay attentive to your breathing. You will find, sometimes, that you become occupied with a thought and lose awareness of your breathing. Release the thought and gently bring your awareness back to your breathing.

- **When the telephone rings:** Instead of always rushing to answer the phone, get in the habit of waiting until the end of the third ring, using that time to practice breathing your awareness to your center. People who acquire this habit find they can answer the phone with a renewed sense of balance and equilibrium.

These exercises are drawn from established mindfulness and martial arts principles. For exercises that draw more directly on Aikido practice, and more information on centers in the U.S. where people are working with through-the-body learning, mindfulness, and aikido practices, visit the Web site: http://www.well.com/~dooley/Aikido.html.

AN UNUSED INTELLIGENCE
by Andy Bryner and Dawna Markova (Berkeley: Conari Press, 1996)

A book by two long-standing "learning organization" practitioners, aimed at managers. It contains safe, simple aikido practices for developing increased skill at transforming aggressive energy into fruitful resolution.

LIVING IN BALANCE
by Joel and Michelle Levey (Berkeley: Conari, 1998)

A comprehensive, practice-filled text emphasizing the value of integrating mind, body, and spirit for wholeness and balanced action in a chaotic world.

LEADERSHIP AIKIDO
by John O'Neil (New York: Harmony, 1997)

Specific applications of aikido principles, skill, and practices to the tasks of managing a business and of leading strategic business initiatives.

AIKIDO AND THE NEW WARRIOR
Edited by Richard Heckler (Berkeley: North Atlantic, 1985)

An anthology of stories about the relevance of aikido practices to everyday life. The individual stories, by leading aikido practitioners, emphasize the lessons of leadership and healing through compassion and interrelatedness. — Jeff Dooley

AIKIDO: THE POWER OF HARMONY
by Richard Moon (San Rafael, CA: Aiki Press, 1997)

Richard Moon, codeveloper of for business aikido practice (with Chris Thorsen, coauthor of this resource guide), offers guidance for bringing disparate groups into one room. (Moon and Thorsen have used aikido principles to develop dialogue between people enmeshed in long-term war, such as those in Bosnia, and Turkish and Greek Cypriots.) How can you deal with someone whom you perceive as an attacker? How can you see what they see? How can you help them, in turn, to see what you see? The practice is not strictly about martial art; it's all about presence and being in harmony. The three lessons are: (1) feel your center, (2) blend harmoniously with others, and (3) make your contribution. — Charlotte Roberts

9 Music, Listening, and Freedom

Some principles for coaching the senses

Miha Pogačnik

Miha Pogačnik, who refers to himself as an "entrepreneur and artist of culture," provides a rare kind of help for executives. Using his own violin playing as a catalyst, he helps them become more aware of archetypal rhythms and hidden emotional structure, in themselves and in the people around them. As founder of the Institute for the Development of Intercultural Relations Through the Arts (IDRIART), based in

Hamburg, Germany, he has also used creativity and music to bridge seemingly unbridgeable gaps among people at war. We think his precepts will help guide any effective coaching—musical or not.

There are manifold attempts in business to help people become creative. But creativity is mostly understood as a problem-solving ability, in the realm of thought. People expect to find an ideal solution by hunting outside themselves, to analyze that solution, and then to imprint that analysis onto the problem they are trying to solve. Creative people, such as artists, know that the process doesn't work that way. This supposedly mysterious creativity is something that everyone already possesses—the ability to approach the world with interest and curiosity.

Keen senses underlie creativity. It is possible to learn perception in a much clearer form than most people are accustomed to using. But the development of the senses, in both children and adults, is seriously threatened today. The electronic media culture, the noise pollution of congested modern life, and the attention-snatching by economic and technological implements all obstruct and blunt our senses. Some people react with passivity and dependence; others, with anger and hostility. Those who can learn to develop and sharpen their senses can avoid either stance, and act instead as leaders.

I have spent a great deal of time, in the last few years, coaching executive leaders and other people to help them develop the sensory awareness that leads to creative thinking. I use music. Even in the midst of noise pollution, staying with a fine-tuned piece of music provides an awareness of pure experience. This is intrinsically beautiful, and it is also useful. It gives people an inner ground for being more creative, and a glimpse of the threshold between perception and thinking.

PERCEIVING QUALITY

Ever since Japanese cars moved on to the American market, managers have been told, "Produce quality!" How do you expect to produce quality if you do not first know how to perceive it?

Quality is perceivable in details. In an automobile, quality does not just appear in the manufacturing process, but in the details of the automobile's design and features, from the doorknob to the way the automobile handles. The same is true in a masterwork of music, but quality in music or art is often easier to recognize. After becoming attuned to quality in music, one can then apply that same awareness to any article.

SEEKING FEELINGS, NOT SENTIMENTS

I might ask people to close their eyes and enjoy the first movement of the sonata: "But let me help you focus your attention very objectively." People listening to masterpieces tend to swim in sentiments, rather than perceiving with their feelings. There is a significant difference. Sentiments are emotions that you have already internalized: sympathy, antipathy, anxiety, confidence, and so on. These emotions come up when you push the right buttons inside yourself. Because they are so well internalized, and detached from pure perception, emotions tend to cut people off farther from an authentic experience of their surroundings.

Perception with feeling intelligence, by contrast, is something new, not yet defined by a person's consciousness. It is perceived by the heart, freshly, in the moment of awareness. Imagine the first time an artist painted a tiger on a cave wall. Before that moment, it was impossible to look at a tiger without being overwhelmed by the immediate emotion: fear. You see a tiger, and you have to run. But in this representation, people could see that tiger and reflect. They could linger, permitting other feelings to form, observing them without being held captive by them. Art is tamed nature.

Like being near a tiger, change is not always a nice experience. Any true change is deeply connected to the sorts of experience that accompany death. That is why preindustrial cultures have initiation ceremonies: to train people's sensitivity so that they can endure harsh experience. People who have not learned this endurance will burst under the pressure of their feelings in situations of conflict. They will try to immediately resolve the conflict, before they have a chance to see where their feelings are taking them.

Effective leadership depends, I believe, on the leader's ability to endure feelings, and learn from them, instead of reacting with immediate sentiments. To build this capability, I try to teach people to endure processes. It can be done with music. You must listen to the end of a musical masterpiece. You can't, in the middle, say, "No! I don't like it!" And if you make it to the end, a revelation may occur.

THE ART OF LISTENING

Learning to listen will, in my opinion, be increasingly important in the business world. When you can give another person the chance to realize what they really want to say, you can accomplish a great deal more in much less time. It is relatively easy to be tricked visually, but if you learn to listen distinctly "between the words," penetrating into the deeper essence of people's speech, then it is much easier to come to the truth of whatever is being said. I often recommend that executives, before a big meeting, stop for a moment and create a "listening space" in their mind; the meeting will have a much better chance of getting to the participants' fundamental concerns. Listen to your listening!

But learning to listen can be awkward. Have you ever been in the presence of someone who listens closely to you? It feels discomfiting, like being stared at. People in society are not used to living at that level of awareness. Who dares inwardness?

That is why one learns to listen gradually. I use music to impart the skill. We may listen, for example, to Bach's Trio Sonata. There are three musical lines, playing at the same time, each rising and falling, all interwoven together. Bach is lovely, and you can simply listen to the motion; you like it. Or you can listen with feeling intelligence, which means following each of the three lines simultaneously. This is awfully difficult. Most people can easily distinguish between two lines of music, but not when you add a third line, especially when the lines shift among the thirty three different "voices" of the instruments of the orchestra. Conscious orientation amid fluidity is the stability of tomorrow!

To develop people's capacity to distinguish among those lines, I ask them to listen closely to the sonata. They follow each of the lines separately, and then build their capability for hearing all three of them at once. They learn to recognize when the quality of a theme changes and it passes from one layer of meaning to another. As they do this, they gain the capability of dealing with multi-dimensional reality—hearing each distinct "voice" while also recognizing the whole, and, once again, not losing themselves while being caught up in the experience.

This skill, which I think of as "transparency," is useful for business leaders. Napoleon Bonaparte had it; he often dictated seven letters simultaneously, cycling from one scribe to another with each sentence so that they would have time to catch up with him. In contemporary business, it helps people build the inner resources for holding their balance amid the ever-more-present "subnature" of the digital world.

LEARNING TO TRUST

People say that trust is essential in business, because controlling people is very expensive. So they seek trust first, and hope to build sensitivity to one another later. This is backward. Trust can only arise where people have deep, intense interest in each other. They must be able to distinguish one another's qualities, to know which aspects of one another are special and worth trusting. I trust my secretary to keep her own expense account; she tells me the amount of money she needs, and I don't ever look in her accounts. I know that she will not spend more than she needs because I know her. I have invested enough attention in knowing her that I can wholeheartedly trust her.

If we truly want to develop trust, we must build unbounded sensitivity first. It is not enough to simply love music; you must engage in music in a way that increases your sensitivity and awakens interest. That capacity, in turn, can lead to an intense interest in other things: In observing the ants in the woods, for instance, it may dawn on you how the natural world is itself an organization of incredible dimensions. If you are truly interested in someone or something, you don't just look at the nice and pleasant aspects of that entity. You look for all you can see, until that person or thing becomes part of your life, necessary to your makeup.

THE FREEDOM OF THE LEARNER

As a coach, I don't tell people what to experience. I play the violin to illustrate my themes; I make jokes; I follow my instincts. I don't stand there with a sour face and say, "Listen to this," or "Here is the point." Who am I to tell other people what they should hear? They must listen for themselves; as a coach, I only help them sharpen their attention. Art is great precisely because it doesn't force people to derive meaning. It leaves them free to learn for themselves.

This freedom should be taken very seriously. All human beings are different; they all bring different backgrounds and capabilities to the work of learning to listen.

When you respect the law of freedom, you know that you cannot sensitize an organization. You can only help individual people, each in his or her own way. If you sensitize only one person, then the composition of the whole organization changes, just as when you take a big bowl of yellow paint, and put in one red drop, everything changes.

LEARNING MASTERY

In the end, the whole of human society is a giant piece of art. The things you do, the places you go, the people you meet, and the ways you spend your time are all lines within the big symphony of humanity. The whole is contained in every one of your actions.

The German scientist-writer Johann Goethe once noted that amateur painters usually complain when their work is praised: "It's not yet finished." And they will never be finished, said Goethe, because they started without awareness. The master's composition is finished with the first stroke; it is clear, from that moment, where the master is going. The same is true of great music. When you hear the first four notes—Da da da DUM—of Beethoven's Fifth Symphony, you are aware of the import of the entire symphony. An awareness of the whole is already contained in the very first step.

Mastery does not mean having a plan for the whole, but having an awareness of the whole. You cannot predict the course of composition, but you can know, from the beginning, the purpose and requirements of the thing you are composing. This is as true for people composing an organizational endeavor as it is for people composing a piece of music. In my work with people, we try to stop and listen for the whole that they are trying to create, in the same way that, before an act of composition, the composer must stop and listen: What is it that is trying to be born?

THE POWER OF MINDFUL LEARNING
by Ellen Langer (Reading, MA: Addison-Wesley, 1997)

One person says, "That way is north." Another says, "That way is probably true north, as far as we know." Which statement sinks in more deeply? Harvard psychologist Ellen Langer makes a compelling case, grounded in rigorous research, that the ambiguous, uncertain, and conditional statement will provoke more people to learn. Rote learning, memorization, and authoritarian delivery of information do not work well. Playfulness, storytelling, supportive coaching, and mutual support don't always make people feel good, but they make people more mindful—less likely to slip into the semiconscious, going-through-the-motions frame of mind that shortcuts learning. Not only does the book help you turn that insight into practice, but it's fun to read. Probably. For me at least. What do you think? — Art Kleiner

THE WEB OF INCLUSION
by Sally Helgesen (New York: Doubleday/Currency, 1995)

Communities of practice can be geared so that people continually learn to help each other. This book by journalist Sally Helgesen shows how. Her "webs of inclusion" are like ongoing processes of creation and mutual aid instilled informally within organizations. One such network developed the "Intel Inside" slogan; another at a Boston hospital invented an innovative support technology for front-line nurses. Webs like these can be stronger than hierarchies, particularly for mentoring and support, because they foster help from unexpected places—like random conversations (which Helgesen calls "the watercooler factor"). This book can help you move effectively from "No Help" to meeting the broader challenge of "Diffusion" (p. 417). — Nina Kruschwitz

THE PATH OF LEAST RESISTANCE FOR MANAGERS
by Robert Fritz (San Francisco: Berrett-Koehler, 1999)

In his book *The Path of Least Resistance*, Robert Fritz articulated the power that people create for themselves by balancing a powerful vision with a clear view of current reality. Here, Fritz applied the same concept to organizational goals, and described a charting approach (with matching working-group software) for helping make it happen. This seemingly simple concept, underlying the learning discipline of personal mastery, is not so simple in practice. This book can help distinguish fruitful progress from mere spinning of one's wheels. — Art Kleiner

CONFESSIONS OF A PHILOSOPHER: A JOURNEY THROUGH WESTERN PHILOSOPHY
by Bryan McGee (New York: Random House, 1997)

The work of organizational change has catapulted many business people into the realms of philosophy: the innate contradictions and ambiguities of human nature and shared reality. This is daunting; few conventionally educated people are equipped for it. Nor have there been any accessible, knowledgeable, personal guides—until now. Written by an essayist/novelist/member of Parliament, this memoir of a lifetime's study guides you through Kant, Heidegger, and the quantum physicists in a way that truly helps build your depth of understanding—like a long letter from a valued uncle who happens to be a philosopher. — Art Kleiner

V. Not Relevant

"This stuff isn't relevant!"

1 The Challenge

"**R**esults need to be visible to the bottom line," commented one manager who had been part of a dialogue initiative in an electronics company. Though he professed support for the initiative, he felt it had not engaged enough people to make a difference. "People wanted to spend time working on the actual issues of the business. [Dialogue] was too abstract, not rooted enough in daily issues. With calendars very full, it's important to connect dialogue with regular work."

Establishing relevance has always been important for any change initiative. But it is, if anything, more important given today's business pressures. As the comment about dialogue suggests, people are so overloaded today, that they are hesitant to engage in anything new. As one employee of a large company put it, "If I had my way, I would never attend another meeting of any kind. While I'm out there, the work stacks up-up-up on my desk. And I keep thinking, 'I need to get back, to clear up my desk.'"

Often, in our experience, failure to develop a compelling business case for change precludes any significant momentum from developing. For example, the electronics company dialogue initiative eventually died out without accomplishing much—even though the senior-most executive in that group, the division president, had enthusiastically sponsored it. People took part in that initiative for over a year, yet many never felt deeply committed because they were unclear how it would impact the business. In other cases, initiatives die out even quicker if people do not

The "results" quote is taken from *The Learning Initiative at Electro Components*, by JoAnne Wyer and George Roth (Cambridge: Society for Organizational Learning Learning History, 1997), p. 30.

The "desk" quote is from *Perspectives on Full-Scale Corporate Transformation: The "OilCo" Learning History*, by Art Kleiner, George Roth, et al. (New York: Oxford University Press, 1999), p. 104.

159

feel there is a compelling case for change and a clear strategy behind the initiative.

Dealing with this challenge doesn't mean focusing on business results exclusively, but it does mean establishing a clear, authentic, convincing story about the relevance of a change initiative. To sustain a commitment over the course of months or years, people must be working on issues that they consider important—not just to themselves, but to customer needs and the business's long-term health. In embarking upon this initiative, are they trying to build a better product? To make a more viable process? To establish a new market? To cut costs without losing capability? Or to fill some other need? If the task of explicitly articulating relevance "slips through the cracks" as individual leaders pursue their own agendas, the entire effort may wither before it has a chance to take root.

THE UNDERLYING DYNAMICS OF "NOT RELEVANT"

Relevance constitutes the third "challenge of initiating." Like the challenges of time and help, it stems from a basic requirement for starting any change initiative—commitment. As investment in the initiative grows, people realize the degree of commitment that will be required of them. At the least, this requires that they be able to "connect" personally to a change initiative. They need to see that there is a focus on key business needs. Second, they need to understand how they fit in, how they can contribute, and how they will benefit. If these needs are not met, a "commitment gap" develops and they will not participate fully. They may participate because they feel they have to, but they will not be genuinely committed. They may pay lip service to the change initiative's goals ("We need this learning stuff to improve communication"), but privately, they will ask each other and themselves: "Why are we doing this stuff?"

Not everyone in a pilot group needs to be committed. To some degree there is almost always a commitment gap. But if only a few zealots are convinced the initiative can make a practical difference, it is unlikely to get too far.

The underlying limit or constraint behind this challenge concerns management's ability to communicate a clear business case for change. In any work setting, people are focused on practical needs. Someone with managerial accountability must make the case that an initiative can help in better meeting those needs. If this does not happen, people will correctly regard the initiative as just adding more work to their already overfull plates.

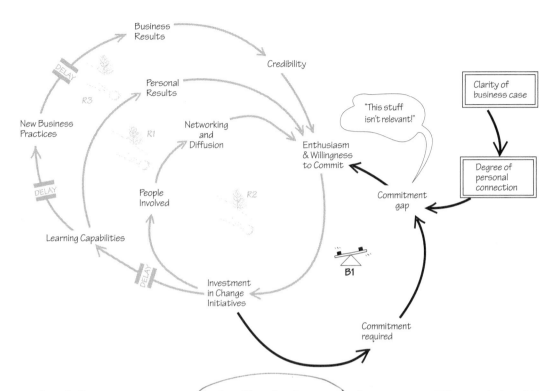

This challenge is one reason why local line leaders are vital to initiating significant change. Only they can "make the case" in a way that will be compelling at the front lines. Conversely, this is an area where executive power is surprisingly limited. Change initiatives championed by executives are routinely undermined when local managers do not see their relevance, and consequently do not communicate a case for change that people can connect to their own jobs. This is often the reason people view top management change initiatives as "management fads."

Investment in change initiatives also requires commitment by members of the pilot group. If the business case for change is not clearly articulated, people do not connect with its aims and a commitment gap results. People may participate because they have to, but there will be little investment and learning.

STRATEGIES FOR MEETING THE CHALLENGE OF "NOT RELEVANT"

High-leverage strategies all involve different approaches to strengthening line leaders' abilities to make a compelling business case for change. It is not possible to delegate the task of "making the case" to staff. If those accountable for business results are not champions, a change initiative will not be seen as credible. Even if staff are focused on business results, they do not have business accountability in the way that line managers do. So they cannot play the role of helping people connect day-to-day activities, business imperatives, and the aims of new change initiatives.

■ **Build strategic awareness among key leaders.** Technical and production-oriented line leaders may have spent their careers ignoring the financial impacts of their decisions; in some companies, that impact has been the exclusive bailiwick of accounting, finance, and planning specialists. But a change initiative, with its unfamiliar new investments and long potential delays before business results improve, requires a critical number of leaders (including line, executive, and network leaders) to learn to "think like business people." They need the kind of business acumen that would allow them to look at their activity and know whether it would be successful or fail as a business.

This does not mean slavishly following bottom line priorities, cutting costs, or laying people off. On the contrary, it may mean adding staff and increasing investment. But until you can justify new efforts in terms of added revenues or lower costs, you can't determine the strategic value of any new investment, or communicate its relevance, especially when the investment involves a long-term payback.

■ **Explicitly raise questions about relevance in the pilot group.** Often, within the pilot group, people need the time and room to come to a common view of relevance. This requires a strong level of trust among pilot group members. Many people on the pilot group will feel accountable to constituencies elsewhere in the organization. They may find it hard to handle the tension between those old loyalties and the new imperatives of the change initiative. Their real opinions of "what's relevant" may not come out at first, until they begin to visibly show the tension, or lose enthusiasm. At that point, many leaders respond by exhorting, cajoling, bribing, or threatening people. These tactics only increase the resistance that people feel. They have little or no impact on the fundamental constraints of this challenge.

If the goals of others on the team don't match your own, and you are attempting to encourage the change initiative, first try to understand how those goals developed. Inquire: What is the reasoning behind their focus? See, from their perspective, the relevance that their goals might have for the rest of the organization. Then, if you wish to advocate your view, make it clear, from your perspective, why the goals are inappropriate. You won't convince them by fiat, but you can make your own reasoning more clear. This is especially important if you have managerial authority, because people want to know how their own actions are meaningful to people of higher status in the hierarchy. Their paychecks, their future in the organization, and their present level of emotional comfort depend, in part, upon continued support from their line leaders and their line leaders' bosses.

■ **Make more information available to pilot group members.** Executive and line leaders sometimes misdiagnose this challenge. It may seem as if the people on the team are not motivated. In fact, team members may be very motivated, both by their personal goals and the aspirations for the organization. But they may fail to see how the change initiative is connected to those goals. If you're a manager, it's your job to give people the information they need about organizational priorities to see the connection.

Often, this means helping people gain a better understanding of their business, the sources of value, and how proposed changes can potentially improve business results. Some large companies, such as Shell Oil, have adopted companywide "business models" that set ambitious financial performance goals for the entire corporation (such as 12 percent return on investment [ROI] and 12 percent market growth per year). Each team within the company develops its own way to meet those goals—often designing their own initiatives to do so. This approach allows people to develop judgment about the relevance of their efforts, the criteria for judging an effort a success or failure, and the potential risks, versus rewards, of new innovations.

⟩⟩ See the story of Shell Oil, page 203; and resources for open-book management, page 181.

■ **Keep training linked tightly to business results.** Many training programs take place in retreat, far away from any actual work setting or business context. Even when people love the material, or find it interesting, they struggle to relate it to their pressing business needs. They may feel more motivated for a few days—but not nearly long enough to develop significant new capabilities or make headway.

⟩⟩ "Practice fields" provide a valuable approach for this; see page 91.

■ **Inquire openly about perceptions that some people are getting "carried away."** Sometimes people defend the work on task forces or change initiatives, simply because they love it. They invest more and more time, and keep it going through flimsier and flimsier mandates. Meanwhile, that time and effort is taken away from more conventional tasks. You can bring these two types of tasks together by deliberately holding shared vision exercises for the pilot group. What investments do you want to make in learning and change? What returns do you expect or want? How do you expect this to occur? How can you adjust the change initiative to meet business goals?

■ **Revisit relevance periodically.** Often, the initial goals of a change initiative are problem-oriented: "We want to make sure we can get our work done without the brutal 'heroic efforts' of last-minute fire-fighting." Or, "We want to stop working at cross-purposes with our own people." Gradually, the team may switch to more long-term or vision-oriented aspirations. As that happens, it is important to regularly recheck that the business case for these aspirations is clear.

2 The Case for Change at Visteon

Robert Womac, Executive Vice President of Visteon Automotive Systems Operations

An enterprise of Ford Motor Co., Visteon combines seven former component divisions into a new global business. Robert Womac offers the executive and line leader's view: How to make the case for change.

Our interest in learning began in 1989, when Russell Ackoff gave a presentation to a group of Ford senior executives. Nobody questioned the fact that the Japanese had whipped us on productivity, especially in the auto industry. Ackoff pointed out that they weren't too proud to learn from us. They had studied our manufacturing methods and improved upon them. I was then the general manager for Ford's Electrical and Fuel Handling Division (EFHD). EFHD's manufacturing manager, Roger Saillant, and I talked about this and read the recently published *The Fifth Discipline*. We agreed that we wanted to learn to learn faster, to improve our competitiveness.

So we sent our operating committee to sessions on organizational learning. Then for eight weeks, we spent two hours every week in dialogue about what to do next. We focused on our problem areas, such as the difficulties we had with new product launches. We put together a team of project managers with different amounts of launch experience, to talk about "what went right, what went wrong, what they'd have done differently." We then created cluster groups—cross-functional teams of managers and hourly paid skilled trades workers and operators, to work on the five major issues that they saw affecting launches at EFHD. We tried to run these as "no-stripes" meetings, where the hourly employee had as much clout as the general manager. We built a pretty good feeling of trust—nobody would get shot for admitting he or she made a mistake. That took some doing, but we made a lot of progress.

Almost immediately, we saw positive results on new launches: less trouble, lower cost, less disruption, higher quality. By 1992, a critical number of people had become believers in the process. From that sprang smaller efforts. Each of us on the EFHD operating committee sponsored a particular learning effort, such as improving the durability of a product. One initiative was set up to improve relations with suppliers. There was a lot of work to do there. We had always said to suppliers, "We're not just trying to take your margin down; we want to work as partners to take out costs, so we can both be successful." But in practice, we pushed for price reductions regardless of costs. Now, for the first time, we began to set up groups with suppliers. This dramatically affected costs and quality throughout the division. In fact, every time we targeted a learning project, it resulted in bottom line improvement.

In 1997, I became executive vice president of Visteon, Ford's new components and systems enterprise. Visteon incorporates seven divisions: chassis systems; climate control systems; powertrain controls (the old EFHD combined with the electronics and sensors for the fuel handling system, from intake to exhaust emissions); glass systems; interior (seats, panels, door trims); exterior (including the lighting, bumpers, and windshield wipers); and electronics, which does audio, multimedia, security, and safety. One of our greatest challenges is to grow our non-Ford business, which represents 9 to 10 percent of our revenue today; our objective is 20 percent. We have to learn to adapt to the way that other customers want us to behave and react. Some of our divisions have had more experience than others with non-Ford customers, and it's very critical to learn to build on one another's knowledge.

EFHD had five thousand employees. Visteon has 82,000 people in twenty-one countries. Of the seven division general managers, two or three are absolutely convinced that it is worth investing the time in organizational learning. A couple are interested, looking for the evidence that it flows to the bottom line. And a couple are probably not there yet.

For more about the EFHD story, see *Learning for Operational Excellence at EFHD, 1992-1996*, by David Berdish, Process Leadership/Learning Organization Manager; Visteon Automotive Systems, Dearborn, Michigan. See *The Fifth Discipline Fieldbook* Web site for information: http://www.fieldbook.com/resources.html. Also see p. 22 and p. 51 in this book.

I don't directly argue for it. I tell them to try it—to set up a team on their most critical issue. I let them design the projects. I ask them to give people the authority and accountability to work on the issues, to make sure they have time to meet, and to measure the results. Within two or three months, they wouldn't see maximum improvement, but they should see some flow to the bottom line; otherwise, they're just wasting people's time or making them feel good about jumping around in circles. Training, in itself, doesn't do any good. Success depends on using what you learn in training, quickly, before you forget it.

My job includes setting up the system so that these general managers can adopt learning initiatives. The survival and success of Visteon is at stake. Competition continuously improves. To be successful, we've got to grow, to stay ahead of the competition, and to catch up in some cases. I personally believe the only way to do that is to learn faster and better.

3 "What Are We Doing This For?"

Questions for planning the transformation focus

Rick Ross, Charlotte Roberts, Peter Senge

PURPOSE:

Articulating the reasons for change.

OVERVIEW:

A series of questions for pilot group discussion.

TIME:

Several hours. Allow time for people to talk through the reasoning behind their answers to these questions, especially when there is disagreement.

1. **Why is change urgent?** Are we driven by external forces? By a crisis? Or by our collective desire to create something together? Why might this effort actually matter?

2. **Who wants it to happen?** Who (in or out of the group) has set change as a priority? Are there clearly defined sponsors of the change effort? Are we aware of their needs and the pressures they feel? What might be the reasoning behind their requests?

3. **What results do we want to produce?** What, specifically, is the change we are seeking? If the change takes place, what will that get us? How will our efforts benefit our customers?

4. **How will we change?** What kinds of new capabilities will we need to develop? And how will we develop them? Which aspects of our current work and practices will be affected by the change? What chal-

lenges do we expect to face? And how could we prepare for them?

5. **Who will be involved?** Will the change initiative mean new activities for everyone on the pilot group? Should other people (inside or outside the group) be included?

6. **Where is our support?** In the organization at large, what is the reputation of our group, and of our sponsor? Will that help or hinder us?

7. **What do I, personally, have to do?** When will the change initiative begin? What steps do I need to take, in which domain? What do I hope to learn? What skills and capabilities would I like to gain? And what do I want to do first?

4 A Light Touch and a Long View

A network leader's perspective on supporting the business case for change.

Vic Leo

Vic Leo, manager of the Executive Development Center at Ford Motor Company, has fostered learning initiatives in a single company more effectively, for a longer period of time, than anyone we know. As a network leader, he has worked behind the scenes at Ford, brokering people's involvement by helping them see how learning might be relevant to their business needs. The questions that Vic poses here can help you work through your own case for change.

For most of the last decade, I've been part of an informal group of internal network leaders and line leaders, promoting "learning" within Ford Motor Company as a key component of our business-related improvement efforts. We are not formally organized, but we talk and meet regularly, and we have gradually built a body of shared experience. These questions sum up the issues that we have wrestled with, separately and together, over the years. They have no easy answers.

WHAT WILL WE CALL THE INITIATIVE?

Let's face it: The term "learning organization" represents a fad. Why hang your reputation inside the company on any particular label? You just set yourself up as a target for resistance.

On the other hand, if you don't label your efforts, others will name them for you. You'll be associated with "the Peter Senge stuff," or "the Steven Covey stuff." Peter and Steven both offer very valuable insights, but to foster an effective effort, we've got to be interested in synthesizing a portfolio of capabilities, and not rely on a single guru's "silver bullet."

Thus, at Ford, we chose to talk openly about the need for "learning processes." We may have turned some people off that way; they might have paid more attention to talk about "change." But a few critical people are interested precisely in the "learning" angle—building competence, for instance, in systems thinking. There's even an HR information technologies project that wants to include a "learning network." Because we used the label, they found us.

HOW CLOSELY FOCUSED SHOULD WE BE ON IMMEDIATE BUSINESS RESULTS?

Our goal was to make learning initiatives sustainable: to help line leaders make a genuine impact on the company. We deliberately designed our efforts so that each initiative could learn from the others, and we explicitly decided to build a body of theory about change at Ford.

Those sound like lofty ambitions. But we think of them in very modest terms. We never think, "Our work will rock the Ford Motor Company." Instead, we keep setting up narrowly focused, local projects, aimed at immediate business results. We look for line managers with some control over their budget and a well-defined project to improve, whether it's an entire factory or a new car launch. We let them assess our potential for helping them, and then wait for them to initiate projects. They play the dominant leadership role and we cofacilitate, research, and document.

This means that we have not ventured into potentially interesting areas like environmentalism, stockholder relationships, or new governance structures. In the abstract, those would probably be valuable; but in practice, they worry me. It would be too easy to get swept away by questions like, "What is the essential purpose of the corporation in society?" That philosophical abstraction would provoke even more cynicism and resistance. Instead, we've worked on material release stability, manufacturing capacity, truck strategy for emerging markets, and the Ford Production System (FPS).

And yet our narrowness may, in the end, be a fatal flaw. No project is as isolated as our approach suggests. For example, inconsistencies in the ordering or billing systems at Ford could have immense repercussions at Visteon, the new components enterprise. Thus, it is strategically important for Ford and Visteon to pursue their improvements together. But given our history of narrow project focus, it may be extremely difficult to make the necessary connections.

HOW FAST DO WE THINK OUR EFFORTS SHOULD GROW?

Not long ago, a vice president asked me why we had less than a dozen projects involving learning. "There are a hundred and eighty sites at Ford; your work is small potatoes. You'll be dead before you see any change on a scale that matters." Then he banged the table with the palm of his hand. "Why not just a few more projects, then boom!" he proposed. "Let's roll it out to the whole company!"

I call that "the boom theory of change." It would follow the model of the management "freight trains" that have roared through Ford over the years: reengineering, restructuring, and business literacy campaigns. Perhaps this model is reinforced at Ford by our distinguished history; after all, Henry Ford invented mass production in our industry. And it provides obvious benefits for network leaders like me—such as a bigger budget and more visibility.

But so far, I'm holding back. "We don't know enough to roll it out," I told the executive. "Every situation is different." Clearly, some ideas about systems thinking or building learning laboratories would transfer easily to plants everywhere from Edison, New Jersey, to Sao Paulo to Germany. But we don't yet know which approaches are universally applicable or have the highest leverage.

Instead, we hang in with a light touch and a deliberately long view. We worry that fast expansion would overwhelm our capacity to provide high-quality help. Moreover, working in depth with one team feels authentic in a way that managing change for 180 teams would not. Subtlety and authenticity are especially important in learning organization work, which requires leaders to internalize new styles of behavior and personal interaction.

We started with just two projects in 1992: the Lincoln Continental and a project at a stamping plant in Woodhaven, Michigan. By now, there are more than a dozen active projects, and many more in the works. The Visteon learning initiative could ultimately involve 82,000 people and seventy facilities worldwide. Is that a comfortable growth curve? Too fast? Too slow? We try to keep rethinking that question as our experience grows.

WHO IS PREDISPOSED?

Since we wait for line leaders to call us, we learn to look for people who are predisposed to new learning methods. This means couching the initiative in terms of people's greatest priorities. We don't say, "D/EW 98 (a current luxury car project) should get involved in learning to make a contribution to society or the company." We offer a way for D/EW 98's managers to deliver on their stretch objectives more easily and effectively. They are predisposed to learning because they see that potential.

Our network of predisposed people has grown both in size and diversity. There are line leaders, network leaders, and a few high-ranking executives. As the number of people grows, we link them in more ways. Some of the networkers here have held "open space" meetings, in which people meet to consider the potentialities, without a rigid agenda. This, in turn, uncovers predisposed people whom we might have overlooked before. At one open space meeting, a manager of a new car launch said, "Why don't we just develop a learning orientation from Day One?" Nobody had ever suggested that before; most learning initiatives at Ford begin midway through a project. This person's chance remark could lead to a highly productive initiative.

⟩⟩ For more about Open Space, see page 484.

WHAT RESOURCES DO WE NEED TO MAKE THE FIRST PILOT EFFORTS WORK?

In general, if people are creative and predisposed, then good ideas and methods will follow. However, some brokering of resources is needed. The task of finding these resources is critically important, arduous beyond belief, and almost invisible to outsiders. There are essentially three types of resources needed:

■ **Brokering resources:** An introduction to a person, an invitation to a key meeting, or an informal conversation between key people, to nudge projects forward in some small way. Simply saying, "Did you know that so-and-so is also interested in seeing this project happen?" can be a powerful brokering move, especially when handled with a light touch.

- **Financial resources:** Recently, I received an e-mail from one plant: "We are hosting a lean manufacturing game workshop this Saturday. Is there any funding available from your group?" The line leader probably didn't know much about me—only that I am a sympathetic person, and there's no other obvious place to turn. Sometimes I put a few hundred dollars together from an alternative source, like my travel budget, just to help keep the conversation going. But I also let the line leader know that part of his responsibility is to ferret out the money he needs.

  We have always funded initiatives with a little bit of seed money, in part because they tend to produce visible savings. Instead of giving me a substantial budget, my boss had the wisdom to say, "Vic, see how far you can get on nothing." I think I have surprised a lot of people by getting pretty far. This "shoestring model" may be a terrible way to sustain initiatives, but it does get them started.

- **Recognition resources:** Imagine that you are a line leader, deeply involved in a learning initiative, and after two years, your boss says, "This doesn't mean anything toward your next promotion." Even if it does not lead to demotion, you may view your efforts as career-threatening, compared to other ways you might invest your time. Unless it's clear that learning-oriented work can lead to advancement, informal networks will not hang together for the long haul. Therefore, a powerful network leader should keep pressing to have learning initiative results recognized and rewarded in performance appraisals and other evaluations.

  By the time you need these resources, of course, it's too late to develop them. It's necessary to identify and cultivate them in advance, so you have them available when needed.

HOW LONG WILL THE PILOT PROJECT TAKE?

Most projects have an ending date—"job one" (the release date on a car launch), or the prearranged end to a research project. Yet most Ford projects last for more than a year; many will last several years. If you are a network leader, you have to discipline yourself to keep from abandoning a team. It's too easy to take them in for three days, get them all psyched up with new ideas and methods . . . and drop them. This work is intensely personal, and we stay with project teams—both as providers of training and as personal coaches—right until the end.

E

WHEN DO WE TALK ABOUT THE INITIATIVE WITH THE EXECUTIVE LEADERS?

As early as possible. The pilot project does not need full-blown corporate support. That would make it another "freight train." But it needs a relationship with the immediate chain of command. If they can't recognize the link between your new methods and the business results, then they and you will start to mistrust each other. By the time symptoms of that mistrust are evident, it's probably too late.

Some line leaders are afraid that executives will cut off their experimentation. But no fair-to-outstanding executive will shut down an experiment. They know how to tolerate exploration—within some limits, at least. To be sure, you may be kept on a short leash. The most effective strategy, then, is invoking curiosity about your efforts—not just from the boss, but at higher levels as well.

I do it by building the kind of relationship with executive leaders in which I can casually (but continually) make them aware of progress in small ways. This type of relationship may be vital, if the learning initiative runs into trouble. At one plant, the manager had invested heavily in a learning initiative . . . and then he was promoted. His successor said, in effect, "All that stuff happened on the last person's watch. I'm not going to invest any more time or resources in it." As a result, the headway that the plant had made was in danger of slipping back.

In a way, it was outrageous. A new plant manager doesn't have the option of saying, "These welding machines were purchased on the last person's watch. So I'm not going to invest in maintaining them." But managers feel free to disregard past investments in the human element, even if that disregard has huge cost implications. It takes a very deft use of the "light hand" to go up to the next level of leadership, explain the situation, and say, "This is your choice, but you should be aware of the investment you are losing." Sometimes a network leader has the responsibility to make that case to executive leaders—ideally before the new plant manager is chosen.

WHAT ABOUT HR?

At Ford, many change initiatives with a human resources sponsorship have been discounted. They carry the baggage of organizational development—seen as ungrounded in business imperatives. "Don't give the learning initiative to HR," people have said. "They'll kill it!"

But I don't like to leave HR out of a learning initiative. HR has capabilities for investment that should not be ignored. They have people who can help with facilitation and coaching. More important, for systemic reasons, the "learning organization" movement needs to build better strategic alliances with HR, quality, process leadership, and finance. If each of these groups were committed to investing a certain amount of inspiration, money, and people's time, then there would be a kind of federation spirit to profound change.

In particular, I would like to see people who conduct learning work be able to advance more easily in the company. Almost the entire network at Ford has taken on "learning initiative" tasks in addition to their official assignments. They are rarely rewarded or recognized for this. In my dark moments, I worry that unless the profession of "organizational learning associates" is legitimized, the work of fostering learning and change will not be sustained.

CAR
by Mary Walton (New York: W. W. Norton, 1997)

This book gives an accurate and interesting picture of the agony and the joy in the creation of a new product—in this case, the 1996 Taurus. *Car* shows how key people in the program coped with difficult personal dilemmas. And it offers the story of growth and change in the life of a company and its people, as they struggle with a management paradigm shift. The Taurus Program Manager, Dick Landgraff, asks the most meaningful question at the end of the book: "What is it that we haven't done right over the years?"

While Dick and his team are at work developing the new Taurus, all of the management reference points are shifting, with the espoused vision of moving from a command and control mind-set toward a culture of empowered teams. The resulting struggles with values and choices can be seen in Dick's admonition to his children: "In a big company, you are dependent on others to do their jobs, which is at best frustrating and at worst a recipe for failure." Within the story of the birth of a new car, this book captures the story of a company in the early stages of a cultural change, and the impact of that change on the team members and the people they touch. This is a powerful story, relevant to us all. — Fred Simon

Fred Simon is a former Ford Motor Company program manager. For more of his perspective, and the story of a car launch involving organizational learning, see "Creating a Learning Lab —and Making It Work," in *The Fifth Discipline Fieldbook*, p. 554.

5 The Pinecone Strategy

Winston Ledet

Winston Ledet, formerly with DuPont, is now an independent consultant who helps organizations with The Manufacturing Game,™ a systems-oriented tool for understanding the leverage in operations. The story he tells here describes how to make a business case for change—not through talk, but through experimentation and action.

In the late 1980s, a small pilot group of maintenance engineers and operators at DuPont developed a counterintuitive but highly effective strategy for maintaining chemical plants. We kept our equipment well maintained, so it would need fewer replacement parts or repairs.

When this strategy paid off in cost savings, we held a party and took in an Astros game to celebrate. We were confident that everyone else at DuPont would rapidly make use of our insights. But they didn't—not even after I wrote up a little booklet with our approach.

So we enlisted champions at several chemical plants, and trained their teams in our new maintenance approach. Now, instead of just one initiative, we had eight. But within two years, all eight of our champions had moved on to other jobs, without really teaching their replacements anything about the new approach. The initiatives died.

It was now 1990, and our pilot group wasn't celebrating any more. We commiserated at a Houston hotel one night—ironically, at a national maintenance meeting devoted to purchasing better replacement parts, the strategy we had rejected. The next day, I looked out my hotel window and noticed that the grass was littered with pinecones. Nature, I realized, doesn't put all its resources into one or two seedlings, and expect them to take root. It drops myriad seeds—like these pinecones—over as broad an area as possible. Most of them may die; but enough survive to generate a whole forest.

In that spirit, we decided to concentrate only on small projects—and chose pumps. They are plentiful, prone to breakdowns, and high leverage, because most people seriously underestimate the problems they can cause. In 1991, we began setting up small, cross-functional teams (including people from operations, maintenance, engineering, and purchasing) to improve maintenance in their ten worst problem pumps. Within six months, we had thirteen teams going, operating in as many

For more about The Manufacturing Game, see "The DuPont Manufacturing Game," by Winston Ledet, in The Fifth Discipline Fieldbook, p. 550. Information about the game itself is available on The Fifth Discipline Fieldbook Web site: http://www.fieldbook.com/software.html.

locations as we could establish. Many of these efforts didn't succeed. Unsympathetic plant managers shut some down, while in other cases people lost interest. But enough lasted to make a noticeable difference in the overall performance of the plant maintenance system.

With so many pumps available to improve, we had new opportunities for learning. For example, one pump that had never been switched off had never given trouble in seventeen years. This led us to see that by keeping pumps running, we could add years to their longevity. We had never seen that before, in part because our focus on problem solving had kept us from looking closely at the parts of the plant that worked well.

As our success with pumps was recognized, we grew bolder. We began making a case for defect elimination in general, not just with pumps—and not just in maintenance. When we developed a board game based on a computer simulation, we called it the "manufacturing" game, instead of purely a "maintenance" game: a decision that represented the beginning of the end for me at DuPont. I was told that our champion, an engineering vice president, didn't have the charter to make a difference from manufacturing—only from maintenance. I found myself losing patience with one aspect of the pinecone strategy: the need to stay insignificant, below the line of visible sight. That's the problem with the pinecone strategy; it takes fortitude to persist. But I still believe that it is a critical factor for building success. In organizational change, as in nature, new developments should spread quietly at first, so they can build both on one another's failures and successes.

Picking promising "pinecones"

Jennifer Kemeny, Michael Goodman

PEOPLE INVOLVED IN LEARNING INITIATIVES OFTEN ASK US: "HOW SHOULD WE pick our battles? How do we decide where to focus our attention?" The short answer is: Start where you will have the most impact over the least amount of time. For many teams starting out, it's relatively easy to talk in abstract terms: "We're developing our personal capabilities for the long run, so we don't have to worry about producing short-term results." As a result, tangible results from learning activities are hard to document. Without visible evidence to convince others, you need to spend more and more time justifying your original "trumpet blasts" of enthusiastic talk—so you devote even more of your time to shoring up your credibility, talking about the philosophies behind the new ideas, and explaining the nuances of the approach you have taken. In the end, this dynamic drives a wedge between the enthusiasts and the people (in the pilot group, or in the larger organization) who care primarily about results. The organization is thus almost compelled to reject your new approach before it has a chance to prove itself.

How can you avoid this trap? By committing to action as a part of learning. Be humble. Start with small steps. Look for relatively minor actions with relatively major impact. Over the years, we've come up with several criteria for promising breakthrough projects:

- **A sense of critical urgency.** Small to medium-sized teams with an urgent project can be an ideal environment. They are usually open, and will readily accept a couple of people with learning skills into the team because the costs of using "this learning stuff" are very small in relation to the overall outputs.
- **Projects where the requisite business skills are already in place.** You risk undermining the opportunity to incorporate learning activities over the long term if, the first few times out, they are linked with projects whose chances for success are shaky. Many companies have not, for instance, made reengineering processes and systems a core competence. All the learning skills in the world can't help a reengineering project if team members can't carry out the necessary work.
- **Authority and autonomy.** Team members must have the ability to implement their own decisions. They need enough leeway to proceed, without having to go through five levels of hierarchy to get permission. Put your effort, in other words, where there is a genuine *chance* to make a difference.
-  **Projects with visibility or leverage throughout the organization.** We sat in on a project where two branches of a company could not agree on their priorities. Everyone in the organization knew about this frustrating situation; it had been going on for years. After a relatively short time, and a minimal exposure to learning and systems thinking tools, they had a breakthrough. News about it spread rapidly through the company: "Toledo and Chicago actually had a pleasant conversation about their priorities!" Organizations will instantly recognize and spread the word about these feats, even as they ignore your talk about the abstract value of "surfacing mental models."

6 Learning What We're Worth

The path to relevance at Shell Oil Company

Linda Pierce

On one level, this is Linda Pierce's personal story: As advisor to the Shell Oil Leadership Council, she dealt with her own feelings about ambiguity and courage as she helped to guide Shell's groundbreaking "transformation." But it also shows how managers throughout the company, from the executive level on down, can build a case for change that does not rely on the head, the heart, or the hands alone— but that integrates all three.

The business benefits of Shell Oil Company's transformation are undeniable, in my opinion. But its greatest benefit is the opportunity that it has given those who work at Shell to become whole people at work. Psychologists would say that more of us are "integrating ourselves," aligning the attitudes and values that guide the transformation with those we hold deeply at a personal level. If we are not sincere, if we do not speak from our hearts, and if we do not mean what we say, then the people of the organization can see through us. At Shell, the people involved in organizational transformation have not reached that level of authenticity all at once. Most of us seem to develop it over time, through an ongoing, three-stage, cycle of learning:

STAGE 1: INTELLECTUAL UNDERSTANDING

When Shell managers first recognized the need for organizational change, in the early 1990s, we approached it as we would any intellectual endeavor. We studied it. We brought in consultants to speak to us. We read books, put on programs, and drew conceptual frameworks. We believed that "change" was a coherent process that we could understand and manage as rational people. We compared theories from Steven Covey, Peter Senge, Noel Tichy, and others. Many Shell people are skilled at the intellectual game, and we enjoy it. At any of our education programs with outside speakers, we would spend the entire question period challenging them, looking for flaws, and trying to prove that our own theories were better. As soon as we found one flaw, then we could dismiss that speaker as "wasting our time."

And as a result, progress was slow. We went through the motions of adopting new intellectual concepts, but that did not mean we had internalized any new ways of doing business. Unless we could develop some emotional engagement between the people and the ideas, it looked like the organization would never change.

STAGE 2: EMOTIONAL ENGAGEMENT

I recognized my own emotional connection to the idea of Shell's transformation in 1993, during its earliest stages. I was assigned to a planning team to help the new CEO, Phil Carroll, investigate ideas for changing the company. After our final presentation, the team disbanded, but I continued to help Phil informally, drawn by my growing interest in his effort. One day I found myself telling him: "Phil, supporting you in the transformation is a full-time job in itself, and I have a different job now."

He sat back and said, "Well, what would you like to do?"

Once before I had given my all on behalf of a leader—but then he dropped the effort without explanation, leaving me feeling like my personal integrity was on the line. I had vowed to myself that I would never again support a leader in a change effort, unless I was convinced, down to my gut level, that the leader would make a full commitment.

Now I heard myself say words different from any I had ever voiced at Shell: "Phil, I have fire in my soul to support this transformation."

Thus I came to my current job as executive advisor to the Leadership Council. It was the first time that I had taken an assignment at Shell that involved an emotional commitment right from the start. As a woman in a highly technical culture, I had been used to avoiding emotional situations, because I wanted to deflect any stereotype that I was "soft" or "flaky." Actually, for anyone at Shell, talking about passion and commitment felt messy. Emotional engagement challenged many of the assumptions that we had taken on at Shell.

For example, I had long ago internalized the importance of appearing competent. Unconsciously, I believed that one visible display of incompetence would lose me my ticket to the privileges of life at Shell Oil. Someone else in our competitive environment would move immediately to take my ticket if I dropped it. Thus I spent every conversation trying to prove my competence, and judging myself relative to others.

This can be a very unhealthy way of thinking about things. It meant, for instance, that I continually looked for more difficult, more complex assignments. To be good, I believed, the work had to be tough—so tough that no one else could do it. I believe this was one reason why the "not-invented-here" syndrome was so common in our organization. No one borrowed ideas, because that demonstrated less competence.

Before the transformation, I would not have been able to recognize this aspect of my thinking. Had I recognized it, I would have thought hard before mentioning it to anyone else. But now, it felt very liberating to realize that I did not have to be tough to be effective. Giving up that "toughness" would not be easy. For example, I would have to learn to say, "I am still thinking this through. Please allow me to be inarticulate for a bit." This in itself was a brave step. In the past, I would have completely prepared myself before saying anything at all.

Unless a sufficient number of people make this type of emotional connection, I don't think transformation is sustainable. But most of us, at Shell at least, have never spent this much time learning about ourselves. The emotional release feels so nurturing, that it's almost like being given a painkiller after years of being in pain. And yet people need to move beyond this phase, no matter how wonderful it feels.

STAGE 3: SUSTAINED ACTION

We used to think, at Shell, that our job was to get rid of ambiguity. We could only act when we knew the absolute right course to take. We've now recognized that our job is to make fundamental business decisions in an ambiguous system, where we will never know the exact right course to take.

Instead, we need to take actions with a learner's lens. We need to find the connection between our newfound internal passion and the value propositions of our business. This concern is particularly relevant at Shell, because we adopted a corporatewide "business model" several years ago. The business model is a highly intellectual, prescriptive set of formulas and guidelines for growing the business and boosting productivity. It functions, in part, like "open-book management": making the financial aspects of our work evident for anyone in the organization.

The business model is so intellectually coherent and new to our culture that part of me believes we must take it as it is given. We can't be trusted to modify and adjust it until we understand it as thoroughly as a finance guru might. But in my heart, I know that we will not be able to use this intellectual theory unless we can make an emotional connection to it, with the same sense of freedom and engagement that we bring to our personal finances. If we try to run our business with the model, knowing that we will make mistakes and being willing to adjust accordingly, we'll develop a much sharper understanding—and better results—than we would ever get by keeping the model on a purely intellectual plane. To make a connection to a theory, I need to be able to adjust it, adapt it, and make it my own. And I can do this while maintaining the integrity of the business principles driving the model.

PUTTING IT ALL TOGETHER

A cycle never ends. If we really want to sustain a profound organizational change, then we don't simply take actions that fly off in an unconnected fashion. The actions must be integrated with the development of new theory. That's why I see this chain of activity, from intellectual learning to emotional learning to action, as a never-ending process.

When I return to the intellectual arena after some sustained action, I do so in a very different frame of mind. I no longer demand, in effect, "Show me the relevance." That's my responsibility. If I am intrigued by someone's methods or theories about business, I will be inclined to experiment with them—first, by seeing how I feel about them upon reflection, and second, by designing some implementation of them.

On any given workday I am playing somewhere in this triangle. So are most of my colleagues. We do not travel around this cycle in lockstep. While some of us try to make sense of the shift intellectually, others are engaged in emotional reflection, and still others are trying things. When I counsel leaders at Shell, the first priority is to help them keep from getting stuck at any of these three points. We will never reach full understanding, so the cycle never ends.

You can sometimes tell, just from talking to people, that they have spent time in each of these arenas. About a year ago, at a retirement reception, I ran into a man whom I had known when I first started at Shell, in the information technologies organization. At the reception, some people were clearly down in the dumps. They had not accepted the shift, and they were obviously wondering, "When will this be over?" And yet in the other part of the room, faces were cheerful, laughter was flowing, and arms waving.

Gene, my friend, was in that group. "Linda," he said,

Intellectual
understanding

Emotional
engagement

Sustained
action

"I'm having a ball." He said he couldn't believe that he had ever been willing to eke out an existence. Now he felt so much more a part of his work.

"Gene," I asked, "suppose someone came in and said, 'Transformation seemed like a good idea, but it didn't work. We have to go back.' What would happen to you?"

"You know," he said, "I couldn't go back. I'm having too much fun." But then he looked at me and said: "Besides, now I know what I'm worth." He didn't just mean that he knew he was marketable. He meant that transformation had shown him some levels at which he was capable, and now he understood, much better than he ever had before, the value of his life and what he could do for the company. He was intellectually stimulated, emotionally engaged, and energized into action.

》》 For more about Shell Oil's transformation story, see pages 115, 203, and 384. Also see 》》 "A personal checklist for change agents facing messy experiences," page 211.

7 Open-Book Management

Tom Ehrenfeld

Writer Tom Ehrenfeld, formerly of Inc. *magazine, knows his way around this management innovation that is percolating upward from small businesses to large organizations. The key principle of this work is relevance: opening up financial information, in innovative and radical ways, so that everyone can recognize the importance of his or her own work (and one another's).*

If learning about finance is like learning a foreign language, open-book management (OBM) is like moving to a country where that language is spoken. Open-book management begins with training in financial literacy, extended to every employee. Typically this is done in the form of a "great game of business," as pioneer Jack Stack calls it—demystifying the arcana of the "numbers," and translating them into vehicles for mutual understanding. Every team keeps track of (and interprets for itself) the numbers that reflect the ways their unit makes a profit. Comparing costs and other numbers on a cross-functional basis allows people with different organizational "turf" to come to mutual decisions.

》》 Also see "Performance Dashboards," page 313, and the challenge of "assessment and
》》 measurement," page 281.

In an OBM system, people assume ownership for their actions—and are paid accordingly. This is done, not through bonuses or incentive pay, but through a genuine stake in the action. This often involves the same kinds of "sweat equity" that you might give people who become partners with you in a new enterprise.

But as workers become increasingly proficient at playing the game of business, they change the game: They set their aspirations higher. First they may focus on making their numbers work at the unit level. Eventually they consider the profitability of the division, or the corporation—and ultimately its ability to care for its employees and community, as if they were responsible for the whole. People begin to ask questions about every cost the company incurs, such as healthcare and corporate taxes. Ultimately, many employees spin out to start their own companies. This family of new companies now networks together—providing support, information, and investment opportunities for one another.

》》 See, for example, the piece by OBM pioneer Jack Stack, on page 380.

RESOURCES FOR OPEN-BOOK MANAGEMENT

■ *Open-Book Management: The Coming Business Revolution* by John Case (New York: HarperBusiness, 1995). Case, who coined the phrase "open-book management" as a senior writer at *Inc.,* provides a general overview of how companies are implementing the practice. This book focuses on small, fast-growing companies like Macromedia, Manco, Rhino Foods—companies that are, in addition to practicing OBM, "reshaping industries, introducing innovations, exploring new business niches."

■ *The Open-Book Experience: Lessons from Over 100 Companies Who Successfully Transformed Themselves* by John Case (Reading, MA: Addison-Wesley, 1997). The leanest of OBM books, designed for people eager to get to work on Monday morning. Alive with well-reported stories and data from companies that have successfully implemented open-book practices, this book will help you learn from the experience of others.

- ***Open-Book Management Bulletin: Resources for Companies of Businesspeople,*** edited by John Case (11 Bay State Avenue, Somerville, MA 02144, (617) 625-7095, Internet: *http://www.open bookmanagement.com.* Subscription $195/year). This monthly newsletter, written and edited by Case, nicely complements his books. It feels like an ongoing colloquy—the kind of useful conversation that might take place in the corridor of a business conference.

- ***Open-Book Management: Creating an Ownership Culture*** by Thomas L. Barton, William G. Shenkir, and Thomas N. Tyson (Morristown, NJ: Financial Executives Research Foundation, 1998, available by calling (800) 680-FERF). This book, based on seven in-depth case studies, shows how OBM plays out in large companies such as GE Fanuc Automation North America, a $515 million (1996 sales) joint venture between General Electric and Fanuc Ltd. of Japan. It provides the best overall context for OBM, tracing its roots back to managerial ideas such as the Scanlon Plan and Douglas McGregor's Theory Y. It also takes advantage of the author's financial backgrounds by explaining the role of finance and the CFO in creating on OBM organization.

Also see *The Great Game of Business,* by Jack Stack (New York: Doubleday/Currency, 1992), reviewed in *The Fifth Discipline Fieldbook,* p. 542.

8 After Fixing the Crisis

Daniel Kim, Nick Zeniuk

Daniel Kim is the founder of Pegasus Communications and The Systems Thinker *newsletter. Nick Zeniuk is the cofounder of Interactive Learning Labs, Inc.*

This exercise is adapted from the "vision deployment matrix," developed by Daniel Kim. See, for example, "From Event Thinking to Systems Thinking," in *The Systems Thinker,* 7(4):6, May 1996.

Crises tend to be perceived as isolated events. If a project is hemorrhaging red ink, or production is in chaos, the team moves to fix the crisis quickly. There is no time to go off on a retreat, reorganize, and rethink the ten-year future. But when the crisis is over, how can teams learn to avoid or prevent the next crisis? We use these questions to help

Purpose:

Investing in pilot group reflection to prevent future crises.

Overview:

Drawing forth the potential leverage in looking under the surface of events to see patterns and structures beneath.

Participants:

An intact team working on a problem.

pilot groups move from an events orientation to a way of working more attuned to systems and fundamental causes.

1. **What are the events going on in current reality?** List the symptoms of crisis as you typically first perceive them: defects going up, quality going down, sales dropping, turnover rising, costs increasing, etc.

2. **What are the patterns of behavior underlying those events?** List the short-term actions that you have taken in the past to respond to crises, perhaps without thinking much about long-term consequences. "We see defects going up, and we adapt by running the factory more hours, so that we get the same level of good products out the door."

3. **What is the systemic structure in this situation?** How might your actions from step two help to perpetuate the symptoms you saw in step one? As you take an adaptive action, such as running the factory more hours, perhaps you are consistently drawing your attention away from higher-leverage actions—such as revamping your own quality or inspection practices.

4. **What mental models keep reinforcing that systemic structure?** How does the way you see the world lead you to the same approaches time and time again? It may take some time and reflection to answer this question, because you're looking for attitudes so prevalent and basic to your thinking that you rarely notice them.

    For instance, you may have justified a computer upgrade in terms of greater productivity. But look at the personal computers in your office. Many people probably still use them as typewriters—entering in page numbers manually, and hitting a carriage return at the end of every line. Assumptions that "most people eagerly want to use computers" often keep technically oriented people from seeing this reality. It might be much more cost effective to spend money on training to help people use the equipment you already have.

5. **What is the espoused vision you want to create?** Up until now, you have considered only current reality—your problems. Now spend some time thinking about the goals and aspirations for your pilot group. What do you really want to create, in business terms? Is it a higher-quality product? Faster cycle time? A broader customer base? A long-standing stable employment base?

6. **What is the vision underlying your behavior?** Consider the answers to the first four questions. Do they "add up" to the vision of the fifth?

If your current actions, responses, systems, and mental models played out, would they lead to your desired vision?

Many people would answer no. At many manufacturing companies, the espoused vision is: "producing high-quality products." But the demand for quantity trumps the wish for quality, every time.

7. **What, then, is the vision "in use" that an observer might deduce from your actions, even if you haven't explicitly chosen it?** In those manufacturing companies, the vision in use might be: "Keeping up production and meeting targets." The mismatch between an espoused vision and a vision in use creates organizational angst, mixed messages, and wasted resources.

8. **If you had an organization seriously aimed at creating your desired vision, what mental models would have to be present?** At this point in the conversation, people sometimes come up with new mental models—"We will all be entrepreneurially minded . . ."—and then try to influence other people to change their attitudes accordingly. This cannot be done; people don't change their mental models under pressure. But gradually, as people reexamine the issues for themselves in conversations like this one, they may see how the mental models of the past reinforce problems, and that may pave the way for deeper changes in attitudes.

9. **Desired systemic structures, patterns of behavior, and events: If you moved toward your vision, what behavior might you see?** How would you know you were doing well? What kinds of systems would you develop, if you wanted to achieve your goal? How could you reinforce the behavior that you wanted to create? What would seem to be the highest-leverage actions?

As you return to this exercise, over time, your proficiency with these questions will grow. One typical story: United Technologies, an automotive component company, had gone through a series of reengineering endeavors to reduce cycle time for new products. Unfortunately, their cycle time and error rates increased. In a conversation based on these questions, they began to recognize that their reward systems only promoted or rewarded people who did not make mistakes in their division. Underlying that system was a mental model that said: "People should not make any mistakes," and a vision in use that said, "Our goal is protecting our own turf within the organization." Only after they recognized this could they begin to put a new reward system in place, based on the desired mental model: "Collaboration is desirable, and by working as a

These questions resonate with some of the exercises and methods in *The Fifth Discipline Fieldbook*. For example, the Acme story (p. 97) provides more perspective on these levels, from events through mental models. Understanding "Fixes that Backfire" (p. 125) and "Shifting the Burden" (p. 135) may help with question #2; "The Five Whys" (p. 108) can be used for question #3.

team, we can cut down our cycle times." They brought the product launch cycle from forty days down to five.

9 The History Map

Rick Ross, Art Kleiner

Every project or change initiative has a history. You will be much more effective at setting priorities, and at making a case for learning to others outside the pilot group (and yourselves), if you can bring that history to light. Typically, each member of the pilot group only knows a piece of it. This exercise is a vehicle for constructing group memory. It focuses your attention on the forces that brought you together in the first place, and on exactly "what those crazy people were thinking back then" when they first confronted the problem you're trying to fix.

⟩⟩ For a broader-scale, more intensive approach, see "Learning Histories," page 460.

On the "time line wall," mark out a time line across months or years, so that everyone can see the chronology from the project's beginning to the present day. Leave some room at the right so that you can continue into the future. Then ask people with firsthand knowledge to answer these questions:

■ **How did this problem or project begin?** Typically, a few people will compare notes: "You were involved in August? Well, I first learned about it in February." As each person speaks, record the event being described on a self-sticking note and post it on the time line. (Move the notes as needed.) If you're good at drawing, or can afford a graphic facilitator, include sketches—they are very effective.

■ **What was it like at the beginning?** If it started with a project or mission, what was the original purpose? Who called it together? What did the founders of this team envision it would produce?

■ **What happened next? Whose idea was that? What was the intended purpose?** Keep moving forward through time, adding new episodes and events to the wall. You may want to draw lines on the time line, showing the trajectories of particular problems, people, teams, or projects. You may even want to call in other people who can provide missing parts of the story.

Purpose:

To create a shared understanding of the circumstances and forces that led to this change initiative.

Overview:

Reconstructing the "jigsaw puzzle" of knowledge held by members.

Setting:

One or more walls covered with a row of flip chart pages, two sheets high and at least ten sheets long, so you can draw a time line across the pages and "read" it from left to right.

Time:

25 minutes to several hours.

Supplies:

Flip chart, markers, and Post-it notes.

Before long, you'll uncover aspects of the original purpose that were lost somewhere. "Oh, those two engineers wanted to develop a new product? But they're no longer here—what happened to them? No wonder we can't get any cooperation!"

This exercise is influenced by the work of Chris Meyer and Louis van der Merwe.

We've seen this exercise take only twenty-five minutes, but it can also take several hours. By the time you're done, you will have created a whole history for yourselves, spanning several walls of writing and Post-its. The storytelling has the flavor of investigative reporting, or tracking down your family tree. You will spend much of your time falling down with laughter, and much of your time groaning.

After this exercise, teams seem to have a keener sense of their common purpose. Finance and production may not have understood each other's business priorities; now they know why the other remains interested. That, in turn, makes them more likely to keep asking at points along the way: "Have we fulfilled our original purpose? What should be our purpose now?"

10 Four Futures for a Change Initiative

Art Kleiner

Your organization's culture and your pilot group members' capabilities are critical driving forces that will help determine the success of your pilot group's efforts. You have limited control over these factors, and you probably don't know, in advance, how they will unfold. Hence the value of this exercise, which I've used to help pilot group leaders come to terms with the difficulty—and promise—of their endeavor. First, answer these three questions:

1. **What are you trying to accomplish?** For example, you may be trying to develop a new profit-and-loss business from a former cost center; or to introduce a new product or service.
2. **When is your deadline?** By when, realistically, must you show results or else the project will be jeopardized?

Purpose:

To help pilot group leaders see their choices more clearly.

Overview:

A simplified scenario exercise, looking at the pilot group's capabilities for change and openness as critical uncertainties.

3. **What new skills and capabilities will be required?** How will people have to change to make the new approach work?

The next two questions ask for predictions of the future. Can you answer with confidence and certainty? Or are the answers unknown?

4. **Will enough people change?** Can a "critical mass," enough to make a difference, adopt the new behaviors in time to meet the deadline?
5. **Will people talk openly?** If people have doubts or concerns, can they raise those issues? Or will they be undiscussable?

If you know the answers to questions 4 and 5 for sure, then you probably don't need this exercise. But if the answers are uncertain, consider four possible outcomes.

THE FOUR FUTURES:

■ Suppose, for example, that a critical number of people change in time, and they "talk about it"—that is, openly discuss the need for changed behaviors (including their own behaviors). In Scenario 1, you move "full steam ahead" toward desired change. Your ability to meet the deadline depends on how quickly and effectively the new behaviors and practices percolate through your organization.

■ What if people don't change—but talk openly about the fact that some of them "need to change and aren't changing"? Scenario 2 ("Lifeboat") is named after the cruel parlor game where players imagine that they are adrift in a small boat together, pursued by ravenous sharks. Each round, players vote to toss someone overboard.

The corporate version is much crueler: Players argue over who is "transformational" enough to stay in positions of authority. Some corporate people refer to this game as "coach, coach, change." They argue that recalcitrant managers should be coached once, then twice, then "changed" (i.e., removed from their position), on the grounds that they are holding everyone else back. To be sure, the judgments for or against any individual may be justified; that's not the point. The discussion itself seems to poison the atmosphere. People sit in judgment of

	Enough people change in time	Not enough people change in time
Enough people talk about it	Scenario 1: Full steam ahead	Scenario 2: Lifeboat
Not enough people talk about it	Scenario 3: Pockets of success	Scenario 4: Authoritarian command and control

one another, with limited data. They anxiously react by trying to "prove" themselves to be "on board," killing any genuine commitment they feel. Talk about "Who stays? Who leaves?" overshadows talk about business concerns.

⟩⟩ See the challenge of "fear and anxiety," page 241.

■ In Scenario 3 ("Pockets of Success"), people change their behaviors on a local level, but are not willing to talk openly about the changes they're making. Leaders from different functions or regions never come together to develop an effective systemwide approach. "We invest a lot in 'learning,'" people grumble privately, "but no one is interested in learning from the other."

If business results grow worse, in an organization under pressure, this scenario can lead to more serious decline. Pockets of "true believers" emerge throughout the organization, suspicious of one another's success. Those who achieve results find themselves ignored, dismissed, or even attacked.

⟩⟩ See the challenges of "diffusion," page 417, and "true believers," page 319.

■ Finally, if people don't change in time, and haven't got the capability or trust for open conversation, then Scenario 4 ("Command and Control") emerges. Success depends upon the competence of authority. Will the senior executives recognize the organization's needs, and direct an appropriate response? Can they do so benevolently and intelligently? Will others implement their demands?

PUTTING THE FUTURE TOGETHER

The real future, unfolding before you, will probably be some combination of these. But by preparing yourself for these four extremes, you prepare yourself for the actual future ahead of you.

If you're heading toward Scenario 1, "Full Steam Ahead," what kinds of initiatives would be most productive to try first? What kinds of training might people need or request?

If you are moving toward the authoritarian future, who will be in positions of authority? What types of help and support will they need?

The two intermediate scenarios (lifeboat and pockets of success) are probably not sustainable. If people figure out how to talk about the issues involved, they lead (as shown by the gray arrows) up into the "full steam ahead" scenario. Otherwise, they drift down toward authoritarianism—or off the grid entirely, into decline. Faced with that dilemma, is it better to pursue the learning orientation? Or is it better to turn over the reins to a strong authoritarian leader, and try to build learning capabilities after the crisis is over? When must that decision be made?

Pick out some early indicators that will help you recognize how the future is going. For instance, if people aren't capable of changing in time, how would you know it early, in your organization? What sorts of failed efforts might you hear about? What types of frustrations might people complain about?

Similarly, if people won't talk openly, are there ways to detect that inability? Can you talk openly about the difficulty of talking openly? If so, you may be able to generate enough inquiry and experimentation to move back up to the "full steam ahead" scenario.

The scenarios make effective arguing points, because they remove the burden of proving that any future might come to pass. "Look," you can say, "no one can say for sure whether we can, or cannot, rise to the challenge. But suppose the worst is true? Are we prepared for it? Suppose the best is true? Are we prepared for that?"

⟩⟩ For more about scenario planning, see page 511.

11 Practicing Relevance

Michael Jones and John Shibley

Pianist Michael Jones and guitarist John Shibley are organizational learning consultants and accomplished improvisational jazz (and classical) musicians. Here they describe how the skillful use of practice (in the way musicians practice) can lead people not just to feel inspired, but to make the case for change.

We're always impressed by the difference between "practice cultures" and "performance cultures." Musicians generally live in the former, and most organizations promote the latter—but each has a lot to learn from the other.

Performance cultures value perfection: You perform once, perfectly. Performances are basically solo events—most people attending are there to witness, not to participate. Practice cultures, on the other hand, are inviting, welcoming, and participative. People in practice cultures do perform, but learning from performance becomes the primary goal.

People who try to make a business case for their change initiatives often start from within a performance culture. There is one presumed answer, and people get one shot with the organization's leaders. They prepare for that shot the way one might prepare to perform an important concert or to open a play. They develop a detailed plan, often in private, and they rehearse "selling" their idea.

But what if, instead, they tried to address their common purposes through a practice approach with one another? Musicians value practice because they recognize that through practice, new possibilities for performance emerge. Could it be that through practice, new directions for a pilot group could be articulated that might not happen otherwise? These principles could be valuable for any pilot group trying to conduct conversations that would lead to a viable direction.

⟩⟩ Also see "Music, Listening and Freedom," page 152.

1. **Articulate individual cases for change before you come to the room as a group.** Musicians spend countless hours practicing alone. Practicing conversation also requires solo practice. Try to understand your own reasoning about the case, really "getting inside" it the way musicians practice a piece until they "have it." People need to be able to listen to and hear themselves before they can articulate their ideas to others, or hear what others are trying to say.

2. **Start meetings without a preconceived agenda.** Classical pieces are usually written by someone other than the performer. While there is room for personal interpretation, the performer can't change a phrase that might improve the piece. Meetings that follow this model are boring: Everyone knows what will be said, who's going to say it, and what decisions will be made.

By contrast, in jazz, a theme is sounded at the beginning of a piece, and then individuals improvise off that theme one after another. If someone is particularly "hot," he takes a longer solo. "Mistakes" can lead you into a new rhythm, a new key, or a new theme that builds on and complements the musical idea you began with. In meetings, give yourself and others permission to make conversational "mistakes." It may be interesting to say "Let's reflect together on the question, 'What have we

Michael Jones and John Shibley maintain Web sites at *http://www.pianoscapes.com* and *http://www.systemsprimer.com*, respectively.

learned in the last year at this company?'"and then allow people to "jam" on the question, so that the conversation, and not the agenda, determines the output and decision. This may require you to become more tolerant of "dissonance" in the conversation, but with time the clash of ideas can become a fertile source of creativity.

3. **Start with "check-ins."** Go around the room once, at the start of a meeting, to give everyone a chance to say the things on his or her mind. In musical practice, the emergence of the group's accomplishment comes from the common "play" space shared between people. Check-ins are a way to build a similar space in conversation. They provide an opportunity for people to "tune up" together, help create an atmosphere that encourages conversation, and often forecast the themes that may come up in the meeting.

4. **Choose a physical space that is conducive to your meetings.** Some rooms have better acoustics for music, and other rooms are more suited for meetings based on attentive listening and thoughtful dialogue. Good natural light, comfortable chairs, an unobstructed view of one another, and amenities like plants make a room more inviting. Becoming sensitized to your physical environment, and how it affects the conversational "music" of your meetings can be as important as becoming sensitized to the conversation itself.

5. **And finally, eternally improvise.** Once you've articulated your business case, don't treat it as a sacred, unalterable, score. Improvisation is a "dance" among musicians themselves, and between musicians and their environment. As your members change, and the context of your initiative within your organization evolves, you may find the skills of improvisation invaluable in making your business case for change.

VI. Walking the Talk

"They're not walking the talk!"

1 The Challenge

There was no question: The company had to change. As a manufacturer of high-tech equipment, they were getting bitter complaints from customers. Sales reps would try to quote prices, but the central office would not back them up. Service reps would make promises, only to have the logistics management say they couldn't follow through. Even some long-standing loyal customers were taking their business to competitors, who seemed to have a better approach to cross-functional teamwork.

The CEO and his executive team finally met together and, in a soul-searching vision session, recognized that there was a company-wide problem with teamwork. They would have to learn to work together more effectively at senior levels, and that new behavior would have to cascade through the company's hierarchy, or they would not survive. They crafted a vision statement saying as much, and held a meeting to announce this before the several hundred top managers of the company. The CEO stood on stage with the new vision statement proudly displayed in huge type behind him. From now on, he said, people in the field would get support from the center; they would not be micromanaged and undermined. The company would reorient itself toward cross-functional teamwork, starting at the top. Then he called for questions.

"I think this vision is great," said a salesperson, nervously, at the microphone. "It lines up exactly with the changes I think we need. But I find myself skeptical about the gap between this statement and the behavior I've seen in the past from the senior management team." Then in a mock-military cadence, he added: "Perhaps even from yourself, sir—respectfully speaking, of course."

The new CEO smiled, as if something had occurred to him for the first time. "You know, you're right," he said. "In making it to the top of this company I've probably operated in ways that directly conflict with the vision we are proposing. But I've looked at this deeply, and I realize I have to change." He paused. "They say you can't teach an old dog new tricks, and I'm an old dog." He was, in fact, near retirement age. "But I'm going to work harder than anybody else, and I need your help." Everyone in the room was completely silent, transfixed, watching him.

"I'll need your help," he said again. "When you see a gap between our principles and my behavior, I want to know. Don't embarrass me in public meetings, or tell me in front of the board." Everyone laughed. "But please take me aside, in the right setting. I promise I'll listen."

Now the energy exploded. If he could be that humble and resilient, so could everybody else. People turned to another, beginning to think that they could finally talk about the problems that had been hidden. The company went through an unprecedented phase of growth and profitability during the next few years. (They also hung on to their new teamwork policies. By now, they are known as one of the most responsive, high-quality service companies in their business.) The CEO retired with a sense of being honored by everyone in the company.

The speech in itself, of course, was not enough. He had to help build capabilities in himself, and in everyone, for developing this new honesty. That's what it took to meet the challenge of "walking the talk."

The challenge of "walking the talk" was first articulated in our research by a group of senior-level executives from Society of Organizational Learning member companies. They wrestled with the dilemma between their own roles, as directly accountable for the organization's performance and strategy, and the need for people throughout the enterprise to take responsibility for changes and new ways of operating.

Eventually, they concluded that the two were connected: Although everyone must be prepared for changes in behaviors and even in values, managers establish conditions that enable such change. If managers are not authentic in their convictions and sincere in their behavior, there will be little trust, and consequently little safety for the reflection that leads to authentic change.

Interestingly, the challenge of "walking the talk" was almost discounted by line leaders in our research groups. They had grown too used to the mismatch between espoused values and bosses' actual behavior. It was not a "challenge" in their eyes; it simply represented business as usual. That is how the challenge of "walking the talk" perpetuates itself, insidiously and unseen, masked by complacency, resignation, and taken-for-granted political games-playing.

Nonetheless, mismatches between bosses' behavior and espoused values do matter. This is true for all three types of leaders, including internal networkers, who do not have formal authority, and therefore whose only authority comes from their personal credibility. And it is especially true for local line leaders. Just as local line leaders must address the challenges of time, help, and relevance, so too do people working for them expect them to set an example. People do not expect perfection, but they recognize sincerity and openness—and their absence. When a local boss relapses from a style of open inquiry into authoritarian behavior, the repercussions can be felt for months. "The [project manager] blew up [at us]," said one subteam member. "He told us that everybody was finding excuses for why our division screwed up. That was the low point of our morale as a team. He apologized [later]. But it happened repeatedly. He would fixate on us as a scapegoat, and a week later he'd apologize one more time. After about three times, I made a joke in front of everybody. I said, 'When am I going to start believing you?'"

None of this is made any easier by the overall climate of distrust that pervades many institutions today. Managers committed to change must be prepared to work through a thick layer of cynicism. This is in part due to repeated downsizings in many firms, and the inevitable fear left behind. It also seems like most everyone has lived through his share of superficial management fads. There is an old saw, "behind every cynic stands a frustrated idealist." In America, this cynicism has been enshrined in "corporate folklore." It resonates, for instance, in the popularity of Scott Adams's *Dilbert* comic strip, which regularly lampoons managers who put forth one new bit of management rhetoric after another, but don't really expect anyone to follow through.

The challenge of "walking the talk" is more complex than it often appears. It is easy to blame cynicism on management hypocrisy, but the roots of cynicism lie in entrenched assumptions that are deeply embedded in industrial-age organizations. "Focusing on the customer wasn't a new concept for me," said one middle-level manager to us. "I always knew who my customer was—my boss. As long as I pleased my boss,

uoted from *A Car Launch With Heart: The "AutoCo Epsilon" Learning History*, by George Roth, Art Kleiner, et al. (New York: Oxford University Press, 1999), p. 34.

everything else would fall into place. So that's where I focused my attention." These assumptions will only change gradually, through reflection, experimentation, and example.

It is difficult to shift those assumptions while working in a system pervaded by them, and yet in organizations undergoing change, the old assumptions are no longer viable. The only way forward is to move forward, with clarity about the dynamics of change and one's own strategy.

THE UNDERLYING DYNAMICS OF "WALKING THE TALK"

This challenge plays out through two interrelated limiting processes, one of which is relatively obvious to most participants in change initiatives and one of which is more subtle. Both may emerge in the earliest initiating stages, effectively keeping an initiative from getting started. But they also continue to play a role *throughout the life of* any change initiative that continues to call for trust and reflection.

As soon as an initiative develops momentum, and people begin to realize that this might involve real change, they begin to ask, "Are these people really committed?" People need to know whether or not those initiating the change are trustworthy, especially if they are in positions of authority. A trust gap only develops when there is an increased level of trust required—when a change initiative "ups the stakes" and leads people to become genuinely concerned about how much they can trust management.

By this definition, low-trust work environments are not necessarily characterized by a trust gap. In a great many work settings, suspicion is high and trust is low and people know it. The trust required to get work done is low, commensurate with the trust that exists. However, when people undertake initiatives that will require personal as well as systemic change, trust required increases and the previously taken-for-granted low trust suddenly becomes an issue. Now those who advocate or mandate change must be prepared to have their own behavior judged. If a trust gap develops, advocates will be perceived as not "walking the talk." This will lessen the credibility of the initiative and make other people feel at risk: They will either not engage at all or they will engage guardedly. Conversely, if advocates are perceived as credible and authentic, the credibility of the initiative will benefit. Indeed, in the early stages of many initiatives, prior to achieving any tangible business results, the credibility of the advocates is the primary source of credibility of the initiative.

As shown in the diagram opposite, profound change initiatives require trust and personal reflection, resulting in two interrelated balancing processes. In loop B1, people feel vulnerable unless they can trust managers championing the initiative. A "trust gap" arises if management values and aims are not clear and credible—resulting in low credibility of the change initiative. Meanwhile (loop B2), a trust gap also generates a "reflection gap": with little safety for reflection and dialogue, people never develop the clarity about their own values and aims necessary to become genuinely enthusiastic and committed.

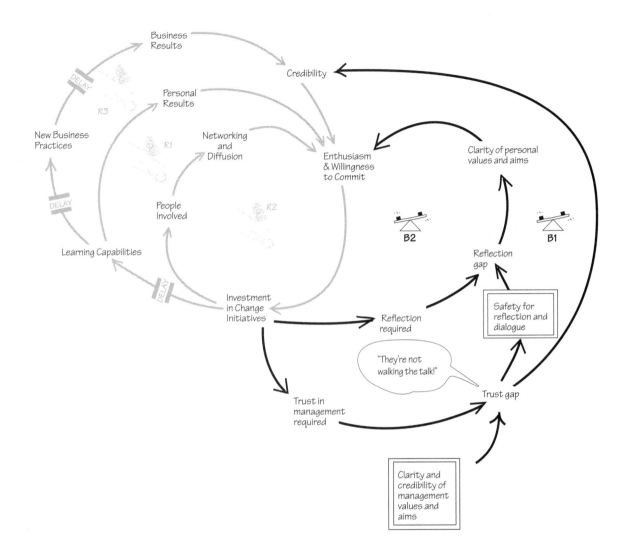

The underlying limit behind this challenge is the clarity and credibility of the management's aims and values. If people feel that their leaders can be trusted to support new values and actions, they will be more willing to commit time and effort and to take risks. Obviously, this is a highly subjective assessment. Sometimes local line leaders truly believe in what they advocate, yet they are still perceived as lacking in credibility. Such perceptions can be unfair, but in our experience they usually have some basis. This is why effective change advocates invariably have close partners, people who can help one another deal with their own shortcomings which could otherwise limit credibility.

There is another more subtle effect of a trust gap. For people to develop personal commitment to a transformational initiative, they need a relatively high level of clarity around their personal values and aims. In effect, change initiatives generate requirements for increased reflection, just as they generate requirements for higher trust. This means that a "reflection gap" develops if people do not in fact become more reflective. This reflection gap will limit the possibilities for genuine enthusiasm and commitment (as shown in limiting process B2).

In turn, deepening reflectiveness depends on trust. This is especially true in a work setting, where much of the reflection that matters occurs publicly. Commiserating with close confidants may release tension, but does little to advance collective capabilities. It's only when we are safe enough to bring our reflections into the open that we may get them disconfirmed. And that's when we start to discover that, "Oh, well, maybe it's not just *them*—maybe, there really are gaps in *my* own reasoning as well." But, in order to engage in such reflective conversations, people need to feel safe. This psychological safety, in turn, is affected by the extent to which management is perceived as "walking the talk." In organizations characterized by perceived hypocrisy and low commitment to espoused values, there will be little safety to reflect. The trust gap influences whether or not there is a reflection gap. Management's commitment to sincerely clarify personal values and aims contributes to a broader environment of personal reflection and genuine dialogue.

The executives who conceptualized this challenge were struck by this insight into how management behavior can subtly encourage or discourage reflection. "Transformational initiatives," commented one CEO, "require people looking at themselves a lot more than looking at the world around them. If their environment is full of games-playing and politics, then they won't have the safety that allows them to do that. And, if people at all levels don't do that as individuals, then we will be unable to develop high alignment of personal and organizational aims."

In fact, the interplay between trust and reflectiveness operates at many levels in an organization. Local managers contribute to safety within the local environment through their clarity and credibility. The top management team can, over time, contribute to reflectiveness throughout the organization through the signals that issue from their own behavior. Over the long term, we have seen organizations develop increased trust and reflectiveness through the concerted efforts of top management to continually explore their own values and aims and face shortfalls in their own behavior.

Trusting people to reflect is a new mandate for many managers. In one instance, a woman operator in a large refinery spoke up and said there were particular technical problems she believed she could help to fix, if given a chance to do it.

"I let her hold up the project—a few days to solve the problem, and six to eight weeks to implement her solution. There would be times when I would go out there and she would be sitting on a brick cement wall, motionless. I was thinking, 'Damn, she's sitting on a brick wall. What are we doing here?' She was thinking about the problem. I had to force myself, personally, to say, 'I'm willing to allow you to do this.'

"In the end, I give her all the accolades. She came up with a process whereby I never lost a barrel of oil! What she did was very, very intelligent—a simple procedure that let us bypass the treater that was causing the problem. She was determined that she was not shutting down."

Quoted from *Perspectives on Full-Scale Corporate Transformation: The "OilCo" Learning History*, by Art Kleiner, George Roth, et al. (New York: Oxford University Press, 1999), p. 76.

It is not enough for people to simply be clear about their values and aims; many people have clear personal aspirations that never connect to their work environment. The important point is to encourage reflective depth at work; only then can people align their personal aims with the organization's values and aims. Only then will reflectiveness contribute to commitment.

Who knows how much of the reflective genius of organizational members is never applied within their workplace? This is an immense loss for them as individuals and for our organizations. It is probably one of the primary reasons that most change initiatives remain superficial and that profound change is so rare.

Last, it is important to recognize just how foreign these notions about reflection on the job are to most people in most work settings. Most people's business careers have never required any of this "values stuff" before. As one executive put it, "In traditional work environments, you needed to understand the job, you needed to understand the business goals, you needed to understand the political environment you were operating in, but you really didn't need to understand what you stood for. In the new type of organization we are now creating, 'knowing what you stand for' is a crucial first step in defining your relationship with your bosses and subordinates, your conception of your work, and your role in the enterprise around you."

STRATEGIES FOR MEETING THE CHALLENGE OF WALKING THE TALK

The executive champions who articulated this challenge concluded that the greatest leverage lies in fostering clarity and credibility of management values and aims.

■ **Develop espoused aims and values that are credible in terms of the "living quality" of the organization.** People will no longer give their hearts and minds to a purpose that consists only of returning net capital investment, or enhancing productivity. "Organizations are ultimately human communities," says former Shell International planning coordinator Arie de Geus, "that either contribute or not to the meaning of people's lives." Similarly, Ikujiro Nonaka writes, "A company is not a machine but a living organism. Much like an individual, it can have a collective sense of identity and shared purpose . . . a shared understanding of what the company stands for." Developing the most credible values will mean learning to listen to the aspirations embodied in the organization as a whole.

See "Asking Big Questions," page 506, and "Strategy as Conversation," page 518.

■ **Build the credibility of organizational values and aims by demonstration, not by articulation.** In other words, this challenge speaks especially to managers who support profound change: Like it or not, you now live in a "glass house." Your inconsistencies of judgment and action are visible as never before. Subordinates will openly critique and evaluate your behavior—not because they're mean-spirited or cynical, but because their own survival depends upon it. Since you and others have apparently changed the "rules of the corporate game," people must test those rules for themselves to see how well they hold up, particularly in moments of stress.

In the end, whether consciously or not, the behavior of people throughout the organization will adjust to match that of their managers. Managers who want genuine information passed up to them must pass genuine information on to others. Managers who want collaboration across organizational boundaries must share responsibility and rewards. Managers who wish to learn how others think and feel must find ways to express their own thoughts and feelings, without retreating behind a corporate mask of inscrutable superiority.

This does not mean that managers should become self-consciously "nicer," or that the working environment should always be smooth and easy. Exactly the opposite may happen; as the environment

The de Geus quote is from talks given by Arie de Geus to the Society for Organizational Learning. Also see "The Living Company," by Arie de Geus, *Harvard Business Review*, March/April 1997, p. 51; and *The Living Company* (reviewed on our page 503). The Nonaka quote is from "The Knowledge Creating Company," *Harvard Business Review*, Nov-Dec 1991, pp. 96–104. Also see "Designing an Organization's Governing Ideas," by Bill O'Brien, in *The Fifth Discipline Fieldbook*, p. 306; and "Building Shared Vision: How to Begin," by Bryan Smith, *The Fifth Discipline Fieldbook*, p. 312.

becomes more genuine, people will become more aware of the organization's hypocrisies and frustrations. When executive leaders (like the CEO at the beginning of this chapter) acknowledge those, people may feel uncomfortable, but at least they will feel that the executive leaders are trying to deal with fundamental issues. Consultant Sue Zupansky worked closely with a company president leading a significant organizational redesign who, every once in a while, would raise his arms to the ceiling in exasperation and remind himself: "Ambiguity is my friend! Ambiguity is my friend!" She would think to herself, "Good. You're sweating with the rest of us."

■ **Don't go it alone—work with partners.** We all have blind spots that limit our credibility and ability to generate safety and trust in others. The thing to remember about blind spots is that we cannot see them! No matter how sincere we are, we may miss the aspects of our behavior that threaten others. We may not see how others see us. Virtually every effective local line or executive leader we have ever seen has had genuine partners—peers, internal consultants, external consultants, or, for local line leaders, executives (provided they are close enough to actually see how the line leader is seen). A partner is a thinking partner, someone with whom we can speak openly and challenge our thinking—a friend who shares our aspirations and is unconditionally supportive. Perhaps most important, a partner practices "ruthless compassion," telling us what we really need to hear but might have the most difficulty acknowledging. Leaders of change without partners are not only blind; they are dangerous, to themselves, to others, and to their dreams.

■ **Cultivate patience under pressure.** When leaders "blow a fuse," lose their temper, and revert to authoritarian habits in tough times, they send a signal that the new initiative was just a "fad" after all. One or two such incidents can compromise the entire initiative. Remember that the crisis itself provides a clue that old ways of operating were ineffective. Otherwise, the crisis might not have happened.

It's very helpful to begin reflecting on your values long before a crisis hits. Ask yourself: "What are my own hot buttons? What would provoke me to 'blow a fuse,' invoke unilateral action, and shut down initiatives? Can I anticipate those provocations, and catch them early enough to sidestep them? Can I find a way to practice enduring them, without losing my cool?"

The good news: By developing this kind of reflective capability in yourself, you can produce a wonderful inner payoff. The greater your personal alignment between your espoused values and your day-to-day action, the less stressed you will feel, and the more energy you will have. Being "out of alignment" in your values can feel as debilitating as having your spine twisted; and if the transformation initiative encourages you to act in greater accordance with the way you'd like to live, it can feel like your vertebrae are popping back into place.

- **Develop a greater sense of organizational awareness.** Much of the difficulty that managers have in "walking the talk" stems from the remoteness built into their positions. This is especially true for executive leaders. Local line leaders, such as plant managers, product development project leaders, or local team leaders, are physically closer to subordinates. They can see firsthand the issues at stake. But an executive leader may be hundreds or thousands of miles away from many subordinates. There is so little face-to-face contact that few people can get a good visceral sense of the leader as a person.

- **Think carefully about your beliefs about people.** Bosses influence a great deal of their subordinates' behavior simply through their expectations. We know bosses who assume that most people are, by nature, too unmotivated to take initiative. These bosses step into the breach because they "know" they must. Their people have learned that if they take initiative, they'll be chastised for "getting it wrong." So they comply by waiting for the direction, thus reinforcing the boss's perception that they aren't ready for autonomy.

)) See "Reflections for an Executive Leader," page 229.

Changing your assumptions about people can lead to dramatic surprises. An Intel plant manager once told us that he was given a factory to close down in two years. "At Intel, you have two choices. You can tell people the truth, in which case your good people leave within four months and you end up closing the sucker down with idiots . . . or you lie and keep your people until the last possible minute. People make different choices. I chose to tell everyone. Sure enough, eight of my best people left right away. I had to give responsibility to people whom I wouldn't have trusted to cross the street with my dog. Now I had to depend on them, and I was too busy to help them much. And yet every one of them delivered."

- **Make room for talk about individual's values.** The executive leaders who identified this challenge stressed the importance of these conversations at all levels of the organization. This is often overlooked. Instead, managers emphasize "rolling out" the planned changes without worrying about the bruising that people may feel when their own personal values and aspirations are disregarded. The deeper the process, the more personal values will be affected by it, and the more emphasis should be placed on clarifying personal values.

■ **Cultivate patience with bosses.** As Jennifer Kemeny notes on page 227, people in the subordinate role can make their own efforts much more effective. There is generally a mental model extant that bosses, with all their capabilities and resources, should be able to change attitudes on a dime, spontaneously and instantly, to match the new imperatives of the change initiative. When managers don't change instantly, it's assumed that they don't really want to. But in reality, managers who have spent their career in organizational environments don't shift immediately.

■ **Practice shuttle diplomacy.** Network leaders may find themselves in a difficult but critical role for this challenge. In the morning, this may mean going to the boss and saying, "You have to back off and change some of your assumptions about your subordinates." In the afternoon, it might mean telling the subordinates, "You'll have to fill this gap yourself, and be more responsible, or the whole operation will move right back to where it came from."

2 The Executive Leader's Perspective

. . . on implementing and leading profound change at Shell Oil Company, 1993–1998

Philip Carroll

For the past six years, a remarkably comprehensive corporate change effort has taken place at the Houston-based Shell Oil Company. Although Shell Oil is part of the international Royal Dutch/Shell group of companies, most of its affairs, for the past half century, have been handled autonomously. The same was true of the Shell Oil "transformation,"—a massive initiative involving hundreds of people directly.

The most visible feature of Shell's transformation is its new governance structure, modeled on principles of "subsidiarity"—moving power, as much as possible, to the local actors in a company. Former cost centers, such as information technologies, are now semi-autonomous businesses (such as Shell Services, now a global enterprise). New alliances (such as joint Shell-Texaco refineries) are prominent. Within the company, old guarantees of lifetime employment have been replaced by a new emphasis on values, vision, and personal authenticity; and continuous learning has become instilled in team practice and a corporate learning center near Houston. These changes, in turn, have shown up in business results, an unprecedented level of entrepreneurial innovation, and in a renewed sense of enthusiasm and commitment.

Five out of the six authors of this book, in one way or another, have consulted to some part of this effort. We have gotten to know Phil Carroll, the CEO of the company during its period of profound change, in part through working with him and in part through seeing his impact on others at Shell. He is also a member of one of the MIT-based working groups that articulated the challenges of this book, and he was directly involved in framing the challenge of this chapter. His story represents a blueprint from the CEO's perspective, for moving forward with a large change initiative in any large organization, while developing a solid, day-to-day sense of the new values of change.

When you find out that you are going to become the CEO of a large organization, but before you actually step into the position, there is a time of real reflection. Thus, for six months in 1993, I asked myself: As CEO, would I simply accept all the nice things that came with higher office? Or would I want to make a significant difference to the company?

I had been in high-level management at Shell Oil for many years, and was thus in a position to assess both my own mistakes and the company's. We had obviously done a lot of things right over time, but in the late 1980s our fortunes had gone sour. In response, we had embarked on a brutal series of layoffs, contractions, and other traumatic cost-cutting measures that were very out of character for Shell. Many people in the company believed that, after we got through the bad patch, we would be all right. But in my view, these traumatic measures were not sufficient to get us to the levels of performance needed to make Shell Oil into an outstanding place to work and a widely respected company.

I have sometimes been credited as the "architect" of Shell's transformation, but that is not accurate. Even before I became CEO, a host of people in the company were predisposed to the idea of revolutionary change, and ready and willing to take part in it. Moreover, it is dangerous to personify any profound change as emanating from the top of a company. If people think that the executive leaders are responsible for success, then they will not embed the change process fully in their own work, and it will not be sustained. If Shell Oil's transformation is robust, it's because many people from around the company have contributed to designing and developing it.

Nonetheless, the members of the Shell "Leadership Council"—the most senior executives in the company, including myself—have had to make decisions every step of the way about the direction of transformation, and the ways that we might implement profound change. Our experience may be helpful to other executive leaders going through similar processes in other organizations. In retrospect, it's clear that four areas were most crucial for our attention.

1. EXTENDING THE BUSINESS MODEL (INTO A NEW GOVERNANCE STRUCTURE)

Organizations are often less resistant to change than people expect. Most managers and employees have the desire and capacity to put their ideas into action. But they get frustrated if their freedom to act and speak out is stifled.

Thus, we wanted to create a structural mechanism to distribute power and decision making to more local levels: to give people the freedom they needed to take control of their job. Shell had evolved over time into a tightly controlled organization. People looked for direction to senior management: "What do we do now, coach?" All my life, I had believed that this is a flawed management style. It had led us to significantly under-use the talents of the organization.

Moreover, under this management style, even senior executives had not been oriented to what it really meant to run a public company. For example, capital was allocated by petition, like lobbying Congress. People took their budgets to the highest levels and said, "We need $750 million for next year, and here's what we'll do with it." Accountability for results was "elsewhere," not felt personally; people knew that those at the top would make the decision and keep score. If they got approval, it simply meant they needed to ask for more money next time.

We shifted to a governance structure in which each part of the company has its own balance sheet and debt. Decisions about how to invest

Shell Oil has used this diagram since 1996 to represent the four critical elements of an organizational change campaign—the four elements described in this article. At the edges of the "transformation triangle" are three types of collective activity: fostering new types of leadership, extending the business model, and engaging the organization in a way that helps develop more energizing attitudes and practices. At the center is the personal work: aligning individual aspirations and attitudes to the goals and vision of the organization as a whole.

Leadership

alignment of individual and organization

Engagement

Extending the Business Model

capital are not made centrally. Executive leaders have the opportunity to speak with local leaders about whether or not a decision is wise. But the local leaders decide; they borrow the money they need at an interest rate from the company, they pay it back, and they pay their dividends. When a local leader wants to buy another company, the governance structure, in effect, says, "Fine. But do you know how much it costs, and how it affects your debt structure? Will you be able to pay it back? It may prevent you from building another plant. But it's your choice."

To make this governance structure work, we needed to develop practical business skills throughout the company. We were surprised to learn that many people at high management levels didn't understand the factors that drive financial success. For example, in 1970, I was the coordinator of the capital budget for exploration and production (the largest segment of our business). Yet I did not know what a write-off was. Our people were capable and knowledgeable, but we never invested much time in training them in business principles.

}} For more about the Shell governance structure, see page 384.

That's always a danger in technocratic industries. The game was technology, all the way up to the highest levels of the company. Building a refinery, for example, was so complex that we assumed no one could make decisions about it without in-depth technological expertise. By contrast, being commercially competent was almost considered intellectually less important. The finance people kept the books, we believed, primarily to make reports to the outside world. Their information wasn't important inside. Nobody went to Finance to find out how the business was working. They went to corporate planning, another group of engineers who had built up a system of operational measures—the number of barrels produced per day, or the cost per barrel versus oil price.

In today's world, we realized, that model is not right. Technological expertise must be coupled with a high level of business skill; people must understand the factors that drive value in their efforts. Therefore, if we wanted people to run their business like a business, we had to put in place the necessary infrastructure: information systems, financial accounts, balance sheets, and accounting data, so that people throughout the company could keep effective score.

The ideas behind the governance structure came in part from an article by British management writer Charles Handy: "Balancing corporate power: A new Federalist paper," in the *Harvard Business Review*, November-December, 1992.

2. LEADERSHIP

The first announcement of our new corporatewide initiative came out in January 1994. It was a simple notice, saying that we would now have "an initiative to strengthen and enhance learning and development," to achieve continually improving performance. Everybody, including very senior leaders, said, "I don't understand. What does this mean?"

It was, in fact, the first statement about the role and purpose of corporate leaders, from the most senior executives on down. To make the new business model work, we had to recast leadership. Our traditional model of leadership had emphasized omniscience, high degrees of control, and a Patton-esque stance in which the leader was always right and was not to be questioned. That had to change. We had to move from seeing senior leaders as decision-making bodies, to seeing them as open to learning and responsible for nurturing the next generation of leaders.

At each meeting, from the senior-most Leadership Council to teams in a refinery or chemical plant, people should ask: What is our program for developing capabilities? How do we develop new leaders—for example, among the operators? What do we do to ensure that people who are running the pump repair shop are able to use and understand and learn the same leadership principles? What types of leadership are good in what types of situations? And people should be rewarded, above all else, for their ability to foster others.

Under the new system at Shell, a position of leadership does not necessarily mean more rights and privileges; it means more obligations. Leaders have to be more careful about their behavior. They are no longer judged by the memos they send out or the presentations they make, but on their actions and results. It is more acceptable for people to draw attention to the gap between a leader's talk and action: "You say you want candid discussion, but you cut everyone off at that meeting."

I recognize that quality leadership is a complex, situational issue. Anyone who tries to describe the characteristics of "good leadership" gets in trouble, because good leadership doesn't emanate from different people in the same way. But if you can articulate the generic shift from "leader as commander" to "leader as servant," people will begin to recognize its rewards—not only in the effectiveness of organizations, but personally. Paradoxically, the "leader as commander" has less freedom and authority. Every commander is usually following directions from another commander; even Patton took his orders from Eisenhower.

A servant leader, by contrast, has the authority to do what he or she thinks is right, and to be responsible for the consequences. This doesn't mean imposing the individual's will in an egotistical, absolute way. It means being as sensitive, open, and engaged in the system as you possibly can, and yet having a sense of where your part of the organization needs to go. It also means being willing to show your vulnerability. If you try to hide your flaws, then you can't provide good leadership.

To make this work, people must have opportunities to stop and reflect on their own development. Status and reward must be unlinked somewhat from hierarchical position and power. For example, people are sometimes promoted into positions where they turn out to be a bad fit, or their performance doesn't meet expectations. Under the current structure of rewards and status, how can they be moved into another position? I don't think anyone knows how to do this well. The most common reaction is to leave them in place, suffering through the results and covering up the error, but that allows the organization to become more and more dysfunctional. I would like to think that under the new governance structure and model of leadership, it will be easier to move people laterally and help them find attractive alternatives that will make better use of their talents.

See stories about developing leadership behavior at Shell, by Linda Pierce, on page 211; and about the "cadre of coaches," by Tom Ryan, on page 115.

3. ENGAGEMENT

When we started in 1993, there was very little belief at Shell that transformation would last. People expected they would have to take part in some meetings about vision and values, and then it would pass, without having much effect on anyone in the end.

Meanwhile, at the top, we articulated a vision and a set of values, and talked about communicating these to our 22,000 people. We didn't use the word "engagement." We felt that if we could explain what we were trying to do clearly enough, in one-way communication, then the design and plan could be implemented and success would be assured. But I don't think an organizational transformation works that way.

Stories came back to us: "I heard you talk and I think the idea of transformation is wonderful, but so-and-so (a member of the Leadership Council) came on a visit, and there was no message about transformation. Why are we getting contradictory messages?" People would throw back comments to us about the ways in which we were not living up to the values we talked about. That's normal human behavior, and in a sense it was healthy: It meant that growing numbers of people were aware of the new ideas and concepts. And once they began talking like that, their leaders would have to respond.

But engagement is primarily a process of listening to people, not communicating at them. Eighteen months into the process, after a series of regular offsite meetings to talk about our values and plan the transformation together, it began to dawn on the members of the Leadership Council: We didn't have the basic skills to listen to people and let their ideas make an impression on us. We had all had supervisory training courses. We had been given coffee mugs that read, "Listen or Shut up." But we could not even engage ourselves in discussion. Some of us shut down in the face of disagreement. Others tried to win every argument: "No matter what you say," they seemed to be thinking, "I will think up an answer that will best your answer."

It took in-depth reflective work and a series of private meetings for us to learn to listen more effectively. As that started to happen, people throughout the organization began to gain confidence in our efforts. I began to hear, for the first time, talk about the process of transformation from people out at offshore drilling base camps, or at refineries. This did not happen in a clean, crisp way. We would make a little progress here, lose a little ground there, and gradually penetrate, in a messy and jagged way, into the organization.

To me, engagement is more difficult than the business model or leadership. It represents a fundamental shift in the relationship between employees and companies. When I went to work for Shell thirty-five years ago, employees were provided security, benefits, and compensation in exchange for a loyalty to the company and obedience to the management system. Today, no company can provide the security implicit in that kind of contract. People recognize that their only security lies in performance—in their ability to add value in an economic system. The transition to this new relationship is very difficult for some people to accept, because it has a higher degree of uncertainty and a higher degree of accountability for each one of us for our own actions and personal development.

Instead of loyalty, we now ask for commitment. It is up to the organization and its leaders to provide the kind of environment where people give that commitment freely. In exchange, Shell is responsible for helping people build their skills to create an environment where they can control whether or not their particular business unit is successful. Until you do that, people will not accept the new employment relationship.

I hesitate to use the word "training" in this context. "Training" takes place through repetition and manipulation; people can be trained to build computer programs and run seismic records, but not to deal with completely unpredictable circumstances.

Thus, we have tried to foster learning instead of training. For example, we have made many of our corporatewide decisions by bringing together initiative teams, composed of people from very different parts of the organization, to look at either business or strategic issues in depth. Looking into issues such as diversity or rewards and recognition, they investigate practices at other organizations and come to solutions not just through their own logic or simple numerical benchmarking, but by bringing in fresh insights from outside.

In addition, establishing our new corporate Learning Center has demonstrated our commitment to building human capability to everyone in the corporation. We use it to orient new people who come to Shell—everyone from file clerks to refinery welders to research scientists. It has allowed us to share best practices by bringing together individuals from different parts of the company to learn from one another. And senior management can put itself on the line there, standing up in front of large segments of the company, articulating their visions, and showing people that they are both vulnerable and committed to our mutual success.

4. PERSONAL ALIGNMENT

A transformational initiative starts and ends with the individual leader's alignment. As leaders, we are called upon to develop a sense of what we think is right, and what we want to do. Then we must ask ourselves: Is this consistent with the good of the organization? Can we get enough people, among thousands of employees, to see things the same way? Are we, in fact, aligned with their interest, their families' interests, and their values? That's the most important element. If there is misalignment between the good of the organization and the values of the leaders—if the leaders' objective is solely to make as much money as possible—then it leads to scandalous stories like *Barbarians at the Gate*.

The wonderful thing about these new forms of leadership is that they get easier as you practice them. Many of the most difficult things that you have to face are things that you fear because you have been taught to fear them in the old culture. Learning to expose your failures is one of the most liberating aspects of the whole journey. If one is no longer required to be perfect, then so many new things are possible. And stubbing your toe is not that painful, as long as you are willing to stand up and say, "I stubbed my toe. Now I am going to do something different."

I am sometimes asked if, after I leave, Shell Oil might revert to a paternalistic, homogeneous, centrally controlled society. It might; but after six years of transformation, I think even the most controlling leadership would find it very difficult to put the toothpaste back in the tube. Nor do I think the organization would look for dictatorial leaders. Making things more possible for individuals has produced enormous success for us, in my view. It makes people more excited about the communities they are in, and it contributes to making an organization into an "employer of choice."

⟩⟩ For the Royal Dutch/Shell transformation, see page 523.

A personal checklist for leaders facing "messy" experiences Linda Pierce

I<small>N</small> S<small>HELL</small> O<small>IL'S</small> <small>TRANSFORMATION,</small> I <small>HAVE FOUND MYSELF IN THREE LEADERSHIP</small> roles: an executive leader creating a context for action, a network leader who coaches and guides others, and a line leader with responsibility for particular projects. Along the way, I developed this checklist of questions to ask myself—both as a check on my own hubris, and a bolster for my confidence. When I find that I'm having a messy experience, I go back and check these principles. If I can't answer these questions affirmatively, that tells me that I need to get myself centered again.

- **Do I have "constancy of purpose"?** This phrase comes from Dr. W. Edwards Deming. I am only effective if I understand, in my own way, why we are investing our efforts in the work of transformation. I need to stay fixed on the desired results and help people remember them.
- **Am I patient enough?** I expect too much if I expect the system to become perfect—today. I can become angry when it doesn't match these expectations, and I undermine my own ability to contribute.

- **Am I too patient?** Do I border on complacency, or collusion with the status quo?
- **Can I muster the necessary courage?** As a change agent, I must give voice to help others hold the mirror to see the warts, gaps, and problems. It's sometimes difficult.

I learned the importance of optimism from a great organization development consultant, Herb Shepard. He embodied, in his words and presence, the power of recognizing the possibility of success. — Linda Pierce

- **Can I keep an optimistic bias?** "Change agents" who don't believe that others can make significant personal progress, because they perceive the system as too biased and corrupt, will not be able to do good work in corporations.
- **Am I opportunistic?** A lot of people think that being "opportunistic" is bad. But if you are opportunistic with good intentions, you are simply prepared to "seize the moment." Since I believe change is mostly an emergent process, I must be alert to unplanned, but well-prepared interventions.
- **Am I approaching people with compassion?** From time to time, I can observe others displaying defensive or bizarre behavior. I have learned that in just about every case, people are being as good as they can be in that moment. If they knew how to be better, they would. It's unlikely that the bizarre behavior is deliberately intended to be hurtful or destructive. It exists for some other reason. So I must be compassionate enough to remember to look for that other reason.
- **Do I conduct my work with love?** I like Bill O'Brien's definition of love: When I love people, I want to help them be all that they can be. If I can bring that attitude to my work, and if I can muster the courage and compassion to act upon that love, then I can be effective.

⟩⟩ See Linda Pierce's "Learning What We're Worth," page 177.

DEEP CHANGE
by Robert Quinn (San Francisco: Jossey-Bass, 1996)

If you find yourself asking, "What am I doing that hijacks change? How can I learn to embrace and model continuous change?" this clear, well-written book will help you reflect on your personal style in the context of leadership. It focuses on the shift from viewing change as an external process—from which you stand back and seek to control—to recognizing that you are part of a wider process, which you can influence but not control. Quinn writes about the reasons why people often choose to hold on to destructive ways of thinking and acting, to avoid the pain and risk associated with change. — Bill Godfrey

SYNCHRONICITY
by Joseph Jaworski, introduction by Peter Senge (San Francisco: Berrett-Koehler, 1996)

Only recently has the idea become acceptable in business circles that our capacity for leadership flows from within our being—our inner journey—more than from anything we do or any bundle of skills. Synchronicity is an autobiographical account of one person's lifelong quest to understand leadership in the context of his own life experiences (which include growing up as prosecutor Leon Jaworski's son, founding the American Leadership Forum, divorce and remarriage, and leading the scenario planning effort at Royal Dutch/Shell in the 1990s). Jaworksi's book focuses on the way a leader can set the stage for "predictable miracles." The leader's job is not to fight for control, but to be a catalyst in the unfolding of meaning. — Bill Godfrey

LEADERSHIP WITHOUT EASY ANSWERS
by Ronald Heifetz (Cambridge, MA: Harvard University Press/Belknap, 1994)

To Ron Heifetz, "adaptive challenges" are the difficult issues that demand changes in attitudes, behaviors, and values. They include complex social and political challenges, like riots and economic crises, where the causes are not clear and the "fixes" not obvious; and they include many business problems. Heifetz asserts that leaders can deal with adaptive issues not by providing authoritative answers, but by asking hard questions that spur the entire community to rethink its assumptions.

Through precepts and carefully interpreted stories of leaders asking people to make difficult choices (ranging from Gandhi to Ronald Reagan to a doctor informing a patient's family that he has cancer), Heifetz develops four key principles of leadership in this book. These represent four sets of key questions that leaders can learn to ask themselves and others with credibility and authenticity. These questions will help you to identify adaptive challenges, to create a "holding environment" for talking about them, to direct disciplined attention to the issues (and to the reasons why people avoid the issues); and to give the work of dealing with them back to the people. — Nelda Cambron-McCabe

SUCCESS ON OUR OWN TERMS: Tales of Extraordinary, Ordinary Business Women, by Virginia O'Brien (New York: John Wiley & Sons, 1998)

O'Brien, who surveyed 700 women and interviewed forty-five for this book, makes a compelling case for the good news that women are succeeding in the corporate world—because of a form of leadership that equates "success" with "personal values." This equation is not without risk, and the decisions, crises, and challenges each woman faces at one point or another makes for a good read. Told largely through conversational quotes and narratives, the experiences of these middle and senior level managers convey the importance of fundamentals like mentoring, diversity programs, and corporate attention to work/life issues. The appendix includes an intriguing job-share proposal modeled on the groundbreaking position created by two women at Bell Atlantic. If work, as former secretary of labor Robert Reich said, is "a moral act as well as an economic act," then the style of leadership described here represents the forefront of organizational change. — Nina Kruschwitz

3 How to "Walk the Talk" Without Falling Off a Cliff

By David Marsing, Intel Corporation

If you are an operational manager or large organization leader undertaking some form of a learning initiative, "walking the talk" probably often means "walking on the fence." On one side are the enthusiastic, loyal people who report to you. The more certain you behave, the more you inhibit the give-and-take that leads to successful learning initiatives. On the other side, your boss, board, or shareholders hold you accountable for performance. They want to feel that you are "in control" of events. Few people have navigated this balance as well as

David Marsing, the Vice President, General Manager of Assembly Test Manufacturing for Intel. Here, Marsing shows us how he learned to conduct himself as a leader under seemingly lethal pressure. Notice the way in which the gradual building of capabilities early on paves the way for remarkable results—not just from Marsing himself, but from everyone involved.

David Marsing's story is also told in "Killer Results Without Killing Yourself," by Michael S. Malone, *Fast Company* premiere issue, p. 124, available at: *http://www.fastcompany.com/online/01/marsing.html*.

For the first ten years of my career, my concept of leadership didn't match the types of management I saw around me—first at Texas Instruments, then at Intel. I was once instructed to lay off 25 percent of the people in our group, with no explanation except that "we had to reduce headcount." The layoff approach was expedient, but brutal on the people; it wiped out any kind of work ethic, morale, or ability to think about quality or safety. I obeyed, along with my peers, but when two of them were laid off immediately afterward, it forced me to think more carefully. Couldn't businesses come up with a more creative approach?

I soon got an opportunity to find out. In the mid-1980s, I became the plant manager of an Intel fabrication plant in Livermore, California—the facility at which we produced the 386 processor, which launched Intel's spectacular revenue growth of that time. This plant was also the site of remarkable technical improvement, but as an eighteen-year-old facility, it could not stay competitive with new, more advanced facilities. In 1989, we were told that we would have to shut the operation down.

I was now in a position where I had to walk the talk. I had to meet our objective in a humane way. We got everybody together to brainstorm possibilities for keeping the facility open, and we exercised the hell out of those ideas for opportunities. People came together with a level of motivation I've never seen before. We set a goal of showing the company that not only could the plant be economically viable, but shutting it down would be dumb. It was black humor, because the shutdown was inevitable; but we kept getting the patient's life extended another year. We held two annual shutdown and closure parties; we literally had plaques with several closure dates etched in and scratched out.

We senior managers made a commitment that whatever we did, everybody working there would have a job. We would find them a job in the area or, if they could relocate, somewhere else at Intel. We spent two years relocating more than seven hundred people. This was a phenomenal task, but it created a core group of people, scattered throughout Intel, who helped do some phenomenal things later. At other facilities, employees would say, "You can't trust management." But people who

For another view of "learning-oriented" change work at Intel, at a testing and assembly plant, see "Skillful Discussion at Intel," by Ed Carpenter, in *The Fifth Discipline Fieldbook*, p. 392.

had been at Livermore would say, "You can trust these managers, because they'll go to the mat for you."

After a brief assignment as the Director of Factory Automation, I became plant manager of FAB 9, outside Albuquerque, the plant that started the ramp of the 486 microprocessor—which Intel was just introducing, with a great marketing campaign to match. But the factory was having serious problems with equipment reliability, and throwing away half of the material they produced. Hell-bent on turning around the plant quickly, I put so much pressure on myself that after a month I succumbed to a heart attack.

While I was healing, the doctor said, "You need to reflect on whether you've chosen the right career." Maybe I should become a forester in a watchtower, he said, or a librarian in a library that's not used much. I thought about it all through my three months of recovery. I knew intuitively that I could do my job at Intel, minimize the pressure, and get even better results. I didn't quite know how, but I knew it could be done, if I could find the right approach to take.

When I went back to work, I felt like I could see and hear things in a way that I never could before, picking up signals from all the people who had a difficult time at work. They were grinding themselves up—in emotional, physical, and spiritual pain. I had never realized the degree to which people all around me were suffering. How, then, could we create an environment for breakthrough performance at every level—not just in traditional work indicators, but interpersonally, and in terms of the individual integration of work and personal life? I believed that part of the problem was our management approach. It was like trying to swim while wearing a set of full weights. It represented a macho achievement, but it wasn't efficient—and if you weren't lucky, you would drown trying. Getting the weights off would require some departures from Intel's traditional thinking and ways of doing things. If I couldn't make it work, I figured, I could always go be a librarian or a forest ranger.

The next year, I became the manager of the startup of FAB 11, next door to FAB 9. This is the world's largest semiconductor fabrication plant, with 200,000 square feet of "clean room." Three or four times a minute, all the air is flushed out of that room; with all the support and construction, the plant at its peak involved 4,000 people with a $2.2 billion capital investment, to produce state-of-the-art Pentium and Pentium Pro microprocessors. That kind of investment meant we had to produce revenue projected at $1.7 million per hour, by the third year.

The names "Pentium" and "Pentium Pro" are trademarks of the Intel Corporation.

With all this at stake, it has always been a challenge to maintain autonomy. A lot of people at corporate headquarters want to help us make decisions. They (and we) are bolstered by a results-oriented, technology-driven, assertive, risk-oriented corporate culture. We teach management classes in "constructive confrontation." Our focus on analytical, rational thinking and decision making is very strong.

Fortunately, we were far enough away from headquarters that we could try new ideas and give them the time needed to produce results. We met the corporation's business expectations, but we also set out to "walk our talk" by creating value in every aspect of the plant—in its work force as a whole and as individuals, in the productivity and capability of its physical assets, and in our relationships with our community, customers, and suppliers.

As I look back, a series of factors made it feasible for us, and for me as a leader, to pursue both our goals in a high-pressure environment.

LETTING GO OF EXCLUSIVE RELIANCE ON ANALYSIS

I've learned to use some dialogue practices based on David Bohm's work, trying to get people to look at the factory from a sensory perspective. In staff meetings we'd say, "How's the factory doing?" Everybody wanted to shoot his hand up with a quantitative indicator. "No," I said. "Don't give me any data. How does it feel on the floor, working with your people? How does it feel to be in some of the key meetings?" The first few times we did this, people looked at me as if to say, "Where is he coming from?" But we deliberately made it a regular practice—conducted with such repetitiveness that it became integrated into our everyday work life. Then they began to look forward to it. They also began to interact differently with their people. This subtle twist, just a simple little thing, started to get people to exercise their observational skills, and use a different part of their brain.

Essentially, we needed to find a way (within Intel's proud, analytical, project-based culture) to tap into people's innate ability and their true essence. Even if it just meant venting their frustration and anxiety, even if we didn't do anything about it but listen, we needed to give them a chance to speak from the heart. We had already tried, starting with the Livermore plant closure, to develop capabilities for good listening. Now, some of our FAB 11 people went through extended training in the five learning disciplines, and we began to adopt some of those practices in a more formal sense. Some took root well; others did

To develop a better understanding of "integrating and embodying these skills," I would recommend two books: *The Tree of Knowledge: The Biological Roots of Human Understanding,* by Humberto R. Maturana and Francisco J. Varela, translated by Robert Paolucci (Boston: Shambhala, 1992); and Cheng Tzu's *Thirteen Treatises on T'ai Chi Ch'uan,* translated by Cheng Man Ch'ing, Benjamin Pang Jeng Lo and Martin Inn (Berkeley, CA: North Atlantic Books, 1985). The traditional teachings suggest that you need to practice something 10,000 times (correctly) before you "know" it. At this stage you have mastered it, and don't have to consciously think about the mechanical execution. — David Marsing

not. We realized that Intel's culture is already predisposed to change; the entire company methodically plans for and executes significant changes in technology every two or three years. As we bundled social and cultural changes with these technology waves, we discovered much less resistance to the "intuitive" practices. Technological change and an increased capacity to learn became complementary parts of "how we're all evolving."

I decided to personally practice enough so that I could integrate and embody these skills in myself. This meant establishing a routine of meshing intuitive and analytical behavior, acting and reflecting, listening and advocating, "task" work and process work, and analytic problem solving and systems thinking, without having to consciously think about it. I now believe that my ability to tap into the organization's potential was a direct result of developing a strong ability to integrate these tools.

ENGAGING THE EXECUTIVE LEVELS

At times I have had to deal with lack of support from my boss. I use an expression that I learned from a United States Navy captain, who had been the commander of the U.S.S. *Kitty Hawk*. When a higher-level executive begins to "micromanage" or do my job for me, I say that I want to clarify what I believe I am accountable for, and then I ask if I'm being "relieved of my responsibilities."

So far they've all said, "No, that's not what I want to do." This focus on explicitly clarifying my role changes the level of the conversation immediately, so that we can talk about the issues that really trouble them. The conversation is confrontational, but it gets them to back off and recognize that they hold me accountable for performance. It helps me understand why they may be uncomfortable, or what problem they are trying to solve. I've only had to use this technique three times in the last thirteen years.

There was a time, three or four years ago, when I took it upon myself to ask difficult questions and challenge the status quo on a regular basis. My boss pointed out to me that this behavior made it harder for people to change, particularly those who were ten to fifteen years my senior. He said something that surprised me—that when I wasn't confrontational, they often looked to me as a role model. In that spirit, I began to learn different approaches. First, I recognized that other people's training and experience was different from my own, and there often wasn't a common basis for understanding. When people sought me out and asked me questions, I engaged with them as much as they would allow. But I've learned not to lose sleep over people who aren't motivated or who have a negative attitude toward what's possible. Once I adopted this approach, I was less of a surprise to my boss in meetings, and he began to view me as a reliable ally in driving and leading change.

I upped the ante with a move that surprised a number of people: In 1992, I applied for the position of Intel's director of human relations. I wanted to formally associate myself with tools and processes that could help Intel tap into the potential of its people. As part of my application, I had to be interviewed by a number of senior managers. Some were surprised that an operations-oriented technologist was interested in human relations. One of them said, "You're a lot more valuable to the company in starting up a $2 billion factory." I replied that was probably true by standard measurements, "but over a longer period of time, you may be making a mistake. Maybe I could position Intel to be very successful as a $40 or $50 billion company."

I didn't get the human relations job, but articulating my philosophy with some of these managers has been immensely valuable. It showed me that I had their confidence and trust to some degree, especially if I continued to meet fundamental business requirements and avoid animosity from other parts of the corporation. This gave me, more or less, a green light to experiment with learning-oriented approaches in FAB 11, without scrutiny and micromanagement from above.

MENTORING AND DEVELOPING OTHER MANAGERS

As part of my strategy, I formally took on the role of developing future managers of future factories. By working with managers as they develop, I could help create conscious awareness of a variety of specific practices—and give them the opportunity to experience a very tight-knit, highly functioning, interactive, cocreating team environment. If they like working in that environment, they'll continue to try to re-create it in their own organizations.

I began promoting people who would experiment and give good (and critical) feedback. I helped people who were not willing to learn and experiment or who had infectious negative attitudes find opportunities in other organizations. I tried to make these decisions based on performance, giving people the space and freedom to heal themselves as a team. At times I have had to convince people to modify their behavior.

In using these tactics, I wasn't looking for immediate results, but for longer-term impact. But breakthroughs sometimes happen. I've seen teams of people who have never worked together demonstrate high performance that might normally take five or ten years to develop, in incredibly short periods of time. In the end, a simple value underlies everything I do: giving people the opportunity to reach the highest capability they can, and recognizing them when they're motivated to try.

HUMAN DYNAMICS by Sandra Seagal and David Horne
(Cambridge, MA: Pegasus Communications, 1997)

Training in human dynamics has been a strategic factor in sustaining our efforts over the years. Once people understand that other people do, indeed, listen and speak with different languages, then they can integrate their own learning styles with the other personalities in a team or a company. Human dynamics is more effective than other "learning styles" workshops and tools because it provides an individual path: a way for people to pull together their own capabilities and make themselves more effective. — David Marsing

Also see the review of human dynamics in *The Fifth Discipline Fieldbook*, p. 422.

The human dynamics approach distinguishes five broad patterns of listening, thinking, and learning that predominate in different people: mentally centered, emotional-objective, emotional-subjective, physical-mental, and physical-emotional. As a tool for exploring leadership values, human dynamics is very helpful, because it shows how different people are drawn to different ways of talking, thinking, and communicating about values. This book, by human dynamics founders Sandra Seagal and David Horne, is the highest-quality introduction we know. — Art Kleiner

4 "... As one of the first black engineers in South Africa ..."

Ehud Nyameko Matya, Plant Manager, Eskom

Just after South Africa's 1994 political transition, Ehud Matya became the black manager of a plant with heretofore "whites only" management. This was the Eskom Corporation's Duvha power station, one of the largest in the world, located about two hours east of Johannesburg. Duvha was in so much turmoil (in both plant performance and human relations) that many observers thought Matya would fail to turn it around. For example, the plant's five labor unions were racially segregated and bitterly antagonistic to one another. Matya had two basic tools: the company's avowed mission of "transformation," and his own integrity and willingness to believe in people. This story demonstrates the distance that a leader can go with those resources.

When I first saw the Duvha power plant, where I am now the plant manager, I was not allowed to eat in the cafeteria. It was 1986. I had just joined Eskom full-time. Since South Africa was still under apartheid, and since I am black, they had had to petition the government to sponsor me at an engineering school; engineering schools were white. In school, I had not been permitted to live in student residences, and I had been continually subject to police checks, which sometimes prevented me from attending classes. At Eskom, I continued to have to fight, because the standard policies for blacks did not fit me. For instance, medical aid schemes were designed for laborers who lived in hostels. I kept asking for proper medical insurance—an ongoing battle.

I came to Duvha initially as part of a team, evaluating the plant as a pilot site for a new software commercial system. One of the managers said, "Our toilets are not open to blacks. You'll have to find yourself a toilet outside the plant. And the main canteen is only open to whites. You'll have to eat downstairs, with the rest of the people."

I replied, "You guys must decide whether you want this team here or not, because I'm part of the team. If you don't want the project, tell us." The team ended up driving to town to eat as a compromise.

We are grateful to Hélène de Villiers, writer/editor and associate of the Centre for Innovative Leadership in South Africa, for developing and facilitating this contribution to this book. We are also grateful to Louis van der Merwe, who established our contact with Eskom and helped arrange the sequence of events that led to this contribution. Today, Eskom leads South Africa in bringing people of color into positions of management; 28 percent of the senior executives of the company are black, including the chairman.

I did not want to deal with this type of environment. I pulled out of that project, and ultimately left Eskom. Then, in 1987, the company's leaders began to transform it, including their attitudes about black managers, and I was recruited back. The chairman, John Maree, was pushing financial performance almost to the point of complete privatization, while the chief executive, Ian McRae, was strongly promoting Eskom's potential role in revitalizing South Africa. As one of the first black engineers, not just in the company but in corporate South Africa, I was highly visible. I knew I could not build a career unless I could be involved in helping to lead the company's transformation.

I felt encouraged by Eskom's new labor agreement, called Unfolding Vision, which came into effect in 1992. This was based on the idea of engaging Eskom's five trade unions and saying, "It's all our future. Let's talk about it first, before we fight." Under this policy, every new change affecting employees would be discussed with them first, and they would have an opportunity to "meaningfully influence it." Everyone understood that it would make the planning and evaluation of options take longer, but implementation would be much quicker, because employees would be better equipped for the change. For people like myself, it was wonderful. It said leadership was not the same as being "the boss around here." And it changed the tenor of meetings with employees. It also provided a reason for affirmative action in South Africa; it meant that people in black unions could now move up into the professional class and gain experience in productive decision making. That was important to me.

At the same time, Eskom had close ties to the national government, and it was home for a lot of conservative people. I was assigned as the chief of logistics at the Bloemfontein distribution business unit, right in the heart of one of the most conservative regions of the country. Nobody was told that I was black before I arrived, or that there were changes coming. One chap turned and walked away, in public, when he learned he would report to me. "I've got nothing to do with him," he said.

I was more relaxed about this than many of the onlookers. I was more worried about the people who seemed easy and open, because I didn't expect many people to accept me at first. But this gave me a wonderful opportunity to test my success. I had the full right to take this chap off the job, but I had the frame of mind that I wasn't there to replace white with black. I was there to run a business. I sought him out to chat with him, and got him to understand that I was not there as a token, or to "prove that change is going to walk over you," but to work with him. He changed around and became very cooperative. I needed him as well, to facilitate interaction with government departments and local farmers. I told him that either he reported to me and worked with me, or he would have to leave Eskom. I worked hard to make sure that he knew he could trust me. It was quite exciting to see that change.

This experience showed me the choice that I would have as a manager at Eskom. In each case, I would be dealing with old hatreds and resentments. I could add to those resentments by coming in and playing favorites. Or I could "walk the talk"—establish an attitude that supported transformation at my level.

In 1994, when the manager of Duvha resigned, they appointed me to replace him. Duvha was one of the toughest sites in Eskom in industrial relations, with a direct spill-off to plant performance. Only two years before, it had been a top power station, winning awards for millions of hours without injury. But performance and morale had dwindled. There were plant failures without any perceivable cause, except political disagreement with the government's policies. Some right-wing trade unions were unhappy with Eskom's support of the new government, and trying to maintain some jobs as all-white. Some of the strikes here became violent almost to the point of people being killed.

THE PLANT'S EXECUTIVE TEAM

In a well-intentioned move, at the time I took this job, three other members of the plant's executive team were replaced. I inherited a half-new team, but I had had nothing to do with choosing them. Nor were they necessarily happy to have been assigned to Duvha. I was still the only black person in top management—and an "outsider" to boot, because I had not come up through the traditional route of power generation management. My boss introduced me to the team and said, "Ehud, good bye, good luck, run the plant, and I demand performance."

Moreover, as part of Eskom's "chief executive challenge," our team was assigned to develop an effective solution to affirmative action that could be tested in plants around the Eskom system. Not only was it difficult conceptually, but it was filled with lots of emotions. The group dynamics broke down. One "old-timer" was absolutely uncomfortable being asked to think about this change. I had to help him find a new job quickly, while making it clear to onlookers that he was not being replaced as a signal of the guilt of the past. The rest of the staff seemed to disagree on everything. We tabled many decisions just for the sake of avoiding chaos.

At times, I felt like the assignment was a setup, a recipe for proving that I couldn't do the job. But when I raised the question, my boss told me that, amid the political transition, this type of situation was taking place all through Eskom. "You fix it," he said. Obviously, it would not be easy—why had I expected it to be? But there was a fortunate aspect: As a plant manager onsite, I would be working fairly independently. I had the authority and opportunity to deal with the challenges directly.

I first tried to understand whether my own personal style was contributing to the problems. I was prepared to change my approaches for the sake of the group. But the problem was not my style; it was people holding to their baggage of the past. One of the managers, for instance, had never accepted the Unfolding Vision approach. He saw it as chaos, as weakening his position. That became a problem. I knew I could not simply say, "Stop everything you've been doing, and do it my way." I had no particular "way" in mind—I was open to anything that would create future business success.

We started with basic team building, to get people unfrozen and willing to talk to one another. We adopted the concept of being "servant leaders," which was useful because it had not come from the past, and it had not come from any one of us. We could talk about it comfortably, which allowed more of the managers to talk about their own labor issues, their unhappiness, and their discomfort. The more candid and relaxed we became, the more that the staff reporting to us began to feel a change.

INSTILLING AN ETHIC OF RECOGNITION

We decided that we needed to instill a culture where employees felt that they were recognized for their achievements. So when people achieved a milestone, such as one hundred days (or one million person-hours) without an injury, we celebrated. Without letting anyone know in advance, the senior managers arrived at work two hours early, at 5 A.M. instead of 7. We had a big barbecue, frying sausages, and we served the staff as they walked into the gate. The staff that worked closely with us could see the difference this made in our executive team atmosphere. The rest of the staff, eating the sausage, could now say to themselves: "What is happening? This is different." Plus, all five unions were now eating together.

It was a matter of pride for Eskom stations to run all six power units as long as possible without a shutdown. In the past, the best record at Eskom for continuous run was forty-seven days. It's very tough to beat that record, but our six units had just come back on line, and I wrote a letter to all the staff: "There's a world record to go for. Let's do it."

To get there, we used every opportunity. We started to hold sessions, once a month, where people could talk about their progress. We began to look for opportunities to mention people's achievement—so that if a fitter, artisan, or technician did something superb, we splashed it up: "This is what we're looking for." Instead of increasing salaries, we relied on community acknowledgment: continuous recognition and having people feeling that we were close to them.

When a unit achieved three thousand hours without a shutdown, we gave everyone in the unit a gift. At five thousand hours, we gave them a more expensive gift. This had the effect of uniting the members of different unions; they now saw themselves as responsible, together, for the success of the unit. When Unit 3 achieved six thousand hours, that made it not just our best unit, but one of the best in all of Eskom. It was approaching winter, and we bought each employee a nice jacket, with the name of the unit embossed on the front. We now have two more units approaching five thousand hours, and they are going for the record. Today, if we try to take a unit down because of a problem, the employees ask why we're doing that. The maintenance staff, instead of taking it down—let alone sabotaging it—now comes up with creative ways to deal with the problem.

We ultimately achieved a record of seventy-two days without a shutdown. We invited the executive director of the company to stand at the gate and shake the hands of all the staff as they came in. By now, during recognition periods, you can see maintenance, engineering, and human resource people all celebrating together. The team has been built across functions, without anyone from the top having to say, "You will be a team."

As an objective measure of success, running hours gave us a way to deflect racial tensions. The measure did not show who was running it, but only that all the systems were operating to support that cause. The measure gave the unions something to talk about openly without any fear of addressing white or black issues. Last year, in an Eskom-wide meeting where we showed our poor performance from the year before, one of the white union leaders stood up and said, "I don't like that slide. You will not see Duvha at the bottom next year." When we broke the record at seventy-two, there was an amazing change in the whole plant. We earned respect, and it wasn't a black or white issue, because we all did it.

The tension and poor morale, in retrospect, actually helped change the climate. It made us reconsider our autocratic ways. Now union members at other plants, including some of the "stars" of the system, are saying, "We want to be more like Duvha."

MANAGEMENT STYLE

When you set tough targets, you have to recognize that you will not achieve them alone. You have to get out of the way and create a climate that allows other people to buy into the objectives and then work on them with commitment.

In meetings with union leaders, I don't take the position on the other side of the table. I walk around and shake the hand of every person in the room. By now, we have developed informal relationships, which means that in a crunch, we can break the tension by talking informally. Sometimes neither side is in control; you're both dealing with the same external environment. It won't help to be the more clever negotiator.

We had a situation like that when Eskom changed its policy on company-supported housing. In the past, this policy had favored whites. Now, if we switched to favoring blacks at the expense of whites, it would disrupt all business performance due to labor tensions. So we had to help the blacks to be patient while incrementally helping them, and getting the whites to understand that they would have to let go of some privileges. You can only do this, as management, if you realize that you are not enough of a genius to dictate what should happen. The people have to be comfortable with the environment.

The closest comparison to my style of leadership and teamwork is one I observed from an all-black power line construction team. Their task was very hard and required full cooperation from everyone involved. Traditional white-supervised construction gangs (in, say, the railways) are very unproductive; the supervisor sits in a truck, watching a team of laborers work, never doing anything physical himself. But with these construction teams, the supervisor is almost always one of the hardest-working people; he might be digging poles himself. Someone else, with an appropriate voice, might spend the whole day singing, so people can keep time to the rhythm. The others are not envious of him. The benefits (including their wages) may be different for different positions, but they achieve their success together.

I've tried to create the same climate with our management team here. As pioneers, we recognize that the change in the environment will come only from our joint efforts. Each of the four functional managers—operations, maintenance, engineering, and human resources—presides once a month over our weekly meetings. They set the agenda, and run the meeting. If I don't agree with their decisions, then I say, "I'd like to influence this decision. Let's think again." As opposed to saying, "You can't do that." Even if I don't attend the meeting, the business continues.

There are still many problems. We rarely get time to sit informally and chat about ourselves. We interact when there's a task; then we disappear. Many of us are still dealing with the baggage of the past.

About two years after coming here to Duvha, for instance, I first told a group of managers here about my experiences back in 1986, when I wasn't allowed to use the restroom. When I finished, there was dead silence as the story sunk in. Then people said, "My, you're so positive about the future." It was almost as if they expected me to be angry, still. There are many other similar stories that black people could tell, but this one struck home because it was about this same station. Now, as the manager, I am responsible for this plant's hospitality to visitors. But I am not responsible alone.

5 "How Are We Hindering Our Management?"

Leverage for getting your boss to "walk the talk"

Jennifer Kemeny, Senior Consultant, Innovation Associates

Time and time again, I have seen direct reports complain about their managers. The bosses have problems with communication. They don't want to let go of power and control. They can't get anything done. People who send such a message assume that management will heed it, and that things will (perhaps) change. But executives feel frustrated with that sort of message. From their perspectives, they are trying to communicate, but no one listens; their direct reports seem to lack initiative; and organizational inertia blocks their actions. The entire situation can become a tragic rat hole of lost opportunity, in which nobody knows what to do, and nobody feels responsible.

Notice the vicious cycle at play. The more frustration executives feel, the more that subordinates resent management for holding them back. And vice versa. Subordinates often assume that management is solely responsible, but *either party can break the cycle.* As a direct report, you may have more leverage than you think for making the first move. Applying the same emotion and passion with which you castigate management, you can set in motion a chain of events that may put a stop to it.

This can start in a meeting with one simple agenda item: "How are we hindering our management from doing the things we want them to do?" In my experience, the answers can usually be phrased in terms of mental models held by members of the team. For example:

- **"We have no right to initiate new activities."** This attitude often leads to a vicious waiting game. Management makes a request, gets an unsatisfactory response, and performs the task themselves. The direct reports assume, therefore, that management is intent on keeping control. So they wait for specific directions. Management interprets this as lassitude and becomes skeptical and doubtful about the direct reports' initiative. And the cycle continues . . .
- **"We can act, but only after the management dictates are fully spelled out."** In fact, management typically can't spell out its strategies and policies without the direct reports' contribution.
- **"You can trust someone completely—or not at all."** Trust actually grows in small, incremental steps. You can build trust over time by thinking about small ways to turn around a relationship.
- **"It's not right for me to challenge my boss."** People with this mental model expect that their boss will often challenge them, but it is disrespectful to do the converse. But a boss who isn't challenged by other perspectives will be ineffective. (If you feel your boss resents being challenged, consider the style of challenge you use.)
- **"Management doesn't tell us what's going on."** When I hear this, I want to know: "How often have you asked them? Do you let them know why it's important that you get this information? Have you explained why the managers' form of communication is not adequate?"
- **"Management can't, or won't, accept any help from us."** One group of direct reports wrote out their view of the management team:

"Incompetent. Incapable. Uncaring. Unaware." Then they talked through these mental models and the "data" they had of specific management behavior, and realized that the management team members were painfully aware of their own inadequacies, under pressure from their own bosses, and feeling stuck. Having seen the management group in that light, it was a lot easier to offer help. It's amazing to see the response when people walk into a boss's office and say, in a friendly tone of voice: "Would you like a little help on this problematic issue?" Nearly every boss responds positively and amiably if the offer is genuine and backed up with capabilities.

■ **"Executives pull the strings and the organization does what they want."** Innovation Associates founder Charlie Kiefer tells a story about a fast-track manager who can't wait to be CEO. He knows that, once he gets there, he will pull all the strings and levers to make the organization finally work. He ultimately makes it to the top. On his first day as CEO, he walks into his big, beautiful, modern office. Sure enough, underneath the huge desk there are dozens of levers and buttons, just as he's always imagined. He starts pulling the levers and pushing the buttons—and they're not connected to anything! (Telling this story to a group of CEOs always elicits fervent groans.)

Consider how you would act differently if you held this mental model of the executive leaders: They want your help but they don't know how to ask for it. You have the information they want but they don't know how to get it. They wield formal power but in practice feel ineffective. Just as an experiment, try on this mental model: "Being led means helping my boss to lead . . ."

6 Reflections for an Executive Leader

Convened by Charlotte Roberts

These executive leaders have been deeply involved in designing and leading profound change initiatives. We asked them to imagine that

If you are an executive leader who has gone through a change process and would like to contribute your own questions to ask oneself as an executive leader, we would be interested in considering them for publication on our Web site. For more information, see http://www.fieldbook.com/exec.html.

someone called them and said, "I'm an executive leader of a corporation. We're about to begin a large-scale learning initiative. What questions should I ask myself, before we even begin?"

PHIL CARROLL, FORMER CEO, SHELL OIL; CURRENT PRESIDENT AND CEO, FLUOR CORPORATION

■ **"Why am I doing this?** Just to do things differently than my predecessor? Is this change for change's sake? What is the fundamental business justification?" It takes a long time, and a lot of personal soul-searching to answer these questions. If you don't have answers—not just glib answers, but responses that inspire your absolute passion about the need for change—then I would not begin. Not every organization needs a process of radical change. If you do not think you have a strong case for the change; if you are not personally convinced that it will produce very positive results in the long term; and if you are not committed, in your gut, to making it happen, then you could waste a lot of time and energy, and divert people's intentions.

I have suggested that executive leaders ask themselves this: "Suppose that some of the company directors said, 'We think you're distracting the organization, and you ought to go back to the old ways.' Would I acquiesce? Or would I say, 'Get yourself another CEO'? If I had to choose between the profound change process and my job, would I give up my job?"

If your answer is, "No," or even "I'm not sure," then you probably ought to go for a more conventional approach: selling off parts of the business, making incremental improvements, or restructuring.

■ **"How and when do we tell the board of directors?"** Ultimately, you have an obligation to inform them. One of the underlying principles of the entire effort is transparency and openness about how companies operate. If you intend to pursue that as a principle and still keep the board in the dark, you have to wonder a little bit about the integrity of your thinking.

At Shell Oil, however, we did not engage the board of directors in thinking about the problems of the company until the transformation was already under way. They have to be prepared first, to have some context and understanding. They need to be sure that the CEO they have hired is stable. So you have to go out and take some risks, produce some results, and hopefully come back with both your failures and some success stories. When you open up to the board, that will be a difficult learning experience for them. They will tend to want to make decisions for you. But you don't want your board of directors voting on whether or not the process of profound change ought to go forward. You want the wonderful insights they can provide, and to learn from their experiences.

■ **"What am I doing?** Is this effort producing results or is it not?" You need to have confidence in yourself, your ideas, and your leadership. At the same time, you need to recognize that you will make mistakes, and to look for ways to correct them. There is an underlying premise that if you create this new world, it will not only produce outstanding results for the shareholders; it will be a better place to work and it will add more value in the communities where it operates. But you've got to have balance; if you are not putting the financial numbers up on the scoreboard for the shareholder, you have to ask yourself, "Am I adding value, or am I burning up resources playing games?"

DON LINDEMANN, CEO, CITIZENS GAS & COKE UTILITY

■ **"Why am I doing this?"** It was obvious fifteen years ago that our industry was going to change dramatically. In our considered judgment, the organization as it was would not be able to cope. Transformation was essential to the continued existence of the organization.

Had we not asked this question, we might have started a transformation just for the sake of transformation, because someone else had been doing it, or because it was the fad of the month. This might have resulted in an unfocused, fragmented approach, and we might not have understood enough about the driving forces to maintain the momentum.

■ **"Do I truly understand what I'm doing, and its consequences?"** When we started, I didn't appreciate how difficult it would be. We knew we wanted to emulate companies like Johnsonville Foods and W. L. Gore, but we had not realized how much baggage we were bringing with us from our previous eighty-five years as a regulated monopoly.

Transforming an organization is like trying to remodel a house as you're living in it. You start with a budget and time frame in mind, but then your spouse has some new ideas; the contractor runs into some unexpected problems; and the scope of the work gets broader. It's not just that the costs get higher; the project takes on a life of its own. Similarly, at Citizens Gas we thought that total quality management principles (particularly those developed by Dr. W. Edwards Deming) would, in themselves, lead us to transform. But reality was not so crisp. Our pay and reward system, and the way we counseled our work associates about the need for development were not appropriate to our new requirements. If we had asked this question in advance, we might not have anticipated all the unintended effects, but it would have helped attune us to the amount of unpredictability we would encounter.

■ **"Am I willing to stay the course?"** Managers initiate many solutions because we think that the answer will solve our problems. Two or three years later, when the problem remains unsolved, we give up and look elsewhere. We need to learn to stay the course. True sustainable change and transformation is very difficult work that almost never ends.

■ **"Is the organization ready for this?"** In our organization, younger front line people seemed to ache for the opportunity to make a contribution. Older employees would say: "I understand why you're changing the organization, and I wish you well, but it's too late in my career. I would rather not be involved." Unfortunately, I think that's the way a lot of CEOs feel, once they get within sight of retirement.

We had the most resistance from the upper levels of management. "I've got a full plate now," they would say. "I can't take on any more, I've got 'real work' to do." In retrospect, I think we were too patient. We should have looked earlier to see how ready people in leadership positions were for this transition. And we should have moved some of the people who weren't ready out of leadership positions.

TRAVIS BURCH, CEO, BURCH-LOWE, INC.

■ **"Am I willing to change?"** If you're a senior leader, you can easily pay superficial attention to a significant learning initiative, without fully realizing that it will require changes in your own behavior to make it successful. You can spend much of your time in a comfort zone that's not very comfortable, but at least it's familiar. So how do you overcome that fear of uncertainty that prevents you from stepping outside that zone? That requires more than a superficial commitment.

For example, the energy is much greater in this company when we've given everyone a chance to have input in our long-term planning and thinking, instead of just involving a cross-section of people without feedback from the organization as a whole. But if you want to create shared vision, are you personally equipped to make space for others to contribute? Will you be ready when they ask for changes in the organization's structure or direction? How will you give people explicit information and the space to respond to it?

■ **"Am I prepared to rethink our organization's purpose?"** My brother Gregg, who is the president and COO of our Highway/Heavy Division, is finishing up his MBA at Georgia State. Not long ago, his finance professor said: "The only strategy anyone needs to know is this: R is greater than K." In other words, if your returns are larger than the cost of capital, you need not worry about any other goal.

But that's a pointless strategy for most of the people here. It's not very compelling to build wealth for shareholders, if you're not a shareholder. We see public companies making stupid decisions sometimes, because they're trying to make R greater than K every quarter. R being greater than K is simply the blood that keeps things flowing so we can accomplish our actual purpose: to develop the organization, to develop solutions for our customers, and to have engaged people here who enjoy what they do.

JOHN LOBBIA, FORMER CEO, THE DETROIT EDISON COMPANY

■ **"Am I willing to accept the ambiguity, and the lack of clarity?"** When we talk to the board of directors or a nuclear review committee about a nuclear power plant that's in trouble, they don't want to hear about transformational learning or empowerment. They want to know, "When the hell are you going to get control of that thing?" But in truth, most of the improvement at our nuclear power plant today is coming from the ambiguous, unmeasurable learning stuff, not the old style of control.

I sit in meetings at the board, and I can't even explain it sometimes. "We've got a transformational plan," I want to say. "But I don't know what to say about it." On the one hand, I can point to successes. For example, we've begun to forge a partnership with our union, moving forward from an extremely contentious situation. We have a long way to go, and I understand that this kind of work goes on forever. But when I see areas where we are making progress, it sustains me, and keeps me going. Often, I've described these efforts as team building, but it is really more about understanding yourself.

I went to a meeting of the top thirty CEOs in the Detroit area yesterday, and when I sat back I could see the level of group-think as they talked about an issue. Yet if I leaned up on the table to get involved, I slipped right into the same mind-set, thinking and analyzing the same way everyone else at the table did. The learning work is about trying to figure how to pull yourself back from that automatic response, to listen differently and hear not just the words someone is saying, but the message that the person is trying to tell you beneath the words.

I keep trying to make things clear and unambiguous. I keep asking, "What are the two or three guideposts in the learning organization work?" If I find them, I can drive the pieces. But I never find them. I find one that works for a while, and takes me through another segment of the process. Then it evaporates, and I have to find a new one. I asked Peter Senge and he said, "If you find a single, central framework that lasts for more than a year, give me a call, and we'll go out and consult together. Because maybe there isn't one."

I stay with it, however, because I've tried enough times to do things the more authoritarian way, and I've seen that way not work.

■ **"Am I willing to keep going, even when I don't get continuous success?"** What happens when I don't constantly see the curve going up? Will I revert to the old style or will I catch myself?

I have learned to be confident by seeing many cases where people slipped on performance or blew their budget—but then came back and rebuilt the results themselves, using the learning orientation to do so. If I could see us go through an economic downturn and sustain our success, I would feel more confident still. I don't know how sour things get when you have to make the decision to cut back and lay people off. Can you build the capabilities, in your people and your process, to get through a period of poor results more effectively?

DR. ROGER GILBERTSON, CEO, MERIT CARE HEALTH SYSTEM

■ **"Do I have the energy and resolve to be fully engaged in effecting this major transformation?"** Recently, the president of another health system told me he had spent $3 million on a consultant to help facilitate an acceptance of change. I said that in my experience you had to do about 90 percent of it yourself. True transformation can only happen from within.

This in turn means trying to understand your own strengths and vulnerabilities, the characteristics that will help you or hinder you. "How committed am I to making this happen? What is my tenacity? How confident am I that I'm doing the right thing? Am I confident enough to accept the input of others, and to trust their wisdom, rather than only my own?"

- **"How am I going to deal with the frustrations and pressures of a change?"** The answer depends on understanding the enormity of the change you are embarking on. If you let yourself get frustrated, you can jump and skip significant parts of the process, and that, in turn, could scuttle the entire initiative. "What resources will I need to sustain myself and manage the stress?" You need to take care of yourself. "Where is my safe haven? Whom can I go to candidly? Where can I have dialogue in a safe environment?"

- **"What major things must I be concerned about to make this work?"** In planning our governance redesign, we set up a system where nearly two hundred people had major input, telling us what worked and what didn't work. That was fine, but we didn't understand that we needed to do the same thing about three or four months into the implementation phase, when people were no longer having a good time.

  We had taken a linear approach to implementation, rolling out the first phase of the change process through the entire organization at once. We did this because I like order. Most people like order. But it doesn't work. I didn't realize I would have to manage that feeling of loss of order. Organizational change is a complex problem, with many interactive things going on simultaneously. I didn't realize how tremendously chaotic and disorderly that can be.

- **"Can the organization tolerate poor performance for a period of time?"** Even in the best cases, performance will decline at first because of the concentration of energy and effort you need with such a huge initiative. The board and top management need to understand this, so you can manage it. The increased efficiencies will emerge over a longer period of time, while your costs increase at the beginning. You need to understand very clearly the time at which you expect to see cost savings and improved performance.

BILL O'BRIEN, FORMER PRESIDENT, HANOVER INSURANCE COMPANY

■ **"What do I believe about people?"** If you have a deterministic view of people—that they come programmed by their genes, there's only a 10 percent margin of improvement and 20 percent of them will screw you if they get a chance—then that belief, in itself, will severely limit your ability to lead profound change.

On the other hand, if you believe, as I do, that there's an enormous reservoir of untapped potential in each person, then you will be better equipped to foster a culture of individual growth. This does not mean holding a naïve view of human nature, ignoring the "devil in people" or letting people take advantage of the company. It means holding the belief, down to the core of your action, that the company's total performance represents the total of the actions and decisions of every employee—not just the upper 5 percent.

In the popular view, the decisions of the upper 5 percent of the hierarchy are most influential. But in today's highly complex, diversified business world, that's bunk. Consider the restaurant on your corner. It may be owned by a conglomerate. But its profit depends on the front line. If the bartender has a personality that makes people feel welcome, it can mean 25 to 30 percent in profitability from long-term, steady customers. The same is true for the quality of service at a gas station, or in a manufacturing business. These days, Shell will not out-oil Texaco. They're both good at technology. DuPont will not out-plastic Dow. But any company could out-socialize its competitors at the point of sale, without any capital investment, simply by recognizing the value of its people.

■ **"What do I believe is the essence of my business?"** The essence of a technology company is inventiveness. Success depends on keeping your product out front technologically. The essence of a transportation company is reliability. People want the plane to take off when they get in. The last thing they want is too much inventiveness.

At Hanover, we asked ourselves: "What's the essence of a property and liability insurance company?" Ultimately, we said it was twofold. In part, insurance depends on the management of probabilities: Would you write a particular insurance deal at 20 cents? How about at 12 cents? In that sense, insurance businesses are like networks of bookie joints, betting on high school basketball games.

But the business also depends upon quality relationships with customers. I have seen insurance companies throw away fortunes by moving into the wholesale use of the telephone to settle claims. This worked all right for small claims, like a broken windshield. But insurance managers who understood the importance of relationships knew when to stop. They knew that a mere telephone response to a bad bodily injury would send claimants running to trial lawyers.

Companies that tried extensive telephone settlement found out the hard way: At first, it was beautiful. They got rid of many high-salaried claims adjusters. But those savings, and then some, got eaten up in litigation costs, lost customers, and expensive settlements.

■ **"What do I, personally, stand for?"** If you are the most senior executive in the company, your personal values represent a major influence on the organization's values. Personally, I believe that God's work can be done in the commercial marketplace. And I believe that personal fulfillment depends on both work and family. That is why, as a leader, I have taken stands for creating a workplace that helps people find fulfillment, get stretched, receive a certain amount of tough love, and raise their families with dignity.

LEADING MINDS
by Howard Gardner (New York: Basic Books, 1995)

Leading Minds is a brilliant analysis of the leader as creator, teller, and actor of stories, of the audiences that leaders must bring along with them and the "counter-stories" they must overcome. Leaders who understand and use this long, fascinating, and readable book will add greatly to their effectiveness. "It is important for leaders to know their stories," writes Gardner, "to get them straight, to communicate them effectively, and, above all, to embody in their lives the stories that they tell." Gardner's earlier works explored child development and learning; he argues that adults have domains in which they are relatively sophisticated and domains in which the "five-year-old mind" continues to reign. The success of the leader will be closely related to his or her ability to link to each of these domains. In carefully chosen vignettes, he shows how a variety of leaders—including Margaret Mead, Robert Oppenheimer, Alfred P. Sloan, George Marshall, Pope John XXIII, Eleanor Roosevelt, Martin Luther King, Margaret Thatcher, and Mahatma Gandhi—succeeded and failed at leadership. — Bill Godfrey

The Challenges of Sustaining Transformation

Sometime during the first year or two, your pilot work probably moves out of the "initiating" phase of profound change. Business and personal results occur and recur reliably enough that, while you can't take them for granted, you can be confident in your ability to create them. Work feels increasingly like a community; your efforts are taking you in an agreeable direction, and you feel that the support you need is available. Your group has clear goals, which everyone finds relevant; and you have discovered, after a while, that your new methods save you more than enough time to put them into practice.

Now your troubles begin. As your original "seedlings" begin taking root, they come into contact with new features of their environment, such as predators, rivals, and other life-forms that will resist the presence of a new entity. Your task is now to sustain life, not just over a few months, but over a period of years. You can't ignore the environment; you must carve out an identity for your pilot group within it.

That is why your concerns turn to boundaries. As in all learning activity, your new endeavors cross "internal boundaries": the individual thoughts and feelings of members of the pilot group. They also broach the "external boundaries" of the group. You are increasingly dealing with organizational culture; you can no longer isolate your team from the larger-scale priorities of your company or agency, from its values (as the organizational leaders practice them), from its ways of measuring success, and from its members' attitudes about you.

Hence the challenges of the next three chapters:

- **Fear and anxiety**: triggered by openness and candor among members of the pilot group.
- **Assessment and measurement**: the gap between your change initiative and the organization's ways of measuring results.
- **True believers and nonbelievers**: the tendency for profound change to fall into an escalating dynamic of perceived threat and siege mentality.

VII. Fear and Anxiety

"This stuff is _____!"

1 The Challenge

Mutual reflection. Open and candid conversation. Questioning of old beliefs and assumptions. Learning to let go. Awareness of how our own actions create the systemic structures that produce our problems. Developing these learning capabilities lies at the heart of profound change. On one hand, they are significant, personally rewarding developments that enhance working relationships and enable people to collectively produce results they truly care about. But learning capabilities are also profoundly challenging.

In most conventional work settings, harmony is maintained through a facade of harmony: "Don't rock the boat." In fact, what passes for teamwork in most work settings is the "smooth surface," the apparent absence of any problems. Everyone sits quietly through the staff meeting, then talks about how they really feel in the rest room afterward, or over a drink that evening. This type of harmony is at risk in any process of profound change. As new learning capabilities develop, people start feeling the confidence to raise challenging, potentially conflictual issues—the issues that must be addressed to make real changes.

Developing collective learning capabilities is like lowering the water level until the smooth surface starts to disappear. The rocks that were previously under the surface appear. They were there all along. Everyone knew they were there. But we colluded to keep them covered up. We colluded by supporting managers who lacked the courage to confront them. We operated in a "silo" mentality in which people handled

Michel's meeting

Finance problems only in their own functional areas, and ignored the difficult interactions between the silos. We covered up past mistakes, including ones that continue to cause problems. And we discussed these issues only in private, in ways that reinforced our resignation and hopelessness and guaranteed that they remained undiscussable. Ultimately, we colluded in our shared belief that all of this would never change, so there was no point in learning how to bring conflictual issues into the open. Now the rocks are starting to show up, and everyone is a bit nervous.

Seeing the rocks start to appear is not equally threatening for everyone. Some people feel relatively little threat; their aspirations of greater openness and effectiveness more or less outweigh their anxieties. But others are more guarded. They may not entirely like the traditional way of working, but they are adept at coping with it. They know what to expect. Some bosses, for example, have lived so long in environments where fear and intimidation are the norms, they can't imagine an alternative. And they don't know if they can handle the change. "We all have our 'gorillas,'" one truck plant manager once put it. "We may keep them in the closet much of the time. But we know how to intimidate people and we know how to deal with being intimidated. In fact, for most of our careers it was the only way we knew."

Fear and anxiety should not be seen as "problems" to be cured. They are natural, even healthy responses to changes in the level of openness. Openness does not merely require the willingness to speak one's mind. It also requires the willingness to listen openly, to recognize the existence of different views—and, if need be, to change one's mind. This is very threatening, because it is harder to cling to a sense of certainty. Life becomes more contingent. People don't just feel more out of control. They *are* more out of control. It's appropriate to feel some discomfort if they don't know where this new openness will take them.

not in MTK's world

In one engineering team, after several months of work, conversations that had formerly been careful, formal affairs, began to shift to the point where people said what they really thought, and hashed out disagreements on the spot. When a newcomer sat in on his first meeting, his immediate response was, "You've got to be kidding." Then he went on to say, "If anybody had said anything remotely like that on [my previous team], he would've been killed. Problems would have to reach a level of disaster before people would ever talk candidly."

To some degree, everyone has fears of exposure, of making a mistake, of showing ignorance and of accidentally hurting others through inappropriate candor and behavior. These are very reasonable concerns in

We have borrowed the "lowering the waterline" metaphor from the Total Quality movement, where people have noticed for years that, once a process is more "in control" when variation is reduced, the more significant, more difficult problems finally become visible.

Quoted from *A Car Launch With Heart: The "AutoCo Epsilon" Learning History*, by George Roth, Art Kleiner, et al. (New York: Oxford University Press, 1999), p. 16.

the new environment of a change initiative. If people believe they have no fear, they are probably very good at denying their own emotions. The essence of the challenge of fear and anxiety lies in recognizing these natural responses and allowing people the opportunity to grow their own capacity for openness.

Fear and anxiety is included in the challenges of *sustaining* change because it only develops after some progress has been made in developing learning capabilities. Often, people are so focused on their progress that they may ignore the problems that are developing as a consequence. Here, more than ever, the words of biologist Humberto Maturana apply: "Every movement is being inhibited as it occurs." Effective leaders learn to recognize growing fear and anxiety as indicators of progress, and they learn how to acknowledge and deal with it, both within themselves and within others.

Indeed, the challenge of fear and anxiety may well be the most frequently faced challenge in sustaining profound change, and the most difficult to overcome. One reason is that it manifests in diverse symptoms. In fact, the authors found it impossible to identify one catchphrase with which to exemplify this challenge, precisely because people express their defensiveness in so many ways.

There is forthright negation: "This learning stuff is a waste of time. We're not here for therapy; we're here to serve customers."

There is objection to its ambiguity and alleged side effects: "You've got to be kidding me. This stuff is out of control. Besides, raising all these negative issues only demoralizes people."

There is superficial support: "This learning stuff is very interesting. It reminds me of a lot of stuff I studied in school." Then in private, the same person says, "But it has nothing to do with the business."

And there is silence. People are afraid to say anything that might be interpreted as countering the "new party line."

This diversity of responses led the authors to simply recognize that there is no one way to categorize this challenge through what people say. So we elected to use the open-ended catchphrase, "This stuff is _____." People may fill that blank with any number of comments that express their fear and anxiety. The first task in dealing with this challenge is to listen deeply to what is being said (or not said) and how it is being said. Leaders must listen to "the music behind the words," ever sensitive to the natural fear that people may be experiencing.

This diversity of responses can also lead champions of change into countless defenses of their efforts and low leverage ameliorations of

The quote comes from: "Biosphere, Homosphere, and Robosphere: what has that to do with business?" by Humberto Maturana; a presentation at the Society for Organizational Learning (SoL), Member's Meeting, Amherst, MA, June 23 and 24, 1998, re-created by Pille Bunnell; available online. See http://www.fieldbook.com.maturana.html.

symptomatic complaints. But it is hard to fight defensiveness with more defensiveness. It is important to recognize that underneath each of these defensive comments, there are generic, recurring questions that arise for us all in the context of deep change, held so deeply that they may not come to the surface easily:

- **Am I safe? Am I vulnerable?** In some companies, people talk about putting on their corporate "mask" when they step in the building, if only to protect themselves. Now they are implicitly being asked to take off the masks and reveal their true reactions—for example, to openly show disagreement with the boss if they feel it, in a constructive manner. How can they be sure that, if they speak openly, this won't be used against them later, by a colleague? How do they know they won't be stereotyped or scapegoated?
- **Am I adequate? Do I measure up?** In the highly competitive atmosphere of many organizations, people succeed by learning to "play the game." Now the "game" may be shifting, and players wonder whether their lack of competence will be exposed. They know they can put on a good slide presentation; but can they really produce results, inquire collaboratively, and learn to listen? And if they fear they can't, then they may be concerned that their career is in jeopardy.
- **Can I trust myself? Can I trust others?** In the past, managers who have lost their temper, taken advantage of people, or acted as a "stooge" have been able to treat these episodes as inconsequential lapses. Now, however, they are expected to practice new values, including the value of treating people with respect and grace. But they know from experience that they can't always control their temper, their abusiveness, or their passive-aggressive destructiveness. They may not trust themselves fully, or they may not trust the people around them. They worry that it's only a matter of time before old abuses resurface.

We want to thank Fred Kofman, Bill Isaacs, Jennifer Kemeny, Joe Jaworski, Sue Zupansky, Michael Goodman, and others for helping to articulate various aspects of this challenge. The questions in the thought balloon ("Am I safe? Am I adequate? Can I trust myself?") are loosely based on David Kantor's three heroic modes. See p. 262.

THE UNDERLYING DYNAMICS OF FEAR AND ANXIETY

As in many limits to growth situations, success creates its own forces of limitation. As learning capabilities develop, candor and openness increase in the pilot group. If *people's* capacity for openness does not grow in parallel, an "openness gap" develops between the growing candor on the one hand and the limited capacity for openness on the

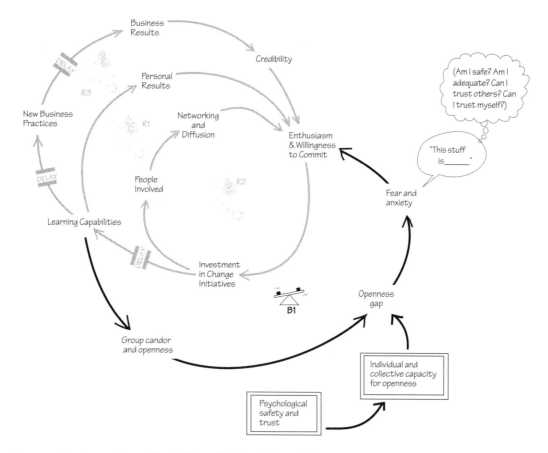

other. People do not have the skills to deal with the difficult issues that are arising. They do not have the confidence in themselves and others to negotiate complex issues that may not have simple answers. They are unfamiliar with how their managers (and others) will react when "diverging subjects" are explored and no action plan is established. This limited capacity for openness results in a gap that can cause the promising movement that has occurred to this point to grind to a halt. When this happens, people do not experience an openness gap. They experience fear and anxiety, which can be expressed in many ways. Regardless of how they are expressed, anxiety and fear affect people's enthusiasm and willingness to commit to any transformational initiative.

The underlying limit that people are bumping into in this process is the capacity for openness and, in turn, the level of psychological safety and trust within the pilot group. According to our theory, there are two

The growth of learning capabilities produces a corresponding growth in group candor and openness. This can create an "openness gap" and resulting fear and anxiety if there is not a corresponding growth in the capacity for openness. Developing new learning capabilities plays two roles in this challenge: as both the source of problems (through increasing candor) and the potential resolution (through capacity for openness).

primary contributors in developing capacity for openness: enhanced learning capabilities and psychological safety. While many individuals and teams strive for openness, most do not succeed because effective openness is not just a matter of intent—it also requires skills. For example, raising difficult issues without invoking defensiveness is a highly skillful behavior. (Many of the skills involved in the disciplines of "mental models" and "dialogue and team learning" directly contribute to the capacity for openness in a team.) These skills develop as part of any effective learning-oriented change initiative. But they are invariably spread unevenly within the pilot group, especially in the early phases of change. Moreover, they are also the source of the increasing candor, which gives rise to the growing openness gap.

For these reasons, developing the capacity for openness, especially in the early phases of an initiative, also depends on the overall environment of safety that the pilot group creates for itself. By safety, we do not mean the absence of risk. All learning involves taking risks. Rather, we mean the conditions which enable appropriate risk taking. Psychological safety depends on finding a workable balance between aspiration and trepidation. Aspiration drives learning—for example, the desire to resolve deep issues, to build new business capabilities to serve customer needs, to shorten time to market through increasing intelligence rather than increasing effort. But, if people perceive that their reputation or well being is at stake in order to learn, they may be unwilling to go forward. Like the young child who swings one arm freely knowing the other is firmly in her mother's hand, so too does all learning involve the interplay of risk taking and safety.

In some ways, this underlying limit or constraint is similar to the limit that drives the "walking the talk" limiting process (Chapter 6). But whereas the "trust gap" was driven by the credibility of management's commitment, the openness gap reflects the ability of management, and other members of the pilot team, to create psychological safety. Many managers are deeply committed, yet don't know how to create safety. In fact, it has been the experience of the authors that many results-oriented managers, trying to drive their agendas forward, have dramatically increased the fear and anxiety on their teams. Moreover, while management credibility is vital in initiating change, safety is significant in sustaining change. The challenge of fear and anxiety often continues to be an issue long after the challenge of "walking the talk" no longer concerns people.

STRATEGIES FOR MEETING THE CHALLENGE OF FEAR AND ANXIETY

Leverage over the limiting process of fear and anxiety can be gained in several ways. These correspond, conceptually, to (1) reducing the openness gap through accelerating the development of safety and the capacity for openness, and (2) weakening the consequences of an openness gap once it emerges. Most of the following strategies deal primarily with the former; the last two deal explicitly with the latter.

- **Start small and build momentum before confronting difficult issues.** As Jennifer Kemeny of Innovation Associates notes, the mere announcement that, "We're going to get to the bottom of the worst abuses around here," can "stress up" the level of fear and anxiety and thus make it harder to deal with the issues in practice. Many people don't know whether they can even handle confronting small, relatively private "little disgraces"; they're even more threatened by the thought of public "witch hunts" around major business blunders. It is much more effective to take incremental steps, dealing with small fears and anxieties, and building up the capability in the long run for handling the large ones. "Working with reflection and inquiry skills," says Kemeny, to "explore simple things, like differences in interpreting one another's remarks, can over time help people become capable of taking on something 'hot,' like the causes of poor performance, in a way that doesn't feel like leaping off a cliff."

- **Avoid "frontal assaults."** Fear cannot be commanded or exhorted away, nor can safety be mandated. One cannot "drive out fear" directly, despite W. Edwards Deming's exhortations to do so. (We wonder if Deming was being deliberately ironic.) The only sustainable way to build psychological safety is to create an environment conducive to safety, in which people gradually feel more and more mutuality and trust with one another. It takes time and dedication to develop these conditions—which may be one reason why fear and anxiety are so prevalent in most organizations. As Fred Simon, former Ford Lincoln Continental program manager, puts it: "Our experience (with a three-year-long learning effort involving hundreds of people) was that real trust only increased gradually over time, as people developed an increasing desire to help one another—and as we evolved a strong psychological safety net. We grew to recognize that, if people offered to help one another, they would not be at risk. The safety net developed as a by-product of really understanding one another. When all is said and done, the bottom line of any real learning process is

[handwritten margin note:] Nice to see Deming critique for a change

This quote comes from an interview conducted in 1997 by Innovation Associates consultant Robert Hanig for a British Petroleum conference.

Quoted from *A Car Launch With Heart: The "AutoCo Epsilon" Learning History*, by George Roth, Art Kleiner, et al. (New York: Oxford University Press, 1999), p. 28.

The Electric Maze is a useful tool for learning to value breakdowns. It sets people up to find a path through a checkerboard labyrinth, where any misstep might provoke a loud buzzer. People can feel paralyzed by anxiety, unwilling to take a step, even though they are penalized for standing still. They learn how their "wrong" answers lead to the discovery of the "right" answer. See *The Fifth Discipline Fieldbook*, p. 403.

trust, but you cannot create trust directly. You can only create conditions conducive to trusting."

■ **Set an example of openness.** Line leaders like Simon, as well as executive leaders, realize that the most effective use of hierarchical power to engender trust occurs when people in leadership positions become effective role models of openness. "Vulnerability is a very important element in leadership," says Fluor and former Shell Oil CEO Phil Carroll. "The truth is that your flaws are there, no matter what you want to say, and if you try to hide them from people's perceptions, it destroys your ability to be consistent. If you don't have a fundamental commitment to the truth and telling the truth, you can't lead. And telling the truth is so much more difficult than just 'not lying.'"

For bosses to exemplify openness means a great deal of unlearning, by bosses and subordinates alike. "It took [us] bosses literally eight months to learn how to quit being bosses," commented a team leader in a multiple-year project. "When we started, we knew all the answers. That's why we were bosses. At least one of us always knew that our answer to the problem was the right answer; and boy did we defend our positions! But as we began to use the [reflection and inquiry tools] and practice with them [we started to listen to the rest of the team members]. Can you imagine the bosses listening? We quit telling them what to do. We started to inquire. We started to challenge their perceptions."

■ **Learn to see diversity as an asset.** In meetings, acknowledge and respect the different views, skills, and learning styles that different people bring. Some people will be enthusiastic; others will be skeptical. Allow both views to be heard. The more people sense that they are heard and recognized, the more completely they will trust their leadership—and one another.

■ **Use breakdowns as opportunities for learning.** For a talented leader, unanticipated breakdowns offer unique, precious opportunities to demonstrate real trust. When people see that they are not punished when a breakdown occurs, that there is a willingness to share responsibility, and that there is genuine curiosity to learn how everyone can do better in the future, it can send a powerful signal of real trust. In the quality movement, people sometimes say, "A defect is a treasure," to indicate the potential learning that can occur when one really comes to understand the source of errors. Developing a similar curiosity about "defects" in our human systems is a hallmark of management transformation.

- **Do everything possible to ensure that participation in pilot groups and change initiatives is a matter of choice, not coercion.** Safety and trust are nurtured by perceived freedom of choice—even though this might appear to slow down a change process in the short term. Admittedly, it may not be practical to let a key team member "choose" to opt out of a particular phase of, say, a process redesign. Effective leaders handle this by holding back on their own coercive power, by allowing people to talk about the reasoning behind their reservations, and by continually checking with people: "Am I doing everything I can reasonably do to respect your choices and allow you to be heard?"

- **Remember that skills matter.** Do what you can to help people develop better skills of openness and inquiry. People who worry, for example, that "I'm not going to be good enough" are putting far more pressure on themselves than anyone else would. They need coaching and support to develop a kind of proprioceptive awareness of their own actions and the ways those actions come across.

   They may also need support to help deal with people close to them who don't want them to change. During one change initiative at Digital Equipment Corporation in the mid-1980s, a number of abrasive, withdrawn engineers became much more communicative and responsive. Then the Human Resources manager started getting calls from their spouses. "Stop messing around with my husband," one wife said. "He keeps coming home and asking how I feel. He's being nosy. I want you to snap him back to the way he was!"

- **As a manager, work to develop a common frame around vision and current reality**. Let people know that you recognize the gap between "where we want to be" and "where we are." Take modest steps to close the gap; let people know that you know it will take time. This is much less anxiety-provoking than having a boss who goes through a sudden conversion and storms into the office saying, "Everything's got to change." Let people know that you expect steady progress, but that you know there will be setbacks and mishaps. Consult with them about how to judge success and failure, and when to look for evidence of success.

- **Don't shoot yourself in the foot.** When they become aware of increasing fear or anxiety, line or executive leaders often respond by pushing harder, thereby increasing anxiety. They talk about why the initiative is important, and remind people "how bad it will be if we do nothing at all." One CEO was so upset to learn that people regarded certain issues as undiscussable in his presence he insisted they all be put on the next meeting agenda of his team. "That will take care of it," he stated. In fact, the ensuing "official dialogue" served mainly to bury people's real feelings even deeper, along with strengthening their belief that nothing would ever really change in their traditional top-down culture.

Some bosses may even demand, in the name of "bringing all our undiscussables to the surface," that people volunteer information about their hidden feelings and past errors. Or they may insist on tackling tough issues, like diversity, environmental damage, or legal charges. All of this simply increases the dangerousness of the pilot group's atmosphere, which amplifies fear and anxiety even more.

■ **Remember, and remind people, that fear and anxiety are natural responses to the precariousness of a learning situation.** One executive, upon being told that his subordinates were saying they felt afraid, snapped, "Nobody in this organization has any fear!" If that was true, it meant nobody was learning. Learning, by definition, implies a willingness to be uncertain, and to figure things out as you go along. "If you feel comfortable," says Robert Hanig of Innovation Associates, "that probably means you're doing it wrong."

Most of these strategies fall into the province of local line leaders. If they are not skillful at building an environment of safety, such as in being a model and in working to reinforce freedom of choice and reducing blame, there is little that others can do to compensate.

However, other types of leaders can provide line leaders with the support they need to create these environments. Internal networkers can play an important part, especially in supporting ongoing capacity building. Executive leaders can play important mentoring roles to line leaders trying to understand the needs for safety and striving to balance pressing business needs with the time needed to build capacity for openness. In addition, effective executives can set a tone of vulnerability and compassion for the entire organization. If bosses of line leaders overreact to emerging fear and anxiety, then it is very difficult for local managers to not do likewise. And if an atmosphere of fear and anxiety pervades the entire organizational culture, then people in any "pocket" of safety will always feel vulnerable.

2 Gray Stamps

Rick Ross

Just about everybody in business has had this experience. A higher-up asks your opinion of a key decision. You figure out your answer, and make a good case. The higher-up listens, and you feel involved—until you find out, later, that the decision had already been made. Your opinion was moot. You were asked as a well-meaning attempt at "participative management," hoping to give you the impression you had a voice.

If you've been in that situation, how did it make you feel? Chances are, you felt foolish and excluded, especially if you gave the "wrong" answer. Next time, instead of answering honestly, you'll spend your time trying to figure out the answer that's already been decided. And you'll chalk up a little "gray stamp" in your mind against that person.

Gray stamps (a concept adapted from transactional analysis) are an all-too-common mental checkmark that people accumulate from all the petty hurts and betrayals that we bury within ourselves. If you ask people to name some things in their "left-hand column," their unspoken reactions when others speak, you'll typically hear about negatively charged emotion: Fury. Upset. Bitterness. Frustration. They can't dump it on the person who provoked it, and they can't forget it, so they save up gray stamps in their minds. Enough gray stamps makes a book, entitling the redeemer to a guilt-free act of abusiveness toward someone else. They deserve it, right? You've taken all their crap for so long.

Most gray stamps are negotiable. You can collect them at work, and cash them in at home—at the expense of the spouse, the kid, or the dog. (The result, of course, is that spouses, kids, and dogs save up their own gray stamps.) But every so often, you may acquire a gray stamp so pernicious, so miserable, that you put a name on it. Your spouse, kid, or dog doesn't get that one. It's reserved especially for, say, the person who asked your opinion without really wanting to know the answer.

Six months go by. In a meeting one day, you smile and let loose with some devastating comment aimed at this person. He or she reacts as if stabbed. Everyone else sits there, wondering, "What's going on here?" The answer is: You've finally cashed in your gray stamps.

Gray stamps are not healthy for individuals, but they're downright deadly for teams, particularly in change initiatives. They can linger for years; I know people who have been exchanging them since the 1970s.

What, then, can you do about it? The first step is to recognize it. Years ago, when I was a university administrator, I had thirty-two books

The discipline of mental models is covered in *The Fifth Discipline Fieldbook*, starting on p. 235. Particularly relevant is the "left-hand column" exercise, p. 246. Also see "Climbing Out of the Muck," on p. 120 of this book.

of gray stamps saved up for Bob, the academic vice president, with his name on every page. I finally redeemed them at a faculty meeting. Bob described a major problem facing the university and asked, "What do you want to do about it?" I knew he was heading for big trouble. The university president had told him, the day before, exactly what to do.

Should I intervene? I decided that, while it wasn't fair to kill Bob's career, I could let him kill it himself. I said nothing. Sure enough, the deans voted the opposite way that Bob had hoped. The following week, he had to announce that the president had rejected their vote, and was going to insist on his way. The faculty was furious. They wrote angry letters, and the episode led to a series of clashes that were thoroughly unnecessary and damaging.

Two years later, I realized I had played a role in allowing this to happen—simply because I had so many gray stamps on Bob. I realized then that, if I wanted any organization to be more healthy, I'd have to learn to talk through my gray stamps openly. (Fred Kofman calls this "processing the toxic waste.") I would have to learn how to recraft my conversations to be courageous and compassionate. That was the beginning of my interest in the discipline of mental models. Anyone involved in a change initiative needs to return to that discipline—because without it, there's little hope of meeting the challenge of fear and anxiety. You'll drown in gray stamps instead.

3 Unilateral Control

Charlotte Roberts

"Unilateral Control" is adapted from an exercise developed by Chris Argyris, Robert Putnam, Diana Smith, and Phil McArthur at Action Design.

When people feel fear and anxiety, their first instinct is to grab "unilateral control"—to do whatever is necessary to take charge of the conversation, to make the threat go away. Often the "grabber" is not conscious of this action. The symptoms are only evident upon reflection.

Most organizational cultures endorse some forms of unilateral control as unofficially sanctioned pressure valves. People can't tolerate open anger and shouting, so they develop a more "respectable" alternative. At a computer company, I sometimes heard people say, "Let's talk about this off-line." I came to recognize this as code for: "I'm stopping this conversation." Other companies use humor; when you hear certain types of jokes, you know that someone with authority is exercising control, preventing the conversation from straying in certain directions.

Unilateral control is counterproductive; it blocks openness. But you cannot get people to stop by preaching at them. They (and you) have to be genuinely interested in changing that behavior, and the group norms that encourage it. The following questions, considered in groups of three to ten people, can help bring unilateral control to the surface.

 This is an effective exercise for a "cadre of coaches"; see page 111.

I. PERSONAL REFLECTION (30 MINUTES):

1. What are my strategies when I feel uncomfortable? Do I get angry and raise my voice? Withdraw? Make wise cracks? Overwhelm people with data? Ask a million questions? Or do something else?
2. Recall times when you slipped into the unilateral control state. What triggered it? What threat did you perceive? For some people, it might be the fear of an angry outburst; for others, the looming but uncertain threat of a pink slip; for others, the double bind of choosing from among too many obligations. Is this trigger typical for you? Is it typical for people throughout the team? Throughout the organization?
3. Why does that particular threat have such an effect upon you? What does it suggest about your own beliefs and attitudes? Each of us has a theory-in-use that prompts us to slip into unilateral control when the trigger appears. For example, someone triggered by too many obligations might feel, "Breaking my word, or not being able to handle this much pressure, are signs of incompetence."
4. What can others do to bring me out of unilateral control and back into the conversation? Try to describe or identify behaviors that the rest of the team can use to help break you of your habits.

PURPOSE:

To help people recognize their habitual defensive strategies for controlling, stopping, or changing conversation.

TIME:

Several hours.

SUPPLIES:

A comfortable room. Be sure that people are prepared for the level of reflection this exercise entails, and comfortable with one another.

II. GROUP DISCLOSURE

Now each person discloses his or her personal reflections and asks for other facets that have been observed. He or she listens and records. Then, he or she discloses underlying fears and beliefs. People listen, asking only questions that clarify—not reacting with objections, protests, excuses, or judgments. Finally, the discloser describes what others can do to bring him or her back into the conversation, possibly role-playing some practice steps. It takes a lot of intimacy and trust to carry off this step, but over time you and your team should learn to manage it.

I have seen this sequence of questions produce seemingly miraculous results. In a corporate executive team of six men and one woman, the chief operating officer had a reputation for sudden rage. Chuck would thoroughly lose control, berating people mercilessly, and shouting in public without apparent concern. Later, he would act as if he had forgotten that he'd lost control. Anyone who worked with him lived in perpetual fear: When would it happen next? Would they be his target?

When Chuck's turn for this exercise came I asked, without thinking: "Are we going to talk about your rages?" There ensued an uncomfortable silence . . . until he smiled and said, "Yes, I want to talk about it."

After acknowledging his mode of unilateral control, Chuck identified the threat behind it. Anytime that the company faced potential embarrassment, he feared he would be blamed. "I am responsible for the company's public image," he said. He only raised his voice when he imagined a negative headline in the newspaper.

Knowing this, and with his help, his team developed a plan for dealing with his temper. When others saw it coming on, now they said, "I can see this is important to you, Chuck. What have we said or done that is concerning you?" That inquiry let him bypass the horror of looming embarrassment.

Two years later, Chuck still rages occasionally, but not nearly as much. His wife says that he has completely stopped raging at home. The shame and embarrassment he felt have nearly disappeared, and he is now perceived as a much more compelling leader.

4 When Good People Do Terrible Things . . .

Addressing the fundamental learning impediments of organizational life

Joseph Jaworski

Joe Jaworski is a former lawyer, a past leader of the scenario planning team at Royal Dutch/Shell, a cofounder of the Centre for Generative Leadership (a consulting firm based in Massachusetts), the founder of the American Leadership Forum, and the author of Synchronicity *(page 213). In this piece he draws upon the "generative interview" form he developed—in which a "peer-advisor" conducts private, in-depth coaching sessions with senior leaders and thereby generates a deeper mutual understanding of the systemic forces at play in the organization. Joe describes a set of principles for intervening to heal innate fear and anxiety—either with an interventionist you trust, or (cautiously and compassionately) as an interventionist in your own system.*

Joe Jaworksi and Kazimierz Gozdz have codified the "generative interview" practice. It is described in a working paper available on-line: "Setting the Field: Creating the Conditions for Profound Institutional Change," by Joseph Jaworski, Kazimierz Gozdz, and Peter Senge, 1997: *http://www.fieldbook.com/fieldspaper.html.*

I've seen the same tension in at least a half dozen companies. The most senior executive—the CEO or equivalent—makes a point of telling me how close he is to the other high-level executive leaders. He golfs with them. He and his wife travel socially with them and their spouses. They share a mutual commitment to the future of the company. But then I talk with those other executives privately—and learn that they are terrified of him. If they speak of any significant change, or confront him with bad news, he'll launch into a tirade or humiliate them before the group. Since they can't be direct with him, they scheme, flatter, and manipulate the situation to try to get the boss to do what they want. (In some companies, this is known as "managing upward.")

Why are people afraid of this individual? It's hard to say, but certainly they react as they might respond to an authoritarian father—or to a dictator. I have known world-class mountain climbers, military heroes, and authors of successful books who cannot bring themselves to talk openly to a boss. Worse still, there is often some highly significant problem in the air, representing a terrible mistake that the boss himself had made, which he continues to defend, or to ignore. No one dares mention it to him; the cost of dealing with it continues to escalate; and the company's business suffers unnecessarily.

I do not mean to imply that executive leaders are bad people. On the contrary, senior executives who behave this way have been among the best people I have known, when considered in their totality. I don't condone this behavior, but I recognize it in many people I respect, including myself, at times. It is a natural consequence of a system in which people are routinely humiliated and beaten down, in which their sense of self is leached or bullied away. Very good people are routinely, systematically destroying other very good people, in a way that replicates itself from generation to generation of managers.

Companies with this problem can ill afford it, for three reasons. First, attitudes are changing about acceptable behavior in the workplace. The best managers and employees will find other things to do than work in an abusive situation. Second, organizations that squelch people can't draw upon their freedom and creativity when they need it to tack into the fast-changing forces of the future. Third, and most compelling, is the inherently tragic waste of human beings.

THE STOOGE'S STORY

To appreciate that waste, consider the story of Mike and Kevin (not their real names). Mike was the chief executive of a division of a large manufacturing company in a painful contraction phase. Kevin had just become his chief of staff, in charge of both finance and human resources.

For each new set of layoffs, Mike decreed the departments to be cut. He then dispatched Kevin to announce the cuts. Each time, people asked: "Will this happen again?" Kevin always said, "No, this is the last time." He asked them to redouble their efforts, to meet Mike's targets and save their jobs. He fired and disciplined people whom Mike pointed out. And in management team meetings, Kevin fiercely advocated the points of view that everyone knew Mike wanted to win.

At one important meeting, Mike spoke for a half hour, emphatically describing a new program. In his exuberance, he knocked over a full cup of coffee, spilling the liquid all over his papers. Mike never missed a beat; he kept on talking. Kevin leapt to his feet, ran for a package of towels, and spent the next few minutes wiping up coffee. Throughout the meeting, Mike never acknowledged the spill, or said a word of thanks to Kevin. In describing the session to me later, another participant said, "That's when I knew our system couldn't make it much longer."

Soon thereafter, Mike retired. The next CEO set a corporatewide change initiative in motion, inviting me to help. It took several in-depth conversations to win Kevin's trust, but then he poured his heart out and broke down emotionally. "I spent my whole career here building relationships with people," he said. "And I threw it all away in the two years I did Mike's dirty work. I didn't think I had any choice; that was the only way to get ahead. Now everybody looks at me like a patsy, a stooge. And I feel the same way about myself. I wish I had the courage to leave, but I don't think anybody else would take me."

BREAKING THE CYCLE

Over the past twenty years, I have developed a deeply personal process for helping organizations stop the dynamic where good people do terrible things to one another. It begins by designating a reputable "peer-advisor" who can conduct in-depth interviews with individual leaders. This person deliberately confronts senior executives with perceptions they don't want to hear, and helps create a field of inquiry to help them deal with such issues as others' fear of them, the squelching of innovation that results, and the consequent risk to the company.

⟩⟩ For more about fields, see page 501.

Raising these issues is itself a deeply fear-inducing experience, even for an independent outsider. It feels like telling a parent that he or she is alcoholic and needs to go for treatment. It may have been years since anyone confronted that executive so directly. And you can often see an immediate reaction in the executive's eyes: "Here's another traitor; someone else I can't trust." But if you wait out their tirade, or through their defensiveness, most executive leaders will come to the point of recognizing the problem. Then they will ask: "What can we do about it?"

The practice then expands into carefully organized small-group discussions (for which we intensively prepare the participants), and gradually builds to collective team dialogues and workshops, incorporating insights about the "undiscussables" and learning impediments that have emerged from the interviews and coaching. Typical impediments might be expressed as "We spend all our time thinking about perks and no time on the business," or, "We don't know how to be civil to one another." Behind each of these simple statements there are rafts of stories, which people gradually begin to tell more openly—first to the peer-advisor, and then to one another.

The specific methodology used here is not important. The most critical element is the deep commitment of the participants and the peer-advisors' empathy, respect, and even reverence for the people they are working with. How, then, can peer-advisors develop the competence to guide people effectively? For me, the key lies in the following assumptions. They define a view of reality as a complex, dynamic, emergent process:

- **Reality wants to unfold.** Nothing in nature stays put. Everything is in a continual process of becoming. Any effective process must explore questions that help people see where they fit inside this constantly changing reality. Thus, people must feel utterly safe. I never use a tape recorder in interviews; it could compromise the field of trust. Instead, a second person takes extensive notes. For the same reason, any peer-advisor must demonstrate the authentic lack of any personal agenda. (That's why it's difficult for internal people to manage this type of intervention on their own.)

■ **There is a primacy to the whole.** People in industrial societies are culturally conditioned to think that parts are more fundamental than wholes, and that objects are more "real" than relationships. But peer-advisors of an effective process must take a kind of "Hippocratic Oath" to commit to the interest of the whole system, beyond the interests of any individual or subgroup, no matter how powerful. If an executive leader's behavior is counterproductive to the interests of the system, then it is the peer-advisor's responsibility to find the courage to inform him or her—or, if not permitted to do so, to find the courage to walk away.

■ **Human beings are predisposed to search for meaning in their lives.** In most organizational systems, people get mired in self-delusion and stories that have been invented to make people feel better. To recover their sense of self, people need to make authentic efforts to understand their own perceptions and articulate their own views. Thus, any effective process must lead people to talk openly about undiscussable issues. This is painful, but it also releases an enormous amount of creative energy. Obscuring reality wastes energy; lie detectors, for example, work by measuring the resonance of that energy on the skin.

■ **The unfolding of reality is not controllable, but it is "leadable."** Peer-advisors need to approach life with a sense of wonder, and to be comfortable with not knowing the answers. Inevitably, there are times of confusion. If that makes a peer-advisor uncomfortable, he or she will no longer be helpful. Thus, part of the task is continually developing the abilities to stay centered, to listen, and to care enough to connect authentically with every person in the room.

■ **Hierarchy is symbolically important.** The ability of executive leaders to drive change is often exaggerated, especially when profound shifts of beliefs and attitudes are involved. But senior executives are important symbolic figures; changes in their behavior can bestow or withdraw legitimacy on systemwide behaviors. An effective process requires partnership with key hierarchical leaders—especially those willing to reconsider their own part in sustaining the organization's problems. This partnership must be continually nurtured, especially when difficult issues come to the surface and place everyone's complacency at risk.

- **People have integrity**. The challenges and dilemmas that confront people in the workplace tend to elevate games-playing and interpersonal artifice. However, beneath any duplicity, people have a basic core of integrity. When individuals are made aware of the gap between their behavior and their espoused values, they are challenged to find that core of integrity. Peer-advisors hear about deeply regrettable acts, which people regard with great shame. It is tempting to think that you would behave differently in the same situation. But you can never know someone's possibilities in a given situation, or why he or she has fallen short of potential. You can only work to create a better environment in which integrity might emerge, knowing that this, in itself, can help people find a better way to handle the pressures next time.

THE HEART AROUSED
by David Whyte (New York: Doubleday/Currency, 1994)

British poet/consultant David Whyte has spent his life adventuring in mountain, ocean, and literary arenas. He writes about the impulse to adventure, and the ways that it twists, when stunted, into fear and anxiety instead. The book's self-aggrandizement is irritating at times, but Whyte speaks directly to the part of us that cowers amid bureaucracy, waiting to make a move. Reading it might spark enough fervor to spur your own adventures, and thereby break the fear and anxiety pattern. — Art Kleiner

DEALING WITH THE PAST: TRUTH AND RECONCILIATION IN SOUTH AFRICA
Edited by Alex Boraine, Janet Levy, and Ronel Scheffer, 1994 (Capetown: Institute for Democracy in South Africa, Albion Spring, 183 Main Road, Rondebosch, Cape Town, 7700, South Africa)

Being in an authoritarian organization undergoing profound change may be somewhat like living in a totalitarian system as it moves into democracy. In countries such as Uruguay and South Africa, forums for "truth and reconciliation" have acted as powerful lightning rods for acknowledging the torture and brutality of the past—allowing the country to begin moving forward, without having to build its future on the repression of past memories. I know of no corporation or similar organization that has established some

One of the contributors to *Dealing With the Past*, *New Yorker* staff writer Lawrence Weschler, describes the heart-rending moral ambiguities of Brazil and Uruguay in another highly recommended book: *A Miracle, a Universe: Settling Accounts with Torturers* (Chicago: University of Chicago Press, 1990, 1998).

kind of "reconciliation" process to help the transition to new values or behaviors. But the reconciliation commission model, for all its political controversy, might provide a useful model to follow— admittedly only with a great deal of care.

This report (of a conference establishing South Africa's Truth and Reconciliation Commission) includes examples of amnesty and reconciliation from around the world. Businesspeople will find this material unfamiliar, but compelling. There is no one standard approach; every circumstance, from Brazil to East Germany to South Africa itself, is different. All unhappy corporations and organizations are probably similarly unalike. — Art Kleiner

5 A Safe Place for "Not Knowing"
"Small Sacred Hour"

Michael Basseches, Harvard Bureau of Study Counsel

This story, by a member of Harvard's clinical/counseling staff, illustrates one effective way to deal with a prevalent kind of fear and anxiety in organizations: anxiety over one's own competence. This is the flip side of arrogance. If they can tackle it in the Ivy League, it can probably be tackled anywhere.

A plaque bearing the image of the Bureau's Coat of Arms hangs on the wall of our main meeting room. The Latin phrase at its center translates roughly to "Nobody else knows either," and the symbolism of the surrounding phrases and images basically means: "It's okay not to know."

It might seem unusual for this kind of ideology to show up at a place like Harvard, but it's very appropriate. The feeling of "not knowing" can kick up a lot of anxiety. As a rule, university culture tends to advocate "knowing": People feel like they need to pretend that they know what they're doing, and then they feel like impostors for pretending. When students come to see us they are often experiencing some kind of distress around what they don't know. It can be anything from not knowing how to study effectively to not knowing how to cope with new social pressures.

Our motto reminds us that there's a relationship between vulnerability and learning. Sometimes, to learn, you have to acknowledge how much you don't know. For example, when students come to see me, I hope and believe that I know something that will enable me to be helpful, but I also assume that I have a lot to learn—about what their experience is like, and about how I can aid them.

Here at the Bureau we put this ethos into practice for ourselves with "small sacred hour." No matter how crazy our schedules get, or how many things come up, we try to keep that hour intact. It's an organizational value that's become institutionalized.

Twice each week the counseling staff meets in groups of three or four for one hour. The participants take turns talking about some work issue with which they are having difficulty—where they have conflicted feelings about what happened, or feel they did something wrong, or just that there's something to learn from others about handling this kind of situation. It's expected that we may encounter difficult or challenging situations, and we see a value in talking about them. A good employee is one who keeps learning from new challenges, not one who already knows how to do everything perfectly.

When I first joined the Bureau and heard about small sacred hour I was a little worried and mistrustful about how dangerous it might be to talk that freely. I think most new staff members and interns also feel anxious initially. But for me it didn't last long. I found the sessions not only safe, but incredibly valuable, both personally and professionally. We keep them safe, in part, by working in small groups—three or four people, small enough to monitor people's reactions. If people wonder about something I said, I get feedback immediately. They won't go off thinking "Why did he do that?" They'll say: "That strikes me as really strange that you did that. How did you get to that point?" I can answer that question, and through articulating my implicit rationale or chain of inner reactions, I usually come to understand the sense of it better. I can also ask, "What would you have done in this situation?"

Not long ago, I had a client who, for some reason, I didn't like. That's very unusual for me; I tend to like people as I get to know them. It was very disturbing to acknowledge my dislike, but I presented this to my

Michael Basseches's related writings include: "A Developmental Perspective on Psychotherapy Process, Psychotherapists' Expertise, and Meaning-Making Conflict within Therapeutic Relationships," 1997, *Journal of Adult Development*, 4(1&2), pp. 17–34 and pp. 85–106; and "Meetings: A Swampy Terrain for Adult Development" (with Ariel Phillips and Abigail Lipson), *Journal of Adult Development*, 1998, 5(2), pp. 85–104.

colleagues during sacred hour and replayed some of my encounters for them. They helped me see that this client and I were interacting at a very superficial level, which I was finding very boring and unpleasant. After that I was willing to take more risks in sessions. We ended up connecting at a much deeper level, I found I really liked him, and we did some very good work together. You have to feel safe—that you are not going to be condemned or made to feel stupid—to work on reactions you wish you didn't have with your colleagues.

Each year when I do my annual review, highlights invariably involve something that I worked on during sacred hour. Having this time each week, knowing one another so well, also affects other kinds of meetings in the organization. We operate more effectively, and are less pressured knowing that a context exists to explore reactions in depth. Not surprisingly, this practice has inspired a sense of loyalty to the organization for me. I have made career decisions to stay here because I value both our ideology and the community of colleagues that practice it.

⟩⟩ Also see "Climbing Out of the Muck," page 120.

6 Heroic Modes

The hidden dynamics of high-stakes situations

David Kantor and Steven Ober

Family systems therapist David Kantor has spent much of the last thirty years building a sophisticated model of human interaction, including the extra turmoil of high-stress conflict. The model has proven highly useful in practice, particularly at Innovation Associates, where Kantor and consultant Steve Ober have used it to break through pernicious impasses that emerge when organizational change threatens the comfortable personae that people have adopted within their long-term groups. In this segment, they introduce it as a vehicle for dealing with "fear and anxiety."

PROFESSOR BRADFORD FEELS HURT

Even before they walk into the meeting, newcomers have been warned about Professor Bradford, the head of the Wrightstown University technology advisory council. "Watch out for him," someone says. "He only hears what he wants to hear." Wrightstown (a real place, disguised here) has been awarded a large grant for economic and technological development by an international foundation. Representatives of the university, local businesses, government, and community groups have come together for this first meeting of the implementation steering committee. The chair is Dr. Archer, the charismatic young university president who initiated the project in the first place.

For the first half hour, the room is full of plans, ideas, and aspiration. Then Professor Bradford gets up. "I'm the only representative here," he says, "of the scientists and technologists who will make this initiative happen. The rest of you don't know what it's like to conduct research. You're not putting the right people on the committees."

Nobody responds at first. They resume talking about their wishes and plans. After another twenty minutes, he repeats the speech. The members politely ignore him once more. So he delivers the same speech a third time and remains on his feet when it's over.

"I'm feeling hurt," he says, his voice shaking. "I say this over and over, and nobody pays attention." All noise in the room ceases.

Finally, Dr. Archer says, "Professor Bradford, we are so sorry." Everyone else nods. But the spirit of the meeting is gone. People drift away without any feeling of consensus, and without the overall plan that proponents had hoped for. During the next few weeks, some people quietly propose taking Professor Bradford off the committee. The scientists and technologists of the advisory council, meanwhile, rally stubbornly behind him. The impasse grows, until a critical deadline is missed, and the grant is withdrawn. Had things gone differently at that single moment of high stress, perhaps the initiative would have been sustained.

On the surface, this seems like a fairly straightforward description of a typical situation, in which nobody gets what he wants. It's one of many meetings where people go in feeling energized and committed, and come out feeling weary, debilitated, and anxious. But underneath the surface, several different cross-currents all exacerbate one another.

Above the committee level, the university governance structure is changing. A political battle brews over whether scientists like Professor Bradford, or administrators like Dr. Archer, should lead innovation.

At the committee level, Professor Bradford sees his influence fading.

The technologists appointed him their representative because of his pugnacious, shrewd, argumentative style. He wants and expects the same kind of appreciation and deference from the committee. But his intensity, which worked so well in the past, now sets people against him. They don't like the way he makes them feel conquered. They gravitate to Dr. Archer's cooler, more inclusive style instead.

At the personal level, Professor Bradford feels hurt—but not entirely in the way that it seems. The first member of his family to go to college, he grew up obeying a tyrannical father, and hiding his inner softness from his family. The adult Bradford has a cunning grasp of other people's frailties, a powerful ability to fix problems, and a deep conflict within himself about showing pain. He can't sway these people through argument or politics, but he knows that they can't ignore the word "hurt." He can use their own language to defeat them.

Just about everybody in the room (including Archer and Bradford) feels caught in a trap, forced into actions that no one wants. Bradford will walk out of the room feeling that he has triumphed. But his victory will be short lived. They will not, in the end, do what he wants. And the community will lose the grant.

How could the group members change these dynamics? They would have to see the structure of interrelationships—not just among Bradford, Archer, and the other individuals, but among the various constituencies and larger forces (the administrators, technologists, and community). They might have to talk openly about the fact that, no matter what happens in the end, Dr. Bradford will not get what he wants.

WHEN THE STAKES ARE HIGH

In calm situations, with low emotional stakes, it's easy to deal with people. They will listen to rational explanations, and offer rational responses of their own. But in high-stakes situations like this one, confrontation—overt or subtle—puts everyone on the line.

Often, people learn about group dynamics and team communication in low-stakes situations, and then try to apply those insights in high-stakes situations. Then they wonder why their efforts backfire. The structure of a high-stakes situation is as different from a low-stakes situation as water vapor is from ice, even when the same people are involved. In a high-stakes situation, the prevailing language shifts to an emotional, symbolic, mythic form: the language of heroes and villains, of confrontation and suffering, malevolence and primal desires. When Dr. Bradford says, "I'm hurt," he is not just voicing his feelings. He is proclaiming himself to be a victim—the shadow image of a defeated hero.

High-stakes situations typically emerge when two different deeply held loyalties or interests conflict, and trap the individual between them. In Bradford's case, success on the committee would mean failure among his "home" constituents, the technology faculty . . . and an even greater failure in his deepest self. Many organizations involved in change unintentionally lead people into this sort of double bind. Formerly people were bureaucratic; now they have to be entrepreneurial. Formerly they were focused on narrow markets; now they have to think globally. The kind of behavior that has always produced success no longer works. In the face of such a trap, people lose their equanimity.

We call these situations "structural traps." When the real Professor Bradford heard this, he said, "My whole job is one big structural trap." He was correct. Anyone who exists in a boundary condition, caught between two cultures or ways of thinking, can be similarly caught.

ANATOMY OF A HIGH-STAKES STRUCTURE

In any human system, one is always three. Each single situation reflects not just the system at its own level (as in the interrelationships of committee members) but the larger system (the technologists and university governing board) and the smaller systems within each person (not just within Dr. Bradford, but within everyone in the room). We generally portray group dynamics in an hourglass-shaped form.

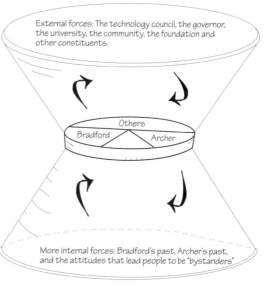

External forces: The technology council, the governor, the university, the community, the foundation and other constituents.

Others
Bradford   Archer

More internal forces: Bradford's past, Archer's past, and the attitudes that lead people to be "bystanders"

The hourglass principle suggests that your understanding is incomplete unless you look at all three levels of a situation. Psychoanalysis failed because it only looked down, within the individual; psychoanalysts did not consider the interplay of families, workplaces, and communities. Group dynamics, on the other hand, looked only upward; it did not consider personal histories and backgrounds. As shown by the thick arrows, each level affects the others, both gradually and in punctuated bursts of change (that generally involve a high-stakes emotional situation).

The hourglass portrays an infinite number of possible interrelationships. By identifying just some of them, your sophistication in the dynamics of the structure can dramatically increase, and you can act

Other levels of this model are described in more detail in *The Fifth Discipline Fieldbook*, in "Reframing Team Relationships," by David Kantor and Nancy Heaton Lonstein, p. 407. As more information about the model is published, our Web site will offer links and information, and details about more "levels" of this model. See *http://www.fieldbook.com/structural dynamics.html.*

more effectively—both in your own high-stakes situations, and those of other people around you. To unravel situations like this committee meeting, where people struggle with emotionally charged issues, one level offers a particularly valuable starting point. This is the "heroic mode," our habitual way of dealing with life when life gets a little too interesting.

WHAT IS YOUR HEROIC MODE?

There are many levels at which subtle forces interact. But to unravel situations like this committee meeting, where people struggle with emotionally charged issues, one level offers a particularly valuable starting point. In high-stakes situations, people tend to revert to one of three ways of experiencing life and interacting with others. These "heroic modes" determine people's habitual ways of struggling for integration and wholeness, coping with anxiety, and trying to reach other people. Starting at a very early age, we summon the heroes within us to deal with the pain and conflict (and the love and freedom) that are part of the human condition. Most people have some combination of these modes in their personae; businesspeople, under the pressure to appear temperate, may find themselves in a constant struggle to keep the modes from coming to the surface. But if you watch carefully, you can see one of these heroic modes predominating in every individual.

Like all categorizations of people, these modes are easy to oversimplify. All three have a light and dark aspect. Experiencing the ascendant side of your heroic mode is one of the things that makes you feel authentic, vital, and fully alive. But there is also a dark, shadow side to each of these heroes: a ghostly demon deep within us, whispering to us that we are hateful, untrusted, and unloved. As adults in high-stakes situations, we may be plunged back into the powerlessness we felt as children, when we could not get our deepest emotional needs met. The shadow side of our heroic mode seems to possess us at such times. Without

	Fixer	Survivor	Protector
Light zone	solves	accepts	shields
	("I will")	("I can")	("I must")
Gray zone	conquers	endures	suffers
Shadow zone	abuses	abandons	is the victim

knowing why, we behave and speak in ways which we would never countenance in our "better moments"—ways that ensure that we will be further misunderstood, dreaded, and unloved by others.

People can swing rapidly back and forth between the light and dark sides of their heroic modes. They may be more or less aware of the modes' influence. But the basic dynamics remain the same for all three types of people:

■ **The survivor ("I accept and endure"):** Survivor-heroes suffer in silence, because they do not want to be exposed. Human pain seems less agonizing to them if it is unwitnessed, even by their innermost selves. They have great capability and power; they exemplify the "pioneer spirit." In their light moments, they seem unperturbed by any crisis, blithely facing (for example) major surgery. Ask them if they are "in touch" with their feelings and they say, "of course," but the expression of feeling discomfits them. They prefer to act according to a code of behavior—a profession (doctor, lawyer, banker) or an outer image ("I'm well organized; I'm wise"). Many survivors use politeness or humor to deflect talk of pain and feelings. They can come across as great listeners; they are curious, detached, forgiving, and unwilling to bring any anger they feel to the surface.

But when the dark side emerges, survivors become rigid. They "abandon" their emotional links with the situation, in effect turning to stone to avoid feeling pain and ambiguity. In the process, they often leave critical issues unaddressed, and the people around them feel unrecognized. Dr. Archer, the university administrator, plays the role of a survivor in this story. He is unhurt and unperturbed, but when emotions start to dominate, he tacitly abandons the group, not rising to the occasion to help it move forward.

■ **The fixer ("I solve and conquer"):** In every situation, the fixer says, "I will do it." They solve problems, restore harmony, and make things all right. Fixers are goal-oriented reformers and visionaries; they are the kind of people who have their "eyes on the prize." They provide energy, insights, and sheer force in overcoming barriers. At their best, they confront and solve problems that seem impossible to everyone else. They make people feel safe and protected. They follow through. They meet emergencies and exercise power. They can be like benevolent conquerors, inspiring everyone around them.

But when they descend into the shadow zone, their power descends as well—from overcoming obstacles to coercing people to

Some of these concepts are described in a popular psychology context in the new book *My Lover, My Self: Self-Discovery Through Relationship,* by David Kantor (New York: Riverside/Penguin/Putnam, 1999).

abusing others. They can be so bent on fulfilling their own desires that they lose sight of the interests, feelings, and autonomy of others. At these moments, fixers can become angry and abusive. If other people refuse their help, the fixers feel their heroic visions of themselves negated. They become engaged and more insistent, at least until the shadow passes. In the deepest shadows of the fixer there resides the child who reacts to imperfect love by throwing a tantrum. The technologist, Dr. Bradford, is clearly a fixer who has stooped to conquer.

■ **The protector ("I shield and suffer"):** The protector says, "I will not stand by idly in the face of suffering, and pretend it doesn't exist." One of the protectors' greatest gifts is the ability to identify areas of pain within themselves and others, and to empathize. They talk with great familiarity about their own inner world and that of others around them. They are often spokespeople for the sick, downtrodden, poor, weak, and abused. They are essential in any group of people, because they operate through foresight; they sense where problems are going to be. They may not act themselves, but they can provide the information needed to correct imbalances or disharmonies, either in relationships or in group settings.

When protectors slip into shadow, they can become maudlin, suffering victims. Life feels bleak and overwhelming. Effort seems pointless. Aware of their own status as victims, and of their own vulnerability, they become ever-vigilant against any evidence that they have played a role in keeping themselves oppressed. They blame the rest of the world, which of course only serves to further alienate those around them. Despite their intimate knowledge of themselves, they have not fully recognized the strength they have to contain their own suffering. The rest of the group, watching Dr. Bradford and Dr. Archer compete, may have been victimized protectors, which explains why Dr. Bradford was so effective in using their own language ("I feel hurt!") to manipulate them.

LEARNING TO HEAR AND SEE THESE SYSTEMS IN REAL TIME

If you are members of a working group, then these distinctions can add depth and breadth to your understanding of one another.

To see such structures more clearly, you need to break out of the "bubble" of daily life: the roles and stances that you assume without thinking, simply because "that's what we're supposed to do to keep rolling along." Ask yourself: "Do I have to act the way I act every day?" You don't need to act differently, but make yourself more aware of the reasons behind the actions you take—the way you say hello to people, the role you take in a meeting, the types of conversations you initiate.

Try to listen, between the lines, for evidence of the structures of interrelationships. Watch faces and posture for clues to the feelings and attitudes that reveal the presence of survivors, fixers, and protectors. Continually ask yourself: "Have I seen what's going on correctly?" Keep monitoring your own ability; test your perception with someone who is less gummed up in the stuck dynamics.

This may feel unfamiliar. Many people in business are used to learning through training programs. They attend a short workshop, and return confident that they can put the ideas into practice. But in complex arenas like this, confidence is a sign that people haven't learned. When learning has occurred, people tend to act uncertain. Their attitude, often unspoken, conveys this thought: "Something has been shaken up in the way I look at the world." There is no moment of insight or "aha" experience—just a gradually building proficiency.

7 Unraveling the Knots from Your "Family of Origin"

Brenda Kerr and Denny Minno

The School for Innovative Leadership conducts a two-year master's degree program for managers, union officials, and other leaders. This program began in 1973 and is currently affiliated with Antioch University in Seattle. Brenda Kerr and Denny Minno (who are married to each other) have been core faculty in this program for over twenty years. A major focus of the program is helping leaders acquire "personal mastery"–style skills—in part, by dealing with deep-seated attitudes and beliefs that develop into fears, anxieties, and other forms of

We first learned of the value of this work from Louis van der Merwe, a graduate of this program.

stuck behavior. The Family of Origin work is effective for this because it reframes psychological backgrounds as part of a system that they can not simply cope with, but change.

Recently we coached Ron, a young manager whose subordinate had challenged his authority on decisions. Although Ron held his ground, he later reported feeling two almost irresistible desires—to discipline his employee, and to just give up and walk away.

Ron had logical reasons for disciplining, firing, or giving in to that employee. But upon reflection, he realized that the logic was all rationalization; his feelings were compelled by an emotional field that he had entered unconsciously. It was as if he stepped back into the contentious family he grew up in—his family of origin. His father had often lectured his mother, always "being right," and his mother had always responded by placating (but resisting, under the surface). Ron would remain silent, trying desperately to think of the perfect intervention that would resolve their struggle, but never saying anything out loud.

Now, as a boss, he was suddenly "hooked" into that old pattern. He knew how he wanted to behave, but in moments of confrontation, he could not seem to draw forth the person he wanted to be.

So Ron went back to talk to each of his parents (now divorced) about their old patterns of behavior. He found out that neither parent had ever felt in control during their arguments; they responded to each other automatically and unconsciously. Hearing this relieved Ron's guilt; nothing he could have done would ever have fixed it. In interviews, his parents told the story of their own upbringing, including the forces in their own families that had helped create his father's rigid arrogance and his mother's placating. As his conversations with them continued, he became more flexible; he saw how each parent viewed the other, and listened without feeling compelled to change them. Thereafter, when challenges to his authority came up at work, he no longer felt blocked; he now knew how to handle himself much better.

Family of origin theory proposes that many chronic problems with human behavior have their roots in the patterns of family relationships. The theory is bold enough to suggest that you can change this behavior, as an adult, by reliving and reshaping some of these relationships in carefully designed ways. For example, if you clear up authority issues with your father, your authority issues could vanish everywhere. If you come to understand the dynamics between you and your brothers and sisters, it may become much easier for you to work effectively on teams and become a more confident and capable leader.

Virginia Satir, a renowned family systems practitioner and theorist, tells a story in which a young couple invites the bride's family for a holiday meal. The bride takes a roast out of the refrigerator, cuts the end off, lays it alongside the larger part, and puts it into the oven. The new husband, observing this unusual process, asks her why she cut off the end.

The bride thinks for a moment and then says, "Well, that's the way I was taught to cook a roast. Isn't that so, Mother?"

Her mother says, "Yes, that's how I learned to do it."

Then the grandmother speaks up. "Yes, that's what I taught you. But we were young and poor, and we didn't have a large pan. I haven't cut the end off a roast in more than forty years." In this way, patterns of behavior are passed on to succeeding generations, and may be intensified each step of the way. The feelings that you experience and behaviors you perform automatically today may be very inappropriate to your current circumstances.

Many aspects of your family history may help determine your responses under stress and anxiety. For instance, firstborn, middle, youngest, and only children (with no siblings) each have characteristic ways of forming relationships, taking responsibility, and responding to authority. Sometimes, for instance, two firstborns fall into rivalry that serves neither of them well, simply because they react competitively to each other as firstborns. Or a difficult relationship with a coworker may bear unconscious echoes of the relationship between a bossy older brother and a petulant younger sister. The following exercise will help you explore your family of origin experiences, both benevolent and bothersome—and begin to change the behavior that stems from them.

STEP ONE: REFLECTION

1. Who, at work, strongly reminds you of someone in your family of origin (including the extended family system)? What physical or behavioral attributes trigger you (i.e., facial expressions or features, gestures, particular behavioral habits, voice tones, etc.)?

2. How do you typically react (inwardly and externally) to that individual? How is this pattern of reacting similar to or different from your pattern of relating with the family of origin member?

3. Is the role you are playing at work similar to or different from your family of origin role? You may not be replicating your family of origin role, but reacting against it. The daughter who was quietly obedient to an oppressive father may become the troublemaker at

The form of family of origin theory to which we subscribe was originally developed by Murray Bowen, and extended into organizational applications by Edwin Friedman. Friedman's most accessible book is *Generation to Generation* (New York: Guilford Press, 1985). This book is well written, deep, and thorough without being too dense. Friedman focuses on the organizations he knew best: churches and synagogues. We also recommend "Reinventing Leadership," a videotape presentation by Edwin Friedman. — Brenda Kerr and Denny Minno.

This introduction and exercise are taken from a much longer, more in-depth piece of writing, with much more material about (for example) the influence of birth order on workplace behavior. For access to that material, see The Fifth Discipline Resource Web page: http://www.fieldbook.com/family.html.

work to make up for the attention she wanted, but never received.

4. Notice your behavior in conflicts at work. When two people disagree, what is your response? Do you want to flee? Do you join in? Do you take the side of the one you perceive as weaker? Do you distance yourself from the fray? Do you mediate? Do you feel sick? Do you become quiet? Identify two or three aspects of your family history that seem relevant. Don't jump to any conclusions about these dynamics. You are still gathering information.

STEP TWO: EXPLORATION

At this point, you reenter your family of origin to build your capacity to make changes in your own present-day responses. We emphatically urge you to make a commitment to the "golden rule" of family of origin work: Its purpose is to change you, not others. As Murray Bowen points out, the process you are embarking on is one of "self-differentiation." By learning to behave more authentically with the people in your family, you learn alternatives to your automatic responses of the past. This does not include blaming, getting even with, converting, or getting back emotional payments from members of your family. Any hint of these kinds of behaviors or attitudes will only cause them to become defensive and you to become frustrated. Instead, it is useful to accept the proposition that your parents (and other family members) did the best they could with what they experienced from their parents, and it is now up to you to create your own desired future.

First, fully identify at least the last three generations of your family: you and your siblings, your parents and their siblings, and your grandparents. To get all of this information you will likely need to call or visit other family members.

Second, write your own autobiography. This five- to six-page document should include descriptions of your relationships (male-female issues, communication patterns, etc.) and significant experiences with your parents and siblings. Also write about the roles you played in your family, important family values and beliefs, and meaningful life events— patterns of illness, family crises (especially concerning loss), dysfunctional family members, and information about the unspoken and spoken family rules. Valuable insights about your life will probably rise to the surface as you write your autobiography. We encourage reading it out loud to a trusted friend, coach, or colleague, to help you think through those insights and make new connections.

To identify the last three generations, we recommend that you construct a diagram of your family that includes names, ages, dates of birth and death, and dates of marriages, divorces, and separations. For complex family trees, you may want to learn the diagramming technique of "genograms." See *Genograms in Family Assessment*, by Monica McGoldrick and Randy Gerson (New York: Norton, 1985).

Third, conduct tape-recorded conversations with family members. Tell your parents and others that you are trying to understand yourself and the history of your family. Most people become eager to share their knowledge about the family, especially when they realize you are not trying to blame or find fault.

Interview by asking questions, not by talking yourself. The more questions, the better—follow their lead and your own nose. Do not challenge or confront people, even if you think they are covering up or lying. If your tone of voice conveys a genuine interest in their account of the discrepancy, then you may discover some very interesting information.

Write down, ahead of time, the core questions you want to ask. Some of the things you might ask about include: early memories of parents, grandparents, siblings, the house, the neighborhood, and playmates. Memories of going to school and the parents' attitude toward school. Discipline in the home. Relationships. ("Who listened to your feelings when you were happy, sad, or angry?") Family squabbles. Family mottoes and rules. Early girlfriends and boyfriends. The ways that spouses or partners met, and their impact on the family.

Do everything possible to be trustworthy. For example, keep every interview confidential. If people ask you about other interviews, respond only with statements about your own perceptions and feelings; don't reveal what anyone else said. Don't challenge, disagree, or condemn family members for what they say to you. People will talk more when you listen with an open, nonevaluative presence. You have asked for their perception of family life, which inevitably will differ from your own perspective. Take on the attitude of an objective researcher; the less debating or criticizing you do during the interview, the better.

These interviews themselves are potential vehicles for change. Instead of lapsing into familiar patterns with your parents (responding to them as their child), arrive with the emotional presence of an adult; a peer who is also their offspring. Many people find that the interview format itself helps put them into this adult-to-adult role.

STEP THREE: CHANGING THE PATTERNS

You can now take the data that you have gathered "back home," reflect on it, and use it to modify some of your behavior in the workplace. While there may be some quick breakthroughs, changes in ingrained behavior won't happen all at once. They tend to take place incrementally. Having recognized the resonance of a "stuck" situation, you will approach it a little differently the next time. It usually goes like this: "They are always

Further reading on "Family of Origin" work:

■

Family Ties That Bind
by Ronald Richardson (Vancouver, B.C.: Self-Counsel Press, 1988). A good primer for lay people.

■

The Birth Order Book
by Kevin Leman (Old Tappan, NJ: Fleming H. Revel Co, 1984). More in-depth theory about birth order positions and their effects on home and work life.

■

The New Peoplemaking
by Virginia Satir (Mountain View, CA: Science and Behavior Books, 1988). An inspiring classical text with general principles about communication.

asking me to take on extra responsibility, and I always acquiesce—just as I did at home, and my mother did in her family. Next time, I'm going to establish clearer boundaries at the beginning." Maybe your new insight will lead to new behavior; but maybe you'll get sucked in to the old familiar patterns again. But now, attuned to how you participate in the conversation, you keep trying new approaches, until you find a response that works for you.

You may wonder if it's safe to experiment in this way, particularly if you are unacquainted with these methods. Having a coach or being in a support group is helpful. In our groups, participants take on roles in one another's dramatic scenes, simulating real-world stress and allowing one another to rehearse new behaviors and respond in a variety of ways.

We believe you can safely explore the "knots" in your family of origin, so long as you bear in mind that you are experimenting. As Ronald Richardson, a well-known family of origin theorist, says: "Most average people with only a normal complement of problems can do this work without involving a third party." We also agree with his warning that, "some people who are deeply troubled or come from families with severe emotional problems should not attempt to do this work without professional help." He adds: "Remember, there is really nothing new here. People have been doing this kind of work in their families for as long as families have existed . . . They have worked at untangling the roots, identifying who they really are, and deciding what they are responsible for."

8 Beyond "Winners and Losers"

Diversity as a learning phenomenon

Toni Gregory

Each of this book's authors has come face to face with the fears and anxieties raised by the subject of "workplace diversity." But we do not have enough experience to feel confident writing about it as authors.

*We know that there are problems with existing diversity training pro-
grams, and we do not want to endorse them; and we also know that
managers and organizations cannot ignore the fear and anxiety that
emerge around race, gender, ethnicity, age, sexual orientation, and so
on. Nor can diversity be treated as a "token" concern, if only because
the corporate world has too much of a history of tokenism here, and
has driven too many people away as a result.*

*As five white men and one white woman, we are aware of our own
lack of diversity. (The contributors to this book are mixed in terms of
gender, ethnicity, and nationality, naturally reflecting the diverse
backgrounds of people who are involved in this field.)*

*For help in reflecting on this issue, we turned to Toni Gregory, a
faculty member/administrator at The Fielding Institute for Graduate
Study and at Morehouse College in Atlanta. As a consultant and
former research director at the American Institute for Managing
Diversity (founded by diversity scholar Roosevelt Thomas), she is
familiar with "diversity training" as it exists, and as it could be. As an
organizational scholar, consultant, and learning historian (on "OilCo,"
page 463), she knows the territory of organizational learning. Here,
she presents a radical way of thinking about both sets of practices.*

Years ago, at IBM, an African-American male was the manager of a
service department with very low status. Fellow employees, including senior managers, often made jokes about his department. He wholeheartedly believed that his ethnicity played a heavy role in the unit's
troubles. But that wasn't the only factor; the members of this department
(all college graduates) were considered more poorly educated and less
valuable to the company than, say, the elite people over in marketing.

When several change initiatives were introduced, the service department's problems worsened. Investment and resources were diverted to
other, higher-status units. People began to pick up signals that associat-
ing with this unit, even informally, could be disastrous to one's career.
Everyone in the department felt the pressure on his livelihood.

The manager had no choice but to act, and yet no actions were available to him within the hierarchy. The only way out was to break the
rules. He got the idea that if he felt marginalized, there must be other
units and people within IBM who felt the same way. He set about finding them, and enlisting their support—not to commiserate together, but
to apply their diverse perspectives to one another's problems. For example, due to budget reductions, the service department had a major prob-

lem supplying parts and service to customers who were spread out geo-graphically. By pooling their budget and their ideas among their new network of colleagues, they developed a fleet of low-cost service air-planes—an innovation that, in the end, saved forty million dollars for the company. This represented an unprecedented bit of "intrapreneurialism" within IBM.

"I had been focused on being a black man," said the manager when I interviewed him. "But this became a learning process. We used our knowledge about diversity to get people involved with one another." In other words, this group of people had felt a tension around diversity—a tension associated with bigotry, prejudice, and being marginalized in both obvious and subtle ways. They'd made it a catalyst for them. It acted as a spark, just as similar kinds of "marginalization" have shut peo-ple out of privileged positions throughout the postwar years and spurred them to create all-new business forms in such industries as music, cloth-ing, and electronic publishing.

If you are facing marginalization from diversity yourself, or if it has come up in the added openness of your change initiative, then you may be drawn to the established ways of dealing with it. There are two pri-mary camps that deal with this problem:

■ The equity school, with roots in the civil rights movement, is con-cerned with the plight of specific groups in obtaining equity, justice, equal opportunity, and the fair distribution of resources. They aim for giving everybody, no matter how disadvantaged, equivalent access to the same opportunities and "stuff."

■ The "business results" school, propelled by Roosevelt Thomas's model of managing diversity, focuses on the impact that structural and cultural change can have on an organization's economic viability. These people say, in effect, "Embrace the differences among people, and you can fix the organization's problems."

For more about the "business results" school, see *Beyond Race and Gender: Unleashing the Power of Your Total Work Force by Managing Diversity*, by Roosevelt Thomas (New York: AMACOM, 1991).

To date, neither camp has been able to produce sustainable results. In fact, they have often either pushed the problems underground, or actually inflamed resistance—at huge expense to the companies. Why? Because both of these practices are based on changing behavior, and only behavior. The equity school holds workshops in which people learn, by rote, new ways they are supposed to treat one another. "Don't say such-and-such. Don't do such-and-such." The business results school seeks to change the culture by focusing on the company's performance.

"Why do we require people to wear business suits instead of ethnic clothing, for example? Does this contribute to business results?"

Neither camp deals with the question: Why is it so hard for different types of people to work together effectively in the first place? Even people from the same ethnic background and gender can feel marginalized. At Western State, an all-white college in Colorado, people complain of rampant "skier bigotry." Nonskiers feel routinely shut out of jobs, tenure, grants, and promotions.

In short, most human societies (and most people, in their deepest attitudes) divide the world into "winners" and "losers." They then choose to see those parts of people that reinforce their conceptions. Racism and the other "isms" will not go away completely, because the mind-set that creates them is probably part of the human psyche. We can't eliminate it, but if we can learn to break some of our habits of thought, then we can learn to deal effectively with the "isms" that appear in ourselves and in others. We can keep the "isms" from blocking us from our goals, and we can build organizations that don't enshrine the "isms" in their policies and practices.

See Gregory, T. & Ouelette, C. (1995): Study examines the issue of competencies for workplace diversity practitioners. *Employment Relations Today*, 22(1), 47–57; and Gregory, T. (1996). Transformative learning: A case study of Thomas's theory of diversity. Ann Arbor, MI: UMI.

WORKING WITH DIVERSITY TENSION

As it happens, the skills and practices of organizational learning give people an unprecedented set of tools for dealing with diversity. Unfortunately, the link between diversity and learning is all too rarely made. On one hand, people assume (wrongly) that it's only appropriate to talk about diversity in terms of ethnicity and gender. As one manager I interviewed about diversity training said, "The idea that diversity was different from equal opportunity or affirmative action was difficult for people to understand. There was too much baggage associated with the word 'diversity.' If I had to do it all over again, I wouldn't call it diversity."

I do not mean to naysay the tragic impact of racism and bigotry, or the devastating effects of sexism. I also do not want to diminish the contribution of my colleagues in the field. But if you want to make organizations less prone to these problems, then the feelings of being victimized by racism, bigotry, and sexism will distract you from the core issue. The core issue is the ability of people not only to learn to be authentic in their interactions and relationships, in the workplace and everywhere else, but also to apply that learning in increasingly effective ways.

On the other hand, leaders of learning and change initiatives, no matter how many difficult issues they have raised to the surface, often seem to stop dead when they come up against the diversity question. It inevitably emerges, precisely because people are learning to reflect and talk about deep concerns. They naturally want to talk about the marginalization they feel, and about whether they are seen as winners or as losers. But leaders and practitioners of organizational learning may have their own blinders. They may even have suppressed bigoted attitudes themselves; most people have. Or they may not understand the link between diversity and organizational effectiveness. Therefore, they don't know how to help people move past the impasse, where some people feel that others are marginalizing them.

The Roosevelt Thomas body of work has produced one very useful concept in this regard: diversity tension. It operates like creative tension in learning organization work: as a signal that, somewhere, somehow, someone's needs are not being met. The "diversity task," in Thomas's eyes, then becomes creative: finding the source of the problem, and redesigning the system to address unproductive balances.

If you respond to diversity tension with feelings of hopelessness, that tends to build on itself and eventually causes stagnation. If you respond to it with integrity, responsibility, and a willingness to work through the tension, then you often get powerful breakthroughs. But these breakthroughs only occur if people learn to recognize the power and capabilities they already have, and stop blocking themselves. This makes it easier to "win"—by any standards of success, but on their own terms.

Nor is this response new. Frederick Douglass was responding to this kind of tension (in a much more extreme situation) when he stood up one day and said, "I am not a slave." Until he was willing to take that stand, he was a slave; thereafter, he was a philosopher and an activist. Viktor Frankl responded to this tension in Nazi concentration camps (again, a much more extreme situation) with the decision to be free, regardless of the worst circumstances imaginable. Maya Angelou responded to the tension by developing a personae that transcended all of the issues of class, gender, background, attitude, and circumstance to become United States poet laureate.

No one, to my knowledge, has studied the factors that allow a Frederick Douglass to develop this kind of response to diversity tension. In the absence of such research, we regard a Viktor Frankl or a Maya Angelou as someone out of the norm, whom nobody else could emulate.

PUTTING IT INTO PRACTICE

What, then, can we do to set up our pilot groups and learning projects to help people resist the hypnotic voice of culture that whispers, "You're not part of an elite, so you can't accomplish what you want"?

You may already be doing most of what you need to do. The learning disciplines of personal mastery, mental models, systems thinking, and shared vision are the same things that will allow you to successfully deal with the dynamics of diversity. But many leaders stop too soon. When diversity tension appears, you must be willing to address questions about rank, power, privilege, and prejudice. These questions might include: Who, here, are seen as "winners"? Who are seen as "losers"? What data is this based on? Is it based on false assumptions? How does this marginalization affect our overall competence and capability? How does it help or hinder us from attracting people? And what would we have to change?

Not long ago, I interviewed the CEO of a large division of a multinational corporation. He talked extensively about how the organization's current change initiative was opening opportunities for a much broader group of people. "The old success model," he said, "was hierarchy—power—presiding over things. Having windows that you could see out of in your office and a secretary were important. But we are attempting to change. We want our practices to recognize that perks and privileges don't add any value to the customer."

On my way in to see this man, I had been greeted by two African-American female receptionists. His white female secretary had escorted me through several locked doors, past several large, traditional offices, all occupied by white males and "guarded" by white female secretaries. His office was the largest of all, with windows all around.

Clearly this CEO, though sincere about his commitment to change, was unaware of the contradiction between his espoused goals and the cultural signals in his immediate workplace. When I talked to others in the division, it became clear that they were keenly aware of it. Without any prompting from me, at least a dozen people raised the question of privilege and indicated that it was a source of contention that kept people from making a commitment to change.

These are the kinds of subtle, hard-to-see issues that get raised by diversity tension. As the biblical injunction against putting new wine into old wineskins suggests, putting new values into old trappings can promote confusion and cynicism. Diversity tension may seem like it makes things harder, but it may actually make it easier for people to productively challenge the status quo by making up their own.

THE PROMISE OF DIVERSITY

edited by Elsie Y. Cross, Judith H. Katz, Frederick A. Miller, and Edith W. Seashore
(Burr Ridge, IL: NTL Institute/Irwin Publishing, 1994)

The forty contributors here nearly all speak personally and directly about eliminating discrimination in organizations. Developed at National Training Laboratories, it's refreshingly short on answers and long on diverse views. If I were a member of a pilot group, feeling uncertain of my sensitivity to any particular category of people, and I felt too shy to ask anyone directly, I'd browse here to find out what people were thinking. Then, at least, I'd have a starting point to seeing diversity issues through someone else's eyes.
— Art Kleiner

⟩⟩ For more about building awareness of cultural issues, including diversity, see page 334.

VIII. Assessment and Measurement

"This stuff isn't working!"

1 The Challenge

As we noted in Chapter II, most innovative managers believe tacitly in the "better mousetrap" theory, which suggests that if an innovative practice produces practical results, it will be seen as successful and "people will beat a pathway to your door." As one line leader said, "We believed that our results would speak for themselves. We knew that there were many things about what we were doing that were not understood by people outside the team, but we tried not to worry about it. We were confident that what we were doing would work and that we would eventually be recognized for that." Unfortunately, our experience suggests that it's rarely that simple.

It is hard to argue with the basic reasoning behind the better mousetrap theory. Surely, if innovative practices never produce practical benefits, it is hard to see why they would spread widely. Indeed, improved business results and enhanced credibility is one of the basic reinforcing growth processes of profound change, as described in Chapter II. The problems arise because there are other limiting processes that prevent this source of growth from operating.

One especially challenging limiting process involves basic problems of measurement and assessment: How do people judge whether something new is working? Expectations as well as observations influence assessments. And new practices result in many changes in traditional measures, some of which will invariably make the pilot group "look bad." In fact, significant new business practices may contradict the

Some papers describing this insurance industry research include: "A Dynamic Theory of Service Delivery: Implications for Service Quality," by Rogelio Oliva (Cambridge, MA: Sloan School of Management, MIT, PhD Thesis, 1996); "Catalyzing Systems Thinking within Organizations" by Peter Senge, in *Advances in Organizational Development*, edited by F. Masaryk, p. 197 (Norwood, NJ: Ablex, 1990); "Developing a Theory of Service Quality/Service Capacity Interaction," by Peter Senge and Rogelio Oliva, in 1993 International System Dynamics Conference proceedings, edited by E. Zepeda and J.A.D. Machuca, Cancun, Mexico. Also see the on-line paper, "Empirical Validation of a Dynamic Hypothesis" by Rogelio Oliva, Sloan School of Management: *http://web.mit.edu/jsterman/www/RO1.html*.

thinking behind many traditional measures. If line managers try to defend their innovations by arguing that traditional measures are wrong, this may be seen as a self-serving effort to shun accountability. Yet, trying to meet these measures may distort and even undermine the very innovations to which they are committed. These problems and dilemmas represent just some of the reasons why assessing success of innovative practices is an inherently complex and ambiguous challenge in sustaining profound change—indeed, one of the most fundamental challenges.

Several years ago, a systemic analysis of the property and liability insurance industry suggested that most competitors were operating at high levels of total cost (and low profitability) because of long-term underinvestment in service capacity. For example, insurance adjusting, once a skilled profession, had evolved into "claims processing," a highly automated process of gathering standardized information and settling claims, overseen by young, relatively low-paid "claims processors." Investigation, negotiation, and qualitative analysis and record keeping, once the forte of the professional adjuster, had becoming virtually nonexistent. (In fact, insurance adjusting had all but disappeared as a credible profession—a young ambitious person went into marketing or finance, never adjusting.) Consequently, the study suggested, fraud, overpayment, and litigation had grown dramatically over twenty to thirty years. Insurance firms were fighting back through inherently low-leverage strategies: by hiring more lawyers to contest litigated cases and lobbying for changes in state regulations to control runaway costs and seek joint management of substandard reserve positions.

This study was controversial because it contradicted mainstream management policies throughout the industry. But it was difficult to completely discount, because its theory of underinvestment had been developed by a research team within a leading firm, which included the firm's claims vice president and other executives. These people had worked in the insurance industry for years, and knew its pressures and culture very well. The team managed to convince many of their fellow senior managers in the firm, including the CEO, and began to implement learning processes to demonstrate this dynamic to other managers, build shared understanding, and (they hoped) change the company's approach.

But little change ever occurred. The reason: Claims organizations throughout the industry are managed according to standard productivity and cost measures. These measures focus on output per adjuster: They include the number of claims settled per adjuster per week, and "expense ratios" (total operating expenses per premium). The core problem was the measures themselves, which had developed over many years as part of the very same fragmented management perspective that focused on increased "productivity" at the expense of long-term profitability. In particular, the measures virtually forbade an alternative strategy for improving total profitability. This "systems"-oriented strategy would have increased adjuster expense ratios to reduce total costs—because the costs of overpayment and litigation were in fact much greater than the costs of adjuster expenses. Yet, the claims organization, including the vice president, were judged based on the reductions in their expense ratios. In the eyes of the management team, the credibility of well-established measures far outweighed that of a radical set of new ideas, embodied in a strange system dynamics simulation model. The systems researchers knew they were in trouble when, in a particularly stressful management team meeting, another of the VPs asked the claims VP sarcastically, "Aren't our claims expense rations already higher than those of our best competitors?"

The authors of this book have watched similar measurement dilemmas cause many otherwise promising initiatives to founder. A sales team invested significantly in developing new learning processes to employ jointly with large corporate customers. The goal: to develop long-term relationships with key customers based on jointly inquiring into complex business issues where the firm's services might be part of more fundamental solutions. But the process was time consuming and increased the "cost of sales" measures by which the team was judged. So the team members lost enthusiasm for it.

Or consider an innovative product development team that succeeded, eventually, in completing a major product introduction almost a year ahead of schedule. A key to their success was developing a norm where engineers talked candidly about engineering problems that they didn't know how to solve, documenting problems early in the company's computer system. "We stopped keeping our problems on the hidden log that every engineer has," said one team member, "so that by sharing them more openly, many people could contribute towards better and quicker solutions." This innovation saved dramatic amounts of time and money, but it also produced high levels of visible "engineering change orders," which sent a message to outsiders that the team was "out of control." Their problems were now more evident publicly, prompting unfavorable judgments from the rest of the company (where people tended to keep problems hidden). These negative judgments about the team had become deeply rooted throughout the rest of the company by the time the product was eventually completed.

Not all the problems with assessing progress occur outside the pilot group. Many occur within. In particular, many team members invariably struggle with long delays between adopting new approaches and realizing tangible business results. Often people within the team begin pointing to the lack of tangible results even before negative assessments arise outside. Some may be uncomfortable with some of the team's new practices, and they express their anxiety by saying, "This stuff isn't working." Others are just naturally impatient, worried about the exposure of investing in new approaches with few immediate "deliverables" to show for their efforts. So many of us in contemporary organizations are inculcated with acting to optimize short-term performance measures that any process that may take months or even longer to realize significant results seems foolhardy, or just plain nonsensical.

Underneath the challenge of assessing progress are deep issues, including some that go beyond any particular organization and its history. In particular, there is a deep belief in Western culture in the legitimacy of quantitative forms of measurement, at the expense of other forms of assessment. This belief stems from the origins of modern science and the industrial revolution. Quantitative measurements, to be sure, are fundamental to the progress of modern life. But as accounting theorist Tom Johnson suggests on page 291, when businesses rely on quantitative measurements so completely, in isolation from other forms of assessment and observation, they fracture people's natural understanding of the ways that processes work. Consider the two schools of thought for managing airline pilots: In the formalistic school, pilots strictly follow rules, procedures, and numerical measurements. In the more intuitive school, pilots are encouraged to use their own innate awareness and judgment, developed through years of simulated and actual flight experience. Pilots who follow this latter approach, it turns out, have a much higher safety record, because they can see the larger picture; they're more resilient in unexpected crises. They sense the flows of forces that will affect their ability to navigate, in the same way that Toyota's production employees are trained to sense the flows of an assembly line, and the impact of those flows on quality.

It is important to remember that the system for measuring success in any organization has evolved over many years. It is as much part of the organization's "culture" as are styles of dress and unquestioned norms of conduct. It simultaneously influences, and is influenced by,

what if there's no system?

every part of the organization. Its tendrils stretch everywhere. Every pilot group is influenced by it. Moreover, the subjective attitudes underlying established measures tend to remain unquestioned, often even undiscussable. Generally, these issues are impossible to address from within the organization, especially by line leaders or internal networkers. The only ones with the authority to question established measures are executives, and often they must do so very carefully, and with effective partners.

THE UNDERLYING DYNAMICS OF ASSESSMENT AND MEASUREMENT

There are two limiting processes at work in this challenge, one primarily within the pilot team and one within the larger organization. Both concern assessments of business results, or lack thereof.

Soon after the change initiative begins, some people expect to see improved business results. However, there are significant time delays—anywhere from a few months to even years—in implementing new business practices and realizing significant improvements from these practices. The "results gap" between expected results and actual results drives negative assessments within the team (loop B1). If observed improvements lag too far behind expectations, then people within the team begin to say, "We've been trying this for weeks. What do we have to show for it? How can we continue to justify the time we are investing?" They may not have expected a miracle cure at the beginning, but the gap created by the delay has raised their concerns, and now, for some, nothing less than a miracle cure will do.

Keep in mind that these concerns will not be equal for everyone. Some will have no problem being patient; they see tangible changes occurring in business practices and they are confident that results will eventually follow. Often, this view holds for the vast majority of pilot team members. But others are much less patient and begin questions about the results gap more quickly. Their negative assessments can undermine the credibility of the initiative.

A similar process arises as side effects of the initiative appear as "negative results" according to traditional metrics in use (loop B2). This process operates primarily within the larger organization, because people within the pilot group do not necessarily view these consequences as negative. Like the increased "expense ratios" for claims adjusting or higher "engineering change orders" in the product development team, these developments are seen within the team as understandable conse-

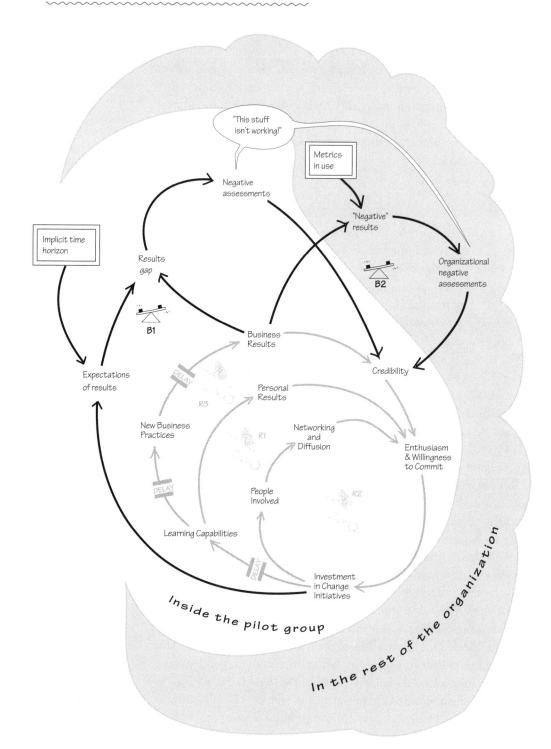

quences of their efforts. But for those looking from the outside, without much understanding of the thinking or approaches in use within the pilot team, these metrics are viewed in well established ways, and thus appear as signs of problems, not progress. People throughout the organization conclude that things are worse. "They've been trying this stuff for months, and look at the problems they have."

If either of these points of view take hold, the credibility of the transformation initiative will decline. It will be more difficult for people to commit, especially those people whose commitment is contingent on evidence of business results. They already have evidence to show that "this stuff isn't working!" There are different underlying limits involved in these two balancing processes. Negative assessments within the team are a consequence of short time horizons. Those involved in significant change initiatives need to cultivate patience commensurate with the changes they are seeking to produce. Negative results perceived within the larger organization are a consequence of traditional metrics in use, which may be inappropriately applied to the pilot group.

In balancing process B1, investment in change initiatives leads to higher expectations for results, influenced by the pilot group's implicit time horizon. The gap between expectations and actual results achieved can cause negative assessments and diminished credibility. In balancing process B2, new business results are assessed negatively by people outside the pilot team (in the gray area) against the organizational metrics in use. This also leads to diminished credibility.

STRATEGIES FOR MEETING THE CHALLENGE OF ASSESSMENT AND MEASUREMENT

Most effective strategies for this challenge focus on high leverage changes in the underlying limits of time horizons, on changes in traditional metrics, or on building the "assessment capabilities" of innovative teams, so they can both better judge their own progress and better communicate progress to those outside the team.

■ **Appreciate the time delays that are involved in profound change.** Don't judge the ultimate success or failure of your efforts based only on early results. Developing new capabilities is a matter of discipline—of regular practice with particular tools and methods, over a course of years. Line managers, by setting an example, can encourage a realistic time horizon for realizing the benefits of that practice.

"I was once a student of the 'old' school of karate," says a local line leader of a long-standing change initiative. "The sensei gave us a basic move and we practiced it ten thousand times until we had mastered it completely. Then he introduced us to another basic move. I guess this gave me a sort of patience. If I believe that our work will make a difference, then I expect it to take some time."

Both local line leaders and executives tend to have a great deal of leverage in managing expectations—leverage that they don't use.

Instead, all too often, managers are their own worst enemies. They promise better results than they need to promise—thus reinforcing expectations of quick fixes and undermining significant change processes that need time to come to fruition. Conversely, they miss the leverage in helping people understand the sources of gestation periods. In so doing, they predispose people to inappropriate assessments, which not only mislead but actively undermine important budding changes. "Managers always want to pull up the radishes to see how they're growing," says Bill O'Brien.

Time delays are not difficult to understand. Why, then, do we so consistently disregard them? Perhaps it is another telling indicator of our deeply mechanical worldviews, worldviews that suggest that change takes time because people are not trying hard enough—when in fact, "trying harder" may cause things to take longer.

■ **Build partnership with executive leaders around assessing the assessment processes.** As former Ford quality strategy director Edward Baker notes, conventional measurements represent a "trap" that can kill change and learning initiatives, by requiring them to report their results in a way that hamstrings future innovation. As measurement is passed up the hierarchy, it usually loses its value to inform about new practices and instead leads to snap evaluations. If costs are higher, or customer complaints have increased, or productivity figures have fallen, senior management often jumps to immediate conclusions that the team is performing poorly.

At its heart, this challenge calls for changing (or at least questioning) the way that traditional metrics are gathered, interpreted, and used. This is often impossible for line leaders. They often have no authority to alter or ignore the metrics, which represent the core of the managerial control systems established by senior management.

It will require ongoing exploration among all types of leaders to deal with assessment structures and systems, and keep them from limiting broader change But some number of key executive leaders must realize that "the buck stops here" with regard to established metrics and performance management practices.

Since most corporations have similar, and therefore similarly suspect, approaches to performance assessment, there is potential leverage in fostering collaboration among multiple organizations around "assessing assessment." This is the aim of the new "assessment initiative" of the Society for Organizational Learning—the first major global research initiative established within SoL, precisely because of the importance of these issues.

See "Springing Ourselves from the Measurement Trap," by Edward M. Baker, in *The Fifth Discipline Fieldbook*, p. 454.

The SoL Assessment Initiative, chartered in 1998, is an ongoing effort to study the relationship between performance assessment and organizational learning. A series of reports and proposals are available on this subject on the SoL Web site. For a reference, see our Web page: http://www.fieldbook.com/sol.html.

- **Learn to recognize and appreciate progress as it occurs.** "One of the most important tasks for any leader of change is to help people feel that they are really making progress," says former IKEA CEO Goran Carstedt. There are several initial steps to help people realistically gauge their progress.

  First, establish interim goals that can help people gauge progress along the way. It might take years to achieve a major breakthrough, but short-term targets make it easier to be patient regarding long-term goals. These might be modest targets: increased openness with key suppliers, for example. But they will be meaningful.

  [margin note: short term goals]

  Second, watch for unanticipated accomplishments. Often, the most important accomplishments are neither predicted in advance nor appreciated when they occur. At one large company undergoing major changes, the senior managers discovered that they had gone two years without a celebration, or even an acknowledgment, of their achievements to date. The subject only came up because someone from a competitor said, "We've heard about all the things you've done there. Aren't you proud?"

  Third, keep a record of the shifts, over time, in people's views. In one learning project several years ago, a consultant asked the same set of questions about the firm's strategy twice—at the outset of the project and then six months later. Several team members' views had shifted so much that they could not even recognize the views they had formerly espoused.

- **Make assessment, and developing new abilities to assess, a priority among advocates of change.** Learning to assess the consequences of significant change initiatives is a complex new territory, often neglected by leaders of those initiatives. In fact, assessment represents an opportunity for those advocating and championing change, particularly for line leaders. If they assume greater responsibility for assessment and measurement of their progress, they can make it a key strategy for accelerating learning. The key shift is to bring measurement and assessment into the service of learners, rather than have it feared as a tool for outside "evaluators." For example, Tom Johnson points out that Toyota, the world's most successful automobile company, has extensive systems of metrics in their production facilities, yet no standardized cost accounting system used for centralized management control. Their entire measurement philosophy is geared to measuring and assessing for learning.

  [margin note: is. to use it!]

  If those who lead change do not assume responsibility for assessing their progress and sharing their learnings beyond the team, they implicitly force those who may be predisposed to negative assessments to bear the "assessment burden." This is precisely the thinking behind the new assessment initiative within SoL. Those involved believe that "there is untapped leverage in change advocates becoming proactive in 'assessing to learn.' But first we must 'learn to assess' before we can better 'assess to learn.'"

Building new capabilities in assessing for learning is a complex territory but there are ways to get started.

First, raise conversations early about the criteria for success or failure. What is the appropriate amount of time before you see results? How will your team know if you have "won" or "lost"? There is much leverage in making these questions explicit grounds for conversation, both within the pilot team and among senior people who oversee the change effort. Managing "up the hierarchy" in this way can lay a foundation for partnership in assessing as a project unfolds.

〉〉 See, for example, "Cracking the Black Box" on page 303.

Second, link business literacy to new thinking about the numbers. Business is complicated. People focus on one or two measures, often collected for arbitrary, historical reasons. "We've always looked at that measure; why stop now?" A business literacy initiative can help break that habit by raising awareness of the many types of measurements to make, and how they fit the goals of the pilot group and the whole organization.

〉〉 See "Open-Book Management" on page 181, the article on Chrysler's ABC system on page 298, and the performance dashboard on page 313.

Third, remind everyone that not all assessment will be pleasant or indicate progress. Innovation means mistakes, and there will be many failures among innovative change efforts. Rather than ignore or suppress these problems, innovators need to continually reassess their own efforts and adjust. For example, a pilot group might learn a great deal from measuring the number of customer complaints, particularly if the complaints go up.

Fourth, don't shoot the messenger. When people within the team raise concerns about the speed of progress, it is important to avoid ostracizing them, criticizing them, or regarding them as not being "team players." The concerns they are raising are almost always valid, and in fact they may help alert the champions of the initiative to concerns that many people share, both within and beyond the team.

When people are ostracized for raising what they regard as legitimate concerns, they take their concerns "underground," reinforced in their criticism by the disrespect they feel.

Finally, mediate and translate explicitly between different interpretations of the same measurements. Michael Goodman, for instance, told us about a pilot group that based its success on "time to market"—except that people at the company interpreted the metric differently. Only after months of being judged negatively by outsiders did the team members recognize the difference in these interpretations and begin to talk openly about it.

If you are a network leader, then you will, by default, become an informal carrier of perception and information between pilot groups and the rest of the company. You will need to inquire on both sides: What reasoning has led people inside the team to reject the conventional approaches to measurement? With what would they replace it? And outside the team, what specific experiences and data have led people to their point of view about the initiative's results? What would have to happen for them to consider the change initiative differently? You are not an advocate for either side. Your role is to make sure that a variety of assessments and points of view are available in a way that balances the emotional turbulence people may feel.

2 Moving Upstream From Measurement

A former management accountant's perspective on the great dilemma of assessing results

H. Thomas Johnson

With Harvard Business School professor Robert Kaplan, Portland State University professor Tom Johnson wrote the business bestseller Relevance Lost—*about the ways that conventional accounting practice had led business people away from learning and improvement. Then he and Kaplan broke up their partnership. Kaplan proposed that*

This segment is, in part, adapted from a talk that Tom Johnson gave at a workshop on assessment research, conducted by the Society for Organizational Learning in January 1998; it also borrows extensively from a work in progress being coauthored with Anders Bröms, tentatively titled *Profit Without Measure*. For details on this book, see our Web site: *http://www.field book.com/resources.html.*

better measurement systems (like activity-based costing (ABC) and, more recently, the "balanced scorecard") could cure the inadequacies of accounting, but Johnson argued that any "cure" would require a thorough rethinking of the premises of the accounting profession . . . and of business. In this segment, Tom Johnson describes the path that led to his point of view, its early exemplars in Toyota and Scania, and its immensely practical and world-shaking implications for anyone who hopes to instill learning or change in a company.

THE DELTA OF DATA

I started my career as an accountant and an academic scholar of accounting history. When I look back, I see myself and my fellow accountants and economists as camped at the delta of a great river, a metaphorical Mississippi of numerical data flowing down from the business world. I spent my time pulling in and "cleaning" the measurements that flowed past me. I felt very comfortable doing this, gained a lot of expertise, and did not question my work until the late 1970s.

But then deep problems began to surface with American productivity, particularly in manufacturing. The companies that had led the world in the early 1900s—Carnegie Steel, Westinghouse, and others—were bleeding red ink and many seemed to be dying by the late 1970s. I was drawn to collaborate on the book *Relevance Lost* with Bob Kaplan because, despite some differences in our background and approach, we both sensed that conventional accounting practice itself was the source of much of the damage.

Accountants would ask why particular costs were so high. The line managers would say, "That cost number doesn't reflect anything real. It's just a measurement we've gathered for the quarterly P&L statement. Don't cut our budget there; we need that investment."

Intellectual influences on the cost driver approaches included: Bruce Henderson of the Boston Consulting Group, Peter Drucker, and Gordon Shillinglaw. See *Relevance Lost: The Rise and Fall of Management Accounting* (Boston: Harvard Business School Press, 1987).

The dispute would rise to the executive leaders of the company, who often backed the cost-cutting accountants. The managers couldn't argue their case effectively, because the prevailing pictures of reality were set by the measurements that the accountants gathered. In the end, however, these companies gave away vital markets and technologies unnecessarily. In exchange, they expected their profitability to rise, but it didn't. Here, too, conventional accounting practice was at least partly responsible. Overhead costs had burgeoned dramatically in business in the 1950s, 1960s, and 1970s, but were allocated in ways that made this difficult to recognize.

In our book, Kaplan and I suggested several ways to help manufacturers clean up the messes that accountants were making. One of our approaches, later known as activity-based costing (ABC), distinguished various drivers of resource consumption (which we called "activities") in ways more meaningful to improving production. For example, in the past the costs of setting up machines, moving materials or making quality inspections might have been included in a blanket accounting of "overhead." Now, they could be spelled out, and give producers a far more fine-grained analytic grasp of the sources of their expenses.

THE FLOWS OF ACTIVITY

After *Relevance Lost* came out, manufacturing engineers and operations managers would come up to me after speeches and say, "This is wonderful. You have told the accountants what we industrial engineers have tried to tell them for decades. Nobody's listened to us."

But then they often added, "We think you could push your argument even farther. After all, doesn't cutting costs mean cutting work? If you cut too many costs, there will be nothing left to do." They referred me to books and articles about Toyota's practices, Japanese management styles, and the quality movement. When you orchestrate work around quality, they said, "costs take care of themselves." Since these guys weren't accountants, I assumed at first that they didn't understand. But as I looked farther into their sources, I found myself drawn to the work and associates of Dr. W. Edwards Deming.

I was now moving farther upstream, looking directly at the work practices that produced all the data at the mouth of the river. Toyota's overhead costs, I learned, were a fraction of those in American companies. The cost savings didn't come from lower pay or tighter inventory, but from the way they organized work. Toyota's production and manufacturing systems made it easy for workers to identify and correct errors as they occurred; and the entire company relied on workers' brainpower to resolve problems and make improvements.

Traditional accountants never looked at work processes; it wasn't considered part of their job. In fact, standard accounting practices made it harder for managers to do so. It was as if the conventional ways of quantifying work had been designed to keep people unaware of the attitudes that would lead to more significant improvements.

See *Relevance Regained: From Top-Down Control to Bottom-Up Empowerment*, by H. Thomas Johnson (New York: The Free Press, 1992), especially Chapter 5.

THE TRIBUTARIES OF AWARENESS

My next book, *Relevance Regained*, expressed some of these points. Soon after it came out, I was invited to join a case study project at the Toyota plant in Georgetown, Kentucky—one of the largest Toyota plants anywhere, and the site of manufacture for their bestselling American car, the Camry. Toyota has an excellent accounting system, but they do not use information from that system to drive day-to-day decisions about operations. Their decision making is guided by a deeply ingrained awareness and sensitivity to the flow of work. They don't need accounting measurements to tell when some work process or material doesn't fit; they sense it immediately. It's as if the organization as a whole had a highly developed immune system, giving it exceptionally high sensitivity to any shift in the quality of the process. This did not happen by accident. When Toyota opened the Georgetown plant, about three hundred employees from Japan spent a year in Kentucky, shadowing and coaching the people there, transferring their ability to recognize when everything was going right.

Around the same time, I began making regular visits to the closely owned Swedish company Scania, the world's fourth-largest maker of heavy-duty trucks. Scania has a highly fine-grained-method of developing collective awareness in product design. At other companies, a numbers-oriented accounting system such as ABC might keep track of the number of different parts used to make a truck. (Parts proliferation is a significant cost factor, because each additional part requires more costs in ordering materials, storing them, inspecting them, and teaching people about them.) But Scania has no objective cost targets to drive design work. Instead, as part of the design process, sophisticated ratios called "structural indexes" represent the continuing advantages and disadvantages of each truck's design. This fosters a greater standardization and interchangeability of parts, without sacrificing product diversity. Among the thousands of variations in the company's truck cabs, there are only one windshield, one driver's compartment, and three door shapes.

Toyota and Scania clearly represented in-depth experiences of organizational learning, which I began to investigate further. Now I felt I was truly moving upstream, to where the water was crisp and clear. I was starting to look for the underlying assumptions that lay beneath the layers of abstraction that conventional measurements had generated.

THE HEADWATERS OF NATURE

I was drawn to the work of epistemologist Gregory Bateson, who argues that many of the world's problems stem from "the difference between the way human beings think and the way nature works." Nature, as Bateson said, doesn't measure. Nature deals only with the "pattern which connects," not with quantification. There is no objective standard for how high a tree should grow, or how fast an animal should run.

Similarly, for most of the history of humanity, people did not quantify their world. Measurement in Aristotle's day had been comparative: "One candle is brighter than the other." Or "One shade of red is brighter," or "One object is heavier," or "One person is bigger." That view of the world changed in the sixteenth century, with Galileo Galilei, who gave us the modern notion of measurement by arguing that the "motion" of any object could be considered separately from all the other characteristics of that moving object, including its weight. When that distinction was clear, then motion could be measured against a scale, and the speeds and direction of movement of different objects could be quantified.

The story of physics goes on from there to Descartes, who plotted motion onto a grid (the Cartesian coordinates); to Newton, who established universal mathematical laws that linked motion to gravitation; and to modern quantified measurement, which depends upon separating, in our minds, the qualities of an object that are inseparable and inherently combined in nature. As humanity got very good at measurement, we reaped the results in technological progress: steam engines, internal combustion, high-rises, and so forth. In this century, measurement came to the human organization—every type of organization, from a church to a business. The practice of measurement leads, over time, to reductionist thinking and then to mechanistic activity—which does an incredible job of destroying nature and the natural sensibility.

If you doubt the degree to which our increased reliance on mechanization has destroyed nature, imagine being dumped in a setting like Idaho two hundred years ago, as Lewis and Clark were, without the machines or tools that people take for granted today. Many people would probably be scared to the point of shock. Then consider the number of people today who blithely ignore the rhythms, limits, and patterns of the natural world, replacing them with the rhythms and patterns of clocks, computers, transit schedules, thermostats, and other quantifying instruments. In a comparatively brief period of time, civilization has become accustomed to "conscious purpose," as Bateson called it—our consciously contrived ends that overrun, instead of emulate, the way that nature develops itself.

Nature has no ends; it builds, continually, upon the interplay of the means of evolution and biology. By contrast, in work based on measurement, the ends justify any perversion of the means, because information

Bateson is quoted in *Deep Ecology: Living as if Nature Mattered*, by Bill Devall and George Sessions (Salt Lake City: Gibbs Smith, 1985). Also see *Mind and Nature: A Necessary Unity*, by Gregory Bateson (New York: Bantam Books, 1979), pp. 53–60.

For more perspective and background about measurement and the evolution of technical thought, see *The Wholeness of Nature: Goethe's Way Toward a Science of Conscious Participation in Nature*, by Henri Bortoft (Hudson, NY: Lindisfarne Press, 1996).

i.e. process is not measured

about the means, the ways in which things get done, and the ways in which people and work evolve, do not show up in the measurements.

Perhaps W. Edwards Deming was resonating with this point when he said that 97 percent of what matters in an organization can't be measured. He added that the result of conventional measurement was "tampering": manipulation without genuine understanding. He seemed to recognize that many of our deepest frustrations come from an inherent sense of the natural way of life, lost in this process. Most of us can't even articulate it, but we've got a gut sense that discovering and embodying nature's patterns is the essence of learning, and the core of our work as human beings. We need to find a way to put ourselves in harmony with these patterns somehow, or dismal consequences will follow.

It is novel to see a respect for the natural way of life embodied in large-scale organizational measurement practice. At Toyota and Scania, the ends do not justify the means. The means are the ends in the making. Given the right means, the ends take care of themselves. I had heard about an example of this in Marcus Wallenberg, the chairman of Scania's board during the years after World War II. A member of the family that controlled Scania and a group of other companies (through a holding company called, simply, "Investor"), he visited all the companies regularly. He did not look at spread sheets; he went into the shops and talked to engineers and operators. When people asked him what he expected to find there, he said, "I listen to the music." He had built in himself the capability for naturally distinguishing harmony from discord.

Assessment in itself is not enough to build this capability. You must be able to continually evaluate and improve your thinking about assessment. Deming wrestled with this issue regularly; when he heard people talk about measuring results, he often asked: "How do you know?" In other words, how can you possibly assess success or failure based on the few miniscule elements tracked by your "measurement machine"? How do you know you have chosen the right elements, and weighted them effectively? If the assumptions put into the measurement model are false, how do you come to recognize the problem? And if the answer depends on regaining some of the insights from nature that were thrown away by the industrial approach to numbers, how do you incorporate those insights back into daily processes?

This message about harmony with nature is not new: We see it in the thinking of Buddha, Christ, Lao Tzu, Plato, all the way through to modern thinkers like Johann Wolfgang von Goethe, Alfred North Whitehead, Paul Tillich, and David Bohm. — Tom Johnson

THE SOURCE OF THE PATTERN

By now, I felt like I was moving still farther upstream, to the source of the "measurement river" in the lakes. Even the lakes, however, aren't the ultimate source. Above them are clouds whose moisture has risen from the ocean, with the rivers' water flowing into it. As T. S. Eliot wrote,

The T. S. Eliot qoute comes from "Little Gidding," pt. 5, in *Four Quartets.*

> " . . . the end of all our exploring
> Will be to arrive where we started
> And know the place for the first time."

I do not advocate eliminating measurement, per se. Although nature does not quantify, nature does count. There are many patterns of two: two eyes for vision, the bilateral system of mammals' bodies, the two genders of sexual reproduction. The plant kingdom is rife with fives, as Bateson pointed out. And there are many ratios in nature, evident in such phenomena as the patterns of shading of light and darkness.

i.e. It's relative— one to another, better or worse

But when measurement becomes a tool for fragmenting our understanding, and assessing one process, or one person, as better than another on some objective scale, then it is inherently unnatural. Accountants and economists regularly operate in this unnatural manner, and when it fails to predict the world's behavior accurately, they refine and redefine the mathematics in their models. But to paraphrase Bateson, describing the world through any mechanistic set of measurements is like partaking of a meal by eating the menu.

What, then, would a system of measurement look like that drew people perpetually closer to the "pattern which connects"? Perhaps one model is the conversations at Toyota. The question, "How are we doing?" is never answered in terms of quantities.

Suppose that you're working a spot-welding machine in a body shop, finishing a small subassembly that may fit underneath the fender. You know exactly where all the components come from, and you can see the person who takes the finished subassembly from you. You also have a clear idea of how the piece fits into the car. Everyone on the line knows immediately, from their own sense of sight, whether or not a piece of work is good enough to pass on. Nobody has to wait for an external measurement system to tell them if something is amiss.

People inform one another not through numbers, but through stories—describing where a piece of work came from, what happened to it, and why it might not be "right." It took years to build the mutual understanding necessary to tell, and listen to, these stories. The company has internalized its measures. People have an innate feel for when the work is on track, just as a medieval artisan knew whether a piece of stone might fit into the wall of a cathedral. There is standardization, but it is inherently flexible; people are always thinking about ways to reshape the work. They are like dancers performing according to a choreographic layout that they choose together at the beginning of the day.

Since people are the measurement system, great attention is paid to respecting people and treating them well. Job assignments and tasks are varied, to keep people feeling alert and comfortable. Toyota employs a large number of ergonomic specialists to continually find ways to overcome stress and strain. One of them told me that, "When workers finish a two-hour stint on one segment of the line, they should come away feeling refreshed. It should feel like coming out of a health club. You know you've just worked hard, but you feel better than you did when you went in." If someone reports feeling uncomfortable, that's a clear signal that something is wrong in the process. Factory workers elsewhere sometimes develop severe carpal tunnel syndrome, and can no longer function. To my knowledge, that doesn't happen at Toyota.

Measurement should flow with the natural sensibility. As Gregory Bateson might have put it: "Are we undoing the way that mechanization leads us to think? Are we putting into place a deeper appreciation of the way nature works?" To ask these questions is to move far upstream, where quality, learning, and performance are facets of the same reality.

3 Measuring to Report . . . or to Learn?

Inside the ABC experience at Chrysler

David Meador

The previous article described the emergence of the theory of activity-based costing (ABC)—and its limitations. Herein, the former manager of the ABC effort at Chrysler Motors shows how work groups involved with new measurement approaches will inevitably move "upstream" as well—or grow moribund. David Meador is currently the manager of the organizational learning effort at Detroit Edison, the electric power company of Detroit, Michigan.

Numbers are the language of business. Changing the way we measure changes everything. That's why it is hard to overstate the magnitude of the change Chrysler initiated in 1991 when it decided to implement activity-based costing (ABC). ABC was a learning system designed to give people at the line level the information they needed to manage their piece of the enterprise. But "measuring to learn" was not part of the Chrysler tradition. "Measuring to report or assess performance," as a means of management control, was the Chrysler way. In that sense, ABC was a direct threat to many of the product line managers and other executives whose performance appraisals were tied to those numbers. Not seeing this in advance, we greatly underestimated the resistance the new system inspired throughout the organization.

We ABC implementation team members had joined up to be part of a leading-edge program. But six months later, we began to question this career move. At the start of our consultation/training projects, the local managers seemed excited. Then the first data on the costs of their processes came out, and their first question was not, "What can we learn from this?" It was: "Who's going to see this?" Many of them quickly lost interest. We gradually realized that the ABC effort was hindered not by plant manager resistance, but by our own approach to working with them. We were asking people to think in dramatically different ways, but we hadn't chosen to do the same ourselves.

With this in mind, we invested time in learning new skills such as systems thinking, effective conversations, dialogue, and stress management. We created an environment where members of our team could surface undiscussables: issues not normally aired at Chrysler. We explored one another's thinking. As boss of the team, I encouraged people to push back when they disagreed with me. We started to feel good about our new way of working through issues . . . and then we began to invite outsiders to participate in team meetings. They saw our open, healthy disagreement, and concluded that we had serious problems getting along with one another. The lesson for us: People would see the nuts-and-bolts of ABC in the light of their existing context. If we wanted ABC to "take," we'd have to give them a new context to consider.

We began by analyzing the old context. At Chrysler—a fear-based, command-and-control culture—management insisted on information being fed to them on a regular basis. When they didn't like the information, they called people on the carpet. Everyone knew how the then-CFO had taken in some ABC information to our former chairman, Lee Iacocca, intending to give Iacocca a candid report on the needs of manu-

The insights here were developed through close association with Fred Kofman, then of the MIT Center for Organizational Learning, who consulted in depth with Chrysler on the design and implementation of the organizational learning aspects of this ABC program. For more about the principles of this approach, see "Double-Loop Accounting," by Fred Kofman, *The Fifth Discipline Fieldbook*, p. 286.

facturing. Instead, the chairman said, "I finally have the data to show that the people in manufacturing aren't doing their job!" In a culture that encouraged yelling, threatening, and swearing, people who didn't make the numbers learned to hide the data . . . or expect reprisals.

Working with ABC required a different style altogether. Managers had to give people the room to make mistakes—and the time to correct them. In the context of Chrysler's culture, this was weakness. And weak people were not taken seriously.

Having articulated all this, the behavior we'd seen around ABC made sense. Setting up an ABC method means interviewing and surveying people throughout a plant to find out what work they do and how they do it. We hadn't realized how vulnerable it made them feel to have their data exposed to public view. For example, one stamping line routinely reported low scrap levels—because they made their scrap disappear by taking it to a recycling center. They looked good, but at a cost: They couldn't use the data to improve their actual scrap rates. Another group had carefully represented themselves as concentrating on preventative and predictive maintenance instead of reacting to events. Our data showed that they spent only 10 percent of their time and resources on preventative maintenance, and none at all on predictive.

The same was true at every level. Individual workers worried about teams having access to the data on their performance; teams worried about supervisors, supervisors about plant managers, and plant managers about the corporate staff. Moreover, people often did not use the information they already had, even when it could help them. We often found plants tracking and charting setup time or cycle time—data that would be relevant at the line level. When we asked why, they said it was gathered for people in corporate. They hadn't considered taking the time to study and talk about the data themselves. But after they learned they could trust us not to pass their data on to the next level, they warmly embraced it. It provided a much-needed feedback loop on their own processes, that they had never had before.

To win people's trust, we had to develop ways to keep measurement away from management. For instance, at one plant, the teams preferred to laboriously enter data into their ABC charts by hand, instead of using computer terminals. This kept the data at their level. They also knew that if they mechanized the process, it would make it more difficult to understand what they had seen. So instead of computer screens, we provided them with whiteboards and greaseboards for tracking measures.

But some of the operations and financial staff wanted us to institute computer screens. They argued that it would help assembly line teams input data and print out colorful graphs, and it would provide consistency to measures around the company. We knew there was a hidden agenda. Some plant managers wanted their data by the hour, instead of at the end of the week. Then they could do what they did best under the traditional system: micromanage. If we allowed those systems to replace the greaseboards, it would undo one of the central purposes of our approach.

At the same time, I sympathized with the plant managers who wanted to understand their operations better. Sometimes a plant manager would tell us, "We only measure six things in this plant, and everyone is aligned with those metrics." Then we would interview people and find hundreds of measures, some contradictory to the direction the plant was trying to move strategically. For instance, the corporate purchasing staff might have asked for the performance metrics on a piece of expensive equipment, so they could negotiate a better price next time. And the plant manager would have no idea that the data was being collected.

REDESIGNING THE CHANGE PROCESS

With a deeper understanding of the structural roots of resistance, we began to redesign our implementation of ABC. We learned to ask for three full days of plant management teams' time for training. This was unheard of; plant management teams never went offsite for one day, let alone three. But much to our surprise, all of the teams agreed to give us the time we needed.

Then, we developed a management "flight simulator"—a software tool to let plant managers experience, for themselves, the operational consequences of the old finance system versus the ABC approach. Much to their surprise, the managers discovered that the old way of allocating costs might lead them to continue investing in unprofitable product lines, or to underinvest in profitable ones. The simulator also gave us a way to talk to them about minimizing the time they spent on the floor fixing problems. "You have been a crutch for other people in the system," we could tell them. "We have to pull you out and build that capability in the team." It sounds easy to say this, but it's very, very difficult to say it in a way that people will hear.

We also created a series of seminars, scheduled throughout the conversion process, to address people's fear and anxiety. The last seminar covered the often overlooked issues of continuing commitment, which

For more about management flight simulators, see The Fifth Discipline Fieldbook, p. 529ff.

had led to many implementation breakdowns—issues such as articulating and agreeing on the "conditions of satisfaction" up front. In all our work, while using "learning discipline" tools, we learned to avoid organizational learning jargon. The language itself increased resistance.

THE HEART OF THE CONFLICT

Several champions in senior management protected the finance team from organizational push-back. As long as we operated within the context of their organizations, we were okay. But when we found ourselves outside of that safe umbrella, we saw our measurements misinterpreted, misunderstood, and misapplied. As Fred Kofman noted, it's very easy to use numbers to stop somebody else's project. Thus, the "good corporate soldiers" would ask questions about organizational learning efforts like: "You're spending a lot of money and a lot of time on this; I don't see the benefits. How do we know we're using the right tools and teachers?" These questions can be raised in the spirit of inquiry, but that wasn't their purpose here.

I also understood they had a legitimate point. Companies spending millions on organizational learning need to know how to leverage their money most effectively. If we went into a management review meeting and said, we won't see results from organizational learning for a year or two, they'd throw us out. They're working on this quarter's results, and they want to know what deliverables you have for them today.

Ideally, the use of better approaches to measurement should make it easier to raise the question of corporate purpose—and how best to support that purpose. When I was a young accountant, a lawyer took me aside and said, "You don't understand the purpose of this company. It's to make a handful of people at the top wealthy beyond their wildest dreams." The highest-level executives live like kings, flying on $25 million jets, with houses around the world, and never spending a penny of their own money. Nobody in the system says, "Should we really be doing this?" They espouse learning and support for people, and challenge to death a million dollars spent on organizational learning. But they don't question buying a $25 million jet. In the end, learning initiatives—particularly those which recast measurement—will raise these types of inconsistencies to the surface. If there isn't a sufficient degree of trust and safety at the senior level, then the efforts will operate at risk.

4 Cracking the "Black Box" of a Learning Initiative Assessment

George Roth

There comes a moment early in any organizational improvement effort, when people inside and outside the pilot group want to know how the effort is doing. A skeptical executive or auditor, for example, may show up with a question: "Are these new team meetings cost effective?" Or "Why are you wasting time on soft stuff, instead of paying attention to the business?"

Questions like these may feel unfair, yet the sentiment underlying them is entirely appropriate. You may have invested hundreds of thousands of dollars and the time and commitment of dozens, or even hundreds, of people. If you can't begin to assess those investments, how can you build your own judgment about the value of your efforts? And if you can't do that, how can you learn from your experience? It would be valuable to communicate your new insights to the whole organization, and tragic to have your efforts misperceived as wasted.

That is why you need to be able to not just endure, but lead the assessment of your learning efforts, with the same hard-nosed rigor that you would use to assess any other type of investment. At the same time, however, you need to set up the assessment so it furthers the learning of your pilot group and, ultimately, the entire organization.

Judging the value of something as intrinsic, subjective, and tacit as learning is a new kind of activity for corporations. In conventional assessments, experts produce their recommendations through a kind of "black box"—a process that others take for granted without having it explained. The evaluators collect the data (the amount you spent and the quantifiable benefits), plug it into formulas (perhaps return on investment, cash flow, or internal rate of return), and produce a quick quantitative judgment, perhaps based on a hurdle rate or ROI calculation.

Unfortunately, the precision of these measurements, even with qualitative commentary, leads to misleading judgments. Worse still, this type of "black box" assessment—and the intervention that the outsiders make—can easily undermine your learning efforts. Conventional assessment will tend to stop, dead in its tracks, the very learning that you are trying to nurture and grow.

HOW ASSESSMENT CAN KILL LEARNING

Suppose you were studying a new skill, such as algebra. In most schools, you would be given a test: a set of problems to solve that required you to use that skill. You would write in the answers that seemed correct, and you would turn in the test.

You'd be finished. But would you have learned algebra? No. Not without feedback. You would need to find out how many answers were right, and whether your approach was appropriate. Until you got this feedback, you would merely have performed. You would have no way to judge your progress, and no guidance for deciding what to study next.

Most "assessments" of organizational learning are like that test. The people on a pilot group are asked to perform, to produce results. Someone in the organization "keeps score"—traditionally the information technology–based accounting systems, whose reports are passed up the line to senior management. Your pilot group may never see that report. Even if you see it, you may have no opportunity to talk with senior managers about its meaning. You never learn the values or judgments underlying management's evaluation. You can't assess your progress.

In the absence of that assessment, you may decide, "Our success stems from our ability to practice systems thinking," but your hypothesis will be, as social scientists call it, "superstitious." Until you get some legitimate feedback that is linked to your activities, you are steering blind, guided by your personal experience rather than the broader organizational information. You will have no idea whether to conduct more systems thinking exercises next time, or less, or how to vary their design.

That is why you need an effective assessment process that engages the collective judgment of the whole organization—and lets you raise questions to build your pilot group's own collective judgment.

REDEFINING "ASSESSMENT"

The words "assessment" and "evaluation" have gotten so muddled in business that, before we can think constructively about them, we need to distinguish them.

Why does being assessed often feel like being persecuted by an auditor? The word itself derives from a Latin root, *assessare*, meaning "to set a rate or an amount," and thus to impose a tax. Today, the word often invokes a strong, gut-level memory of being graded in school, and then having your opportunities determined by those judgments. Naturally, people feel anger and resentment when they think of being "assessed."

Evaluation comes from another Old French verb, *évaluer*, "to be worthy" (or to have value and valor). To evaluate means to determine the worth of an effort, or to appraise it. Since judgment is often subjective and capricious, many people expect "evaluations" to be flawed and biased.

Organizations have tried to compensate for these biases by carefully quantifying assessments, using tests, surveys and numerical rankings to measure the progress of learning. ("Employee satisfaction scored 3.2 this year, compared to 2.7 for last year. We must be learning.") But in day-to-day organizational work, people recognize that this type of "bean counting" does not reflect any authentic change in the organization's capability. It merely indicates which type of "beans" are valued.

Some people try to eliminate all judgments, evaluations, and assessments. But that makes them doubly vulnerable—to outside criticism, and to the loss of their own judgment. They need to learn not to throw the "assessment" baby out with the "evaluation" bathwater. Assessment needs a new definition: the gathering of information about results, the comparison of those results with the results of the past, and the open discussion of the meaning of those results, the ways they have been gathered, and their implications for your next move.

~~~~~~~

PLANNING THE STAGES OF ASSESSMENT

How can you tailor your investment in new capabilities so they'll be robust—even in a business downturn?

To answer that question, you need to understand the complex, long-term nature of the link between learning and business performance. Your assessment strategy needs to somehow indicate, through short-term measures, that you are probably on the road to improving profitability in the long term.

This chart is a device for planning that sort of assessment strategy. It helps you distinguish the cause-and-effect relationships between your learning effort (input), your actual new capabilities and skills (learning output), and the results you visibly produce.

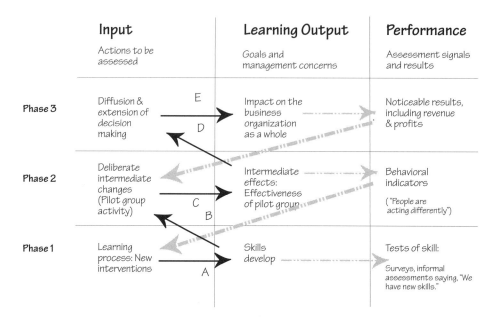

The chart shows the learning initiative taking place in three distinct phases. They overlap somewhat, but in most learning efforts, they will occur in order. Each might take several months, a full year, or even longer.

This chart was first developed with Peter Senge in a research effort at the MIT Center for Organizational Learning, and later expanded, in a *Dance of Change*-related initiative, by George Roth with Art Kleiner and Amy Fiore.

■ Phase 1 (shown in the bottom left-hand corner of the chart) begins with a "new intervention," such as a new training course that fifteen or twenty people take. You invest in their skills and capabilities, both individually and collectively, using some learning orientation (such as the five learning disciplines).

  If you're the manager designing this initiative, then you probably aspire to "noticeable business results": the final performance signal at the top right-hand corner. But during phase 1, you probably don't get there. Instead, your surveys or informal assessments tend to focus on people's new skills: "I completed the course, and now I know how to use system archetypes." Why focus there? Because that's the only tangible result that can be measured so far.

■ In phase 2, you apply those new skills and get a "pilot" action under-way: a process redesign, new product development, or business-related project. You may still continue the phase 1 training efforts, but you also shift business practice. And the measurable results shift. You assess the effectiveness of the pilot group in terms of behavioral indicators. People act differently. They build relationships with key suppliers. They manage their time more effectively. They may report that the atmosphere has changed, so that they can think more creatively and speak more candidly.

- In phase 3, your efforts begin to change "business as usual." Operations within the pilot group will improve, and the new methods may filter out to the rest of the organization. (There may, for example, be a series of cross-functional systems exercises set up for teams around the organization.)

Now you may finally see an impact on the business as a whole. You may begin to achieve some of your most desired goals: fundamental, long-term improvement in organizational achievement, performance, profit, and revenue.

But then, after a short, happy period of self-congratulation, along comes that skeptic from outside: "How can you prove that these 'noticeable results' have anything to do with your training efforts?"

So, in an effort to justify your time and expense, you set out to trace the causal relationship between the bottom left- and the upper right-hand corner. You soon discover that you can't prove that link. So many other factors have operated in this system, you cannot say for sure that the learning effort, across all three phases, has definitely led to the results you claim.

So what can you prove? The black arrows represent five different documentable relationships that, over the course of the project's first several years, give you a generic way to test the progress of your activity.

Assessment A: During phase 1, you can assess the link between the learning process and new skills, by asking people to rate their own improvement when they return from training.

Assessment B: Later, you can track the number of new innovations and activities within the pilot group, developed by people who have been trained (or people they work with) versus those who have not been exposed to new training.

Assessment C: Beginning in phase 2, you can measure the impact of new behaviors, by looking for observable behavioral indicators. In surveys, do people report that their meetings are more productive? Does decision making happen in a more collaborative fashion? Do people perceive one another less negatively, and blame one another less frequently?

Assessment D: Gradually, you can begin to trace pilot group members' influence on the work of the organization. Some, no doubt, will be frustrated in their attempts to gain responsibility and achieve results; but others, often quietly, will show up in new areas of innovation. Simply listing these new activities demonstrates the diffusion and extension of decision-making prowess.

Assessment E: Finally (and only in phase 3), you can point to the "noticeable results" that each of these efforts have produced. How do they compare to the "noticeable results" of other projects, which don't have people involved from the original learning effort?

This approach to assessment gives you a reliable set of measurements that anyone in the organization can agree is significant. It will help you deal with the skeptics, both inside and outside the pilot group. But it still represents a generic "black box"—an evaluation without any effort to build judgment and learning. Fortunately, however, this "assessment by stages" is only a beginning. With this framework in mind, you can engage executive leaders and other line leaders each step of the way, in developing collective judgment about the purpose of your effort and the meaning of success.

DEVELOPING JUDGMENT WITHIN THE PILOT GROUP

Many pilot group members, at various times along the way, intuitively seek an answer to the question, "How are we doing?" They also want to tell their story to help others make sense of their experience. But they're typically too busy to write down their thoughts about the new approaches they've learned or developed, and they are often reluctant to invest a day or two in describing the details of their progress. So their story is lost, or drowned in a mass of hurriedly gathered quantitative "data" that does not really represent the team's experience.

However, you can set up a project so that gathering and assessing data is a collective act within the pilot group—not assigned to an individual, but conducted by the team as a whole. When that happens, the assessment process becomes part of the pilot group's innate capabilities, and it reinforces (and accelerates) the group's improvement.

As members of a pilot team, beginning the phase 1 level, you should already be talking together about the criteria for assessment: "How will we judge our success? What criteria will we set to know we're doing well?" Look at the various types of data that you have assumed you would collect: for example, the cost of the training, the time spent in training, and the results of surveys you expect to make. Ask: "Why should we collect this particular data? What do we expect it to show? And what assumptions are embedded in it?" With questions like these, you tackle the difficult task of talking about the values that you tacitly attribute to the data.

What observable behaviors should you see, for instance, after training people in "the ladder of inference"? Perhaps you'd agree that people would distinguish their observations from their interpretations, and regularly seek to understand one another's points of view—not just in easy times, but also in moments of stress. "If our competitor starts eating our lunch," you might say, "we'll know we're really doing well if we don't revert to our old backbiting behaviors."

Develop your own criteria for success, based on the results that you care about. And continue engaging everyone who joins the effort. In every training session or practice field workshop, for instance, the leader could ask: "If you applied these skills, how would you know it was making a positive difference?"

It's also important to engage in candid conversations after you collect your assessment data. The U.S. Army's after-action reviews (AARs) are based on this principle: Starting with "ground truth" (the relatively objective record, gathered by computers and video cameras, about some recent training exercise or battle), teams of participants meet to come to a mutual understanding of the reasons why a particular campaign worked—or did not. The ability to lead a good after-action review has become a critical skill for leaders.

≷≷ See page 473 for more on the army's after-action review.

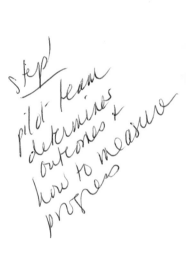

ENGAGING OTHER LEVELS OF THE HIERARCHY

Even while you are still in phase 1, still getting your pilot team going, you need to begin talking with the management higher up in the organization about their criteria for judgment. These conversations are shown in the diagram on page 306, by the lower gray dotted arrow.

You might begin by saying, "Boss, we don't know exactly how this will turn out. We have our own ideas, of course, and we are monitoring our results very closely. But we need to know, before we go any farther: In this unprecedented effort, how would you define achievement?"

Then, ask them to think about the future with you: "If the learning effort truly made progress, what kinds of measures or tangible evidence might you expect to see?" Then ask, "What is a reasonable time frame in which to expect progress, and bottom line results?"

These are not easy questions to ask. Your bosses know that this new learning initiative will be closely scrutinized by everyone in the organization, if only because it's different. Moreover, your bosses are ultimately accountable for its results. Now you're saying that it's an experiment, and you're not sure it will work! By asking for your bosses' judgment, you are overtly asking them to take on part of the risk and responsibility for your success or failure.

In the long run, you will make yourself much less vulnerable by raising these questions. Your bosses may hold a "theory in use," not even consciously articulated, that "success" does not only mean producing better results. It also means having your practices adopted by other groups throughout the organization. As a result, though they intellectually support your experiments, they may send mixed signals if you contradict too many established practices too visibly. They may speak of commitment to learning, but demonstrate, if only through side comments and critical lapses in support, that they really expect the new efforts to fail.

The earlier you can raise questions about assessment, the more likely you are to break such patterns. What dangers and opportunities do your bosses see, which are not so obvious to you? You may only get an hour or two on the bosses' calendar to talk about this, but even that short conversation can invite them to feel genuine responsibility in the effort—as not just objective "judges," or benign paternalistic parents, but as sincerely engaged individuals. You can also use this conversation to lay the groundwork for behavioral changes to come: "People by this time next quarter or next year will probably act differently. What types of new behavior would represent a step forward, in your view?"

Note that you are not asking your bosses in advance for approval. You are making a sincere inquiry about judgment: What will constitute success, as this innovation evolves? One team I worked with told me they could never go to their boss to discuss setting up measures and criteria. They said, "Our boss doesn't want to have that kind of conversation." If that's true for you, then it's all the more important to persevere—to find a way to get the issues of assessment out on the table.

After your initial conversations with the boss, six months or more might pass. At some point, you will move up to the next rung of the ladder: to phase 2, the stage of "pilot unit" activity. Now there is some middle-range group of people, perhaps twenty-five to three hundred people, who have begun to accomplish miracles. (Anyway, they think they're miracles.) The emphasis within the group has shifted, from marveling at the skills they've learned, to marveling at the results they can produce.

Now, in a carefully timed conversation, it's vital to raise the question of criteria for success again—not just with the boss, but with other senior people and peers outside the effort, who will be inevitably watching, and judging, its progress. (These conversations are shown in the diagram on page 306 by the upper gray dotted arrow.) "We are continuing to try new things," you might say, "and some of these are stretching over to include people in your department. What kinds of success might you be looking for? How will you judge that the learning effort is effective?"

MAKING IT FUN

I've noticed that when an assessment process seems like a lot of work, it tends to be on the wrong track. The question "How are we doing?" is nearly always interesting. The question, "How can we present our progress to the boss?" is nearly always deadening.

To be sure, most teams want to win. A good assessment process lets them see the scoreboard while they're playing—to develop their own standards, and to recognize the standards of the overall organization. Once those standards are visible, then the pilot group members can direct their energies and efforts appropriately. If people feel safe, they can initiate and use assessment processes to raise questions not just about results, but about the worth and value of their efforts. That leads, quite naturally, to the kind of eye-opening storytelling and conversation that helps people make sense of their lives. In the end, that's how you build capabilities that could lead to a better "score" next time—or, if not a better score, a better understanding of the score's meaning.

Measuring the Unmeasurable David Meador

SOME "SOFT" RESULTS ARE ALMOST IMPOSSIBLE TO QUANTIFY—ESPECIALLY IF we hold to the conventions of traditional financial analysis. How can we measure diversity, employee satisfaction, or personal change—the most important factors in predicting organizational change?

But not measuring such factors could lead to people excluding them from consideration at all. I think a chairman or president should be able to sit back and say, "We did well with employee satisfaction this year," and feel confident in the validity of that assessment.

In that spirit, let me propose some of the "unmeasurables" that I have considered measuring, or actually implemented, to open the door to better conversations:

■ **Open inquiry about difficult issues:** If you survey them, can people tell stories of breakthroughs? "I've been able to explore a controversial business issue, and stay whole in the process. Here's how it happened." Are the number of positive stories increasing over time? Also, are the amount of employee litigation or union grievances decreasing? By how much?

■ **Treating people with dignity and respect:** Do we have a hostile environment? I would ask people for their assessment of the company, and specifically ask them to ground those assessments in observable data. Then I would see if that data could be independently verified and even tracked in some kind of measurement. This would be a challenging survey, but it would help us understand the drivers behind employee commitment. It would help us answer the question: As a management team, are we doing the right things?

■ **Advocacy, inquiry, and effective conversation:** We could tape-record some meetings and conduct a word analysis. How many times do people say, "I propose we do this now," versus "Could you explain your reasoning?" You could probably weight different phrases according to the level of advocacy versus inquiry. For example, "I don't know" would indicate a high degree of openness. This would also provide valuable feedback to the members of the team.

■ **Care for the employee community:** On some level, the question "Should I get involved with organizational learning?" is a question of belief and values. I grew up watching my father struggling with several careers, and ultimately seeing him lose his job as a high school auto mechanics teacher. It has stuck in my mind all my life; the experience, for instance, of going to a surplus food bank to get powdered eggs and Spam for our survival. And seeing the effect on our family of my father's loss of dignity. As a result, I have an ongoing problem with companies that permit traumatic things to happen to their employees who come to work with passion, commitment, and the will to be their best. The organization has to show, through some measurable and verifiable way, that it is walking the talk on commitment to its people. Chances are, this can be done through an analysis of the history of the company's layoff practices.

5 Performance Dashboards

Indicators designed by employees for learning, rather than designed by the central organization for control

Chris Meyer and Rick Ross

Silicon Valley–based consultant Christopher Meyer is the academic director of Stanford University's Fast Cycle Time Strategy Program. Here, he and Rick Ross present a hybrid, proven in the field, of reflective inquiry skills and high performance process measurement.

This graphic tool for managers and teams is based upon two powerful assumptions. First, learning efforts in corporations depend upon good performance measurement. Without clear and consistent feedback to help monitor your progress toward your goal and the effects of your actions, there is no way to learn.

Second, measurement is meaningless without interpretation and judgment, as practiced by the people who will make decisions and learn through implementation. Unfortunately, in many companies, there is a tacit "measurement mind-set" that treats measurement and judgment as synonymous. According to this mind-set, once you agree, as managers, upon a number, you can rush to make a decision about it, without considering the quality of that number: where it came from, how it was measured, or why it was chosen.

For instance, many managers read budgets by looking immediately to the variance column. If the number is negative, that's "bad." They spent more than they predicted. If the number is positive, that's "good." But in reality, a negative budget variance is not always bad. Maybe the budget projections were too low; or maybe the project didn't invest enough, which means that it will be consistently underfunded. Underfunding might, in turn, delay the release date for several months—which, in a

These concepts owe a great deal to the influence of Russell Ackoff.

fast-moving industry like high technology or fashion, could result in 30 percent lower profits. In that case, the "good" budget number might actually be devastating. To reach a truly viable judgment, you would have to consider this number in light of several other measures—including, perhaps, your staffing levels and progress toward your deadlines. You would have to think through the ramifications of those interrelated measures in terms of your own goals and objectives.

The "measurement mind-set" has been in place so long that, even in companies which espouse learning, few offer alternatives. Hence the value of the performance dashboard. It is a device for escaping the measurement mind-set, by displaying information relevant to a working group or team in a graphically meaningful way. The "gauges" and "indicators," which are designed to resemble the dashboard of a car, are kept up to date by the people who need the information. They can be displayed on a computer screen (using any graphics program), or simply drawn by hand and posted on the walls. Either way, the people closest to the daily work decide which information is relevant, and how to portray it. The result is a visual representation of progress and potential trouble spots, and a valuable set of tools for sustaining a learning effort.

THE DASHBOARD'S DESIGN

We find the dashboard metaphor useful because running a team without a good, simple guidance system is like trying to drive a car without a dashboard. You might try it in a pinch, but not as a matter of practice, because you'd lack the necessary information—the speed, the amount of fuel, the engine temperature—to ensure that you reach your destination. The dashboard is a key feedback mechanism that makes you (as the driver) and the car part of the same transportation system. If that system broke down—if you no longer had the information you needed to drive it—then the car would crash, or roll to a halt, or simply run out of fuel.

In a performance dashboard, as in an automobile dashboard, one or two instruments won't do. You need a variety of gauges and indicators. Some, like a speedometer, provide real-time data, showing the rate of performance at any time. (These might include the week-by-week levels of overhead, or the competitive product quality). Some instruments, like an odometer, keep cumulative track of progress. (These might include progress toward a project milestone, or the number of people hired for a start-up.) And then there are the warning lights, which simply indicate that a big problem is brewing. (These might include a gauge of team morale, as measured by team leaders' judgment.)

Displays like these have the virtue of simplicity. Other participative measurement systems, like activity-based costing, open up financial information and cross-functional process data to everyone. But they are often so elaborate that they require a complex infrastructure (and the cooperation of professionals) to get started. In practice, they often lack the kind of direct involvement that builds judgment. Performance dashboards, by contrast, can be designed in a day or two by a small team of people, ideally with a sympathetic sponsor at a more senior level (who is needed, in part, to protect them from stray tendrils of the measurement mind-set.) The multiple-gauge format makes it easier for people to comprehend their own most critical parameters in a single glance—thus subtly inclining them to use these measures for systemic learning instead of merely reporting up the hierarchy.

Graphic tools like the Operational Dashboard are particularly important for multifunctional teams, which have no common language for coordinating action. Members of such teams often end up tracking the numbers relevant to their own function, at the expense of the team as a whole. Team members from finance focus on cost per product. Manufacturing and operations people look at measurements related to quality control and process speed. Marketing people track the evolution of new features compared to past models. And the team leader watches the mounting level of errors and rework. Until you collectively create a common set of measures (the dashboard) and a common language (relative to the project) you will find yourselves misunderstanding one another and working at cross-purposes.

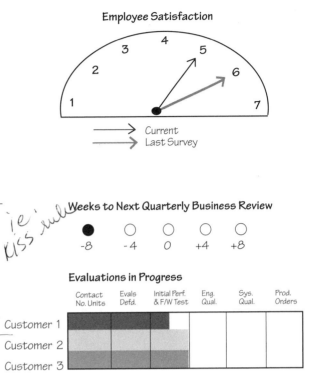

Some sample gauges from a prototype "performance dashboard": The top gauge shows employee satisfaction, which (in this case) has decreased from the last survey taken. The middle gauge shows the team's deadlines at a glance, and the bottom gauge indicates progress in testing the reliability of products for various industrial customers. A typical business performance dashboard might have anywhere between five and fifteen such gauges, all chosen for the benefit of the team which designed the dashboard.

DEVELOPING A SET OF INDICATORS

First, gather all the team members for an extended "skillful conversation." (Remember that a team includes all the people who need one

For more on "skillful conversation," see *The Fifth Discipline Fieldbook*, p. 385.

very interesting I do

Parts of this segment were adapted from "How the Right Measure Help Teams Excel," by Christopher Meyer, *Harvard Business Review*, May/June 1994, p. 95. For more detail on the performance dashboard, including other examples of gauges and metrics, see *Relentless Growth: How Silicon Valley Innovation Strategies Can Work in Your Business*, by Christopher Meyer (New York: Free Press, 1998), chapter 7.

How do you track morale?!

another to accomplish a task, so include essential people from different functions.) Move toward a clear common understanding of the goals of your team: To develop a new product or service? To produce a result?

After the goals have been confirmed, each member should develop two or three gauges that he or she considers most effective for monitoring his or her functional area. Avoid defaulting to conventional "standard company measures," for they are often carriers of the outdated measurement mind-set. Instead, ask yourself: What hypothetical measures could you use to track your business results? What indicators do you already turn to, informally, to track your progress (or lack thereof)? What are the most revealing measures in your present work?

Look for "process" measures that tell you how you are progressing as you try to achieve your goals. For instance, some teams might choose to track how long it takes to resolve customers' service calls. This is a more meaningful measurement than a snapshot survey of customer satisfaction might be. The most effective process measures are often those that express relative terms. For example, a measure that tracks the percentage of new or unique parts is usually more valuable than one that tracks the absolute number.

Include the "soft" measures along with the "hard" measures. Many variables cannot be measured precisely: motivation, commitment, ownership, and resistance to change. Often, these are the most critical variables for feedback that can help a team reflect, learn, and move forward. "Soft" variables will demand more scrutiny and judgment, because they are measured less precisely. However, tracking trends such as morale can be very helpful. It can also be helpful to track ratios between two "soft" (human-oriented) characteristics—such as the number of people on a committee or board versus the number of people required.

Pick measures that you believe will count for key constituents. These are probably your team members and the sponsor—the executive, network, or line leader who "chartered" the team. What measures will these people find meaningful? If they are not in the room during your meeting, you may have to ask them.

COMBINING THE MEASURES INTO A DASHBOARD

Each member should explain his or her proposed measures and their relevance to the rest of the team. Some measures will be either eliminated or agreed on very quickly. The hard work will be assessing those that fall in between. Make no final decisions until you test all the gauges against the following criteria:

Are critical team objectives tracked?

Are all "red alert" conditions (in which the team runs into trouble serious enough to trigger outside attention) monitored?

Are "drivers" of results (indicators that show ongoing fundamental factors) tracked as well as the results themselves?

Are the critical variables required to reach the goal (like having enough skilled personnel to run an order-entry system) tracked?

TRANSFORMING YOUR INDICATORS INTO A DASHBOARD

Once you have a number of potential indicators, reduce them to a few key measures. If you could track only six or eight things, what would they be? The point is to avoid devising so many numbers and gauges that your dashboard looks like a 747 cockpit. Otherwise you'll spend all your time looking at the dashboard and forget to "look out the windshield"—to actually implement the work.

Next, test the dashboard prototype with a few key sponsors at higher levels of the organization. These individuals should be asked: Do these measures fit with the goals that our management wants to achieve? Are they consistent with our strategic imperatives?

Done w/ Board

It is criticial that the measures don't lose their meaning at this juncture. Some senior managers tend to get so enamored with this process that they usurp the tool from local teams by adding additional measurements that are not relevant at a local level. The team's sponsor in a shipping company, for instance, might want you to switch from measures of tonnage shipped from various locations per day (so you can compare your processes at these locations) to an overall aggregate of tonnage shipped per quarter. Suddenly, the numbers shift; they may be useful for your sponsor, but you can no longer use them for learning at your level. The purpose of your dashboard will be defeated. Thus, work closely with your sponsor to help him or her see the need for focusing on process as well as results.

After you get agreement on the particular measurements in your dashboard, use intranets (e-mail, electronic note systems, and internal Web sites) or other forms of open space (posted workspaces, learning laboratory rooms) to make the dashboard visible to all. Then meet regularly, perhaps every two to four weeks, to review the measurements. Prior to each meeting, update the dashboard so that you can discuss the new measures. Look first for variance between targets and the indicators you chose. Are you higher, or lower, than the numbers you had expected? It's vital to consider this variance without seeing it as neces-

New idea "closed" curchive in a "closed" curchive

sarily "bad." Try to avoid language such as, "How far below our goals did we hit?" or "Why didn't we measure up?" Instead, see the numbers on the dashboard as an opportunity to explore your work without rushing to judgment. Where are the results different than you wanted or expected—and, most important, why might they be different? What factors from the outside are at play? What factors are at play within the team? As you talk about these issues, you will hopefully bring to the surface your mental models about the business, the team, and the external environment. Rather than merely providing data, the performance dashboard sparks conversations that build managers' own capacity to learn.

At times, you may want to recalibrate or reconfigure the dashboard, to redesign some of your indicators to focus more closely on your meaningful measurements. This step should be taken with care; do not redesign your instruments until you have used them for a long enough time (ideally, at least six months) to be sure that they need changing.

With innovative graphic measures like dashboards in place, it's much easier for the team to look ahead and say, "If we want that indicator moving up six months from now, what kinds of things should we be doing now?" Simply posing this question, with the dashboard in front of you, allows you to act more proactively. That, after all, is the purpose of a good measurement system. It tells you about potential potholes in the road before you hear the ominous thud of a breakdown.

IX. True Believers and Nonbelievers

"They don't understand us!"

1 The Challenge

Several years ago, a production team at an oil refinery in the United States reoriented their plant's operations around continuous learning. The results included a series of self-generated improvements and innovations, including a new equipment maintenance system that saved $1.5 million annually, and a tremendous leap forward in morale and commitment. The team's leaders didn't stop there; they set down a record of their innovations in an in-depth report, and that report sparked further performance improvements and learning efforts inside the refinery. "John," a key instigator and leader of the initiative, hit the lecture circuit. He spoke inside the company and out in public, eager to help the rest of their corporate parent learn from his team's experience. An engaging and earnest engineer in his thirties, he had no doubt that the results they'd achieved would provide compelling evidence for anyone.

It didn't work out that way. Many people inside the company but outside the refinery—executive and line leaders alike—ignored John's efforts to tell his group's story. At first, he tried to make his case with greater fervor. He began to blame and resent the corporate culture for being misguided and politically biased against his plant. Meanwhile, one of the authors of this book interviewed a corporate executive and asked casually about John. "We think he's made some good technical innovations," said the executive. "But I'm not going to sit through any more meetings with those missionaries."

A few months later, John inadvertently learned of that comment. At first, it shocked him a bit. He saw himself as an adventurer, trying to move in pioneering directions. Yet, they apparently saw him as "over the top." At the same time, he had begun some in-depth work on reflection and inquiry skills, and he thought carefully about the number of assumptions that people were making, on both sides, about one another. His approach and ambiance changed. He became lower-key; he began to spend much more of his time inquiring about the needs of the other refineries. He became less of an advocate, trying to be right, and more of a deliberately open-minded internal consultant. Today, he visits people in the company only by their request—and these visits, fueled by requests, have become a full-time job that keeps him traveling around the world.

The True Believer: Thoughts on the Nature of Mass Movements, by Eric Hoffer, 1951, 1963; second edition (New York: Harper & Row and *Time*), p. 165.

In his classic book *The True Believer*, philosopher Eric Hoffer analyzed the mind of the fanatic. He showed how easy it is for any change-oriented movement to draw people across the thin line from certainty to fanaticism. "At the root of the fanatic's cockiness," wrote Hoffer "is the conviction that life and the universe conform to a simple formula—his formula." Once people become convinced that they are absolutely right, their mind become closed to the voices of others who disagree.

Many of the most committed leaders skirt the edge of fanaticism—even more are seen that way. The more time a pilot group spends only with one another, and the more they develop their own unique ways of operating, the more isolated and distanced they can become from the rest of the organization. Dynamics on both sides of the gulf reinforce this isolation, and make the gap wider. Both sides feel an almost irresistible pressure to defend themselves: They are right, and the other side is wrong. If the pilot group stumbles, that will be seen as evidence that they have been taken in by a misguided management fad. If they continue to gain momentum, their success will be seen as an implicit criticism of more established ways of working. Either way, they become "strangers in a strange land"—finding themselves increasingly at odds with the larger organization.

From the perspective of the pilot group, it feels as if they have been rejected by the larger organization, like a foreign body rejected by an "immune system" built into the organization's culture. They often feel unappreciated and misunderstood. They can easily develop a "siege mentality," pitted against enemies, even some of whom were former colleagues. Many innovative components of staid organizations have become famous for falling into this pattern: Saturn and NUMMI (the GM–Toyota partnership) within General Motors, the IBM personal computer group within IBM, the original "skunk works" within Lockheed, and the Topeka dog food plant within General Foods. Underlying this challenge is a core challenge, not just for pilot groups, but for organizations in general: How can they remain attuned to fringe and counterintuitive ideas and perceptions, without risking their core values?

In many ways, zeal and isolation are the most insidious unintended consequences of profound change initiatives. The deeper and more effective the changes that occur in a pilot group, the more easily they can come into conflict with the larger organization. The more people do change, the more different they become, in their thinking and acting, from the mainstream culture. The more they do succeed in producing significant advances in practical results, the more potentially threatening they become to others competing with them for management attention and reward.

Ironically, the more personal and business results they achieve, the more arrogant, and intolerant, they can become. As one pilot group team member put it, "It has taken a lot of effort to get to the point where we can openly and effectively talk about issues which other teams handle in private. When I see other teams working, they seem closed and very political to me. Yes, it does make me feel a bit isolated—sort of like waking up behind enemy lines."

As Art Kleiner shows in *The Age of Heretics*, these dynamics have existed throughout the history of industrial corporations—and perhaps throughout the history of organizations. Time and time again, corporate innovators are exiled, ignored, or frustrated (if only because they see others get credit for their ideas). Curiously, despite abundant evidence of these problems, innovative line leaders invariably seem to believe that they will never happen to them. We're not entirely sure why innovators so frequently discount these risks. Perhaps the "better mousetrap theory" is so deeply rooted in their minds that they cannot believe that their work will not be appreciated. Perhaps they are so focused on their own passionately held dreams that they cannot see beyond them, to see how they may affect others. Perhaps they, like us all, underestimate their own potential for reacting defensively, especially when unappreciated. Regardless, blindness to the issues of believers and nonbelievers, in the judgment of the authors, is often the "Achilles heel" of otherwise brilliant organizational innovators.

⟩⟩ For more about organizational "heretics," see page 346.

The Topeka Gaines dog food plant story, in particular, is an archetypal story of "believers and nonbelievers," taking place in General Foods between 1969 and 1975. See *The Age of Heretics*, by Art Kleiner (New York: Doubleday, 1996).

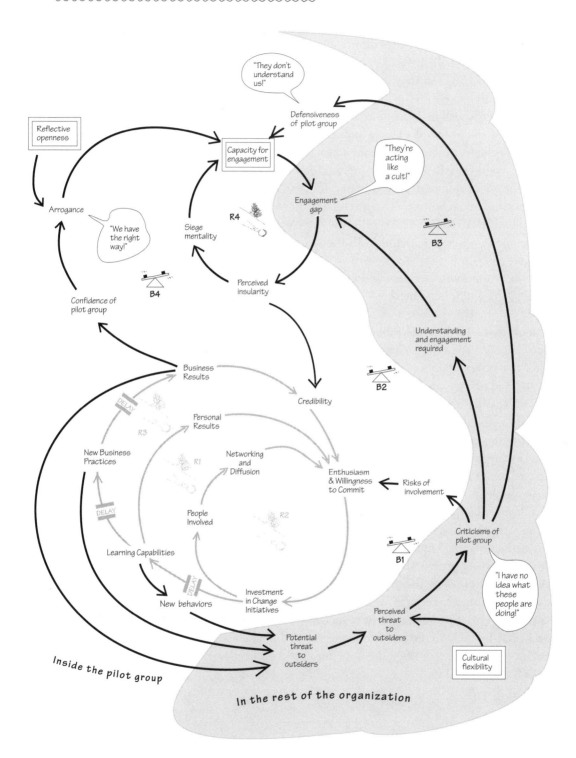

THE UNDERLYING DYNAMICS OF "TRUE BELIEVERS AND NONBELIEVERS"

In this challenge, several different balancing processes come into play and interact. As in the challenge of measurement and assessment, these processes arise as the pilot group interacts with the larger organization. Here they concern the growing split that can develop between the pilot group and the larger organization, each developing differing views of one another. Moreover, there is a vicious cycle that can exacerbate problems once they start to develop.

It is important to understand the variety of forces at play here, all of which must be considered in developing high leverage strategies for dealing with the challenge of "believers and nonbelievers."

■ **Perceived threats to people outside the team (loop B1):** Perceived threats can arise from three aspects of a pilot team's endeavors: new behaviors, new business practices, and improved business results. In many situations, any one would be potentially threatening. The combination can be overwhelming.

Profound change initiatives, more than other types of change processes, nurture new ways of thinking and visibly different forms of behavior. When viewed from the pilot team's perspective, these new behaviors are valued expressions of new learning capabilities. But from the perspective of individuals embedded in the traditional organizational culture, they can be threatening.

The pilot group members talk more candidly. They display less fear of the "boss." They ask "real questions"—questions that are not thinly veiled statements, questions that expose their ignorance. They may talk differently, using strange jargon like the "ladder of inference" and "structural causes of problems." They don't seem as concerned about the organization's traditional measures or symbols of success. And in many different ways, probably without intending to, they sometimes convey the impression of being "legends in their own mind," presuming themselves superior to more established practices in the larger organization.

When these behaviors threaten people outside the pilot group, the threat will surface first in comments like these: "I have no idea what these people are doing." Or "They seem to spend a lot of time on this learning stuff rather than their business." A perception may grow in the rest of the organization that the pilot team members are going overboard or just plain losing their focus. Others may grow jealous and unsettled by the enthusiasm of pilot group members: "Those

The diagram on the opposite page, the most complex in the book, shows four complementary balancing processes and one reinforcing process at play. Balancing processes B1, B2, and B3 depict the potential threat to outsiders from new behaviors, new practices and improved results, which provoke greater criticisms of the pilot group. These increase risk of involvement(B1), while simultaneously raising the amount of outside understanding and engagement required if the pilot group is to be successful (B2), and reducing the group's capacity for engagement through increasing defensiveness (B3). Meanwhile (B4), the pilot group's own confidence and arrogance increase, further lowering capacity for engagement. B2, B3, and B4 all interact in a "vicious spiral," reinforcing the insularity of the pilot group (R4).

people are strange; work just isn't that much fun," commented one salty manufacturing veteran.

When the pilot group adopts new business practices, like including customers in "learning laboratories," the potential threat increases. If the pilot group achieves significant business results, the potential threat is likely to increase still further. In particular, if pilot group members trumpet their new practices as superior methods that lead to significantly better results, this can be seen as an implicit challenge to competing units. In one case, dramatic improvements in particular process measures were met with accusations that the group distorted their results. "We heard a few things about their timing results, but none of us took them too seriously," commented another team leader. The greater the degree of improvement, the greater the potential threat felt elsewhere.

If something is not done to respond to these growing perceived threats, an air of critical disapproval starts to develop in the larger organization around the pilot team's efforts. This increases the risks of commitment and lessens enthusiasm to participate. It distracts those already engaged, leaving less of their time and energy to invest in the initiative, and discourage others from getting engaged.

■ **The Engagement Gap, or, "They're acting like a cult" (loop B2):** Growing criticisms of the pilot group can also be seen as requests for greater understanding. Often they are not expressed in those terms, and in fact, some of those who are critical may not be interested in understanding more. But many outside the pilot initiative are open-minded and genuinely curious to learn more about practices that might benefit their operations as well. Either way, if the need for increased understanding outside the pilot group is not met, an engagement gap develops which further limits the initiative's credibility. As one manager put it, "Many of us aware of [that pilot group's] new processes were really interested, but when we tried to learn a little, all we got back was jargon and theory that was pretty hard to make sense of." Innovative teams who cannot explain themselves effectively to others often end up being seen as insular. This lessens their credibility and acts as another limiting process reducing enthusiasm for the initiative.

As the understanding and engagement required goes up, the key question is: Does the pilot team's capacity for explaining their efforts go up as well? The engagement gap is generated by the required engagement relative to the pilot team's capacity for engagement. The

Quoted from *A Car Launch With Heart: The "AutoCo Epsilon" Learning History*, by George Roth, Art Kleiner, et al. (New York: Oxford University Press, 1999), p. 3.

capacity for engagement is the fundamental constraint in this limiting process. Usually, the members of the pilot team are so focused on their own changes, they invest relatively little in learning how to help people outside the team understand what they are doing.

- **"They don't understand us"** (loop B3): Developing capacity for engagement is nontrivial: Responding effectively to people who have not invested time to gain firsthand knowledge of a pilot group's innovations is challenging. People tend to interpret whatever information they receive in the light of their established mental models. If one group begins to operate from fundamentally different mental models, their efforts can be truly puzzling to others. As one beleaguered local line leader put it, "I remember a meeting where a vice president listened to us present the reasons for our success: team leadership, and the fact that everyone had the same goals and knew that they depended on one another. 'That sounds really great,' he said, 'but what did you do?' He finally said that it must have been a fluke, and that was the end of it."

  Unfortunately, at the same time that greater engagement with others is needed, pilot group members are often becoming more defensive, as a result of external criticisms. In other words, just when increased capacity for engagement is needed, forces to reduce that capacity develop within the pilot group. As the earlier quote illustrated, it is easy for team members to feel misunderstood and frustrated after repeated encounters with people holding very different mental models—after all, they are innovating in the first place because they want to demonstrate new possibilities based on new assumptions.

  But becoming defensive and withdrawing is dysfunctional relative to the team's goal to build momentum for their efforts. When they withdraw, the engagement gap increases and pilot group members become seen as insular. To some degree, this perception is valid because they are cutting themselves off, emotionally and practically.

- **"We have the right way"** (loop B4): Pressures for withdrawal and disengagement are also building within the pilot team, as a side effect of their success. These come from growing confidence, based on both their learning capabilities and the evidence they perceive, of improved practical results. Confidence is vital to sustaining innovations, but it can also have a dark side, breeding arrogance and a feeling that, "our way is the only right way." People rarely recognize when they cross this line. The members of a successful, innovative team can easily begin to believe (with plenty of evidence, as they see it) that their way is unquestionably superior to more established practices. When that happens, their capacity for engaging outsiders declines even further, and their perceived insularity increases further, lowering their credibility further.

■ **The trap door—"siege mentality" (loop R2):** As the engagement gap grows and the team is seen as being insular, they can become even more so. They feel unappreciated and misunderstood. When this attitude takes hold, the innovators can become psychologically isolated from the mainstream organization. They can develop a siege mentality, where team members feel that the rest of the organization has placed them under attack. When this develops, local line managers see themselves as buffers, protecting and sheltering the team from unpleasant and defensive disdain. The team members come to believe that those on the outside "will never understand what we are doing. If only they did, then we wouldn't have these problems." Anticipating even more isolation, they become less and less willing (and less able) to explain their efforts to outsiders. The growing siege mentality leads to still lower capacity for engagement and a still larger engagement gap. The attribution that the team is more interested in themselves and their own process than in the larger organization becomes a self-fulfilling prophecy.

The existence of this vicious cycle is one reason that the challenge of believers and nonbelievers is so dangerous. Small imbalances, once they develop, can feed on themselves and create larger imbalances. The vicious cycle of a festering siege mentality, once it sets in, continually expands the schism between the pilot group and the larger organization. It is a kind of trap door, from which it can be difficult to escape once you fall through.

Two comments from the most senior managers in one pilot team under attack illustrate the siege mentality mind-set—the boss of the team manager, who viewed himself as a supporter: "I think one of the reasons that we didn't spend more time trying to get management support is because . . . it (our process) could be viewed as 'soft.'" And the team manager: "I tried to be the buffer for the team. I said, 'Wait until the results come in. When they see the results, they're going to start asking, "How did they do that?" Then they'll be ready to listen.'"

Two primary underlying limits lie behind these balancing processes: cultural flexibility within the organization, and reflective openness within the pilot group. In some organizations, people are more prone to be threatened by groups that work differently. There is a pervasive attitude that, "things should be done the way we have always done them." This affects both members of the pilot team, who find themselves implicitly battling to prove there is another way; and people outside the pilot team who find themselves automatically judging others who are different critically.

This notion of cultural flexibility is closely related to what writer and former Royal Dutch/Shell executive Arie de Geus has called "tolerance." In studies conducted at Royal Dutch/Shell, tolerance was a consistent feature of those companies that had survived one hundred years or longer. Tolerant companies recognized that the organization was a loose confederacy of sorts. While there existed a "mainstream" business focus and style, they accepted that different parts of the organization would pursue different market opportunities and operate by somewhat different norms. This tolerance, de Geus argued, was a key feature that made such organizations more adaptable. When their environment changed, they had a diverse "internal ecology" capable of diverse responses. Businesses and subcultures that had been marginal might, within a few years, become mainstream if they were more harmonious with new requirements in the larger world. In effect, tolerant organizations are continually experimenting with next year's possible "seed crops," while they continue to reap the harvest from their current businesses.

See *The Living Company*, by Arie de Geus (Cambridge, MA: Harvard University Press, 1997), p. 142–143.

However, developing cultural flexibility is a long-term proposition. Like any deep feature of an organization's culture, the degree of tolerance has evolved over many years and is not something that anyone, including top management, can change quickly.

The second underlying limit, reflective openness within the pilot group, represents the capacity for people to continually question their own assumptions. This is the great safeguard against certainty and arrogance in any social body. To what extent can the members of any group, however successful, continually challenge their own thinking? To what extent can they "hear" comments from outsiders as possible sources for their own learning? To what extent are they inherently skeptical of any set of ideas, especially their own, as explanations for why things are the way they are?

In truth, no one can ever say with certainty to what factors any group's accomplishments should be attributed. We are all constructing hypothesized explanations, looking for interpretations that best fit our experience. The more complex the change, the more this is invariably the case. An innovative group that can develop the capacity to continually test their own thinking is less likely to confuse confidence with certainty than one that does not. Nurturing reflective openness also represents an important strategy for leaders who seek to balance passionate commitment to new innovations with respect for the mainstream culture and ways of doing things.

STRATEGIES FOR MEETING THE CHALLENGE OF "TRUE BELIEVERS AND NONBELIEVERS"

Seeking leverage amid the complex forces posed by this challenge is not easy. It requires understanding the different limits that are operating, the different time frames under which they develop, and the ways that the respective balancing processes can be mitigated. For example, increasing cultural flexibility may be the single point of highest leverage, because it conditions the extent to which any innovative practice becomes potentially threatening. But knowing this does little good for the local line leader or internal networker trying to help an at-risk pilot group, because it may take several generations of management to help an organization develop greater cultural flexibility. On the other hand, for those executives who see themselves building an organization over the long term, understanding the importance of tolerance is critical. Last, for everyone concerned with fundamental innovation, it is vital to understand the dynamics whereby pilot groups become isolated and arrogant, where they unintentionally create threats—and where others respond to those threats, productively or unproductively.

All of the strategies below focus either on the limits directly (reflective openness, capacity for engagement, and cultural flexibility) or on mitigating specific reactions within the balancing processes set in motion by encountering the limits.

■ **Become "bicultural."** The most effective local leaders seem to be those who learn to "live in two worlds"—the world of their innovative subculture and the world of the mainstream culture of the larger organization. They realize that innovative practices need "incubators" to develop and that, to some degree, these new practices must be protected. But they also value the knowledge developed through experience that resides in the mainstream culture. They seek to cultivate both, and they do so by developing their own abilities to be effective in both environments.

In a sense they become "bicultural," just like someone who lives in two countries with very different cultures. They become adept at crossing the numerous, often subtle, cultural divides between the two worlds. When they interact with their "bosses" they do so on the bosses' terms. Yet, at the same time, within their teams, they are developing their abilities to extemporize, to challenge assumptions, and to trust—the requirements in a more learning-oriented culture. Perhaps most important, they continually develop their awareness of the boundaries between these different worlds, knowing when they are in which domain and what it requires of them. Virtually all local managers engaged in workplace innovations operate in two cultures—yet, relatively few actually understand this and come to appreciate, even thrive, on it.

For example, one especially effective manufacturing manager developed a strategy he called "stealth transformation." His aim was to keep the transformative efforts in his facility "below the corporate radar level." When he reported up the hierarchy, he made every effort to focus on the same metrics as used in assessing all similar facilities. The goals upon which he and his team were focused aligned with the corporation's priorities. He didn't go to extremes to hide the innovative processes being employed. "I just didn't talk about them unless someone asked," he said.

Developing this sort of biculturalism is challenging. Successful line leaders in transformational initiative naturally identify deeply with the new subculture they are helping to nourish. It represents, no doubt, many of their own core values. It is their "baby," and not only are they predisposed to protect it, but to defend it (and one another) as well. This is one reason that having mentors is so vital.

■ **Mentoring.** Many otherwise talented local line leaders are blind to the issues of the organizational immune system, or somehow believe they won't affect them. Executives and internal networks can help by serving as mentors to local line leaders, helping them appreciate and deal with unintended misconceptions about their efforts. They can offer feedback when communications are swamped in jargon, or when local leaders become defensive. They can help local leaders learn to recognize when outsiders are raising legitimate questions, instead of simply throwing rocks.

Executive and network leaders can also act as interpreters and "diplomats," bridging misunderstandings among local pilot groups, their bosses, and other line managers. Line leaders facing this challenge sometimes need help learning to explain their innovations, without threatening people on the outside. This is important because, ultimately, line leaders are needed to give credibility to new business practices. Only line leaders can explain what they are doing and why. Executive leaders are less effective when they "jawbone" than when they encourage peers to learn from one another—and then get out of the way. "Often, when people start to complain about our organizational learning experiments," says one executive, "I simply say, 'I too have my questions, but we have to experiment. If we don't make some fundamental improvements, we will not be able to achieve our overall business goals in the coming years.'"

⟩⟩ For more on mentoring, see page 128.

■ **Build the pilot group's capability to engage the larger system from the beginning.** MIT's Deborah Ancona has shown that the most effective product development teams deliberately develop their abilities in "ambassadorial scouting"—placing themselves, and their team, in a compatible context with the rest of the organization, and building those links as strongly as possible from the very beginning. "Contrary to much of the literature, with its emphasis on team building, these studies suggest that the most critical characteristics of successful innovative teams came from their 'external orientation' rather than being focused on their internal development."

This does not necessarily mean that everyone must become equally effective ambassadors, but at least a few team members must be actively engaged in this role. If only a single team leader falls into this role, she or he will typically find themselves becoming the "protector" of the group. This is a taxing job and we have seen many talented innovators burn out trying to continually defend their people, and in the process becoming more and more defensive.

For example, one effective strategy is to regularly invite in key suppliers, customers, and peers to share what the team is doing, to invite their comments and suggstions. Team members might ask, for example, "How can our new processes help address your needs?" Such regular contact can go a long way to developing the capacity of team members to continually question and explain their thinking. It can also help in focusing their aims in ways to serve key external constituencies.

⟩⟩ See, for example, "Cracking the Black Box of Assessment," page 303.

■ **Cultivate reflective openness.** Whether or not confidence becomes arrogance in a pilot team depends on subtle distinctions often

See "Demography and Design: Predictors of New Product Team Performance," by Deborah G. Ancona and David F. Caldwell, *Organization Science*, 3 (3), August, 1992. p. 321–341. Also see "Bridging the Boundary: External Activity and Performance in Organizational Teams," by Deborah G. Ancona and David F. Caldwell, 1992, *Administrative Science Quarterly*, 37 (4), December 1992.

ignored by change advocates. Many pilot teams who invest heavily in new processes are predisposed to becoming true believers. Yet a few do not. Where is the difference? It appears to lie in whether or not the team also develops the capacity to continually challenge their own thinking, and in whether or not they can simultaneously develop confidence and humility.

Interestingly, a foundation can be established by focusing on how the group deals with the conflicts that arise internally. In many ways, the pilot team is a microcosm of the larger organization, even if its members do not see this. The key is to not strive to get all the members of the pilot team to buy in to a single view of the world, but to learn how to work productively with a diversity of views within the pilot. Can team members learn how to see differing views as an opportunity to broaden their own thinking, as opposed to an opportunity to defend their own thinking? If they can, then they will be more likely to confront qualms from people outside the team with curiosity rather than with hostility.

■ **Respect people's inhibitions about personal change.** Often, when pilot group members start talking about the power of the personal changes they have experienced, there is an unintended (or tacit) message: "You must change, too." This message is a time bomb in any work setting and leads members to inadvertently increase the potential threat they pose to people outside their team. People understandably resent the uninvited intrusions of business pressures on their personal attitudes and beliefs. They wonder if something is wrong with them in the eyes of the company, or how safe they will be if they refuse to go along with pressures to change.

If enough people feel this way, there may be a groundswell of reaction against the pilot group, no matter how well intentioned its members are. "We had a great session with forty leaders at [a lake resort]," recalls one senior manager. "Three months later, we had another session for one hundred and eighty people, where we kept talking about [the lake resort]. People started resenting this: 'We weren't there. Quit beating us over the head about this "mystical experience" you had.' Finally, someone raised his hand and said, 'We're here now, not at the lake resort.' The room erupted into spontaneous applause."

Ironically, for leaders committed to learning who value freedom of choice, such perceptions of their testimonials are the farthest thing from their mind. Yet, they forget that organizations are traditionally coercive systems, where people are regularly expected to change to accommodate the organization's needs. Consequently, their own

Quoted from *Perspectives on Full-Scale Corporate Transformation: The "OilCo" Learning History,* by Art Kleiner, George Roth, et al. (New York: Oxford University Press, 1999), p. 133.

statements will often be heard against this backdrop—even if it is the opposite of what they intend to communicate. It helps to remember organization development pioneer Dick Beckhard's aphorism—"People do not resist change; they resist being changed"—and expect that you, too, will often be seen as someone trying to change them.

■ **You don't have to convince people.** As pointed out by Howard Gardner, in his book *Leading Minds*, several different interpretations of reality can readily coexist within a single society or organization. In fact, working with "multiple realities" can be an artful leadership strategy. For example, when Alfred Sloan came to the fore at General Motors, in the auto industry and in society at large, it was believed that organizations had to be run by a single top guy (like Henry Ford) or authority should be scattered among components of the organization (as Billy Durant, the original founder of General Motors, had decided). Without directly refuting either view, Sloan told a story of an organization that could grow to unprecedented size by coordinating centralized and decentralized authority, with the help of highly skilled experts. His successes with General Motors were built, according to Gardner, on the foundation of his ability to get people to consider this different story.

When communicating with people about new ideas and new business practices, it is not necessary to absolutely convince them. It is important to help them see that the story you are telling is "on their side," and therefore worth listening to. It need not align perfectly with their point of view. But it needs to show that their point of view is treated fairly, and that they are not cast as an outsider. If you can tell the story of your team's efforts, showing that you understand how it is seen from a variety of perspectives, then you have gone a long way to breaking through the challenge of believers and nonbelievers, while keeping your aspirations and sense of purpose.

See "Learning Histories," page 460, as one technique for telling a story through multiple perspectives, and the history map, page 186, for another technique.

■ **Deploy language consciously.** One of the most effective strategies for exclusion is to use language that others do not understand. When people hear others speaking in jargon, they often get turned off even before they know what people are speaking about. "There's a bit of cliqueishness," said one manager in a learning history. "You hear it in the jargon: 'Share your left-hand column,' the 'ladder of inference,' and 'take off the masks.'"

See *Leading Minds: An Anatomy of Leadership*, by Howard Gardner with the collaboration of Emma Laskin (New York: Basic Books, 1995), pp. 140–145; pp. 310–313.

Quoted from *Perspectives on Full-Scale Corporate Transformation: The "OilCo" Learning History*, by Art Kleiner, George Roth, et al. (New York: Oxford University Press, 1999), p. 133.

One's own jargon is hard to recognize because it is always "in the eye of the beholder." Once new terms and idioms become used regularly within a team, team members come to take them for granted. Then, when they use these terms with others, they are unaware that they are "speaking in tongues" as far as the uninitiated are concerned. This is why developing awareness of one's language is a high leverage strategy in becoming effectively bicultural. It is also why explaining complex ideas in the most simple and accessible manner has always been a hallmark of great leadership.

■ **Lay a foundation of transcendent values.** As discussed earlier, there are no magic pills or other short-term fixes to evolving more tolerant, flexible organizational cultures. But, there are approaches that have stood the test of time and should be considered seriously.

A second feature of the long-lived companies, according to de Geus, is a strong sense of identity, of "knowing who they are beyond what they do." This strong sense of identity based on values enables them to identify less with current markets, current products, and current business practices. Having a stable foundation in terms of underlying values, paradoxically, makes them more flexible. "Members know 'who is us,'" writes de Geus, "and they are aware that they hold values in common. In a very real sense, they belong to one another . . . The company is clearly a unit, with a single identity; but the people and substructures within that unit show a rich variety."

See *The Living Company*, by Arie de Geus (Cambridge, MA: Harvard University Press, 1997), p. 103–4.

Innovative executives may also be able to take advantage of developments unfolding in the larger business environment to nudge their organizations toward greater tolerance and flexibility. "The day when everyone who matters to your company is an employee are probably gone forever," says Shell's Phil Carroll. "The transition to a new employer relationship is very difficult for some people to accept, because the new model has a higher degree of uncertainty and accountability for our own actions and personal development. We no longer ask for loyalty . . . what we want from people is commitment. And it is up to us as leaders of organizations to provide the kind of environment where people give that commitment. It's got to be given freely, though. A deeper sense of identity will be needed than was the case for the traditional 'company man.'" This is why Shell's evolution toward a "network of relationships of ambiguous identity," as Carroll once described Shell's multiple alliances, was guided by deep work on purpose and values.

This quote comes from an interview conducted in 1997 by Innovation Associates consultant Robert Hanig for a British Petroleum conference.

In effect, executive leaders like Carroll realize that the brave new world of the "networked enterprise" will be a low trust, low learning environment if it is based exclusively on transactional relationships. If everyone is focused only on what they can get in exchange for what they give, there will be no mutuality and willingness to undertake the risks required for deep learning. On the other hand, if people are connected by a common sense of purpose and core values, the networked world may indeed encourage the type of flexibility that has long eluded traditional hierarchical organizations.

2 How to Set the Stage for a Change in Organizational Culture

Edgar Schein

Since his early research on the impact of North Korean "brainwashing camps," Edgar Schein has been a leading researcher of the interplay between the individual conscience and the collective consciousness, particularly in organizations and business. His books on process consultation, career development, and organizational culture have defined the practice of "change-agentry" around the world, (for example, in helping interventionists avoid the seduction of their own biases). A professor of management at MIT, Ed was one of the founding governors of the Center for Organizational Learning and has been an ongoing friend and guiding spirit for the Fifth Discipline books.

People who try to change organizations often run up against attitudes that seem unchangeable. "We can't make any headway," they decide, "unless we can create a new culture around here." Already, they have made an irreversible mistake. You cannot create a new culture. You can immerse yourself in studying a culture (your own, or someone else's) until you understand it. Then you can propose new values, introduce new ways of doing things, and articulate new governing ideas. Over time, these actions will set the stage for new behavior. If people who adopt that new behavior feel that it helps them do better, they may try it again, and after many trials, taking as long as five or ten years, the organizational culture may embody a different set of assumptions, and a different way of looking at things, than it did before. Even then, you haven't changed the culture; you've set the stage for the culture to evolve.

This process may sound painfully slow and uncertain. But many people prefer it to the alternative approach, the approach made famous by wholesale change artists like Al Dunlap. They come into an organization with approval from the board, wipe out the senior layers of management, and impose a new set of rules. This produces a rapid culture destruction—amid an atmosphere of crisis, with the potential for suppressed resentment and backlash. If the cost of that backlash is too great, or if you want people to grow more capable, instead of merely changing, then you have a long, incremental, and very fascinating task ahead of you. And you have not created a new culture, only destroyed the old one.

To help make sense of this cultural evolution, I have laid it out as a series of steps. But the steps need not be followed in rote form. As in all processes of inquiry, the steps and precepts will gain value with the insight, thoughtfulness and flexibility of the people practicing them.

1. CLARIFYING YOUR PURPOSE

First of all, why do you need to change your culture at all? I sometimes hear managers say they want to change because "a learning organization should have a more open culture," or because "it came back in the benchmarks; everybody else is doing it, so we'd better do it, too." Those are not reasons for change; they are statements about an idealized workplace that you imagine in the abstract. Starting with that kind of purpose will simply lead you farther and farther into abstractions.

Instead, try to articulate the concrete business problems that have brought you to a cultural impasse. What will learning or openness get you? More likely than not, people in your organization feel that the unspoken rules of the game have shifted. In a self-managing team environment, being a foreman is no longer a position of authority. In a company being downsized, a manager's career is no longer defined by a guarantee of lifelong employment. Globalizing companies no longer maintain the same kinds of relationships between the field and the home office. Possibly, a legal or PR crisis, or an external threat from a new competitor, has made it clear that you can't go on with your existing cultural values. After the Bhopal chemical plant disaster, Union Carbide's

The approach in this article was adapted, in part, from Chapter Eight, "Deciphering Culture for Insiders," in Edgar Schein, *Organizational Culture and Leadership*, 2nd edition (San Francisco: Jossey-Bass, 1997), p. 147. Several other books by Ed Schein are relevant to learning cultural exploration. *Process Consultation*, Vol. 2: "Lessons for Managers and Consultants" (Reading, MA: Addison-Wesley, 1987), lays out a concise approach to noncoercive intervention. *Strategic Pragmatism: The Culture of Singapore's Economic Development Board* (Cambridge, MA: MIT Press, 1997), uses the methods described here to investigate the culture of Singapore's Economic Development Board and its implications for the Asian "tigers" and all developing nations. *Career Anchors* (San Francisco: Pfeiffer, Inc., 1990) and *Career Survival* (Pfeiffer, Inc., 1993), provide further insights into corporate cultures and their impact on the individual.

culture underwent dramatic change. Maybe you simply need to understand why marketing is always fighting R&D; why can't they get along?

In such ambiguous situations, people become aware that their own collective shared assumptions no longer seem to fit reality. That's why they turn to changing culture. A "culture" is a pattern of shared basic assumptions that have been learned by the members of their group. These assumptions stem from people's experience, as they conduct their business successfully over and over again.

Suppose, for instance, that a company has succeeded by producing medium-quality, medium-price products. If the market suddenly changes, so that more people hold out for higher quality products, even at higher prices, then this company will be in trouble. Their worldview might still hold that "our customers want quality, but they won't pay more for it," and they will literally have a hard time seeing the market shift—until a precipitous drop in their sales volumes makes them see it.

Cultural assumptions provide meaning to daily events for people inside a group; they make life predictable, and therefore reduce anxiety. They are taught (in both explicit and tacit ways) to new group members as the "correct" way to perceive, think, and feel about all aspects of daily life. To change an organization's culture is thus to change the basic attitudes that members have developed over the years of their career. That's why cultures resist change: Resistance is a natural response to an aggressive attack against one's values.

2. ASSEMBLING A GROUP OF CULTURAL "STUDENTS"

You cannot detect cultural assumptions through the devices of individual inquiry, such as surveys, questionnaires, and/or interviews. Cultures are held by groups, not individuals, and you can only diagnose them in groups. An optimal group might include ten to fifty people, chosen to represent a cross-section of the organization as it relates to the problem at hand. If the problem is a conflict between marketing, purchasing, and production, make sure people from all three areas are present.

Be aware that your preconceptions, no matter how well informed, may be wrong. In the early 1970s, I consulted with Digital Equipment Corporation. Managers there fought constantly; meetings moved from argument to bickering to outright shouting. At times, I tried to tell them how much more constructive they could be if they were nice to one another. They would compliment me on my insights, and ignore me.

Finally, I gave up trying to reform them. And then I saw it. They weren't fighting because they were rude or angry people. They were fighting over ideas that might determine the fate of the company. I saw a way to be helpful, by writing down some of the ideas that emerged, and were lost, amid the melee. This turned out to be useful for them, and it allowed me to enter the culture, instead of imposing my views upon them. Once inside, I could begin to have an influence.

One way to keep your inquiry relatively bias-free is to penetrate from the visible surface inward: looking first at artifacts, then at espoused values, and only then at the underlying assumptions that make up your group's culture.

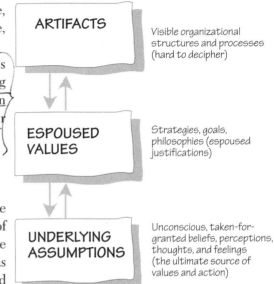

ARTIFACTS — Visible organizational structures and processes (hard to decipher)

ESPOUSED VALUES — Strategies, goals, philosophies (espoused justifications)

UNDERLYING ASSUMPTIONS — Unconscious, taken-for-granted beliefs, perceptions, thoughts, and feelings (the ultimate source of values and action)

3. ARTIFACTS: LISTING THE VISIBLE

I vividly remember the chaotic scene that engulfed me whenever I walked into DEC headquarters outside of Boston. Casually dressed people rushed past one another through thronging open spaces. The floor was crowded with cubicles; people constantly interrupted one another; and none of the offices had doors.

That same year, I consulted with Ciba-Geigy, a European chemical company. What a contrast! After being admitted by a security guard, I walked down hushed, elegant corridors into a formal waiting room. Finally, a secretary summoned me into an elevator, from which I exited into another long corridor on the third floor. On each closed door, a mounted gold name plate included a cover panel concealing the name of the person inside. Above each door, a small lamp glowed either red or green. Once, I broke the mood of silence to ask the secretary about the lamps. "If the light is off," she said, "the occupant is out of the office. If it's green, you may knock. And if it is red, he is in but doesn't want to be disturbed."

All of these signals are artifacts: observable signals of the organization's way of life. Everyone can agree that they exist, although your team might not agree on their significance. At Ciba-Geigy, I assumed that the covered name plates indicated that these managers were very private people. It turned out that there had been a terrorist attack on some managers, and the name plates were a safety measure. Since you don't know what the artifacts mean, you should start simply by listing them on flip charts as they occur to you. Fill the room with chart pages. You can jump-start the list by asking yourselves these questions:

- When you first joined this organization, what details struck you?
- What aspects of the workplace typify, to you, "the way we do things around here"? What rules? What procedures? What habits?

4. ESPOUSED VALUES: THE ORGANIZATION'S RATIONALE

Still as a group, try to establish the reasoning which underlies the artifacts. What has led the people of this organization to do things this way?

At DEC, for instance, I asked why there were no doors on the offices. "That's the way we work," people said. "We like a lot of interaction." I also learned that, for the sake of open conversation, the founding CEO had personally insisted on removing the doors.

At Ciba-Geigy, I asked why everyone worked behind closed doors. The secretary looked at me as if I were stupid. "That's the way we work," she replied. "How else could anyone get their work done?"

Both organizations had a well-articulated set of principles and values, expressing how work should be done and how people should relate to one another. In other companies, I've heard people say, "We value problem solving more than formal authority," or "We think that a lot of communication is a good thing," or "We don't believe that bosses should have more rights than subordinates."

Put the espoused values of your organization up on another set of flip charts. With each new phrase, check to see whether the other team members agree that this, in fact, represents a core espoused value.

5. CULTURAL ASSUMPTIONS: SOURCES OF MEANING AND CONTRADICTION

With a list of artifacts on one set of flip charts, and a list of espoused values on another, you're ready to delve into the deeper assumptions ingrained in the culture. Start by pointing out the inconsistencies.

A computer company had a strongly espoused value: "We make our decisions through teams and consensus." And, indeed, most decisions were the product of intensive group deliberation. At the same time, however, the artifacts included pay, appraisal, and career development systems that recognized only individual achievement. Nobody could quite figure out why the culture was resisting teamwork so hard. Yet when I suggested instituting team incentives and accountability, as a vehicle for realizing their ideal, their faces froze. "You can't be serious," they said.

As we talked through the contradictions, it became clearer that people had worked out, over time, a fairly well-entrenched way of working that no one had ever articulated. "You know," a participant said, "I've just realized that the consensus decisions are only a starting point. Nobody is sure whether a decision will stick. So if you want it to stick, you have to line everybody up, and make sure that you have the approval of anyone who can kill it. If you can do that, you'll be treated as responsible for the decision, and you'll become an individual hero."

Every organization has its own such hidden dynamics. Your challenge, in an exercise like this, is to bring to the surface the hidden attitudes that trigger your "you-can't-be-serious" knee-jerk reflexes. As you sift through the contradictions that you see, questions like these may help you maintain a clear perspective:

- **How does your culture define "truth"?** Each organization has its own assumptions about the correct way to reach a common understanding of reality. For instance, at DEC, "truth" was determined through argument. If you proposed an idea and your boss disagreed, it was culturally acceptable to take the risk of trying it anyway. If you were wrong, you were put in a kind of "penalty box," but you weren't fired or excommunicated. And if you were right, you would be a hero. At Ciba-Geigy, by contrast, truth was the province of scientific credibility. If you were a Ph.D. with patents and papers, your statements were automatically taken to be true.

- **What does your culture believe about human capability?** Some organizations are Promethean in spirit: Human willpower, if pushed hard enough, will always prevail over any obstacles (including nature). Another belief, more common in Asian organizations, puts less faith in human willpower. People get farther by harmonizing with the forces around them, by attuning themselves to the bigger picture, and by "going with the flow."

- **What does your culture believe about human nature?** In 1960, Douglas McGregor articulated two beliefs still common today.

  Theory X, as he called it, posits that people are basically lazy and uncommitted. Give them responsibility, and they'll mess up. Managers must take on the burden of creating rules, rewards, and punishments to stop the inherent badness of people from bankrupting the company. This view of human nature often turns out to be a self-

Theory X and Theory Y are articulated in *The Human Side of Enterprise* by Douglas McGregor (New York: McGraw-Hill, 1960, 1985).

fulfilling prophecy. "The bosses mistrust me," employees think. "They make me punch a time clock and watch my every move. What's the point of trying anything different?"

McGregor's other proposed view, Theory Y, suggests that human beings are more complex. If someone messes up, the fault lies (at least in part) in the structure around them. Give them the benefit of the doubt, and you may be able to tap into their inherent creativity and commitment. McGregor observed that most of the effective managers he knew held Theory Y beliefs.

A third view, held by many people in learning organization circles, holds that human beings are basically good and trustworthy. If there's a problem, it's the fault of the system, not of any person.

■ **What does your culture believe about social organization?** Many people still hold the traditional view, that people can only be managed in strict hierarchies, where the lines of authority and accountability are clear. Another point of view, formerly influential as part of Communism, suggests that the individuals should sacrifice themselves for the good of the group as a whole. Another view, prominent in the United States, places the value of individual expression and opportunity above the strictures of any group or hierarchy. People should govern themselves and work out their differences in some kind of transactional marketplace. Your culture will hold assumptions about many other things—the nature of time, space, authority, openness, gender differences, and so on. Explore whatever dimensions seem to be important to the problem you are trying to solve.

6. NARROWING DOWN THE CULTURAL DIAGNOSIS

Now that you have some of the contradictions of your culture written out, try to get as clear a collective understanding as you can. You may want to adjourn, conduct some individual investigation, and then return to consider your findings together. These techniques may help:

■ Listen to yourself explain your culture to newcomers, telling them: "What you have to learn to get along in this organization."

■ Seek out informants—thoughtful people who know subcultures within the organization that you don't know well. Say, "I don't understand why such-and-such is going on. Explain it to me." The explanation process reveals more perceptions, thoughts, and feelings than you would ever discern by simply observing the company directly.

- Explore similarities and differences between your organization and others. Look for organizations that "think alike," and for those where people do things that you feel are absolutely crazy. Then inquire: "How did this practice originate, and what keeps them going at it?"
- Pose hypothetical conflicts. Suppose your boss stood up at a meeting and said, "We want to send everyone in the organization to a training course." Or, "We want to change our core business." What would happen? How might the culture respond? By talking through plausible scenarios of what might happen, you can get a much better idea of what will happen when your culture is actually challenged.
- Avoid unilateral interpretation. Sooner or later, you will act on your insights. At that point, if you have only articulated one or two people's views of your culture, you will get into trouble. People will see through your biases, recognize your errors, and ignore you. An accurate diagnosis depends on the interplay between all the viewpoints of members of your "cultural study" team. It's particularly important that an outside facilitator or consultant, if you have one, not impose his or her viewpoint on the group.

7. FORMAL INTERVENTION: INITIATING CULTURAL CHANGE

Now the team is ready to wrestle with the bottom line issue:

- What results and new ways of working do you want to create?
- Which characteristics of the culture (especially cultural assumptions) are most likely to hinder the change?
- Which characteristics are most likely to help?
- Finally, in order to develop the results you want, what attitudes would have to shift? How much of a change of viewpoint would that require from the average employee? How much from the average manager? How would their self-image shift? How would their concept of their place in the organization shift?

In many organizations, the "change leaders" have not asked themselves these questions. As a result, they tend to minimize, in their minds, the adjustment that is needed. They downplay it and assume that adjustment will not be difficult. Then they get angry when they discover that people aren't adjusting that easily.

Focus on the positive. It's much easier to change people by accentuating the qualities that seem close to the ones you want to promote.

One further avenue of investigation is the three clashing occupational subcultures that exist in most organizations. The operators, close to the work, recognize that people are a resource. The engineer/technologists responsible for designing products and systems understand the potential in systems design, see people as a problem. And the executive community recognizes both people and technology primarily as costs. Anyone who cares about an effective organization should not take sides, but should work on getting these three cultures to understand one another's priorities more clearly. See Schein, E. H., "Three Cultures of Management; The Key to Organizational Learning," *Sloan Management Review*, 38:9–20, 1996.

This article is dedicated to the memory of my parents, who filled my life with rich stories. — Marty Castleberg

GETTING STARTED

If there are steps missing, be sure to work first on filling them in. People need role models and new heroes with whom to identify. Successful changes always involve the creation of new myths built on the heroic stories of new ways of doing things.

A final thought: To do all of this without some outside help can be very difficult. It is hard for insiders to see their own culture's strengths and its limitations. The culture change projects that work best always involve at the outset a team of insiders and outsiders working together. Each has a key perspective to bring to bear on the situation. But the outsider need not be an anthropologist or high-priced consultant. A good organization development (OD) professional from one part of the organization can often fulfill the role of "outsider" for another part of the organization.

If all this seems complicated and time consuming, you are perceiving it correctly. But there is no substitute for the trouble. Culture is complex, powerful, deep, and stable. It can be evolved—if you think clearly about it and understand its dynamics.

Kick-starting cultural exploration at Harley-Davidson Marty Castleberg

WHAT MESSAGE IS THE CULTURE OF YOUR ORGANIZATION TRYING TO TELL itself? For the past four years, I've found myself asking this question as a consultant, reflective analyst, and learning historian at Harley-Davidson. My work has involved listening to the stories and metaphors that people use naturally, and playing them back in a more formal way (sometimes in written memos or "reflective notes" that get talked about in a team). In this way, we've raised issues that might never have come to the surface otherwise, issues for which there wasn't a very good analytical language.

For example: I met once with a group of product testers, "old union" men who worked in a spartan basement facility with no windows, just across the street from the newly remodeled corporate headquarters. They were last in the flow of work, never involved with planning; a few complained endlessly through the meeting while the rest simply sat, silently and sullenly. The constant rehashing of gripes and resentment, the grimy walls, even the smell of burnt coffee pots all produced a kind of queasy feeling, which (from their perspective) echoed the way most of the rest of the company seemed to feel about them.

Then one employee said something that caught my attention: "Down here, we suck the hind titter." Having grown up on a farm, I knew immediately what he meant. Orphaned calves, unfavored by any cow, must compete for mother's milk to survive. Often, they wander around the herd trying to find an udder they can feed from. They learn to sneak behind a cow while she is nursing another calf, and tap into some of the rear, untapped udders. This works until the cow discovers what's going on and irritatedly kicks the "hind tit" calf into the next pasture.

I replayed this image to the group and a number of dynamic issues began to surface. They said they felt as though they were often forced to scrounge for resources; their work was rarely planned with them in mind, or communicated to them effectively. When a project failed, they often felt they were made the scapegoat.

Of course, the conversation had its share of attributions, but the image led to a moment where they talked about reality differently. I would not claim that this episode was the deciding factor, but the group's image began to change, both to each other and to the rest of the company. As I write this, they have moved into a new state-of-the-art facility. They have also implemented new processes that require more up front collaboration and are planning with those in charge of development projects to more effectively manage the flow of work through their area.

Another significant image at Harley had a great deal to do with the company's history. The Harley mystique of its designers as "rebel artists" goes back to its origins, when William Harley and the Davidson brothers founded the company. Harley, a gifted painter, won awards for his paintings of wildlife. In product development, they were known for their ability to craft a machine out of any piece of material that could be remotely construed as a motorcycle part. (The story lingered, be it myth or true, that they made the first carburetor out of a tomato can.)

That legacy bore fruit in the mid-1980s when the company had to meet the quadruple challenges of a declining market, Asian competition, a cash crunch, and a sudden reputation for diminished quality. Harley met all of these challenges by embracing Total Quality techniques, by lobbying the Reagan administration for higher tariffs, and by the creative use of merchandising. They also cut back the product development community. Facing austerity, the remaining product development people pulled together to do what they could to stay in business. Stories abound of ways that the company's "rebel artists" made do with limited resources and people. You need to develop a new fairing? How about splitting a gas tank in half and filling in the rest with bondo to create a

The cultural exploration practice described here was influenced by a body of work on organizational intervention; particularly, *Fostering Critical Reflection in Adulthood: A Guide to Transformative and Emancipatory Learning*, by Jack Mizerow and Associates (New York: Jossey-Bass, 1991); and *Images of Organization*, by Gareth Morgan (London: Sage Publishing, 1997).

model? As one engineer said, "We learned a lot of tricks in those days."

But the downsides to this operating style became more apparent as the company recovered and customers' expectations grew. For example, while one newly recruited engineer waits patiently for a part requested some weeks prior, having followed the formal process, his counterpart, a veteran of Harley crises, gets a similar part in a matter of hours. While the latter gets touted as a hero, the former is perceived as ineffective. But the "informal, heroic" mode means the system is in perpetual havoc; exceptions are always being made; and the company's ability to develop new products reliably is threatened, if only by the lost time spent "breaking in" to the ordering supply line.

As people talked about these issues, they kept referring to their tradition as "rebel artists." Talking about this allowed for a richer conversation that transcended personalities. Instead of "old guys versus new guys," the image helped people see that they were talking about two modes of operating.

3 Infectious Commitment

Andrea Shapiro

What can be done to spread the passion for profound change throughout an organization? Andrea Shapiro, an internal consultant at Nortel Networks, a leading telecommunications company, brought the eye of a cognitive psychologist and systems thinker to the problem. She designed "Applying the Tipping Point to Organizational Change," a computer simulation, as a tool for inquiry among team members faced with this dilemma.

What if ideas and patterns of behavior move through human communities the way infectious diseases do? It is intriguing to think that the same mechanism that governs the spread of, say, a flu virus, also governs the dissemination of ideas. Evidence is mounting that this may be the case.

For example, sociologist Jonathan Crane has studied the effect of positive role models in a neighborhood—professionals, managers, and teachers—on the lives of nearby teenagers. When the number of these "high-status" workers dropped below 5 percent, teen pregnancy and school dropout rates doubled. At the 5 percent "tipping point," neighborhoods go from relatively functional to wildly dysfunctional social patterns virtually overnight. There is no steady decline: a little change has a huge effect.

At Nortel Networks, I wondered if an organization could "catch" commitment in the same way. With the input of change agents, I designed our tipping point computer model around a principle of epidemiology: When more people are getting a disease than are being cured of it, the disease will tip into an epidemic. The speed at which the epidemic spreads depends on the all-important ratio between the number of people being infected and the number of people being cured. If slightly more people become ill than are cured, and if nothing else changes, the disease will slowly become an epidemic. By contrast, if many more people get sick than are cured, the disease will spread like wildfire. In this simulation, the "disease" is the strongly held belief that a particular change will transform the organization for the better. The means of infection is exposure to committed change advocates.

The simulation begins with an organization of 20,000 people, of whom the vast majority are apathetic. Five hundred people advocate change. Another five hundred are "incubating": They have been exposed to new ideas, and are testing them against their own experience on the job. The goal of the simulation is to get all twenty thousand people to become advocates—in the shortest time, at the lowest possible cost.

In the game, players manipulate on-screen levers to do the kinds of things that executive and line leaders can do: They can hire new advocates; expose employees en masse by sending people to one-size-fits-all training classes or conducting poster and tent-card campaigns; increase the time available to advocates for contact and conversation with others; provide financial incentives for altered behavior; improve the infrastructure for supporting the change; or change their own behavior, to lead by example and "walk the talk." As in real life, each lever has a cost, and there may be delays before the effects are felt in the organization.

All of these factors increase the number of advocates in the short run, but some have side effects that end up reducing the number of advocates in the long run. For example, massive training investments, if ramped up too quickly, will produce resistance in people that undermines the entire effort. I weighted these factors in the model based on continuing conversation with change advocates in our organization—and we keep revising

The simulation described here, "Applying the Tipping Point to Organizational Change," is available as a tool for inquiry from GKA Associates. For more information, see *http://www.fieldbook.com/resources. html*. Also, see "The Tipping Point," by Malcolm Gladwell, *The New Yorker*, June 3, 1996; Gladwell is currently writing a book about this subject. Another good reference is *Micromotives and Macrobehavior*, by Thomas Schelling (New York: W. W. Norton, 1978).

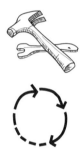

The figure of 500 "advocates" in an organization of 20,000 prople has been criticized by some "Tipping Point" model users as too optimistic. — Andrea Shapiro

the model to reflect the experiences and reactions of people who play "Applying the Tipping Point to Organizational Change."

As with all management simulations, the value of the model is not in its predictive power but in its power to catalyze reflective conversation. Nonetheless, a number of surprises have emerged. Conventional thinking tells us that great changes have great impact. But nonlinear systems such as change initiatives don't work that way. A big change, such as hiring a large number of new advocates, can have a frustratingly small impact. And a small change, such as increasing the amount of time that leaders spend setting a good example ("walking the talk") can make a dramatically large impact, by pushing the flow of new advocates past the tipping point in a way that permanently affects the population.

This simulation is most effective when used in group interventions. The teams talk about their assumptions about organizational change and commit to a strategy. Then we try each team's strategy on the simulation to determine which team can make the change in the shortest amount of time, for the least amount of money. Dealing with the model helps people re-evaluate with their own situation. One leadership team, planning a "tent card" campaign, rethought their approach after an hour and a half working together on the simulation.

The simulation, and the tipping point idea that underlies it, provide an opportunity to articulate your own mental models about profound organizational change. What factors do you believe make a difference to the spread of new ideas? How do those factors influence one another? Why would you choose some factors and not others? And what could be done to increase the power of particular factors that seem to "tip over" the balance from apathy to interest?

For information on how to facilitate this kind of conversation, see "Using Microworlds to Promote Inquiry," The Fifth Discipline Fieldbook, p. 534.

4 Heretical Tactics

Bill Godfrey, Bill Harris, W. M. Deijmann, Cliff Havener, Dave Buffenbarger, Iva Wilson; edited by Art Kleiner

Heretics are people who take a stand in a way that challenges conventional wisdom, but who remain loyal, in their own mind, to the organization they are challenging. (They may not be loyal to the man-

agement, but they recognize the value of the organization.) Organizations may shun their "heretics," but without them it is much harder to adapt to a changing world. In 1997, I convened some organizational "heretics" via electronic mail to consider: How can people fostering change from within become more tactically effective? As these stories suggest, fierce opposition is counterproductive; but empathy, engagement, imagination, and gentle persistence are surprisingly powerful.
— *Art Kleiner*

Bill Godfrey (consultant, former executive of the Australian Tax Office): The aim of a heretic should not be to impose a contrary truth, but to open minds to new possibilities. Too many heretics forget that and fall into the same trap as their opposition. While we were going through a monumental information technologies change initiative, I adopted the heretical view that networks and terminals, not mainframes, should be regarded as the core of the system. I never had a prayer of "winning" this discussion, nor did I have the knowledge to deal with the technical arguments. My purpose was to ensure that no decision got made without considering the impact on LANs and local users. If I had played to win, I would have lost the decision. By playing to "question," with as much humor as I could muster, I believe we made some modest gains in the responsiveness of the system as a whole.

Bill Harris (former Senior Process Consultant, Hewlett-Packard): Being effective means eschewing actions (or language) that isolate me from the company's mainstream. I feel I must take responsibility for presenting my ideas in ways that don't just express them, but can help the orthodoxy improve.

For example, I've tried to introduce new ideas by sending books or articles up and down the management chain. Only rarely has that been successful. I was astonished when a colleague told me that other people saw my penchant for crediting sources (which I regarded as honesty and humility) as intellectual browbeating. They felt they couldn't keep up the pace of reading, and I was making them feel inadequate. She encouraged me to have the courage to state ideas as simple, authentic statements from me. If anyone asked, I could give them more background.

W. M. Deijmann (Partner in DIALOOG Consultants in Holland): One powerful tool that heretics have is the "act of irreversibility." I invite people to describe an ongoing problematic situation and propose an "irreversible act" that would benefit the individual, the area of

We would like to thank and credit participants who contributed to the discussion leading to this article: Doug Carmichael, Myrna Casebolt, Benjamin Compton, Sam Cruce, Jeff Dooley, Jim McAbee, Douglas Merchant, Tom Petzinger, Harriet Rubin, Dan Simpson. A longer version, including more material on the conceptual approaches useful to "organizational heresy," is available on our Web site at: *http://www.fieldbook. com/ heresy.html.* We also want to thank Rick Karash for helping organize the electronic newsgroup that led to this article. Rick maintains an ongoing "learning-org dialog on learning organizations." For more information, visit his Web site at *http://world. std.com/~lo.*

For more examples of "irreversible acts," see the Web site: *http://www.come. to/dialoog.*

responsibility, and the organization as a whole. Once executed, the act could not be taken back.

A manager from a travel agency couldn't send bills to his clients (including the local army base) because of organizational rules that required a controller from the head office to visit their remote site and verify all bills. This sometimes took two months, and clients complained. So the manager sent a letter to all clients, saying that henceforth they would receive all bills within a week. The same day, he faxed a copy of the letter to the head office controllers' department, accompanied by another letter explaining the situation and why he had done this. Within three days, a central office controller had visited the agency and they came to an agreement that everyone could live with.

Cliff Havener (consultant, former General Foods marketing executive): If you're uncomfortable with the term "heretic," how about "deviant"? Dr. Everett Rogers's "norming" theory suggests that innovation tends to originate within a statistically very small group (Innovators, representing as little as 2.5 percent of the total), and moves to the Early Adopters (who might represent 13.5 percent). Once they have put their stamp of approval on it, it is adopted by the Majority (the 68 percent in the middle of the bell curve). Eventually, Laggards (the remaining 15 percent) adopt it. When anyone comes up with a significantly different view of "reality," by definition they find themselves in that first group of 2.5 percent. That makes them "deviants" of the highest order.

Most old company cultures are disproportionately populated with Majority and Laggards. Dr. Rogers concluded that the only way an Innovator can influence the adoption of a new idea is to link up with Early Adopters. He characterizes them as people who recognize that something is wrong, but don't know what to do about it and are actively seeking a "better way." The Majority and Laggards will not accept a new idea directly from an Innovator. It has to go through the "sanctification" process of Early Adopter endorsement first.

Not surprisingly, my biggest client over the last twenty-three years has been 3M—not because of its mainstream culture, but because there is a large "secondary culture" of people dreaming up new products, hoping to turn them into operating divisions that they would then head up. This culture encourages Innovators and Early Adopters.

Dave Buffenbarger (recently retired from Dow Chemical): Two of my friends would claim to be heretics. Same organization. They both use laughter, silliness, craziness, quick wit in an attempt to garner support. One of them makes it work. The other does not. The difference? The

S ee Everett M. Rogers, Diffusion of Innovations, (New York: Free Press,1983, 1995); or books by George Land (Grow or Die, 1974 and 1986; Breakpoint and Beyond with Beth Jarman, 1992). For information about Cliff Havener's books— Meaning–the Peaceful Revolutionary's Guide to Quality of Life, and Value Based Business—see the Web page http://www.fieldbook. com/resources.html.

successful one "wears his heresy on his shirt sleeve," voicing it visibly and continuously, but is not offensive about it. The other is a closet heretic, voicing his beliefs only when out of the sight of management.

Iva Wilson (former President, Philips Display Components Company, U.S.): I was born and raised in the former Yugoslavia. I came to the U.S. in 1968, in the midst of the Vietnam War. I immediately recognized one big difference. In Yugoslavia, you could say whatever you wanted about your boss, but to say something negative about President Tito could be life-threatening. In America, you could freely vent your frustrations about the President, but talking openly about your boss could have a serious negative impact on your livelihood. This recognition stayed with me throughout my life. That's why I tried so boldly to make change happen in corporate America; the repercussions were not life-threatening, as they had been in Yugoslavia.

THE AGE OF HERETICS
by Art Kleiner, (New York: Doubleday, 1996)

When I first heard the title *The Age of Heretics*, I envisioned a book about people who had been exiled, tortured and even put to death for their beliefs and choices. But the heretics in this book are the heroes, outlaws, and forerunners of corporate change from the preindustrial years up to 1982. Punishment still existed for them, but it came in the form of betrayal, fear of office politics, and giving up one's life to a job. Do not despair! There is far more about life and opportunity in this book than about death and loss. The people presented in this book (Kurt Lewin, Douglas McGregor, Robert Blake, Eric Trist, Ed Dulworth, Edie Seashore, Jay Forrester, Chris Argyris, Warren Bennis, Pierre Wack, Amory Lovins, and many more) made passionate choices. Their stories bring possibilities to the foreground and provide new energy to readers as we develop our own capacities for fostering change within a larger organization that may not always be ready. — B. C. Huselton

The "heretical" story of GS Technologies is told by B. C. Huselton and others in "The Cauldron: Heat and Light Between Labor and Management at G.S. Technologies," by Gary Clark, John Cottrell, Rob Cushman, B. C. Huselton, and Phil Yantzi, in *The Fifth Discipline Fieldbook*, p. 364.

5 The Perils of Shared Ideals

William Isaacs

Bill Isaacs is the proprieter of DIA•logos, a consulting firm based in Cambridge, Massachusetts, a lecturer at MIT's Sloan School of Management, and the director of The Dialogue Project at MIT. In this contribution, he delves beneath the surface of the relationship between true believers, nonbelievers, and the habits of thought that drive them.

The material in this article owes much to David Bohm—to the published material that Bohm made available, to the transcribed conversation published as David Bohm, "Thought as a System," and also to the unpublished work that he and I developed together as we considered how to articulate a "theory of thought."
— William Isaacs

For information about dialogue, see the DIA•logos Web site: http://www.dialogos-inc.com. Also see *The Fifth Discipline Fieldbook*, p. 357.

See *Leadership Is an Art*, by Max de Pree (New York: Doubleday/ Currency, 1987).

At the heart of organizational change is a heartbreaking paradox. On one hand, we cannot instigate change without an image of our longing and aspiration. In companies today, for example, people hunger for a sense of belonging and an opportunity to produce meaningful work—ideals that seem sorely lacking in modern civic life. Unfortunately, ideals are dangerous. As we become involved with the abstract image of our longing, we run the risk of losing touch with the real opportunities to get what we want. When we fix our attention on an ideal, even a lofty one like "vision," "openness," "learning," or "natural processes," then we serve a cut-and-dried image, a way to impose order on the world. Ultimately, that imposition will produce consequences we do not intend or want. The ideal itself becomes a trap. Ideals become external standards, used to punish noncompliance, instead of inspirations for new action. Idealists assume that people need "a new way of thinking," as if they did not already have their own way of thinking. Corporate vision statements lock in attitudes, keeping the company from being alive to the ever-changing realities of the market. Heavily ideal-led systems seem to have a great tendency to get paralyzed by their own ideals, as if blinded to their experience by the images they seek.

One organization which has dealt courageously with these issues is the Herman Miller Company. Founded by people steeped in the egalitarian attitudes of the Dutch Reformed Church, this manufacturer of office furniture was renowned for its innovative approaches to participative management and employee stock ownership. In 1987, the CEO and board chairman, Max de Pree, published a popular management book—*Leadership Is an Art*—conveying the idea that a corporate leader should be not just a chief or a "number-cruncher," but a creative inspiration and steward. Herman Miller's furniture was exhibited in the Museum of

Modern Art; their invention of the "action office" revolutionized workplace layouts. (This included the invention of the now-infamous cubicle, which ironically had been invented as an idealistic way to give people a more flexible, vibrant workplace.) The people at Herman Miller were (and are) among the brightest and most creative of any in the corporate world. Yet in the early 1990s, the entire company struggled and lost considerable strategic momentum because of the fallout from its own cherished "participative" ideal.

The first signs that something was wrong appeared in the mid-1980s. Competitors, which had always "knocked off" the company's designs for resale to cheaper markets, began to drain away its premier customers. Market share and profitability eroded. Competitors grew in size. Within Herman Miller, true to the ideals of the company, all employees were eager to play out their role, to help turn things around. But they found themselves in conflict. Artisans and designers argued that the company needed to return to its roots of design leadership. Other voices insisted that the key to the future lay in improving business and marketing operations. Over the next few years, as the company followed both directions, tensions grew deeper. There were endless abstract conversations about the company's management philosophy, but little agreement about setting immediate priorities.

Nor did anyone talk about their factionalism. They *couldn't* talk about it—because the ideal of participation made it almost impossible to see that they were factionalized. After all, "everyone had a voice." But the company lacked any way to translate that voice into action. Participation became paralysis, where no decisions were made without extensive consultation. Critical decisions were held up for months. The company could not seem to adjust the meaning of participation to mean "appropriate" participation without seeming to violate the original ideal.

Eventually, a cultural transformation began to bring many of these points to the surface (which is why they can be written about now). But this happened at great cost—erosion of market share, high turnover at the top, and unnecessarily low morale.

On a broader level, the Herman Miller story shows an attempt to reconcile one of the most troubling tensions in industrial society—between the isolating, competitive, insecure free market, and the community-based commitment needed for high performance. Managers often deal with this uncomfortable tension by trying to "have a vision": to find a cohering meaning that will unite everyone in a common goal that will serve both institution and individual.

like Michel's Era [handwritten marginalia]

However much energy such efforts temporarily stir up, they also have a shadow side. They encourage people to rule out certain behaviors while praising and including others. People, however, cannot simply legislate out certain parts of themselves. The more they try to hide the bureaucratic, authoritarian or customer unfriendly side of themselves, the more they intensify the power of the unwanted behavior, until it leaks out at inopportune moments. At Herman Miller's lowest moment, some of its people were known for promising things they could not deliver, and then acting as if the problems were beyond their control.

THE FACES OF FOLLY

There is a word for this condition: "folly." Folly is a common phenomenon not only in corporations, but in governments and individual behavior. It is so prevalent and so important as a force in human affairs that some thinkers and historians have attempted to categorize it. The problem is not ideals, per se, but the way we think of them. The ecology of our thought—the inherited network of ways of thinking, speaking, and acting in the world—induces us to make idols out of our ideas. Until we find a way to think together and inquire together about these habits of thoughts, we may be condemned to re-create the conditions we struggle to change. For Herman Miller's managers to break free of their impasse, for instance, they had to learn to see their most cherished value and the damage it did to them. Only then could they confront the downside of their own idealism and rebuild their market position.

In the discipline of "mental models," based on Chris Argyris's theories of "double-loop learning," people practice reflection and inquiry skills to bring these sorts of hidden attitudes and intentions to the surface. But simply retraining ourselves, as individuals, doesn't help alter the shared ideals that collectively sustain folly. A group of people following a common vision will almost inevitably become true believers together: They will unwittingly reinforce one another's views and ineffectiveness.

Some people have predictable patterns of behavior and action around them—patterns that are reflective of the local ecology of their thought. Picture the cloud that followed the cartoon character Pigpen everywhere he went. He carried his own ecology. Most people do the same thing. I recall one senior manager who seemed surrounded by people with doubts about him. It was said that he was in line for a senior job, and then was passed over. "You know," people added knowingly, "now he

The sociologist Robert Merton began his career with a paper on folly: "The Unanticipated Consequences of Purposive Social Action," *American Sociological Review*, (1936: Vol. 1 pp. 894–904); Barbara Tuchman devoted a book to folly: *The March of Folly, From Troy to Vietnam* (New York: Knopf, 1984). She noted there how, throughout history, groups pursued "a policy contrary to the self-interest of [their] constituency." Policy makers and leaders, she said, often "continue down the wrong road as if in thrall to some Merlin with magic power to direct their steps" (p. 383).

is not all that effective." The story had a certain magnetic quality to it; it organized my thoughts, even though I had never met him. And when I met him, I discovered that he, too, had accepted this story. The ecology of his world, including his own thoughts about himself, reflected this pattern. The world that surrounds this fellow seemed somehow dampened, without energy.

Groups also carry their own ecology. A pilot group planning a change initiative will establish a certain presence for itself, within the organization. That presence is composed of their own thinking, along with the thinking of others around them. If the pilot group and the organization seem to repel each other in a counterproductive but unstoppable way, then there is probably a problem with the ecology of thought in that system. If you are a member of the pilot group, there is little you can do directly to change the thought on the other side. You can only start on your own side, unilaterally, by "trying on" some new thoughts that may help you develop new capabilities for coping with the perils of your own shared ideals. Here are four such sets of thoughts.

ABSTRACTION, FRAGMENTATION . . . AND PARTICIPATION

Intellectually, if we think about it, we know that the human body has made no division between our fingers and our hand, or our hand and our wrist. But for most people, if someone asks, "How many fingers am I holding up?" our first reflexive thought is to consider the "finger" as a separate thing. The idea of a "finger" is an abstraction that we have made into an object. Similarly, when we hold up our organization, we see different teams, divisions, functions. We intellectually recognize that they are still connected, part of a larger whole—but on the level of our thought, we act as if the divisions are real, and thus make them real. The boundaries between nations are similar lines, created only by thought, and yet made so real that it is virtually impossible to forget that they are there. When the first astronauts went into space and looked back upon the Earth, they were struck by the fact that, unlike their mental image of the planet, this one had no lines between nations!

One common form of abstraction is "fragmentation," a word whose roots mean "to smash." In fragmentation, we create divisions and then forget we have done so. Fragmentation is useful for focusing on a narrow purpose, but it causes us to lose our awareness of the connection between the parts and the whole. (This is part of what David Bohm meant when he wrote, "thought creates the world, and then says, 'I

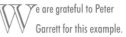

We are grateful to Peter Garrett for this example.

didn't do it.'") When pilot group members presume that, "We are not like the rest of the organization," they are creating an abstract image of themselves that will lead to further abstraction and fragmentation.

To heal the problems of abstraction and fragmentation in thought we pay attention to the details of our experience: seeing our environment as directly and closely as we are able. In truth, the group is both like and unlike the rest of the organization—in ways that you cannot fathom until you learn to look at things without automatically referring to the names you have in your head for those things.

Practice looking at a tree without the name "tree." You may find that associations occur to you—the wish to be outdoors, the kind of tree, thoughts about the health of the tree. As they occur to you, notice them and let them go. Look instead at the tree with your eyes, your body. See if the tree becomes more unfamiliar and strange to you, more like an unnameable living thing. Give it no name or description: Just see it.

Direct experience of the world is a remedy for the problem of abstraction. This is also what the zen Buddhists call "beginner's mind": a fresh perception with many possibilities, while in the expert's mind there are few.

Zen Mind, Beginner's Mind, Shunryu Suzuki (Trumbull, CT: Weatherhill, Inc., 1970).

MEMORY, IDOLATRY . . . AND THINKING

Imagine yourself walking down a dark street. You see a shadow, and imagine it is an assailant. Your heart starts to race; you look for the nearest escape. Then you realize that it was only a shadow, perhaps your own. You relax. The thoughts and feelings triggered by that shadow were not new thoughts; the danger came from your memory. (There may also be a real assailant, but your alarm makes it difficult to tell.)

Idolatry is the perception of memory as thought. Like sounds from a tape recorder, the thoughts and feelings in our memory are instantly ready to overshadow any new, fresh thoughts we may have. We think of idols as the false gods of ages past, but our current age is rife with idols—images that we have accepted, that blind or limit us to other possibilities. Herman Miller's managers held an idol of "participation" in their minds; other companies have "idols" of their customers—jealous, capricious beings who don't appreciate the company's offerings.

People often do not recognize the way that they collude in creating these sorts of idols, nor can they quite bring themselves to see how their own behavior, and the behavior of the world around them, fails to live up to the ideal. The system drives them to blame one another instead.

This example, first proposed by David Bohm, reveals the flight or fight reaction in memory. It is arguable that this reaction is "instinctual," and so in a way part of a social or even biological memory pattern, one that comes preinstalled in the package, as it were. — William Isaacs

When the idolatrous values include tolerance and openness, the results are particularly ironic: "open" cultures that close themselves to anyone who doesn't quite seem "open" enough, or tolerant cultures that close ranks to protect themselves against the intolerant.

We can only remedy these problems of memory, idolatry, and thinking with the principle of articulation. This involves the gradual process of learning to tell the truth about what you feel. This principle for dialogue is based on a premise which physicist David Bohm spoke of as the implicate order—the idea that there is an invisible, patterned reality waiting to unfold into present, visible form. Nature, Bohm said, constantly unfolds and folds back again—not just in plants and animals, but in human thought as well.

Bohm called the habitual reactions of memory "thoughts"; to him, they were leftover artifacts from a previous "thinking." Thinking takes a longer time, and emerges more gently; it appears sometimes in the kind of simple, quiet idea that stands out among the crowd of passing thoughts, that contains a surprise, that includes things we have not thought before, that has the potential to change us.

To learn to think, instead of following thoughts, we listen to our own automatic reactions and gain perspective on them. "Why," we ask, "did I just do that?" Ralph Waldo Emerson once said, "Trust thyself. Every heart vibrates to that iron string." Trusting ourselves means doing the hard work of listening and giving voice to the truth as we see it, continually listening to see if we are still paying attention to our memories instead of the thoughts that unfold within us.

CERTAINTY, STASIS . . . AND MOTION

A woman I met recently found it intolerable that some people hunted and killed bears in New England—especially when human actions had all but eradicated them from that part of the world earlier in this century. She saw people who disagreed with her as "Neanderthals" and others who shared her views as "sensible." At the same time, she wanted to learn how to influence people who disagreed with her, and she recognized that learning to change them would mean changing herself first. While it was painful to know that bears suffered and died, it had become equally painful to hold on to a belief that caused so much polarization between her and other people.

But then came a much more startling realization. "If I do not hold on to this belief," she said, "what else is there? I may be left with nothing."

Many of us develop partial understandings that we see as complete. Juanita Brown calls these rigid views "noble certainties." The more certain we feel of them, the more they limit our freedom to think. We may have spent years building up these certainties, and beneath the fear of letting go of them is indeed the fear of having nothing underneath.

The overall problem of certainty can be remedied with an awareness of the motion of change. This takes place through "reflection-in-action": deliberately training oneself to see the flow of activity that underlies all things. This embodies the ability to let go, to "suspend" our certainty, to see things from another point of view. The notion that everything is in motion, in process, can relieve us of the pressure to have everything fixed and worked out, since the only reliable thing we can know is that this situation, too, shall change.

JUDGMENT, VIOLENCE . . . AND INCLUSION

A final problem of thought relates to judgment. We decide things are one way or another. We defend our interpretations, looking for evidence that we are right, ignoring or discounting evidence that we are wrong. Then we impose our judgments on others. We cannot see any possible logic or validity in their views. Therefore, either they must change—or they "obviously" are acting from malicious intent, and must be stopped.

At the ArmCo steel company, during dialogues among managers and steelworkers, the two groups defended themselves, not against each other, but against the saber-toothed ideas that sat behind them. One union man put it well: "We hear the word, 'union.' You think, 'ugh.' We think, 'ahh.' Why is that?" Just the sound of those ideas had triggered a "fight-or-flight" reaction.

Maintaining defensiveness of this sort leads directly to violence. The word "violence" comes from roots that mean "the undue use of force." Without violence of thought—the attempted imposition of logic, judgment, and values on others, even in perceived self-defense—there would be no violent action. Violence begins between our ears.

What remedy could exist, however, for judgment of the outside world? Only the recognition that the boundary between ourselves and the rest of the world does not exist as we perceive it. Most of us generally experience ourselves as simply living "in" the world. We say, "I am here, the world is out there around us." But it is more accurate to say that the world is in us. Everything that happens to us takes place in our consciousness. As you read these words, they will become part of your awareness. You may think about them, discard them, or ignore them, but they have already become part of you.

Think of people who matter to you. Their influence does not leave you simply because they are not physically present. They continue to live in you, active forces that guide you.

Initially, it is somewhat challenging to think this way, but there is some real power and potential in it. In practices such as dialogue, people can learn to look for the ways we connect, as well as the ways we pull apart from one another.

DIALOGUE AND THE ART OF THINKING TOGETHER
by William Isaacs (New York: Doubleday, 1999)

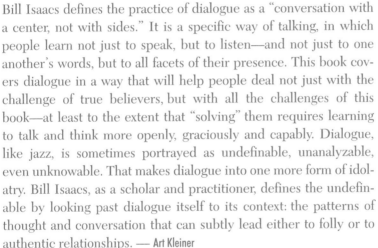

Bill Isaacs defines the practice of dialogue as a "conversation with a center, not with sides." It is a specific way of talking, in which people learn not just to speak, but to listen—and not just to one another's words, but to all facets of their presence. This book covers dialogue in a way that will help people deal not just with the challenge of true believers, but with all the challenges of this book—at least to the extent that "solving" them requires learning to talk and think more openly, graciously and capably. Dialogue, like jazz, is sometimes portrayed as undefinable, unanalyzable, even unknowable. That makes dialogue into one more form of idolatry. Bill Isaacs, as a scholar and practitioner, defines the undefinable by looking past dialogue itself to its context: the patterns of thought and conversation that can subtly lead either to folly or to authentic relationships. — Art Kleiner

The
Challenges
of Redesigning
and Rethinking

Our concept of emergent design comes from management theorist Karl Weick, who writes, "Design, viewed from the perspective of improvisation, is more emergent, more continuous, more filled with surprises, more difficult to control, and more tied to what people pay attention to than the designs implied in [formal] architecture." See "Organizational Redesign as Improvisation," by Karl Weick, in *Organizational Change and Redesign*, edited by G. P. Huber and W. H. Glick (New York: Oxford University Press, 1993), pp. 346–379.

Successfully dealing with the challenges of sustaining profound change opens up a broader set of challenges. These tend to not only be frustrating but enervating—because they are impossible for committed local line leaders and internal networkers to confront alone. They concern fundamental issues facing all industrial-age organizations—issues for which imaginative, courageous executive leadership is needed:

- **Governance:** As pilot groups expand their reach, how can they develop the legitimate autonomy they need to act in tune with existing power and accountability structures?
- **Diffusion:** How can the entire organization (and its external partners) learn from the experiences of profound change initiatives? What infrastructures and practices can help prevent organizations from continually "reinventing the wheel"?
- **Strategy and Purpose:** What does it take for an organization to continually reinvent itself as its world changes? How can new ideas about purpose and strategy that emerge from innovative pilot groups potentially influence thinking more broadly?

Meeting these challenges involves understanding the need for both *formal design* (the conscious, intentional architecture of organizations, such as guiding ideas and strategies, established structures, and policies and rules) and *emergent design* (the ways that people naturally "redesign" the organization as they live in it). Efforts to meet these challenges seem to be effective to the extent that the formal and emergent designs are harmonious.

The material in these last three chapters is more speculative than for the preceding challenges. Our experience with them is more limited, because fewer of the pilot groups we know have reached the point of dealing with them. But these challenges are too significant, too unavoidable—and too rewarding—to ignore.

X. Governance

1 The Challenge

The business world today is gripped by tremendous cross-currents concerning the philosophy and practice of governance. Traditional industrial corporations concentrated power in top management; yet many of the most successful corporations in recent years have implemented radical changes in governance systems.

Visa International, for example, would have a market capitalization twice that of General Electric, were it traded as a conventional stock ownership corporation. But it isn't, because Visa is incorporated as a member-governed corporation. Its 20,000-member financial institutions are simultaneously one another's customers, suppliers, and competitors; they "own" not stock, but perpetual rights of participation. This prototypical networked organization is more than an alliance or consortium: It has a coherent identity of its own, and it is permanent (outlasting any members who drop out or dissolve). Six hundred million consumers used its product to produce $1.3 trillion of business in 1998. Most important, Visa's 3,000-person central administrative staff does not set strategy and business direction; that comes from the network, through a system of overlapping, elected governing boards.

At the same time, many corporations in the U.S. and elsewhere have been gripped by a different type of governance crisis in the past ten years—demands for increasing accountability to shareholders. This movement has sprung from the growing proportion of shares held by institutions (such as pension funds); from two decades of highly publi-

Sources on the turmoil in governance structures include: *Ownership and Control: Rethinking Corporate Governance for the 21st Century*, by Margaret M. Blair (Washington, D.C.: The Brookings Institution, 1995), pp. 1–2; and "The Eclipse of the Public Corporation," by Michael Jensen, *Harvard Business Review*, September-October 1989, p. 61.

The reference on marketing strategy is: "Changes in the Theory of Interorganizational Relations in Marketing: Toward a Network Paradigm," by Ravi S. Achrol, in *Journal of the Academy of Marketing Science*, 1997, Vol. 25, No. 1, p. 58.

but there's a lot of confusion counterproductive

Our use of "dependence, independence and interdependence" is borrowed in part from *The Seven Habits of Highly Effective People* by Steven Covey (New York: Fireside/Simon & Schuster, 1989), pp. 185–203.

cized takeovers, leveraged buyouts, and corporate mergers; and from growing concerns about self-serving, inward-focused management who neglect shareholder returns. The business press regularly celebrates the current pantheon of CEOs who "deliver for shareholders," powerfully reinforcing the perceived value of strong management control.

The struggle over corporate governance is playing out against the backdrop of accelerating technological and geopolitical change. The industrial-age world in which authoritarian, centrally controlled organizations developed and prospered no longer exists in most global markets. As one prominent marketing strategist put it recently, traditional hierarchical governance structures "are likely to prove hopelessly inadequate in the knowledge-rich environments of the future." Self-contained global enterprises, owning every part of the value chain from raw materials to retail, are giving way to networked organizations: enterprises that operate at high speeds, building relationships and controlling only part of a business niche or even only part of a brand name. With no one at the center, there is no one to fight for centralized decision making. Local decision making is growing, even in large organizations. Its advocates argue that it is faster, more adaptive, and builds commitment. At the same time, skeptics (including many senior executives accountable for the performance of the whole company) worry that strengths of effective hierarchical management, such as balancing short-term and long-term and focusing on integration of diverse processes, are being discounted in the headlong rush to empowerment and networks.

Our own view of these cross-currents is that organizations of all sorts are in the midst of fundamental evolution from governance systems that reinforced dependence on the central authority, to those that encourage more independence among local units, toward governance processes for increasing interdependence, balancing central and local decision making. Traditional authoritarian hierarchies fostered dependence by placing concentrated decision-making power in the hands of a few and demanding compliance from the majority.

But traditional hierarchical governance systems also managed interdependency, and this capacity can be easily lost with increasingly autonomous, disconnected decision makers, each pursuing their own independent self-interests. In a world of increasing interdependence, decision making based solely on local self-interest may be expedient; but it may only go half way toward the governance structures and practices that organizations most need.

This view of the cross-currents of change in governance leads to a core dilemma: how to gain the advantages of local autonomy and decision making while increasing the ability to understand and manage interdependence. We believe that those organizations that learn how to walk this tightrope will build unique competitive advantages.

Regardless of how one interprets the winds of change swirling around corporate governance, innovative pilot groups sooner or later find themselves caught up in issues of accountability and power. It may happen when they find higher level managers questioning how they make decisions and wanting to know "who is in charge." It may happen when they cross organizational boundaries—for example, initiating changes to integrate across functional areas to better serve customers, but inadvertently undermining established practices that other managers rely upon. Or, it may happen when a pilot group tackles a problem or opportunity, and then discovers that achieving their goals will require a decision or change of direction for the company as a whole. From the standpoint of pilot groups, the timing of the challenge is not predictable. It could come at the beginning of a pilot group's endeavor, or much later. But the challenge of governance will surface in "power clashes" around autonomy and integration, as surely as "cultural clashes" will arise in the challenge of "true believers and nonbelievers."

When this happens, pilot groups can feel like victims of power dynamics they neither anticipated nor brought about. Their reactions often then make matters worse. But neither victimization or overreaction is necessary. If they can understand the underlying dynamics at play, pilot groups can adopt far more effective strategies.

Issues around governance are not just vital for pilot groups—they also occupy the time of many executives concerned with designing enterprises better suited to today's marketplaces. Indeed, the "pilot group" may be the top management team, wrestling with such design issues. They may believe that more flexible, adaptive firms are critical to delivering shareholder value. And they may see rethinking and redesigning governance systems as a cornerstone in building such firms.

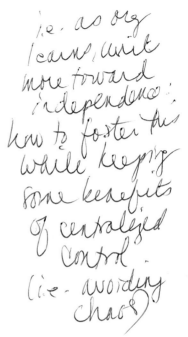

"We're not trying to eliminate control in our organizations," says former Hanover Insurance CEO Bill O'Brien. "The movement to increasing localness is really about replacing hierarchically imposed control by increased self-control. This is a far more difficult challenge than merely giving people authority to make decisions."

"People incapable of self-governance are incapable of being governed," says Dee Hock, founding CEO of Visa International. "The function of the 'core' (central management)," says Hock, "is to enable its

The quotes from Dee Hock are derived from talks he gave at the Systems Thinking in Action conference, 1996; and at the Society for Organizational Learning annual meeting, 1997.

Two leading thinkers on localized governance, whose ideas we draw upon, are Russell Ackoff and Charles Handy. Ackoff offers a variety of systems-oriented governance redesign approaches, including "internal markets": creating market economy relationships among corporate sub-groups. Charles Handy's "corporate federalism" develops the principle of "subsidiarity"—that decisions should be made at the lowest level of the hierarchy at which people are competent to make the decisions. See *The Democratic Corporation* by Russell Ackoff (London: Oxford University Press, 1994) and *The Age of Unreason* by Charles Handy (London: Business Books Limited, 1989).

constituent parts." Like O'Brien and other corporate radicals, Hock takes his inspiration from trying to understand what it would be like to build "organizations based on biological precepts, not mechanical concepts." He suggests that such organizations would distribute power and function to the maximum degree, and seek "infinite durability, malleability, and diversity."

Such ideas are not only radical but have proven practical, at least for some organizations. Hanover rose from the bottom of the property and liability insurance industry in 1970 to become a top performer for the decade of the '80s. Hock's thinking lies at the heart of Visa's "chaordic" ("producing order out of chaos") governance system, which many regard as a key to its phenomenal success. In the mid-1990s Shell Oil borrowed from innovations tested at Hanover by establishing "internal boards" to push decision making, including capital investment decisions, down to four newly formed autonomous business units: upstream operations (exploration and production), downstream operations (distribution, marketing, and sales), chemicals, and "services" (primarily IT—information technology)—with dramatic increases during the next four years in profits, growth, and innovation. Even military organizations, such as the U.S. Army, are evolving away from a tradition of "just follow orders." Starting with the Gulf War, a practice called "directional intent" has become accepted, in which commanders set up units with broad objectives, and the units make decisions semiautonomously and learn as much from checking with one another as from central command.

This does not mean that making locally controlled governance systems work is easy. Failed corporate efforts to break down centralized control are legion. "Matrix" organizations, intended to free people from the arbitrary whims of a single boss, often trap them between the inconsistent demands of two or more bosses. Decentralization often gives people decision-making authority beyond their business judgment. This can demoralize the local managers that it is meant to empower; they are afraid to ask for help lest they communicate lack of confidence. It likewise places senior managers in a double bind; they are accountable for the results their subordinates produce, and yet wary of intervening lest they communicate that they do not trust local managers. Lastly, very few models of successful alternative corporate governance structures exist to study and learn from. There are a plethora of novel ideas and several interesting examples of new practice. But connections between new theory and new practice are only now starting to be articulated, and, by contrast, established mechanisms of centralized control and power have had many years to become entrenched and understood. It is sobering that a savvy practitioner of redesigning governance processes, Dee Hock, believes we are just at the very beginning of a fifty-year journey in reinventing industrial-age command and control management.

Nor does it mean that hierarchy will disappear. On the contrary, if hierarchy is to have a future, and we believe it will, it will be necessary to rediscover the fundamental reasons for its existence in the first place. As management theorist Elliott Jaques has pointed out, the fundamental function of managerial hierarchies is to differentiate accountability over differing time horizons. He argues, based on extensive analysis of hierarchies in diverse settings, that there are seven levels of "requisite organization." The most local level should be focused on processes with time horizons up to three months; the seventh and most senior level on time horizons of twenty to fifty years. Obviously, management hierarchies in most contemporary organizations bear little resemblance to Jaques's theory. Rarely are there as few as seven levels, and senior management is often obsessed with very short term issues. Creating workable new governance systems will mean rethinking hierarchies so that they can be more functional in a world of increased interdependence and change.

See The Requisite Organization by Elliott Jaques (Arlington, VA: Cason Hall & Co., 1996). Also see p. 390 of this book.

The challenge of governance appears differently for local line leaders and networkers on the one hand, and executive leaders on the other. For leaders in pilot groups, it often appears as conflicts with an existing management system that they believe is constraining them. For innovative executives, it appears as the challenge of guiding the orderly distribution of power and authority. Only by understanding the dynamics of the challenge of governance from both perspectives can we see the variety of high-leverage strategies available for both groups to share power effectively in an increasingly interdependent world.

goal

We believe one key to achieving this lies in understanding the interplay between "design and emergence." Executives have unique responsibility for designing formal governance mechanisms. But everyone in the organization, including executives but also middle and local managers, enacts the organizational practices that shape how governance processes actually work. New, more flexible formal governance mechanisms can be readily undermined by contrary day-to-day organizational practices. From this perspective, innovative local pilot groups and imaginative executives are important allies for each other: the one developing new practices based on new self-governing capabilities, the other new governance mechanisms that rely on those capabilities.

Governance systems designed with overly rigid command and control structures predominating are like sailing ships designed so the rudder requires a heavy hand. On well-designed sailing ships, by contrast, the fore and aft sails can be trimmed so that they balance each other. These vessels get to their destinations efficiently with only light guidance to the rudder. The interplay between the human and mechanical systems allows more flexibility in control, leading to entirely new, emergent sailing strategies.

LEXICON

GOVERNANCE

The verb "govern" derives from the Greek *kubernán*, "to steer a ship." ("Cybernetics" comes from the same root.) In its Latin form, *gubernare*, it came to mean "to guide or rule" (as in, "maintaining control of an empire"). Then, during the industrial revolution, it acquired a machinelike connotation. People began to speak of the "mechanisms" of governance: the rules, decision rights, privileges, rewards, and channels of authority.

In modern organizations such as corporations, governance is often defined as the Romans did: as the arrangement of power for directing and controlling other people. People say "I direct you to . . ." or "He controls whether or not we can . . ." and understand this as talk about the governance system.

But that is not the only definition. Alternatively, *directing* can mean orienting, in the sense of setting a direction; and "controlling" can mean adjusting, in the sense of adjusting the speed or the rudder. Obviously, which of these two sets of definitions is adopted says a great deal about whether "governance" is seen as the imposition of one group's will upon another or, as is closer to its Greek roots, the process of continually orienting and adjusting.

We use governance in this later, older sense, because we regard it as the more fundamental definition. Once that is established, there are many options for orienting and adjusting: Concentrating power may be appropriate in some situations, while distributing power may be more appropriate in others.

In corporations, formal governance mechanisms include boards of directors, management structures (such as the hierarchies of accountability in an organization chart), reward and recognition policies, and more novel developments like internal boards. Such formal mechanisms define who has power to make particular types of decisions.

Just as steering a ship does not take place unless there is a chosen destination, governance is meaningless without including an awareness (tacit or explicit) of the purpose and direction of the organization, while taking into account the current reality along the way. Conversations about power structures or control, without including consideration of where the organization needs to go, are counterproductive. They lead to organizations where control itself becomes part of the organization's purpose.

THE UNDERLYING DYNAMICS OF THE CHALLENGE OF GOVERNANCE

The challenge of governance arises through three interrelated limiting processes driven by three underlying limits.

Often, this challenge arises for pilot groups first through clashes over their autonomy (balancing process B1 in the diagram on page 368). As such groups develop new learning capabilities, they gain confidence, a sense of increased power, and a greater capacity for self-governance. They become more able to resolve conflicts, more consistently focused on their purpose and vision, more aware of how they fit within the larger system, and more capable of producing intended business results. All of this tends to lead naturally to acting with higher levels of autonomy; to self-determine more and more of their direction and accomplishments. Pilot group members might expect to hire their own people, set their own strategy, develop their own business opportunities, implement new processes, and perhaps even make capital investment decisions.

However, the larger organization is often not prepared to grant this increased autonomy. When this happens, an "autonomy clash" develops, and management imposes greater control on the group. Members of the pilot group may feel that management is trying to control them arbitrarily. Those imposing control, on the other hand, often feel that the pilot group doesn't understand the larger business context and strategic impact of local decisions they are making. For both groups, the result is less enthusiasm and willingness to commit to the pilot group's efforts. The pilot group looks less attractive to its members, especially for potential newcomers. Senior managers resent being labeled "authoritarian" and "controlling" when they raise their concerns and likewise may feel less supportive of the pilot group's initiatives.

The underlying limit for this balancing process concerns the organization's "tolerance for independent self-governance." How flexible are

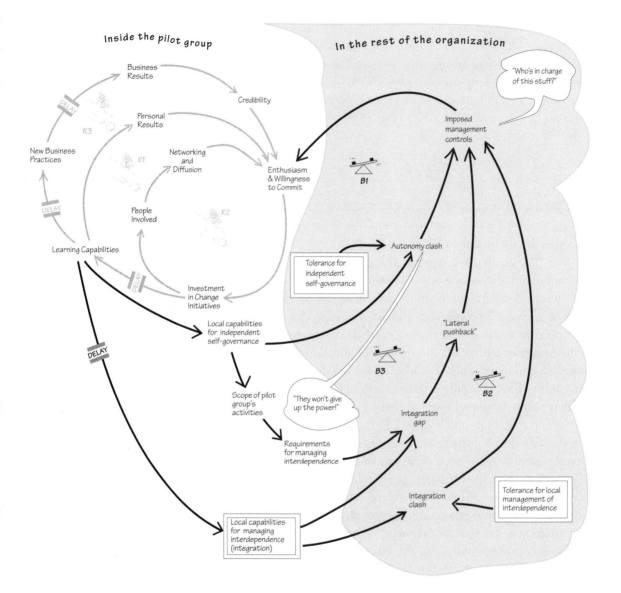

formal governance systems in allowing more decision-making authority to migrate to capable local units? How capable is the organization's management in dealing with creative, self-confident local units? How able and willing is management to assess the capabilities of local pilot groups to manage themselves effectively?

Even if management tolerance for local self-governance is high, there are other ways that pilot groups can run afoul of existing governance processes. One occurs when pilot groups extend the scope of their initiatives (limiting process B2). This could occur through overt changes like involving suppliers in redesigning procurement processes, or through subtle changes like expecting people in other functional areas to be comfortable with the high-trust, high-responsibility style of management that has developed within the pilot group. Or it may occur when pilot groups, exercising their natural propensity to look ahead, inadvertently enter the domain of strategic planning for the organization as a whole. As the pilot team expands the scope of its activities, it may underestimate the increased interdependence of its activities with other groups within the organization. In effect, requirements for managing interdependence are increasing more than the team's capabilities for managing interdependence. When this occurs, an "integration gap" develops. The pilot team finds itself at odds with other groups or with senior management, resulting in increased management control.

For example, one innovative product development team gradually replaced the corporate ethic of formal reports with informal communication and high candor. But when they approached their launch, they found themselves in trouble. They had to "hand off" the job to manufacturing counterparts who operated more traditionally, with a strong emphasis on formal reports and management approval for local actions. The head of the manufacturing facility interpreted the product development team's willingness to deal more openly with problems as evidence that they were poorly managed. "I rate projects as red, yellow, or green," he said, "and that team is purple. They are completely out of control." The result was that senior management, who resented being brought into the whole matter, had to impose more "discipline" on the product development team—causing the team to lose face and straining their relationship with their manufacturing counterparts.

It was easy for the team members in such a situation to blame this clash on the manufacturing people or on senior management. But, in truth, had the two units found a way to talk about and integrate their two different approaches to management, they might have had a smoother product launch.

This sort of integration gap will occur, sooner or later, for most innovative pilot groups, leading to strained relationships and "push back" from other parts of the organization. The underlying limit concerns the team's own capabilities to manage interdependencies with other teams or units. It is easy for innovative pilot groups to neglect such interdepen-

As learning capabilities develop in the pilot group, the group's local capabilities for independent self-governance rise. If the organization's tolerance for independent self-governance does not increase, then this leads to a clash over autonomy between the local group and the larger system (loop B1). After some delay, the pilot group's capabilities for managing interdependence (more integrated relationships with others in the organizaion) go up; if the rest of the organization does not tolerate this interdependence, then there is an "integration clash" (loop B2). Finally, as new capabilities cause a broadening of the pilot group's scope of activities, its requirem4ents for managing interdependence go up. If the new capabilities of loop B2 do not keep pace, then there is an integration gap and "lateral pushback" from others around the organization (loop B3). All of these balancing processes may result in an increase in imposed management controls, which in turn reduces enthusiasm and willingness to commit among everyone involved.

dencies. Their focus is often on their own processes, relationships, goals, and problems. Even if they are developing greater understanding of the larger systems of which they are a part, they still may not develop much skill or credibility to address issues that involve other groups. After all, this has traditionally been the responsibility of those farther up the hierarchy and probably exceeds their business mandate.

Finally, pilot groups who develop capabilities for managing across boundaries with other groups sometimes find themselves amid another set of problems. Senior management may not be ready for them to do this, especially for key interdependencies. (This is limiting process B3.)

Senior managers are often wary of problems like the integration gap. They have seen pilot groups who successfully innovate in their own processes cause problems for other groups. They appreciate the blindness pilot groups can have around issues of interdependence. Moreover, managing interdependencies is traditionally one of senior management's key roles. Lastly, key interdependencies often arise out of strategic goals and plans. For example, many firms are seeking more integrated product development and manufacturing processes—so-called "concurrent engineering" or "design for manufacturability." Some are even pursuing what manufacturing expert Charles Fine calls "three-dimensional concurrent engineering," focusing on joint development of product, manufacturing process, and supply chain. Such strategies are complex, highly interdependent, and often not even widely communicated within the company for fear of divulging key information to competitors. Under these conditions, it is easy to see how senior managers could be extremely concerned about local management of key interdependencies.

See Clockspeed: Winning Industry Control in the Age of Temporary Advantage by Charles H. Fine (Reading, MA: Perseus Books, 1998).

If senior management has relatively low tolerance for local management of interdependence, a different type of power clash can develop—an "integration clash." Local management feels that it is capable of managing cross-functional issues. Perhaps they even have a track record of successfully doing so. They feel they need to exercise this capability to continue to pursue new business opportunities. Senior management differs and imposes increased control to limit such boundary crossing. Just as in the earlier situations of increased management control imposed on the pilot group, the results are reduced enthusiasm and willingness to commit to the group's endeavors.

It is important to distinguish the sorts of conflicts that arise in the challenge of governance from those that arise in the challenge of believers and nonbelievers (discussed in Chapter 9). The two types of conflict may interact—for example, clashes over power may feed the attitudes of isolation and defensiveness developing within a pilot group. But in the challenge of governance, conflict arises from the pilot group's way of managing itself, not from new behaviors within the pilot group. If its self-governance processes have drifted far away from the governance processes of the larger organization, the stage is set for power clashes, around autonomy, or integration, or both. The challenge of governance will arise even if problems created by believers and nonbelievers are resolved. Moreover, the leverage in dealing with this challenge is quite different.

Key

Viewed from the perspective of executives attempting to innovate through implementing more flexible governance systems, all these same problems arise, although their symptoms differ. If executives succeed in implementing alternative governance mechanisms with greater tolerance for both self-governance and local management of interdependence, but local capabilities are inadequate in either of these areas, increased localness will result in poor decision making. It will produce anxiety among managers, customers, suppliers, and perhaps even shareholders. Eventually, either business results will suffer or there will be push-back from other parts of the organization, and the only recourse will be increased management control—perhaps by a new generation of executives who rise to their positions in reaction to a governance system seen as out of control.

The three balancing processes underlying the challenge of governance can play out in many ways, but the overall consequences are always the same. Little lasting change occurs if only local innovative teams succeed in developing new capabilities. Little lasting change occurs if only courageous executives implement more flexible governance mechanisms. Either both must occur, or the status quo is likely to prevail. This is why high-leverage strategies must attend to both local and global capabilities, and why both local and executive leadership is critical to pursue such strategies.

STRATEGIES FOR MEETING THE CHALLENGE OF "GOVERNANCE"

This challenge requires two sets of strategies. One set is for the change initiative pilot group working within the current governance structure. Leverage for them lies with building their own capabilities—for self-governance, for managing interdependence, and for dealing with potential power clashes that can arise with formal governance structures.

The other set of strategies is for executive leaders, who can potentially initiate governance redesign. Their leverage lies in increasing awareness of design possibilities, to develop governance structures that balance local autonomy with systemwide interdependence.

While pilot groups and executive leaders require different strategic orientations, they need each other to sustain lasting changes. The most promising strategies help people at different levels look at the future of the business together, to educate each other, and to increasingly appreciate each other's aspirations and dilemmas.

Strategies for the Pilot Group

Pilot group members, facing resistance from other parts of the company, sometimes assume that the only way out is to propose a wholesale redesign of the governance structure. But there are no perfect governance systems that eliminate all conflict. Instead, learning to deal with actual and potential conflicts early on can be vital for local line leaders.

■ **Pay attention to your boundaries, and be strategic when crossing them**. Pilot groups often get involved in projects that seem to demand changes beyond their own areas of accountability and authority. It is important to recognize this when it happens. It is easy to get caught up in the group's enthusiasm and ignore the boundaries that differentiate the group from others.

If your team is trying to make something new happen across boundaries, you will need sponsors with authority to help ensure that you can carry the endeavor to fruition. Don't shortchange your vision, but recognize that part of the task of expanding your vision is finding links to the existing governance structure. This, in most organizations, will mean gradually expanding your sphere of influence, rung by rung, as you build credibility and capability.

If the pilot group is a cross-functional team composed of people from different parts of the organization, then there should be a clear line of accountability to each member's manager, who should approve of his or her participation in the group, and who should be kept aware of the group's work.

Engage openly with the people who are accountable for other parts of the larger system that your efforts might affect. Enthusiastic pilot group members are often blind to the effects they are having on other groups because they take little time to inquire about them. When you start to realize you may be about to cross delicate boundaries, invite the people from the other group to a meeting (or to a meal) and lay open the reasons for your project to them. "We have these plans in mind; they overlap with your area in these ways. What is your reaction? How might developments like these help with your problems? What can and can't we do, from your perspective?"

- **Articulate the case for change in terms of business results.** As proponents of a change initiative, you are responsible to people in your group, and to the organization as a whole, to make sure your effort is not wasted. If you pretend that "good results will speak for themselves," you risk the credibility and effectiveness of your project. Instead, you will need to make a clear, compelling business case for change, especially to people with accountability for other parts of the system you're dealing with. The more practiced and capable you are at meeting the challenge of "relevance," the more effective you will be here. In making a business case, it's most effective to "work from outside in": talking about meeting outside market demands, or new competitive threats, as well as fulfilling internal personal aspirations.

i.e., talk the traditional talk

- **Make executive leaders' priorities part of your team's creative thinking.** Develop the ability to understand and internalize the pressures that they feel and the opportunities they perceive. Avoid attributing the reasons for resistance to a leader's personality (or to anyone's personality); look for systemic causes instead. This may require getting time with the executive leaders, interviewing them about "the things that keep them awake at night," particularly where the problems exist in the boundaries or connection points of the current governance structure. Recognize the executive leaders' concerns about balancing immediate business quarterly performance with long-term growth. Inquire into the needs they see for integration across business units, especially when related to overall business strategy.

  As you internalize these priorities, your pilot group helps to transfer some of that pressure off the CEO and his or her direct reports. It is unhealthy for any group, no matter how central, to concentrate accountability on only a few people, but that is how most organizations are structured. Outward-looking pilot groups can share that pressure.

- **Experiment with cross-functional, cross-boundary teams, if you can get them sponsored by the hierarchy.** This can be a very good mechanism to demonstrate the value of new forms of governance. You can prototype more permanent cross-boundary connections without having to sell them at a conceptual level: "Customers are demanding better integration. Let's start a team to respond to that, and use that to create temporary examples of how better cross-functional lateral connections might create business value." Avoid talking of creating permanent connections or any sort of matrix; that could scare people. Demonstrate results first, and later negotiate a transition from the temporary cross-functional group to some more permanent arrangement, if one is needed.

A good example of all of these precepts took place in the late 1990s at Kredietbank, a Brussels-based bank, well-known in Belgium and employing more than 10,000 people. Needing to revamp the bank's credit processes, an elaborate internal "skunk works" was formed, centered around a new pilot group called the "Core Team," which was charged with redesigning the credit process. There were two other panels: a "Decision Group" formed of senior executives, and a cross-functional advisory "Checking Group," which served as a kind of volunteer bridge to many of the managers with decision-making authority under the old system. Some of these managers began to suspect the Core Team members of "not really listening"—of having their minds made up in advance. The Core Team members did not realize for a long time that their own practices were part of the problem. Their feedback to the Checking Group was too slow, and neither systematic nor explicit.

For the full Kredietbank story, see "Blending formal and informal decision-making: How process redesigners at a Belgian bank came to understand the two parallel forms of authority," by Carl Rossey and Wouter van den Eynde, Kredietbank (1998), http://www.fieldbook.com/k-bank.html.

"The result was a painful loss of confidence and an increase in mistrust on all sides," notes Carl Rossey, the Kredietbank general manager who led the Core Team process. Eventually, the Core Team members, who still held their process redesign mandate, responded by making a business-oriented case for more involved sponsorship. It was no longer acceptable for key leaders to hold themselves aloof from the Checking Group and other advisory roles—and Core Team members and process designers could no longer "work around them" or ignore them.

In the end, Rossey says, "We have learned that there are two power structures in the organization: the top-down (formal) authority of the management hierarchy and the bottom-up (informal) authority of pilot projects where new work processes have been invented. Neither form of authority—formal or informal—can be overcome through brute opposition. And neither can be neglected. The ongoing challenge is to get the two structures working together."

Strategies for Executive Leaders

》》 Also see "Redesigning an Airplane in Midflight," page 404.

■ **Begin at the beginning: with governing ideas.** "We hold these truths to be self-evident . . ." With this simple phrase, the drafters of the U.S. Declaration of Independence established what they regarded as powerful guiding ideas, deeply held convictions upon which an equitable and workable system of governance might be built. Two hundred years later, might the same philosophy of governance—based on guiding ideas people are prepared to live by—enter the world of institutions?

"The design of governing ideas is the most important aspect of organization design," says Bill O'Brien. "It is much more important than the typical reorganizations that most executives regard as redesign. These often leave little changed because the underlying values which guide the organization are unchanged. The problem with designing guiding ideas, and why most executives shy away from it, is that it creates a mandate for those same executives to change their own mental models and their own behavior—otherwise the new ideas will have no credibility."

Developing a set of governing ideas is one of the few activities that can penetrate to all levels of an organization, because it is one of the few ways to reach the hearts as well as the minds of an organization's members. "The biggest problem with most corporations today," according to O'Brien, "is that they are governed by mediocre ideas." A mediocre set of ideas, to O'Brien, reflects lack of conviction. Governing ideas that do not evoke passion, that do not inspire imagination and excitement can never be the basis for "an organization worthy of people's commitment," in the words of former IKEA president Goran Carstedt.

From the standpoint of governing, of orienting and adjusting, the primary function of such ideas is to establish a common set of aspirations and guidelines for everyone in the enterprise. Ultimately, they define who "we" are and how "we" operate. They are guidelines, not rules. But as such, they are potentially more powerful than rules because they can influence a broader array of behaviors. "All men are created equal" does not prescribe any particular behavior, but it establishes a foundation for a vast array of judgments, and ultimately sanctions, on behavior.

Two key governing ideas we have seen articulated in many settings are localness and merit. The first encourages local, individual decision making; the second stipulates that the criterion for good decisions was what most benefited the business as a whole. The tension

Thoughtful executives around the world are wrestling with the orderly distribution of power and authority in the service of developing more competitive and responsible enterprises. This is a vast subject about which current knowledge is woefully limited. In organizing these suggestions, we have drawn on a few examples with which we have firsthand knowledge. This is not to discount the many other corporations that are equally pioneering, nor is it to hold up these few examples as paragons of perfection. Rather, we simply want to illustrate the depth and breadth of changes that are occurring and acknowledge a few pioneers worthy of serious study.

For more about "localness" and "merit," as they were developed at Hanover Insurance during the 1980s, see *The Fifth Discipline*, p. 181ff.

CVC: 1) "open" mgmt
2) standardize where possible

This concept of "the source of power in ideas" stems in part from *Sources and Uses of Power* by Bill O'Brien (Cambridge, MA: Society for Organizational Learning, 1998). Also see "Designing an Organization's Governing Ideas," by Bill O'Brien, in *The Fifth Discipline Fieldbook*, p. 306.

created by this juxtaposition forces decision makers at all levels to wrestle with unavoidable trade-offs, rather than leaving management with the sole responsibility of aligning local and global interests.

How are "governing ideas" different from the commonplace mission statements, vision statements, and value statements? The answer lies in how they are used. Ideas become "governing ideas" when they form the foundations for a system of governance. They matter, because they are a source of legitimate power in decision making. For example, Shell Oil's reorganization into autonomous business units, including the formation of its internal boards, helped make tangible some of its newly articulated core values, including "belief in people," "innovation," and a "sense of urgency." Visa's purpose and guiding principles are integrated throughout its constitution, which is part of its legal articles of incorporation. They set the framework for designing its policy-making apparatus—notably, spelling out the powers and limitations of its elected governing boards. If these powers are superseded, Visa's members can elect new governing board members. In this way, Visa's member organizations have recourse to abuse of power, just as do the citizens in a democratic society.

For more on the governing ideas of Visa, see page 391.

It is much too early to say if Visa's constitutional approach will have broad applicability. But one aspect seems universal: If the primary source of power in a system is a set of governing ideas, then by definition that source of power is not any particular set of individuals. This is exactly the opposite of most traditional industrial-age organizations, where power flows from people in positions of power. It's worth noting that in totalitarian systems power is also grounded in a set of people, while in democratic systems of governance power is grounded in ideas.

■ **Develop specific structures that guard against "authoritarian drift."** Considerable forces emerge in almost all organizations to push tough decisions up the hierarchy. Even after governance systems have supposedly "localized," these forces can arise, coming both from fear of making mistakes on the part of those who have not traditionally had such decision-making power and fear of losing control on the part of those who had lost decision-making power.

When U.S. Shell Oil reorganized into four autonomous profit and loss businesses in 1995, it also established "internal boards" for each of those businesses. These boards comprised Shell Oil's most senior executives. They became, by design, structural blocks to guarantee that the individual business's management teams, in conjunction with their local boards, would be able to make virtually all key decisions regarding that business's future. Without these boards, there would have been unavoidable uncertainty as to whether certain decisions, like capital investment decisions, could be made by the business unit or had to be referred to corporate management. Given this uncertainty, and Shell Oil's traditions of central control, sooner or later, issues would probably have come along that the local managers would have felt were too risky to tackle themselves. Once some decisions were referred upward, others would have probably followed. With the boards available for consultation and oversight instead of for micromanagement, this did not happen, and the individual business units rapidly grew into true profit and loss businesses, releasing enormous energy and innovation.

⟩⟩ See "Interdependence at Shell," page 384.

∎ **Deploy new rules and regulations judiciously.** "Rules change behavior," writes systems author Donella Meadows. "Power over rules is real power. That's why lobbyists congregate when Congress writes laws, and why the Supreme Court, which interprets and delineates the Constitution—the rules for writing the rules—has even more power than Congress. If you want to understand the deepest malfunctions of systems, pay attention to the rules and to who has power over them."

See Donella H. Meadows, "Places to Intervene in a System (In Increasing Order of Effectiveness)," *Whole Earth Quarterly*, Winter 1997, p. 78.

Meadows's insight suggests that those with power over the rules have special responsibilities. Yet executive power to reorganize and change governance systems is often exercised with little attention to the many effects the reorganization and change will have on many people. Some companies reorganize every year; some even more frequently. When people complain, "All this restructuring is just a power game," they may be correct.

∎ **Never underestimate the power of small changes in complex situations—if they are the "right" changes.** Governance issues, like many social change issues, seem daunting because they are full of "detail complexity." Dozens of factors could be included in any description of a governance system: channels for participation and resolving conflict; external sources of authority, including shareholders, government regulators, and customers; traditional forms of privilege, ranging from the massive and undiscussable (immense pay disparities between senior-level managers and employees) and the small but highly visible trigger points (such as executive parking spaces); special cases of "single-point" authority, such as members of a founding family who still wield influence over the company, or a proprietor who has his or her name on a line of credit; patterns of information flow; reward structures, and the methods and rules for determining promotions, recognition, bonuses, options, and other compensation; the intangible, but very real, boundary between those who are considered lifelong "members" of the organization, to whom it has made an implicit commitment for life employment, and those who are considered "employees"; the established customs of compliance, or noncompliance, with laws and regulations; and many more.

Yet there are many examples where a simple rule change has made a big difference. One company we know has two manufacturing plants next door to each other. Both plant managers initiated learning-oriented maintenance projects at the same time. But there was one key difference between them. The successful plant manager had the authority to write checks up to $25,000 without getting them approved. This meant he could set up training sessions in system dynamics and other learning disciplines, and he could fund small experiments, without the delaying, demoralizing step of submitting his ideas for approval. This small boost in local autonomy led to millions of dollars in savings and a "work-styles" renaissance that continues to this day. In the other site next door, the project withered.

■ **Be prepared for a long journey and don't embark alone**. No individual has unilateral power in establishing significant changes in governance systems. Even CEOs who carry out reorganizations by fiat encounter much more difficulty if they try to alter significantly the real design and functioning of the governance system—that is, the distribution of power.

Developing a vision-based governance system is an arduous consensus-building process. It is pointless to even start off without at least a few staunch partners. If you're a CEO, this may look like an advisory group to help you think through design issues and widen your perspective.

Building an initial consensus usually starts with the top management team or with some cross-section of senior management. It is very difficult to proceed without this. But it is important to remember that the first definition of consensus is not agreement, but "harmony, cooperation, sympathy, and group solidarity." Building genuine consensus

This definition of "consensus" comes from *Webster's Third New International Dictionary* (New York: Merriam-Webster, 1971), p. 482.

on governing ideas, on systems of checks and balances, and on blocks against authoritarian drift does not require unanimity. It does require people willing to find common ground in principle and practical solutions that everyone can live with. It also requires a group of people who collectively have the power to take action in designing governance systems. In a corporation this means the CEO and some significant percentage of senior managers. Depending on how sweeping the changes are, it may require involvement of board members as well.

Set up any governance redesign process so that it is difficult for anyone to stack the deck in his or her own favor. To the extent possible, make sure that the principal designers do not know in advance what role they will play when the dust clears. Otherwise, there will be an irresistible temptation to enhance that role.

Everyone involved must be prepared for an arduous journey. We have rarely seen significant redesign take less than a year, and often considerably longer. When Visa International was being founded, it took over two years to articulate a statement of purpose, to be "the world's premier system for the exchange of value," and an initial set of guiding principles. At Shell Oil, the top two hundred managers were involved for over two years in developing the core ideas that guided their "transformation process." When the "design team" seeking to recreate the MIT Center for Organizational Learning as a self-governing network started off, Dee Hock warned the group that "Coming to real consensus on purpose, principles, and structure is the hardest work you will ever do." Two years later, no one questioned his admonition.

Moreover, developing new governance systems is only the first step—implementing them is no easier. Be prepared to receive, and feel, a great deal of emotional heat. Most people have developed their innermost attitudes about governance from early experiences with authority figures, going back to their relationships with their parents. Shifting to a more nonauthoritarian governance structure can involve a great internal shift, as usually occurs in giving up control. Even when governance structures change, many accountabilities will not. For example, a CEO still has to deal with shareholders, other owners, and a board, and they may not recognize the value of the shift at first. Customers and suppliers may also be perplexed by changes that affect them but that they do not understand fully. Most of all, many in positions of hierarchical authority find that they must confront complex reactions from within the organization. Some managers will openly or quietly oppose any move that involves losing control. Some local units will be eager to have more control of their destiny while others will prefer to keep the authoritarian system they know, understand, and can maneuver within.

Remember that, ultimately, real change in governance practices is connected to capacity building—and this takes time. Expect delays. "Most systems of governance are based on external control," says Bill O'Brien. "But people thrive, in the long run, on a system based on self-control. Moving to self-control is a process of advancing to maturity—not just among individuals, but on the part of an organization." That is why, even after a change in the governance structure is put in place, there may be months' or years' delay before people are able to consistently deal with the responsibilities of increased autonomy and increased management of interdependence.

Even given growing maturity and local capabilities, there still may be a slow adjustment in people coming to believe things have really changed. Keep in mind that most people in organizations have lived through a long history of management control, and gone through cycles of relatively more tolerant systems followed by relatively more intolerant bosses. They naturally take any change as more likely than not to be reversed in the future. There is no substitute for patience and perseverance, along with compassion for those who seem to "not be on board."

2 Community of Companies

Jack Stack

This is both the most radical and the most down-to-earth governance model in this book. Raconteur, JFK look-alike, and outspoken CEO, Jack Stack is probably best known as the original developer of the "Great Game of Business," the first example of open-book management and a pioneering effort to build financial literacy (page 181). This article, edited near-verbatim from a conversation with him, gives hope to those of us who, like Jack, follow the "Moe, Larry, and Curly" school of management. And it demonstrates an approach to gover-

nance that sets dozens of people free to create remarkable results—in
a way that any organization, no matter its size, can implement.

The story of our most innovative governance structure began with a decision made to improve community, though we didn't call it that at the time. In 1981, a group of International Harvester managers engineered a leveraged buy-out of a troubled truck engine remanufacturing plant in Springfield, Missouri. We created a new Springfield Remanufacturing Company (SRC). We did it, frankly, because this town was (and is) a phenomenal place to live, and we didn't want to take away people's jobs—or move away ourselves.

Right away, we did two innovative things. We knew we could never pay back our debt load unless everyone in the company understood the fundamentals of the business and had a stake in our financial success. Thus, we created the "Great Game of Business."

Second, we put every employee into an Employee Stock Ownership Plan (ESOP). We had no idea what we were doing; it's as if the Three Stooges had decided to start a company. At first, we had wanted to provide stock to all employees. Then somebody told us, "No bank will lend money to three hundred people." And we found out that the SEC wouldn't let us do it, so we said, "Let's go public." But that would have cost $250,000 in filing fees and expenses. We stumbled into the ESOP approach as the last alternative we could find; the only way we knew to give everyone a financial stake in the business.

When you teach people the business, they ask questions—and when they own some of the stock, you'd better have answers. Around 1983, a janitor stopped me in the hallway. "You're telling us that once we pay back our debt, we'll be secure," he said. "But I looked at the balance sheet, and seventy-six percent of our receivables are in the truck market. That market has a recession every six years. If we don't diversify, we'll have to lay people off." I looked up this guy's background. He was a former stockbroker who had gotten tired of the stress on Wall Street. (You never know who you'll find out is working for you.) So I called my senior management staff together and we spent hours trying to figure out a solution. Finally, somebody said, "Why don't we diversify out into a business that goes up in a recession?" The automotive parts aftermarket seemed like a good bet; in bad times, people hang on to a car for nine years or more.

So we tried it. By 1988, we were up to $40 million in sales. The company was privately held, with employees holding 15 percent of the shares, and the rest in the hands of managers. The value of our shares was extraordinary. Morale was high; we loved all of this. Then, at a meeting one day, a manager named Steve Shadwick said, "I'm going to retire soon, and I don't want to live on crankshafts and camshafts. Where's the money going to come from to buy back all our stock?"

Sure enough, we had made no provisions for this. Hello again to Larry, Moe, and Curly. So we ran the numbers. It turned out that we would have to sell the company to pay all of our stock options. Did we really want to sell? And if not, did we want to turn the company over to our kids? Or to our employees? We couldn't answer these questions, and we couldn't ignore them, either, because our job as leaders was to answer the tough questions that we have trained people to ask us. We ultimately decided we didn't want to sell, so as a last-ditch alternative, we came up with a crazy idea: "Why don't we start building mini companies as separate limited liability corporations or partnerships? If we need to raise money to buy out the original shareholders, we can sell off these little spin-offs, and we won't have to sell our core business."

Soon after that, some people in the plant suggested that we get into a new line of work: rebuilding and reselling the engine coolers that we had been discarding. We invited them to create a business out of it. We gave them 22 percent of the new company in exchange for their full-time sweat equity, and Springfield Remanufacturing kept a majority interest of 78 percent. We explicitly stated that we might sell our shares at any time. We invested about $60,000, along with some of our expertise and advice, and the new company, called Engines Plus, started with about $286,000 in sales. Within a year it developed a major contract with J. I. Case, a Fortune 500 company. Later, Engines Plus developed a thriving business in irrigation equipment, and grew to be worth about $2 million.

We continued to spin off new companies, so that by 1996, there were twenty-five independent organizations in our family. We have had to sell none of them. The revenues coming in from them has more than covered our costs in buying back stock and growing the businesses. We discovered that, within our community of companies, we could help one another enormously—in ways that ranged from lending one another forklifts to supplying engineers on temporary projects. Being small and owner-owned, the new companies tended to be passionately devoted to their customers and their businesses.

Now some truly incredible synergies developed. Overachievers who had reached the top of their pay scales at SRC had an entirely new set of opportunities. They didn't have to live with the frustration of no promotion opportunities. We could give them new challenges in their own businesses that would provide a chance to make four or five years' worth of raises. We could painlessly replace them with lower-paid people, which lowered our overhead rates. Accidentally, we had solved a perennial problem of industrial society: that there is not room in the hierarchy for all the people who have worked long enough to be chiefs.

In effect, we had become our own venture capitalists. But most venture capitalists want to get out in five years or less, with a high return. We wanted to build up companies with equity ownership. It turns out, to the people who started these companies, the financial aspect of ownership wasn't as important as the freedom to make their own decisions. They did excellent jobs, better than they had done at SRC in many cases, because they understood the responsibilities and their need to get the job done. I think this is the true meaning of equity.

Eventually we would like to test our concept by taking some of these companies public. If the market rewards people who are truly focused on the future, then adding the feedback level of the stock market could become part of our education process.

The result of all this is a system of governance that doesn't just let us grow and thrive but also lets us give people opportunities and watches out for them. In one company, a guy in the maintenance department set up an emergency fund for people who run out of workmen's compensation. Most of the people in the business have donated one hour's pay per week into this fund, and he's set it up to be payroll-deducted. People who didn't contribute at first were allowed to tap into it—with the result that they, eventually became the biggest advocates of contributing. At a Christmas party several years ago, a man who had had a brain aneurysm stood up and told everyone how he could never have survived without it. This form of community represents the kinds of things that people in organizations should always do for one another. But they won't—until the governance system of the organization, or group of organizations, encourages it to take place.

INNOVATIVE REWARD SYSTEMS FOR THE CHANGING WORKPLACE by Thomas B. Wilson (New York: McGraw-Hill, 1995)

Today's compensation and performance appraisal methods emerged in the 1950s and 1960s, intending to get employee pay variability "under control." No wonder they turn people against one another, promote games-playing, and kill collaboration. How, then, could you develop alternatives? An erudite and savvy rewards consultant named Tom Wilson, familiar with the disparate territories of conventional compensation and organizational learning, shows how. Under headings called "What's Wrong with This Picture?" Wilson describes how stock options can distract, instead of motivate, executives; or how recognition programs can breed cynicism. Then he suggests alternatives, in detail. — Art Kleiner and Charlotte Roberts

3 Interdependence at Shell

Tom Botts

Shell Oil went through one of the most abrupt, full-scale shifts from centralized to decentralized governance in recent memory. Here, one of the architects of that shift describes the inside story—not just what happened, but what they learned along the way.

As in the introduction to the governance chapter, the use of "interdependence" in this contribution is borrowed in part from *The Seven Habits of Highly Effective People* by Steven Covey (New York: Fireside/Simon & Schuster, 1989), pp. 185–203.

During much of Shell Oil's history, the company's governance structure was based on dependence on authority. Senior managers were accustomed to telling subordinates what to do. Subordinates knew how to function in a system of top-down controls and expected their managers to tell them what to do. Starting in 1994, we made a big shift to independence: to a system where local, autonomous businesses within the company made their own decisions with their own profit-and-loss accountability. We moved away from the controlling corporate center, and pushed decision making lower in the organization. At the time, as Shell Oil's manager of corporate planning, I was right in the thick of the change. And I had big concerns.

In early 1994, then-CEO Phil Carroll called a meeting of the top ten executives, called the Leadership Council, to discuss how Shell Oil should be governed in the future. To prepare for the meeting, my corporate planning group worked with a management consultant to develop a model of various governance structures, which I presented to the Leadership Council. Shell's choices ranged from a loose "holding company" framework to a tightly centrally controlled "operating company." Based on the difficult business we were in and our own top-down leadership style of the past, the model indicated a centrally controlled governance structure would be appropriate for Shell Oil.

But Phil Carroll stopped me midway through the presentation. He said it was obvious where this was going—a recommendation for Shell to continue its "control from the center" tradition. "I don't think it has to be that way," he said. "I give much more weight to a leadership style based on what we want to be, not what we are."

I was devastated at first. I hadn't delivered the "right answer." And I wasn't sure that a radically different governance structure would work in Shell. But the meeting turned into an energetic and exciting dialogue about "what could be." The Leadership Council members began to enthusiastically envision a new Shell, where they ran their businesses with a lot more autonomy and were held accountable for their performance. They talked about the benefits of devolving decision making deeper in their organizations, and how that would unleash more human potential. Afterward, one of them told me it was the best conversation they had ever had as a group.

Now the intensive work began. We began grappling with the key questions: How would work get done? How could we ensure that the newfound freedom of the businesses was accompanied by appropriate accountability? We studied companies like Emerson Electric and Frito-Lay, that seemed to have found ways to balance central alignment and local autonomy. Maybe, I realized, it wasn't so important to get the "right" governance model, *per se*. It was more important to make sure that the governance model we chose had structures and processes that were clearly aligned with our leadership style and guiding principles.

MOVING TO INDEPENDENCE

We chose a federalist governance model. Power was held as much as possible by independent entities with profit-and-loss accountability, but they still had interaction and responsibility to one another and to the center. No longer would the businesses come on bended knee to the center, begging for capital and taking direction on detailed operating activities. They would now have their own capital structures and internal debt levels. If they chose to invest capital, they would be held accountable for providing an adequate return, just like a publicly held company. For the major businesses, internal boards of directors were established for advice and oversight. These boards, with interlinking membership, served as the common genetic code that enabled learning and idea sharing among the businesses. In addition, other structures and processes were put in place to achieve business alignment: an overarching mission, vision, and core values; a revised planning process; a Shell Learning Center; and a Corporate Leadership Group made up of the top 150 executives from across Shell Oil's businesses.

Several of our businesses joined with other companies such as Amoco, Mobil, and Texaco to form new independent joint ventures. In general, these new ventures, as well as the newly independent 100 percent Shell businesses, rejoiced in their freedom to run like real businesses. They were like sons and daughters of the old system, now old enough to strike out on their own, still somewhat apprehensive, but convinced that without the oppression of the parent center they could be much more innovative and productive. The Shell employees finding themselves in these independent businesses and joint ventures were generally enthusiastic, but they also wondered who they now "belonged to." What was their connection to Shell in this evolving governance structure?

Late in 1997, I visited one of our big California oil fields. A few months earlier it had been swept up in our new joint venture with Mobil, becoming part of an independent company called Aera. We got several people from the venture together in a conference room at the field office. At first, I couldn't tell the former Mobil people from the former Shell people. Then I asked what they were struggling with and one guy started to answer, saying, "I worked for Mobil for twenty years . . ." Then he stopped and looked at me, almost with tears in his eyes. "I'm not even sure I can say that anymore."

I thought to myself, "God, why shouldn't you say that?" We were looking forward to a different future, but we should be able to be openly proud of our past. You could tell this guy felt apprehensive that his co-workers wouldn't like him bringing up his past company affiliation. I asked more about the barriers people felt. "I get sick and tired of seeing these Shell interoffice envelopes on my desk," someone said. "This is not Shell." Someone else said, "I'm tired of seeing hats with the Mobil logo on them. This is not Mobil." Small things stuck in people's craw, but everyone I met seemed determined to overcome the everyday frustrations and get on with creating something new. Several people told me that, yes, they were walking around conflicted. Which company did they belong to? But they could talk openly about their dilemma; they could see the opportunity to build something that was more competitive and sustainable; and that meant they could tolerate the confusion over creating a new allegiance.

COMPLETING THE CYCLE TO INTERDEPENDENCE

My early concerns had been based on an old paradigm—that better business performance would come from tighter control and top-down instruction. As it turned out, Shell Oil's performance blossomed beyond everyone's expectation in the years following the governance shift. It's hard to imagine that the same dramatic improvement would have been realized with the old command-and-control structure. In 1998, business performance across our industry has been disappointing, largely due to a very difficult business environment of low prices and margins. Still, I shudder to think what the results would be looking like if we were still trying to call all the shots from the top.

I believe that if Shell's businesses remain completely independent, the best they can hope for is parity with their smaller independent competitors. We will excel when our businesses are nimble and effective but can also leverage the knowledge and scale across all our businesses to make the whole greater than the sum of the parts. To make this work, businesses in the network share resources (for example, people moving between the business boundaries), share best practices (being willing to learn from both successes and failures), and align around common business principles and behaviors (agreeing to adhere to a few big rules).

I believe Shell is in the process of completing the cycle to interdependence. We clearly don't have all the answers and are feeling our way along. This new networked community begins to feel more like a living organism, capable of unexpected growth and innovation. It feels much less like the rigid machine that had worked well in the past but that became too slow and unimaginative for today's dynamic challenges.

At the end of the day, the change boils down to getting people excited to come to work, feeling a strong affiliation and passion for their business unit, and at the same time, feeling like they are an important part of something bigger. I remember early in my career as a young engineer with Shell, I was coordinating a big, critical, capital-intensive project and given the authority and responsibility to make it happen. I felt very connected to my coworkers and to my business unit—and to the broader Shell organization. What we were doing and learning would have an impact on other Shell companies. That feeling of connectedness and purpose left me so excited to come to work, I literally had trouble sleeping on Sunday nights. The organization of the future must replicate that feeling of connectedness, and maybe even the sleepless Sunday nights.

4 From Control to Clarity

The case for Elliott Jaques's "accountable hierarchies"

Bill Brenneman

There is a natural inclination among people involved in profound change to bemoan hierarchies. But instead, it behooves us to try to understand why hierarchy might be important, and which principles might guide leaders in distinguishing functional from dysfunctional hierarchy. No one has done better thinking on this subject than researcher/writer Elliott Jaques. Bill Brenneman, internal consultant at Shell Oil Company, has been a long-standing implementor of Jaques's ideas within large organizations. We asked him to describe the value of this unconventional approach and how it can make a difference in work at the line leader and internal networking levels.

A widely held concept of hierarchy derives from the divine right of kings. God grants power to the king, who further grants power to the princes and nobles, who in turn give power and control to the dukes and sheriffs, who ultimately control the serfs. Similarly, the board grants power and control to the CEO, who controls the vice presidents, who control the GMs, and so on down to the operating floor. Aside from being open to abuse, this "command-control" model of hierarchy is a poor path to high performance in contemporary industrial settings.

In my experience, a more powerful concept for driving organizations toward higher performance—along with learning and effective empowerment—is Elliott Jaques's model of "accountable" hierarchy. A strong focus on accountability and stewardship provides an antidote to "command-and-control" abuses of power. When I apply Jaques's perspective, I recognize that instead of divine rights, authority figures have divine obligations: to their owners, their peers, their colleagues, their subordinates, their constituents, and the organization as a whole.

Jaques has a fully thought-out conceptual structure—grounded in forty years of in-depth research on psychological testing, pay scales, and the measurement of results—that doesn't fuzz accountabilities in loose or ill-defined ways. This sets Jaques's approach apart from many efforts to achieve "self-management" or "empowerment," where everyone becomes responsible and therefore no one is responsible. In Jaques's framework, hierarchy ensures organizational accountability.

Suppose, for instance, that you need to develop an operating plan for a manufacturing plant. In a traditional plant, everyone looks to the plant manager for direction. But under a Jaques model, the senior manager holds conversations with each of his or her direct reports, spelling out the boundaries of their work and the resources available to them. "I will hold you each accountable for your work and your subordinates' work, including finding ways to work together to optimize the whole plant," the manager might say. "It's my obligation to create the conditions that allow you to do that. Similarly, I expect you to be constantly attentive to the conditions needed to support your subordinates' performance."

When a sufficient clarity of goals, roles, and expectations is established, including making people clearly accountable for the learning and performance of their subordinates, then learning is virtually automatic. Conversations no longer focus on "what the boss wants," because that has been made clear. Instead, people work out the answers to their obligations. Was the data from last year's preventative maintenance program made available to operations? Who is accountable for making it happen? The plant manager, freed from micromanaging or trying to control others, spends his or her time managing the system—paying close attention to the career development of people two levels below.

Much of my work involves helping managers and their management teams move toward this sort of accountability. I've learned, the hard way, that the first step is to enlist the people with organizational power and authority. Peer group commitment, even with trained facilitation, is not enough, and task forces cannot, in themselves, solve performance problems. When the task force's work is finished, the responsibility for implementation passes to the line organization. The senior line leader in an organization can create the necessary conditions for success, as no network, team, or staff personnel can, if he or she accepts accountability for implementation. This in turn means putting authority "on the table": talking openly about different levels of authority and accountability, and about whether the authority is being used responsibly.

I spend a lot of time in conversations with people about their relationships with their bosses. You can always tell when people are working for a respected, accountable boss, who (in Elliott Jaques's terms) "fits" the stratum of the job. People say that such a boss:

- Cares about their success and makes sure they are clear about their expectations;
- Expects them to be accountable for results;
- Listens to and thinks things through with them;
- Sets context, letting them know what's coming and helping them see ahead of the wave;
- Makes certain they have the skills and resources they need, and spurs them to work up to capacity;
- Requires that they collaborate authentically with colleagues.

Managers who cannot behave this way, unsurprisingly, are less well regarded by subordinates, even if *they are pleasant and supportive as individuals.* Espousing ideals and values turns out to be unimportant; fostering a structure that supports them is critical. Jaques's research and insights have led me, and others, to learn how to do this, in a way that resonates with managers of hierarchies in the real world.

REQUISITE ORGANIZATION
by Elliott Jaques (Arlington, VA: Cason Hall & Co., 1988, 1996)

In many organizations, people flail and flounder because they do not have clearly defined boundaries for their job, their authority, and their careers. Jaques's work helps explain why. Often misinterpreted as mechanistic or as pigeonholing people, it provides enormous predictive and conceptual power for helping you design an organization where everyone, not just a core group of "approved" people, fits in and makes a contribution.

Jaques's most controversial aspect: He ranks people according to "strata" based on the number of months or years into the future they intuitively consider when making a decision. Then he argues that different "strata" fit best with specific levels in a management hierarchy. In employee surveys, for instance, CEOs are routinely rated worthy of their pay if they are seen to be operating at twenty to fifty years ahead. When CEOs make decisions based on a two- to five-year time frame, people around them tend to intuitively feel that there is a mismatch; that the person doesn't "deserve" the post. Fortunately, "strata" aren't fixed. Most people naturally seem to grow in cognitive complexity throughout their lives (at a rate of about one stratum every fifteen years).

It's fascinating, and eye-opening to see how Jaques links these observations to organizational design. He sets out chains of deliberate relationships in which managers are not just accountable for work, but for the well-being of people in their part of the structure. In practice, when these ideas are implemented, people tend to feel not pigeonholed, but comfortable and relieved. They are no longer shoehorned into a job that doesn't fit them. If the transition is handled well, the culture stops dividing people into "winners and losers" based on their level in the hierarchy. Instead, it recognizes the value and dignity of people performing at every level.

It takes a while to grasp the full "requisite organization" theory. This book, written for CEOs, provides the clearest, most coherent overview. — Art Kleiner

5 Visa International
A "Chaordic" Design in Practice

Emily Breuner

As a corporation owned by its members, Visa may be a prototype for new types of emerging corporations that need to foster collaboration and competition, simultaneously, within themselves. Emily Breuner, a former student at MIT's Center for Coordination Science (now at Intelligent Systems for Retail, Inc.), researched and put together this story, based on interviews with Dee Hock, the designer of the governance structure, and other key figures. Each section of this piece lays out one of the guiding ideas underlying Visa's design.

We would like to thank Professor Thomas Malone, Director of the Center for Coordination Science and co-Director of the 21st Century Initiative at the Sloan School of Management at MIT, who brought this research project and this contributor to our attention.

From the moment that the Bank of America (BoA) launched the world's first bank credit card in Fresno, California, in 1958, the value of the BankAmericard depended on the size of the network. But the bank was limited, both by banking laws and the huge funds a national network required. Thus, BoA licensed its card to one bank in each state, and a rival bank confederation, MasterCharge, did the same. In their race to build networks quickly, BankAmericard and Master-Charge began mailing out cards indiscriminately. The result was massive credit card fraud and losses due to bad credit risks.

In 1968, BankAmericard's problems, including complaints about administrative practices, were serious enough that many franchisees threatened to bolt to MasterCharge. An executive from the National Bank of Commerce in Seattle, Dee W. Hock, provided a glimmer of hope. He suggested that the BankAmericard organization could take on a democratic, membership-based governance structure radically different from anything that had been designed before, which no one entity—including the Bank of America—could dominate.

An avid reader of poetry, philosophy, and science, Dee Hock had been marginalized by companies in the past when he tried to institute some of his more innovative organizational ideas. Yet suddenly he found himself in a position to invent an organizational structure designed "to enable the exchange of electronic value." (He would eventually call this structure a "chaord," a structure combining the maximum chaotic behavior with the minimum hierarchical order necessary for stability.) The new entity he conceived of would be equitably owned by all participants, with power and function distributive to the maximum degree; he aimed for it to be "infinitely malleable yet extremely durable."

Visa International (originally called National BankAmericard Inc., or NBI) opened for business in 1970 with 243 charter members. According to Hock, "It took six months to get the principles and two years to get the organization right." Since then, Visa has grown to handle approximately 50 percent of credit card transactions, way ahead of both American Express and MasterCard. As a single commercial enterprise with a self-organizing structure, Visa may be unique. But its elements are applicable to other companies, and many aspects of its design seem to be highly desirable features, if not requirements, of any successfully decentralized organizational structure.

■ **A network of independent agents.** Ask any Visa cardholder what Visa does, and you will most likely get the answer, "They issue credit

For more details, see the MIT master's thesis on which this article is based: "Complexity and Organizational Structure: Internet and Visa International as Prototypes for the Corporation of the Future," by Emily Breuner (MIT Sloan School of Management, 1995), available at http://www.fieldbook.com/breuner.html. Information about chaordic organization structures, and about Dee Hock's own writings (including a book in progress) is available at the Chaordic Alliance Web site, http://www.chaordic.org/.

cards and sign up merchants to accept them." But it is the member banks who issue cards, produce statements, collect payments from customers, and deal with merchants. Visa's product is coordination—aligning the efforts of hundreds of member institutions, leaving no one entity in charge.

In legal terms, Visa International is a zero-profit corporation owned by the member banks. Its board of directors is a group of representatives, elected (like most political legislatures) to represent different regions. Its income is provided by service fees, paid by member banks, based on the volume of their transactions with merchants and cardholders. Its "outgo" is spent operating the Visa funds-transfer network and marketing the brand name. The structure is so loosely defined that the by-laws are only 62 pages long, and most of that is composed of rules for meeting and voting procedures.

Visa gives great autonomy to member banks. They can devise and market any products, so long as they conform to the by-laws and operating regulations (which, in practice, means that the cards must bear the Visa logo and hologram). By leaving much of the power and authority at this level, a great deal of coordination and consensus building is avoided while the benefits of competitive forces, such as diverse and rapid product innovation, are preserved.

At the same time, Visa incorporates a hierarchy of regional, national, and international organizations, each (in effect) chartered by approval of the members. This insulates different parts of the organization from disparate regional concerns. For example, the banking industry is changing much more quickly in the U.S. than in Europe, and that change occurs more smoothly for Visa than it would if Europe and the U.S. had to both adopt new procedures together.

The interaction of these separate but interdependent entities creates stability, in the same way that the chaotic, unplanned behavior of interacting species leads to the stability of an ecosystem in nature.

■ **A Federalist structure with checks and balances**. The parallels between Visa's governance structure and the principles of federalist government are unmistakable and intentional. Dee Hock and Visa General Counsel Bennett Katz relied heavily on the example of the U.S. Constitution in particular. In a federalist structure, as Dee Hock put it, the role of the government is to manage the conditions of the system, but not necessarily the behavior. Authority is shared between a central governing body and its constituent parts, which give up some of their sovereignty in exchange for the benefits of cooperative behavior. The constituent parts agree to abide by certain commonly held and supported principles. The role of the governing structure is simply to mediate in matters of dispute and to act as a steward of the common good.

A series of checks and balances ensures that neither the central organization nor any member bank can dominate. Why isn't Citibank "running the show" at Visa? As its largest card issuer, one would think it would be in a position of power. But Visa's by-laws are laid out such that there is fair representation. Voting rights are based on sales volume, but only to a certain point. Thus, the large players are kept in line by the power that is distributed to end-users.

The central organization, Visa International, does not issue cards itself. Therefore, it is not in competition with member institutions, as was Bank of America. Moreover, the banks are not required to buy any services from Visa International. This keeps the central staff from becoming complacent and gives them an incentive for innovation. Also, the members themselves sit on a board at the top of the organization, performing somewhat the same role as a Supreme Court.

But Visa International does have the power of the purse; money from the service fees gives it the autonomy it needs to develop strategic initiatives, such as the central interchange system or new technologies, without having to build consensus from the bottom up each time. And the central body sets the voting rights of members and specifies who has the right to make decisions.

The people at the top are stewards, judging the merit of issues and solutions that emerge at various parts of the organization. They do not manage operations; they manage the conditions through which growth can occur. They are not chosen for their ability to plan or execute, but for their ability to coordinate, govern, coach, and judge.

■ **Balancing cooperation and competition.** The Visa founders also incorporated less linear (Western) and more holistic (Eastern) philosophies. Instead of following linear concepts ("If we give a bonus for product development, we'll get product development"), Dee Hock mindfully sought to leverage the natural push and pull between the yin of cooperation and the yang of competition. Because there is competition among member banks, new products are rapidly produced. Because there are rules and a structure that foster cooperation, powerful banks cannot gain local monopolies; therefore, the size of the credit network is ultimately maximized, making all Visa members better off.

■ **Unplanned innovations.** By relying on the diversity of agents to create emergent, incremental solutions to Visa's problems, the organization can adjust along with the environment. "Grown" solutions may not be perfect or elegant, but they tend to be applied more quickly than engineered solutions, and with application comes feedback. The feedback serves to further refine the solution and to adjust to new environmental conditions that have arisen in the interim.

When deciding on which technology to use to encode information on the Visa card, many technologies superior to the magnetic strip were available, yet not all countries had the electronic infrastructure in place to make use of them. Thus Visa decided to go with an incremental solution—magnetic strips—rather than embedded chips. At the same time, Visa France wanted to implement embedded chip technology because France had the infrastructure to support it. French Visa cards thus included both technologies in one card, providing the system with another opportunity to gain experience with a new technology without endangering the viability of the entire network on a single-technology bet.

■ **Self-policing behavior.** When people have power and authority, they are unlikely to give it up. Member banks acted as policemen early in Visa history, when Dee Hock made a special agreement with JCPenney to accept Visa cards. Hock allowed JCPenney to connect directly into the Visa system without going through a bank. The member banks violently reacted to Hock's move because they knew that one of their rights had been violated: Visa had gone into competition with banks in a sense, cutting them out of the transaction fees from JCPenneys. The result was an explicit by-law making such future agreements "illegal."

■ **Power to the end-user.** By leaving power, control, and authority at the periphery of the Internet and Visa, the end-user has acquired the most power. Cardholders can choose whichever card product gives them the options they want, whether award programs, low interest rates, or high credit limits. They may complain about getting so many card offers in the mail, but they nonetheless have great power in the marketplace.

Some articles about Visa include: Russel Ruthen, "Adapting to Complexity," *Scientific American*, January 1993, p. 132. Jeffrey Kutler, "Metal Plates to Duality: The Shaping of an Industry," *American Banker*, September 9, 1994, p. 9. Steve Green, "Power pyramids falling: Founder of Visa speaks of future," *Ogden Standard-Examiner*, June 14, 1994: Section A, p. 5. Dee W. Hock, lecture, "15.563: Inventing Organizations of the Future," MIT, September 28, 1994. Dee W. Hock, "Out of Control and Into Order," seminar, MIT Center for Coordination Science, September 27, 1994. Visa International By-Laws and Regional Board Delegations, Visa International, November 15, 1994.

I also developed some of the insights in this piece with reference to: Karl E. Weick, *The Social Psychology of Organizing* (Reading, MA: Addison-Wesley Publishing Company, 1979); Peter Senge, *The Fifth Discipline* (New York: Doubleday, 1990); Joseph Nocera, *A Piece of the Action: How the Middle Class Joined the Money Class* (New York: Simon & Schuster, 1994). And from interviews with Dee Hock, Charles Osborn, John Rugo, Tom Flanagan, Deborah Rossi, Fred Luconi, David Wagman, Scott Loftesness, and Bennett Katz. — Emily Breuner

■ **A fractal, flexible hierarchy.** Because Visa International can create new levels of hierarchy, different regions and subregions can be raised or lowered to appropriate levels. For example, Visa Europe may soon be split as Eastern Europe and Western Europe because the volume in Eastern Europe has put it on a par with the other regional levels. Because the goal of hierarchies in a decentralized organization is based on managing participation of many agents, they tend to be fractal in nature. That is, the shape and format of each level of the hierarchy are similar, and each level of the hierarchy has a similar relationship to the levels above and below. This design reduces risks by insulating subassemblies from one another's failures, while making it easier to pass information through the system (for example, between one region and another).

The structure and nature of the operational information that is passed between agents (i.e., packets of digital information) is highly unequivocal and thus there are precise rules about how and when it is passed. This precision ensures that everyone understands how decisions are made and issues resolved, and enables the interoperability that Visa needs to be successful.

How resilient will Visa be as the world continues to change? Imagine, for example, what would happen if cardholders gained the ability to both make charges and accept payments—turning Visa into a complete substitute for cash, even between individuals. This is technically feasible (through embedding computer chips in the cards), but it would mean new operating procedures and further responsibilities for member banks and for the central Visa governing body. Visa would be well positioned to operate such a service without any changes in its structure. The member entities would simply make the necessary incremental changes. Other, more hierarchically managed systems would have to thoroughly reconfigure their systems, and they might have a much more difficult time making the switch.

6 "Learning Shareholders..."

... and the companies they seek to influence ...

Nell Minow

Nell Minow is a prominent corporate gadfly. She and her partner, Robert Monks (principals at the LENS, Inc. investment fund) have spent much of the last decade deliberately purchasing stock in moribund companies, hoping to make their investments pay by influencing the managers of these companies. First implicitly, and then with greater deliberateness, the Monks/Minow approach has adapted the idea of "building learning capabilities" as a source of growth. Nell, who is also a writer and film critic, provides the first serious, experienced answer that we have seen to the question: How can shareholders and companies abet each other's learning capabilities?

Shareholders are typically seen as silent partners—the more silent, the better. But over the long turn, any shareholder who can help improve the company's capability will improve its performance—and thus increase the shareholder's own return. This requires that management sees active shareholders not as outside predators, ready to pounce and destroy, but as an inherent part of the "checks and balances" of the company's governance structure. In every company, the shareholder and corporate executives should oversee each other and keep each other honest. In a learning organization, they should also take part together in improving the long-term performance of the company as a whole.

But how might that work in practice? Based on my experience, there are five overlapping themes that illustrate the kind of mutually advantageous relationships that shareholders and managers could build. Because each of these themes represents a different form of leverage, I address them to different groups of people: shareholders, board members, financial auditors, chief executives . . . and, finally, to all of us.

■ **Shareholders: Influence through inquiry.** If you are a long-term shareholder, your most valuable contribution is to question the assumptions of corporate leaders. This is exhausting, but businesses need it, and the best opportunity comes from you, as a shareholder, because your day-to-day livelihood does not depend on the boss's approval. The reason you are raising questions is, after all, directly related to learning: The company has a deep systemic problem that has moved past the immediate capacity of its leaders to solve.

As an outsider, you can see the forest instead of the trees. It is not your place to micromanage what kinds of new products to create, how to market them, or where to build a plant. But you can be useful on large-scale or long-range issues involving succession, money, and investments—issues where the company can benefit from your clear-eyed, unsentimental perspective. You can bring out the issues that are creating impossible double binds and mixed messages, where no one else has the power to force the company, as a whole, to pay attention. You can say, "You may have been in the basket-weaving business for centuries, but your little computer chip–making subsidiary is generating 150 percent of your profit. Could it be time to spin off the basket weaving, or donate it to a museum?"

Shareholders can also act as a check when managers might otherwise take advantage of a system. Last year, our firm invested in a company where a CEO was replaced. We noticed a number of asset sales below market rate to people with whom the ex-CEO later found employment. So we wrote and said, "This company has had a long tradition of bidding out the sale of assets. Could you either bid them out or put all further sales on hold until the new CEO comes in?"

As you develop relationships with managers, you will learn that there is a way to help executives raise these questions for themselves. You will typically not be welcomed at first, but you can overcome that with personal charm, persistence, and the credibility that you can only get from knowing what you are talking about. Before my partners and I invest in a company, we always design a restructuring plan, just to satisfy ourselves that the values we expect to find are there. Then we can sit down and say, "Look, you know more about the industry than we do, but based on our knowledge and perspective, we think you can create more value in another way." Because we're shareholders, we can at least insist that they answer.

Occasionally, I run across a management that is interested in learning, and my job is easy. George Fisher, then-CEO of Motorola, and Jack Welch, CEO of General Electric, have both come up to me and said, "I know who you are. If you ever have a problem with my company, come and see me and we'll talk about it." When I hear comments like that, it spurs me—and other informed shareholders—to buy their stock and hold it.

■ **The board: Creating your own legacy.** In some companies, CEOs have quietly arranged pay packages for themselves that are so exploitative that angry insiders have leaked them to us. We understand why CEOs try to keep such things hidden. But why do boards approve them? What are they thinking?

If you are a member of a corporate board, you have enormous leverage to help the company's executive leaders avoid these destructive actions—and to help question the values underlying them. Tragically, however, you will probably not feel much of an incentive to exercise that leverage. Dissident shareholders like me often find that their most bitter fights come not with managers, but with board members—who seem, from our perspective, to have little interest in the future of the company.

Why would board members show such little interest? Perhaps because they have little incentive. Shockingly few corporate board members are compensated with stock. They are compensated with money, awards, grants, and status. One disgusting incentive package endows a university chair in their name after they die. The inventor of this package told me, "Sometimes it takes a little Christmas ornament to get these big, famous people onto a board."

However, this "ornament" has no relationship to their performance as directors. If you are a board member, think carefully about the legacy you are creating through the impact of your advice on a company that employs hundreds of people and plays a role in the world's economy. The best answer to the question, "What can we do to get you on the board?" is to say, "Pay me in stock because I think this is a great company. It's doing the right things, and it will make a lot of money for me. I'll endow my own school."

■ **Financial managers: Providing information on human capital.** Financial author Richard Crawford has pointed out that most modern accounting conventions are based on nineteenth-century corporations whose primary assets were machinery and real estate. Today, the primary assets in large corporations are brains and the people who own them. But there are no financial data available to shareholders that really give us any kind of useful information about human capital—and how the skills and learning, available to the company, are expanding over time.

One regulatory proposal that makes sense to me is a requirement for disclosure of "human capital" data: Amount spent on employee education and training, rates of employee turnover, and data on employee satisfaction. There is no need to wait for regulation. I think that companies that revealed that data, in clear, coherent form, would have tremendous competitive advantage. They would not influence the numerically oriented investors who dominate the rapid movement of capital. But they could influence the single largest pot of capital in the market: pension funds. These long-term repositories appreciate the importance of employees, and they have thirty-year–long investments to maintain. They would be natural customers for this data, and especially for relationships with companies that were willing, over the long term, to continue providing it.

■ **Executive leaders: Setting an example with your own investments.** Suppose that you were trying to change a company for the better from the executive level. Sooner or later, you would need to make the case for impressing a more patient kind of capital. And, in fact, after the 1987 stock market crash, seventeen American CEOs testified before Congress that it was caused by the short attention span of institutional investors.

But my partner and I computed the amount of money in the pension funds controlled by those same seventeen CEOs. If they followed their own advice—if they kept their money in companies longer and tried to influence those companies to perform better—then that change, in itself, would flood the market with patient capital. Apparently, most CEOs (or the people who make decisions in their names) seem to have as little confidence in patient capital as the "fickle" investors they complain about.

If, as a senior executive, you wish to set a different example, you could simply index some of your investments to the market as a whole. This would be financially and legally prudent. Indexing has been the best long-term performance strategy for more than a generation. It would also free enormous amounts of time that you and your employees currently spend on asset allocation and investment decisions. Finally, indexing would provide enormous amounts of patient capital to companies around the world, including your own company.

We suspect that most CEOs, whatever they may espouse about patient capital, actually have a "theory-of-use" in mind: Patient capital means outside control. That may be true for a conventional company. But in a learning organization, input from long-term investors is no longer "control." It is one more source of knowledge, exclusive to you, that may turn out to be remarkably useful.

■ **All of us: Encouraging employee ownership.** The conventional corporate governance structure has outgrown most of the political structures designed to control it. Accountability must therefore come from within. Thus, a number of prominent people, from Louis Kelso to Margaret Blair, have proposed more creative use of employee stock-ownership plans as a vehicle for organizational learning. My partner and I agree. We think ESOPs represent a natural stage of corporate evolution. As Bob Monks puts it, after John D. Rockefeller gets $1,000 for every dollar he invested in the market, it's time for someone else to make the money. And in my view, once a corporation reaches a certain size and degree of learning, the employees are in the best position, as a whole, to make ultimate decisions.

I base this view on the principle that decisions should be made by those with the fewest conflicts and the most information. People who work in a room are best suited to decide what color to paint the walls. They have no "agency" costs, they are not acting on behalf of someone else, and they know what color suits them best. But they may not be best suited to decide how often to paint the walls, or how much money to spend. Only if they are meaningfully responsible for budget allocation will they "feel" the impact of the decision enough to align their interests with those of management.

Effective governance depends on the alignment of information, incentive, and capacity to act. The challenge is aligning the responsibilities and authorities of all of the various constituencies to achieve the best possible conditions for learning, growth, and renewal. Employee ownership is not perfect, but in the end, it probably does the best job of joining the interests of all of the participants in the corporate structure.

For more about Lens, Inc., and the work of its cofounders, Nell Minow and Robert Monks, see their Web site at *http://www.lens-inc.com/*. Also see *The Emperor's Nightingale*, by Robert Monks (Reading, MA: Addison-Wesley, 1998), which approaches corporate governance structures as emergent systems, in light of complexity theory.

RESOURCES ON CORPORATE GOVERNANCE

Consider a hostile takeover. The management is accused of empire building and self-indulgence, at shareholders' expense. The takeover artists, and their shareholder backers, are accused of short-term thinking at the expense of the company's long-term survival. From a learning orientation, who is right? Neither. Long before it reached the point of crisis, a learning orientation would build capabilities for effective governance that would prevent "barbarians at the gate." These books and resources have helped me get an overview and introduction to the issues, and they may help build that capability in others.

■ *Power and Accountability*, by Robert A. G. Monks and Nell Minow (New York: HarperBusiness, 1991): Probably the best single starting point, grounded in the rise of institutional investors as a systemic force.

■ *Ownership and Control: Rethinking Corporate Governance for the Twenty-First Century*, by Margaret Blair (Washington, D.C.: the Brookings Institution, 1995): An erudite textbook introducing the legal background and context for corporate governance and employee participation in management.

■ The Corporate Governance Web Site: Continually updated with pointers to books and articles: *http://www.corpgov.net*.
— Art Kleiner

~~~~~~

7 Cultural Due Diligence

Sue Thomson

Innovation Associates consultant Sue Thomson delves beneath one of the most critical governance issues: the power clash in a merger or acquisition. A little cultural leverage can pay great dividends.

Merging two organizations, it is said, is like mating two elephants and hoping to produce a gazelle. In the 1990s, only 30 percent of the corporate mergers in the U.S. realized anticipated synergies, even two years after the transaction. Thus, while looking after the financials of the deal, it's also important to exercise cultural due diligence: examining the way each organization does things, to see if, when they net out culturally, they might diminish or even negate the apparent value of the deal. In essence, this challenges the way many deal makers use the word "synergy." To them, it means the ability to remove costs by eliminating duplication, but it really means setting up two groups so they can, together, produce and develop capabilities that they might never have developed on their own.

This represents a wonderful opportunity for dialogue, if the conversation is designed to help make each side more aware of themselves, and the others. In a "fishbowl" format, people from each of the merging organizations can talk among themselves in turn, while their new compatriots from the other organizations listen as the audience. Later, the listeners will reflect back what they heard and learned. The purpose of these conversations would be to understand each other's culture—where each other is coming from, the commonalities and differences, and ultimately the qualities that people wish to see in the future organization, borrowing from all the merging parties. Some of the issues worth covering in these conversations include:

- **Identity.** How will each subgroup's culture influence the new entity? What values will the new entity respect? What values are worthy of respect in each of the existing partners?

    And on a more personal level: "Will I still have a job? And will it be something I can be proud of?"

- **Control.** Which subgroup's culture will dominate? Whose leaders will determine what decisions are made? Will one culture automatically take precedence, or will we forge something new out of our separate approaches? Who's in charge now and what do they want?

    It is said that there is no such thing as a merger of equals. Pretending that merger partners are equals can lead to awkward decision processes and suboptimal outcomes. For example, working hard to split key positions evenly between the merging partners can lead to situations where jobs are filled politically, rather than by qualifications. Then, when consequences inevitably arise and the senior partner steps in to set things right, the dominant partner will be seen as reneging and "proving that they cannot be trusted."

    By contrast, explicitly talking about control can allow leadership roles to be defined up front. One group's approach can be planned to prevail in certain categories of decisions, or certain business domains, while the other partner's ideas can lead the way in other arenas. If worked out and communicated ahead of time, staff on both sides will see that their ideas are valued and the number of confused or mixed messages will be reduced.

- **Action.** What is the destiny of the new organization? Who participates in developing that vision? And how will we get there? The key here is to talk about a shared vision for the newly merged company, first among the senior team and soon thereafter throughout the whole organization. It's important that espoused vision and values match the ways that the new senior team members behave and operate. This is a signal that others in the organization will be waiting for.

It is important to hold these conversations at all levels of the organization so people can get to know and appreciate one another. In many mergers and alliances, people at lower levels are regularly in touch with one another, and they understand one another's cultures far more completely than the people at the top. The people at the top may have golfed together, but they haven't called one another's companies and tried to place an order, or dealt with frustrated customers. When those types of perceptions come forward, placed on the table for all parties to hear and think about, then the chances of success for the learning or change initiative are much, much greater.

8 Redesigning an Airplane in Midflight
Letter to an executive leader

Arun Maira and Bryan Smith

Arun Maira is Chief Executive of Innovation Associates, the consulting firm founded by Charlie Kiefer and Peter Senge (and now part of Arthur D. Little). In coauthoring this contribution with Bryan Smith, he draws on his experience as a board member and a managing director at Tata Engineering and Locomotive Co., Ltd. (Telco), a truck and car manufacturing company that is a key part of India's largest business conglomerate, and also on experience with helping clients in many industries all over the world to implement organizational change.

"**P**eople are advising me to decentralize this company; and to empower small teams to function independently. But this advice ignores the fundamental challenge of maintaining coherence among these teams. Our company has many aggressive opponents who are nimble and formidable in their piece of the jungle. I fear we'll end up as a company of small teams, competing in hand-to-hand combat, without the advantages of efficiency, lower costs, global scope and collective know-how that we have in our current organization. How can we become more innovative and nimble without jettisoning strengths that we've taken years to build?"

This statement reflects the concerns of many CEOs we talk to, who are grappling with the core dilemmas of redesigning their organizations to be more effective in a rapidly changing world. So if you are an executive leader and you feel this way, you're not alone. The principal strategic challenge for global companies, as recently reported in a survey of 2,700 senior executives, is the reconciliation of seemingly conflicting goals: thinking long-term while delivering short-term results, developing global scale while being locally responsive, learning to collaborate across internal boundaries while keeping a competitive edge, and investing in innovation while increasing operational stability and efficiency. In each aspect of these challenges there is a tension between two necessary but apparently opposing goals, which can't be resolved, only managed over time as an ongoing dilemma.

The root cause of these dilemmas can be found in three prevailing mental models about business governance. First, most business managers have been schooled to define precise fit of resource to purpose and to avoid redundancy of resources in the pursuit of efficiency. They divide their organizations into parts, each part aligned with one "accountability" to one purpose or boss, and they dedicate their resources to achieving those compartmentalized responsibilities. The boundaries between the parts go up, reinforced by powerful incentives for individual performance, severe penalties for poor local performance, the application of skills and techniques dedicated to each part's performance, and the development of unique practices and cultures oriented to local achievement.

Second, most executives seem to believe that governance is a matter of "hard" structures alone: the ownership of resources, decision rights and boundaries, performance measures, and economic incentives. This mental model ignores the fact that organizations, in reality, are formed by a blend of "structures": some "hard" and some that are often seen as "soft." The soft structures are people's motives and aspirations, underly-

The survey was conducted in 1997 by the International Council of Executive Development Research jointly with Arthur D. Little's School of Management; respondents were senior executives in 28 global corporations with headquarters in North America, Europe, Asia, and Australia.

In writing this article, the authors drew on ideas from an article by Arun Maira, "Connecting Across Boundaries: The Fluid-Network Organization," which appeared in the 1st Quarter 1998 issue of PRISM, a management journal published by Arthur D. Little. The "fluid network" concept and the premises about governance in this article are grounded in an ongoing exploration of the qualities of "governance in nature." More research and writing about the application of these qualities is being developed at Innovation Associates; for more information, see the Web page http://www.fieldbook.com/ia-gov.html.

ing beliefs and mental models, and competencies and skills. The way people think and behave in an organization is affected by both types of structures.

Unfortunately, the management disciplines associated with change have become split into two schools: those who emphasize the hard economic aspects and hard performance management disciplines, and those who advance the softer cultural and behavioral views of the organization. The advocates of each of the two schools are all too often insufficiently informed about the other, and sometimes even denigrate the other approach. This does not help leaders of business organizations, some of whom often feel that one school is telling them that they have only bones in their body, and the other that it is only flesh, whereas they can feel that they have and need both!

The third mental model suggests that, although there are many imperatives from the outside world, and all of them command the attention of top executives, only one of them may take precedence at a time. We call these imperatives "dimensions," because they line up the organization's resources and decision-making rights as the leaders organize to fulfill their accountabilities. One dimension might be functional capability, which ensures technical competence; another might be regional and local market presence; a third might be product/category management, to reflect key market segments. Different organizations will choose different "dimensional" imperatives, which in turn determine how divisions are organized, how decisions are made, and the ways that resources and rewards are allocated. Typically, organizations are set up to optimize one dimension at the expense of all others. Then, as teams deny or ignore the existence of a dimension, they eventually get in trouble in the territory they are ignoring.

These three mental models contribute to the governance dilemmas by keeping different characteristics of the organization apart and, in essence, pitting them against one another. Thus, "changing the governance structure" often simply means reassigning power and resources from one external dimension to another—for example, from a "functional" structure of decision rights to a "regional" or "product-based" structure. This provokes more thrashing and emotional heat than in any other management decision-making process. People form armed camps around their preferred way of organizing, with battle cries of "Decentralize! Autonomy! Growth Through Innovation!" from those seeking a shift to a new design. These are met with equally forceful calls for "Renewed Controls! Rationalizing Our Business! Centralize!" from those who feel accountable to the status quo. These "abstraction wars" often have a deep-seated intractable quality. And to add to the heat governance conversations include emotionally charged issues like personal accountability for results (and failure), trust, power, authority, rewards, and status.

If you are serious about breaking out of these ingrained dilemmas, you will need a new approach to the design of your organization. By following the example of biological and ecological systems, you can replace fragmented, compartmentalized governance designs with interdependent, systemically aligned structures. By integrating "hard" and "soft" structures in a common design, you can reunite organizational "bones" and "flesh." And by developing the thinking and acting capacity of your executive and line leaders, you can help your organization meet the multidimensionality of the outside world.

SETTING UP A PROCESS FOR REDESIGN

These fundamental changes will almost always have to be brought about while the organization continues to meet its commitments to customers and the expectations of investors. The business cannot be stopped while it is redesigned. Hence we describe this process as "redesigning an airplane in midflight"—a process of learning amid action.

The unusual intensity, effort, and care that this will require from you, in your capacity as CEO, should be measured against the central importance of this undertaking. While building alignment around shared vision is a core process for mobilizing people's energy, designing an organization's governance structure is the central means for channeling that energy to achieve results. We see faulty design as the most potent limiter of an organization's ability to realize its purpose and potential. Talented race-car drivers and sailors can make poorly designed cars and yachts perform well in short bursts, but they will eventually lose to competitors with better designs. And the challenge here is not just to create an optimal design on paper, but to engage yourself, your executive team, and managers in the ongoing challenge of making it work every day.

Do not conduct this redesign work alone. The governance system exists to contain and buttress enormous pressure, from outside the organization (for example, shareholders, the board of directors, regulators, customers, and suppliers) and from within (functional groups, members of the executive team, line leaders, labor unions, staff, and influential internal networkers). All have something legitimate to say about the

This diagram represents the six key elements of a governance redesign. At the front of the "aircraft" are the shared aspirations, drawing it forward. The other four elements, involving different combinations of interrelated "hard" and "soft" governance structures, are all aligned to the organization's articulated purpose. Thus, the arrows are all shown facing in one direction. In many organizations, which do not go through a process like that described here, the arrows all point in different directions, and the plane wobbles dangerously among its various orientations. A special case, shown at the "back" of the airplane, is the set of permeable boundaries—represented here as a dotted line between the organization and its environment. Openness to strategic influences, shown as arrows crossing boundaries, helps develop an "airplane" structure that can follow multiple orientations without losing coherence.

direction of the enterprise, and they may all disagree. In typical business organizations, the board of directors, the shareholders, and a myriad of outside groups like environmental organizations hold the CEO solely accountable for delivering consistent short- and long-term results. CEOs also face rising expectations for flawless leadership from below—they are expected to be decisive yet democratic, tough yet compassionate and all-knowing, while drawing out every insight from below, to name a few typical expectations! No individual human being can survive for long as the single fulcrum for this pressure in a situation of substantial change, without either backing down from change or blowing a fuse.

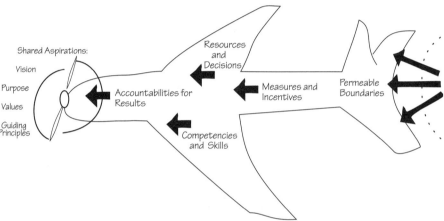

Thus, your first step is to develop the capacity of your top leadership team to metabolize these pressures collectively. Working together to design the governance system is a powerful vehicle for developing this capacity. Find a capable facilitator you trust, who can help your team conduct the necessary conversations through this entire redesign process, and free you to think and participate.

SHARED ASPIRATIONS

As you and your executive team engage in intense dialogues around governance, it is essential that each of these conversations occur in a relevant context. It would be unproductive, for example, for your team to talk about the distribution of authority or the establishment of rules (both "how" issues) without the reference point of clear accountabilities for results (the "what"). Therefore, begin by holding in-depth conversations in your executive team on the organization's purpose, vision, values, and guiding principles. Be wary of stopping short in this difficult endeavor. Don't settle for superficial vision statements written to motivate others. Focus on what really matters to members of the team, individually and collectively. Many executive teams reach some conceptual agreement but miss the potential for becoming deeply aligned partners through this work.

The context for work on vision, values, and purpose is the external environment of the business. Business organizations need to accomplish things—their purpose can't be entirely esoteric. Your job as CEO is to ensure that the context of external environments is used to its fullest in maintaining focus and relevance in the conversations that follow.

Aligning people to a shared set of aspirations (vision, purpose, values, and guiding principles) can be a lot of work. Why put in the effort? Because the results are worth it. If people are going to the same place, share the same values, and work within the same guiding principles, these shared aspirations can take the place of other means of ensuring coordination and alignment, such as top-down supervision and rules. When shared aspirations exist, it is possible for executive leaders to responsibly ease up on these other power and control mechanisms, and for people to give each other latitude in their local domains.

Aligned aspirations are also the reference point that give you constant orientation and focus, and allow you to redesign the airplane as you're flying it—it is this orientation that provides the stabilizing effect while you do this redesign work. This is much like an aircraft engine and propeller pulling the aircraft forward—if they are properly designed and installed in relation to the rest of the aircraft, they help to keep the aircraft in dynamic balance, in part as a function of its momentum.

For more about the kinds of conversations to hold around shared vision, see *The Fifth Discipline Fieldbook*, pp. 297–347.

ACCOUNTABILITIES FOR RESULTS

Once the initial vision, values, and other guiding ideas are formulated, they can be used to surface the strategies and specific results that must be accomplished. As in the previous step, the process of building alignment, ownership, and partnership is as important as the outcome. As much as you can, let people step forward and ask to be accountable for specific results that matter to them as individuals. Avoid assigning accountabilities unilaterally if at all possible. Accountability means "to freely stand and be counted"—as when Roman senators stood and walked across the floor of the senate to cast their affirming vote for a measure, simultaneously demonstrating their "stand" and commitment to carrying out the measure if it passed. Let people stand for accountabilities that matter to them on their own steam; encourage them to tell the team why it matters to them and voice their commitment to achieving the results. This approach is feasible only because of the investment made in a coherent, grounded set of aspirations.

Once accountabilities for results are clear, the goals and realities for each member of the team need to be fully internalized by all other members of the team. This is the basis for a true partnership on the team. Then each partner can act creatively and innovatively, but always mindful of the visions and concerns of the others, taking them both intuitively and explicitly into account as they optimize both their part of the business and the larger whole.

RESOURCING AND DECISION MAKING

Within an executive team, this partnership around accountability for results becomes the foundation or context for designing the authority systems—the systems that enable your team to mobilize the necessary resources and make the "steering" decisions needed to accomplish the results they are accountable for. Coach members of your team to work together as partners and build a web of lateral connections, first at their level, then below, to optimize the use of resources while "steering" the organization to achieve specific results. If these peers can build positive synergies around the interdependencies among them, then you can reverse the common habit of "shifting the burden" of difficult decisions up the hierarchy to the CEO.

This is good for all concerned. Most executive team members would prefer to make these decisions themselves, if they can learn the skills to do it without resorting to the overuse of formal authority and the resulting frustrations of authority clashes and gridlock. And if they can learn to work collaboratively, the quality of solutions and decisions will be higher and you won't be cast in the role of Solomon: using your chief executive power to decide among alternatives.

Besides being exhausting, the "Solomon" role tends to lead to arbitrary and uninformed decisions, because the underlying complexities are not addressed in the information brought up the hierarchy; these decisions can create havoc and misalignment at lower levels. Even at best, you can expect low commitment from the side that "lost" in your decision—which, in turn, will translate into ineffective implementation of your decisions.

Finally, building the habits of cross-boundary decision making can directly contribute to breakthrough innovations that can't be realized without greater interaction.

Two mechanisms can be used to help build a "fluid-network" organization design that reinforces the web of lateral connections. The first is governance councils: involving relevant other members in the effective multidisciplinary steering decisions that are essential to success. These governance councils can help to further distribute and metabolize the pressures on you as CEO beyond you and your executive team. For them to be effective in this role, you have to tell them what those pressures are (start with the things that keep you awake at night!). The support you'll get is well worth the risks of disclosure.

⟩⟩ Shell Oil used governance councils in its redesign; see page 384.

The second is a minimalist approach to rules. Historically, large organizations have relied on the propagation of rules and standard operating procedures to maintain the efficiency and productivity of their various systems, from R&D and manufacturing to sales, service, and logistics. But as Dee Hock and others have pointed out, specifying many detailed rules intended to cover all situations can lead to behaviors that often appear ridiculous to customers and other outside observers, because employees at all levels feel obliged to stop thinking, and to apply the rules arbitrarily. In rapidly changing or globally dispersed operating environments, the benefits of efficiency (defined here as doing things one way, the right way) should give way to effectiveness (defined here as doing the right thing to achieve the result using many different ways, tailored to the unique situation).

Demanding work is required of executive teams to develop and refine a small, essential set of guiding principles that can then guide the creation of minimal critical rules. This work is so tough that many teams abandon it and leave a large set of rules in place, with consequent arbitrary responses by members of the organization. In addition, the organization will need channels for assessing rules and policies at a local level, relating them to the strategic direction and core values of the organization, and critiquing or commenting on them in a way that can be heard up the hierarchy. Ideally, there would be a great deal of excitement in your organization around designing new rules and the guiding principles behind them, because they would be vehicles for providing new feedback. And in some organizations, rules do, in fact, work this way.

At W. L. Gore, the manufacturers of Gore-Tex, the vision of "Freedom," led to a single minimal rule called the "waterline" principle. Employees envision their enterprise as a ship on which they all sail together. If someone occasionally bores an accidental hole above the ship's waterline, it's not calamitous; after all, innovative organizations must make allowances for some mistakes. A hole below the waterline, however, could sink the ship. Therefore the waterline principle states that on "any action that might seriously harm the success, the reputation, or the survival of the enterprise, the associate will consult with appropriate associates who might share the responsibility of taking this action." No other rule is necessary.

COMPETENCIES AND SKILLS

Many executives, would consider any discussion of skills and capabilities irrelevant in a conversation about governance. We see extraordinary relevance. Without this nucleus of skills and capabilities, the other design elements deflate like punctured balloons to flat, mechanical elements.

The highest leverage for this development of skills and capabilities is with you and your executive team. If you don't grow and change, don't expect much change below you, other than increased frustration and cynicism. In fact, don't go public with any of this without considering the sometimes daunting task of changing your own learned behaviors.

⟩⟩ For an amplification of this, see "Reflections for an Executive Leader," page 229.

Leading companies such as Coca-Cola, Shell Oil, and British Petroleum have recognized this and are providing their managers with the new tools they need. Many of these tools are associated with the five disciplines of organizational learning. The objective is to enable managers to go beyond tolerating ambiguity to understanding its root causes and discovering the high-leverage actions they can take to influence the behavior of the system.

MEASURES AND INCENTIVES

As you've undoubtedly noticed throughout your career, misalignments abound in this aspect of governance systems. The most common ones that can undermine redesign efforts are:

- individually focused measures and rewards that pull people away from even acknowledging team and organization interdependencies, let alone acting on them!
- discrepancies between the stated measures and incentives and "what you really need to do to get noticed and get ahead around here" (the "unwritten rules" of measures and rewards).

■ measures and incentives that focus only on short-term performance, punish mistakes, and leave little time, money, or space for learning, collaboration, or exploration, which can include some mistakes as part of learning.

Be prepared to be bold in redesigning the measurement and incentive systems. Be particularly thoughtful about how much formal external control you really need. The financial function of a Fortune 500 company we worked with once did an estimate of the cost of their financial control systems against the risks they were attempting to control. They estimated that the cost of their controls was five times the cost of the risks they were attempting to cover! As you might suspect, they radically reduced their investments in controls, and in doing so, achieved significant improvements in performance and ownership within business units.

〉〉 For some approaches to redesigning measurement and incentive systems, see Chapter 8
〈〈 (page 281) and the review of Thomas Wilson's book (page 383).

However, there is a relatively straightforward way to make progress here as part of the governance redesign process. First align the other elements (accountability, decisions, skills, etc.). Then do a good first draft of what you think an aligned measurement and incentive system should look like and put it out for comment. Let people tell you where the further misalignments are (they will—in far more detail than you may need, but that's fine). Gather all this feedback and put a system in place. Let people know it won't change for at least two full review cycles. That will normally be at least a year. Make it clear people can continue to tell you what's wrong with the system (and they will) but that you'll only collect their feedback, not act on it—until the year is up, when it will be redesigned again. This stance reduces the ongoing fretting and complaining that can undermine progress.

PERMEABLE BOUNDARIES AND MULTIPLE ORIENTATIONS

All of these elements, if well-designed, can help create an organization that naturally produces alignment and commitment. But something more is needed to master the multiple-dimension nature of reality: the need to fulfill functional, regional, product-oriented, and other imperatives all at once. We have seen organizations successfully address this issue by establishing "permeable boundaries." They deliberately create dense, horizontal linkages that cut across internal boundaries and stimulate regular two way communication and learning. Asea Brown Boveri

(ABB), for example, is a network of sixty companies. This network is connected by many councils, including an executive committee at the apex, country structures to connect all companies in a country, a board for every business area, and functional coordination teams across a business area. In addition, people are connected by exchanging visits regularly, by a staff of veteran executives who travel constantly to drive the coordination, and by ABB's worldwide Abacus information system.

Similarly, in an effort to shave precious weeks and months from their time-to-market, companies such as Hewlett-Packard, Honda, Johnson & Johnson, and Sony routinely assemble cross functional teams with clear charters but small budgets—forcing them, in effect, to find ways to uncover and share resources that might otherwise have been "owned" by one group or another. Other firms, such as Chrysler, have gotten exceedingly good at creating symbiotic relationships with their suppliers —to such an extent that vendors literally move into Chrysler factories for the life of their contracts. European companies such as Hoechst, Philips, and Volkswagen have demonstrated great skill in using intellectual exchange with universities and technical institutes as a stimulus to their own product development and R&D efforts.

Your success with permeable boundaries depends, once again, on the flexibility of your mental models about business. For example, you may hold the view that, for every new important dimension of performance you add, you need a new component in the governance structure: an executive solely responsible for that dimension, or a separate department dedicated to it, or both. This is the approach taken by many organizations when they decide to improve along a particular dimension such as Quality, or Information Technology Management. Organizations also use this approach when they wish to emphasize product management along with market management, and perhaps with functional management (such as manufacturing and R&D): They create separate executives and departments accountable for each of the dimensions. That is all very well for the performance of each of the parts, but it results in many problems for the whole system. Overhead costs go up with the number of senior positions. Interdepartmental coordination becomes more complex as the number of departments to be coordinated increases. Further, it becomes more difficult to change the organization to focus on new dimensions should the strategy require it, because the people presently dedicated to other dimensions often feel insecure.

Instead of investing in new structures, you can invest in new skills: specifically, skills such as systems thinking, which help people manage along many dimensions without dropping the ball on any one. If these skills are coordinated with measures that track coordination among various dimensions, and incentives that reward it, then the organization can be aligned towards not just one, but a variety of simultaneous accountabilities.

Many executive teams successfully pursue multidimensional goals by having members wear multiple hats. One hat is the accountability for a business or region—that is a part of the whole. Another hat is typically the accountability for a process, or strategic project, that cuts across the whole organization, such as the installation of an enterprisewide information system, or a quality improvement process. In this way, not only does every executive see the whole through the lens of the organizationwide activity, but the executives also have to rely on each other since the organizationwide activities benefit all the parts.

This mutual dependency through the distribution of accountabilities is a big step in the right direction. But even with this there can be conflict, since executives may end up competing with each other to show better results from their respective organizationwide accountabilities also! Thus, executive teams we have worked with have used a "two flag" technique in their meetings. Every member has two flags—perhaps one green and the other red. The green flag represents a truly organizationwide perspective going beyond the requirements of any of the accountabilities of the executive, whether for a part of the organization or for an organizationwide activity. The red flag represents perspectives from the specific accountabilities of the executive. The executives use the flags to signal their desire to speak, instead of raising their hands. But they must think before they ask to speak: Are they speaking from a whole organization perspective over and above their accountabilities or from their accountabilities? Of course, they are expected to represent the perspectives of their own accountabilities, so there is no criticism if they raise red flags. But the team as a whole must see many green flag views also so that it can understand the interaction of the various pieces in the whole. It is remarkable how, with this simple device, the conversation becomes much richer and less confrontational as the team looks at the situation from multiple perspectives.

The capacity for working in an interconnected and interdependent network of people and resources is becoming more essential as business organizations deal with rapid change in a world in which the boundaries of geography and industries are blurring. Competitors can also be partners, markets can be found in unexpected niches, and better sources of supply can be brought into the network as people work across boundaries. Like biological and ecological systems, effective organizations must learn to work with increasingly permeable boundaries—both internal and external. By helping your organization develop the capabilities described here, you can set your organization up for its next evolutionary steps and provide people within it with invigorating challenges, to create the future of your company backed by an inspired organizational design.

XI. Diffusion

"We keep reinventing the wheel!"

1 The Challenge

The problem of diffusing innovative practices is more prevalent than many people realize. For example, one of the most common laments heard from CEOs is the difficulty of helping the organization learn from its own members. "We are better at benchmarking other companies than learning from ourselves," said one executive. "The NIH ('not invented here') mentality seems to reign supreme." There are numerous examples of "skunk works" in American corporations—small, dynamic, semi-isolated teams that produce genuine breakthroughs in product development or process design. But far fewer companies have taken successful methods and tools developed by their skunk works, and diffused them throughout the organization. Some companies have seemingly hundreds of pockets of pilot activity and intense problems communicating from one to the other. Even when executive and line leaders are sympathetic, it often seems like they do not know where to begin to enable useful knowledge to travel better across the boundaries of individual working groups, divisions, departments, and functions.

Much of the interest in "knowledge management" springs from these concerns. But many of the investments in knowledge management made in recent years—particularly investments in new information systems to capture and spread "knowledge"—have had disappointing returns. "I can't tell you how many millions we have spent on our 'lessons learned' database," commented one executive recently. "Our benchmark studies have shown that this is important at our primary competitors, but we still struggle with getting people to enter their lessons and to make use of what is there."

Symptoms of the challenge of diffusion go beyond failures of "knowledge management" information systems. They include the isolation, competitiveness, and distrust experienced by so many working groups toward one another—especially the disheartened attitude of pilot team members who feel unappreciated, misunderstood, and angry that others seem so disinterested in their accomplishments. In many ways, the evident symptoms of this challenge are similar to those seen in pilot teams facing the problems of "believers and nonbelievers" (Chapter 9). This occurs because the underlying causes are similar: the designed isolation of working groups from one another, and management practices that pit teams against one another in internal competition. But there are other symptoms of this challenge as well, which arise even for teams that deal effectively with believers and nonbelievers. Such symptoms include:

- **"Reinventing the wheel"**: One team, after an arduous struggle to develop a new design methodology, finally receives word of another team that accomplished the same thing six months before.
- **"Not Invented Here (NIH)"**: Members in another team hear of a new innovation, but dismiss it automatically as inapplicable to them. "Sure, the idea is interesting but it's a manufacturing project. It would never work here, in sales."
- **"Underwhelmed"**: It is simply not possible to digest and really understand, let alone implement, complex new ideas and practices based on reading a memo or Web page summary, or listening to a one-hour presentation. "We were interested, so we went to a meeting," people say, "but it didn't seem to add up to anything for us." They may even attempt to put the ideas into practice, but in a halfhearted way that provides only the most superficial assessment: "We tried talking about our 'mental models' at a meeting. Sure, we had a nice conversation, but I honestly don't see what all the fuss is about."
- **Failed attempts of "fast followers"**: Teams convinced of the value of another team's approach undertake their own implementation, but doom themselves through a combination of unrealistic expectations and insufficient guidance and help. "That pilot group took two years to transform their conversations and get at the systemic causes of their problems," they say. "We'll do it in three months. We're much smarter, and we don't have two years." Then, when no results are apparent after three months, they feel disillusioned and give up the undertaking.

- **Arrogance:** People assume away any need for learning because they already know everything they need to know. "I read about this systems thinking stuff when I was in college. It's nothing new."

- Last, and perhaps most important, are the **"invisible symptoms"** of the challenge of diffusion: the absence of vigorous internal learning communities, the lack of confidence among innovators that their ideas will elicit curiosity and broader testing, and the pervasive paucity of genuine curiosity among the organization's members about what one another is learning. All of these symptoms are easy to overlook because they are evident only in the fact that something significant is missing. Many people don't even register this deficiency consciously until they are part of another organization with vigorous learning communities. They're like the constable in the Sherlock Holmes story who protested when Holmes mentioned the curious incident of the dog in the nighttime. But the dog did nothing in the nighttime, said the constable. It didn't even bark. "That," responded Holmes, "was the curious incident."

i.e. lack of creativity

See "Silver Blaze," in *The Complete Sherlock Holmes*, by Sir Arthur Conan Doyle (New York: Doubleday, 1930), p. 347.

It is important to realize that, despite all the difficulties of diffusion, new ideas do sometimes spread, and innovative practices do sometimes start in one part of an organization and eventually end up almost everywhere. Perhaps the best research on the cases where diffusion does work has come from studies of "communities of practice," originating at Xerox's Palo Alto Research Center in the early 1980s. These are the natural internal mechanisms whereby ideas spread in work settings. These informal webs of people who work together regularly—a group of clerks in an insurance company, a set of purchasing people along a supply chain, a network of people involved in maintenance for a factory—have their own cultural attitudes and habits, relationships, and levels of recognized authority and expertise, all gradually accruing over time. Though they tend to exist outside the bounds of the formal hierarchy, communities of practice represent the way in which ideas, information, and new practices spread most rapidly and efficiently through organizations. They are powerful precisely because they are informal.

"Attempts to introduce 'teams' and 'work groups' into the workplace to enhance learning or work practice," writes Xerox chief scientist John Seely Brown, "are often based on an assumption that without impetus from above, an organization's members configure themselves as individuals. In fact, people work and learn collaboratively and vital [communities of practice] are continually being formed and reformed. To understand the way information is constructed and travels within an organization, it is necessary to understand the different communities that are formed within it and the distribution of power among them."

Seely Brown and his colleagues have focused most of their studies on diffusion of technical engineering innovations. Their work leads to two questions: (1) Do such naturally arising communities of practice operate to diffuse work process and managerial innovations, as they do for engineering innovations? and (2) Can naturally arising communities of practice be enabled and made more effective? Recent research suggests that the answer to both questions is yes. As researcher Dennis Sandow notes, there is growing evidence that "embedded in our organizations are self-organizing social networks of mutual assistance, maintained through people's recursive interactions while getting their work done. These social networks are a primary means of learning about our capacity to support each other, our community as well as our companies' financial goals."

Improved diffusion of knowledge won't just happen because the CEO says it should, or because new information technology is "ordered up" by management. As Nancy Dixon and Rick Ross suggest on page 435, designing effective cross-organizational learning infrastructure will be more complex than designing infrastructure for team learning—which itself lies beyond most organizations' capabilities—and much more challenging than the typical information technology approach of the "knowledge management" fad. Effective organizational learning infrastructure will need to augment the natural workings of the informal communities of practice that already exist, just as effective team learning infrastructure must augment the day-to-day needs of working teams.

Ultimately, meeting the challenge of diffusion effectively depends on developing organizational cultures that continually encourage people to cross "walls and stovepipes" (functional boundaries), not just to tell each other their news, but to inquire and come to greater levels of mutual understanding. Increasingly, this challenge involves bringing together diverse people, not just those with different practices or professional training, but from different countries and with different cultural values. To do so requires a common sense of purpose, a common valuing of inquiry into the "whys" as well as the "whats" of their actions.

The Seely Brown quote is from "Organizational learning and communities-of-practice: Toward a unified view of working, learning, and innovation," by John Seely Brown and Paul Duguid (1991, *Organization Science*, available on-line at *http://www.parc.xerox.com/ops/members/brown/papers/orglearning.html*). The Sandow quote is from correspondence. Also see *Communities of Practice* by Etienne Wenger (New York: Cambridge University Press, 1998).

INFORMATION VS. KNOWLEDGE

Unless we have clear, grounded definitions of key terms like information and knowledge, how can we hope to make progress in dealing with the challenge of diffusing new innovations? Information is data with relevance to the receiver's situation, or in Gregory Bateson's well-known definition, "any difference that makes a difference." When people come across a datum, they instantaneously interpret it as either "noise" (to be ignored and discarded) or as information, "important to me" in some way. As soon as data hits your sensory apparatus, you've probably already attached some meaning to it. This shows the important role of the human being in converting data into information.

The word "know" derives from the Latin *noscere*, also meaning "to know"; the words "gnosis," "cognition," and "note" come from the same source. The suffix "ledge," may have originally meant "process" or "action." Today, there are many definitions of knowledge, but in our work, a definition that has proven useful is "the capacity for effective action."

This is an unusual definition for those familiar with more "intellectual" notions of knowledge as "accumulated information." By our definition, a statement such as "We know all about our competitors' new products, and we're not worried," does not represent knowledge. "Knowing about . . ." concerns information. Whether or not it leads to effective action depends upon people's capacity to interpret the information, generate meaningful options for action, and implement an action that leads to desired results. As the biologist Humberto Maturana says, "All knowing is doing. All doing is knowing." Westerners, in particular, tend to consistently confuse information and knowledge because knowledge is not linked to action, even by "knowledge management" experts.

Much of the confusion and disappointment today around knowledge management, for example, comes from this lack of clarity. People are investing in systems to capture, organize, and disseminate information, and then calling it "knowledge." But knowledge cannot, by definition, be converted into an object and "given" from one person to another. Knowledge only diffuses when there are learning processes whereby human beings develop new capacities for effective action. Information technology, while critical for enabling the spread of information, cannot "capture and store" knowledge. Only people can do that.

This definition of knowledge, borrowed from linguistic philosopher John R. Searle, has become widespread among many organizational learning practitioners through the work of Fred Kofman.

66 The myth of synthesized knowledge ... is just the latest in a long line of nonsense, of 'knowledge engineering,' 'data mining' and 'inference engines,' that has been inflicted on a world made gullible through ritualised technology. Mega-millions of dollars have already been wasted in the 'knowledge scam,' the futile quest to categorise commonsense knowledge in this daft way. Thankfully it will soon be dumped in the garbage bin of technological history." — Ian Angell, London School of Economics, "The Knowledge Scam," in *Information Strategy* (http://www.info-strategy.com), July/Aug 1998.

LE XI ON

See *The Knowledge-Creating Company*, Ikujiro Nonaka and Hirotaka Takeuchi (New York: Oxford University Press, 1995). Also Michael Polanyi, *The Tacit Dimension* (London: Routledge & Kegan Paul, 1966). Nonaka and Takeuchi's discussion of Polanyi is on pp. 59–61. The example of the young lawyer was suggested by Nancy Dixon, and adapted from an unpublished draft by her.

As the illustration on the opposite page shows, increased new business practices and business results mean greater potential benefit for the larger organization. But there is a limit: the capacity to diffuse new organizational practices, which in turn depends upon the level of infrastructure for community building, and the organizational capacity to appreciate different world views. If the potential benefit outstrips the capacity, then the diffusion gap grows, leading to diminished effectiveness of change initiatives throughout the organization —and thus to a decrease in organizational learning capabilities.

TACIT KNOWLEDGE

"We can know more than we can tell," wrote the philosopher of science Michael Polanyi 50 years ago. In their book, *The Knowledge-Creating Company*, As Ikujiro Nonaka and Hirotaka Takeuchi build on Polanyi's notions of "tacit knowledge" to distinguish between explicit and tacit knowledge—a useful distinction for anyone designing infrastructure for organizational learning. As Polanyi, Nonaka, and Takeuchi use the term, "explicit knowledge" is spelled out in language and numbers; it can be codified and transmitted, precisely because it has been analyzed and broken down into discrete parts. A legal casebook, laying out precedents in a precise order, with indexes and cross-references, is one example.

Most crucial for getting things done are mental models, assumptions, skills, and capabilities—about which we are often quite unaware, and which Polanyi calls tacit knowledge. The word "tacit" comes from the Latin verb *tacere*, to be silent. (The words "taciturn" and "reticent" come from the same root.) A young woman just out of law school who has recently joined a firm may find herself "acting like a lawyer" without ever making a conscious decision to stop "acting like a student." She learns the behaviors of her new profession by picking them up, both deliberately and unconsciously. She watches other lawyers; she notes the moments of her own success; and she continually draws conclusions about the "ways that lawyers do things."

All of this represents a critical component of her knowledge as a law professional; as vital to her success as her knowledge of cases. She could never learn this kind of tacit knowledge in a classroom or from a book. She can only learn by being a part of a community of practicing lawyers, trying new behaviors, seeing the results, and gradually assimilating that knowledge into her own behavior until she is not even consciously aware, anymore, of why her behavior has changed. This illustrates the way in which knowledge is generated within practicing communities—the source of the notion of "communities of practice."

It is important to understand that tacit knowledge can never be reduced to explicit knowledge. In fact, talk of "converting tacit to explicit knowledge" reflects a superficial grasp of the very notion of tacit. As one researcher put it recently, "I understand at XYZ corporation, the management says they are collecting the organization's tacit knowledge. I hope they have a large bag." Ultimately, contemplating the deeper meaning of tacit knowledge leads to recognizing subtleties in what it means for humans "to know."

THE UNDERLYING DYNAMICS OF THE CHALLENGE OF DIFFUSION
This challenge does not start until the growth processes of profound change have operated for long enough to build up substantial experience

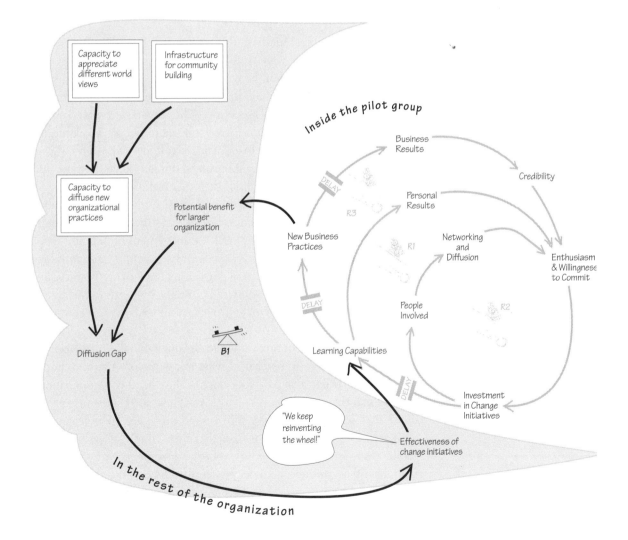

with new business practices and evidence of business results. At this point, there exists significant potential for the larger organization to benefit from the insights, experiences, and new practices generated within the pilot group. Realizing this potential, however, requires the organizational "capacity to diffuse innovative practices." If this capacity is lacking, a "diffusion gap" develops, which limits broader implementation—either by limiting the number of people who become interested and willing to commit to their own experiments, or by limiting the effectiveness of those who do try to adopt the new ideas, or both.

An organization's capacity for the diffusion of innovative practices depends on:

- **Coaching capacity:** Much of the most effective diffusion occurs through giving people opportunities to cross traditional boundaries and work with one another. New innovators need access to someone who has "been there and done that," both for substantive insight and for moral support and perspective. The organization's coaching capacity reflects the number of knowledgeable people available for coaching, mentoring and help—particularly those who have direct experience with the relevant pilot groups, but also have the time and capacity to help others throughout the organization.

- **Permeability of organizational boundaries:** Organizational boundaries are a fact of life. All organizations create them. The real question is: To what extent do they limit the movement of people, ideas, and the formation of communities of inquiry around systemic issues that cross boundaries? Biological organisms have many boundaries, such as cell walls and the epidermal boundary, but a common feature of all biological boundaries is their permeability, allowing a continual flow of energy and matter.

- **Information infrastructure:** People throughout the organization need to know whom to reach and what to ask, before they can begin to learn from other groups' experiences. They need communications channels so that inquiry can be easy. And they need someone on the other end who is accessible. Many innovators are so beleaguered with inquiries by phone or e-mail that they simply stop answering them. There is a need for media—reports, documents, videos, or simulations—that can help give people an introductory overview of new ideas and practices.

- **A learning culture** that encourages mutuality, collaboration, curiosity, and reflection across both internal and external boundaries and effective learning infrastructure. Once diffusion is seen as a challenge of people learning from one another, and not just using technology to exchange information, it is clear that qualities of the overall organization environment influence both the quantity and quality of diffusion. The sense of mutuality and genuine concern for one another determines the extent to which people want to help one another, and the genuine interest they have in what others are learning. Conversely, organizational environments characterized by intense personal competition and political games-playing have lower capacity for diffusion.

Learning infrastructures—ways of organizing resources and opportunities to promote regular reflection and sharing—both make a learning culture real and enable it to continually grow. For example, over the past ten years, the United States Army has institutionalized "After-Action Reviews" (AARs), the Army Center for Lessons Learned, and many other successful learning infrastructures. Through these changes, a cultural shift has been occuring gradually, at least in the eyes of some army veterans. "I think we have begun to see a shift from a 'culture of reports' to a 'culture of review,'" says recently retired General Hal Nelson. Traditionally, in the army, as in most hierarchical institutions, people focused on managing the flow of information up the hierarchy. People were good at making reports to their bosses because this was the primary way to influence how your unit was viewed and how you were evaluated. Today, a set of norms is emerging that emphasizes everyone's part in continual review of "how we are doing." Says one insider, "It doesn't matter where you sit in the hierarchy. You can expect to participate in reviews aimed at learning and improvement on an almost daily basis."

}} For more on the army's learning infrastructure, see page 470.

STRATEGIES FOR MEETING THE CHALLENGE OF DIFFUSION

High-leverage strategies for dealing with this challenge concentrate on building the different dimensions of an organization's capacity to diffuse innovative practices: coaching capacity, permeability of boundaries, information infrastructure, and a learning culture and infrastructure.

- **Learn to legitimate and value network leaders as carriers of new ideas and as coaches.** "One Hugh Smith [senior executive] on board is worth one thousand John Hollands [internal networker]," commented a senior executive in a Fortune 50 company. His statement was directed at the importance of senior management buy-in. But it also reflected the widespread devaluing of internal networkers.

This devaluing is unfortunate because, without effective internal networkers, little significant new knowledge spreads. In many ways, network leaders are the keys to enabling informal communities of practice to function effectively. They are crucial to getting predisposed local line leaders of common mind talking with one another, perhaps even helping one another. They are also pivotal in helping leaders develop the ability to appreciate different worldviews and new ideas. If anything, the importance of effective internal network leaders may be growing.

mediators

One reason is information availability. In companies where all information flows up and down the hierarchy, bosses can control subordinates' learning by controlling the information to which they have access. But this is less and less feasible in today's world of intranets, e-mail, and the World Wide Web; and it will become even less feasible in any organization that invests seriously in infrastructure for systemwide knowledge sharing. Network leaders are the human part of such infrastructures—the generators of coherence and alignment.

Internal networkers also play a vital role when team-based work arrangements, in concert with information technology, leave people overwhelmed. We often hear comments like this: "I've just been made part of two new projects. Each one sends out fifty e-mails and twenty voicemails a day. If I don't find a way to prioritize them, I'm going to snap." More and more people, in situations like this, will look for help for filtering, prioritizing, and sense making in rapidly changing work settings. Computer/communications systems cannot handle that task; they simply swamp people with information and data. But network leaders have always monitored information and knowledge for relevance on an informal basis. They are well equipped to help shunt information to the places where it will do the most good.

Finally, network leaders will become increasingly critical in getting people the help they need to be effective. Previously, help came primarily from the boss; if you needed an increase in your training or consulting budget, you'd have to ask for assistance. Now, internal networks provide much of that help themselves, through one-on-one coaching and mentoring. Increasingly, help will come through networks of mutual assistance, inside or outside the company; internal networkers will help people join, contribute to, and gain benefits from those networks.

■ **Pay explicit attention to existing communities of practice.** The theory of communities of practice has coevolved with a form of innovation diffusion that accepts the informal webs of people in an organization as channels for diffusing knowledge and information. As Etienne Wenger, one of the originators of this body of research, puts it, "The existing set of interrelationships gives people a context for exchanging information. They know what information is relevant; and they know how to present it so it will be heard, because of their past history. And they have already established relationships of trustworthiness. They don't have to establish credentials as propagators of new knowledge. The function of brokering—of passing knowledge across community boundaries—is based on membership in multiple existing communities."

Wenger observes that organizations seeking to instill new knowledge often inadvertently disrupt the communities of practice on which the spread of knowledge depends. For example, General Motors and Toyota established the high-performance-team-based NUMMI plant in Fremont, California, with hopes that NUMMI's innovations would spread back into the GM mainstream. But the rest of GM picked up very little new practice from NUMMI. "GM sent individuals to spend a year there," Wenger notes, "disconnected from their former jobs at GM, without knowing in advance where they would end up when they returned. If they had gone in groups, learning together and coming back together to work at GM, or if they had kept up their membership in their existing communities of practice back in Detroit, then the innovations of NUMMI would have had a much better chance of being adopted at GM. It is not enough to go back and say, 'I learned the right thing to do here.' Those who learn new things must simultaneously maintain connectedness with their old communities."

■ **Release information about new innovations with less constraint.** When you make information available openly, potential boundary spanners can seek you out. This creates an "open market" for innovation that takes advantage of the natural competitiveness among potential partners, by making you equally available for collaboration with all of them.

The highly innovative environmental research center, Rocky Mountain Institute, has used this approach in its partnerships with private corporations to develop new technologies. For example, in

For a more in-depth guide to the use of communities of practice in fostering organizational change see *Communities of Practice: Learning, Meaning and Identity,* by Etienne Wenger (Cambridge, England and New York: Cambridge University Press, 1998).

For more about Hypercars, see "Hypercars: The Next Industrial Revolution," by Amory B. Lovins, in Proceedings of the 13th Electric Vehicle Symposium (EVS-13), (1996: Osaka, Japan), published as Rocky Mountain Institute publication #T96-9, available at www.rmi.org/hypercars/osaka/index.html. Other publications of RMI's Hypercar Center are available at www.hypercar.com. "Hypercar" is a trademark, and The Hypercar Center a service mark, of Rocky Mountain Institute.

For the full story about P&G and Wal-Mart, see "Accidental Adversaries" in The Fifth Discipline Fieldbook, pp. 145–148.

1991, RMI and some senior General Motors managers began talking about setting up a "Hypercar" project, to develop an ultralight, low-drag, hybrid gasoline-electric, highly energy-efficient vehicle. When the project encountered resistance from some GM managers, the Institute decided not to seek an exclusive relationship with GM or any other automobile company, but rather to publish their technical information openly, thus implicitly inviting any company to compete in exploiting the concept—with RMI's help if desired. As a result, thirty companies (including Toyota, Volkswagen, Chrysler, Ford, Volvo, Honda, Subaru, Mazda, Daimler-Benz, and General Motors) have invested more than $6 billion among them—far more than any one company would invest on its own. As competitors, they may be reluctant to work together, but RMI serves as a collaborator with many of them, and a clearinghouse for research information on technical issues such as fuel cells and lithium batteries.

"The open competitive model has been a runaway success, in stimulating all the companies to important efforts," says the Institute's cofounder and research director, Amory Lovins. He quotes one company's head of advanced materials and manufacturing, who was asked if he wasn't concerned that someone else might make Hypercars first. "Yes, we're absolutely terrified," said the executive. "That's why we're working so hard on it!"

■ **Get "the system" in the room.** One powerful strategy for working together across internal or external boundaries is to gather people from the entire system for collective inquiry, especially inquiry into how they collectively are creating outcomes where no one wins.

In the mid-1980s, Procter & Gamble and Wal-Mart were caught in an adversarial spiral, where each company's efforts to "fix" its business problems hurt the other. Both sets of managers, well known for their fierce organizational pride, had to recognize that they needed the other, even though they perceived the other as aimed at exploiting them. In a joint working session, they began to see how each party's actions were causing problems for the others. Jennifer Kemeny, a systems thinking facilitator of the session, wrote: "Once in the room, they discovered that the other organization's strategy seemed perfectly rational and reasonable from their local perspective. There was no 'treachery' afoot. There was simply a larger system whose pieces didn't work well together."

■ **Design more effective media for internal information exchange.** Sooner or later, any pilot group activity reaches a limit to the number of people who can communicate on a face-to-face basis. Several hundred people, for instance, will not all know one another by name or face; so they can't take part in ongoing, casual conversations. If they need to communicate regularly, they need to do so through some sort of mediated channel of communications: e-mail, computer conferencing, memos, reports, videotapes, or other forms of documentation.

All of these artifacts differ from face-to-face conversation. They are full of potential misunderstandings and miscommunications. Most reports, for instance, end up skimmed and put into a drawer. Many stories that travel by e-mail communicate the moral that "it's so- and-so's fault," and make it easier for organizations to fragment.

Mechanisms for diffusing information can be designed effectively, but this is not primarily a matter of better information technology design. Most of the faddish recent interest in knowledge management seems to miss this point: that information technology systems are designed to carry data and information, while people are starving for knowledge they can use.

As an illustration, consider the case of two software companies, Microsoft and "MarvelWare," a rival word processing program developer during the early 1990s. Software companies depend on the quality of their help lines—the people who answer questions from frustrated customers with problems. Both Microsoft and MarvelWare invested in recruiting and training extensive help line staffs, and both companies set up computer systems with technical information they could call up on computer screens. But MarvelWare's infrastructure designers stopped there.

"As MarvelWare grew," Dan, one former help line manager told us, "our intelligence was taken for granted." He saw this most clearly, he said, when he left MarvelWare for a similar job at Microsoft. Microsoft set up a "knowledgebase" that allowed service representatives to regularly query and learn from each other, and from software engineers throughout the company. This helped them continually make sense of not just technical information, but ways of improving their service; and it gave them an easy, organizationally embedded way to offer comments and knowledge back to the software developers. The Microsoft service representatives came to feel that it was wrong to help customers without using the knowledge base—because then they would be helping from their individual perspective, without the expertise of the whole company implicitly behind them. MarvelWare also had an on-line data knowledge base, but few people used it, because "it was all crap anyway," according to Dan. Nobody maintained it. Nobody used it for communication between people. It was seen only as a vehicle for canned "knowledge." Ultimately, MarvelWare's software sales declined, due, at least in part, to inferior customer support.

In some cases, the narrowness of the "bandwidth" on a computer-based system makes some forms of reflection and inquiry easier; people may talk candidly about work matters via e-mail in a way they would never dare in a meeting. At Chrysler, for instance, all the accountants are linked in a computer conferencing system that is set up for serious inquiry. If they have questions about the meaning of a number, they can raise that question "publicly" and invite a wide variety of comment from Chrysler people around the world.

Effective use of information technology for sharing knowledge depends on give-and-take among people, building various forms of on-line coaching, mentoring, guidance, and inquiry into the fabric of the media itself. People need to feel that they always have an opportunity to speak and be listened to. Knowledge should be seen not as static information, to be "accessed," but as dynamic, generated in its use and continually altered through use. For example, a key to the Information and Knowledge Exchange (IKE) intranet system developed for the business markets division of AT&T is the creation of full-time "knowledge community facilitators." As AT&T Marketing Vice President Patricia Traynor describes it: "The first time a salesperson directs an inquiry or a question through IKE, they typically receive a rapid and concise response from another salesperson (or from us) within twenty-four hours. If they don't, they may not return to the system. IKE's value depends entirely on the interaction and two-way sharing of ideas and information among our sales executives."

■ **Cultivate "Appreciative Inquiry": other people are probably not as crazy as they seem**. Often, the "rubber meets the road" in relationships across boundaries when the "others" say or do something which truly seems inexplicable. At this point, all your worst fears seem about to be confirmed. The potential for suspicion and distrust which has lurked below the surface seems about to become fully realized. At these times, without genuine inquiry, you may make costly, unnecessarily harsh decisions based entirely on misinterpretations of the others' intent or meaning.

This anecdote, by an engineer in the "AutoCo Epsilon" learning history, demonstrates the leverage of even modest inquiry when external partnerships are at risk:

One of my suppliers . . . mentioned under his breath at the end of a meeting that a part would be two weeks late. He didn't want anyone but me to hear him. I gathered my wits for a minute, because it was really a shock. We hadn't had any problems with that part. I asked why it would be late, and he said, "I'm not sure."

I could see everyone's eyes in the meeting hitting the roof. They were saying to themselves: "God, Bob is an idiot. What's wrong with him? We thought he was a good guy."

. . . After a lot of prodding and pleading, it came out that he thought it was a problem with paperwork that we [at AutoCo] had lost, and he didn't want to be the one to tell us. So I went back and checked. AutoCo's system had misplaced not only his paperwork, but a lot of paperwork. It was causing parts to come in a little later than anticipated, just enough to mess up the [car launch]. Bob's honesty allowed us to make sure everything coordinated on time.

Traditionally I would have thought, "I don't want to hear about Bob's problems. He is an idiot." I wouldn't have checked the reasoning which led me to that assumption. I would have said to him, "Just make sure the part's on time." There would be nothing he could do about it.

An especially relevant body of practice for external partnerships is "appreciative inquiry," developed by organizational change theorist David Cooperrider. "Appreciative" interviews draw forth images and ideas from people's peak experiences and aspirations, which in turn can help people articulate the propositions that they agree upon, despite their differences. This approach has been very useful in helping people deal with explosive boundary-crossing issues, such as sexual harassment in the workplace.

Appreciative inquiry constitutes a method for bringing empathy into day-to-day practice. Empathy does not mean sympathy. It means developing an understanding of another so intimate that the feelings, thoughts and motives of one person are readily comprehended by another. To be empathetic means to "try on" different perspectives and assumptions, temporarily suspending your own in the process, so that you can inquire into the reasons why people hold them. This requires the willingness to believe that people aren't inherently vicious, mean, or crazy, but that the world looks very different to them, and that you could appreciate it if you took the time to see it from their point of view. Good negotiators are masterful at this skill —they step into the shoes of different people, whether they agree

See *A Car Launch With Heart: The Story of the Autoco Epsilon* by George Roth, Art Kleiner, et al. (New York: Oxford University Press, 1999), pp. 42–44.

requires good listening/probing

See, for example, "Appreciative Inquiry in Organizational Life" by David L. Cooperrider and Suresh Srivastva, *Research in Organizational Change and Development*, 1987, Vol.1, pp. 129–169; and "An Interview with David Cooperrider on Appreciative Inquiry and the Future of OD," *Organization Development Journal* (1995, vol. 13, no. 3), pp. 5–13; http://www.appreciative-inquiry.org/AI-Life.html. For more information, see David Cooperrider's Web site at: http://universe.cwru.edu/Faculty/Profiles/07-04.html. We are grateful to Nancy Dixon for suggesting some of these references.

with them or not, and then in turn help others to do the same. Developing the capacity to cross organizational boundaries is very much like being a good negotiator.

■ **Make research part of executive accountability**. There are a great many innovations going on simultaneously in any large organization. How can management help people gain insight into those innovations, beyond simple "best practices," personal anecdotes, and "war stories"? While storytelling is critical to put a "human face" on new ideas, it also can be misleading. People can attribute dramatic improvements to their pet ideas, with little critical judgment. Potentially significant innovations that fail to lead to dramatic business results can be incorrectly discredited. The missing link is organizational research.

Few organizations today would expect to prosper without significant investments in research capabilities: market research, product development research, and engineering process research. Yet none of these types of research will add value to customers unless new ideas and practices can be implemented. That capability, in turn, depends on investing in ongoing research in new management processes and ways of working together.

The famous "Team Taurus" of 1980 to 1985 was arguably the most effective car development team in Ford's history. The product they produced became one of the bestselling cars in automotive history. Yet Ford managers undertook little serious study of the reasons why the team was so effective. "Ford learned very little from Taurus," said one Ford executive familiar with the Taurus story. "The team broke many rules, but no one ever came back afterward and analyzed which rules were broken and whether or not some of those rules should have been changed." Team members who went on to other Ford car programs took their experiences and beliefs with them, but there was no systematic attempt to tap their knowledge base.

Ford is hardly unique in this respect. This lack of capability to learn—even from your own successes—is unlikely to change until there is clear managerial accountability for research. We believe that this accountability should be placed primarily at the executive level. There exists great uncertainty about the future role of executives. Traditionally they made the major decisions, but an increasing amount of decision-making responsibility is being pushed throughout the organization (Chapter 10). Traditionally, they created the strategy, but many argue that strategy in today's dynamic business marketplaces needs to engage people at all levels (Chapter 12). One critical area of new work for them is ensuring that the organization can learn from its most innovative practitioners. This will require study, translation of idiosyncratic practices into potentially general tools and processes, and eventual creation of appropriate standards.

It may turn out that an organization's ability to extend its knowledge depends upon the capability of managers at many levels to conduct such research: to identify, codify and build judgment about emerging new tools and methods and to look for the communities of practice where the knowledge of work practices is embedded. As executive accountability for organizational research becomes established, some of this responsibility will naturally filter down to local line managers, where most of the actual experimenting is taking place. Thus, it will become important to also . . .

■ **Develop the managerial ability to conduct research, especially by line leaders.** For example, Intel fab managers "ramping up" a new manufacturing facility are responsible for generating a variety of data during the ramp up. They must trade off getting the facility up to full volume production as soon as possible with running experiments that will provide other fab managers with information they can use. In this way, they are conducting research on their own facility, while simultaneously managing the facility.

Some of the most innovative diffusion mechanisms, such as learning histories and after-action reviews, represent efforts to systematically increase the organization's managerial research capabilities. Consulting firms often build up research libraries of frequently encountered business situations; at Innovation Associates the library also involves systems archetypes that apply to different cases. If firms are indeed becoming more and more "knowledge based," might not they build up similar libraries?

See page 460 for more on learning histories.

There is still a long way to go to make "research" a word that sits comfortably with "management." "Research" sounds like a dry activity, far removed from day-to-day concerns—in part because it has been traditionally conducted by academics, brought in from the outside, often focused on very narrow problems, who write up their results for journals, and often provide little concrete help. Today, there is a growing interest among academics and corporate practitioners alike in better connections between research and practice.

Information about Intel came from conversation; a similar approach is described in "Web Technologies for Technology Transfer and Organizational Learning in a Production Environment," a master's thesis by Greg Gunn of MIT (1998).

For more information about the Innovation Associates library of systems archetypes, see the Web page: http://www.fieldbook.com/ia.html.

For the first several years at the MIT Organizational Learning Center (now the Society for Organizational Learning, or SoL), company managers would "tolerate" or "humor" our desire to study projects in their companies. "That's okay—that's your MIT thing." But when the impact of studies began to be demonstrated—including the impact of some of the reports in *The Fifth Discipline Fieldbook*—that attitude began to change.

Today, many managers are commissioning studies of internal social networks and of communities of practice, as well as learning histories, as part of change initiatives in order to better understand how learning is occurring and how it can be enhanced. This represents a refreshing shift from the tendency toward "quick fix" consulting. The key will come with how such research is used. Does it contribute to creating communities of inquiry where people working together step back from day-to-day pressures and really learn to reflect and conceptualize? Or will it produce reports that sit on shelves? The difference will probably depend on the type of overall climate for inquiry and learning that an organization creates.

■ **Remember that all boundaries are ultimately arbitrary.** Organizational boundaries have a way of seeming more tangible than they are. Ultimately, they, like all boundaries created by human societies, are artifacts of how we choose to organize our lives. They serve a purpose, but they can also outlive their purpose. When they are reified and people stop realizing that they are human inventions, they can become prisons that limit who we are and what we might achieve.

For example, when you have worked for an organization for a long time, it seems like being a member of the organization defines who you are professionally. This label can be more limiting than you realize. As one Shell executive put it, "Most of us at Shell had been career employees. We were 'Shell men and women' first and foremost. Today, after several years of Shell's transformation, many of us feel a much clearer, deeper sense of personal identity. It feels more like we are standing on our own. We can then make a more conscious choice to be here at Shell; and if we make that choice, it paradoxically gives us a deeper commitment to Shell, to each other, and to our communities, than we had when we were all just Shell employees in the traditional employment relationship."

2 The Organizational Learning Cycle

Turning knowledge creation into a self-changing system.

Nancy M. Dixon and Rick Ross

George Washington University professor Nancy Dixon asks not how teams might learn more effectively. She asks how learning might be embodied in the large-scale channels of communication of any major enterprise. In this article, she and Rick Ross begin to flesh out the question of implementation: how to bring an organizational learning cycle to life. This article, which emerged early in our editorial process, was a pivotal influence on the challenges of profound change, helping us see how the challenges continued to emerge even after learning initiatives moved beyond the pilot group to the organization as a whole.

Years ago, one of us (Nancy) belonged to a singing group that sang early Baroque music. Each member of the group sang beautifully alone, but the group made a wonderfully complex sound together, truly more than the sum of its parts. In retrospect, there was more going on in that group than anyone realized. The singers, over time, developed a collective knowledge—not stored in any individual's mind, but in the practices that they used for improvement. They listened regularly to recordings and each other; they helped each other in systematic ways. They talked regularly about where lines needed to stand out, or how to alter the phrasing. The beautiful sound got better all the time, in a way that might have seemed uncanny if it didn't feel so naturally right.

What if an organization could work that way—not just at a team level, but across internal boundaries? What if there were processes and infrastructure in place for building large-scale knowledge? People all through the organization would naturally move to help one another become more capable. They would continually develop their collective knowledge throughout the organization rather than passively receiving and implementing someone else's information.

Unfortunately, many business people seem to think that "generating knowledge" is just a matter of hiring the best people, giving them training if necessary, and then getting them to stay out of one another's way.

This article draws upon concepts and examples developed in *The Organizational Learning Cycle: How We Can Learn Collectively*, by Nancy Dixon, second edition (London: Gower, 1999). We recommend this book for more in-depth descriptions of both theory and practice, that could help executive and line leaders, and internal networkers, set up "organizational learning cycles" in their organizations.

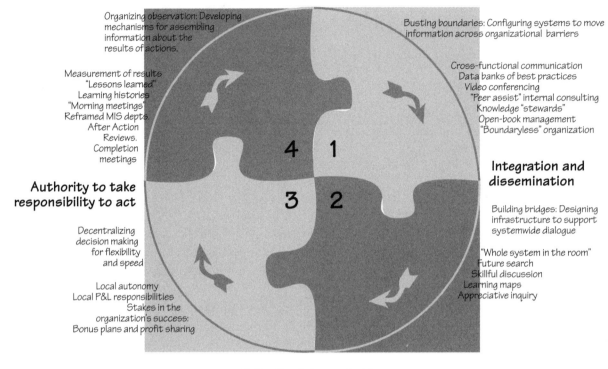

Widespread generation of information

Organizing observation: Developing mechanisms for assembling information about the results of actions.

Measurement of results
"Lessons learned"
Learning histories
"Morning meetings"
Reframed MIS depts.
After Action
Reviews.
Completion
meetings

Busting boundaries: Configuring systems to move information across organizational barriers

Cross-functional communication
Data banks of best practices
Video conferencing
"Peer assist" internal consulting
Knowledge "stewards"
Open-book management
"Boundaryless" organization

4   1

3   2

Integration and dissemination

Building bridges: Designing infrastructure to support systemwide dialogue

"Whole system in the room"
Future search
Skillful discussion
Learning maps
Appreciative inquiry

Authority to take responsibility to act

Decentralizing
decision making
for flexibility
and speed

Local autonomy
Local P&L responsibilities
Stakes in the
organization's success:
Bonus plans and profit sharing

Collective interpretation

It's as if they believe that, simply by putting the experts together, their accumulated skills and capabilities will combine naturally. But knowledge doesn't work that way in real life. It tends to stay put within the various internal "silos." Organizations suffer an enormous amount of duplicated and even conflicting effort—unless they operate in a deliberately designed large-scale cycle for sharing and developing knowledge. Hundreds of people, as natural parts of their jobs, would take part in different parts of this cycle, and the organization's processes and capabilities would continually improve as a result.

I. WIDE-SPREAD GENERATION OF INFORMATION

Shown at the top of the cycle in the "twelve o'clock" position is the stage of gathering and creating knowledge. Many companies conduct their information gathering through specialized research teams which report their findings to decision makers. But in this cycle, the people who can act on the information do the collecting. Everyone in the organization—line workers, managers, salespeople, senior executives, customer service reps, accounting professionals—spends part of his working time focused on acquiring and generating new information that will help him understand and conduct his work better.

Johnsonville Foods, a family-owned sausage company based in a small Wisconsin town, has mastered this part of the cycle. CEO Ralph Stayer, seeking to galvanize employees, set in place a new performance evaluation system, oriented from the customers' perspective. Employees were asked: "For your specific product or service, what does great performance look like to the customer?" Teams who shared a task went to their customers, either internal or external, to ask that question—and then wrestled those answers down onto paper in a way that identified specific measurable results.

■ **Infrastructure for moving forward:** To move from collecting information to integrating and disseminating it as knowledge, organizations can invest in "busting boundaries": configuring systems that move information across organizational barriers. Electronic communication has greatly enhanced people's ability to communicate, but it's not always obvious how to use this wizardry wisely and judiciously. Thus, it is also worth considering familiar techniques: multifunctional project teams, technology fairs, collocation of project members, and face-to-face meetings of networks of committed people. All of these can serve as integrative mechanisms.

Ernst & Young (E&Y) requires its consulting teams to submit their work products (such as reports and slides) to a common database at the end of consulting engagements. Senior consultants sift through those submissions to cull out those that are exemplary. These become part of special electronic packages, "Powerpacks," that other teams can use with clients. By making use of this shared knowledge, a consultant can reduce the time it takes to develop a customized proposal for a client from three weeks to three days. This infrastructure involves not only the databases but the knowledge stewards who sort and manage the submissions, the laptop computers that every consultant carries, plus easy worldwide voice telephone access to the databases, frequent network meetings that bring together consultants who are doing similar work, and the commonality of software, so that learning one database gives easy access to all others.

The theory of knowledge creation underlying this cycle is based on the theories of David Kolb, Reg Revans, Chris Argyris, and Jean Piaget; and on close observation of organizations that have, in one way or another, embedded knowledge creation into their everyday activities. It is now well understood that learning from experience takes place in an ongoing cycle. For example, people may take action, observe and reflect upon the results (Reflecting), draw conclusions (Abstracting/Connecting), choose a new action to execute and learn from (Deciding), and then once again move back to the action stage. There are many individual "wheels of learning"; for more about them, see *The Fifth Discipline Fieldbook*, p. 58. Also see *Organizational Learning: A Theory of Action Perspective*, by Chris Argyris and Donald Schon (Reading, MA: Addison-Wesley, 1978); *Experiential Learning*, by David Kolb (Englewood Cliffs, NJ: Prentice-Hall, 1984); *ABC of Action Learning*, by R. Revans (London: Chartwell-Bratt, 1983); *Action Learning: New Techniques for Management*, by R. Revans (London: Blond & Briggs, 1980); and *The Developmental Psychology of Jean Piaget*, by John Flavell (New York: Van Nostrand Reinhold, 1963).

References on the widespread generation of information include: "Beyond Team Work" (Johnsonville Foods), Training, vol. 2 no. 6, pp. 25–32; "Wide-open management at Chaparral Steel," by Alan Kantrow, *Harvard Business Review*, 1986, 64 (3), p. 96; "Chaparral Steel: Unleash Workers and Cut Costs," by Brian Dumaine, *Fortune*, 1992, 125 (10), p. 18; *Open Book Management*, by John Case (New York: HarperBusiness, 1995).

Similarly, Chevron has established an infrastructure that uses internal consultants as human links, referring project managers to managers who faced similar issues on other capital projects within Chevron (at any time there may be over two hundred). Although there are numerous databases available to these project managers, the real benefit lies in having a human mind that fully comprehends the specifics of the context of a project, is equally aware of the specifics of other projects, *and* has the time and energy to make the connections. Sometimes all that is needed is a document that can be pulled up on the computer, other times the needed knowledge requires a site visit, a conference call, or a shared resource. The internal consultant works with a project manager off and on, over the life of a project, which might be up to two years, and is eventually able to use that project as a source of knowledge for newly developing projects. Chevron says that making these internal connections can save up to 20 percent on the cost of a project. In the downstream operation, between 1992 and 1997, those connections resulted in 816 million dollars in savings, a testament to the ability of learning to impact the bottom line. Although the internal consultants were originally carried as overhead, their "Project Resources Group" has evolved into a profit center that holds best practice seminars, manages the databases, and keeps up on the latest technology in the industry.

"Open-book management" is a vital form of infrastructure for moving information up and down the hierarchy. Thus at Manco, a consumer-products manufacturer, there are several key business indicators, including manufacturing direct support, dollars, and percent of net sales, displayed on running electric signs posted throughout the facility. Hewlett-Packard puts its key business indicators in a database that is open and accessible to all organizational members on their desktops. At Pace Industries, a maker of die-cast metal parts, inventory accuracy and scrap reduction are posted on the shop floor.

See material on on-line infrastructure, page 456; and open-book management, page 181. Another example is British Petroleum's Pacesetter system on page 444.

In all these systems, it's important not just to make key information (such as financial numbers) available to everyone, but to provide the training and conversation to give people context for that information, and to encourage them to share their perspective with others. This sets up in the next part of the cycle . . .

II. INTEGRATION AND DISSEMINATION: REFRAMING INFORMATION IN CONTEXT

Information that teams and individuals have generated cannot be fully understood in isolation from the rest of the system. To be a full partner, each individual and team has to understand the whole organization's task as well as the relationship of each subtask to the whole.

The World Health Organization (WHO) learned the importance of this phase during the 1960s, during its worldwide campaign to eradicate smallpox. Experts assumed that the vaccination techniques which worked in the first locale, Tonga, could easily roll out to the entire planet. But in various countries, caseworkers needed a variety of strategies to work effectively with shortages, community attributes (some countries had extensive midwife networks), media (some countries had radio networks), and other local practices (like tattooing or nomadic water holes).

All of their varied approaches were systematically recorded, and fieldworkers received summary reports and supplemental papers every two or three weeks. Requests for help from the field got the highest-priority responses at the central office. Staff people were expected to visit each country in their regions, at least once and preferably twice a year. Even embarrassing news, such as the politically sensitive locations of new outbreaks of the disease, was openly shared. Since everyone had access to all this information, WHO fieldworkers continuously compared notes. They discovered, for example, that adult women rarely contracted smallpox; they did not need to be vaccinated, thus saving precious expense. This sharing of knowledge was critical to the ultimate success of the campaign, and the last case of smallpox occurred in Somalia in 1977, just ten years after the effort began.

- **Infrastructure for moving forward:** There are a variety of ways to construct such an infrastructure. Some of these are "whole system in the room" processes such as General Electric's Work Out, search conferences, or open space technology. These processes bring from eighty to three hundred organizational members together with representatives from suppliers and customers for a three to five day meeting. Much of the work is done in small groups alternating between functional and mixed groups. Facilitated by outside professionals, people at the meetings systematically generate and test ideas.

  In 1993, the Whole Foods grocery chain brought together more than seventy people, representing, store managers, employees, customers, and suppliers, in a three-day event. Many of the current store

References on integration and dissemination include: "Death of a Disease," *Science News,* 107, Feb. 1975, p. 74; "The Eradication of Smallpox" by D. A. Henderson, *Scientific American,* 1976, vol. 235, #4, p. 25; "The Eradication of Smallpox," by J. W. Hopkins, *The Journal of Developing Areas,* 1988, vol. 22, p. 321; *Participative Design for Participative Democracy,* edited by Merrelyn Emery (1993, Australian National University Centre for Continuing Education); *Real Time Strategic Change* by R. Jacobs (San Francisco: Berrett-Koehler, 1994); *Riding the Tiger* by Harrison Owen (Potomac, MD: Abbott Publishing, 1993); *Discovering Common Ground* by Marvin Weisbord (San Francisco: Berrett-Koehler, 1992); and "Skillful Discussion," by Rick Ross (*The Fifth Discipline Fieldbook,* p. 385).

managers were opposed to the chain's continued expansion, valuing the benefits of a relatively small-sized organization. However, as the store managers worked through discussions with other voices in the conference they came to their own realization that continued growth was essential to the long-term viability of the chain. This was reflected in the target the conference set: one hundred stores and $1 billion in sales by 1998.

Teams can also serve as the primary unit of discussions that move towards collective interpretation. We have seen such conversations take place with a variety of facilitative tools. For instance, the protocols of "skillful discussion" (balancing advocacy with inquiry, paying attention to your intentions, etc.) are specifically designed to help a team make shared meaning and explore, instead of avoid, impasses.

To provide value, these processes must be clearly recognizable as part of the culture of the organization—not onetime events, used only once to remedy a specific problem, but embedded in the organization's cultural DNA. When GE began to use Work-Out in the early '90s, it was considered a "special event" at most sites. Now, after ten years of use, Work-Out is simply a way to get work done.

Also see "Culture Change at General Electric," page 74; "Watershed Events," page 480; Open Space," page 484; "Search Conferences", page 486 and "Asking Big Questions," page 506; and the article on scenario planning, page 511.

III. COLLECTIVE INTERPRETATION: MEETINGS OF MANY MINDS

Individuals make sense of life based on personal experience. But that's not easy in an organization, where "experience" has been dispersed among all the employees. Some have been collecting information by talking to customers; others have been experimenting; others have been analyzing mistakes and successes; and still others have been interacting with suppliers. All of these many perspectives can be brought to bear on critical organizational issues, but only through deliberate conversation.

This process can occur between two people, within a team, between two teams, among everyone in a division, across the whole of the organization, and with external stakeholders. But it has a substantially different character than most meetings. It represents a time of dialogue, not speeches; of egalitarian participation, not polite response to authority. Participants bring the data they have generated, and the conclusions they have drawn from their own experience—not reports from others.

As the primary sources of the data, they expect to challenge each other and conventional wisdom, because the organization's knowledge will emerge by making sense of conflicting frames of reference. Finance sees one "story" behind the loss of a key supplier relationship; purchasing sees another; and operations sees yet another. So what single story can explain how each of these perspectives might make sense to the people who hold them?

Not only must differences exist, but the sense-making process must sustain the talk of differences, instead of restraining it, to allow organizational members to wrestle with their own assumptions. Many of these dialogues do not result in consensus, but participants come to understand the reasoning and data that others are using to arrive at their meaning and thereby understand others' meaning more fully and, by comparison, understand their own more completely.

A story from Johnsonville Foods illustrates the power of this stage. In 1985, company president Ralph Stayer received an offer from a food-processing company, to buy more sausage, on a regular basis, than Johnsonville could easily produce. Rather than calling together the top six or seven people, to decide whether or not to expand for this client, Stayer called a meeting of the whole organization. With more than two hundred people in the room, he said something like this:

"We have two weeks to think this through. First, what would it take to make this new account work? What would we have to do differently, in order to take on this new account? What would it mean for shipping? For manufacturing? For billing? Second, is it possible to reduce the down side? Third, in the end, do we want to do it?"

For two weeks, people met in teams to answer those questions. They wrestled with the considerable risks, and developed their own points of view. In the end, they almost unanimously decided to take on the new business. Since they had all been part of the sense-making process, they could all naturally implement it; they had already thought through the necessary changes that each of them would have to make. This use of collective intelligence was very different from having someone at the top say, "Now we're going to take this contract, and do whatever we have to do around here to meet it."

References on collective interpretation include *Beyond Certainty: The Changing Worlds of Organisations*, by Charles Handy (London: Random House United Kingdom, 1995)

- ■ **Infrastructure for moving forward:** The third quadrant provides the infrastructure needed to translate the collective interpretation into local action—decentralizing decision making for flexibility and speed. Two critical elements seem necessary. First, if self-managed or autonomous teams can act on their observations and reflections, in a way that is aligned with the organization's overall goals, then they become much more capable at contributing to those goals. Second, employees need a stake in the organization's success. As participants in this cycle of collective knowledge building, they will tend to view themselves as partners in the enterprise, and will expect to be compensated when their efforts bring about exceptional results. This can be accomplished by a variety of group incentives such as bonus plans, profit sharing, and stock distribution. However, for any of these to function effectively: 1) the members of the unit must clearly understand how their actions relate to the payout; 2) they must be able to affect the outcome by their own efforts; and 3) the goals must be tracked in public, according to criteria that everybody understands.

The Baltimore plant of Chesapeake Packaging Company makes corrugated boxes. It is made up of eight internal companies: Quality Trucking handles shipping, Chesapeake Maintenance Services maintains the machinery, Corrugator Specialties Unlimited is responsible for the corrugating process, and so on. These internal companies compile their own operating information and are responsible for managing their own affairs. Once a month everyone in the plant meets to review the numbers and build an income statement (collective interpretation). If the plant hits a certain target level of earnings, profit sharing kicks in and employees receive a bonus of at least 5 percent of their gross monthly income, with the percentages rising as the profits rise.

⟩⟩ Also see Chapter 10, Governance, page 361; and governance resources, page 401.

IV: AUTHORITY TO TAKE RESPONSIBLE ACTION: DESIGNING EXPERIMENTS

Experience with the "wheel of learning" makes it clear that individuals can only learn when they can take action based on their own experience. But for organizational learning, individual experience is not enough. The organization cannot learn if individuals or groups act only on their own conclusions, uninformed by the knowledge and perspectives of others. That is why, if organizational members are to act responsibly, they must have enough autonomy to make changes when and where they are needed.

Thus, at the World Health Organization, fieldworkers took the authority to act on the insights that they had gained from sharing one another's data about smallpox. They varied their practice according to local conditions, and they involved the local population in their decision making. As they wrought new variations on the practices they had learned, they continued to take note of their results and to share their notes back with other fieldworkers around the world.

- **Infrastructure for moving forward:** For this stage to be fruitful in generating new knowledge, the people who take action must also capture, observe, and reflect on the results. Thus, it's necessary to develop an infrastructure for measuring results and capturing lessons learned—which, essentially, returns the leaders and members of this organization back to the first stage, to start the cycle over again.

Unit members themselves are the people best able to design the ways that their own processes are measured, so they can use those measures to decide new actions and correct their course. These measures are not reporting tools to higher management. The "performance dashboards" developed by Chris Meyer are an excellent example of this type of self-generated measurement system.

To develop the measures that will inform their actions, teams may need the help of measurement experts or some basic training in the construction of useful measurement systems. At Johnsonville Foods, Management Information Systems was renamed "Member Information Systems." The name provides a constant reminder that the staff reports to local units, not to senior management.

The U.S. Army has led the way in this quadrant with its "After Action Reviews," meetings held after a campaign or practice session to draw forth key observations and indicators. British Petroleum has a similar process, called "completion meetings." A project is not considered "done" until people have articulated the lessons learned, action points for the future (with a person assigned to be accountable for each), and quantification of key internal measures (completion time, degree under budget, satisfaction ratings, and time spent for critical path items). Discussions of these items include all team members, the project leader, and often a key customer. These facilitated "lessons learned" meetings last from half an hour to half a day, depending upon the number of people and scope. When projects are lengthy, BP holds these meetings every six months.

⟩⟩ See "Performance Dashboards," page 313 and the Army's After-Action Reviews, page 470.

Rerferences on authority to take responsible action include "Organizational learning: A guide for executives in technology-critical organizations," by G. P. Huber (1996: *IJTM Special Publication on Unlearning and Learning* Vol.11, Nos. 7/8); and "How the right measures help teams excel," by Chris Meyer, 1994, *Harvard Business Review*.

PUTTING IT ALL TOGETHER

Many organizations already pursue some parts of this cycle in isolation. They set up an intranet, "so everyone can learn from everybody." But then they don't set up a governance structure that allows people the autonomy to act on what they've learned. Only when the full cycle is connected together, can an organization-wide system emerge that embodies learning in the way it changes itself.

This "self-changing" system operates very differently from the typical ways that most people expect companies to change. The organizational members are all involved in generating information, integrating it into the big picture, making sense of it, and deciding how to act. They instigate change, because they are themselves the learners, rather than being the passive recipients of someone else's learning. The system helps them continuously develop the judgment to handle complex situations, without waiting for instructions from above. The system also provides the checks and balances that keep unrealistic or frivolous ideas from sweeping the organization. Ideas are subjected to multiple perspectives; they are challenged and assessed, no matter what their origin. They come to fruition as the collective "makes sense" of them.

Organizational learning is powerful precisely because it represents a fundamental change in our beliefs about who holds knowledge—and, by extension, about who holds power. There are no more thinkers, separate from doers; all doers are thinkers. Just as the individual learning cycle is a gateway to a more effective, more enjoyable life, the organizational learning cycle provides organizations with a far more healthy, and self-generating, way to be.

3 BP's Pacesetter Network

British Petroleum's global infrastructure for learning across five continents

Humberto Vainieri, Robert Hanig, Rick Porter, Alan Thomas, Paul Monus

We wish to thank John Williams and Colin Reid, business unit managers at the Grangemouth (Scotland) refinery, who contributed their time to helping shape and develop this article.

Linking refineries on six continents, the highly innovative British Petroleum "Pacesetter" program is a global infrastructure for generating and sharing knowledge and information for performance improve-

ment, closely linked to BP's new governance structure for refineries. It provides a way for people throughout the BP system to build upon one another's successes with change, learning, and quality initiatives. All of the refineries choose the depth and breadth of their involvement. In this roundtable, we hear from five people: Humberto Vainieri, vice president at British Petroleum, architect of the Pacesetter program; Robert Hanig, the Innovation Associates consultant who helped develop Pacesetter's approach to organizational learning; Alan Thomas, business unit leader of Nerefco, the refinery in the Netherlands, and convener of the European peer group; Rick Porter, business manager at BP's Toledo, Ohio refinery; and Paul Monus, one of the members of the Pacesetter coaches team.

SETTING UP THE PACESETTER NETWORKS

Humberto Vainieri: 1995 was a very bad year in the refining industry, with worldwide overcapacity. Our only viable alternative was to find a way to turn all our refineries into "pacesetters"—an industry standard term for the highest-performing plants. In a strategy session with the Executive Committee, we agreed to a concerted effort to change our working practices at the fourteen refining sites that BP operated around the world. BP had already achieved some success with organizational learning in our exploration and production businesses, but this would take place at a much larger scale. The committee gave us approval in July 1996, and asked me to lead the Pacesetter project.

We started by convening the refinery managers in London. There was little buy-in for Pacesetter or for organizational learning. Yet the refinery managers all had a powerful incentive to be interested. Shortly before, there had been a major governance restructuring; instead of being cost centers, refineries would now be business units, with bottom line responsibility for all the returns on their investments. They needed help making this transition, but they were also under such short-term financial pressure that it was easy for them to refuse any training or consultation we offered.

But they unanimously agreed that they wanted ownership of change efforts at their sites; they wanted to tailor and control them. This led to our proposal: For the first year, we would provide and pay for training, coaching, and consultation by request. If they didn't want it, that was fine; they would have to come up with their own way of boosting performance. If they invited us, we would come to their facility. Now I found myself in an uncomfortable position. The executive committee expected results, but I was not in control. I had to create pull, relying on the personal relationships that I had developed with the business unit leaders, and on my ability to exercise influence. I visited each refinery with a presentation for the management team, hoping to break the ice.

Robert Hanig: Most of these sessions at the refineries were spent in conversation, working with the management teams figure out their priorities. I think we gave an honest impression that: "We don't know for sure if this is the right thing to do. However, you do need to boost performance in some way. Let's find out together if this approach will work." We thus consciously emulated the kind of reflective, participative process that we were recommending. Our level of availability—we were ready to travel at short notice to any location—also showed our level of commitment.

Vainieri: There were three groups of people, all interrelated:

1. The core team was composed of two or three representatives from each refinery; they had to enroll not only their business unit managers, but their peer groups. In effect, each site had its own core team. They all met together, once or twice a year, in a network to support each other.
2. The central support team consisted of the facilitators and internal consultants who were involved in training and other support.
3. The Global Refinery Network (GRN), composed of all the site managers from around the world, was first a vehicle for mutual support and gradually for governance. Managers at refineries are jointly accountable for their performance, and they use GRN to keep each other aware of new approaches and to put pressure on one another. The GRN evolved into peer groups, which are the core of the performance management process for refining in BP.

Paul Monus: Each site developed its own pilot projects. Some plants discovered that painting, cleaning, paving potholes, and making the equipment tidy was the highest-leverage action they could take. Others focused on the behavior of the supervisors as a group. And at other sites, like Kwinana in Australia, they began looking systematically at the tension between the central control building and the rest of the refinery. (One factor turned out to be the physical distance of the various parts of the plant from one another.)

Hanig: The GRN members wanted to get to know one another as a group of peers. So we met in situations where they could spend social time together. This began to enhance their level of communication, not only at their meetings, but throughout the year. They agreed to always be available to one another, whether in a meeting or for visits and phone calls in between, so that they could behave more and more like a team of people, even though each had a separate refinery to lead.

THE VIEW FROM THE REFINERIES

Alan Thomas: In 1996, within my first three months of being business unit leader, we decided to close two of our three sites. This was a considerable challenge: Lay off 350 people, move three sites into one, and keep everybody in a reasonable frame of mind and looking forward. About that time, we got our offer to take part in Hum's Pacesetter project.

We applied the techniques and methods we learned from Pacesetter to our negotiations with the union, and the Dutch Works Council. We closed the site approximately twelve months sooner than we'd hoped, without loss of business opportunity. We have found jobs for 140 people of the 200 that we laid off and continue to work with the remaining people to find suitable new jobs. We got agreement from the government to make voluntarily redundant a group of ninety-odd people—no mean achievement in this part of the world. And we are commissioning a new hydrofiner that will come in 10 percent under budget and six weeks ahead of the original Pacesetter schedule. We haven't killed anyone, we haven't blown anything up, and we set the seeds for a positive commitment to the future, despite all those changes. I would say, we've had a bit of success.

Had we not had the Pacesetter infrastructure—both the training and the contact with other managers—we would have progressed toward the same goals at Nerefco. But we wouldn't have been aware of the techniques of organizational learning, and we would certainly not have spent as much time engaging the total organization in producing a vision. I think the process would have been a lot more difficult.

Rick Porter: Most needed, here at Toledo, was the idea of looking outside what we were doing—looking at other people's ideas and trying to incorporate the things that would work here. In the past, our culture never looked outside the refinery for ways to do things better. Instead, all the energy here was spent defending our current approaches. This is a truly high-tech refinery, and most of our people had tremendous levels of technical training and experience; they could not be replaced. They had to be induced to change themselves.

Many "silver bullet" programs had been attempted in the past: culture change, reengineering, reorganizations. I had to bring in something more fundamental. To make it work, the other senior leaders and I had to first earn some respect in order to get our people to listen to our ideas.

We billed Pacesetter as low-key training: "This is not a significant change; we're just going to give people new skills for the way they interact with people, or how they approach their job." Our management team went first. The union would not initially participate, because they assumed we wanted to increase productivity so we could cut jobs. We had to be explicit about our goals: to create a work environment that people would want to come to. Once the union started participating, they discovered that the reflection and inquiry tools are effective in managing meetings, and they are now using them. We now have a variety of teams using these tools, from shut-down teams to union committees, all setting an example.

Knowing that I'm one of BP's best experts on refinery operation, it's hard for people to believe that I'm not going to give them the answers. But I try very hard not to. I tell people, "I don't run anything here. Give me some guidance on how I can help you be effective, and I'll do whatever I can, but it's your job, not mine." Obviously, if I see something done wrong that's significant, I will stop it. But in most cases, I'll let wrong answers occur for a while, as part of a process for developing the capability of the people.

Over the past four years, this refinery has sustained improvements of around $100 million. Over the next couple of years, we hope to generate another $70 million. Is it because of Pacesetter, *per se*? We don't care. We're in touch closely enough with the organization that precise measurements about the Pacesetter program would be a hindrance.

THE FIVE PACESETTER "KEY SUCCESS FACTORS"

Several Innovation Associates consultants took part in the development of these key success factors: Michael Goodman, Cliff Bolster, and Sue Thomson.

Monus: What would we actually measure if we wanted to know whether Pacesetter was making progress? These five domains of change seem like the most compelling factors:

- **Pull.** How many people are asking for help? How eager are they to pay for it beyond their established budget?
- **Spread.** What percentage of people have been exposed to concepts such as the learning disciplines? Two? Eight? Twenty? Forty per cent? This measure doesn't tell whether people like the ideas or found them convincing; only that they have been exposed to them.

- **Internalization.** This is a measure of capacity development, gathered primarily through surveys and interviews. Someone might say, "I liked the idea of talking about assumptions, but I wasn't very graceful. I was like a bull in a china shop, and I made people angry." That person would score 2 or 3 on an internalization metric. To develop this metric, you need to give people a guide to different levels of proficiency, so they know how to score themselves.

- **Alignment.** Are people pulling in different directions, or moving together? This can be measured through diagnostics: for instance, if the site leadership team can (or can't) agree on critical priorities. If disparate working teams start to blend into cross-functional teams, that's another sign of alignment.

- **Sustainability.** You know that a project is no longer "flavor of the month" when you can count incidents of people incorporating new techniques into their work.

⟩⟩ Also see Chapter 8, on measurement and assessment, page 281.

THE FUTURE OF PACESETTER

Vainieri: At the end of 1997, Pacesetter became self-supporting; local sites must pay for all costs, including training, themselves. In retrospect, we did not prepare people enough to manage this in a smooth way, and some training projects were abruptly cut. But the Pacesetter infrastructure does continue, the support remains enthusiastic, and the improvements have continued to be dramatic. In our first year, 1996, we barely exceeded our performance target; in 1997, we doubled it. Now, in 1998, we're averaging well above 20 cents per barrel improvement per year, which means $50 million annual net income gains.

Under the stress of the 1998 drop in the price of oil, we will undoubtedly revert in some places to old behaviors. But by and large, our behavior under stress shows that we are a very different organization than we were three years ago. The Pacesetter project in itself is not spoken of as a project anymore; it is part of what we do. As refinery business units report their performance, they include a line item describing their pacesetter improvements. The most important factor remains the same: to create an environment, systemwide, in which people do it themselves.

This article was developed and completed before the British Petroleum/Amoco merger, which was announced as we were going to press.

4 The School for Managing

Peter Block

Bestselling author of Flawless Consulting, The Empowered Manager, *and* Stewardship, *Peter Block has reinvented himself throughout his career, from manager to trainer to consultant to author. Now, he's reinvented a way of bringing people together across the boundaries of their organizations. Block is the codeveloper of a school where people can go to study emerging approaches to management as part of a living, learning, cross-organizational community of practice. Organized under the auspices of the Association for Quality and Participation, the school takes life wherever its students and faculty can come together. Anyone developing an effective infrastructure for learning across organizational boundaries will deal with the issues that Peter and his colleagues are dealing with here.*

After twenty years in the consulting field, it seemed to me that most change efforts were cosmetic. I had seen too many times when consultants believing in empowerment would develop communication and team skills without ever talking about the real issues preventing change—the distribution of wealth and power in the system, or the prevalent unwillingness to question the organization's purpose. Consultants aligned with top management were like missionaries who went into native regions and taught them Spanish or English so they could adapt more easily to the conquering colonial powers.

I had an image in mind of genuine empowerment. It would begin with an organization's executives telling the truth. They would say, "We know that we senior managers are partly responsible for creating the problems here. But we don't quite know what to do about it. And we don't know what's going to happen. We're going to start by giving you choices over aspects of the business you never had before, and the information you need to understand the business a little bit better." It would then move into a form of democracy—a genuine self-organizing system, in which new projects emerged naturally and spontaneously, in which people were treated like adults, and were capable of exercising control over their lives. This organization would not be composed of leaders and followers, but of self-aware, committed citizens who came together to work together.

See Flawless Consulting: A Guide to Getting Your Expertise Used, *by Peter Block (Los Angeles: Pfeiffer & Co., 1981);* The Empowered Manager: Positive Political Skills at Work, *by Peter Block (San Francisco: Jossey-Bass, 1987); and* Stewardship, *by Peter Block (San Francisco: Berrett-Koehler, 1993).*

For more information about the School for Managing, contact the Association for Quality and Participation, Cincinnati, Ohio, at 1-800-733-3310 or http://www.aqp.org/sfm.html.

I knew, of course, that most senior executives, subordinates, and consultants are not prepared for an organization that functions as a democracy, any more than citizens of a totalitarian state are prepared for a rapid transition to a republic. Most subordinates, for instance, don't want to hear that the boss doesn't have the answers. They want to be told, "We have a plan for you. We can't reveal it at the moment, but we will take care of you." When they are urged to communicate and learn with their peers, instead of waiting for information to travel up and down the hierarchy, they say, "We didn't come here to pool ignorance." (And why, I want to know, does everyone in that organization think their peers are ignorant? Where does that dark view of people come from?)

So I decided to create a school that would teach people how to create a different kind of organization by being an example, in itself, of one. Cathy Kramer of the Association for Quality and Participation suggested that it should be an in-depth school for self-organizing management skills, and we started by enlisting a faculty. I made ten phone calls, and nine people said they would take part.

Our first rule flew in the face of conventional training practice: *Require a long-term commitment.* Workshops would take place over nine months, not one week. The skills of freedom and citizenship can't be learned quickly, or in an isolated, fragmented fashion. This meant we had to hold sessions where we had extensive interest, and where people were willing to return month after month.

During our first year, we fell prey to the structure of our profession. Each of the ten faculty members parachuted in, one after another, to teach their part of the school. None of us learned anything. "For me to get interested," said Kathie Dannemiller, one of the faculty, "I need to do this *with* someone." This led to our second rule: *Do not segregate the "experts" from one another.* The faculty must show up for all others' sessions, be willing to integrate their thinking with that of others, and be willing to change their minds.

For years, all of us had preached that whole teams should do whole work, without fragmenting into silos and stovepipes—and yet in our teaching and consulting, we were all over the management map, with very little communication among us. Some of us taught self-organization systems, others taught empowerment, others taught structure and systems, others taught business literacy or deep personal destiny. Now, with all of us together, we had the moral authority to insist on a third rule: *Tie all our endeavors to real-life needs.* Students could only attend as part of a team working on real issues, with at least three levels (executives, managers, and workers) represented on each team. Organizational citizenship could not be practiced only by one or two levels of society; managers could not learn to manage without workers in the room. Our teams now became microcosms—grains of sand that contained the universe of work that people were learning about.

A fourth rule naturally followed: *No one is exempt from learning.* The faculty must go through the course as participants every time. Whatever we had students do, we would do ourselves. To be sure, I've grown tired about talking about my personal ups and downs, but if we demand personal introspection from the students, I've got to take part myself. This also helps us avoid the terrible professional trap that Ivan Illich and John McKnight have noted, in which professionals conduct needs analyses, identifying other people's problems as "needs," in a way that creates more reliance on the professionals.

With all of this give and take between faculty and students, a fifth rule became essential: *The school must demonstrate the principles.* If we were to teach the ambiguity of democracy, and the messiness of self-organization, then we would have to experience it ourselves. As part of our courses, we held continual dialogues about the purpose of the school. What were we here for? What mattered to us?

By the second afternoon of class, students realize that this is not a typical school environment. They've paid good money, ostensibly for training in management skills, but none of the teachers have the answers. They're in a messy, self-organizing learning structure, which likely as not is not going well. We aim for an environment where people feel safe having the kinds of "airplane conversations" in which you bare your soul to a stranger whom you will never meet again—like a seatmate on an airplane flight—but, in this case, you will be working with your "seatmates" for months and maybe longer.

We explicitly recognize that building a capacity for change means recognizing, at times, the tragic aspects of work life: Failure. Burnout. Losing people. Stress. When things change, something is going to die. If you don't have room to give up parts of life, you can become a prisoner of your own success. And if some amount of frustration or discomfort is not present in the classroom, then people will not learn to deal with the emotional tension. *As educators, we can't ignore the realities, but we can give people a safe place in which to talk and think about them.* No one in our class can expect to be told, by an instructor, "Don't worry; you're going to be okay. It's going to work out." If they turn themselves over to that kind of reassurance, how can they be truly free?

See, for example, *Toward a History of Human Needs*, by Ivan Illich (Berkeley: Heyday Books, 1977).

We agonize about marketing the school, precisely because it is so authentic. How do we describe it? Can we tell people the truth about the school and get people to come? How can we tell them that democracy doesn't produce predictable outcomes? Perhaps there's another implicit rule: *Only people who deeply want to attend should attend.* We want people to attend despite the fact that they know, sometimes, they won't be comfortable.

To be sure, we do have results to point to. A team of "graduates" from Blue Cross/Blue Shield went back and convened 200 people to talk about customer service quality, with highly powerful results. On the other hand, some "graduates" report that they have, indeed, changed their behavior, "but it hasn't touched the organization yet."

But the more significant result (as we enter our fifth year) is the change in the school itself: Faculty and student members feel responsible for the overall well-being of the enterprise. You can see it in the way people complain, speak up, and stand up: "This isn't right." They no longer passively accept our "teaching." They devise tasks; they set the school's direction. They demand our best.

5 Bootstrap Principles

A set of guiding ideas for designing computer-based systems to scale up the learning organization

Douglas Engelbart and Christina Engelbart

The technological innovations developed by Douglas Engelbart— including the "desktop" graphic user interface, the mouse, and the computer conferencing system—were all originally conceived as tools that would make human beings become more effective learners. In this contribution, Doug and his daughter, research scientist Christina Engelbart, apply their combined 70 years of experience with "augmenting learning" to the problem of scaling up innovation.

The Engelbarts have created and direct the "Bootstrap Institute," a research center for fostering networks of improvement: For more information, see the Institute's Web site: *http://www.boot strap.org*. The issues and principles dealt with here are discussed there in much more depth.

As computer technologies continually become smaller, faster, and cheaper, organizational leaders are going to try to expand the "reach" and "breadth" of their systems accordingly. But this will often lead to counterintuitive, unintended consequences. Imagine a mosquito expanded to ten times its original scale. Instinctively, we assume that it would continue functioning as a mosquito, only larger. Perhaps it might buzz off to terrorize a dog. But in fact, the creature would instantly collapse as different aspects of its body expanded with different effects. Its muscles, whose strength depends on their two-dimensional cross-section area, would become 100 times stronger. But its overall cubic body volume (and, thus, its weight) would increase by 1,000. The mosquito could no longer carry its own weight. Nor could it count on finding the same type of food with a stinger magnified at least tenfold.

We've already seen a similar dynamic in the explosive growth of e-mail, voicemail, and the World Wide Web. People can now reach 100 times more people in the course of a day. But the skills of social bonding —the skills needed to have a high-quality conversation in a team producing result—have hardly increased at all in many organizations. The result is disproportionate increases in scale, with more and more people contacting each other, but less and less chance to think and reflect.

The development of knowledge infrastructure can't ignore these kinds of subtle realities. Here are some principles for designing and using technologies in ways that augment human capabilities, instead of undermining them.

The Engelbarts and others are developing a prototype conceptual model for this kind of knowledge base. It is called CoDIAK, which stands for Concurrently Developing, Integrating, and Applying Knowledge. They are interested in colloquy with others around the potential mutual influence of organizational learning and dynamic libraries. For an overview and further reference, see *http://www.fieldbook. com/engelbart.html*.

- **Support the transition from passive "documents" to active "knowledge bases."** Reports, Web sites, project plans, and other documents are evolving into dynamic knowledge bases. These will rove the networks, picking up and filtering knowledge from the outside world relevant to their workgroup's purpose, integrating that material into a continually evolving library, and continually learning from their users. The choices that members of the group make, the topics they choose to look at closely, and the questions they ask of the document will all continually refine the knowledge repository's internal commands. The knowledge base will become a mirror for self-knowledge and a form of living memory. It could help people see patterns in the information requests that they, and their group, have made over the past year. The net result could be far greater longevity, diversity, and value in a workgroup's collective thinking.

- **Build in bootstrapping capabilities.** An information exchange system should handle three types of management activity. First, there's the activity needed to run the organization: product R&D, marketing, manufacturing, sales, accounting, and so on. Second, there's the work needed to improve the organization's capabilities. Much of the work of the quality movement, of *The Fifth Discipline* and *The Fifth Discipline Fieldbook*, falls in this domain. But there's also a third category, overlooked in most organizations: improving your ability to improve. This might involve developing a series of pilot group experiments with various organizational change strategies, to see which one has the greatest leverage for success. If you are a line leader or an executive leader, it's helpful to ask yourself: "What percentage of my organization's resources do I want to spend on each activity?" Is it appropriate to spend 20 percent improving your ability to produce results? Can you afford to spend less than 5 percent improving your ability to improve?

- **Provide real-time reflective feedback.** Research on voice recognition suggests that computers will be able to recognize and record natural speech to a startlingly accurate degree within a few years. This offers enormous potential for transcribing meetings as they take place, and recouping missed connections and unpursued "undiscussables." This technology would provide enormous value for coaching, mentoring, teaching, commenting on the past, collaborating on documents, or simply learning from observation of one another's actions.

- **Include outsiders.** During the mid-1980s, while helping some McDonnell-Douglas executives reconsider their information system designs, I saw that tens of thousands of separate companies—joint-venture partners, subcontractors, suppliers, and customers—were intimately involved in knowledge exchange around the aircraft they were building. Why not include them in the "knowledge base?" McDonnell-Douglas didn't take that unconventional step, but it might plausibly have saved millions of dollars in billing and information costs and led to unprecedented innovation. Today, the need to include these "outsiders" in "in-house" knowledge exchange is even more compelling. Companies that think of themselves as self-contained will not be able to compete. It is particularly important to include the first tier of suppliers, who actively contribute to the design of new technology. This means promoting high "interoperability": your computer system works effectively, at high speeds, with the greatest number of computers, workstations, servers, software, and communications devices owned by your many partners.

- **Make information more transparent.** Innovation often comes from taking an idea across disciplinary boundaries. Yet, as one Rand Cor-

As an example of interoperability issues: If any one software package (such as Microsoft Word) dominates a technical category (such as document development), this could make it difficult to guarantee future openness to the range of companies and individuals who need to join a knowledge base. For more about the implications for (and of) interoperability, and for more on other issues raised by this article, also see *http://www.fieldbook.com/engelbart.html*.

poration study of multidisciplinary research discovered, the conceptual barriers against this type of innovation are immense. Bring professionals from different backgrounds and fields of study together, and they all look at the problem differently, with no common language for bridging the gap. But you can design your systems to make it easier to develop that common language, continually incorporating and updating definitions and commentary that help people come up to speed when they enter, and express their insights coherently.

■ **Encourage research-oriented links between high-performance teams and the outside world.** Management research should not take place in remote universities, but in experiments on real business issues. That sort of research happens rarely now, because there is no infrastructure for communicating among the pilot outposts, and keeping them in touch with each other on an ongoing basis. Experimenters have no easy way to compare notes with each other, and with academics, to generalize from their activity. They need to establish links with people in other organizations and with some oddballs who do not work for any organization at all.

All of the technologies described in this article exist in incomplete or prototype versions today. All of them will be increasingly prevalent. Will they be used to help networks of committed people bootstrap their collective capabilities? Or will they be used to reinforce entrenched and outmoded organizational methods and practices? In the choices you make today, you can shape the way they evolve.

6 On-line Engagement

Managing computer networks for "the dance of change"

Lisa Kimball, Eric Best, Howard Rheingold, Liz Rykert, Rick Karash, Graham Galer, and Art Kleiner

Computer-mediated communication—electronic mail, computer conferences, Web sites, intranets—seems like a natural way to build bridges between far-flung people in an organization. People can "log in" whenever they want, from anywhere in the world, at any time of day or night, keeping up with group ideas and feelings in depth. It costs far less—in both money and time—than travel. And it gives people a chance to raise issues at a more leisurely, thoughtful pace than most face-to-face meetings permit.

As an active computer communications user since 1979 (when common modems ran at1/100th of today's speed), I've seen firsthand the power of electronic discussions. But I've also seen the pitfalls—for instance, the hyped-up ways that computer technology is sold, the thoughtless ways it is often implemented, the lack of attention to helping people get used to the new media, and the sheer drain on people's time. Many business people now average 120 to 150 e-mails on a heavy day, and some receive as many as 1,000!

How, then, can a pilot group (or a company) design and implement its electronic media to foster genuine communication—the kinds of in-depth conversations that bridge the "chimneys and stovepipes" of an organization—or in the world at large? With the help of Rick Karash, I convened an on-line roundtable of computer network luminaries, all with years of in-depth experience linking people together. Here are some of their suggestions. — Art Kleiner

Lisa Kimball (computer conferencing designer and facilitator, Metasystems Design Group): Being on-line was never about accessing information for me, no matter how much great stuff gets loaded up on the Web. It's about access to people.

For the on-line facilitator, time serves some of the same functions that physical space provides in a face-to-face meeting. For example, we organize seasonal "salon" conferences (one opens on the first day of each new season). We have an introductions ritual in that conference. We have other monthly and yearly events. People can engage at different levels of intensity at different times and still feel like full members of the community, without a guilt trip about not logging on "enough."

Eric Best (scenario planner, Morgan Stanley): Success with "virtual teams" depends a great deal on whether face-to-face work is well integrated into the on-line work. Otherwise, a distributed, discontinuous conversation becomes truncated chatter.

Howard Rheingold (author of *The Virtual Community* and *Tools for Thought*, founder of the Electric Minds Web-based community): The best possible scenario: A group with a common purpose and well-defined common goal meets together in person first. They meet in per-

This is a brief excerpt from a much longer roundtable, available on-line at: *http://www.field book.com/online.html*. In this excerpt, we focus primarily on nontechnical issues of interest to a general business and learning-oriented audience. Thus, we don't go into the relative merits (for example) of electronic mail and computer conferencing for learning-oriented discussions. We would like to thank the participants in the original roundtable: Jennifer Stone Gonzalez, Lisa Kimball, Howard Rheingold, Liz Rykert, Rick Karash, Graham Galer, Peter and Trudy Johnson-Lenz, Eric Best, Jessica Lipnack, and Jeffrey Stamps. We especially wish to thank Rick Karash, host and moderator of "learning-org," for helping to design and organize the e-mail system that supported this conversation.

For further information on networks within organizations, see *The 21st Century Intranet*, by Jennifer Stone Gonzalez (Englewood Cliffs, NJ: Prentice-Hall, 1997). For the use of on-line networks with teams located across great distances, see *Virtual Teams*, by Jessica Lipnack and Jeffrey Stamps (New York: John Wiley & Sons, 1997). For an in-depth introduction to facilitation, especially for nonprofits, see *Working Together Online* by Maureen James and Liz Rykert (Toronto: Web Networks, 1997, http://www.web.net). And for a general guide to the on-line world and its ramifications for community and discourse, see *The Virtual Community* by Howard Rheingold (Reading, MA: Addison-Wesley, 1993). On-line networks mentioned in this article include Metasystems Design Group (http://www.mdg.net), the Whole Earth 'Lectronic Link (http://www.well.com), the River conferencing system (http://www.river.org), and "learning-org" (see page 459). Since this field changes so rapidly, we have opted not to include reviews of books or other resources in this book. See our Web page, http://www.fieldbook.com/online-revs.html for more detail.

son again, every six or twelve months. In between face-to-face meetings, having some knowledge of one another as flesh and blood humans, a great deal can be accomplished on-line. They can become great information hunter-gatherers for one another, finding and posting links and tidbits that they think would benefit the group.

The facilitator, moderator, or host will be perceived as an authority figure, and will be challenged. How the host deals with early challenges determines how the rest of the discourse will go. And of course, real-world power dynamics don't disappear on-line. If your boss or your subordinate is in the conversation, then there are real constraints on how open you will all feel about frank discussions.

The limitations of the medium, in which people communicate only through their words, mask a great deal, including their assumptions. This masking can be beneficial. It enables people to state things they might be too timid to state in person, and to take their time and think about their contributions. But it is very easy for people to misunderstand one another. People can be ruder to one another than they would be in person. A good on-line conversation requires attention by someone who is experienced in this kind of discourse, and committed to painstakingly work through the obstacles.

Liz Rykert (on-line designer/facilitator, coauthor of *Working Together Online*): As an on-line facilitator, I write occasional postings designed to bring newcomers up to speed, saying "Welcome," and "Here is what has transpired so far." People need to feel safe in an on-line discussion area. I try to surface the implicit aspects of group behavior and help them tap into the "know" of the group—what is expected of them, who to turn to for advice, and how to join in. For example, in busy on-line workspaces, people agree that silence on a proposed action means agreement—if you don't speak out, you agree. This saves multiple "yup" postings and time. But it also means that those who fail to read and respond must learn to "live" with the final approval of decisions.

Graham Galer (developed the on-line conferencing system at Royal Dutch/Shell Group Planning): You can keep in touch with each member of the group individually by the on-line equivalent of "passing notes under the table." Handled with tact, this is a very useful skill in keeping the group together.

Art Kleiner: On the WELL computer conferencing system, there is a "politics" conference rife with adamant libertarians, Berkeley liberals, neo-conservatives—every political stripe. Amid vicious debate, people would occasionally reveal the underlying assumptions that led them to their positions. It occurred to me that a skillful on-line moderator, using the inquiry skills of the "mental models" discipline, could bring the assumptions behind many "hot" topics—like, say, racism, education reform, or the free market—to the surface. People would respond with more depth and reflection than they ever would in a face-to-face debate, with its limited "air time" and need for instant response.

Inspired by that idea, Faith Florer and I started a conference called "inquiry" on the River conferencing system in 1993. This self-selected group of about thirty people discussed anything under the sun, always seeking to understand the forces, attitudes, and reactions, that had led us to our points of view. We resolved not to pass judgment on each other. Instead, we tried to "suspend assumptions" and deliberately asked questions like: "What leads you to believe . . . ?"

"Inquiry" lasted two years. It was fascinating; I've rarely learned so much from a single experience, about myself or other people. But it was an exhausting conference to run, requiring hours of time each week. As moderators, Faith and I had to provide an ever-present model of "reflective inquiry," even when we had to deal with "hijackers" who wanted to impose their bullying on the conference. The approach worked—as long as someone was willing to keep returning to the technique, consistently prompting people to listen and go deeper, instead of "spouting off" from the top of their heads.

HTTP://WWW.LEARNING-ORG.COM

Probably the most effective place to raise questions, or test ideas about the concepts in *The Fifth Discipline*, *The Fifth Discipline Fieldbook*, this book, or organizational learning in general. About a dozen messages will arrive each day in your e-mail queue, with a readership of several hundred people, all vetted by Rick Karash, who eliminates duplication, chastises the disrespectful, and adds occasional references. People who feel lonely in their organization will find compatriots here. — Art Kleiner

7 Learning Histories
Creating a reflective infrastructure

George Roth and Art Kleiner

How many times have organizations innovated locally—yet, despite enormous expenditures in training and development, failed to "roll out" those innovations? How many times have organizations let promising new techniques and capabilities, developed within the company, slip away without replicating the innovators' success? It's hard to know the answer, because most lost opportunities remain undocumented. The innovations become unintentional secrets, known only to close associates of the people involved in these initiatives. This is deeply unfortunate for companies as a whole. If people could build upon one another's collective experience in some reliable way, then new groups of innovators could stand on the shoulders of those who had gone before.

Learning histories were developed to address this fundamental need, in a way consistent with the nature of organizational learning. A "learning history" is a document that tells a critical organizational story in the words of many of the people involved, each with his or her own perspective. The document, whether available on paper or over an intranet, is a "transitional object"—an artifact that helps spark open-ended reflective conversations throughout the rest of the organization.

We create learning histories through a rigorous, multifaceted approach to story "getting" and storytelling. This approach brings together techniques and theories from social science research, theater, anthropology, oral history, process consultation, and journalism. We gather material primarily through reflective interviews, glean the themes of the story from the interviews, and painstakingly check quotes (although they are all anonymous, they must appear credible to readers.) The writing weaves together people's comments in a flow that calls to mind a tribal gathering—a group of people sitting around a campfire, each with his or her own piece of the narrative to offer. We use a two-column format so that we can place this narrative side by side with critical commentary and questions, written to help the reader think about why these particular quotes were chosen, and what they might mean.

After the document is finished, we do not hand it out as a report, to sit on a manager's shelf. Instead, we take advantage of the gossip and buzz that have been building through the organization during our interviewing phase. We conduct "dissemination" workshops, somewhat like reading groups. People who are trying to undertake change efforts meet together for two or three hours in a reflective conversation, talking about the pitfalls and challenges that faced the group whose story is told in the learning history. Because they have a common in-depth record in front of them, they can talk about not just what the innovators did, but what they were thinking, how they felt, how they perceived their challenges, and how they responded. They can create their own theory about the critical factors in the story. They can ask questions like these: "Which influences, decisions, and actions made the most difference, positively or negatively, in the story we've read? Which would make a difference in our situation? And how might we do things differently?"

A learning history may be used to assess the impact and value of a profound change initiative, but it is more elaborate than a conventional assessment. It is more like a full-scale strategic consultation, except that the organization is consulting to itself. Most organizations, we have found, already know the answers to the problems facing them. The answers are told in stories—at the water cooler or coffee pot, in the rest room, in late-night "watering holes" and in the car pool. Unfortunately, the stories that pass around informally only provide one or two points of view. With learning histories, organizational stories are told in depth from a variety of perspectives, with various listeners distilling their own theories and precepts for action from the "data" of the narrative.

Learning histories are so elaborate that they are often overkill for pilot groups—who can reflect together with an exercise like the history map (page 186). Instead, we aim them at the rest of the organization, particularly at managers who would like to foster a similar approach elsewhere. We also try to make them useful to researchers and students of management outside the company, eager to learn from stories of genuine innovation told in depth.

Since 1994, learning histories have been undertaken to recount and evaluate a variety of episodes: team learning efforts, corporatewide "transformations," consulting efforts (evaluated by major consulting firms), government-funded programs, and international political movements. Each new learning history produces its own new "themes"—its own story lines about the dynamics of that organization. But some themes continue popping up, again and again, common to a wide variety of change and learning initiatives. Here are two of the most common and (to our mind) the most interesting:

For the full theory and method of learning history work, see *Field Manual for a Learning Historian*, by George Roth and Art Kleiner (Cambridge, MA: Reflection Learning Associates, 1997); http://www.fieldbook.com/rla-manual.html.

The learning history form emerged from a group of researchers at MIT's Center for Organizational Learning, starting in 1994. We would like to credit and thank all the members of the group. We also wish to thank Peter Senge, Ed Schein, John van Maanen, Chris Argyris, Don Schön, and Anthony DiBella for their interest, critique, and encouragement; and we wish to thank the following learning historians who helped develop the practice and process: Linda Booth Sweeney, Hilary Bradbury, Marty Castleberg, Brenda Cruz, Faith Florer, Robert Frick, Judy Gilbert, Rik Glover, Toni Gregory, Hans Houshower, Terry Johnson, Nina Kruschwitz, Virginia O'Brien, Eric Siegel, Ann Thomas, John Voyer, Diane McGinty Weston, Kenlin Wilder, and JoAnne Wyer.

This excerpt is from *The Learning Initiative at Electro Components*, by Joanne Wyer, George Roth, and two "Electro Components" internal people, edited by Virginia O'Brien (Cambridge, MA: Society for Organizational Learning, 1997), pp. 37–39 and 50–53. Note: In adapting this excerpt for this book, some of the commentary notations (in the minor column) have been changed, and the quotations in the wider column are not necessarily in the original order.

"The Glass House"

During a transition from a hierarchical "command and control" organization to a more open enterprise, people naturally look to their bosses for direction—especially when it comes to implementing the new behaviors of profound change. But the bosses themselves are also wandering into uncharted territory. Not just the leader's actions, but his or her attitudes and conversations, are fully in view and open to critique, in a way that had never been an issue under the old system.

In this situation, leaders have to invent a kind of authentic, reflective, self-aware behavior on the fly, knowing they will be judged accordingly. In this story from the "Electro Components" learning history, a new course in dialogue skills is seen as the "president's baby." Its credibility rises and falls with the president's own level of openness. In this episode, he tries to force one of the factories to take part in a new learning initiative—in a way that backfires.

How much "backsliding" will subordinates accept from the leader of an organizational learning effort?

Management team member: There's been a tremendous change in the [president's] way of dealing with people. I have never seen anyone in my life change to the extent . . . He was a command-and-control manager and he has moved very hard to become a participative manager . . . It was very difficult for him to move toward true delegation of authority and decision making and let people make mistakes.

Another management team member: [The president's] own personal change process lagged behind what needed to happen. He takes a tremendous amount of coaching and facilitating on-line, to keep him from dominating. When people raise issues, if they're controversial to his own, he overreacts. Since he's been involved in learning work, he's listening better.

President: I believe the only way to build an infrastructure for organizational learning is to build it in the workplace, in the area where you want learning to occur. This means that if I didn't engage people in the factory, but only engaged people at headquarters, it would never happen. I insisted people at the factory be exposed to the work. In the beginning, the [factory manager] wouldn't let me. There was no time.

Note how the president's attribution of the factory manager's reason ("there was no time") was different from the factory manager's actual reason ("This would take us in the wrong direction"). Despite all the emphasis on open communication, the president may never have heard that comment from the factory manager directly.

I didn't want to push. It was always voluntary. But [later,] we had a pretty heated argument. He said to me, "It isn't that I don't want to do it. I just can't."

Factory manager: Getting involved with [the learning effort] might set the organization on its ear and take it in a totally wrong direction. I tend to deal in reality, and the reality of the situation is that we are an action-oriented organization. We're here to do the right thing for the organization, but I don't think [the learning organization consultants] know [our company], or vice versa.

Management team member: [The president] was giving [them] very significant autonomy in [managing the business] down there. On the other hand, he was driving these [new organizational learning] projects out of headquarters, which were perceived as evidence of either a conflicting or disingenuous position: "You say I'm empowered," the factory manager said, "but then you have guys coming down here and telling me exactly what I have to do, things that I'm not comfortable with, like learning. And on top of that, I've got to produce, more than I've ever produced." So there were a lot of conflicting messages.

President: [In retrospect,] I was still driving the learning efforts forward instead of saying, "Okay, let's just quit for a while and see what happens." I had had such a strong belief in the [learning methods]. If this kind of work is stopped, restarting it is more time consuming, and the chances of success are going to be diminished.

The president's last comment implies that he now feels that "quitting for a while" would have been a better solution than the rancor that erupted, despite the diminished chances of success. Is that true? Were there no alternatives besides browbeating the factory manager or giving up? In the president's position, what might you have done?

"The Three Siblings"

When an organization undergoes sweeping change, we identified three types of reactions as people are asked to change. These are not to be confused with three types of people: Indeed, the reactions may coexist within a single person, among all age groups and all levels of the hierarchy. We label these reactions as if they were members of a single family:

1. The eldest sibling: Ambitious and responsible, climbing on the bandwagon of change (as soon as it becomes the established order), receiving rewards and recognition for new innovations.
2. The middle sibling: Committed to the idea of change, if only because "things will at last get better around here"; willing to take risks and experiment; but feeling, in the end, unrecognized and unrewarded.
3. The youngest sibling: Expecting to be protected, conscious of human needs and community, and resisting the upheaval of change.

Organizations in change, the learning histories suggest, can find huge leverage in recognizing the ideas and efforts of middle siblings. They are often cast, or cast themselves, as "cynics." They may not be as easy to

These excerpts from *Perspectives on Full-Scale Corporate Transformation: The "OilCo" Learning History,* by Art Kleiner, George Roth, Ann Thomas, Toni Gregory, Edward Hamell, and seven "OilCo" internal people; forthcoming in 1999 (New York: Oxford University Press), pp. 102–106. Note: In adapting this excerpt for this book, some of the commentary notations (in the minor column) have been changed, and the quotations in the wider column are not necessarily in the original order.

deal with as the "eldest siblings," who know how to "talk the talk" more consistently. But they often appear in the midst of change, trying to create good effect for the organization as a whole. They and the "elder sibling" achievers, often operate at one another's expense. How can they best be seen, heard, recognized, and involved—and what will be threatened in the process? A large leverage point in transformation exists as organizations are able to support, rather than undermine, the "middle sibling's" personal change process. Here are some excerpts from the "OilCo" learning history that reveal this dynamic:

This quote, from a refinery manager, describes one view of the three sibling attitudes: first the "lastborn," then the "middle," and then the "first-born" siblings. Other views might disagree, finding the "lastborn" more heroic—or might disagree that these three categories apply at all.

Manager, Oil Refining, OilCo: There are a few folks in OilCo that don't get it and don't really want to make an effort . . .

There's another group of folks who don't quite understand the corporate change yet. They would like to be there, but don't quite know how to get there. I worry for that group, because I get the feeling that somehow they will be left behind.

Some of those who "get it" might think they've got a corner on the knowledge, and that they know how to do it better than anybody else. This group will become the target of that feeling of superiority, which will split the company and really slow the transformation.

Manager, OilCo Consulting Services: We wanted to learn more about what it was like to win and keep business. So I worked at an [external] computer consulting company; OilCo paid my salary. The umbilical cord was cut to the point where I wasn't allowed to use OilCo resources, even to make sales. "What you have in your head is yours, but everything else is off-limits." I learned the power of my own network, being out there on my own trying to make business happen.

Sometimes, the perks and rewards granted to people with "firstborn" attitudes seem remarkable and refreshing; the old OilCo culture would never have permitted them.

Our current corporate travel policy says that we can't be reimbursed for health clubs or dog sitting. As we get into [new onsite] situations, long distances away, management is being receptive to these kinds of requests that a normal consulting firm grants. Five years ago, I would never have made those requests.

This manager felt subtly tracked into the "middle sibling" role. He faces a dilemma: How can I choose my fate at OilCo, when people have already decided who I am?

Manager: I think I have a good vision. But ultimately, no amount of arguing or logic will convince other people. There's so much ego, and when one person initiates something there tends to be an immune reaction, so I give up. After a while, you tend to push less, because you don't get positive response. There are a few other people I resonate with, people with creative ideas—and they're pushing less, too.

Grade 5, OilCo Consulting: William [a pseudonym] was my "answer person." I went to him whenever I needed to know something:

"William, what is this? William, what year did that happen?". . . He was a rock, the one who remembered the lawsuits and the old deals, and why they were important. There is nothing written down. All you have is people who remember.

But then William didn't get along with a new manager, and she traded him down to another office. And the work was graded lower than his current salary, so he's had to decide whether to leave or take a pay cut. He's in his fifties; he has one or two kids.

What are they going to do when they get rid of the "Williams" and nobody else remembers what they know?

Many people with "lastborn" attitudes have traditionally filled the informal role of providing "institutional memory." Now they are leaving. In their absence, who or what fills that role? Is it filled by information systems?

Research, mythic and pragmatic credibility

Themes like these are developed from the "ground up," in a process of distillation that involves three separate ways of looking at the world:

- **The research imperative:** Cultivating "loyalty to the data." In the highly charged political atmosphere of large organizations, the bias of any document—real or perceived—casts immediate doubt on its credibility. Thus, learning history work draws heavily upon social science traditions to establish the same sort of research legitimacy that would be expected from any academic study. For example, learning historians read through all documents and interview transcripts, coding "concepts" that emerge from the text and grouping them together in a way that draws key themes from the interview transcripts instead of from the biases of the learning historians. We also allow interviewees to choose the topics that they consider most important to talk about, which further frames the document as a work "by" the organization, not by the learning historians.

- **The mythic orientation:** Tapping into the heart of the story. Every story of significant change entails joy, anxiety, humor, honor, betrayal, grief, dignity, shame, and respect. These emotions need to come alive in the document, or it will not be meaningful. This is particularly important in corporations and large bureaucracies, which tend to be "mythically deprived"—starving for ways to make sense of their situation. In creating documents that people will read, we try to "step back from the facts" at various times, to appreciate the evocative heart of every theme. We write, read aloud, and revise vignettes and ask ourselves: Does our story ring true? Does it move us?

This approach to qualitative research is derived from the "grounded theory" research methodology, as described in *Basics of Qualitative Research: Grounded Theory Procedures and Techniques*, by Anselm Strauss and Juliet Corbin (Newbury Park, CA: Sage Press, 1990).

■ **The "pragmatic" orientation:** Developing sensitivity to the audience. People believe the best of themselves, no matter how others see them. They will not learn from a story that casts them as a villain, labels them as ignorant, or downplays their perspective. They will only draw value from the lessons they see as relevant. Thus, the learning historians take responsibility for the reactions of the audience. We try to orient ourselves to the values, needs, and reactions that people in the company will bring to the document. That's one reason why we include "insider" learning historians in all our interviewing, distillation, and editing. They know the organization's culture intimately. They can draw attention to seemingly innocuous phrases that will powerful reactions among the audience, and they can help us tone down (or tone up) the likely response.

We have learned, in creating learning histories, that it is extremely difficult (if not impossible) to hold more than one of these imperatives foremost in mind at any one time. Each requires a different way of thinking. You cannot focus on the heart of a mythic story—with no holds barred, as if it were written for your private journal—at the same time that you are pragmatically concerned about helping managers deal with their resistance. It is similarly difficult to focus on the minutiae of "research," triangulating the perspectives of many sources, at the same time that you are trying to distill a sense of the whole "mythic" forest. And when trying to take a "pragmatic" stance—to cater to the business audience, with its demands for brevity and directness—it's almost impossible to be fair to the wealth of detailed "research" data that you have uncovered. Thus, in learning history work, we "listen with three ears"—cycling steadily and regularly among all three perspectives. The more we practice them in succession, the stronger you become in each.

The learning history represents a bridge between disciplines that may, in the long run, make business management research more effective. Academic organizational researchers (whose work follows the research imperative closely) typically produce very reliable findings—but it is almost impossible to put them into action. Consultants (following the pragmatic imperative) know how to tell people "what they want to hear," but do not necessarily have much valid support for their recommendations. Literary artists, channeling the mythic imperative, tend to stay far away from corporate storytelling, because they assume they will not be heard. And managers look wherever they can for "answers," because they do not seem to have time to listen to the stories they need to hear.

Learning histories involve managers in all these ways of thinking, in a relatively painless way. They link the need for business results directly to the ability to generate a deeper understanding of "the forces at play in the system."

Using learning histories

You don't need to wait for a learning history about your own company. Indeed, some of the most effective sessions have used a relevant document from a different company. Because people feel more detached and remote from that group, they're more apt to feel comfortable applying insights from the learning history to their own situation. Pick one or two sections of a document relevant to your situation, ask everyone to read them, and then spend a half day talking through questions like these:

■ What happened? What is going on in this story? Who were the protagonists? What do you see taking place "between the lines"? What surprised them? What snared them? What propelled them? What are the critical comments in the story that can help us understand our own situation?

■ So what? How are this group's challenges similar to the challenges we face? How might we be surprised, snared, or propelled by similar forces?

■ What next? Seeing our own story from the outside (as if it were in the Learning History), what could we invent or create next? What criteria do we set? (How long to allow before seeing results, what results we expect to see, etc.) How will we know (feel, think) if it's going well? How will we know (feel, think) if it's going badly? How much do we care?

The learning history experience at Ford

Betsy Maxwell, Organizational learning manager, Ford and Visteon: I first noticed the value of learning histories when I was assigned to distribute one to new employees, to help orient them to a car production project. Their appreciation of it surprised me. For the first time, they felt forewarned about the steep challenges ahead of them. They were attuned to the importance of "walking the talk" as managers, and they knew better how to recognize trustworthiness in their own bosses.

The Learning Initiative at Electro Components, by Joanne Wyer, George Roth, et al. (Cambridge, MA: SoL, 1997). Tells the story of a dialogue project in an American subsidiary of a European company. Deals with the challenges of "Walking the Talk" (Chapter 6) and "True Believers and Nonbelievers" (Chapter 9).

Perspectives on Full-Scale Corporate Transformation: The "OilCo" Learning History, by Art Kleiner, George Roth, Ann Thomas, Toni Gregory, Edward Hamell, et al. (New York: Oxford University Press, 1999). Describes three years of full-scale organizational change, dealing with the challenges of "Relevance" (Chapter 5), "Governance" (Chapter 10), and "Strategy and Purpose" (Chapter 12).

The Learning Initiative at Mighty Motors, Inc., by Marty Castleberg, George Roth, et al. (Cambridge, MA: Society for Organizational Learning, 1997). Valuable for facing the first four challenges of this book ("Not Enough Time," "No Help," "Not Relevant," and "Walking the Talk," Chapters 3–6).

The learning history introduced them to some technical processes, such as prototyping. It made them feel (and act) less naïve.

We distributed the same learning history among a group of network leaders, reading one "bite-sized chunk" every other week and meeting to talk about it. We had expected the document to give us insight into the rest of Ford, and it did. There was also one chapter about the design of a learning lab, which only a few of us had been exposed to.

But the learning histories also surprised us by unearthing dysfunction in our own group. We, too, had leaders who sent ambiguous signals, and colleagues who were driven, by systemic forces, to work at cross-purposes. Talking about someone else's story, in that document, gave us a way to get outside our own emotions and go to a neutral spot and begin dealing with our own issues. We had more satisfying dialogues and fewer undiscussables.

Vic Leo, manager of the Ford Executive Development Center: The learning histories were important to Ford because very senior management read them, page by page. When I look back, they are the only reports we sent to senior management that I know were read in their entirety. That has helped us sustain our learning initiatives. We are not looked at as amateurs. There were no moves to limit our activity, and there were occasional episodes of mysterious support from the top. I believe the learning histories contributed to that.

This was particularly important because the documents looked at things gone right as well as things gone wrong—warts and all—in a documented way. They represented a kind of full disclosure. And even at their most telling, there was nothing in them to suggest that the company was out of control, or that it intentionally didn't produce the finest product it could. They portrayed spectacular results sometimes, but they didn't show flawless work; they showed the company having problems and dealing with them. They made our efforts credible in that way.

For information about other available learning histories, including the new Oxford University Press learning history series, see *http://www.fieldbook.com/lh.html.*

HARLEY-DAVIDSON'S SYSTEMS LIBRARY

In July of 1997, the product development team at Harley-Davidson surprised themselves—and others—with a new vehicle launch that had noticeably less turmoil, stress, and confusion typically experienced in the chaos of meeting launch deadlines. This was due to changes in policy and behavior resulting from work begun several years before. With the help of many managers and engineers, MIT system dynamics professor Nelson Repenning and Harley-Davidson Director of Program Management Don Kieffer had developed a series of system diagrams that articulated the forces that kept product development from improving.

The system loops drew attention to the way that the interaction of formerly valuable policies and behaviors caused problems in the aggregate. For example, during the years when the company was fighting for financial survival, it was very effective to have product engineers familiar enough with the production processes that they could make late changes effectively. But later, when the company was trying to establish a system for bringing new products and features to market, this caused expensive turmoil late in the product development process. That turmoil, in turn, caused the company to focus its resources even more on the ability to make late changes.

Since 1997, Kieffer, Repenning, and others have been developing their own library of systems diagrams. This represents an equivalent to the "ten challenges" of this book—a set of system diagrams that constitute the "engine of improvement" for product development that, when completed, can be applied at any company. Based on their studies of the quality movement at Harley-Davidson, Ford, and AT&T (work funded through the National Science Foundation), these system dynamics models provide a very nice starting point for experiments in any company, and will help line leaders make a case for change.

The story of the project can be found in papers by Repenning et al on the Web site *http://www.sysdyn.mit.edu/s-group/home.html.* The Harley/MIT material may be published next year; see our Web page: *http://www.fieldbook.com/engineimprovement.html* for ongoing information. — Nina Kruschwitz

8 A "World-Class" Reflective Practice Field

Simulations, observations, and "After-Action Reviews" at the global-scale U.S. Army

The author wishes to thank Col. John O'Shea, Director of the Strategic Outreach Program at the Army War College for the opportunity to visit the National Training Center and observe AARs.

We would like to thank Hal Nelson for his assistance in assembling this material. For more about the history of the U.S. Army approach, see "The U.S. Army Reflection-in-Action: A Brief History," by Hal Nelson, available on-line at http://www.fieldbook.com/army-nelson.html.

During the last few years, the United States Army has begun to institutionalize collective reflection, in a highly intensive, systematic way. Not only have they achieved unprecedented operational success (for example, in Operation Desert Storm and Haiti), they have satisfied themselves (and outside observers) about the link between their learning efforts and their improvements in performance.

To be sure, armies are unique organizations. Yet businesses and other organizations can learn a great deal from the army about diffusing innovations in management practice throughout a large, global organization. Moreover, the army has faced changes and pressures in recent years that echo the challenges of its civilian counterparts. It has taken on new types of work, such as peace-keeping missions, amid severe budget reductions; it has seen its workforce change dramatically, not just in gender and ethnicity, but in the move from a draft army to an all-volunteer force. And it has embraced new technologies that quickly make traditional skills and capabilities obsolete.

In the following articles, several army officers provide insights from their experiences in promoting learning and leadership for learning. Although these leaders are all now retired from active army service, we hope the passion of their convictions is as clear to readers as it was to me, when I interviewed them and compiled this material. They all continue to pursue activities that develop and promote learning in civilian and military arenas. — George Roth

Beyond "Number 26, you're dead."

Dr. F. J. ("Rick") Brown (Lt. Gen. U.S. Army Ret.), Neale Cosby, and Lt. Col. Jim L. Madden (U.S. Army Ret.)

IT HAS LONG BEEN RECOGNIZED THAT SOLDIERS NEED TO PRACTICE ENGAGING THE enemy before they actually get to the battlefield. But traditional training for soldiers has been conducted through lectures, books, tests, and critiques from commanding officers in the field, and it had always reached a relatively small group of people. After Vietnam, we began to see the remarkable advantages in learning through simulation. For a while we used a system called SCOPES, in which a 10-power telescope was attached to every soldier's rifle, and everybody's helmet had a number. If you saw another soldier in your scope during a training exercise, you could mention it to a facilitator, and he could get on his radio quietly and say to that soldier, privately, "Number 26, you're dead."

This was far more effective, especially with the least motivated, least educated soldiers in the army. They'd come back singing; the number of delinquency reports dropped dramatically. And their skills kept improving. Kids who knew nothing about military tactics were firing shots and running for camouflage simultaneously, as sharp as anything you've seen in the movies, just because they'd been caught up in the combat and wanted to beat the other squad.

Our current approach is far more sophisticated still, both in the technology we use and in the group dynamics for helping people make sense of their experience both individually and collectively. The Tactical Engagement Simulation combines four major components:

1. A simulated free-play battle. In units ranging from platoons to brigades, trainees spend two weeks at one of three National Training Centers in the United States. Each is a mock battlefield site, where soldiers preparing for combat missions go through all the maneuvers of combat, but don't actually kill each other. To create this experience, we have developed "hard" technologies, such as the laser weapons used to simulate "kills," along with "soft" technologies, such as techniques for involving people in role-play. The army has long had simulations where soldiers fired on the enemy; but this is the first where the enemy fires back. Players who don't have their act together get "wasted": tagged as dead, and evacuated as "casualties." The genuine risk and excitement represent the same cues that soldiers would receive interacting with the enemy.

2. Feedback, if only to know: "Did that shot kill the target, or not?" The National Training Center is suffused with large, elaborate data-collecting instruments that track the movements of each soldier, even in the confusion and heat of battle. The instruments must be sophisticated enough to be believable, so that people can't argue about the validity of the data. After the battle, we hold in-depth discussions called After-Action Reviews (AARs). In those sessions, we refer con-

tinually to the "ground truth" (as we call it)—the inescapable, verified data gathered from the monitors and instruments.

3. An observer-controller (OC) monitoring the battle: someone trusted, respected, knowledgeable, and capable of saying "You screwed up" to officers and soldiers without offending them. In the AAR sessions that we hold later, the OCs pick out the four or five critical events in a battle that really made the difference. Then they get soldiers from both sides to talk about those key events as they experienced them. Similar discussions take place between senior commanders and their subordinates.

The quality of a tactical engagement simulation depends on the capability of the observer-controller. Some of the early OCs were authoritarian in outlook; in this role, they tended to infuriate people and cut off conversation. If we hadn't changed to a nonauthoritarian style, that in itself would have killed the project. The observer-controller must also have enough seniority and experience to understand the battle and the military dynamics, and to help keep discussion on track. We choose OCs carefully, and train them in depth.

4. Time and facilities for repetition of the battles. Once people have the intellectual knowledge of how they can fight better, you have to let them go out and fight another battle. That's why people spend two weeks at the National Training Center.

These simulation-trained units expand beyond greater numbers of "kills" into capabilities we've never seen before. For example, we've had young, inexperienced soldiers in remote parts of the battlefield who called in to ask their command to send in artillery to counter an offensive. They hadn't yet been trained to phrase the request properly, but they already knew how to think tactically and plan ahead at their level. The net result, in our view, has been between a three- and fivefold intensification of the learning process. During Desert Storm, and our recent operations in Haiti and Bosnia, many senior officers said privately that the soldiers exceeded their expectations. All of the things that might typically go wrong just didn't happen.

In Haiti, the first unit came in with an observer-controller, who noted what was happening, captured it, and designed training packages that were shipped back to the U.S. When the second unit arrived, 85 percent of the soldiers said, "Hey, I've done this, I've been there. I'm doing this for the fifth, or the tenth or the fifteenth time"—because they had in fact learned lessons from the experiences of the first unit.

By now, most of the army's senior commanders have been through the tactical simulation process as subordinates. They have seen the benefits for their units. But it took us ten to fifteen years to get here. Along the way, there were many doubts about these uncomfortable, expensive "learning" environments. Without the threat of the Soviet Union and the high military funding of the Reagan years, this program never would have seen the light of day. We had help getting over these hurdles because key people in senior leadership were willing to invest in this type of learning.

What corporations can learn from the After-Action Review George Roth

THE ARMY DEFINES AN AAR AS "A PROFESSIONAL DISCUSSION OF AN EVENT, FOCUSED on performance standards, that enables participants to discover for themselves what happened, why it happened, and how to sustain strengths and improve on weaknesses." Formal AARs are scheduled after each mission, requiring detailed planning and preparation. One-and-a-half to two-hour discussions take place at platoon, company, and then task force levels, a system that allows each level to build on the lessons learned at previous discussions. Informal AARs take place after single critical events, usually called by an "observer-consultant" (OC) who is working with an individual soldier or unit.

The purpose of an AAR is always the same: to help soldiers discover what happened in a critical event, why it happened, and how it might take place differently next time. To accomplish this goal, AARs have several critical features:

- Performance standards are general and well defined, so everyone knows explicitly how they will be judged.
- The ground rules for the AAR are deliberately designed to lead to a relatively democratic process, so that people feel comfortable speaking openly and candidly about their own, and one another's mistakes. People are told to "leave their personal problems at the door," to "speak loud and clear," and to have "no thin skins"—setting a norm of candor and detachment.
- Reviews always include the mission and concept of both individual units and the full force on both sides, so participants can judge real performance against objectives.

- The discussion stays close to "ground truth" (observable events, as reported by both instruments and human observers. Three key questions are considered in order: "What happened? Why did it happen? What should we do about it?" Events are considered in chronological order, to encourage storytelling and avoid confusion.
- The facilitating observer-controller is carefully trained and charged with ground rules of his or her own: Seek maximum participation, maintain focus on training objectives (so that the group doesn't become sidetracked), constantly review key points, and record key points (on flip charts, so that the group develops its own evolving "institutional memory").

The U.S. government has made a tremendous investment in AAR. Fort Irwin in California, one of the army's three national training centers, has over 600,000 acres. It required more than one billion dollars in capital investment, and operates at a cost of one million dollars per day. This gives the army an incredibly powerful incentive to be sure that people are learning from their experience.

Yet AARs are in themselves not sufficient for sustaining learning processes. In the army, the AARs are part of a larger infrastructure for learning that includes training simulations (perhaps the equivalent of managerial practice fields), the national training centers and their instrumentation (an equivalent to learning histories), and observer-controllers (an equivalent to the coaching and mentoring relationships and the development of individual's skills for effective engagement and communication). You can't produce the army's kinds of results by implementing techniques like these in isolation; they are most effective together, as an integrated, self-reinforcing system.

This level of integration doesn't happen over night. It took a generation of leadership changes for the army to institutionalize its learning approach. Paradoxically, the long time frame allowed greater sensitivity to early results. As young officers advanced to senior leaders, their early personal experiences with AAR and lessons learned translated into a passionate commitment for learning. Meanwhile, senior leaders had their own "practice fields" called the Louisiana Maneuvers (see page 476). In this way, the army established a consistent chain of performance reviews, from the "point of the spear" all the way up through battalion command to the army's highest levels. The learning efforts at different levels in the army can also be seen as a deliberate attempt to develop line and network leaders into future executive leaders, who then, in turn, create the opportunities for developing new line and network leaders.

As a joke I heard recently goes: "If the army is an organization in training, waiting for action, then corporations are organizations in action —waiting for some kind of effective training." With all the reverence that people in corporations have for the military (and the number of military alumni in prominent positions in companies), it's startling how little of the army's integrated approach to learning has carried over to the business world. Perhaps as the army's experience becomes more visible, the benefits of an integrated approach will be clearer, and more organizations will begin to follow this example.

HOPE IS NOT A METHOD:
What business leaders can learn from America's Army
by Gordon R. Sullivan and Michael V. Harper (New York: Times Books/Random House, 1996)

This book provides an intriguing view of a large institution learning to do more with a lot less. Over the past thirty years, the U.S. Army has developed an amazingly thoughtful and careful infrastructure for building the capabilities of its people, both officers and enlisted men. The story told here includes the imperative for change after Vietnam, the creation of a learning-oriented team of top leaders, and the transformation of the organization. It was not an easy task. But it provides lots of examples that can help other organizations with similar levels of large-scale change. The strongest aspect of the book is the relationship between the commitment of a leader—a co-author, General Gordon R. Sullivan— and the organization's capacity for implementing new ideas.

— George Roth

Interpreting the Fray General Gordon Sullivan, U.S. Army (Ret.)

EXECUTIVE LEADERSHIP IN AN ORGANIZATION REDEFINING ITSELF

For most of my career, I was part of an organization with a single-market focus: "Beat the Russians." But on November 10, 1989, that focus began to change. Why, my fellow generals and I asked ourselves, did the United States need an army in a post–Cold War world? We came up with four reasons: to compel another nation (or group) to do something; to deter a nation or group from doing something; to provide support during catastrophes; and to reassure friends and allies. (By sending troops to the Gulf, for example, we reassured allied nations that we were still "in the fray," and they could rely on us.) These concepts had been secondary since the 1950s; now they would be primary.

I had been a hands-on leader in the field—unaware of the complexity of the political environment of Washington and the pressures that executive leaders feel. Then I became Army Chief of Staff in 1991. Almost immediately, someone told me: "Look, you've got a leadership challenge." It took me about six months to come to grips with that statement.

In the army, as in most organizations, the most senior executive leaders were perceived as being positioned "above the fray"—outside of the day-to-day events that everyone else in the organization had to deal with. We had to find a way to put ourselves visibly "in the fray" with them: to stop holding ourselves aloof or above the organization's main activity. And we had to accomplish this without undermining the middle-level ranks who had traditionally kept the senior levels of command insulated from the fray.

The kinds of issues we were dealing with required a different depth of involvement. For instance, it had formerly taken eight minutes to fire an artillery round at a target effectively. New technologies had reduced that to three minutes. What would we do with the remaining five minutes?

That's a big question. The shorter time frame presumably means far less ammunition. This means fewer ammunition plants, ships, and trucks —and in turn, major changes may take place in logistics, coordination, and organizational training. Dealing with that simple case of a five-minute savings would involve everyone from the soldier on the ground to the most senior people in the organization.

At the same time, the most senior generals faced an enormous leadership challenge around trust. We had to find a way to build trust not just by opening up communication at lower levels, but by engaging the middle-level ranks as well.

We started by deliberately developing a series of sessions called the Louisiana Maneuvers. They were named after a set of practice maneuvers that General George Marshall conducted just before the Second World War. Our own version were dialogues among senior leaders about how the army might move forward into an uncertain future. The organization had trouble with this. People kept coming back and saying, "Just tell us what you want us to do." But we saw that the people at the top were so far removed from day-to-day experience that it would be illogical to presume that they will understand the nuances of it. We settled on our give-and-take collaborative process at these meetings, and the army continues to run such meetings several times a year.

This principle has also led to a culture in which even very senior officers take part directly in AARs; it puts them "in the fray" directly, in a way that everyone in the army can see, and in a way which keeps everyone learning.

Once people buy into the process of learning this way, some very interesting things happen. We see it when people from other countries observe the Training Engagement Simulations. They are shocked; they can't imagine sitting in on an After-Action Review and hearing a corporal tell a colonel, "Well, that's a terrific concept, sir, except nobody told me anything I needed to know to implement it."

If you are an executive leader in an hierarchical organization, it may be challenging to understand that even your smallest teams can feel comfortable enough to conduct their own little AARs to improve their performance. If the culture begins to accept this approach, you can begin asking from your level: "How did you guys do this? What did you learn as you were doing it? How did you overcome the obstacles?" Those lessons can become part of the infrastructure for learning that has emerged, as the teams with their own individual AARs gradually create the new organizational culture.

For those interested in a real look at the underpinning theory and approach that has been a large part of the transformation, look at the *U.S. Army in Transition II*, by Lt.-General Frederick J. Brown, PhD. (retired) (Washington, D.C.: Brassey's, U. S., Inc. — a division of Maxwell/Macmillan, 1993). It's a detailed view of the strategic environment that the U.S. Army faced, their approach to training and education and its revolution, and the role of information technology in warfare.

9 What Are "Communities of Practice"?

Chris Turner

Until recently an internal networker at Xerox Business Services, Chris Turner is now a consultant whose experience includes this in-depth story of in-depth community building.

In 1993, trying to create a strategy to position Xerox Business Services for growth, I went to visit the Institute for Research on Learning in Palo Alto. IRL had evolved, from work done at the Xerox Palo Alto

For an in-depth look at this subject, with examples drawn from "communities of practice" in the insurance industry and their effect on performance and organizational effectiveness, see *Communities of Practice*, by Etienne Wenger (New York: Cambridge University Press, 1998).

Research Center, a method for studying organizations the way that anthropologists study cultures—looking for the socially constructed reality inherent in the "constellations of interrelated communities of practice," as IRL's Etienne Wenger puts it. Over the next three years, we worked at Xerox to create an environment for nourishing communities of practice. I have since left the company, but I carry with me an appreciation for how significant this work can be, and how difficult it is in the ordinary corporate environment.

IRL didn't offer the quick fixes that we were accustomed to getting from consultants at Xerox. Instead, they said, our organization's existing informal networks had their own tacit, unvoiced knowledge of what needed to be done for growth. If we could make the invisible visible, then we could tap into a resource that we already had, but weren't using —the knowledge and initiative of our people.

Selling the concept of an ethnographic study to senior management wasn't easy, especially at a cost of $1 million. But as part of my preparation, I had made a list of all the failed programs I could remember that Xerox had invested in, trying to change operations and marketing, and how much they had cost. That list made a compelling argument to one key senior executive, a former Marine who was considered a very scary individual. "Will we find out why nothing works?" he asked. "Exactly," I said. He then bullied the rest of the executives into the project. I learned, from that experience, always to get a "scary guy" on your side —an example, in itself, of how powerful informal communities can be.

We began in late 1993 with four field ethnographers, divided into two teams. One team observed meetings and other activities at headquarters; the other did the same at three remote field locations. After a few months, we began to see patterns emerging. The most critical had to do with formal versus informal communication. "Official" information traveled either by "cascade" (dispatches from headquarters to the field organizations) or by "suck-up" (in which headquarters called the field and asked them to send information up). But none of this information was very useful for helping people get their work done more effectively, in part because nobody was willing to question or think about it much.

The information that really helped people survive moved laterally, from one field office to another, despite the fact that there were no formal lateral channels of communication. Much of it traveled through communities of practice. By definition, communities of practice are *not defined*. They have no names, no formal memberships, and no status. But they move information. For instance, the smokers who grouped outside the building at breaks all knew each other. The people who used a particular type of computer software regularly got together to share technical notes—and then talked about other things as well. It took me years to discover one of the most influential communities of practice: a group of people who all bet on the lottery together. They didn't have meetings, but they all crossed paths regularly and exchanged information. Most people didn't even know this group existed.

Once we had made people aware of the ethnographers' findings, of course, our real work was just beginning. We needed to find a way to harness and build upon these existing communities. Some Xerox people started forming groups they called "communities of practice." They didn't see at first, that any community you have to deliberately form isn't a community at all. It's a team or some other kind of formally defined group. We gradually realized that the "community of practice" work would be an ongoing effort to build webs of relationships, by bringing people together in ways that would encourage them to get to know each other informally.

The variety of methods we used for this would take a book in itself, and some of them might not sound like much. In fact, some of the smallest interventions made the biggest difference because of the ways they disturbed the system. For example, simple gatherings where people left their titles at the door, and related to each other as humans, were very effective because they took hierarchy out of the relationships.

As people get involved in ethnographic self-examination, and then in community building, they open up to the understanding that, simply because they have something in common, they have a great reason to get together. They can organize themselves; they don't have to have a schedule or agenda to meet, or a hierarchical set of relationships to get things done. In one case, a group who met for lunch, regularly but informally, became the linchpin for Xerox's successful effort to win the Baldrige quality award.

In the end, community of practice work expands the possible range of acceptable "ways of being" in a corporation, even a corporation with a very conformist culture. And that may be the final challenge for this work. For example, I had spent my entire career at Xerox, starting as a sales rep in Fort Worth, Texas, and I ultimately realized that, for most of that time, I had not felt able to be myself. As I reflected on the ethnographic work, I began to realize I didn't feel comfortable anymore "walking and talking" like everybody else at Xerox. I had two choices: to leave, or to wait for the company to grow in my direction. (I chose to leave.) I don't know whether that choice is inevitable for most people who get involved in ethnographic self-examination. Will they feel stifled by the culture that they are changing? The challenge for community building work is to help people find a way to move toward common goals informally, without having to think and act like everybody else.

10 Watershed Events

Louis van der Merwe

Louis van der Merwe's work has focused on helping leaders at all levels find the authenticity within themselves. To accomplish this, he draws upon two and a half decades of experience and theory building in facilitation and coaching, scenario planning, restructuring large organizations, and organizational learning work, in Africa, Europe and the United States. During the 1970s and 1980s, he was a key figure in the remarkable turnaround of Eskom, Africa's largest power utility company and one of the most influential companies in the transformation of the southern African region. For this book, we asked Louis to draw upon his extensive knowledge of community and organizational learning in indigenous and business cultures, to describe the rites of passage and significant events that can allow everyone in an organization to see their common values more clearly, and that can accelerate the process of reconsidering and reforming those values.

When children reach puberty, in many of the tribes of southern Africa, they are isolated for a three- or four-month period in groups of up to five hundred. Their faces are painted ceremonial colors. They speak an ancient language, in which a few elders teach them the skills of adulthood. When they return to the tribe, there is a celebration of reentry. The children are now adults, ready for marriage, travel, and community participation. They are given symbols of their new adulthood; Sotho tribespeople, for instance, might be marked with a lion one year. Thereafter, in a strange city, if they can find someone who "dances the lion," they know that they have found someone who was in the same cohort group during this ritual.

In modern business organizations, many people believe that values are difficult or impossible to change; they seem too ingrained and entrenched. But the tribal rites of passage demonstrate that, in the space of several weeks, a person's values can change completely. And the same archetypal process takes place even in our own society. You can see echoes of Sotho induction, for example, in boot camps, MBA programs, and orientation programs for new corporate recruits.

All of these are "watershed events": vehicles for deeper individual learning through some kind of group or organization experience. As systems psychologist Murray Bowen has noted, the system of a family opens itself up to the adoption of new sets of values during specific transition points in the family's life cycle: birth, rites of passage into puberty, marriage, and death. Families turn to initiations and ceremonies at these times to help trigger the shifts in values and attitudes that their members will need. Similarly, during periods of great organizational and community transition, people become more receptive to new ways of thinking, as long as there is some ceremonial "watershed event" to provide a visible acknowledgement and symbol of the emotional nature of the shift. By raising awareness of the values of a large organization or nation, these events can permanently influence the behavior of thousands of people.

Organizational watershed events can be as simple as meetings to talk about performance appraisal; they can be as far-ranging, and complex as the moment when businesses recognize that their existing products or services can no longer compete. (The onslaught of Japanese cars and consumer electronic devices in the 1970s provoked hundreds of watershed events in American companies, leading to the acceptance of the quality movement of the 1980s.) They provide an ongoing infrastructure in which "moments of truth" may occasionally occur. These are the moments of heightened awareness, when "things come together." A leader makes a statement, or a person from the back of the room puts in the words an idea that everyone has been thinking, and suddenly, the frightening, awful, great, and inspiring nature of the organization's new reality stands out in sharp relief. People walk away saying, "My gosh! I never saw things clearly until this moment."

You cannot manipulate "moments of truth," even by creating watershed events. If the events are to be authentic forges of values, then they will get their power from the collective realization that people already feel. But you can learn to develop watershed events, and to be prepared for the moments that do emerge.

There are two types of watershed events: organizational rites of passage, which occur regularly throughout an organization's life cycle, and onetime spontaneous events whose timing cannot be predicted.

ORGANIZATIONAL RITES OF PASSAGE: MANAGING THE SUCCESSION PROCESS IN ORGANIZATIONAL LIFE-CYCLE EVENTS

Whenever a CEO celebrates his or her fifty-seventh birthday, the atmosphere changes. The succession of the next executive leader takes center stage in everyone's mind. Anxieties heighten. Rumors and speculation run rampant. In corridors and carpools, people ask: "What's going to happen? How will it affect me?"

In this context, setting up an effective plan for choosing a successor is not just smart business practice. It is an organizational rite of passage, a deliberate and almost ritualistic event to mark and make sense of this highly emotional moment. By visibly offering ceremonies and public statements at key moments, the succession plan reassures people and signals that the transition is understood, and is a natural part of the organizational life cycle, no matter how worrisome it may seem.

Shaping and structuring rites of passage is an extremely high-leverage place for a change agent or leader to intervene. By anticipating these moments before they happen, and preparing for them, leaders can articulate the collective issues at hand, and design different types of conversations and practices to bring out the issues in each. For example:

- **Looking to the future:** Periodically, organizations hold strategic conversations, bringing people together to plan the medium- and long-term future: Where are we going? What will happen when we get there? What plausible futures might occur?" This conversation becomes a galvanizing, commitment-building rite of passage if it is opened up to a relatively large number of managers and employees, and if it is designed to engage ideas about a number of different possible futures and alternative views of the future.

- **Reviews of accountability and performance:** When teams and groups meet to jointly assess themselves, if they are encouraged to talk through their job descriptions and performance in the presence of their colleagues, it seems to force honesty, openness and authenticity in a very special and moving way.
- **Firings and downsizing:** A 10 percent reduction in staff would constitute a huge life cycle event—equivalent to losing 10 percent of the members of a community in a catastrophic accident. The emotional

pressure placed on the system opens people up to new ideas and insights: "What must we take notice of now?" People who remain after a downsizing tend to see themselves as survivors. The way the reduction is handled, the acknowledgment of grief, reasoning behind it, and the allocation of the remaining work will have a very strong influence on the values of the remaining organization.

■ **Leadership development:** The training and recruitment process may include looking back at the roots of the organization, and learning from the "wisdom of the elders." The Disney Company's orientation for new recruits, for instance, includes a session where people "study Walt." When people see their passage into leadership roles as a kind of organizational initiation, they feel, more strongly, the need to be trustworthy and to follow through on their promises. They recognize that they have not just been placed in their positions by the board or CEO, but also by the ethos of the organization as a whole.

SPONTANEOUS WATERSHED EVENTS: REACTING TO UNANTICIPATED CRISES OF THE HEART

Several years ago, the executive leaders of a large commodities trading company designated all 350 managers above a certain grade level as "change leaders," gave them a sizable bonus, and charged them with promoting the new values of the organization. Almost from the beginning, people elsewhere in the company questioned the legitimacy of these 350 "change leaders." Grumbling and doubt simmered below the surface for three years, unaddressed in any public forum.

Then a vice president, one of the highest-level female executives in the company, instituted a review of the dozen or so "change leaders" who reported to her. If they were obviously not contributing as a change leader, she demoted them. These demotions were private, but word leaked out—and it triggered a watershed event in the company, She became anointed, as a kind of "Joan of Arc" figure—the only senior official courageous enough to deliver a signal that said: "We demand certain qualities from the people who will take us into the future." The executive leaders of the company realized that they had to make a public stand, or visibly be seen as losing their way. Within a year, they disbanded the "change leader" group entirely.

Events like these are not repeatable, naturally occurring processes. They occur when circumstances (such as the death of a leader, the loss of a customer, or the rise of a competitor) demand them, or when a decision by a key individual suddenly crystallizes the growing internal tension.

These events take the measure of an organization's leaders. If you are alert to them, you can construct your response in a way that provides symbols that can shape the organization's values for the better.

These questions may help executive and line leaders frame an appropriate response when a spontaneous watershed event occurs:

- How well do you understand the signals that you send? For example, if you arrive late for a meeting, and do not acknowledge the time others have been waiting, does that get noticed? Is it a signal about seniority, or about coordination? Does it matter to people? How could you find out effectively?
- What symbolic gestures do you have available to you, and how can you use them? Phil Turberville, the President of Shell Europe Oil Products, occasionally pumps gas with other senior managers in service station forecourts to engage with customers directly. Each time, he rolls up in an open-necked shirt. Something as simple as the clothes you wear to a public event demonstrate how open you are and how seriously you take the group.
- Can you hear the "unspoken voice of the organization"? If a spontaneous watershed event is rolling toward you, how can you learn what the organization is trying to become?

When you conduct a watershed event, you are a host: inviting people in to a transcendental space. Issues will rise about ethics, power, and life purpose, issues that many people relegate to the spiritual realm. People will be intensely creative together. They may feel elated and uplifted, just from the opportunity to contemplate the future and their role in it together. For the heart of this practice is celebration: recognizing the joy and awe embodied in the cycles of life.

One watershed event that I attended was a picnic at a large corporation, in which people brought their families. Nothing much seemed to happen at that event, but during the weeks afterward, people couldn't stop talking about it. "I've got seven kids," someone said to me. "My kids said, 'Dad, now we understand why you work for this company. And we're proud of you.'"

OPEN SPACE

A few weeks before the Olympic games, the AT&T pavilion was moved to a more prominent spot. The design they'd worked on for years had to be drastically changed. The organizers abruptly pulled architects, technical people, and managers together in a single room. In a couple of days, they redesigned the building, planned the logistics, and got the teams under way. In retrospect, they accomplished in a couple of days a feat that would have taken many months with conventional planning. They used Open Space, a viable way to bring people together when there are high levels of complexity, a great deal of time urgency, and an openness to unpredictable outcomes. If you're an executive leader who already knows the solution you want people to come up with, don't use this technique. But it's valuable for any group with passion and responsibility for some impossible goal—even for warring factions who must come together for a common purpose, without knowing in advance, how they'll do it.

Open Space seems very loose in execution, but it requires a lot of thoughtfulness in planning. There are only four "rules": Whoever comes are the right people. Whatever happens is the only thing that could have. Whenever it starts is the right time. When it's over, it's over. That means that, if at any time in an Open Space meeting, you discover you're not contributing or learning, then you use your two feet and move on. Being in Open Space makes me wish that every organization were set up so that people who weren't learning or contributing would feel free to leave. How much less time and effort would people waste on meetings where they really had no interest . . .

Harrison Owen, the originator of Open Space, has written several books. *Open Space Technology: A User's Guide* (San Francisco: Berrett-Koehler, 1997) describes the process in detail, including the methods for setting it up and facilitating it. I truly admire Harrison's willingness to explain the nuts and bolts, in ways that encourage people to experiment without trying to control the way it is used. *Expanding Our Now: The Story of Open Space Technology* (San Francisco: Berrett-Koehler, 1998) provides stories and reflections about the beliefs and principles that underlie his approach. There is also a Web site: *http://www.tmn.com/openspace*. I continue to support and promote Open Space, not just because it works, but because of the "connection with the human spirit," as Harrison puts it, that resonates through it. — Ruthann Prange

SEARCH CONFERENCES

Search Conferences are a form of large-scale meeting design that bring together the talents and insights of "the whole system," while leaving differences of rank at the door. Shuffling back and forth between agreement and disagreement, between vision and current reality, between large plenary and small subgroups, and between long-term and short-term priorities, a group of thirty to 250 people can develop a kind of shared awareness of one another's aspirations and gifts, even if they don't know one another directly. After forty years of work on various search conference techniques, there is now ample evidence of how powerful these methods can be.

The theory and practice of the techniques and their similarities and differences are covered in three major books. They are:

■ *Large Group Interventions*, by Barbara Benedict Bunker and Billie T. Alban (San Francisco: Jossey-Bass, 1997). The place to start. It concisely compares the full range of related techniques and their uses. It shows which technique is appropriate to what situation, with brief case studies, without seeking to promote any one technique. It is clearly written and has an appendix with an excellent listing of useful books, videos, training, and other resources in the field.

■ *Future Search: An Action Guide*, by Marvin R. Weisbord and Sandra Janoff (San Francisco: Berrett-Koehler, 1995). If you need to run a search conference, go straight to this incredibly detailed "how to" book. It tells you who should be invited, how to prepare, how to choose facilitators, and how to set up the room and the equipment—right down to how many flip charts and what sort of marker pens. The agenda, facilitation, and follow-up are also covered. It is based on lots of experience in a wide variety of situations.

■ *Discovering Common Ground*, edited by Marvin Weisbord, (San Francisco: Berrett-Koehler, 1992). A very useful anthology for people looking to broaden and deepen their search conference facilitation practice. The contributors have all designed or taken part in search conferences in a wide range of circumstances. They offer plenty of case examples, covering a broad canvas of related techniques and applications. — Bill Godfrey

XII. Strategy and Purpose

"Where are we going? What are we here for?"

1 The Challenge

See *The Ecology of Commerce: A Declaration of Sustainability*, by Paul Hawken (New York: HarperCollins, 1993).

"When I read Paul Hawken's book, *The Ecology of Commerce*, it was a spear in the chest for me," says Ray Anderson, the founder and chairman of Atlanta's Interface Corporation. Interface is the United States's largest carpet and carpet tile manufacturer. "I realized just how destructive our entire business was to the natural environment. I knew we had to change the way we do business, even the concept of the business. We had to get out of the 'take/make/waste' economy and into a restorative economy."

In the last few years, Interface has pioneered a host of innovations based on its new sense of purpose: to lead American industry toward an ethic of "100 percent recycling," starting with the recycling of Interface's own carpet materials. The company has designed and developed an increasingly popular program for leasing office building carpets, instead of selling it. Customers' carpets are replaced, tile by tile, as they wear out, and Interface recycles old carpet tiles into new carpet, instead of seeing the carpet dumped. Meanwhile, Interface's plants are increasingly solar powered; and the company has invested in closed-loop manufacturing processes that won't produce emissions or use fossil fuels.

The environmental focus has been not just financially viable for the company, but profitable. As many companies discover, it leads to great savings on materials costs, energy costs, and dumping fees, simply because all of these resources are used more frugally. It becomes a vehicle for energizing employee involvement; Interface employees have had

Ray Anderson's quotes appear on "Corporations and the Environment," National Public Radio Talk of the Nation, December 15, 1997, moderated by John Nielsen and Ray Suarez; Transcribed by Federal Document Clearing House, Inc. under license from National Public Radio, Inc. Other information comes from: "CEO Seeing Green With Rented Carpet," by Karen Hill, Associated Press/Los Angeles Times, Thursday November 13, 1997, and from Anderson's speeches.

Isenberg's paper was "The Rise of the Stupid Network," by David R. Isenberg, 1997, published at http://www.isen.com. Some of this story is told in "The Stupid Network," by Thomas Petzinger Jr., *Wall Street Journal*, Feb. 20, 1998, p. B1; "The Dumb Network Paradigm," by George Gilder and David Isenberg, *Gilder Technology Report*, January 1998; and "Former insider aired AT&T's 'obsolete' ways," by Scott Moritz, *Bergen Record*, April 26, 1998.

thousands of suggestions for cutting waste, adding up to savings of $43 million over three years. And it helps to sell carpet, in part because customers who lease carpets develop an ongoing, long-term relationship with the company, purchasing a growing array of services in addition to carpet rentals. All these factors make the environmental effort viable at Interface, but they are not driving the effort. Interface has taken on this role because Anderson and his colleagues see restoring the environment as part of the reason they are in business. "I see this whole effort as a mountain to climb that's taller than Everest," says Anderson, "and I know that we're just on the lowest slopes, but we have found the direction of up, and we're moving in that direction. Sometimes it seems very rapid; other times, it's slow—but it began frankly, in the heart, not in the mind. And I suspect that that's where the next industrial revolution has to begin: in the hearts of people to do the right thing."

Profound change initiatives invariably lead people to a heightened sense of meaning and aspiration. From the outset of such initiatives, people ask (through personal mastery and shared vision exercises), "What do we want to create?" As they proceed, the questions become increasingly refined and focused: What is our purpose? Why is that a worthy purpose? Whom do we serve? How can we generate unique value? How do we need to change to create that value ? What should our relationship be to people in our community—and how broad is our community? What about the other people in our industry? What kind of example do we want to set? What about the people of my children's time, or their children's time? How will this company be seen by historians? What part will I be remembered for? What legacy do we hope to leave?

But engaging people around deep questions of purpose and strategy is fraught with challenges because it opens the door to a traditionally closed inner sanctum of top management. One such case occurred in 1996, when AT&T Labs researcher David Isenberg, in a scenario project on the future of telecommunications, questioned whether the company's strategic direction fit the technological changes going on around it. AT&T was building increasingly sophisticated digital communications networks, to provide unprecedented kinds of telephone services through its central offices. But Isenberg could see that the company had more potential market leverage, not by building an "intelligent network," but by embracing the Internet with a "stupid network"—providing a reliable, simple, ubiquitous, fast, international digital pipeline through which independent companies and customers could easily connect.

Isenberg published a small paper about this idea on the Internet, and soon the paper was circulated back within AT&T. Some at AT&T saw it as a useful synthesis of the dilemma facing the company, and others as a "glass of cold water in the face." When the writer George Gilder invited Isenberg to talk about the "stupid network" at a *Forbes* magazine conference, AT&T's executives refused to let him speak, because, they said, he wasn't high enough in the hierarchy to "represent the full range of the discussion within AT&T."

To be sure, Isenberg may have acted like a "true believer," raising some management hackles within the company. But he felt that the issue was important enough to continue raising it, especially after dozens of people from inside and outside AT&T sought him out by e-mail. Unfortunately, Isenberg's resignation after the Gilder episode sent a signal that open discussion about this issue would be discouraged. AT&T thus lost an opportunity to raise critical questions about its strategy in an open, nonthreatening fashion. The point is not to single out AT&T; few organizations have an effective way to handle these types of strategic questions when they bubble up from within. But those that do may find themselves tapping a source of energy, creativity, and responsibility unavailable in traditional organizations.

One oil company division discovered this in 1996. The "OilCo Consulting Group" had only been created one year before. It was a new freestanding profit-and-loss business comprising previous staff services, including accounting and information services. It was a daring venture for former staff operations that had previously operated as cost centers. Now, in a major closed-circuit teleconference before 2,000 people, the top forty managers of the new company unveiled their "noble purpose"—to become technological leaders in moving the oil business forward. This in itself represented a strategic leap forward.

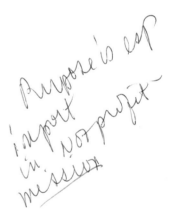

Initial reactions to the noble purpose during the teleconference were favorable, but then it was questioned by a junior-level employee from a remote location in the U.S. He stepped into the soundproof booth to speak into the videoconference microphone and posed a question to the CEO: "I like the idea of a noble purpose. But I don't think [the purpose you've described] is noble enough. What do you have to say about that?"

He later explained that the noble purpose he had heard from the stage (and in preparatory sessions at his office) was just a great way to make money. "A noble purpose, to me, would address concerns larger than profits. It would allow me, as an individual, to get up and say, 'I'm going to work today because I feel good about it. I know that OilCo is contributing to the world, the nation and the community, and it cares about people.'"

See *Perspectives on Full-Scale Corporate Transformation: The "OilCo" Learning History*, by Art Kleiner, George Roth, Ann Thomas, Toni Gregory, Edward Hamell, and seven "OilCo" internal people; forthcoming in 1999 (New York: Oxford University Press), p. 55ff.

When this comment came through the videoconferencing monitor, nobody knew how the CEO would respond from the stage. He was known for his quick temper. The people watching the executive half-expected him to explode back in anger. But instead, after a minute's pause, he said, "I'm going to have to be honest with you. I just hadn't thought about it that deeply." Later, the CEO said, "I was caught right there, with no other answer to give. He had asked a great question. I had been at the meetings where we had worked that noble purpose. I had accepted it. But I had not thought enough about it."

People were stunned at the CEO's response. Later on, an observer commented, "There was a remarkable catharsis in that moment, because the executive did not react, as everybody had feared, in the old punitive way. He simply listened. And empathized. The incident caused a quantum shift upward in his leadership credibility."

The junior-level employee didn't hear the CEO's response; technicians had cut the sound in that closed-off room. "When I came back out," he later recalled, "they told me that the audience had cheered and clapped, and they were still discussing the noble purpose. I didn't feel like much of a hero. I wasn't the first one to ever notice that there was no definition behind 'noble.' I was just the first one to say it out loud. For weeks thereafter, people I didn't know would stop me and shake my hand. That made me feel like I had done the right thing."

In the years since that episode, many more conversations about the "noble purpose" have taken place at the "OilCo Consulting Group." The official corporate purpose is still closer to "making money" than it is to "contributing to the world"—but that is appropriate. The goal, in meeting this challenge, is not to turn one's back on making a profit. Accomplishing business results is a necessary precondition for organizational survival. But, when he posed his question, the employee suggested that, in some fundamental way, the company's financial purpose was not enough. In turn, when he respected the question, the CEO acknowledged the legitimacy of questioning what the company stood for. And by continuing to consider the question, the audience of managers and employees had taken a major step toward developing shared responsibility for thinking about purpose and strategy.

Today, the field of strategy and strategic planning is in a state of turmoil. Traditionally it was the domain of top management, strategic planners, and strategy consultants, but there have been "barbarians at the gates" for a decade or longer. Organization theorist Henry Mintzberg began arguing twenty years ago that strategy is as much "emergent" as planned and that managers needed to learn about "crafting strategy," not just setting strategy. A growing number of voices have urged breaking up the power monopoly that top managers hold around strategy. Gary Hamel, who, along with colleague C. K. Prahalad, has developed highly influential ideas like "strategic intent" and "core competencies," says that "the bottleneck is at the top of the bottle." He argues that "strategic orthodoxy" is the greatest enemy of new strategy and that senior managers are often the primary "defenders" of this orthodoxy. Others have argued that the real leverage is not in creating the "right strategy" but in increasing managers' capabilities to surface and test the assumptions that lie behind the strategies they advocate. The real territory for strategic dialogue, according to this view, concerns the "mental models" managers hold. Indeed, a recognition of the importance of mental models to strategy provided the core of Royal/Dutch Shell's famous "planning as learning" philosophy in the 1980s, and directly influenced the emphasis on "mental models" as a discipline in *The Fifth Discipline* and *The Fifth Discipline Fieldbook*.

Yet, despite its articulate critics, by and large, strategy remains the province of planners and top managers. Most companies still focus on "the plan," and the "budgeting and planning process" remains essentially mechanical and static. Few people in most enterprises feel they have any opportunity to even ask deep questions about the firm's strategy and purpose, let alone have any influence whatsoever on them. This is why innovative pilot groups who articulate imaginative new aspirations for the business often find little apparent interest in their ideas.

One possible resolution to these conflicting views could come from an idea Peter Drucker has advocated for many years—operating from a more explicit "theory of the business." When people ask, "What is the essence of our business?" they call into question fundamental assumptions about the organization's value to its customers and society. For fifty years, General Motors's theory of the business involved producing a car for every income level. Marks and Spencer's involved creating a classless department store in Britain. And AT&T's was to provide universal quality service. If the company's capabilities, its markets, and business environment all align with its prevailing theory, then the company is likely to succeed.

But Drucker also writes that, "The theory of the business has to be tested continually. It is not graven on tablets of stone. It is a hypothesis. And it is a hypothesis about things that are in constant flux—society, markets, customers, technology. And so, built into the theory of the busi-

The Mintzberg reference is "Crafting Strategy," by Henry Mintzberg, *Harvard Business Review* July-Aug 1987, quoted in *The Rise and Fall of Strategic Planning* by Henry Mintzberg (New York: Free Press, 1994) p. 110; the Hamel quotes come from "Strategy as Revolution," by Gary Hamel, *HBR*, July-Aug 1996, p. 69; Also see "Strategic Intent," by Gary Hamel and C. K. Prahalad, *HBR* May-June 1989, p. 63; "The Core Competence of the Corporation," by Prahalad and Hamel, HBR May/Jun 1990, p. 79; and *Competing for the Future*, by Hamel and Prahalad (Boston: Harvard Business School Press, 1994). Finally, the concept of "Planning as Learning" was developed in "Planning as Learning," by Arie de Geus, *HBR*, March/April 1988, p. 70–74, and in *Learning to Plan and Planning to Learn*, by Donald N. Michael (Alexandria, VA: Miles River Press, 1973, 1997).

See "The Theory of the Business," by Peter Drucker; *Harvard Business Review*, 1994, reprinted in Drucker, *Managing in a Time of Great Change* (New York, Truman Talley Books/Dutton, 1995). The quote comes from p. 31.

ness must be the ability to change itself." The practical question then becomes: How does this "testing" of the theory of the business go on? Who can participate? What happens to people who challenge prevailing orthodoxy? How can organizations build the capability to engage people's imagination and intellect in testing and improving prevailing theories of the business?

Perhaps Drucker's idea could become part of a larger synthesis. "A fundamental shift is arising as leaders come to understand that the process of strategy is not just about ideas but about releasing energy," says Joe Jaworski, formerly head of Royal/Dutch Shell's scenario group. "The key is the willingness to see yourself, and even your enterprise, as part of larger forces that can shape new realities." When Ray Anderson says, "I have asked my people to join with me in leading the second industrial revolution because the first is not sustainable," he is seeking to harness such forces—through infusing strategy with a deep sense of purposefulness.

Drucker described the "theory of the business" as the focus of a highly significant, but primarily intellectual task: to define the environment of the organization, the mission of the organization, and the core competencies needed to accomplish that mission But the reflection and inquiry required in creating this theory can also tap people's deepest aspirations. If the attitudes brought forth are genuinely heartfelt, if managers and especially top managers can increase their vulnerability by exposing their own deepest aspirations and assumptions, if people can feel part of a larger creative process shaping their industry and society, and if all this can be tied to people's commitment to creating a future about which they deeply care—then intellect and spirit align, and energy is not only released but focused.

THE UNDERLYING DYNAMICS OF STRATEGY AND PURPOSE

When pilot groups succeed in sustaining profound change for some time, invariably, new aspirations emerge. These arise because of increased competence, and confidence, but also because of increased reflectiveness. As pilot groups develop learning capabilities, they spend more time questioning basic assumptions, including assumptions about the nature of their business and marketplace. They also begin to live with the basic questions of the creative process: "What do we want really to create?" "Why is it important to us?" "How will it contribute to others?" Sooner or later, these questions crystallize into new strategic ideas: "We'd like to start this business, or reach this customer . . . why can't we?"

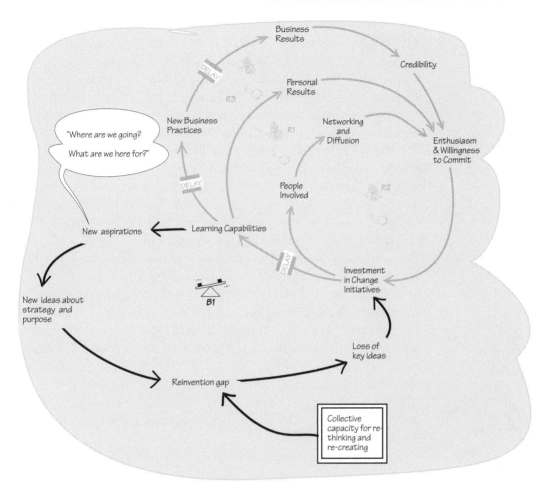

Business
Results

Credibility

DELAY

R3

Personal
Results

New Business
Practices

Networking
and
Diffusion

"Where are we going?

What are we here for?"

Enthusiasm
& Willingness
to Commit

R1

DELAY

People
Involved

R2

New aspirations

Learning Capabilities

DELAY

Investment
in Change
Initiatives

B1

New ideas about
strategy and
purpose

Loss of
key ideas

Reinvention gap

Collective
capacity for re-
thinking and
re-creating

But new ideas about strategy and purpose typically bump up against limits that are both subtle and unyielding. To some extent, these relate to the limits involved in the challenge of governance: for local groups to artic-ulate new business visions can be seen as significantly overstepping their mandate. In other words, there may be little management tolerance for this level of autonomy. This is especially true in companies where the strat-egy process is seen as the unique province of senior management. New strategic ideas from elsewhere are not especially welcome, especially when articulated publicly. But there are also other limits at play. Pilot groups may challenge assumptions about markets, technology, competi-tors, or regulators—assumptions that no one had thought to question before. The response is often not a negative reaction from management but no reaction at all.

The same may happen around questions of purpose. For example, what happens when pilot groups develop new ideas about the organiza-

As learning capabilities develop, new aspirations increase, lead-ing to more new ideas about strategy and purpose. The organization's collective capacity for rethinking and re-creating its strategy and purpose acts as a constraint. If that falls below the level of new ideas, then a "reinvention gap" will be apparent. The quality of individuals' contribution to the organization will go down, deflating enthusiasm and willingness to commit, and potentially curtailing business results.

tion's potential role and contribution, which question the official "statement of corporate purpose"? This is less a challenge to the existing strategy than to still deeper assumptions about why the organization exists in the first place. Typically, such issues are undiscussable, not because management has said they cannot be discussed, but because no one even recognizes the assumptions they reflect and thinks to question these assumptions. Consider, for example, the generally unquestioned belief that the purpose of the business is the maximization of shareholder return. When people's aspirations deepen, they often feel unaligned with this purpose. It is not that they are disinterested in business results—on the contrary, many pilot groups like the "OilCo Consulting Group" are much more focused on overall business performance than ever before. But they see business results alone as "too small" a purpose. They see profits as more of a consequence of creating unique value than as an end result that has primacy over everything else.

For example, in a global oil company where management recently adopted the "triple bottom line" as its focus—shareholder value, community value, and environmental stewardship—one senior manager reflected quietly that, "It was just growing increasingly uncomfortable for us to have a strategy based on denial." As individuals, people cared about the company's environmental impact. But by keeping it as an "EH&S" (environment, health, safety) issue, it never commanded the strategic attention needed to release imaginations and passions of people throughout the company.

Such radical questioning of purpose and strategy creates significant potential for both change and disillusionment. In effect, it calls into question the capability of the organization to "reinvent" itself. The challenge of strategy and purpose arises for innovative pilot groups when this capability is low. If deep questioning about the organization's purpose and strategy is pushed down and never given a serious audience, internal innovators often disengage emotionally or leave. They conclude that their ideas "will never have a chance around here." They get frustrated because they can't exercise their strategic thinking in service of their career. "There's nowhere for me to move. The company is closed to my insights. Only those at the top know where we are going." The consequence is a loss of imagination and passion, and eventually a decline in the willingness of people to commit to new learning initiatives. But, if this "reinvention gap" is met, it can lead to significant increases in the quality of the organization's contribution in the world, and consequently to its business results.

This does not imply that all new ideas that bubble up from innovative pilot groups are good. Many are not. But if groups that prove their mettle by producing significant improvements, and who truly have a deep sense of responsibility for the business, do not have the "space" to expand their thinking toward fundamental new ideas about strategy and purpose, a significant source of innovation is lost.

The underlying limit here is the "collective capability for rethinking and re-creating." This capability lies at the heart of great strategy. It goes beyond cleverness, or recognizing changes in the environment. It derives from a critical mass of leadership who can truly question and potentially upturn previously unquestioned assumptions and then take actions based on fundamentally new views. It is extremely difficult to express this collective capability in words, and we hesitate to trivialize it by trying to reduce it to a few concepts. But some organizations seem to have this capacity, at least for a time—the ability to truly reinvent their strategy and, in the process, rediscover or extend their sense of purpose.

IBM did this in the early 1960s, when it abandoned its major new computer series after only three sales. Thomas Watson Jr. and his colleagues became convinced that this machine, code named "Stretch," which had been the primary focus of the company's strategy, was simply not going to fulfill the primary needs of IBM's customers. Watson told an industry group that Stretch never met more than 70 percent of its specifications and that "We're going to be a good deal more careful about what we promise in the future." Three years later, IBM had developed the System 360, which became the platform for the company's extraordinary growth over the next ten years.

Intel did something similar twenty years later when middle managers lobbied CEO Andy Grove that the future of the firm rested on microprocessor—not its current product, memory chips. Grove, like Watson before him, listened to the type of disconfirming argument that often gets squelched in most corporations, challenged it, and eventually came around to agreeing with its merits. Over the next few years, microprocessors became the core of Intel's strategy.

This does not mean that all new strategic ideas need to turn around a business. On the contrary, many of the most important occur "on the margin," and only accumulate into significant business impact over many years. Some companies like 3M even make a business of continually reinventing themselves through pursuing a great many new product ideas in new markets all the time. What matters fundamentally is whether or not companies have the capacity to challenge orthodoxy and

See "IBM's $5,000,000,000 Gamble," *Fortune*, September 1996; "IBM Unwraps Its Billion-Dollar Gamble," *Business Week*, April 11, 1964, p. 67; "Fading memories: a process theory of strategic business exit in dynamic environments (Intel)," by Robert A. Burgelman, *Administrative Science Quarterly*, vol. 39, March 1994, pp. 24–56

i.e. don't have to be big idea

reinvent themselves, either in a few big steps or many small ones. That is the essence of the "collective capacity for rethinking and re-creating."

STRATEGIES FOR MEETING THE CHALLENGE OF STRATEGY AND PURPOSE

Effective leverage for this challenge lies with increasing the organization's capacity for rethinking and re-creating, and with improving the processes of conversation that lead people to articulate and refine their aspirations and strategy.

- **Use scenario thinking to investigate blind spots and signals of unexpected events.** All organizations have blind spots. One of the core challenges of rethinking is: How do organizations avoid decline? Partly, this involves learning to keep aware of external signals, especially those which tend to be systematically ignored. It is important for executive leaders, in particular, to develop ways to introduce potentially threatening ideas into the decision-making and planning processes without invoking people's defensiveness.

  Scenarios are not predictions. This gives scenario thinking one of its great strengths: the ability to engage a diverse group of people in thinking about multiple possible futures. If you predict that someone's current strategy will fail by asserting that it is based on a false perception of the future, that person will have a strong tendency to defend that view. If you can engage that same person in thinking about a variety of plausible futures, he or she will often see very quickly how his or her "preferred" strategy is based on one set of assumptions among many. This can create greater openness of mind without forcing people to defend their current decisions.

  "If I had predicted to a South African gold-mining executive in 1985," notes Louis van der Merwe, "that Nelson Mandela would be released, the ANC would be legitimized, and there would be a multi-party democratic country with a market-based economy in ten years, it wouldn't change his thinking one bit. However, if I presented that as one possible scenario, alongside the expected futures which most people anticipated—bloodshed and bloodbath—there might be a little more willingness to do something about it."

- **Combine scenario thinking and explorations of organizational purpose.** Conventional planning processes typically ignore the future people truly want to create. But the combination of scenario thinking (thinking in depth about external forces that may affect the future) and shared vision (thinking in depth about the collective aspirations of people in the organization) can bring into relief the choices facing the organization and the impact those choices might have.

"If people are shown a 'high road' and a 'low road' in contrast to each other," argues van der Merwe, "they will gravitate toward the high road." In fact, that's exactly what happened in South Africa—a series of scenario exercises laid out the choices for the country as a whole, first before high-level corporate executives in the mid-1980's, then before other groups of citizens, and ultimately before the formerly banned political groups as they moved into their legitimate roles as government leaders.

For more about scenario planning's role in the South Africa transition, see page 511.

■ **Develop stewardship as an organizational ethic and practice**. Ryuzaburo Kaku, longtime president and current honorary chairman of Canon, describes this strategy as a way of thinking called "kyosei": promoting the welfare of all components of society whenever possible, including that of your competition, as a way of achieving business health. Attuned to the value of kyosei, Canon eschewed R&D investment in memory chips, because other companies were already investing in that technology and Canon's leaders did not want to steal business. Instead, they developed the inkjet printer, which turned out to be a highly successful investment.

Similarly, instead of looking for help with trade deals, Canon urges global governments to rectify imbalances between rich and poor nations. And the kyosei value drives Canon to set up R&D facilities in non-Japanese countries. "By training local workers and introducing them to new technology," Kaku wrote in the *Harvard Business Review*, "corporations can improve the standard of living of people in poor countries. And by developing and using technology that reduces or eliminates pollution, companies can help preserve the global environment."

Quote from *The Path of Kyosei*, by Ryuzaburo Kaku, *Harvard Business Review*, Jul/Aug 1997, p. 55. The concept of stewardship is vividly expounded in *Stewardship: Choosing Service Over Self-Interest*, by Peter Block (San Francisco: Berrett-Koehler, 1993).

Doc. strategy - don't copy

See "Conscious Oversight," by Charlotte Roberts, page 545; and on the dangers of idealism see "The Perils of Shared Ideals," page 350.

Even if such a philosophy is articulated by a CEO, it is still necessary to . . .

■ **Engage people continually around organizational strategy and purpose.** Involve people throughout the organization in developing a clearer view of options and constraints. This will build the capability for strategic thinking and thinking about purpose throughout the organization. It does not mean that top management abdicates. In many leading firms, executive leaders maintain responsibility for strategic direction, but do so by remaining open to ideas from throughout the enterprise.

Management theorist Gary Hamel suggests engaging three particular constituencies normally excluded from conversations about strategy and purpose: young employees, people at the organization's geographic periphery, and newcomers. Hamel argues that the young members of the organization who "live closer to the future" have "the biggest stake in the future." He asks: "When was the last time a Generation X employee in your company exchanged ideas with the executive committee?" Likewise, those away from corporate headquarters often have a very different view of the world; yet their voices are also usually disenfranchised from the strategy process. Lastly, people who have entered the organization recently "have not yet been co-opted by an industry's dogmas."

See "Strategy as Revolution," by Gary Hamel, Harvard Business Review, July-August 1996.

In conversations about the organization's purpose, in particular, continue to look for the deeper purposes that underlie immediate needs and goals. "Profitability and profit," for example, often stand in for values that matter very deeply: the ability to raise a family with some level of security and comfort; the establishment of a new industry; the creation of long-term wealth.

■ **Expose and test the assumptions behind your current strategy.** Conventional strategic planning is typically an exercise in prediction: extrapolating from present figures to project next quarter's or next year's revenues and gains. But this is typically like saying that the future will look like the past, only more so. Even when there is interest in looking more deeply, people find it difficult; a typical strategic plan is based on dozens of implicit assumptions about the forces of the business environment, the needs of the market, and the impact of the organization's actions. It is difficult, if not impossible, to make all these assumptions clear, let alone to test their validity or applicability. There are simply too many "interdependent and unknown moving parts" to sort out cause and effect in our heads.

This is why there is so much "magical thinking" in conventional corporate strategy. After the market sorts out the winners (e.g., FedEx, Microsoft, Schwab, Intel) from the losers, we attribute causality to "Mission-Vision-Value-Strategy" factors that the winners claimed were the reasons for their success. We never go back and look at all the failures to see how many had the same "Mission-Vision-Value-Strategy" elements.

One potential alternative is the use of computer simulations and microworlds to model the effects of different strategic alternatives. The point, with computer simulations, is not to find the right "strategy," but to bring to the surface the assumptions underlying each strategy, and to give people the chance to experience the potential impacts of their proposed strategic choices in a safe environment, with fine-grained detail, and with quick enough results (since several years of real-life experience can be simulated in a few hours) to provide useful feedback.

For example, a few years ago, when managers of the highly successful Ford Explorer developed a system dynamics microworld to explore alternative overseas marketing strategies, they eventually concluded that their basic strategy was not feasible because it was based on contradictory assumptions about the demand for light trucks in various markets, and how that demand might change over time. The microworld didn't tell them what they should do. But, according to program manager Dave Boerger, "it sure helped speed up the process and clarify the thinking that went into the strategy we have pursued."

The technology and design of microworlds is more than two decades old, but it is still comparatively undeveloped as a means for developing strategic thinking capability and formulating more rigorous theories of a business. We expect much more significant work to emerge in this area in the future.

■ **Focus on developing better strategic thinking and ethical thinking capabilities.** Detroit Edison CEO John Lobbia notes that, when he set up broad-based discussions around corporate strategy, involving several hundred people, it was the "highest high I think I've ever personally seen in thirty-four years around here. On an emotional, spiritual, and energy level, it was great." However, in terms of usable ideas, "the hit rate was pretty low. People still don't have the other tools to turn their newfound energy and enthusiasm into results that dovetail into the business." In other words, it's easy to involve people in strategy conversations *per se.* It's hard to develop the capabilities that allow a lot of people to add value to an organization's orientation. The critical part is not bringing strategy into the learning process, but bringing learning into the strategy process.

His candid assessment of the current strategy suggestions has not

For more about microworlds as strategic tools, see *The Fifth Discipline Fieldbook*, p. 529 and p. 536.

One detailed, in-depth, high-quality source on microworlds as strategic tools is *Modeling for Learning Organizations*, edited by John D. W. Morecroft and John Sterman (Portland, OR: Productivity Press, 1994).

Sort out assumptions

shaken Lobbia's faith in the value of a participative strategy process, because he sees it affect people's day-to-day capability. "Most of the time now, I don't react to [the low hit rate]," he says. "I try to coach and train people around the business issues. I say, 'Make a mistake this week.' I admit I'm scared of the mistakes people will make. But there's no going back. Even if we turned around and became more authoritarian, again, society would keep opening up around us. People would continue to experiment more. We can only decide what resources are needed to successfully support and nurture this new way of working."

We've seen two approaches taken to this challenge, each of which complements the other. One focuses on developing "business literacy," helping people to understand the basics of their business, how value is generated and the factors that distinguish their organization from competitors in trying to create customer value.

⟩⟩⟩ See, for example, the "open-book management" resources on page 181; the material on Shell Oil's business model, on page 203; Jack Stack on page 380; "Performance Dashboards" on page 313; and "Conscious Oversight," on page 545.

The second approach focuses more on collaborative thinking skills, including the "learning disciplines" (particularly systems thinking and mental models skills) along with training in logic, philosophy, mathematics, or theology: Learning to think more precisely and effectively is essential to learning to think more strategically.

The Covenant Insurance Group, for example, offers a series of courses for all employees, on subjects that range from Applying Values ("we discuss ways to narrow the gap between actions and intentions") to the philosophy of technology at Covenant. The oldest course in the series is "Thinking About Thinking," a course in philosophical history and its implications for practical, day-to-day life, taught by philosophy instructors at nearby universities, and originally offered to employees at Hanover Insurance in the 1980s. The Covenant Learning Center brochure describes the course as "Sandpaper on the brain . . . Few who take it ever forget it."

■ **Learn to pay attention to subtle shifts in the sense of possibility**. Over the past 150 years, Western science has gradually shed its view of nature as comprised primarily of "things"; instead, it has begun to recognize the primacy of relationships and the effects of "fields," such as gravitational and electromagnetic fields and more recently quantum fields. Little of this thinking has penetrated into the arena of management, where, by and large, we still think in a sort of New-tonian "billiard ball" universe of things affecting other things—like dollars paid affecting effort expended and managers directing subor-dinates. No wonder it's so difficult for them to conceive of a coherent process of large-scale change, when we can only think in terms of one thing affecting another—for after a while, the interactions of all those billiard balls becomes pretty random.

An alternative is the view that behavior within large organizations is infuenced by subtle fields of thought and emotion, and that these fields are susceptible to change—indeed they are continually unfold-ing. According to this view, social realities, like physical realities, are not fixed but continually unfolding, and that this unfolding is influ-enced by these subtle fields. Just as fear can pervade a team or an entire organization, causing people at all levels to withdraw and become self-protective, so too can hope and a sense of possibility. The presence of fields, influencing behavior and capability, explains the many accounts of performing or sports teams where people feel the entire team is "in the zone" or "in the groove," accomplishing extraordinary performance. People often report similar phenomenon in times of war or other situations of life-or-death urgency. The ancient aphorism, "There is nothing as powerful as an idea whose time has come" speaks to the power of a shaping field of thought in human affairs. Leaders in the arts and sciences, like Picasso or Ein-stein, demonstrate the way new visions create new fields of possibil-ity. Occasionally, political leaders similarly capture the hearts and minds of people in a way that legitimizes what seemed previously impossible. Both Vaclav Havel of the Czech Republic and Nelson Mandela of South Africa emerged from extended periods of suffering to give voice to timeless truths that transcended everyday concerns and energized their countries.

It is not important to establish whether "fields" literally exist in social systems like organizations. It is important to recognize, how-ever, that for introducing new ideas about significant subjects like strategy and purpose, there may be extra leverage in cultivating fields. This would mean deliberately developing new patterns of interactions, extending through wider and wider circles, in which new ideas are discussed and thought about. The Industrial Revolu-tion itself was created this way. There was no central plan, but over time diverse autonomous activities became coherent around a few guiding ideas. There is no reason to expect the fundamental dynamics of change to be any different for any genuine revolution in thinking and action.

"If you assume that fields exist," says Joe Jaworski, "then our intention and state of being as individuals are of prime importance. They affect our actions as leaders, and the way we see ourselves as leaders. This sets the tenor of the field." Jaworski points out that while people in positions of power and authority have strong influence over fields, so can the rest of us: "In any setting, in any room, any single person through his or her intention and way of being in a way can reset the field and change the orientation of the whole."

The problem with this view is that most of us have not seriously cultivated the "state of being" needed to work with fields, and there is nothing in our development as professionals that has aided this cultivation. Seventy-five years ago, the philosopher Martin Buber said, "What is to come will only come when we decide what we are able to will." But Buber distinguished two types of will. He said that we must surrender "our unfree will which is controlled by things and instincts for our grand will, which quits defined for destined being." In doing this, a person starts to "listen to what is emerging . . . to the course of being in the world, not in order to be supported by it but in order to bring it to reality as it desires."

Very few of us have given much thought to the distinction Buber makes, between "unfree will" and "grand will." For this reason, it is difficult to understand the kind of "intention" that Jaworski is referring to. The intention that allows a leader to work with an emerging field is different than just having a personal goal or ambition. It depends on one's cultivation or maturity, aspects of leadership that are often neglected today. The connection between personal maturity and leadership capacity is one of the oldest strands of thinking about managerial hierarchies. Plato discussed it in terms of the "philosopher king." On the other side of the world, Plato's contemporary Guanzi, a Chinese sage, advisor to the Emperor, and precursor to Confucius, wrote: "To place the state on a firm foundation means to entrust (government) to men of virtue."

While all of us have the potential to "listen to what is emerging," few have worked to develop this capability. The work of Jaworski and his colleagues suggests that the capability to work with emergent fields seems to be accessed through two ways: through deep personal reflection about one's own sense of purpose and deepest aspirations and through cultivating individual and collective responsibility for

---

J aworski's point draws on a quote from physicist David Bohm, whose concept of "the implicate order" suggests that fields as active social influences are directly linked to a primal reality enfolded within our own. For more about Bohm's concepts, see *Wholeness* and *The Implicate Order*; Bill Isaacs's book, *Dialogue and the Art of Thinking Together*; Joe Jaworski's book, *Synchronicity*; *The Fifth Discipline Fieldbook*, pp. 46–47. Also see, *I and Thou*, by Martin Buber (New York: Scribner, 1970).

S ee Guanzi, *Political, Economic, and Philosophical Essays from Early China*, translated by Allyn Rickett, (Princeton, NJ: Princeton University Press, 1985) pp. 55, 100–1.

the future. This is neither easy nor fast. But, it is possible to create a conducive organizational climate that can accelerate such development: "When enough people start to authentically examine their deepest hopes, and tell the truth about the problems that exist and their own part in creating those problems, the field starts to shift," says Jaworski. "I have seen this many times, and although we are still a long way from understanding fully how it happens, I have seen the consequences, and I am convinced it is possible."

So have we, the authors. When people bring their "grand will," as opposed to their "unfree will," to authentic inquiry into the questions, "Where are we going?" and "What are we here for?" it can breathe life into an organization. This is the power that people like Ray Anderson discover, when they reconnect purpose to strategy. It is the key to the future of strategy in an interdependent world.

i.e. maturity is required to work w/ "fields" for greater good of org + society

THE LIVING COMPANY by Arie de Geus
(Boston: Harvard Business School Press, 1997)

This is a book of practical philosophy. At its heart is a simple question with sweeping implications: What if we thought about a company as a living being, instead of as a machine for making money?

Seeing a company as a machine implies that it is fixed, static. It can change only if somebody changes it. Its only sense of identity is given to it by its builders. It exists for a purpose conceived by its builders. To be effective, it must be controllable by its operators—ie., "managers." It will run down, unless it is rebuilt by management. Its members are "human resources," waiting to be used. And it learns only as the sum of the learning of its individual employees.

Seeing a company as a living being means that it evolves of its own accord. It has its own sense of identity, its own personhood. It has its own goals and purpose, and its own capacity for autonomous action. It is capable of regenerating itself, of continuity as an identifiable entity beyond its present members, who constitute human work communities. It can learn as an entity, just as a theater troupe, jazz ensemble, or championship sports team can actually learn.

The machine metaphor has become so increasingly powerful throughout the industrial age—to the point that, whether or not we are aware of it, most of us think of our organizations in this way most of the time. And this thinking shapes how they operate.

So, our first mandate is to shift our thinking. Arie's book suggests that doing so will reveal four characteristics of "long-lived companies," companies that have survived for hundreds of years: sensitivity to the environment, cohesion, tolerance, and frugality.

Arie's view of companies as living might seem radical at first, but it is in fact quite old. The oldest term for "business" in Swedish is *nârings liv*, literally, "nourishment for life." The ancient Chinese characters for "business" can be translated as "life" and "meaning."

It is also quite practical. Thinking of your organization as a living entity, as a human community, will shift the way you see every challenge in this book—and your capacity to meet those challenges effectively. — Peter Senge

2 Managing the Horizon

BRYAN SMITH

In looking ahead, what percentage of your time do you spend talking about long-term plans, three to five years away? What percentage do you spend talking about plans for the next month or quarter? The proportion between these two types of conversation should be a matter of choice, and not a habitual practice. That's particularly true when a change initiative is brewing that will affect the business priorities of a significant part of the organization.

Draw a diagram on a flip chart that looks like the one following.

The semicircle depicts you standing on the surface of a planet, looking forward at the horizon. Under your feet is current reality. There are four plausible visions for your organization's future in front of you. Each has implications for your current strategy.

On self-sticking notes, write out individually the vision that you see for the organization: Where is it going? What results do you aspire to create? Choose a future that you feel genuinely excited about, and that you feel the team is capable of creating.

Then, all at the same time, walk up to the flip chart and attach your notes to the horizon diagram. Arrange them relative to each other, so the most immediate aspirations come early (Vision 1 or Vision 2), and longer-

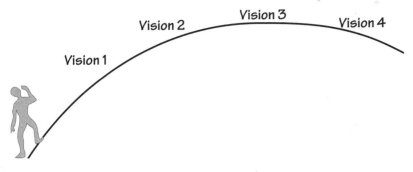

PURPOSE:

An organization's future vision is not static. It can evolve over time. This exercise focuses attention on the evolving goals and priorities held in mind by different members of a strategy-making team.

OVERVIEW:

Placing themselves on a continuum, team members consider the relevance of their different "desired futures" to immediate results.

TIME:

An hour or more.

SUPPLIES:

Flip chart, self-sticking notes.

term aspirations come later (Visions 3 or 4). Sort them until you feel you have them in order from shortest- to longest-term.

Now you have a snapshot of the "horizon focus" of your strategic group.

I conducted a workshop in this fashion with a management team at Xerox several years ago, during a period when they were encroached upon by newer, cheaper, highly competitive photocopier rivals.

Vision 1 represented a fast profitability turnaround. Team members imagined "getting out of the hole" by any means possible. In practice, that would mean pushing promotions to generate new business. Implementing that future would require team learning among the components of the copier business.

But to the proponents of Vision 2, Vision 1 was dangerous. It represented a "promotions spiral," in which promotions to new customers would make existing customers feel ignored, and diminish customer loyalty. Xerox would be increasingly forced to compete on price. Instead, the Vision 2 proponents noted that customers most wanted fast, reliable machines with easy repairs. "What if we really got good," asked the Vision 2 proponents, "at providing high-quality machines and service?"

The proponents of Vision 2 recognized that they couldn't just ignore Vision 1. Given the competitive pressures on cash flow, they would need to carefully maintain their sales momentum, while investing as much as possible in Vision 2. Since they would be under constant temptation to drop back to Vision 1, they would need to keep mutually aware of their values and the unintended consequences of their actions. There would be some tight moments, but they would end up on steady footing.

"And we would just be another photocopy company," said the proponents of Vision 3. The greater opportunity, they realized, would exist for "document management." With their capabilities in electronic storage, and the emerging need for communications between scanners, data banks, copiers, and computers, they could take on storage and retrieval for banks and other companies that were drowning in documents. There was a ready market for this, but it would require redefining the service function toward new customer needs.

Vision 4 did not get expressed until after the meeting. "If we can do all this," one team member said privately, "we might reshape the publishing industry." It might take years, but by preparing the right kinds of relationships with other companies ahead of time, Xerox could take advantage of the trend towards "quick-print" books and (ultimately) "instant books" downloaded into handheld portable reading machines.

This range of futures—from next quarter to years later—is typical. You may be surprised at the divergence. But in fact, it's healthy for a team to have diverse vision horizons among its members. People with a short-term focus are cautious, and they may miss long-term opportunities and directions as they try to solve the problems in front of them. Their colleagues with a long-term horizon may have trouble keeping track of resources and immediate business results. If both views are seen as legitimate, the two groups can work together to fulfill all their aims.

I'll often coach CEOs that, especially at first, they should conduct their Vision 4 conversations privately with one or two hand-picked people, or with outsiders, to keep from blowing credibility with the people whose attention is focused on Vision 1. Sooner or later, many people will get to Vision 4, but they may need time to work their way into it.

3 Asking Big Questions

A Catalyst for Strategy Evolution

Juanita Brown, David Isaacs, and Nancy Margulies

"Stop asking so many questions," many children hear at home. "Don't give me the question, give me the answer," many students hear at school. "I'm not interested in hearing what you don't know . . . I want to hear what you do know," many employees hear at work.

The injunction against discovering and asking questions is widespread in today's family, educational, and corporate cultures. That's unfortunate, because asking questions that matter is one of the primary ways that people have, starting in childhood, to engage their natural, self-organizing capacities for collaborative conversation, exploration, inquiry, and learning. Asking questions is essential for coevolving the "futures we want" rather than being forced to live with the "futures we get."

Our experience confirms that strategic learning can occur through webs of informal conversations and networks of relationships, both within the organization and among key external stakeholders. We are also discovering that choosing to ask and explore "big questions"—questions that matter to the future of the organization—is a powerful force. When people frame their strategic exploration as questions rather than as concerns or problems, a conversation begins where everyone can learn something new together, rather than having the normal stale debates over issues. In effect, people begin looking at "the map of the territory" together. The questions encourage them to wonder "What is the map telling us?" rather than to push preconceived ideas.

> " A vital question, a creative question, rivets our attention . . . the creative power of our minds is focused on the question. Knowledge emerges in response to these compelling questions. They open us to new worlds . . ." — Verna Allee, *The Knowledge Evolution: Expanding Organizational Intelligence*

> " Because questions are intrinsically related to action, they spark and direct attention, perception, energy, and effort, and so are at the heart of the evolving forms that our lives assume." — Marilee Goldberg, *The Art of Asking Questions*

"WHAT WOULD IT MEAN TO BE THE WORLD'S BEST INDUSTRIAL RESEARCH LAB?"

One of the best corporate examples of the way a "big question"—a truly strategic question—can galvanize collective conversation, engagement and action, has occurred at Hewlett-Packard (HP). The director of Hewlett-Packard Laboratories wondered why HP Labs was not considered the best industrial research lab in the world. As he thought about it, he realized that he did not know what being the "World's Best Industrial Research Lab" (WBIRL) really meant.

One key staff member was charged with coordinating the effort. Instead of looking for "answers" outside the company, she encouraged the director to share his "big question" with all lab employees around the world. Instead of going on a senior executive retreat to create a "vision" and then "rolling it out," she encouraged organizationwide webs of inquiry and conversation, asking people what WBIRL meant to them, what it would mean personally for their own jobs, and what it might take to get there. She invited the entire organization to join in exploring the question, through informal, ongoing conversations; and she took advantage of the more formal internal survey and communication infrastructures. When the lab director acknowledged his "not knowing"—an uncommon stance for a senior executive—an open field was created for multiple constituencies and perspectives to be heard.

> For more detail and perspective, see the article by the initiator and coordinator of this effort, Barbara Waugh, the worldwide personnel manager of HP Labs. The article is: "The Self-Organizing Transformation of Hewlett-Packard Laboratories," by Kristin Cobble and Barbara Waugh, available at *http://www.cobbleand company.com.*

The conversation continued for several months. The WBIRL leader developed a creative "reader's theater" piece which reflected eight hundred survey responses, detailing employee frustrations, dreams, insights, and hopes. Players spoke the key themes as "voices of the organization," with senior management listening. That made a difference to everyone's thinking by literally putting a variety of points of view on stage together. But it wasn't the only venue in which the "big question" was explored. Senior management met in strategic sessions, using approaches such as interactive graphics and "storytelling about the future" to see new opportunities that crossed functional boundaries. In these strategic conversations they considered core technologies that might be needed for multiple future scenarios at HP Labs to unfold.

People throughout the labs, meanwhile, were initiating projects at all levels, resulting in significant improvement in key areas of the lab's work. Weekly Chalk Talks for engineers, "coffee talks," an Administrative Assistant Forum, and a Community Forum created opportunities for ongoing dialogue, listening, and learning. A WBIRL Grants Program provided small stipends for innovative ideas, enabling people to act at the corporate grassroots level, taking personal responsibility for work they believed in.

In all of these efforts, the leader of the WBIRL project spent most of her time "helping the parts see the whole" and linking people with complementary ideas together. The rich web of connections that these informal efforts fostered were critical. They enabled the collective knowledge and competence of HP Labs to become increasingly visible, to itself, to the rest of HP, and to the outer world.

And yet, while productivity was improving rapidly, something was missing. During an informal conversation while planning for a "Celebration of Creativity" to acknowledge what had already been accomplished, one of the lab engineers spoke up. She wondered what was really different about HP that distinguished it from any other company who wanted to be the best in the world. She said, "What would get me out of bed in the morning would be to become the best *for* the world."

Suddenly a really "big question" had emerged. What would it mean for HP Labs to be the best both *in* and *for* the world?

A senior engineer created an image of what "for the world" meant to him. It was a well known picture of the founders of HP looking into the backyard garage where the company began. He added a beautiful photo of planet earth placed inside. This picture became the symbol of "HP for the World." A "town meeting" of 800 Palo Alto employees with live satellite hook-ups enabling a global conversation focused on the question, "What does 'HP for the World' mean to you?" The "HP For the World" image has now spread throughout the company—appearing in lobbies, featured in recruiting brochures, and offered as executive gifts. More than fifty thousand posters have been purchased by HP employees around the world, stimulating a growing network of conversations about the meaning of the big question for the future of the company.

In the course of this exploration, people rediscovered that the company founders, Bill Hewlett and Dave Packard, had always maintained a commitment, as Packard put it, that "the Hewlett-Packard company should be managed first and foremost to make a commitment to society." Now growing numbers of people throughout HP are reconnecting to that founding governing idea—stimulating investigations into break-through technologies for education, remote medical care for third world nations, and a sensor net for global environmental issues.

As part of this effort, the same senior engineer who had created the "for the world" poster image was persuaded to pursue a twenty-five-year-old dream: To create a mile-long educational diorama, placing human life in the context of evolutionary history. In 1997, this work—*A Walk Thru Time: From Stardust to Us*—was featured at the annual State of the World Forum. There, the question of what it means to be for the world was posed to global leaders gathered from every continent. Public and private partnerships are now evolving from these conversations. Clearly, this is a powerful question that "travels well."

BIG QUESTIONS AND STRATEGIC THINKING

This approach to discovering and asking the "big questions"—strategic questions for which we truly do not have answers—is grounded in the assumption that stakeholders in any system already have within them the wisdom and creativity to confront even the most difficult challenges. Given the appropriate context and support, members of an organizational community can often sense where powerful strategic possibilities and opportunities for action may lie.

Is it simply "luck" that enables us to stumble onto questions that really matter for strategic thinking? Or can we actually design processes that make it more likely for those questions to emerge?

"Discovering strategic questions," says one colleague, a senior executive at a major multinational corporation, "is like panning for gold. You have to care about finding it, you have to be curious, and you have to create an anticipation of discovering gold, even though none of us may know ahead of time where we'll find it. You head toward the general territory where you think the gold may be located, with your best tools, your experience, and your instincts."

To evoke strategic thinking based on discovering powerful questions, several activities may be useful. They may not apply to all situations and they may not always follow the same sequence——but they suggest ways that formal and informal processes can coevolve to support individuals as well as teams in discovering "gold" for themselves.

■ **Assessing the landscape:** Get a feel for the larger context in which you are operating. Scan the horizon as well as the contours of the current business and organizational landscape, at whatever level of systems or project you are working with. Like trackers in the mountains, look for obvious and subtle signals. Notice indicators that point to storms as well as to sunny skies. Allow your curiosity and imagination to take the lead as you begin to identify the many questions that the business landscape reveals. It will be tough, but important, to frame your findings as questions, rather than as concerns or problems. To help in framing those questions, ask yourself: "How does A relate to C and what questions does that suggest? If X were at play here . . . what would we be asking? What is the real question underneath all this data?"

■ **Discovering core questions:** Once you think you've posed most of the relevant questions (and there may be many of them), look for patterns. This is not a mechanical process, even though it can be disciplined and systematic. You are on a treasure hunt, seeking the core questions—usually three to five—which, if answered, would make the most difference to the future of your work. Cluster the questions and consider the relationships that appear among them. Notice what "pops up" in order to discover the deeper themes that the initial questions reveal.

■ **Creating images of possibility:** Imagine what your situation would look like or be like if these "big questions" were answered. Creating vivid images of possibility is different from pie-in-the-sky visioning, especially if people with a variety of perspectives have participated in the earlier stages of the conversation. This part of the conversation can also provide clues for evolving creative strategies in response to the "big questions." It often reveals new territory and opportunities for action while remaining grounded in real life.

Ray Kroc, the founder of McDonald's, launched his company to its preeminent market position by posing a simple but powerful strategic question— a "big question" to his colleagues: "How can we assure a consistent hamburger for people who are traveling on the road?"

A POWERFUL QUESTION . . .

• Is thought provoking
• Challenges assumptions
• Generates energy
• Focuses inquiry and reflection
• Touches a deeper meaning
• Evokes related questions

■ **Evolving workable strategies:** Workable strategies begin to emerge in response to compelling questions and to the images of possibility that these questions evoke. Of course, the cycle is never complete. Relevant business data, ongoing conversations with internal and external stakeholders, informal conversations among employees, and feedback from the environment enable you to continually assess the business landscape—revealing new questions.

Many organizations are stuck in a "problem-solving orientation," when it comes to strategy. They can't seem to shake the focus on fixing short-term problems, or seeking immediate (but ineffective) solutions. Simply by moving their attention to a deliberate focus on essential questions, they can develop an inquiry-oriented approach to evolving organizational strategy. In a knowledge economy, this approach provides an opportunity for developing the capability of strategic thinking in everyone, and for fostering sustainable business and social value.

4 Scenarios for Changing the World

Adam Kahane

A significant debate has taken place during the past decade over scenario planning—the methodology developed in part at Royal Dutch/Shell, for creating a series of imaginative but plausible and well-focused stories on the future, thus putting the choices of the present into better perspective. Should scenarios be used purely as a "reactive" tool, opening one's eyes to the forces coming in from the environment? Or should they be used in a "generative" way, to help people better recognize how they could contribute to changing the world? Leading scenario planner Adam Kahane, founding partner of Boston's Centre for Generative Leadership describes his own odyssey in using scenarios to "make a better world" —and shows, in the process, how strategy efforts at corporations and other organizations can balance the needs to both aspire and react.

We wish to thank Napier Collyns, principal of the Global Business Network, for helping to arrange and develop this material; and Kees van der Heijden and Steve Rosell, for their comments and suggestions.

The *Fifth Discipline Fieldbook* contains a blueprint for a scenario-based internal consultancy by Kees van der Heijden (p. 279) and a generic scenario planning exercise (p. 275). For more resources on theory and practice of scenario planning, see http://www.fieldbook.com/scenarios.html.

The approach to strategy in corporations is at a crossroads, where each of us has a choice to make about the way we look at the future. Will we be most effective by trying to adapt to what is happening in the world around us? Or by choosing to participate in shaping the future?

Looking back on my own career, I can see that I have been working on this question for the past fifteen years. From my journey so far, four lessons have stayed with me. They have come from experiences in the cauldron of public conflict, but I think they are particularly pertinent for corporations and other organizations creating strategy for themselves.

1. THE MAN WITH THE ANSWERS

In the early 1980s, I arrived at the University of California at Berkeley, eager to learn to use policy to make the world a better place. The professor who had invited me there, John Holdren, taught a course called "Tricks of the Trade," about influencing the world. The essence was having the right answer quickly, so that when testifying before a Senate Committee (which we all aspired to do), we could say, "Well, Senator, that's a good question, and I think that the right answer would be exactly 3.2 terajoules, and that's why you should support this legislation."

When I graduated and joined Pacific Gas and Electric, the Northern California energy utility company, I learned more of the same. The way to be a star was to have quick answers to your boss's questions: "Well, boss, I think the rate of return on this project would be 15.2 percent and that we should go for it." Then I was recruited to work at Royal Dutch/Shell in London in Group Planning Coordination, eventually to head up the social-political-economic-technological scenario team. For somebody interested in strategy and scenarios, this was the pinnacle. By this time, I had lost most of my interest in changing the world. I was dispassionate, even cynical. At the same time, I loved the Shell environment. I found the people incredibly smart and knowledgeable. If they were arrogant, it was because they were the best. I admired them and was proud to be one of them.

I learned the scenario method there. My teacher, the Group planner Kees van der Heijden, taught me that the purpose of scenario planning was to observe the world and to help the organization adapt to it. Talking from the stance of idealism about the things we wanted to see happen was not just improper, but dangerous. Thinking about their desired futures, people might miss important signals that didn't fit with their desires. As Kees says, "If you're in a hang glider, you only have scenarios for the direction of the wind. And if you start talking about options for wind direction, as if your wishes about wind direction could influence it, you would get terribly hurt."

I was not completely happy with this approach. It implied that Shell, one of the largest corporations in the world, didn't and shouldn't really have much influence on the world. Except in matters that directly affected the business, our task was to observe and adapt as best we could. This is the dominant paradigm in most thinking about corporate strategy. But I wondered if it was a responsible stance.

When Kees retired from Shell, he was replaced by an outsider, a visionary lawyer and businessman named Joseph Jaworski, who had founded the American Leadership Forum and is now my partner in the Centre for Generative Leadership. Joe caused a ruckus at Group Planning; he wanted the scenario work to be activist, and to try to contribute to shaping a better world. This stance sparked deep disagreements in Group Planning, but it struck a deep chord within me. I found my energy, which had been sapped, coming back.

In 1991, Shell was invited to send a staff member to South Africa to facilitate a series of workshops at a conference center near Cape Town called Mont Fleur, and Joe encouraged me to go. South Africa had just begun the transition from apartheid to a democratic government. It had only been a year since Nelson Mandela had been released from prison and the left-wing opposition legalized; the first all-race elections would not be held for two more years. There were many activities where people who had been in deep conflict were getting together to try to find a collaborative way forward.

The Mont Fleur scenario team included twenty-two members from across the spectrum of South Africa's diverse constituencies: community activists, conservative politicians, African National Congress officials, trade unionists, mainstream economists, and senior corporate executives. Our objective was to develop a set of alternative stories about what might happen in South Africa, to provoke debate and forward movement. One scenario, called "Lame Duck," envisioned a weakened transitional government that "purports to respond to all, but satisfies none." This was an important scenario because a coalition government was in the midst of being negotiated, and now participants could see the potential danger of languishing growth and drawn-out uncertainty. Another scenario, called "Icarus," suggested that a black government could come to power on a wave of public support, embark on a huge, unsustainable public spending program, and consequently crash the economy. For the

For more about the Mont Fleur scenarios, see "Scenarios for Building Community," by Adam Kahane, in *The Lost Chapters of the Fifth Discipline Fieldbook* (Niagara Falls, NY: Resources Connection, 1994), or on the fieldbook Web site: *http://www.gbn.org/scenarios/ fleur/fleurIntro.html*.

first time, a team that included prominent left-wing economists discussed the possibility of government trying to do too much.

The Mont Fleur project was influential. It contributed to the building of a common language for talking across different groups about the opportunities and challenges the country faced. This shared understanding—together with the fruits of countless other workshops, meetings and negotiations—eventually helped lead to the unprecedented "miraculous" transition in 1994 from minority to majority rule.

Personally, I was overwhelmed by this experience. I liked the South Africans. I found them warm and I admired their extraordinary capacity to listen to one another. And I respected the sacrifices that these people had made to bring their country to this transition. I was also struck by the fact that I was more effective in the Mont Fleur project than I had ever been before. Clearly, I had done something right, but I didn't know what it was.

Eventually I figured it out. In Mont Fleur, I had had almost no time to prepare. With more time, I would have done my normal Shell thing: reading up on the problem, forming opinions, and coming in with a recommendation. I was effective because I arrived in ignorance and respect. One of the participants said afterward, "Adam, we couldn't believe anyone could be as ignorant as you. We were sure that you were manipulating us. But when we realized you really didn't know anything and you were really there just to support us, we decided to trust you."

This was my first lesson: I was much more effective when I gave up the stance of knowing and arrogance and replaced it with one of wonder and reverence.

2. THE MESSY GRAY ZONE

Mont Fleur was the start of a series of love affairs for me. I fell in love with the country, with this new kind of "servant consulting" work, and with Dorothy, the project coordinator. I ended up marrying Dorothy, resigning from Shell, moving to South Africa, and starting to work internationally as a strategy consultant to both private companies and public institutions. But I wondered about a comment made by Rob Davies, a member of the team. "The exercise was very good," he said. "But I felt that I had to compromise." Why, I wondered, did he feel dissatisfied?

In the work that followed, I forgot the first lesson almost immediately. My old arrogance came back, my learning slowed down, and I began to consider myself the north's gift to South Africa. In 1994, I began working on a scenario project for the Canadian government. Like most public enterprises, the Canadian government had never done scenario work. Why do scenarios when you control the fate of the country and can simply choose the future you want? But now this assumption of control was being questioned. "We have these levers that as civil servants we've been trained to use," one of the government people said, "but the levers don't seem to be connected to anything anymore."

At the same time, I was working in South Africa with various collaborative "forums," composed of businesses, government, opposition parties, trade unions, and community organizations, sitting together trying to find a way to reshape the country's institutions. People in the forums joked that there was both "a practical and a miraculous solution. The practical solution is that we all get out of our chairs, get down on our knees, and pray for a band of angels to come and solve this problem. The miraculous solution is, we stay here, work together, and find the solution ourselves."

I learned my second lesson from the contrast between these two experiences. People seemed much more effective when they gave up the illusion of being in control, and instead tried to work things through with others. When they held on to the need to deal only with what was under their control, they weren't effective. They operated in an all-or-nothing, black-or-white, win-or-lose world that didn't reflect the way the world really works. The South Africans, by contrast, were playing in a gray zone between complete control on the one hand and no influence on the other: a "generative domain" where they had less control than they wished but more influence than they expected.

3. THE DIMENSION OF THE HEART

Some time later I became involved in another, larger scenario project on the future of Canada, in the context of fierce debates over economic and social policy, Quebec secession, and other issues. I found this project difficult. I felt fogged in, as if I couldn't see clearly the picture we were trying to create. As a Canadian myself, I certainly had strong feelings about the subjects we were discussing, but I didn't pay much attention to them and certainly didn't articulate them. Most members of the group behaved in the same way. So although the rational arguments often had an emotional edge, people's feelings were rarely put on the table. Somehow this slowed things down.

Around the same time, in South Africa, Dorothy Kahane and I facilitated a strategy session for the Synod of Anglican Bishops. Archbishop Desmond Tutu had retired and Winston Ndungane, his successor, wanted to make plans for the future of the Church. We knew this would be a very special workshop within the first fifteen minutes, when we were putting together ground rules for the meeting. Someone suggested that "We must listen to one another." So far, nothing out of the ordinary; that rule was usually suggested. But then a second bishop said, "No. I think we must listen emphathetically." A third bishop said, "No, we must listen to the sacred within each of us."

In corporate strategy sessions, we have to downplay the spiritual dimension of the work. That wasn't necessary with bishops. Although there were many clashes during the workshop, people dealt effectively with difficult and important issues, including some that had been undiscussable for decades.

I learned my third lesson in contrasting these experiences. Strategy work is not only work of the mind—which was the only training I had ever had for it—but work of the heart and spirit as well. Without open acceptance of that heart and spirit, you cannot have true connection. Now I had a clue to Rob Davies's meaning about compromise. To compromise means to give in; he had been hoping for a consensus, a true accord. The bishops had the capacity for true consensus because they were able to evoke more than only the mind.

4. CHANGING THE WORLD

If ever I faced a "supreme ordeal" in my own work—a peak experience, after which one is never the same—it was the scenario project I facilitated in Colombia in 1997. Back at Shell, "Colombianization" had been our metaphor to describe everything going wrong: the drifting of an economy into a downward spiral of criminality and impoverishment. This scenario exercise would take place in a country in the middle of a guerrilla war with tens of thousands of people under arms, with one of the world's largest drug-trafficking operations, under a corrupt political and economic system. One of the jokes told at the workshop summarized the mind-set: "In Colombia, the optimists say, 'The way things are going here, we're all going to end up eating shit.' And the pessimists say, 'Yes, and there won't even be enough to go around.'"

At the same time, the forty-four members of the scenario team were wonderfully intelligent, sensitive, humane, and diverse. We divided our evenings between earnest debate, personal storytelling, and singing.

There were academics, business people, and trade unionists; rebels and members of the militia who were fighting them; retired army generals and environmentalists; peasant community leaders and newspaper owners; representatives of black people, indigenous people, and youth. I think that about a third of the participants had lost an immediate member of their family to the conflict that they were discussing: somebody's father had been assassinated, somebody's sister had been kidnapped, somebody's son had been killed in the conflict. They weren't just observing this situation; they were as intensely engaged as you can imagine.

Technically, it was a challenging project. The top leaders of the left-wing guerrillas were either in hiding, prison, or exile. Four of them participated via speakerphone. One called in from a different Costa Rican phone every workshop. Another once called from a prison pay phone, saying, "I only have a few coins, but I really need to give my input on scenario 'B.'" If that sounds too strange to be true, remember that this is the country that produced the Nobel Prize–winning surrealistic novelist, Gabriel García Márquez.

One thing I noticed was that those people who had suffered most in the war were, in many cases, the most humble, open, and respectful of the others. I had seen the same phenomenon in South Africa: In these terrible, terrible situations, the people who are not destroyed by the conflict are purified by it—touched by grace. These Colombians realized that they were in a war that nobody could win, and that they had to struggle together to resolve.

I returned, in my mind, to my argument with Kees. Were these scenarios or options? If they were only scenarios, only efforts to develop better ways of coping with outside events, then why was there this energy in the room? Why were these participants so passionately engaged? Why did they come at all?

Then I realized that this project was not really about understanding and adapting. People come forward to influence and improve the world, and for no other reason. The fourth lesson from my journey, then, is this: We must give up the assumption that we are powerless, that we can only react to the world, and that we are passive in its face. If we have the courage to step forward, we can participate in helping the future be born. We can create generative scenarios and strategies, in the sense of helping articulate the future that accords with our highest aspirations, and that we can see trying to come forth.

I see these four lessons as a kind of gift from the activists, bishops, and guerrillas to corporate strategists and leaders. We can be more effec-

For more information, see the Centre for Generative Leadership's Web site at *http://www.cgl-leadership.com*. Also see the following: For Canadian scenarios see *http://scenarios.competitor.net/*; for Cyprus scenarios see *http://www.igc.apc.org/imtd/NL.HTML#cyprus*; for Colombia scenarios see *http://www.gbn.org/scenarios/colombia/*.

tive, if we let go of the arrogance of knowing and move toward wonder and reverence; if we move away from the black-and-white, secretive approach of trying to try to keep things "under control," toward the gray zone of greater openness and influence; if we engage not just our minds but other parts of ourselves, including our hearts and spirits; and if we move away from a passive attitude of only adapting and reacting, toward intentionality and generativity. Of course, all of these lessons are easier to talk about than to practice. But I think they carry a prize worth struggling for: the capacity to make the world a better place.

SCENARIOS: THE ART OF STRATEGIC CONVERSATION,
by Kees van der Heijden (New York: John Wiley & Sons, 1996).

Kees van der Heijden distills the essence of scenario planning and strategic conversation from Royal Dutch/Shell's Group Planning department and his subsequent experience as one of the world's preeminent scenario planners. Properly used, this material has the potential to transform the effectiveness of strategic management in most organizations. The author lays out an explicit process for scenario building, integrating three schools of strategic practice: "rationalist," "evolutionary" (intuitive) and "processual" (learning through experimentation). — Bill Godfrey

5 Strategy as Conversation
An organizationwide path for learning to be strategists

Andy Thomas and Charlotte Roberts

Andy Thomas, who is currently director of strategy and business development at the W. W. Grainger, Inc., draws upon his experience creating learning-oriented strategic processes at a variety of companies for this contribution. It shows that strategy need not be a "finished" endeavor, but that it can emerge, organically, if you put the right conversations in place. In the process, it will build the organization's capability for higher-quality conversations. This piece resonates with the "organizational learning cycle" (p. 435), another design for instilling learning in the regular processes of the organization.

Most organizations exist in tension between innovating some new business and preserving their old success. In the past, senior executives and strategic-planning departments set the strategy, generally erring on the side of stability. In more recent years, as that has led to stagnation, boards have invited in new, charismatic, firebrand executive leaders—who err on the side of change. They start "with a blank sheet of paper," consuming assets like crazy, forcing new ideas on the company, and often exhausting the organization. Both approaches are rooted in a command-and-control view of Strategy as Direction: that only the person at the top can set the course for the organization. Organizations can thus end up at war with themselves, with the visionary "generals" on one side and the implementing "troops" on the other.

An alternative view is Strategy as Conversation: based on the idea that organizations are already populated with intelligent and aware people, engaged in a collective search for meaning about the direction of the organization. It engages many more minds to be "at cause" in their industries looking for new ways to define and create customer value, seeking out and preempting new competitive space, finding ways to change the rules of the game in their favor, and raising the bar for themselves and their competition. But how do you get to that point, from the traditional top-down strategic approach?

In a variety of organizations, we have seen executive leaders wrestle with this question. We believe they all need the same thing: a developmental path that can build strategic skills throughout the organization. This process can't be divorced from the real work of the company; it can't be delivered, for instance, in a three-day workshop. It can only be built by engaging key people in five key activities:

- **Scanning:** In this activity, people throughout the company are set up to continuously "read the world": building and maintaining an objective awareness of their organization and environment, looking for signals in the words and actions of customers, suppliers, or interesting organizations that could have strategic implications.

    Designing a process for gathering useful information means giving those people who are in a position to pick up early signals some con-

I have found these books useful in the strategic thinking process—for giving you more to think about as you scan, and for approaching issues in other parts of the process: *Competitive Advantage,* by Michael Porter (New York: Free Press, 1998) shows how to pull together a picture of your organization's position in its business environment. *The Discipline of Market Leaders,* by Michael Treacy and Fred Wiersema (Reading, MA: Addison-Wesley, 1995) describes three fundamentally different ways to compete, based on technical excellence, customer intimacy, or operational excellence, and the importance of choosing and following through with one. *Leadership and the New Science,* by Meg Wheatley (San Francisco: Berrett-Koehler, 1994) shows the organic, nondeterministic relationship between any business and its environment, and the need for strategy to allow for change driven from outside. Finally, the papers of W. Brian Arthur (such as "Increasing Returns and the New World of Business," *Harvard Business Review,* July-Aug, 1996), propose a new economic model to explain the emerging information economy, and show how strategy is becoming a battle between competing visions for the future. — Andy Thomas

text to help tune their "antennae" to relevant frequencies. It does not mean telling them exactly where to scan; they may do the most good by following their own noses. Have a diverse enough group of people scanning that you are sure of covering all the bases—predictable and unpredictable. And make sure they have a vehicle to succinctly report back on what they have found, and a forum to pool and discuss their findings regularly with the rest of the core strategic team, if not the entire organization.

■ **Thinking:** The activity of pressure-testing current explanations of reality and models of the business, and developing and exploring alternatives. How does the new data (from scanning) fit into current business models? If the data doesn't fit, then the model of the business should be questioned. This process depends on melding different types of thinking. People inclined, respectively, to intuitive, creative, lateral, and rational thinking should all be included together. Teams may decide they need to bolster internal perspectives by inviting remarkable people who know the business well or are great thinkers in their own right. Outsiders may be better positioned to challenge the interpretation of the data and prevailing assumptions.

Thinking processes need not be formal. Network leaders, for instance, can conduct a lot of shuttle diplomacy among the emergent thinkers within the business, building a multidimensional consensus without necessarily bringing everyone together for a meeting. In one-on-one and small group conversations, an informally drawn systems model of the business might emerge. It can then be discussed in financial terms with finance people, in technical terms with technological people, and in human-resource terms with HR people. People may say things that seem unrelated at first, but as the network leaders mull them over, it soon becomes clear that each provides the missing part of the other's conundrum. As the picture evolves, people start to understand the context of one another's issues.

■ **Choosing:** The most critical step in strategy, and perhaps the least understood, this involves deciding on a view of the future of the marketplace, and how best to compete in it. When you choose, you take accountability by placing valuable resources on the table in a well-considered wager. This activity is not for the reckless or faint of heart, because choices can have a life or death impact on the organization.

Many organizations "let the CEO choose"; people are not willing to be visibly accountable, especially if the choice turns out to be a "mistake." But these organizations may end up with no one choosing. Any single individual, no matter how competent an executive leader, cannot consider all the options in the crush of other concerns, particularly those options which nobody has taken the trouble to elaborate in detail, or options that don't fit the existing business model. Those options are automatically foreclosed to the organization, and the capability for choosing among a wide range of options does not get further developed.

The alternative is to instill choosing as a conversational process. Having come this far in Strategy as Conversation, you already have a much bigger basket of options to choose from. You therefore need to spend more time in explicit dialogues, where you consider each of the options in detail, and perhaps inquire into the assumptions underlying one another's preferences. This can often take place in small groups, linked through another "shuttle diplomacy" effort, so that the decision gradually emerges from the interplay among the conversations. The participants are self-selecting: They are the people who show up, who care, and who are accountable for the related results. We've never found an issue where no one shows up. The rest of the organization will typically go along with a brokered consensus among these individuals, because they represent an organized, thoughtful body of opinion. It helps to make sure that these people represent a balanced cross-section of the business, with members from finance, systems, sales, marketing, and production.

■ **Planning:** Now comes the tension of operationalizing the choices. People come together to say, "We know where we're going. But how will we get there?" This activity is characterized by hope and practicality, where the strategic choices are translated into actions.

The planning activity will fail if there is too much focus on deadlines and reporting up the hierarchy. "We must produce a fully documented action plan to the board by December 6. We will need a powerpoint presentation for the president by November 30." This kind of talk will ensure that attention stays focused on the bureaucratic form of the presentation, instead of the quality and integrity of the content. The endpoint of planning is not a document; the value is in the process that people engage in. If that process is healthy, then any document is a nonevent. There already is alignment and concerted action in the best interest of the organization's future.

Planning as conversation means opening up the plan to anyone who might benefit from involvement. This means coming to terms with confidentiality. Often organizations are so concerned about confidentiality that their own people don't know the strategy. This is more threatening to the long-term health of an organization than having the strategic plan get in the hands of competitors. Or as a banking CEO put it: "The fact that we have done all the up-front thinking and have engaged the organization gives us a head start on anyone who gets a copy of our plan. By the time they understand the choices, we'll be on the next round of strategy development. I'd rather have everyone in our bank know the strategy and be focused on implementation, realizing there may be a leak, than hold our plan for executive eyes only and hope they can mastermind the execution."

- **Implementation** is not about mindlessly following orders. It's about playing "heads up" ball: intelligently executing the actions that the organization has agreed to as documented in the strategic plan. No doubt some accountants would like to see that plan as a definitive prediction of the future. But things will not turn out exactly as planned. Variances from expected results are not bad news, to be denied or explained away; they are delicate and precious evidence from the real world that a key assumption or strategy may be wrong.

All participants in the plan, therefore, should be trained and given the support they need to monitor and evaluate the effects, as far as they can see them. This means people must understand, and be prepared to question, the assumptions and action plans that took great effort to develop in earlier stages. At the same time that they stick to the plan, they measure their progress and success. They may deliberately deviate from the plan, in some deliberate and controlled way, to see what happens—to see why some part of the plan didn't work. A business initiative that is not playing out as expected may be the result of local disturbances in the marketplace, erroneous assumptions in the model, inaccurate feedback, or other causes. The deviators' job is to research and inform.

In the end, implementing leads right back into scanning—monitoring the impact that your actions, and the actions of others have on your customers, marketplace, and community.

⟩⟩ Tools like the "performance dashboards" are very helpful in this stage. See page 313.

WHO DOES STRATEGY?

Not everybody can learn to follow these steps. Some people may never be interested in or capable of working on strategy. They remain valuable to the organization, particularly in implementation. But if you ask them to think about where the organization should go, they can't. They will simply reply, "Tell me what you want me to do, and I'll do it."

Another group of people are natural strategists, born into that mindset. They are drawn to all these activities—and will not thrive unless they can take part in strategy. Not to involve them would represent a tragic waste.

The largest group of people is strategically dormant. They can learn to be effective strategists, but they never have tapped that part of their skills, at least not within this workplace. Involving them in one or more of these activities will instill a strategic awareness and competence throughout the organization.

6 Strategic Transformation at Royal Dutch/Shell

Cor Herkströter, former chairman of the Committee of Managing Directors, Royal Dutch/Shell; Mark Moody-Stuart, current chairman of the CMD; Gary Steel, LEAP team

This organizational change story is so large and multifaceted that it cannot be relegated to pilot group activity. It describes a strategic shift in the orientation of one of the largest companies in the world. The Royal Dutch/Shell Group is composed of 165 semiautonomous operating companies worldwide, linked by a common brand name (the largest, and best-known, is the American operating company, Shell Oil). It is both a relatively conservative company, and an enormously diverse one, with a long-standing tradition of local decision making by operating company managers in Malaysia, New Zealand, Houston, Spain, Nigeria, Brazil; in fact, just about everywhere.

Royal Dutch/Shell was doing exceptionally well in 1995, when this story begins. But the leaders of the company were dissatisfied, and decided to change the governance structure, to reframe the ways in which people engaged one another and their customers, and to focus intently on the process of leadership development, as a way of revitalizing people's initiative, innovativeness, and financial accountability throughout the group. They made this decision not out of desperation, nor out of anticipation of a future crisis, but out of aspiration: deciding that the capabilities and direction that had made them successful in the past would not continue to produce that level of success.

Unlike its semiautonomous American operating company Shell Oil, whose transformation preceded it by several years, Royal Dutch/Shell has only begun to put its changes in place. We cannot tell much of its story yet. But we can show how the leaders of the company made a case for change, and established the learning organization as the central metaphor of that change. We are privileged to have this story told by its two chief architects: Former chairman of the Committee of Managing Directors Cor Herkströter (who retired in mid-1998), and the current Chairman, Mark Moody-Stuart. (The CMD is the worldwide governing body for Royal Dutch/Shell, equivalent to a committee of CEOs.) In addition, we have asked Gary Steel, a key member of the Leadership, Improvement and Performance Operations (LEAP) team that has organized and coordinated much of the group's new training and coaching, to add comments. As the LEAP team's story suggests, Shell's leaders chose deliberately to build capacity to transform, even from the beginning.

Note also that the transformation included a vision-based response to the damage to Shell's reputation from the Brent Spar and Nigeria controversies of the late 1990s. This took place after, not before, the emphasis on improving performance and transforming the business mind-set. The business shift gave Royal Dutch/Shell an effective context for drawing people together to talk about their broader vision for the future. — Rick Ross

NOTHING FAILS LIKE SUCCESS

Cor Herkströter: One of our largest problems was success. We did not have our backs against the wall financially. We were growing and respected; we treated our shareholders well; everybody was relatively happy. There was one small problem—profits were not forthcoming in the short term.

The need to do better had come up in chairman's letters, annually published in our shareholders' reports, for at least seven years in a row before I became chairman. But we had been unable to get the message across within the Group, even after a major organizational restructuring. We could see a situation approaching where everybody was happy about our core purpose and corporate identity, but the return on capital was forgotten. I remember a delegation from a Shell operating company saying: "Look at your results. They are higher than ever before." That was true, in terms of nominal dollars. But our returns didn't meet the performance criteria that we had set for ourselves.

Soon after I became chairman, I had to go to New York to talk to financial analysts. Our investor relations department prepared a presentation which repeated the same information that we had announced a few weeks before. Bored with that idea, and assuming that the analysts would be equally bored, I said that I would talk about "ten areas that are not going so well at Shell." This created an upheaval in the investor relations and public relations departments. But I gave the talk anyway, and it went down very well. The analysts said that they had always gotten a story from Shell that we didn't have problems. They appreciated being talked to honestly for a change. But during my flight back, I realized that it was easier to talk openly about our financial issues to one hundred outsiders. We didn't have a structure in place to allow me to get the same kind of message across internally.

After looking into our options for communicating internally, I decided to begin with an article for the in-house Shell magazine. "You can't get in the next one," I was told, "but it will be in an issue that comes out in six months." I could not believe it would take me six months to begin this dialogue within the company. I called a meeting of thirty-five senior executives, and we began to talk about the message. Was there a need for significant organizational change? No one present at that meeting could remember a time that anyone in the history of Shell had held such a meeting before. Reluctantly at first, people began to see the value in learning to conduct our business more effectively

THE ANATOMY OF THE RESTRUCTURING

We began with the service companies at London and the Hague—the "central offices" that handled the coordination among operating companies and provided worldwide services to them. We at the central offices were very good at telling the operating companies how their performance was not satisfactory, but (from their perspective) we seemed to feel that the same performance needs didn't apply to us. So we knew we had to bring the service company in line with what the operating companies had been doing already: being more effective, more efficient, with more productivity and less bureaucracy,

But as we reviewed our central activities, we saw we needed to change other parts of the organization as well. For example, there were technical research activities going on both in the service companies and locally. We began to feel that there should be a much clearer guidance for the operating companies to understand what we (at Shell's central offices) expected of them, and what we felt we could do together to improve the businesses. That led to the abolishment of Shell's complex matrix structure—a structure that had incorporated shifting responsibilities among business sectors, regional sectors, and functional groups. Many people in Shell agreed that this structure, which had been in place for thirty-five years, was far too complicated, slow, and bureaucratic. And it provided the organization with ample places to hide. If something went wrong, the sectors, regions, and functions could all blame one another for it. If nothing went wrong, all three claimed credit for it.

In part following the example of Shell Oil, we replaced that bureaucracy with a structure in which individual businesses had a fairly high level of responsibility and accountability. We could no longer make the mistake of sitting in our central offices in London and the Hague thinking we could run the operating company in Australia. We would always be too late, and always too involved in second-guessing the guys on the spot. We wanted to develop a structure that reflected our intent: to develop a clear-cut relationship between our thinking and the people who are in touch with customers and doing the job.

As early as 1996, we saw that the people in the organization needed assistance to cope with the process of organizational restructuring. We already knew that this was an ongoing process rather than a project with a beginning, a middle, and an end. It would not stop the way most restructuring projects stopped; it would be with us forever. Moreover, people weren't prepared to accept all of this change under a commonplace label such as "restructuring." The attitude we heard was: "If you want to apply the process of constant change successfully, then the company's mind-set has to change. That process takes time, so we have to transform." We would not only have to give people the intellectual and financial tools required to meet the future approach to business, but help them begin to "see" and think about the world differently. And we would have to develop the capability to do this in house; we could not rely on external consultants to catalyze the transformation.

Gary Steel: Consequently, Cor determined that there was a need for a work unit within the corporate center to accelerate transformation across the entire Group. LEAP was created in July of 1996 with the specific objectives of accelerating transformation, supporting and enabling the achievement of aspirational (stretch) goals, seeking synergies and sharing knowledge among operating units (which had previously been done in pockets of isolation), and fostering learning.

LEAP began with ten full-time staffers, mostly operating out of a "learning center" in the Hague. Today, there are forty-five full-time members, all networked together, moving among various operating companies within different countries as needed, providing ongoing courses in leadership development, business improvement strategies, and value creation. Orientation of new Shell employees also takes place through LEAP, which establishes organizational learning as the basic introduction to a Shell career.

As part of LEAP's planning, we met with Rick Ross at a site overlooking the California shoreline. Rick suddenly pointed to the ocean, where eight dolphin were swimming in perfect synchronous form, and where they remained for almost an hour. It was quite an inspiration, seeing these individuals moving in powerful alignment. That image will stay with me for a long, long time. It prompted us to make alignment among the leaders within Shell one of the areas of focus.

We want to thank Mac MacDonald, the director of LEAP, for his help with this article.

SOME REQUISITE SHIFTS IN MINDSET

Herkströter: Transformation requires constant coaching, because while people like the additional authority they get, they don't always realize that it carries with it responsibility and accountability. Today, I think if you wake up any Shell employee in the middle of the night and say: What is the minimum return on capital employed that we should make? He or she will know. Three or four years ago that wasn't the case.

Visibility is also important. The Committee of Managing Directors is much more directly in touch with the organization. This is helped by the fact that all of my colleagues on the CMD have a business responsibility, so they have to be in touch with the business. It isn't a free-for-all. The buck stops somewhere. But at the same time you can't allow authority to take over again, because then you are back to square one.

Another shift in mind-set was extremely important for us—from a focus only on shareholders to an awareness of stakeholders.

Steel: In 1995 two events took place that eventually made a significant impact on our changing attitudes: The Nigerian government's execution of activist Ken Saro-Wiwa (which critics said Shell could have intervened to stop), and Shell's decision, later rescinded, to dispose of its enormous Brent Spar oil platform by dumping it in Atlantic deep water. As the public reacted against Shell after these events, the company became an uncomfortable, disappointed, disenfranchised, negative place to work. It got to the point where at dinner parties, some of us were reluctant to say we worked for Shell. There was a growing awareness in a painful way that a company's reputation is the sum total of the way it is perceived by different peoples. We also realized that there are huge returns to be made on a high-quality, grade 1-A reputation. We developed the concept of a reputation "bank account," or reservoir. We saw we would need to make deposits there because, from time to time, there might be unavoidable withdrawals.

Herkströter: In 1998, we created and launched a core purpose statement for the Royal Dutch/Shell Group of Companies. We asked ourselves: Shouldn't we have done that earlier? Shouldn't we have done it before the restructuring, the evolution of LEAP, and our other shifts in mind-set? Personally, I'm convinced we did it in the right order. The previous work focused the minds of people on the key essentials that had been neglected, for whatever good reason, far too long. We have to make certain that when people wake in the morning, they don't get the feeling: "This feels cozy, and now I can forget the world around me."

Ultimately the customer determines your success or failure. The structure of the business has changed, and continues to change, so dramatically that we can't rely on technical superiority anymore. For the first time in our history, we have begun to talk about these issues.

TRANSFORMATION: NEW MINDSETS NEED NEW METRICS

Mark Moody-Stuart (current chairman of the committee of managing directors): People often ask me, "How do you know if the transformation is working?" I always say that within Shell there are three ways. First, you should see an impact on financial performance if part of the organization has really changed and is applying these things effectively. You can clearly see that already in some areas of our business.

The second comes through sensing. If I visit an organization in some part of the world and spend a day talking to people, at the end of the day I have a very strong feeling about the atmosphere. Is there a feeling that creativity within that piece of the organization is released? What is the reaction of people in a wide sweep of the organization? I think that sometimes we underestimate this type of managerial sensing. To me, it's very important, but it's totally qualitative. It's very personal and judgmental, so if somebody else does this, you have to really trust him and value his judgment.

The third method is to ask people what they think through surveys throughout the organization. We have done that in some parts of Shell.

Cor and the rest of us on the CMD realized early on that transformation would not only mean a significant change of mind-sets within the company, but would literally mean continuous learning and change. It also meant that people would need to learn how to build and lead groups of people of differing cultures and perspectives from around the world.

I remember thinking that there seemed to be three phases of team leadership that I personally passed through in Shell. First, there were the times when my technical expertise—in my case in Geology—was enough to help me lead a team's effort. But on cross-functional teams, technical expertise wasn't enough. Being a team leader meant that I had to blend the multidisciplinary expertise of the team members, tapping their technical competencies toward a shared goal. The most difficult was the third phase where I needed to engage the team members themselves in managing the team and setting the direction. That has been a difficult lesson for me to learn—one I am still learning. It is absolutely critical to liberate the creativity of teams, and yet not just have chaos. Leadership is often expressed as the self-confidence to navigate the unknown waters of the future.

7 Sustainable Innovation

Bryan Smith and Joel Yanowitz

In developing a coherent sense of organizational purpose, environmentalism always arises—if only because long-term purpose requires a sense of sustainability, of feeling responsible for the impacts of organizational action into the future. In this piece, Bryan Smith and Arthur D. Little Vice President and Innovation Associates Managing Director Joel Yanowitz sum up the "business case" for organizational change in the environmental arena. Both Smith and Yanowitz have extensive experience in implementing large-scale change initiatives, especially in working closely with executive leadership teams.

Examples of companies using the Natural Step framework were provided by Brian Nattrass and Mary Altomare, coauthors of the book *The Natural Step for Business: Wealth, Ecology and the Evolutionary Corporation* (Gabriola Island, B.C., Canada: New Society Publishers, 1999). This article also benefited from in-depth research on other environmental issues, and on corporate environmentalism in general, from environmental researcher/writer George Mokray.

The idea of sustainable development is still relatively new to the corporate world, and only limited evidence exists so far about its business impact. However, a growing number of studies and stock

The references and quote come from "From Wall Street, Increasing Evidence that Green Begets Green," by Claudia H. Deutsch, *New York Times*, Sunday, July 19, 1998, p. BU-7.

performance appraisals are highlighting the business value of new strategies and practices that reflect broad environmental issues and concerns. Companies that act on these approaches have been consistently outperforming the broader market by about two percentage points. In the face of this evidence, according to the *New York Times*, investment analysts are rethinking their traditional resistance to corporate environmentalism. "An eco-efficient company is making efficient use of its resources," suggested the Swedish investor Ingeborg Schumacher of UBS Brinson, "and that's probably a strong signal that it's well managed as a whole."

But efficient management alone doesn't explain why environmentally motivated companies prosper. There are many well-managed, efficient companies without much environmental awareness; and there are companies with great environmental awareness that, nonetheless, do not succeed in business terms. Some other ingredient is needed to catalyze the interrelationship of environmental innovation and business growth.

The experience over the last few years suggests that the key catalyst may be the development of learning capabilities. The disciplines of organization learning, when practiced over time, have proven very effective in bringing about the kinds of fundamental innovation that lead to compelling breakthroughs in new products and processes, as well as cost savings from energy efficiency and reduced materials use and waste. At the same time, the assumptions behind sustainable industrial design—such as dematerialization, cradle-to-cradle product responsibility, and "natural" strategies (following the example of nature's processes) for growth, cooperation, and competitive success—have proven very effective "boosters" for organizational learning initiatives. The concept of sustainable development shakes up existing industrial habits of thinking and doing, and spurs people to fresh solutions. In short, environmental innovation and organizational learning reinforce each other.

In our experience, three elements of organizational learning are essential to success with sustainable development:

■ **Shared vision and personal mastery**. A compelling vision that connects with what people care about is a powerful ingredient for change. And employees strongly identify with the values represented by sustainable development. Thus, when sustainable development objectives become part of a corporate vision, this creates a "pull" for change rather than the "push" dynamic of traditional, highly directive management. Because sustainable development often aligns personal values with business goals, people bring exceptional energy to driving efforts forward in this area.

IKEA, a global furnishings company headquartered in Sweden, with over $6 billion in annual revenues, tapped into this reservoir of energy for change when the world around them shifted. The use of formaldehyde in furniture manufacturing came under media scrutiny after Denmark issued tough new regulations on its use. To promote compliance, the government decided to prosecute IKEA, even though consumers had expressed no concerns and the quantity of formaldehyde used by IKEA only slightly exceeded the new limits. The press treated the prosecution as a major story. IKEA soon experienced a one-third drop in its Danish retail sales. To IKEA, whose mission is to make life better for its customers, the adverse publicity and lost sales were genuinely shocking.

IKEA's president, Anders Moberg, responded by convening a task force under the company's Quality Division to examine how environmental issues would affect IKEA in the future and how IKEA was likely to affect the environment. After conferring with numerous organizations, including environmental, government, business, and academic groups, the task force engaged the assistance of The Natural Step, based in Stockholm. IKEA decided to adopt the four "system conditions" for sustainable industrial activity posited by The Natural Step (see p. 535) as part of their business approach. The company embarked on a series of rapid innovations, culminating in the production of an "eco-plus" line of furniture. Although the "eco-plus" line was generally higher in cost than other IKEA lines, it was priced to be the "lowest-cost environmentally friendly furniture available."

The energy and pull for this type of activity does not have to be created. It is already there in the form of people's deep concern about the environment. Leaders can legitimize the effort by clearly affirming, in a vision or value statement or business rationale, the link between the company's core mission and sustainability—which works best if the issue is personally motivating to them as well. Forums must then be established where people can come together to creatively understand the implications for their part of the business. These meetings should be structured so that people can articulate their own values and aspirations and begin to organize themselves around the new opportunities. Finally, leaders must reinforce the message through speeches and memos and through tangible support of early initiators' efforts and results.

■ **Team learning and mental models.** Companies that align with sustainable development will need new mental models for thinking about their business and new ways to reach across internal and external boundaries. This is hard work, particularly because the "pull" power of sustainable development as an aspiration may bring diverse groups of people together in collaborations that require breaking down old boundaries.

Hyde Tool, a Massachusetts-based family-owned business that manufactures hand tools, gained a competitive cost position in its market by relentlessly focusing on pollution prevention. Environmentalism galvanized a spirit of organizational learning and experimentation across traditional boundaries. A purchasing department employee suggested a change in the display of putty knives that cut annual paperboard purchases by eight tons, reduced distribution box sizes by 12 percent, saved the company $40,000 per year, and increased the enthusiasm of retailers (including Wal-Mart) for the product. The company cut its annual discharge of process wastewater from 29 million gallons to 1 million—moving on the way to zero. Hyde Tool also reduced its potential future liability by diverting 1,000 tons of solid waste generated by its tool-grinding operation from a landfill to use as an ingredient in the production of blacktop.

The Scandic Hotels story comes from *The Natural Step: Good Examples; Business Case Study, Sweden,* by Change the Way Foundation, 1996. Available from Change the Way Foundation, P.O. Box 375, Inverlock, 3996, Australia.

Employee teams at Scandic Hotels have embarked in the past two years on an environmental initiative called the "Resource Hunt," which seeks to reduce water and energy consumption by 20 percent and unsorted waste by 30 percent. Breakthroughs include a computerized system for tracking energy and emissions per guest, allowing Scandic to give discounts to guests who used less energy. They have saved 17 percent of their annual laundry costs by reducing their use of energy, water, and detergent—enough to recover the cost, within a year, of their new equipment. Because its environmental sustainability goals are so much in line with those of its employees and guests, these innovations consistently reinforce its image as a company that cares about people. In 1997, for the first time, Scandic was placed on the list of the 100 most desirable companies to work for in Sweden.

On the surface, getting people to collaborate in ways that generate new ideas and add real value to the enterprise seems straightforward. In reality, it is difficult to sustain. Many collaborative efforts fall prey to divisive, competitive behaviors and falter before they produce any results. Rather than learning from their differences, groups often settle for superficial agreement, or polarize into different camps, reinforcing existing preconceptions and approaches. Team learning skills in areas such as dialogue and the effective use of advocacy and inquiry, along with protocols for collective reflection, enable groups to quickly turn diverse perspectives to their advantage.

■ **Systems thinking.** Sustainable development is shaped by an innate appreciation for systems: particularly the mutually sustaining interdependent causal relationships among the economic, environmental, and social spheres. Actions to meet goals in one of these spheres affect the others and are helped or hindered by them. One chemical company, for example, while siting a facility in a town in India, undertook to train not just new employees in environmental mangagement techniques, but to support an educational infrastructure. The company reasoned that its facility would flourish better in an environment with enough trained workers to attract other similar companies and develop a center of manufacturing competence.

As IKEA worked through its experience with formaldehyde and rolled out its new "environmental" line of furniture, it learned a powerful lesson about systems and unintended consequences. By creating a new, more "environmentally friendly" line, IKEA inadvertently divided its customers into those who could afford the better line and those who could not. In addition, because IKEA provides detailed information to its customers about the contents of its products, information about the new furniture line potentially raised questions in customers' minds about the contents of the other product lines. To remain consistent with its core business vision, IKEA rethought its strategy and decided to approach *all* of its product lines from an environmental perspective, starting with the bestselling lines.

Looking back at these events, people at IKEA view them as pivotal to a shift in providing customers a higher quality of life. IKEA is developing systems to account for closed-loop, "cradle-to-cradle" product accountability, covering dematerialization, design for disassembly, and recycling. In some countries, IKEA is experimenting with furniture recycling, partnering with firms that will distribute old furniture for reuse, or disassemble and recycle old furniture components.

This systems-oriented, proactive approach has helped IKEA regain market share and continue its global expansion. Today, it is the largest interior furnishings company in the world, with over US $6 billion in revenues.

The best source on "green buildings," with dozens of in-depth examples from around the world, is *Green Development: Integrating Ecology and Real Estate*, by Alex Wilson, Jenifer L. Uncapher, Lisa McManigal, L. Hunter Lovins, Maureen Cureton, and William D. Browning (Snowmass, CO: Rocky Mountain Institute and New York: John Wiley and Sons, 1998). Also see the CD-ROM *Green Developments*, by the Rocky Mountain Institute and the Center for Renewable Energy and Sustainable Technology (Windows 95, Windows 3.1, and Macintosh compatible), Snowmass, CO: Rocky Mountain Institute, 1997.

Leading commercial developers are now demonstrating that they can design and build "green" office buildings at costs that are competitive with conventional construction, but with operating costs that are half that of conventional buildings. This requires a total systems view of the building—recognizing the interactions of physical systems such as windows, lighting systems, heating, ventilation, and air-conditioning, while rethinking the ways that these systems best support the needs of the occupants. These buildings have many tangible benefits, such as natural lighting, increased air flow, personal control of lighting, and the right balance between individual work areas and areas for collaboration—factors that have been shown to contribute to marked increases in productivity and job satisfaction. Thus the initial investment in design and construction repays itself over and over, in both substantially lower operating costs, and in the value of work accomplished in the building. To make this innovative design and construction process work, developers and owners have had to create new levels of collaboration and teamwork across all of the disciplines involved—for example, to provide incentives for builders linked to operating costs, not just construction costs.

■ **Measurement and feedback.** Knowledge and skills in these new areas may bring awareness of the larger systemic impacts, but will not necessarily lead to action. Most organizations still maintain measurement and feedback systems that reinforce a short-term focus and reward actions that optimize the parts (e.g., department or functional goals) rather than the whole system. But companies that have changed their approach to measurement have often gained significant insights that have led to new innovations.

Beginning in the early 1990s, British Petroleum has been broadening their sphere of measurement to include monitoring changing public perceptions of BP's contribution to the economy, environmental protection, and social responsibility. They have also maintained similar public perceptions of the oil and chemical industries. Insights gained from seeing these public sentiments change has been a significant factor in BP altering their strategy and public leadership stance on global climate change, and increasing their investments in renewable energy technologies.

Interface's comprehensive "take-make-waste" approach to analyzing their environmental impact led them to invent attractive new designs for their carpets that use less materials and that can be more easily recycled into new carpet. And, as they measured and began to understand the impact of customers disposing of old carpet to land-fills, they invented an "evergreen" lease for their carpets, with take-back and remanufacturing of old carpets. They expect this lease program to drive new growth for the business while significantly reducing their environmental impacts.

A condensed version of this article, by the same authors, appeared in the 4th Quarter, 1998 issue of PRISM, a management journal published by Arthur D. Little.

REACHING FOR SUSTAINED LEARNING AND SUCCESS

These stories illustrate the rewards and challenges facing any company attempting to realign its principles and business activities with sustainable development goals. Their key to success has been the willingness to keep learning from the experience of pursuing a sustainable goal. In the end, sustainable development can't be achieved without innovation, and innovation is best achieved in a culture that embraces and fosters learning and change.

THE NATURAL STEP

Swedish physician Karl-Henrik Robèrt founded The Natural Step in Sweden in 1989, as part of a personal effort to enable that country to move toward becoming a sustainable industrial economy. The Natural Step has brought together an international network of experts focused on moving beyond debate on policies and costs to see how much can be accomplished through a rigorous process of consensus building.

To accomplish this, Robèrt and his colleagues embarked on a search for principles that would garner the widest possible agreement while providing unambiguous, clear direction toward achieving a sustainable society. After a lengthy consensus process in Sweden, they articulated four key principles: Substances from the earth's crust must not systematically increase in nature. Substances produced by human society must not systematically increase in nature. The physical basis for the productivity of nature must not be systematically deteriorated. And the use of resources must be efficient and just with respect to meeting human needs.

In Sweden, the first Natural Step report was endorsed by the king and by many national leaders, and 4.3 million copies were distributed—one to every household and school. The network has grown to include scientists, economists, teachers, environmental activists, politicians, business leaders, artists, and others. Natural

For information about The Natural Step, and for links and recommendations of other resources on corporate environmentalism, see the Web links kept updated on: *http://www.fieldbook.com/natstep.html.*

Step organizations are now active in the Netherlands, the U.S., the U.K., Canada, Australia, and New Zealand. — Bryan Smith

~~~~~~~~~~~~~~~~~~~~~~

THE TIMELESS WAY OF BUILDING
by Christopher Alexander (New York: Oxford University Press, 1979)

"A system is given its character by those events which keep on happening there most often." This has serious implications for the leader who sees the need for change. Walk around your organization and observe the physical, social, and informational flows, and the behaviors and events that keep repeating. Which support the future vision of your organization? Which need to be designed out, by having attention flow in another direction?

The author may not know it, but Christopher Alexander's architecture book is a must-read for any leader who wants to support an organization's capability to sustain itself as a living system. This book, written in 1979, is also timeless for its observations and suggestions in designing systems which work. Be sure to read his instructions on how to read his book. — Charlotte Roberts

~~~~~~~~~

8 After the Rainforest

Tachi Kiuchi, John Savage, and Takashi Yoshida, Mitsubishi Electric Corporation

Tachi Kiuchi, Chairman of Mitsubishi Electric America, Mitsubishi's American subsidiary, until 1997, is known for his persuasive vision for combining economic imperatives and environmentalist ideals. His speech, "What I Saw at the Rainforest," is one of the best-known environmental statements by a prominent corporate leader. In 1992, he describes how he had been targeted by a letter-writing campaign in which elementary school children, mistakenly assuming that he was connected with a Mitsubishi trading company, pleaded with him to stop destroying the rainforests. Though the two Mitsubishi companies had been sundered 46 years earlier, Kiuchi's curiosity was piqued, and

he made an in-depth visit to the Malaysian rainforests. When he returned, he entered into partnerships with the Rocky Mountain Institute and the Rainforest Action Network, but he also came back intent on transforming Mitsubishi Electric into an environmentally conscious company. As he noted in the Rainforest speech:

"A rainforest has almost no productive assets as we know them. Its soil is thin; it has few nutrients. Yet rainforests are incredibly productive, more than any business in the world. They are home to millions of types of plants and animals; more than two thirds of all biodiversity in the world, so perfectly mixed that they sustain themselves and continuously evolve into an ever more complex form.

"Imagine how creative, how productive, how ecologically benign we could be if we could run our companies like the rainforest," Kiuchi continues. "How can we begin? By operating less like a machine, and more like a living system. An industrial ecosystem. That is why, at Mitsubishi Electric, we have begun to adopt an environmental management system founded on principles of industrial ecology. For us, this means two things: First, we must have our eyes wide open, and see the environmental costs and benefits of our business. Second, based on what we see, we must take action . . . We must take responsibility for the impacts of our products, from cradle to cradle. From now on it is not just quality of product. It is quality of the Earth."

Many other companies are following similar paths, and thus the Mitsubishi Electric story provides a fascinating model—not just of corporate environmentalism, but of the aftermath to an ideal. How can executive leaders translate a vision from the rainforest back to local action? We asked Mr. Kiuchi for his perspective, and we also asked two of the people who have been called upon to create Mitsubishi's environmental practice: John Savage, Executive Vice President of Mitsubishi Electric America, the corporation's American subsidiary; and Takashi Yoshida, Manager of Strategic Planning for Mitsubishi at their central offices in Tokyo. Together, drawing upon Mitsubishi's experience, they suggested these principles:

For more about Mitsubishi Electric's activities, a transcript of Mr. Kiuchi's speech, and other relevant documents, see the Web site http://www.globalff.com. We also wish to thank Bill Shireman of Global Futures for his help in arranging and developing this article.

SPEAK PERSONALLY

Tachi Kiuchi: Unless people have a strong interest in learning, it doesn't work to try to motivate them. That is why I continue to speak personally, about my experience at the rainforest, and about the big picture as I see it. People would not be enthusiastic if I talked about environmental issues in general terminology.

Savage: It takes someone stepping forward to take a leadership role and be willing to shoulder the risk. Otherwise, environmentalism remains a compliance function, as opposed to a business management function. It stays outside of the mainstream.

Today, some people still go through the motions because we have a written policy that says we'll have an environmental committee; we'll meet twice a year, and so on. But Tachi's rainforest visit and the authentic energy he brought back from it transformed us. There's a real sense that we are doing this because it's the right thing to do, not because we have a mandate from Tokyo that says, 'This is what thou shalt do.'"

Tachi invited Randy Hayes, head of the Rainforest Action Network, to come in and talk to us in our North American Presidents' Meeting about the issues of the rainforest in terms of the impact on the ecosystem. It helped to take the idea of environmental responsibility from the realm of a politically correct activity, on the order of using recycled papers, to an activity that had real world validity. Even folks on the East Coast started saying, "Save a tree," in passing, whenever we did something that would reduce paper usage.

BRING THE INSIDE OUT

Yoshida: Before the current managing director, Mr. Mitsuhashi, took office, he had little or no information about environmental issues. I knew that he needed to become much more aware about the environment. Otherwise, we would not be able to achieve our environmental goals.

I tried several approaches, but the most successful was to encourage him to participate in outside, environmentally oriented meetings. On several such occasions he was asked to explain Mitsubishi Electric's approach to a particular environmental problem. He had to answer questions in public. This experience encouraged him to learn more.

At first, he was forced to get some knowledge about the environment to answer the questions. But in a few years, he himself was very, very much involved and interested in the environment. And now he's one of the most environmentally conscious managing directors in my company.

INTEGRATE ENVIRONMENTALISM INTO THE WORK

Savage: We moved from talking about environmental practice because the law requires it to talking about the return to the corporation in terms of value. For example, a company in the Atlanta area told us that if we shredded our styrofoam packaging materials, they'd buy it from us, reprocess it, and turn it into styrofoam again. So we put in a styrofoam shredder. We saved a huge amount on the cost of our waste stream, and we got a twofold impact from the environmental standpoint: Styrofoam does not biodegrade, and we were in a rural area of Georgia where there was a significant concern about the landfill being filled up.

We used to just throw corrugated into the compactor. We analyzed this from an economic standpoint and decided to invest in a baler, bale the corrugated, and have it hauled away by a recycler. They didn't pay us anything for it, but because of the reduced waste stream, there was an economic payback.

In each of these areas, we identified places where the managers could say, "This makes good business sense, too." This is the best way to overcome the negative knee-jerk reaction many business managers have when you say "environment" or "ecology." They think, "EPA, fines, regulation," or they think "tree-hugger."

You also need to make the people with environmental responsibility accountable as business managers, not as staff people or even as environmental managers. My own background was human resources. But for a long time I have acted as a business manager with some expertise in that area. Similarly, environmental practice will be conducted not by staff people, but by line managers who can learn environmental principles. These managers will have as much accountability to the bottom line success of that corporation as anybody else does. But they will now be in a position where they can better effect change in the organization.

9 Electricity for All

Learning to rethink the purpose of a major utility

Dr. Ian McRae, former CEO, Eskom, South Africa

When apartheid fell in South Africa in 1990, the managers of Eskom, that country's premier power utility (and the largest electric power company in Africa), had to rethink their company's purpose. This meant undoing the ingrained habits of power-company practice

throughout the world. Dr. Ian McRae, the author of this piece, was CEO of the company during that time. A lifelong Eskom employee, he is generally acknowledged as the custodian of the company's spirit throughout the South African political transition away from apartheid. He retired at age sixty-five, to become the chief of South Africa's National Electricity Regulator Board in Nelson Mandela's government. He was the recipient of the first Servant Leadership award from Sanford University in Birmingham England.

I keep a mural-sized reproduction of a photograph in my office. It shows a small isolated farmhouse on a South African veldt, without water or electricity, and a small tree in its front yard. Behind it, visible not too far in the distance, is a very big power station—one with six six-hundred megawatt generators, enough to supply electricity to several countries at once. But none of that power, produced so near, reaches that house. The wife in that family might have had to walk fourteen hours to fetch their wood. If they remain much longer without electricity, the tree will disappear. And the environment around the house will turn into a desert.

When I was CEO of the Eskom power company, I used to show this photograph in speeches to our managers. Then I would ask: "If we wish to bring electricity to this house, what do you think we should do first?"

Eskom was a company of technologists and engineers, and people had a variety of solutions to propose. But I was always waiting for one answer: "We should go up to the door, knock on it, and ask them what they want."

Over the years, Eskom has developed a new kind of culture. We are now more willing to go and ask people what their needs are. This practice has made a great difference to those of us within the company, who have had to learn how to ask and to listen.

LEARNING TO ASK

I first began to understand this practice in the early 1970s, when I was put in charge of all the power stations after a reorganization. I had spent my entire career at Eskom, working my way up from a position at the bottom of the ladder as an apprentice fitter artisan, and I could see that we did not have enough skills for the future, and would have to begin to train blacks for some skilled jobs.

But legal restrictions existed, preventing blacks from entering many skilled jobs. Trade unions were all white; black trade unions were prohibited. And many blacks were illiterate, because apartheid also restricted their education. If they were to fill skilled jobs, they would have to become literate. We would have to train them to read thermometers and pressure gauges, and to keep written records of the equipment they were operating.

So I went around asking people what they thought of this shift—presenting my view, and listening to theirs. I went from power station to power station, talking to trade unions and managers alike. Most of them did not agree with me; but I kept asking for their concerns. One of the most conservative power station managers phoned me at home. "You keep me awake at night," he said, "and I'm starting to think you're right." Now he accompanied me when I spoke to Eskom managers and engineers. What better consort could I have, in that political environment, than a right-wing leader? I also had to talk to the black staff members, who said, "What if we fail at these new opportunities? What will happen to us then?" I would have to support the measure, I realized, with good training and ongoing development.

We started to introduce blacks into traditionally white skilled jobs for the first time, calling them "operating assistants." It was not good enough, but it was a start. And I had learned the value of going personally to ask people what they wanted from the company.

VISITING THE TOWNSHIPS

I became chief executive of Eskom in 1985. By that time, like many South Africans, I could see that a dismantling of the apartheid system was inevitable. I hoped, of course, that it would come through negotiation and not armed struggle. And I believed that Eskom, in its own little way, could play a role as a catalyst—because our product, electricity, was a critical factor in improving people's ability to deal with poverty.

At the time, black people in urban areas were confined legally to settlements called "townships," without shops or banks. People migrated there to find work, sleeping in shacks, shanties, and plastic bags. These townships had their own separate governments, cut off from the South African infrastructure. Electricity in most townships was bought in bulk from Eskom and disbursed by local councils. Very few people could afford electricity there. And I had been told by some whites that black people did not want electricity. They felt it would be window dressing that would uphold the apartheid system.

Even before I became chief executive, I resolved to learn directly from the people: I must go and ask them. But the townships were under the influence of the African National Congress and other political parties that had been officially banned. If I went in, I would have to deal with them, which I could not do officially as a senior executive of Eskom. So I would have to go in undercover. I did not know anyone who could help me do this. Then, one Sunday night, at the suggestion of a house guest, I went to a church to which I had never been before. The minister was a long-standing white activist named Peter Storey; in his sermon, he said that everyone had to do what we could to help people who were suffering under the apartheid system. After the service, we had a cup of tea, and he agreed to help me set up a meeting.

I brought only one Eskom manager with me; no one else knew I was going. That way, if the police picked me up, people could say that "This guy McRae's lost his head," and I would not put the company into any difficulty. Peter Storey introduced me by saying he believed me, which opened the door for me to ask my questions: "Do you want electricity? Why do you want it? Can you afford it? Will you pay for it? And what do you think of Eskom?"

An old black man at the back replied. "Before we answer," he said, "I want to ask you: What is your relationship with the government?" I explained how Eskom reported to a government but was financially independent. I said I had come because I wanted to be there; no one in government knew I was there. The man at the back was an ANC leader, and I learned later that, if I did not answer sincerely, he was prepared to close the meeting down.

I learned a great deal in Soweto that night, and in the many visits and meetings that followed (and that continued after I became CEO of Eskom). Yes, people wanted electricity. Their first requirement, every time, was a light bulb. Secondly, they wanted something they could cook on without having to gather fuel. For most urban blacks, electricity would save them money, rather than cost them money. But they had no confidence in the local councils that dispensed electricity. Meters were placed outside the homes, and often no one read the meters—so people were billed arbitrarily, sometimes for phenomenal amounts. No one kept track of who paid and who did not. Unlike other products, such as bread, there was no way to tell, ahead of time, what the electric bill would be. There was no way to govern your own use, to make the most of your power. You simply got a bill at the end of the month. That's why people couldn't afford electricity.

They said that all they wanted was a utility with good service, one that they could trust. "If we get that," they added, "we will assure you that you will get paid [for your power]." I asked for time to think about it and return with more developed thoughts. That was the most I could do. The Electricity Act prohibited Eskom from providing electricity directly to the townships. And no one at the meeting had told me that, even if the laws changed, they wanted us to enter.

Yet I had no doubt that Eskom had to try to provide electricity for all South Africa. Otherwise, we would be blamed in the future when the government changed, even if we did not think it was our responsibility now. Moreover, I felt a moral responsibility toward this problem which, it seemed to me, no one but Eskom was in a position to address.

TWO VISIONS FOR ESKOM'S FUTURE

Through the late 1980s, we debated the matter at Eskom. The company chairman, John Maree, and many senior managers, already had a vision: That Eskom would be a "top utility," meaning an organization with world-class performance. We were, in fact, making great strides in getting our numbers of people down, improving our bottom line, and supplying our industrial customers. But as chief executive, I began to propose the idea of "Electricity for All"—a phrase proposed by one of our staff members. And a few of us also began to talk about "Electricity for Peace"—because we had learned, once again by going into seemingly unfriendly territory and asking, that we could use our primary energy supplies as a basis for collaboration between South Africa and its communist or hostile neighbors.

First in small gatherings, and then at our top-30 managers' meetings, I began to talk about these ideas. At first, the majority of people answered no. It would be risky to get involved in social issues; it would impact the bottom line; and it was not our concern. John Maree argued that it would take our focus away from being a top utility. However, I felt that there had to be a greater or superordinate reason why we wanted to be the top utility. Around that time, I attended a dinner for Florida Power & Light, when they won the Deming award, the Japanese award for superior quality. They had put everything they had into the competition, and it had drained them. The chairman said to me, "I don't know what's going to happen to us after we get this award. We need the kind of vision that you are developing."

Gradually I discovered that a great base of support had developed, within Eskom, for the idea of "electricity for all." We began to change our policies to support this. When the government insisted that we shut township people off for nonpayment, we refused. We knew that shutting off electricity to towns and large areas put undue pressure on both the people and their township governments; sometimes it provoked violent riots. We insisted, instead, on investigating the reasons for nonpayment—which often had to do with the local township councils' service quality. We worked to help the local councils improve their service, and put pressure on them to comply.

Then, in the 1990s, we developed a technological innovation that addressed the problem directly: the prepaid meter. Someone in the townships had inspired this, by telling us, "When I put petrol in my motor car, I can actually see it going in. I know what I will be asked to pay, because I can see it in a gauge." Even with a pile of wood, you can see how much fuel you have left, before you run out. So we designed a box, about the size of a small shoebox, with a light bulb socket and a plug for, say, a hot plate. We put a little meter on the side, to show them how much electricity they were using—and then we incorporated an electronic card slot. They could buy cards with an allowance of so many units of electricity, whose usage they could control. Later, we added refinements, such as a yellow light that would warn people to go buy more electricity.

Electrification, we have learned, means much more than simply stringing wires. In the township of Tembisa, where they have wires but no prepaid meters, the level of payment is about 10 to 15 percent. In Ivory Park, where the meters are in place, there is an 80 to 90 percent payment rate, and usage is high. This means that quality of life is higher; people can read at night, cook without carrying fuel, and look for work more effectively.

To achieve this sort of thing, you must start in small ways. It took us more than twenty years to prepare for our "overnight" transition. Having the experience, all the way back in the mid-1970s, of asking people about how they felt about training blacks, gave me the confidence to pursue bolder visions later on.

If you are a senior manager, and you want to know what people will need from your company, there is no shortcut to an authentic answer. You have to go and ask them yourself, long before things come to a crisis point. Ask your employees, ask your customers, and ask those who might become your customers—and then, most importantly, listen to them. If you wish your organization to survive the crisis, whenever it may come, you must be prepared to act thoughtfully on the answers you get.

The corporate initiative described here has been continued and amplified by Dr. McRae's successors: Eskom chief executive officer Allen Morgan, and Eskom chairman Reuel Khoza. We wish to thank Louis van der Merwe, CEO of the Centre for Innovative Leadership (Johannesburg) for making this segment possible.

10 Conscious Oversight

A discipline of organizational stewardship

Charlotte Roberts

In early 1998, British Petroleum CEO John Browne said that a central concern of the company's board of directors is to nurture the social and economic health of the villages, towns, and cities in which BP does business. So strong is his belief, he reportedly has made "social investment for the long term" an important variable in compensating BP employees around the world.

Some of the resulting projects include developing computer-based technology to control flood damage, replanting a forest around the Black Sea, donating two hundred solar-powered refrigerators to help doctors store anti-malaria vaccines, and turning BP's waste material into local home-building materials. "These efforts have nothing to do with charity," said Browne, "and everything to do with our long-term self-interest. I see no trade-off between the short term and the long. Twenty years is just eighty quarters. Our shareholders want performance today and tomorrow and the day after."

The quote comes from "Globalism Doesn't Have to Be Cruel," by Jeffrey E. Garten, *Business Week*, February 9, 1998, p. 26.

This action taken by a global corporation—to see a wider system with more than just fiscal boundaries, existing in a much longer span of time than just a quarter or a fiscal year—points to the existence of a discipline of complexity for leaders: conscious oversight. When people ask if there is another body of study and practice besides the five "learning disciplines" of *The Fifth Discipline* that is crucial for organizations, I point to this one. People who develop competence and skill in the five learning disciplines will naturally find themselves drawn into the practice and study of conscious oversight, just as people who develop competence in personal mastery find themselves drawn into shared vision. Like the other disciplines, conscious oversight requires deliberate study and practice throughout the organization, hopefully modeled and coached by the executive leaders.

Conscious oversight is a discipline of care and nurturing of people and systems with an eye toward the impact on generations who come after them. The discipline encompasses the ability to see and understand the system at hand as part of a nested body of larger systems, and to make thoughtful decisions about matters that will have significant consequences across many years. Decisions made as part of this discipline are full of respect—for the traditions of the past (while distinguishing those parts which are still important), for the realities of today (from a variety of points of view), and for the sustainability of life for generations who come after. When practicing conscious oversight, people focus on insuring congruence and viability of a system larger than themselves, in service of a purpose larger than themselves.

It is not an easy discipline to master; as I write this, for instance, British Petroleum has just announced a merger with Amoco. Based on the priorities of both companies, there is reason to think that the emphasis on "social investment for the long term" will survive the pressures of the merger. But when conscious oversight is recognized as a discipline, then "impossible" missions like social investment for the long term become more feasible. They do not have to be mastered immediately because people learn to master them over time.

THE CONTEXT OF CONSCIOUS OVERSIGHT

As it happens, there is a long tradition of conscious oversight in organizations. It is a significant, though often unvoiced, aspect of any community's life where the community is expected to last beyond the life or tenure of any individuals.

For instance, not long ago I was riding in a van with a group of students and faculty members from a small, closely knit college. The students began talking about a rival college, whose students' politics they didn't agree with, with whom they would be attending a college leadership conference. "What if they show up at our presentation and picket us?" one of the students asked.

"If they do," said another student, "We'll take 'em out."

For a moment, there was laughter. Then one of the adults said, in a light and gentle tone, "I hope you are using the phrase 'take them out' to mean, 'invite them to a social gathering.'" Everyone in the van knew the point; in this closely knit community, everyone was affected by a joke about doing violence to another person. The student had not committed a major offense; anything more than a gentle comment would have been inappropriate. But to leave the remark hanging with no response would have sent the message that the adults didn't care about the person that the student would become, or the fact that as an alumnus, he would be linked with the college's reputation forever.

Knowing how to take that kind of action, in any situation, and feeling that sort of responsibility for the future, are two facets of conscious oversight. The word "conscious" suggests "deliberation." The practitioner slows down the hubbub of daily activity to reflect on the system and situation from a variety of perspectives, and in a variety of ways of thinking. In addition, this discipline seeks to make the organization conscious—to bring an ongoing deliberation into everyone's frame of reference, and to give them time, permission, methods, and support to take the long view in the midst of making decisions and generating business results.

The term "oversight" is borrowed from a group with a rich tradition of sustaining community responsibility—the Society of Friends (Quakers). Historical writings recorded in *Faith and Practice* describe part of the practice of oversight as building and sustaining relationships throughout the system.

In any Society of Friends community, there is an oversight committee, whose purpose is to enhance the total health and sustainability of the community. Many decisions in a Society of Friends community are made through meetings and consensus. But sometimes there isn't time for consensus. If the members of the oversight committee believe that a change is needed with urgency, they may move forward in the decision without waiting for everyone's agreement. It should be clear to all, from the way they exercise this move, that they are acting out of deep discernment for the welfare, present and future, of the community.

In early Quaker communities (and in some that exist now), there were no ministers. No individual leader was responsible for the community's well-being. The care of the community was shared. Early writings about oversight stated, "Desirable as it is that some should be specially entrusted with these (oversight) duties, an earnest concern has prevailed that all may take their right share in the privilege of watching over one another for good." Through the rotation of the membership on the oversight committee, the community developed the practice as a part of their character and genetic code. "Watching over one another for good" became a natural awareness and capability of individuals and the community at large.

Conscious oversight is relevant for an increasing number of organizations in our time. Leaders want to develop the agility and flexibility of their teams, departments, or companies, so they can act autonomously and quickly to adapt with the marketplace. I have heard this called, "creating a virtual organization." To act with autonomy and flexibility, you need to feel as if you belong to a purposeful organization. That, in turn, requires developing an organization with an innate sense of community.

Most organizations already do have a sense of community—but it

66 "The life of the community consists in something more than the body of principles it professes and the outer garments of organization which it wears. The spring of life that often escapes recognition is in practicing fellowship to build unity of spirit among the community. This unity allows the members to mold organization into the fresh forms demanded by its own growth and the changing needs of the time. Where there is not this freedom, the community has its life cramped by ill-assorted clothes and its work becomes dwarfed or paralyzed." From *Christian Faith and Practice in the Experience of the Society of Friends*, London Yearly Meeting of the Religious Society of Friends (Richmond, Indiana: Friends United Press, 1960), Chapter 7.

works at cross-purposes to the organization's direction. When a teenager comes to work in a plant for the summer and wants to make as much money as possible, he or she tends to work very hard for the first day or so. Then the community kicks into gear. Soon, one of the permanent workers will pull the teenager aside. "Look, you don't have to work here for the rest of your life. We do. So we don't want you working so hard and making it hard on us. Slow down and be a part of the team." That's an example of oversight, but with a different outcome than most leaders desire in the workplace. This type of oversight fills the gap when the official leadership is "unconscious" to community issues.

When conscious oversight becomes a part of the genetic code of a community, there will be a "leaderful" organization (as Meg Wheatley calls it). The community speaks through all of its members, and any of its members may step forward as needed to lead.

SIX INTELLIGENCES

The practice of conscious oversight rests on this principle: being responsible for large systems requires the exercise of multiple intelligences. Human beings are, in fact, intelligent in a variety of ways, but most of us have not learned to exercise all of them at once. If we can learn to do so, then we can become more comfortable and facile with complexity and ambiguity.

To describe these intelligences, I use the metaphor of an office building with six floors. The first two floors are easily accessible. Almost all managers and leaders have had some formal learning experiences with fiscal and social intelligence. The latter four floors are more obscure. Some leaders and managers have been exposed to noetic, environmental, emotional, and spiritual intelligence, but rarely in any deliberate way that draws all of them together and increases the mastery of conscious oversight.

■   By **fiscal intelligence** I mean the ability to understand and act upon financial flows, processes, and procedures—for example, to recognize the types of external pressures embodied in the oscillation of supply and demand, or the changing costs of raw materials, and to recognize the internal leverage that an individual manager or team has to affect the company's global profitability. Financial intelligence can be employed mechanistically and even cruelly, but it doesn't have to be. At its best, it is a critical tool for placing value on people's time, assets, and relationships, and for learning how the business creates financial viability.

See for example, articles by Phil Carroll, page 203; and Tom Botts, page 384; about fiscal intelligence at Shell Oil; and the article by Jack Stack, page 380, about fiscal intelligence at Springfield Remanufacturing Corporation.

■ **Social intelligence** too often gets labeled as the "soft, touchy-feely stuff." However, it has long been proven, first perhaps by Kurt Lewin, that the quality of relationships directly impacts productivity. Out of their discomfort with touchy-feely matters, some leaders prefer to delegate the responsibility for social health, either to formal positions such as human resources or informal positions, a charismatic or affiliative team member. But this delegation always backfires. Leaders don't have the luxury of saying, "The quality of relationships is not part of my job."

Social intelligence allows a leader to choose the appropriate social form for teams and departments—committed work teams, self-directed teams, work groups, task forces, etc.—and to coach people in their new relationships. By understanding the demand of the work and the current group's social capacity, a leader with social intelligence can intervene more effectively. Social intelligence also allows leaders to sense where in the organization there is a social problem and whether people are ready to face the issue. Leaders can frame the issue to bring the right parties to the table for dialogue about their issue. This type of intelligence attunes people to social issues that are brewing, and will surface in the near future. Corporate leaders, for example, who were attuned to the emergence of single-parent women in the workplace were first to recognize that onsite daycare would help them retain talented employees.

Two good sources for building social intelligence are *Leadership Without Easy Answers,* by Ronald Heifetz (Cambridge, MA: Harvard University Press, 1994) and *Seeing Systems,* by Barry Oshry (San Francisco: Berrett-Koehler, 1995).

■ **Noetic intelligence** focuses on the capability for thinking and learning, particularly in groups—and thus continuously raising the collective IQ. If an organization is survive and thrive long term, people must have the ability to perceive changes in the environment in a timely way, to build shared understanding of the incoming data, and create knowledge throughout the organization.

When executives have asked for help in building a learning organization or establishing a knowledge management system, they have recognized a need for developing this type of mental, noetic capacity throughout the organization. Much of *The Fifth Discipline Fieldbook* is dedicated to tools and techniques for developing noetic intelli-

Ron Nahser, author of *Learning to Read the Signs*, offers pragmatism, a form of practiced self-awareness, as another method to develop noetic intelligence. See *Learning to Read the Signs: Reclaiming Pragmatism in Business*, by F. Byron Nahser (London: Butterworth-Heinemann, 1997).

See *Executive EQ: Emotional Intelligence in Leadership and Organizations*, by Robert K. Cooper and Ayman Sawaf (New York: Putnam, 1997). This book is good for executives and managers who are trying to develop more emotional intelligence.
I particularly like the opening, which considers the value of emotional intelligence and leadership in organizations. — Charlotte Roberts

gence, individually and collectively. This requires patience, willingness to engage, and the skill of reflection. Too many times I have heard people complain that they are wasting time if they aren't doing something; thinking about thinking just isn't part of the culture of many organizations. But the growth of noetic intelligence requires sustained reflection.

■ **Emotional intelligence** has been given attention in the last few years. This intelligence focuses on sensing and surfacing emotions in real time and identifying the "message" they are conveying. You may have had the experience in the past of explaining to someone, "I can't describe to you rationally why I'm doing this. I feel it strongly and yet can't give it words. I just know it's the right thing to do." Emotional intelligence is an inner compass to sense what we know to be right.

Conscious oversight depends on leaders who can sense the emotional health of the community so the community will not be blocked or sabotaged by inarticulated, suppressed, or mistargeted emotions. Emotional intelligence can also help people pick up on weak or oblique signals in the community and environment. However, emotional intelligence is rare in organizations, because most of us have endorsed in our work cultures the discouragement of the experience or expression of emotions. We have created our own organizational disability by making emotions undiscussable or inappropriate.

Robert Cooper and Ayman Sawaf offer a significant contribution in this arena. In their book, *Executive EQ*, they not only describe the four cornerstones of emotional intelligence (emotional literacy, emotional fitness, emotional depth, and emotional alchemy), they have developed and tested the EQ Map Questionnaire, for mapping your emotional intelligence.

Emotional intelligence is closely related to two other intelligences. Social intelligence has a close tie because emotional intelligence is needed for creating trusting relationships. It is also being closely associated with noetic intelligence. The head of neurology at the University of Iowa College of Medicine stated, "In truth, reasoning and emotion intersect in the brain. Feelings and emotion have a powerful influence on reasoning. Feelings retain a primacy that pervades our mental life. Their influence is immense."

■ **Environmental intelligence** represents attention to the physical environment—an obvious element of the total well-being of a group of people and yet often ignored. Managers plan for and measure safety, examining the ways that the physical environment and management practices support safe behavior—but we don't often think of the air we're breathing in a closed building or the quality of light around our open work spaces.

Recently, a newly appointed CEO inherited a corporate move from a suburban setting to a center-city office building. He was told it was a great financial move with many incentives offered by the city. The office space was more plush and in a high-status location. However the overall environment made people feel sick. There were long hallways and doors behind doors. The physical barriers for able people were noticeable, and required a great deal of effort from physically challenged people. During the first winter, there were more flu cases than expected, which led people to investigate the air filtration system. Employees have begun to voice concern about their safety in the underground parking garage, originally considered a perq.

The simplest application of environmental intelligence could have avoided all this. Leaders need to sense what it feels like to work in the space provided. Is it too open? Too crowded? Too spread out? Too intellectually or emotionally sterile? Engaging members of the organization to help in the healthy design of their environment can lead to incredible results.

}} The Natural Step is a good starting place for environmental intelligence. See page 535.

■ **Spiritual intelligence** may well be the aspect of conscious oversight that makes leaders the most uncomfortable. And yet I have found in the last two years, it is the one subject that leaders most eagerly want to talk about. Consultants and other people are writing books and articles, holding seminars, and designing internal management retreats—all dealing with soul and ethics at work.

Yet we are also told that this subject is off limits in the workplace. The reason given is the separation of church and state—the unwillingness to create an atmosphere that might exclude "nonbelievers." That's the first misunderstanding surrounding this intelligence. Spirituality is not about religion. It is about the space, freedom, and safety to bring our whole beings to work. When we work in an organization without much spiritual intelligence at play, we become tired, fractured, and dissatisfied. We feel invisible, as if no one sees us.

In 1997, two organizations asked me to lead spirituality retreats for their top 250 managers. When I asked them what outcomes they were hoping for, both leaders said that they wanted people to know they were valued and respected, that they belonged to a community

A Tibetan elder described spirituality as authentic presence. "When people are able to live from their heart and soul experience, we are able to talk openly and honestly with each other, say the things we deeply feel, even when it's hard to say. We can hold ourselves and each other accountable to our best effort in all things. We can search for our calling, for the path we are born to take. We can take the chance to keep learning from whatever is here now." The quote is from the preface to *Executive EQ: Emotional Intelligence in Leadership and Organizations*, by Robert K. Cooper and Ayman Sawaf (New York: Putnam, 1997).

Other useful sources on spiritual intelligence include *Business As a Calling: Work and the Examined Life*, by Michael Novak, (New York: Free Press, 1996) and *Towards a Theology of the Corporation*, by Michael Novak (Washington, D.C., AEI Press, 1991); and *Stewardship*, by Peter Block (San Francisco: Berrett-Koehler, 1993), p. 6. *Stewardship* was reviewed in *The Fifth Discipline Fieldbook*, p. 68.

and were not alone, that they could help create a culture that let them bring their whole selves to work, not just their hands or their backs or their brains. To create such an organization without spiritual intelligence would be impossible.

The spirit of an organization is palpable. When you walk into a restaurant, hospital, or manufacturing plant, you can sense the spirit of the organization. You can feel if people are hassled or supported, trampled or developed, used or valued. What did you see or hear to draw you conclusion? You probably can't answer precisely and yet you know what you feel. Your emotional intelligence informs your spiritual intelligence.

One simple example sums up conscious oversight. I spent most of one wintry Sunday night at a crowded airport in Charlotte, North Carolina. With snowstorms raging across the U.S. Atlantic seaboard, there were delays on top of delays. Irritable people wanted to get home from their vacations or reluctantly start their business week.

Finally our plane to Boston boarded. We sat for thirty more minutes on the plane. Then the captain came out of the cockpit, stood in the aisle in the front, and began talking over the flight attendant's microphone. He introduced himself—Orlando Haynes, pilot for USAir.

Then he said: "I'm standing so you can see me. I want to talk with you honestly. Tonight the weather is bad all up the coast and the ride will be bumpy. There will be no cabin service as we go. The weather in Boston is bad and I don't even know if we'll be able to land. We may have to turn around and come back here. If we land, I can tell you, it will be original. You need to know what to expect. Now . . . I have a wife and children and I won't put my life in danger; I want to live to be an old man. I won't land if I'm not confident. You deserve to have all the facts as I know them now. We will be pushing back in five minutes. Think it over. If you aren't comfortable with the situation as I described it, then you may want to wait until tomorrow to fly up. The storm will have passed and Boston will be ready for you. It's your decision to make. If you need help getting your things off the plane; our attendants will help. We want you to make the right choice for you." Several people got off, including me. I could wait until the next day. The flight did land safely that night, although in the wee hours.

I didn't fly with him, but Orlando Haynes had given me, and everyone else on the plane, a rare gift. He had demonstrated that he authentically cared for each of us, including himself and his family. (Have you ever had the pilot leave the sanctuary of the cockpit to engage personally with the customers about the circumstances of the flight? I never have, before or since that incident.) He knew his actions would impact that flight's profitability and also people's impression of his leadership and his company's, long-term financial consequences. He knew people needed to know how scary the flight would be and he honored those emotions. He let every person consider the known facts and make the best decision for him- or herself. He provided us with an everyday example of conscious oversight in practice.

THE INNOVATOR'S DILEMMA
by Clayton M. Christensen (Boston: Harvard Business School Press, 1997)

Books on strategy are most valuable for becoming aware of possibilities that might otherwise never occur to you. This much-praised book by a Harvard Business School researcher does exactly that, debunking the idea that being "responsive to your customers" is a prescription for success. Responsiveness to customers can prevent a company from reinventing itself, precisely because the best, highest-margin customers continually demand stability in their purchases. Clayton Christensen demonstrates all this through a detailed and fascinating study of the computer disk drive industry, the business equivalent to geneticists' fruit flies (because hard disk technology evolves so quickly). — Art Kleiner

RED MARS, GREEN MARS, BLUE MARS
by Kim Stanley Robinson (New York: Bantam Books, 1993-1996)

Ending this chapter with a review of a science fiction trilogy may seem odd, but few books I've seen display as many strategic ramifications for the long run. This is essentially a single scenario for the twenty-first century, with four plausible "critical uncertainties": Mars is slowly colonized and made habitable, the human life span is doubled, global crowding surges (as a result), and corporate governance continues in its current mode. Against that backdrop, the first colonists of Mars and their progeny deal with the same kinds of moral dilemmas and strategic choices that business people must cope with today, rethinking all of their institutions' purposes, and living long enough to see the environmental (and human) impact of their deeds. — Art Kleiner

Endnotes

Endnotes

1 Leadership in the World of the Living

Peter Senge

When all is said and done, there is a central message that underlies the specific details and strategies of all the different challenges of this book. Meeting the challenges of profound change does not represent a set of separate tasks, a sort of checklist of problems to be solved by aspiring leaders. Rather, these challenges—of initiating, of sustaining, and of redesigning and rethinking—arise and present formidable barriers because the world in which we are seeking to sustain profound change is a living world.

We tend not to see it that way. Our personal history in institutions, starting with school, has conditioned most of us to see a mechanical world—a world of measures, plans, and programs, a world of people "in control" and leaders who "drive" change. This leads us to be blind to critical features of the living world that shape whether or not we ever have any success in actually sustaining change.

The Nature of the Challenges

THE TEN CHALLENGES OF PROFOUND CHANGE ARE DYNAMIC, NONLINEAR, AND INTER-dependent. They are dynamic because they arise from balancing processes that naturally "push back" against efforts to produce change. They are "nonlinear," in the sense that you cannot extrapolate reliably from one experience to another. In a different setting, with only a few small distinctions, a given challenge may play out entirely differently. Last, they are interdependent. Addressing one can increase the challenge of addressing another. Or, in other cases, make it easier.

APPRECIATING BALANCING PROCESSES AND COMPENSATING FEEDBACK

Self-proclaimed "change agents" often complain that "people resist change." But the people or groups typecast as resistant rarely see themselves that way. Often, instead, they believe themselves to be quite open. From a systems viewpoint, it is not the people "who are resisting"— rather, it is a system functioning to maintain its internal balances, as all living systems function. Just as all growth in nature is achieved through self-reinforcing growth processes, "homeostasis"—maintaining balances critical to survival—is accomplished through balancing processes.

"History is a process of transformation through conservation," according to biologist Humberto Maturana. In our efforts to produce change, we often forget how important it is to pay attention to what is being conserved. Balancing processes are not the enemy. They are neither inherently good nor bad. Whether or not we value a particular balancing process depends on how much we value *what it conserves.* Balancing processes that conserve financial cash balances, adequate production capacity, technological know-how and innovation, or committed customers are not problems. Indeed, many of the change strategies at the heart of developing learning organizations hinge on conservation of personal purposefulness, honesty, love of inquiry, and the quality of relationships. But, balancing processes that conserve inflexible cultures, outmoded centralized styles of management, defensive routines that stifle innovation, misleading metrics, organizational "stovepipes" that thwart knowledge diffusion, high levels of stress, and fragmented ways of thinking are problems.

The flaw in most leadership strategies stems from fighting blindly against balancing processes, rather than seeking to understand what is being conserved. When this happens, leaders of all types become the victims of "compensating feedback."

Compensating feedback arises when people attempting to produce change do not see the balancing processes that are conserving the status quo. When they encounter difficulties, they "naturally" work harder to overcome them. But "the harder they push, the harder the system pushes back."

Compensating feedback is what happens when a person enters a room with no knowledge of the thermostatic heating system in place.

The quote from Humberto Maturana is from a talk given at the Society for Organizational Learning's (SoL) annual meeting, July, 1998. A transcript edited and expanded by Pille Bunnell is available through SoL; for access, see *http://www.fieldbook.com/sol.html*.

Imagine that the thermostat is set at 90 degrees. You open a window to cool down the room. It works for a short while, until the heater comes on and it starts getting warmer again. You then open another window, with the same results. After a while you have opened every window there is and you can't understand why the room will not cool off. In this case, there is no leverage in opening the windows. Achieving lasting change requires understanding the thermostatic balancing process in operation; You need to either alter the balancing process (for example by turning off the furnace) or reset the thermostat.

Exactly the same happens with each of the limiting processes underlying the challenges of profound change. For example, a local line leader fails to understand why people seem uncommitted to a new initiative. He entreats them to the task, telling people how important it is. Yet the harder he tries to convince them, the less convinced they seem. Somehow "pushing harder" on commitment is not making people more committed. In fact, the harder he pushes, the less committed people seem to be. He fails to see that his own credibility is the real issue—people do not trust that he himself is prepared to change. The more he exhorts them, the more they hear "you must change." Until he addresses the limiting process at play, the "credibility of his values and aims" (Chapter 6), the balancing process will keep compensating for his efforts.

If leaders do not understand the balancing processes and limits underlying each challenge, they do not understand what the system is *trying to conserve*. Each of the individual limiting processes works to conserve some aspect of the status quo. For example, the limiting processes underlying the four challenges of initiating conserve a low rate of successful initiation. They do so through conserving low effectiveness of such initiatives (because pilot groups have neither the time nor help they need) and through conserving low commitment to them (because they are seen as not relevant or because their advocates are distrusted). Each of the challenges of sustaining conserve a high rate of premature mortality of otherwise successful initiatives. For example, the limiting processes of "true believers and nonbelievers" conserve irresolvable differences between innovators and the mainstream by reinforcing each's stereotypes of the other. The same can be said of each of the challenges of rethinking and redesigning, only more so: These limiting processes conserve both low initiation and low sustaining. For example, underlying the challenges of governance are balancing processes that conserve centralized decision-making through conserving low tolerance for local control and conserving low decision-making capabilities of local actors.

Once leaders begin to appreciate these limiting processes and what they are conserving, they can begin to identify higher leverage strategies. In each case, this starts by seeing the balancing process that is at work and what it is trying to conserve. This is why virtually all of the suggested strategies for the challenges in the preceding chapters focus either on weakening those balancing processes or altering the underlying limit or constraint. Otherwise, we will just keep "opening windows," rather than sustaining profound change.

NONLINEARITY

Understanding limiting processes and principles like compensating feedback is very different from having a list of "how to's." Yet many managers seek just these types of answers, and many management books endeavor to provide them. The only problem is that most "how to" books are not very practical.

Generalizing from one situation to the next can be logically sound in a system like the solar system. If you know the location of Pluto today, you can extrapolate its position for the next 2,000 years. This is because the laws of motion that govern the planets are linear laws, where each incremental change in one variable causes a constant incremental change in another. But extrapolation is a fool's occupation in a nonlinear world, where even "perfect knowledge" leads to highly imperfect predictions.

Effective leaders know this intuitively. They know that it is tempting to say, "This is how we did it over there and it worked. So, we should follow the same rules here." But "here" and "there" are never identical and even small differences can alter the outcome of so called "tried and true" formulas. If you have ever worked for a manager who knows "exactly how things should be done," you know what I mean. He or she is trapped in a futile struggle to make today's reality fit yesterday's answers, and everyone suffers as a consequence. This does not imply that there is no learning from experience, but real learning is more subtle than can ever be captured in simple formulas or rules.

This is why we repeatedly emphasize intuitive appreciation of the different challenges to profound change, and reflection on their meaning in your own context. Only through deep understanding of these issues can you lay a foundation for real learning. Only through practice, and continuing reflection, will practical know-how develop. There are no answers. But there are ways of looking at reality that are higher leverage than others.

INTERDEPENDENCIES AMONG THE CHALLENGES

There are three different types of interdependencies, each presenting both problems and opportunities.

1. **Shifting dominance:** when efforts to address one challenge shift pressures to others, so that they require more attention. This is akin to compensating feedback; only here the interaction among different limiting processes generates the difficulties. The more that any one limit is relaxed, the more that others come into play.

   For example, this operates among all four of the challenges of initiating. A profound change initiative will never get too far if there is no compelling case for change (the challenge of "not relevant"). But if there is "relevance" but not enough time, people will be overloaded and their initial commitment will be replaced by frustration at lack of progress. The more management aggressively "makes the case" for change being important to the business, the more frustrated people will be. If there is "relevance" and time *but* no help, the time spent will be unproductive. Pilot group members will use the time to deal with problems as they have always dealt with problems. They will get frustrated because this time is taken away from more urgent problems.

   If all of these first three challenges of initiating are met, then, often for the first time, questions will start to arise about management's values. Such questions might have been there all along, but they will become more important in people's minds if they start to believe that a change initiative might actually be serious—both in terms of the potential benefit and risk.

   Similar shifting dominance interactions operate for all the challenges—progress with each creates conditions that make the others more problematic. For example, from the pilot group's perspective, the challenges of sustaining and of redesigning and rethinking exist only as intellectual problems until the group has generated sufficient momentum and progress that they pose real barriers.

   Shifting dominance is important to understand because it is easy for leaders to feel like "I've fixed the problem that was holding people back; now we'll really make progress." Given this attitude, it is easy to be surprised when new problems arise. But those new problems are suddenly evident precisely because an earlier problem was fixed. Conversely, leaders who understand shifting dominance continually guard against this sort of complacency and are always strategizing about the next challenges, even before they arise.

2. **Related capacities** exist when different constraints underlying different limiting processes stem from similar capabilities. Where there are related capacities, progress with one challenge can carry over to benefit another.

For example, the challenge of fear and anxiety arises to the extent that candor and openness develop more rapidly than a group's capacity for openness (Chapter 7). The key in addressing this challenge lies in building "capacity for openness," the ability to hear one another and tolerate multiple views. These same capabilities play a role also in dealing with the two others challenges of sustaining: measurement and assessment (Chapter 8) and "believers and nonbelievers" (Chapter 9). Both concern confronting problematic views of pilot initiatives, especially views held by people outside the team. In "believers," problems arise when confidence turns to arrogance within a pilot team. When this happens, it is easy for them to become isolated and disengaged when confronting criticisms and misunderstandings from people outside the team. The underlying constraint in this limiting process concerns the team's capacity for "reflective openness," the ability to remain humble and continually question their own assumptions and ways of doing things. If they can do this, they are also more likely to productively engage questions and concerns from outsiders concerning measurable results. In this way, the capacity for openness aids in all three of the challenges of sustaining: being able to really listen to team members who are concerned and being able to reflect on our own assumptions when challenged by outsiders, rather than to simply defend them.

Other cases of "related capacities" include:

■ The role of effective coaching and mentoring ("No help," Chapter 4) in dealing with virtually all the challenges of initiating and sustaining;

■ The benefits of investments in strategic thinking capabilities and developing useful "business models" ("Not relevant," Chapter 5) for the challenges of governance (Chapter 10), for crossing organizational boundaries ("Diffusion," Chapter 11), and as a type of "help" for all pilot groups (Chapter 4);

■ The benefits of a tolerant, flexible culture (Chapter 9) in dealing with questioning and improving metrics (Chapter 8);

■ The benefits of reflective openness for dealing with fear and anxiety (Chapter 7), as an antidote to arrogance ("True Believers and Nonbelievers," Chapter 9), and for the challenges of diffusion and crossing organizational boundaries (Chapter 11).

Leaders who understand related capacities can see how some developments are more fundamental than others because they can benefit multiple challenges. Those who do not understand related capacities see each challenge as unrelated to the others. This is one reason that effective leaders continue to emphasize the core learning capabilities of aspiration, reflective conversation, and understanding complexity. As we showed at the very outset (in Section 2 of Chapter 1), low collective learning capabilities can be a fundamental constraint for any change initiative. Conversely, continually developing these core capabilities lays a foundation for fostering many related capacities. This is also why we regard pilot groups as so important; they are the incubators for developing such learning capabilities.

3. Last, there are also **"fractal relationships"** among particular challenges. In these cases, local challenges constitute microcosms of more global challenges, and local successes may establish a foundation for global change.

For example, the experience of developing time flexibility in a pilot group (Chapter 3) will be very useful in the complex time coordination that goes into, say, a governance structure based on increased local responsibilities and lateral organizational processes (Chapter 10). In this increasingly "networked world," goals, work tasks, and time deadlines are not handed down from bosses and then controlled by traditional management control systems. People continually form and re-form working groups to meet emerging market opportunities and organizational needs. Their skills in prioritizing and coordinating their efforts grow directly from learning to increase time flexibility in pilot groups.

Similarly, coaching skills, the ability to mentor and guide others' development in the context of facing practical issues ("Walking the Talk," Chapter 4), can prove foundational for designing learning infrastructure for community building (Chapter 11). Today, Ford's Visteon is developing learning infrastructure for a global enterprise of over 80,000 people. "What we have learned over the past eight years about coaching is a foundation for what we are doing today," says Visteon's process leadership/learning organization manager, David Berdish. "Our whole approach is based on not having 'learning organization' be another program. Everything we do is aimed at application, helping people do the work they need to do anyway for the business. Using organizational learning tools is one way we do it. My team of thirteen internal coaches and facilitators has only one person with an HR background. Everyone else is from production, finance, purchasing, and industrial engineering. We now have to extend this coaching network to a global scale."

Likewise, pilot groups that successfully address the challenge of "not relevant" are learning to tackle a set of core questions underlying large scale change, albeit on a more local scale: "Why are we here? What are we seeking to accomplish specifically? How do we intend to do it?" and "What do we need to pay attention to in order to assess progress?" Effective local line leaders invariably have a keen focus on key business results, but they also typically don't "drive results." They tend to believe that developing new capabilities and new business practices will lead to better results, so long as people have a clear idea of the results desired. In effect, they learn to "dance" with the paradox of focusing on results and yet not focusing on results.

The same issues operate within larger organizations. For example, thoughtful executive leaders wrestling with strategy and purpose (Chapter 12) invariably start to ask whether or not focusing on shareholder value may be a poor way to generate shareholder value. They appreciate the energy, commitment, imagination, patience, and perseverance needed to build superior shareholder value. "The entrepreneurs whom we work with do not focus on value," says German consultant Thomas Leder of Hirzel, Leder, & Partner. "They, of course, understand the value concept well, since entrepreneurs know that value is future profit. But in their reality, the concept doesn't seem to mean anything in terms of action—it doesn't energize them the way interactions with people or dealing with tasks do." Similarly, they understand that assessing progress is more complicated than simply looking at formal metrics. As managerial accounting expert Fred Kofman once put it, "Managing by the numbers is like trying to coach a team by looking at what is on the scoreboard rather than how the action is unfolding on the field." Such understanding can eventually shape how executives think about measurement systems (Chapter 8) and governance structures (Chapter 10).

One last fractal relationship has to do with authenticity and "walking the talk." Line leaders who inquire effectively into their own values and behaviors at the pilot group level become more reflective and credible. In effect, they become models for the integrity and interpersonal trust needed to explore a host of organizationwide issues. These qualities can help other pilot groups become more open to learning from one another (thereby helping meet the "chal-

See "Double-Loop Accounting: A Language for the Learning Organization," Fred Kofman, *Systems Thinker*, vol. 3, no 1, Feb. 1992, Pegasus Communications, Waltham, Mass.

lenge of diffusion," Chapter 11) and can be invaluable when the time comes to explore potentially volatile countercultural approaches to governance and strategic dilemmas (Chapters 10 and 12).

Communities of leaders or no leadership at all

It would take a genuine flight of fantasy to both take seriously the multiple, interdependent challenges involved in sustaining profound change and still hold the view that change happens because great men "drive" change from the top. How could one or a small number of people at the top of a hierarchy possibly deal with the range of challenges presented in the preceding pages?

Undoubtedly, the diversity of people who lead in addressing these forces exceeds the simple categorization we have used in this book: local line leaders, executive leaders, and internal networkers. But these three types of leaders still represent a good place to begin in thinking about the constituents of a healthy "leadership ecology," an interdependent human community commensurate in diversity and robustness to the challenges of profound change.

- **Local line leaders**. These leaders are vital to initiating significant change. The four challenges of initiating: "no time," "no help," "not relevant," and "walking the talk"—constitute a litmus test for the effectiveness of local line leaders. Unless they deal successfully with all four of these challenges, they will not create conditions where the growth processes of personal results, networks of committed people, and business results can develop momentum. Likewise, local line leaders are vital in addressing the challenges of sustaining change, which play out both within innovative pilot groups, such as the challenge of "fear and anxiety," and between those pilots and the larger organization. Experience has shown again and again that without committed and talented local line leaders, little significant change ever gets initiated and takes root. Value is actually created at the front lines of all organizations, where products and services are designed, produced, marketed, and sold, where customers are served, and where the practical problems impeding these processes are addressed. In a fundamental sense, organizational learning involves the enhancement of capacity to generate value—hence, all organizational learning, ultimately, involves front line people and core business processes where value is created. This is why local line leadership is so essential.

But the strengths of great local line leaders are also their limitations. They are vitally committed to their units or teams, but they tend to pay much less attention to how others might learn from their efforts, or how they might learn from others. They can easily develop disdain for other groups less innovative than theirs. They can run afoul of organizational measurement processes and cultural taboos. They often disregard how their innovations affect other groups. By themselves, they can do little about the challenges of redesigning and rethinking. They depend on internal networkers for mentoring and to connect them to other, like-minded leaders within the larger organization. They depend on executives to develop an overall organizational environment conducive to innovation, and often for mentoring as well. By themselves, effective local line leaders generate tremendous energy, but more energy will ultimately produce more frustration without effective partnerships with internal networkers and executive leaders.

■ **Executive leaders**. Unlike many theorists of leadership, we do not regard executives as the *sine qua non* of organization change. We do not believe "all change starts at the top" and that "little can happen if the CEO is not on board." We have seen too many counterexamples of significant change started and sustained for some time with little or no executive leadership, and conversely too many examples of aggressive executive leadership that results in little lasting change. But sooner or later executive leadership becomes crucial, especially in sustaining change that can have organizationwide impact. The real role of executive leadership is not in "driving people to change," but in creating organizational environments that inspire, support, and leverage the imagination and initiative that exists at all levels.

Executive leaders do this in at least three ways.

They are designers in the sense of having unique responsibilities around the formal structures within organizations—such as the infrastructures of performance measurement, assessment, and reward, formal governance structures, and the infrastructures that support learning communities. Good design will not create commitment and innovation, but poor design will surely thwart them. If executive leaders do not help in meeting the challenges of formal design, the possibilities for emergence will be limited, and innovators throughout the enterprise will be continually frustrated.

As teachers, executive leaders mentor local line leaders, especially guiding them in their interactions with those outside their teams. This is vital in meeting the challenges of "believers and nonbelievers" and in dealing with the potential power clashes that the challenge of governance can bring.

Last, effective executive leaders serve as role models. They can embody genuine commitment to change through their example of "walking the talk," through their efforts to transform the functioning of top management teams, and to demonstrate genuine commitment to values and purpose. In these ways, the symbolic role of executives as stewards for the organization's long-term contribution can be as important as what they do. This stewardship extends to being convenors of strategic conversations. The real work of strategy, we believe, is less about setting "the strategy" than creating forums, both formal and informal, for addressing deep strategic issues that otherwise would become undiscussable, and for cultivating the collective capacity to rethink and re-create.

In general, as you progress from the challenges of initiating and sustaining to the challenges of redesigning and rethinking, executive leadership becomes more and more important. But, redesigning and rethinking always require initiating and sustaining, and it is always important to remember how limited executive leaders are in their ability to genuinely initiate change. They can encourage. They can provide a compelling business case for change. They can continually work to reduce barriers to change, but they depend critically on committed local line leaders to integrate new ideas into business practices and on effective internal networkers to support and interconnect those line leaders. Likewise, their ability to really understand the "current reality" of the organization—how people are thinking and feeling about difficult issues and challenges—is limited. Hierarchies distort information, and they have limited usefulness in spreading new knowledge and practices. On the other hand, information that travels laterally tends to be less distorted, and most knowledge sharing occurs through informal networks. These are domains where effective network leaders are vital allies to executives in organizationwide learning.

▪ **Network leaders.** Many of the most crucial issues that determine the long-term course of organizational change occur at interfaces— between pilot groups and the larger organization, across functional boundaries, and between the organization and its surrounding envi-

The counter examples of change without executive leadership have been demonstrated by many experiments within the SoL consortium over the past 10 years, as born out by many "learning histories." In no SoL member companies has any degree of organization-wide change been achieved without effective local line leadership, while there are several examples of executive-led initiatives that accomplished very little.

See *The Fifth Discipline* and "Leader's New Work," *Sloan Management Review*, 1990.

ronment. If anything, learning across such interfaces is becoming increasingly important in an increasingly interconnected world. This is why the role of internal networkers is growing in importance.

As we seen over and over in the preceding chapters, internal networkers play critical support roles in facing the challenges of initiating and sustaining within pilot teams. They are guides, advisors, active helpers, and "accessors" in the sense of helping pilot group members access resources outside the team. In challenges of sustaining they help connect local line leaders to one another, thereby reducing the isolation and misperceptions that fuel "believers and nonbelievers," as well as lead to power clashes. Since the challenges of design are as much about "enacted designs" as formal designs, internal networkers are vital at bringing new organization-wide structures, like improved community-building processes and more effective governance processes, to life.

But because they have little formal power or business accountability, they only provide leadership in partnership with line managers at all levels—local, middle, and senior managers. In this sense, the internal networkers are the penultimate example of the community of leadership that fuels all profound change. They can ill afford to live under the illusion that "they are doing it." They know they depend upon others. They know that they must develop genuine partnerships in order to be effective. Ironically, those with the least formal organizational authority may hold many of the keys to better understanding the leadership communities that will determine organizational vitality in the future.

Organizations will enter a new domain of leadership development when we stop thinking about preparing a few people for "the top" and start nurturing the potential for leaders at all levels to participate in shaping new realities. There is no real option. The re-creation of industrial-age enterprises can only happen through countless actions of thousands, indeed millions, of people.

Creating the Future

THE CORE LEADERSHIP CHALLENGE OF OUR ERA LIES IN ADDRESSING CORE ISSUES FOR which hierarchical authority is inadequate. Contemporary society is afflicted with deep problems like environmental destruction, decline of community and family structures, deterioration of systems of public education, and inequity. None of these problems will be "fixed" by a few great leaders. They have arisen, or been exacerbated, as a by-product of the industrialization process. The primary agents of the industrialization process are us, our collective decision making, mediated through the large institutions of the industrial era—in particular, corporations, school systems, and governmental institutions.

It is easy for individuals to feel powerless when we confront such global problems. Perhaps this is one reason we feel that we need to wait for leaders to emerge. It is pointless, we feel, to start on our own.

But organizations, and pilot groups within them, provide a way to start together. Learning to build and sustain momentum in the face of challenges like those examined in this fieldbook will build confidence and practical know-how. Eventually it may build momentum beyond individual organizations.

In novelist Daniel Quinn's *My Ishmael,* the protagonist, a twelve-year-old girl, inquires of her mentor Ishmael, a lowlands gorilla with whom she communicates telepathically, how present human society can possibly accomplish the sweeping changes needed to begin living in more harmony with nature and with one another. His simple response: "Be inventive." When she asks, "What do you mean?" Ishmael responds, "When was your greatest period of inventiveness, the greatest period of inventiveness in human history?" After some pause, she offers, "I'd have to say this . . . is it," meaning the Industrial Revolution. "That's right," Ishamel responds and then asks, "How did it work? . . . Did an Industrial Revolution Army move into the capital and seize the reins of power? Did it round up the royal family and guillotine them?

" . . . You've asked me what do to, Julie, and I've given one blanket directive: Be inventive. Now . . . I'm trying to show you how the greatest period of human inventiveness worked: The Industrial Revolution was the product of millions of small beginnings, a million great little ideas . . . It didn't proceed according to any theoretical design, (it) was not a utopian undertaking . . . it didn't depend on people being better than they are . . ."

Gradually, after much give and take, Ishmael suggests that the revolution needed today:

"won't take place all at once . . .

"will be achieved incrementally, by people working off each other's ideas . . .

"will be led by no one . . .

See *My Ishmael,* by Daniel Quinn (New York: Bantam Books, 1997), pp. 198–208.

"will not be the initiative of any political, governmental, or religious body . . .

"has no targeted end point . . .

"will proceed according to no plan . . . (and)

"will reward those who further the revolution with the coin of the revolution . . ."

And the coin of this revolution is a better way of living.

To Quinn's list, I would just add that such a revolution will also be guided by a few core images, shared metaphors or pictures of the world people are seeking to create. Such images enable diverse actions to become coherent in ways that no plan can accomplish. I believe that the industrial age has been dominated by two such core images—the image of the machine and the belief in material progress, especially of individual material gain.

Laying at the root of the profound inventions ahead, I believe, will be a slow, gradual process of rediscovering how the natural world, the living world, operates, and reorienting our institutions to embody this knowledge. The guiding image might be that of the Earth itself, as the living system which is our home.

Thirty years ago, the biologist, anthropologist, psychologist, and pioneering systems thinker Gregory Bateson claimed that the source of most of our problems is "the difference between the way man thinks and the way nature works." It is the fervent hope of the authors and contributors to this book that it enables a small step in closing this gap.

Quoted from *Deep Ecology: Living as If Nature Mattered*, by Bill Devall and George Sessions, (Salt Lake City: Gibbs Smith, Publisher, 1985), p.1.

2 Acknowledgments

The Dance of Change, like all fieldbooks, would not exist without a great deal of time and attention from a great many people. The efforts that we wish to acknowledge took place over the course of the last several years, as first the premises, then the project, then the challenges, and finally the book itself took shape.

First acknowledgements must go to Nina Kruschwitz, the managing editor of this book. She organized and carried out the complex tasks of editorial management, deadline coordination, and page production—tasks which are normally kept separate, but which, in this book, were integrated together so we could write and produce this book in camera-ready computer form. Her capabilities, dedication, concern for quality, and feeling for the reader made a difference to every page.

Roger Scholl, editor at Doubleday/Currency, inherited the Fifth Discipline resources from his predecessor, Harriet Rubin. He took on this project with enthusiasm and grace, and we benefited greatly both from his working relationship with us and his editorial insights. Michael Palgon, Paula Breen, and Steve Rubin at Doubleday played key roles in developing the concept for this book (and another "Fifth Discipline Resource" to appear soon, a Fifth Discipline-oriented Fieldbook on Education). Nicholas Brealey, publisher of this book in the United Kingdom, was a source of valued comment and help.

Joe Spieler, literary agent, played an adroit and active role, with much appreciated "enthusiasm and willingness to commit," to this book and the series of which it is a part. We benefited from the help of Ada Muellner and John Thornton at the Spieler Agency, from the consulting editing of Jon Beckmann during the proposal stage, and from the global reach of international literary agents Paul Marsh and Abner Stein. We drew on the publishing industry expertise of Lorraine Shanley and Constance Sayre of Market Partners, as well as that of Tom Wohl. Naseem Javed of ABC Namebank in Toronto contributed expertise and perspective to the selection of the book's name, as did Diane Senge. We are grateful for the legal advice of Renee Schwartz, the business advice of Jim Roberts, and the counsel of George Claseman.

Terry Karydes served as Doubleday's production liaison, making it possible for the book to proceed through a rigorous and time-bound production schedule. Chris Welch designed the compelling and innovative "Fieldbook" graphic format. Kim Cacho managed the production process at Doubleday, always with an eye towards the value of this book, and Harold Grabau and Maureen Cullen ushered us through Doubleday's impeccable copyediting process.

The illustrations in this book were created and produced by Karyl Klopp, who worked to our rigorous and often-changing specifications with diligence. We were grateful for the consulting-editorial assistance of writers Virginia O'Brien, Amy Fiore, and Janet Coleman, along with that of Tom Ehrenfeld and Lillie Mikesell. A few readers provided critical encouragement at a crucial moment: Michael Goodman, Vic Leo, Bill O'Brien, Linda Pierce, Louis van der Merwe, and Tim Savino.

Colleen Peacock and Josie Ford handled successively and successfully the difficult job of being the book project's "business manager." Debbie Federico provided much-appreciated early editorial assistance.

Ben Florer was a stalwart, constant source of office and logistic help. We relied upon the quality and flexibility of Purple Shark Transcriptions, Brooklyn, and particularly thank its proprietor, Sharon Harkey; we also drew upon the talented typing of Judith Webb, Timothy Conway, Margaret Bonnano, Laura Martocci, Terese Brown, Wendi Denman and Anita Brown. The book's public presence was defined by a team of people that included: Suzanne Herz and Laurie Matranga at Doubleday; and Gail Rentsch and Jill Danzig of Rentsch Associates.

Travis Burch, Ed Dulworth, Betsy Jacobsen, Joan Kelly, Charlie Kiefer, Randy Kubota, Carl Rossey, Peter Stroh, Ann Thomas, and Hardin Tibbs made insightful contributions to drafts of various segments of *The Dance of Change*; Jose-Elias Alvarez, Bill Holmes, Eamonn Kelly, Oliver Markley, Alberto Saldarriaga, and Francisco Santos participated in editorial development with us. Our material on the U.S. Army was made possible by John O'Shea, Mike Harper, Neal Cosby, Jim Madden, Rick Brown, Gordon Sullivan and Hal Nelson. Janis Dutton, Nelda Cambron-McCabe and Tim Lucas offered encouragement and help from "across the wall" of the Education Fieldbook (Janis took part in some of the early development of this book). Rick Karash produced the "listservs" that led to two critical roundtables, and we are grateful to the participants there who joined us online. Harry Schessel goaded and produced the website that galvanized some of our research (*http://www.fieldbook.com*); contributions to it were also made by Adam Engel, Jamie Biggar, Ed Kleiner, Joshua Ross, Robin Sacrafamilia, and Annette Weintraub. The site exists on a server at Digital Telemedia, Inc., New York City.

This book benefited from the support and encouragement of the following organizations:

■ The Society for Organizational Learning, Cambridge, Massachusetts. The Society is a consortium of researchers, consultants and organizational practitioners, all working to advance the foundations of theory, methods and understanding that can make learning organizations a way of life. We particularly benefited from the insights and work of Goren Carstedt, Edgar Schein and B. C. Huselton and from the support and help of Jean McDonald, Judy Rodgers, Steve Buckley, Nadine Chase, Vickie Tweiten, Jane Punchard, and Angela Lipinski.

■ Innovation Associates, Waltham, Massachusetts. A division of Arthur D. Little, Innovation Associates offers consulting and training services to enable clients to collectively create the results they most care about. The system archetypes featured in the "Fifth Discipline" series were developed at this organization, which was co-founded by Charlie Kiefer and Peter Senge. Michael Goodman, director of the Systems Thinking practice at Innovation Associates, helped coordinate and guide the contributions by Innovation Associates's people. We are also grateful to Arun Maira, Joel Yanowitz, Robert Hanig, Jennifer Kemeny, Charlie Kiefer, and Sue Thomson; and to Diane Nakashian, Lindsay Price, Sue Bedrossian, Shirley Stahl and others.

■ Innovation Associates of Canada, Toronto, Ontario. The work of this branch of Arthur D. Little provided a key laboratory for the evolution of some of the ideas in this book. We want to thank Susan Zupansky, Daniela Kasper, and Frances Spatafora.

■ Ross Partners, Encinitas, California; Bluefire Partners, Sherrills Ford, North Carolina; Reflection Learning Associates, Cambridge, Massachusetts. These three independent consulting firms, each associated with different authors of this book (Rick Ross; Charlotte Roberts; and George Roth and Art Kleiner, respectively), provided necessary financial, logistic, intellectual, and "ground truth"-building support.

■ MIT's Sloan School of Management: This was the original home of the Center for Organizational Learning, under whose auspices much of this work began. Its intellectually rich, (although sometimes controversial) environment provided a continuing institutional base for Peter Senge and George Roth, along with faculty colleagues (Ed Schein, John Van Maanen, Wanda Orlikowski, Robert McKersie, Lotte Bailyn, Jay Forrester, John Sterman, Nelson Repenning and John Carroll) whose work and insights influenced our thinking about the ideas of learning and change in organizations. Without an "incubator" where these ideas have found a supportive environment to grow over the years, many of the experiments that led to this book wouldn't have taken place.

■ The Resources Connection, Mt. Albert, Ontario. This "access-to-tools"-oriented enterprise is a purveyor of books and other resources for people working to change organizations. They have helped our colleagues and clients get the resources they needed, and we have benefited from the work and insights of proprietor Robin Sacrafamilia and others there.

■ The Learning Circle, Sudbury, Massachusetts. This partnership-oriented organization develops and fosters a variety of projects and joint ventures, dedicated to fostering learning organization concepts and practice. We benefited from the encouragement, and suggestions of Judy Rodgers, Anne Starr, Sandy Billings, and Rita Cleary.

■ Pegasus Communications, Cambridge, Massachusetts. Publishers of

The Systems Thinker newsletter and other publications (p. 136) and conveners of the annual Systems Thinking in Action conference, this organization provided a context or starting point for some of the insights covered in this book. We are particularly grateful to Daniel Kim and Kellie Wardman.

■ Global Business Network, Emeryville, California. Once again, this organization helped develop some of our material on scenarios and strategy. We wish to thank Nancy Murphy, Napier Collyns, Katherine Fulton, Peter Schwartz, Kees van der Heijden, Roberta Gelt, Stewart Brand, Sean Baenen, Lynn Carruthers, Eamonn Kelly, Chris Ertel, Alan Steed and Laura Likely.

■ New York University Interactive Telecommunications Program, New York, N.Y. This center for research and graduate study in new media has helped us develop the "fieldbook" sensibility and form, and provided a base for thinking about moving forward more effectively into the information age. We wish to thank Red Burns, George Agudow, Midori Yasuda, Martin Elton, Tom Igoe, and Gilles Bersier.

■ The Centre for Generative Leadership, Hamilton, Massachusetts; Action Design Associates, Newton, Massachusetts; the Centre for Innovative Leadership of Rivonia, South Africa and the Hague, Netherlands; DIA•*logos*, Cambridge, Massachusetts; The Bootstrap Institute, Fremont, California; The Institute for Research on Learning, Menlo Park, California; Metasystems Design Group, Washington, D.C.; Interactive Learning Labs, Inc., Farmington Hills, Michigan. These and other private consulting organizations, each with its own body of knowledge and practice, represent the "early exploring ships" that first navigate the coastlines of uncharted organizational change territory.

All of the organizations listed in these acknowledgements, if accessible through the internet, can be reached through *http://www.field book.com/organizations.html*.

Others whom we wish to single out for their help, insight and encouragement include: Pille Bunnell, Nancy Dixon, Paula Edmund, Ruth Hansen, David Haughton, William Isaacs, Katrin Kauefer, Fred Kofman, Hunter Lovins (and our hosts at the Rocky Mountain Institute), Wendy MacPhedran, Will McWhinney, Dave Meador, Doug Merchant, Don Michael, Paul Monus, Mwalimu Musheshe, Jr., Jose Pacheco, Susan Price, Chrissi Rohn, Otto Scharmer, Howard Schultz, Bill Shireman, C. Sam Smith, Rich Stiller, and Iva Wilson. We would also like to thank all of the organizational practitioners whom we have worked with, who have had the courage to stick with it, and from whom we have learned. Though we cannot list them by name, we also wish to thank the attendees at the various working sessions whose deliberations led to the original versions of the balancing processes of *The Dance of Change*, and to other concepts that made it into this book.

We produced *The Dance of Change* as camera-ready copy, using Apple Macintosh computers, Microsoft Word, Macromedia Freehand 8, and Quark XPress 3.32. Our "lexicon" etymologies derive from two primary sources: *Dictionary of Word Origins* by John Ayto (New York: Arcade, 1990) and *Origins (A Short Etymological Dictionary of Modern English)* by Eric Partridge (New York: Greenwich House, 1958).

Creating a book of this size and scope inevitably involves the support and attention of the people with whom we are closest in our lives. Therefore, we particularly wish to acknowledge, with love and appreciation: Faith Florer, Frances Kleiner (who was born during this book's production), Joyce Ross, Jason Ross, Jessica Ross, Joshua Ross, Linda Rafferty, Erika Roth, Maggie Roth, Diane Senge, Nathan Senge, Ian Senge, Anthony Smith, and Michael Smith.

3 About the Authors

Peter Senge is a Senior Lecturer at the Massachusetts Institute of Technology where he is part of the Organizational Learning and Change group. He is also Chairperson of the Society for Organizational Learning (SoL), a global community of organizations, researchers, and consultants dedicated to building knowledge about fundamental institutional change. He is the author of *The Fifth Discipline: The Art and Practice of The Learning Organization*, identified by the Harvard Business Review in 1997 as one of the five most influential management books of the past two decades. He has lectured extensively throughout the world, translating the abstract ideas of systems theory into tools for better understanding of economic and organizational change. His work articulates a cornerstone position of human values in the workplace; namely, that vision, purpose, reflectiveness, and systems thinking are essential if organizations are to realize their potentials. He has worked with leaders in business, education, health care, and government, and has authored many articles in both academic journals and the business press on systems thinking in management. He received a B.S. in engineering from Stanford University, and an M.S. in social systems modeling and Ph.D. in management from MIT.

Art Kleiner is a writer, consulting editor, educator, and the editorial director for the Fieldbook projects. His book *The Age of Heretics* (Doubleday, 1996) was a finalist for the Edgar G. Booz award for most innovative business book of 1996. A faculty member at New York University's Interactive Telecommunications Program, he has a Master's of Journalism from the University of California at Berkeley. Writing on technological, cultural, management, and environmental topics, he has contributed to *Wired*, the *New York Times Magazine*, *Fast Company*, the *Harvard Business Review*, *Across the Board*, and many other publications. He was a contributing editor to *Garbage*, for whom he wrote an ongoing series on corporate environmentalism, and a former editor of the *Whole Earth Catalog* and *CoEvolution Quarterly*. He is also a developer, with George Roth, of the learning history form. He lives outside New York City.

Charlotte Roberts is an executive consultant, speaker and writer. She specializes in working with executives on creating a learning culture and modeling learning. Her articles have appeared in the *Journal for Quality and Participation*; the *Journal of the American Compensation Association*; and in a variety of academic and business publications and newspapers. She serves on the board of trustees of Guilford College, a private liberal-arts college in Greensboro, NC. She has also served on the advisory council of the American Compensation Association. She is currently a project facilitator for a five-year research study by the Danforth Foundation on the new leadership model for public school superintendency. She has worked with a wide range of organizations, from manufacturing to hardware and software design to healthcare to local community groups. She completed post-graduate work in management at the Wharton School of Business and has served on the faculty of the International Institute for Management Development in Geneva, Switzerland. She is one of the pre-eminent storytellers and innovative designers in the learning organization movement. A native of North Carolina, she lives near Charlotte, N.C.

Richard Ross is a motivational speaker, trainer, and organizational consultant who consults to numerous Fortune 500 and international corporations. Rick has been a member of the faculty at the University of Southern California in Los Angeles; his published research in psychology concerned the neural substrates of cortical learning. He has been licensed as a clinical psychologist in California, and has also held senior line management positions. His work focuses on the ways in which teams and organizations can gain competitive advantage by increasing the organization's intelligence through knowledge management. Rick's speaking topics range from "Winning in the Global Knowledge Economy" to "Leading Winning Teams" and "Applying the Principles of the Learning Organization." He received his doctorate in neuro-physiological psychology from the University of London. He lives near San Diego, and is on the board of directors of The Women's Resource Center.

George Roth is a researcher and lecturer at MIT's Sloan School of Management, and Executive Director of the Ford/MIT Collaboration—a multi-million dollar alliance between MIT and Ford, emphasizing learning, change and knowledge creation activities in environmental policy, engineering education, and research. He is also a faculty member at the University of New Hampshire, and a past Research Director for the MIT Center for Organizational Learning. Founder of Reflection Learning Associates, he co-developed the learning history form. He is the author of numerous academic and professional journal articles on learning and change, and is (with Art Kleiner) coeditor of a series of learning histories published by Oxford University Press. Prior to his academic career, he spent ten years at Digital Equipment Corporation. His work experience included advanced product development, strategic planning, business development, operations, marketing, and sales in the U. S. and Europe. He has an MBA in finance, BS in Mechanical Engineering, and Ph.D. in Organizational Studies from MIT. Born in Germany, he currently lives in Southern Maine.

Bryan Smith is an international speaker and consultant to executive teams. He is President of Innovation Associates of Canada and a Vice President of Arthur D. Little, Inc. He has been a central contributor at Innovation Associates to the development and application of organizational learning strategies over the past eighteen years. Much of his current work is helping client firms build innovative sustainable development strategies to create distinct competitive advantage. He does this by developing the synergy between organizational learning tools/disciplines and sustainable approaches to business. He has worked for over twenty years with senior managers and executives in business and government to develop inspired leadership capabilities, and help clients apply them to innovative strategy, organizational design, and the creation of profound change. As part of his doctoral research, he carried out the first empirical study of charismatic leadership in business, which has informed his work with leaders worldwide. He received his MBA and Ph.D. in Organizational Behavior from the University of Toronto, and lives in Toronto, Canada.

4 How to Get in Touch with the Creators of This Book

- **Comments:** If you have found this book valuable and would like to tell us why, or if you have responses or suggestions of any sort, we are interested in hearing from you at The Fifth Discipline Fieldbook Project (creators of *The Dance of Change*). Please write to us at the addresses given below or visit our website at: *http:/www.fieldbook. com.*

- **Credit:** We have done our best to track down and credit the sources of all the material in *The Dance of Change*. However, we recognize we may have inadvertently omitted some important sources or credits. If you feel someone is not properly acknowledged, please let us know and we will do our best to correct future printings.

- **Contributions to future Fieldbooks:** We are interested in continuing to gather and disseminate information about ongoing learning organization initiatives. It's possible that we may produce future Fieldbooks incorporating this material. If you would like to contribute a description of your experience, or if you know someone we ought to know about, then please write a letter to us at the address below.

- **Contributor information**: We maintain an up-to-date list of contact information for contributors to *The Dance of Change* (and *The Fifth Discipline Fieldbook*) at: *http://www.fieldbook.com/contributors.html*.
- **Mailing list:** We are continuing to produce materials that may be of value to people wanting to change organizations, or foster learning in them. If you wish to be informed (as an individual, an organization, a team, or a study group) of these Fieldbook Project developments as they unfold, please send us your business card, use the reply card on the last page of this book, or visit our website.
- **Resource**: If you would like help obtaining any of the resources that are reviewed or identified in *The Dance of Change* (including books, videotapes, computer software, or programs, with volume discounts), we suggest that you contact the Resources Connection at: 1-800-295-0957.
- Contacting us:

The Dance of Change
The Fifth Discipline Fieldbook Project
PO Box 943
Oxford OH 45056-0943
United States

or:

The Dance of Change
The Fifth Discipline Fieldbook Project
PO Box 602
Mt. Albert, Ontario, L0G 1M0
Canada

Or visit:
http://www.fieldbook.com.

Index

The Dance of Change
Owner Registration Form

Mail to:
The Fifth Discipline
Fieldbook Project
PO Box 943
Oxford, OH 45056-0943
USA

or:
The Fifth Discipline
Fieldbook Project
PO Box 602
Mt. Albert, Ontario, L0G 1M0
Canada

or you can fill this form out electronically on our Web site at http://www.fieldbook.com/danceform.html.

Thank you for your interest in *The Dance of Change*. Use this form to stay connected with new developments, tools, and resources as they emerge. People who respond with this form will receive an electronic copy e-mailed to them of *The Lost Chapters of the Dance of Change*, a compendium of additional material on meeting the ten challenges of profound change. If you cannot receive e-mail, please indicate that on this form.

My preference is:
- ❏   full-length "Lost Chapters" e-mailed in Adobe Acrobat (.PDF) format
- ❏   shorter paper "Lost Chapters" by postal mail.

Name _____
Title _____
Organization _____ # of Employees _____
Type of Organization _____
Address _____
City _____ State/Province _____
Zip/Postal Code _____ Country _____
Is this your home or work address? _____ Phone # _____
Fax # _____ E-mail _____

- ❏   I would like to be informed of new developments and resources for organizational learning and change. I'm particularly interested in _____
- ❏   Please inform me about the forthcoming Fieldbook on Education.
- ❏   Here are my comments on *The Dance of Change*: (use back of form)
- ❏   I would like more information about speakers, seminars, consultants, or other "in-person" resources on learning organizations and organizational change.